THE CHRISTIAN BED & BREAKFAST DIRECTORY

2002–2003 Edition

BARBOUR
PUBLISHING, INC.

Published by Barbour Publishing, Inc., P.O. Box 719, Uhrichsville, Ohio 44683
http://www.barbourbooks.com

 Member of the
Evangelical Christian
Publishers Association

Printed in the United States of America.

THE CHRISTIAN BED & BREAKFAST DIRECTORY

2002–2003 Edition

PROFESSIONAL
Association of
INNKEEPERS
International®
ASSOCIATE MEMBER

Table of Contents

How to Use This Book

Have you ever dreamed of spending a few days in a rustic cabin in Alaska? Would you like to stay in an urban town house while taking care of some business in the city? Would your family like to spend a weekend on a Midwestern farm feeding pigs and gathering eggs? Maybe a romantic Victorian mansion in San Francisco or an antebellum plantation in Mississippi is what you've been looking for. No matter what your needs may be, whether you are traveling for business or pleasure, you will find a variety of choices in the 2002–2003 edition of *The Christian Bed & Breakfast Directory*.

In the pages of this guide you will find over 1,200 bed and breakfasts, small inns, and homestays. All of the information has been updated from last year's edition, and many entries are listed for the first time. Although not every establishment is owned or operated by Christians, each host has expressed a desire to welcome Christian travelers.

The directory is designed for easy reference. At a glance, you can determine the number of rooms available at each establishment and how many rooms have private (PB) and shared (SB) baths. You will find the name of the host or hosts, the price range for two people sharing one room, the kind of breakfast that is served, and what credit cards are accepted. There is a "Notes" section to let you know important information that may not be included in the description. These notes correspond to the list at the bottom of each page. The descriptions have been written by the hosts. The publisher has not visited these bed and breakfasts and is not responsible for inaccuracies.

General maps are provided to help you with your travel plans. Included are the towns where our bed and breakfasts are located, some reference cities, and major highways. Please use your road map for additional assistance and details when planning your trip.

It is recommended that you make reservations in advance. Many bed and breakfasts have small staffs or are run single-handedly and cannot easily accommodate surprises. Also ask about taxes, as city and state taxes vary. Remember to ask for directions, and if your special dietary needs can be met, and confirm check-in and check-out times. Whether you're planning a honeymoon, family vacation, orbusiness trip, *The Christian Bed & Breakfast Directory* will make any outing out of the ordinary.

ALABAMA

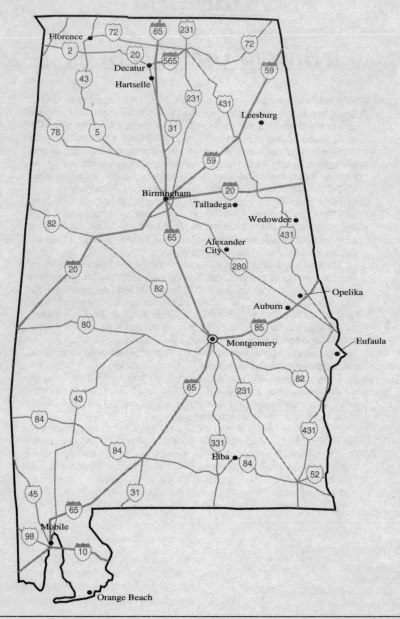

NOTES: Credit cards accepted: A Master Card; B Visa; C American Express; D Discover; E Diners Club; F Other; 2 Personal checks accepted; 3 Lunch available; 4 Dinner available; 5 Open all year;

Alabama

DECATUR

Hickory Hill Bed & Breakfast

224 Hagood Drive, Somerville 35670
(256) 584-6972; E-mail: kkjh1@aol.com
bbonline.com/al/hickoryhill

Hickory Hill is a very quiet inn in the country, atop a mountain with views of city lights at night. Flowers abound every season. You can take a quiet walk in the woods or sit in one of our sitting areas outdoors or swing in one of our antique swings while reading or just relaxing. We are located near historic towns noted for their historic areas and antique shopping. There are several golf courses nearby. We are near Huntsville (20 minutes away) with its Space and Rocket Center, Botanical Garden, Art Museum, and restored historic district. We are located five miles east of I-65 near Huntsville, Decatur, and Hartselle.

Hosts: Joyce and Ken Helphand
Rooms: 3 (2PB; 1SB) $75-85
Full Breakfast
Credit Cards: A, B, C, D
Notes: 2, 5, 7, 8, 9, 10

FLORENCE

Wood Avenue Inn

658 North Wood Ave, 35630-4608
(256) 766-8441
E-mail: woodaveinn@aol.com
www.woodavenueinn.com

This 112-year-old Victorian mansion offers Southern hospitality in the heart of Dixie, just 13 miles off the Natchez Trace and two miles to Florence marina harbor on the Tennessee River. Enjoy a romantic weekend; walk to restaurants, art galleries, and antique shopping; or sit on porches and watch song birds build their nests in the wisteria gardens. Business guests welcome!

Wood Avenue Inn

Hosts: Alvern and Gene Greeley
Rooms: 4 (PB) $75-110
Full Breakfast
Credit Cards: A, B, D
Notes: 2, 5, 7, 8, 9, 10

HARTSELLE

The Oden House

201 Main Street East, 35640
(256) 751-2933; fax: (256) 751-2933
bbonline.com/al/odenhouse/

We invite you to relax and enjoy our lovely Victorian home, where we have held onto the best of the past that makes this home and Hartselle one of

---

6 Pets welcome; 7 Children welcome; 8 Tennis nearby; 9 Swimming nearby; 10 Golf nearby; 11 Skiing nearby; 12 May be booked through travel agent

The Oden House

the most beautiful places to visit in the state. Just a short walk to over 30 antique and speciality shops. Choose from three beautifully decorated rooms; enjoy a delicious gourmet candlelight breakfast. The well known hymn "Leaning on the Everlasting Arms" was written in our home.

Hosts: Ann and Ray Hill
Rooms: 3 (SB) $85
Full Breakfast
Credit Cards: A, B
Notes: 2, 3, 4, 5, 10

LEESBURG

The Secret Bed & Breakfast Lodge

The Secret

2356 A.L. Highway 68 West, 35983-4000
(256) 523-3825; fax: (256) 523-6477
E-mail: secret@.tds.net
www.bbonline.com/al/thesecret

At the Secret B&B Lodge, guests have a 180-degree panoramic view of seven cities and two states, overlooking Weiss Lake from the Lookout Mountain Parkway. Rooftop pool. Vaulted ceiling in lodge area and bedrooms. The lodge offers king/queen beds, TVs, VCRs, private baths, Jacuzzis, fireplace, and balconies. AAA-star rating. A special place—a secret with a view as spectacular in the day as it is enchanting at night. Come. Discover. Enjoy!

Hosts: Carl and Diann Cruickshank
Rooms: 8 (PB) $95-145
Full Breakfast
Credit Cards: A, B
Notes: 2, 5, 8, 9, 10, 11, 12

MONTGOMERY

Red Bluff Cottage

551 Clay Street, P.O. Box 1026, 36101
(334) 264-0056; (888) 551-2529
fax: (334) 263-3054
E-mail: redblufbnb@aol.com
www.bbonline.com/al/redbluff

Share the comforts and pleasures of Red Bluff Cottage, high above the Alabama River in Montgomery's historic Cottage Hill District. Red Bluff is a raised cottage, built in 1987 as a B&B inn. The guest rooms are on the ground floor, with easy access from the parking area, gazebo, and fenced play yard. The kitchen, dining room, living room, sitting room with TV, and music room with piano and harpsichord are on the second floor for guests to enjoy. A deep upstairs porch offers a panoramic view of the river plain and downtown Montgomery, including a unique view of the state capitol. Each guest room is furnished with family antiques.

Red Bluff Cottage

Hosts: Mark and Anne Waldo
Rooms: 4 (PB) $75
Full Breakfast
Credit Cards: A, B, D, E
Notes: 2, 7

ORANGE BEACH

The Original Romar House

23500 Perdido Beach Boulevard, 36561-3007
(334) 974-1625; (800) 847-6627
fax: (334) 974-1163
E-mail: original@gulftel.com
www.bbonline.com/al/romarhouse

Wake up to rediscover romance in a charmingly historic atmosphere, as the sun streams through the stained glass windows of your art deco-furnished room. After breakfast, take a morning swim or stroll along the beach collecting seashells, curl up in a cypress swing or hammock and read a book, or relax in the hot-tub whirlpool spa. You are only minutes by car to gift shops, golf courses, seafood restaurants, and entertainment. Break away from your everyday world. Come, be a part of the history at the Original Romar House bed and breakfast inn.

Hosts: Darrell Finley, Manager / Jerry Gilbreath, Owner
Rooms: 7 (PB) $79-129
Full Breakfast
Credit Cards: A, B, C
Notes: 2, 5, 8, 9, 10

VARIOUS CITIES

Natchez Trace Bed & Breakfast Reservation Service

P.O. Box 193, Hampshire, TN, 38461
(913) 285-2777; (800) 377-2770
E-mail: natcheztrace @worldnet.att.net
www.bbonline.com/natcheztrace

This reservation service is unusual in that all the homes listed are close to the Natchez Trace, the delightful National Parkway running from Nashville, Tennessee, to Natchez, Mississippi. Kay Jones can help you plan your trip along the Trace, with homestays in interesting and historic homes along the way. Many locations of bed and breakfasts, including in the cities of Ashland City, Columbia, Fairview, Franklin, Hohenwald, and Nashville, Tennessee; Florence and Cherokee, Alabama; and Church Hill, Corinth, French Camp, Kosciusko, Lorman, Natchez, New Albany, Tupelo, and Vicksburg, Mississippi. $60-125.

---

6 Pets welcome; 7 Children welcome; 8 Tennis nearby; 9 Swimming nearby; 10 Golf nearby; 11 Skiing nearby; 12 May be booked through travel agent

ALASKA

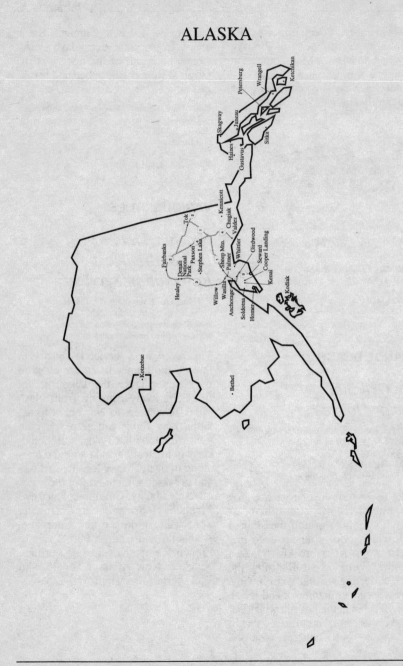

NOTES: Credit cards accepted: A Master Card; B Visa; C American Express; D Discover; E Diners
Club; F Other; 2 Personal checks accepted; 3 Lunch available; 4 Dinner available; 5 Open all year;6

Alaska

ANCHORAGE

Camai Bed & Breakfast

3838 Westminster Way, 99508
(907) 333-2219; (800) 659-8763
fax: (907) 337-3959
E-mail: camai@alaska.net
www.camaibnb.com

Achorage's premier B&B offers spacious suites with private baths and many amenities. We are located in a quiet neighborhood on Chester Creek's greenbelt. Moose are frequently seen nibbling in Caroline's flower garden. The hosts are active in church. Craig is the Missions Committee Chair and Caroline is the organist and youth/children's bell choir director.

Hosts: Craig and Caroline Valentine
Rooms: 3 (PB) $45-110
Full Breakfast
Credit Cards: None
Notes: 2, 5, 7, 8, 9, 10, 11, 12

Elderberry Bed & Breakfast

8340 Elderberry Street, 99502
(907) 243-6968; fax: (907) 243-6968
E-mail: elderberry-b-b@gci.net
www.alaskan.com/elderberrybb

Elderberry B&B is located by the airport and has three guest rooms with private baths. We cater to each guest on an individual basis. Situated on the green belt in Anchorage where moose can often be spotted. We serve full, home-cooked breakfasts. The hosts love to talk about Alaska and are very active in their church.

Hosts: Norm and Linda Seitz
Rooms: 3 (PB) $70-90
Full Breakfast
Credit Cards: A, B
Notes: 2, 5, 7, 8, 9, 10, 11, 12

FAIRBANKS

7 Gables Inn & Suites

4312 Birch Lane, 99708-0488
(907) 479-0751; fax: (907) 479-2229
E-mail: gables7@alaska.net
7gablesinn.com

Luxury accommodations at affordable rates. Our rooms and suites have private baths with Jacuzzi tubs, cable TVs/VCRs. A full gourmet breakfast is included in the room rate. We offer laundry facilities and complimentary canoes and bikes. Spacious suites/apartments include full kitchen and living room areas. Central to major attractions: UAD Museum, Riverboat "Discovery," Alaskaland, etc.

Hosts: Paul and Leicha Welton
Rooms: 20 (PB) $50-180
Full Breakfast
Credit Cards: A, B, C
Notes: 2, 5, 7, 9, 10, 11, 12

Pets welcome; 7 Children welcome; 8 Tennis nearby; 9 Swimming nearby; 10 Golf nearby; 11 Skiing nearby; 12 May be booked through travel agent

HOMER

Beeson B & B

1393 Bay Avenue, 99603-7941
(907) 235-3757; (800) 371-2095; fax: (907) 235-1491
E-mail: b-b@beesons.com
www.beesons.com

1992 custom-built for B&B. Comfortable rooms, apartments, and bunk rooms, all with private baths, cable TV, and phones. Individually decorated with comforters and quilts. Breathtaking view of Kachemak Bay, mountains, glaciers, and famous Spit. Nestled in wooded acreage; minutes to fishing, theater, shops, restaurants. Scumptious breakfast; Jacuzzi and exercise equipment in gazebo, 52-inch TV in common room.

Host: Doni Beeson
Rooms: 11 (PB) $90-130
Continental Breakfast
Credit Cards: A, B
Notes: 2, 5, 7, 8, 9, 10, 12

Fernwood Estates Bed &Breakfast

Fernwood Estates

P.O. Box 900, 99603
(907) 235-2070; (888) 788-2838
fax: (907) 235-2838
E-mail: fernwood@xyz.net
www.fernwoodestates.com

Fernwood Estates is a perfect blend of remote elegance. This brand-new home is just minutes from downtown Homer and fishing spots, yet has the air of rural Alaska with all its charm. Take in the incredible, unobstructed view of Kachemak Bay or simply watch the eagles soar above you. Either way you're sure to enjoy your stay here.

Hosts: Bob and Leah Handley
Rooms: 4 (PB) $90-95
Full Breakfast
Credit Cards: B
Notes: 2, 5, 7, 8, 9, 10, 11

Three Moose Meadow Bed & Breakfast

P.O. Box 15291, 99603
phone/fax: (907) 235-0755; (888) 777-0930
E-mail: 3moose@xyz.net
www.threemoose.com

Spirit-filled couple invites you to enjoy your own log cabin in a serene wilderness setting. We offer two log cabins that overlook beautiful, snow-capped mountains and glaciers. Both cabins are fully equipped with kitchen, bath, living room, and a bedroom with a queen bed. Covered porch with swing!

Hosts: Jordan and Jennie Hess
Rooms: 3 (PB) $80-110
Continental Breakfast
Credit Cards: A, B
Notes: 2, 5, 7, 10, 11, 12

NOTES: Credit cards accepted: A Master Card; B Visa; C American Express; D Discover; E Diners Club; F Other; 2 Personal checks accepted; 3 Lunch available; 4 Dinner available; 5 Open all year;

JUNEAU

A Cozy Log
Bed & Breakfast

8668 Dudley Street, 99801
(907) 789-2582; fax: (907) 789-3617
E-mail: cozylog@alaska.net
www.cozylog.net

Imagine sitting on the porch of your Alaskan log home in the heart of Juneau's recreation area, just five minutes from the airport and shopping, and 15 minutes from the city. The quiet of the forest and majesty of the Mendenhall Glacier are only heartbeats away. From cozy beds to all the little extras, your stay will be a relaxed and memorable one.

Hosts: Bruce and Judy Bowler
Rooms: 2 (SB) $65-99
Full Breakfast
Credit Cards: A, B, C, D
Notes: 2, 5, 6, 7, 8, 9, 10, 11, 12

KENAI

Eldridge Haven
Bed & Breakfast

2679 Bowpicker Lane, 99611-8835
phone/fax: (907) 283-7152
E-mail: lridgebb@ptialaska.net
www.ptialaska.net/~lridgebb

Eldridge Haven B&B is hospitality at its best: peaceful, clean, friendly! Excellent food includes giant Alaskan pancakes, steaming gingered bananas, stuffed scones, and more. It's in a wooded area surrounded by prime habitat for moose, caribou, bald eagles, and waterfowl. You can walk to the beach. Cross-country skiing is convenient. The lodging is close to all Peninsula points, including Seward and Homer. So eliminate packing and unpacking; stay with the best and visit the rest. Children are treasured; guests are pampered. Eldridge Haven B&B is open year-round. We've been serving satisfied guests since 1987.

Hosts: Marta and Barry Eldridge
Rooms: 2 (1 PB; 1 SB) $65-80
Full Breakfast
Credit Cards: A, B
Notes: 2, 5, 7, 10, 11, 12

PALMER

Abbey On The Lake

HC 01, Box 6312-H, 99645
(907) 357-6332; fax: (907) 357-6333
E-mail: abbeyonthelake@compuserve.com

Beautiful cedar home situated on five acres. Finger Lake is right out your door and the fishing is great! We are approximately an hour's drive from Anchorage and on your way to Denali National Park. We have plenty of pets to greeet you and open arms to welcome you into our family. Also lots of good food and conversation.

Host: Jackie Williams
Rooms: 2 (PB) &55-120
Full Breakfast
Credit Cards: A, B
Notes: 5, 7, 9, 10, 11

Hatcher Pass
Bed & Breakfast

HC 5 Box 6797D, 99645-9611
(907) 745-6788; fax: (907) 745-6787
E-mail: cabins@hatcherpassbb.com
www.hatcherpassbb.com

---

6 Pets welcome; 7 Children welcome; 8 Tennis nearby; 9 Swimming nearby; 10 Golf nearby; 11 Skiing nearby; 12 May be booked through travel agent

Stay at Hatcher Pass B&B where you will experience Alaska's finest log cabins with all the modern conveniences of private bath, kitchenette, phone, and TV/VCR. Nestled at the base of beautiful Hatcher Pass, Alaska, home to a variety of outdoor activities in any season, and only 50 miles north of Anchorage and eight miles from Palmer. Relax in the comfort and beauty that is yours at Hatcher Pass B&B.

Hosts: Dan and Liz Hejl
Rooms: 3 (PB) $70-80
Continental Breakfast
Credit Cards: A, B
Notes: 2, 5, 7, 8, 9, 10, 11, 12

SEWARD

Bell-in-the-Woods Bed & Breakfast

P.O. Box 345, 99664
phone/fax: (907) 224-7271
E-mail: bellwoodbnb@juno.com
www.bellinthewoodsbnb.com

A full hot breakfast awaits you when you stay in one of our five guest bedrooms or two family suites during your visit to the Pristine Kenai Peninsula in the heart of south central Alaska. Nature cruises out of Seward, and hiking and fishing are nearby.

Hosts: Jerry and Peggy Woods
Rooms: 7 (PB) $99-170
Full Breakfast
Credit Cards: A, B, D
Notes: 2, 5, 7, 11, 12

SITKA

Alaska Ocean View Bed & Breakfast

1101 Edgecumbe Drive, 99835-7122
(904) 747-8310; fax (907) 747-3440
E-mail: alaskaoceanview@gci.net
www.sitka-alaska-lodging.com

This popular lodging is rated one of "Alaska's Best!" Drift to sleep in an exceptionally comfortable king/queen bed under a fluffy down comforter after a relaxing soak in the patio Jacuzzi. Wake to the wonderful aroma of a delicious, generous hot breakfast. In-room cable TV/VCR, stereo, refrigerator, microwave, coffeemaker, and phone are provided. Enjoy the extensive library, beautiful fireplaces, lush rock gardens, magnificent view, and gracious, genuinely warm, cheerful hospitality. Centrally located, all nonsmoking, concierge.

Hosts: Bill and Carole Denkinger
Rooms: 3 (PB) $79-179
Full Breakfast
Credit Cards: A, B, C
Notes: 2, 5, 7, 8, 9, 10, 12

SOLDOTNA

Affordable Bed & Breakfast

P.O. Box 1476; Penny Lane Sterlin Hwy. 89, 99669
(907) 262-9578; (888) 705-9578
E-mail: abnb@alaska.com
www.home.gci.net/~abnb

Our B&B is within easy walking distance to Longmere Lake and five minutes from the world-famous Kenai River where you can catch your own world-record king salmon. It's also two miles from a golf course. Choose from three bedrooms; there is a nice guest living room with a refrigerator and microwave for your convenience. Children are welcome.

Host: Valya Zumwalt
Rooms: 3 (SB) $50-110
Full Breakfast
Credit Cards: A, B
Notes: 2, 5, 7, 10

Ingrid's Inn Bed & Breakfast

51810 Ariels Lane, P.O. Box 967, Kasilof, 99610
(907) 262-1510; (888) 422-1510
fax: (907) 260-5810
E-mail: ingrids@alaska.net
www.alaskaone.com/ingrids

Ingrid's Inn

Ingrid's Inn is a traditional, colonial home secluded on seven acres of tranquility. Our guest rooms are large and comfortable, with sitting areas and vanities in each. We maintain a smoke-free, alcohol-free facility for your comfort, as well as a private entry. Our rooms are beautifully decorated, highlighting some of Alaska's finest artists. Ingrid's Inn is located close to the Kenai and Kasilof Rivers for salmon fishing, and near the Deep Creek area for Halibut fishing. We love Alaska and look forward to sharing it with you.

Host: Ingrid Edgerly
Rooms: 4 (2 PB; 2 SB) $72-95
Full Breakfast
Credit Cards: A, B
Notes: 5

J C's Bed & Breakfast

P.O. Box 1761, 36885 Beau Circle, 99669
(907) 260-3856; E-mail: jcbb@ptialaska.net
ptialaska.net/~jcbb

Regal Alaskan setting overlooking Whisper Lake and Alaska Mountain Range. Fabulous sunsets! Our beds give you Alaskan Bear Hugs. . . You'll want to hibernate. Fishing on the Kenai River, floatplane adventures, golf, and much more just minutes away. Start your day with an Alaskan-style breakfast and end it with a soothing soak in the outdoor hot tub. Handicap friendly.

Hosts: Jack and Cheryl Page
Rooms: 2 (1 PB;1 SB) $60-180
Full Breakfast
Credit Cards: A, B
Notes: 2, 5, 7, 9, 10

WASILLA

Snowed Inn

495 South Begich Drive, 99654
(907) 376-7495
E-mail: snowdinn@mtaonline.net

---

6 Pets welcome; 7 Children welcome; 8 Tennis nearby; 9 Swimming nearby; 10 Golf nearby; 11 Skiing nearby; 12 May be booked through travel agent

Snowed Inn is located in pristine Matanuska Valley just 40 minutes north of Anchorage. The Inn offers two large suites with private balconies and spectacular mountain views. Enjoy a hearty Alaskan sourdough breakfast prepared on a wood stove. Salmon fishing excursion may be booked on the Little Susitna River with a lifelong Alaskan. Experience the Iditarod Race Headquarters, walk on the Matanuska Glacier, go flight seeing from Talkeetna for awesome views of Denali.

Snowed Inn

Hosts: David and Charlotte Crockett
Rooms: 2 (1 PB; 2 SB) $75-125
Full Breakfast
Credit Cards: A, B
Notes: 5, 7, 8, 9, 10, 11, 12

Yukon Don's Bed & Breakfast Inn

1830 East Parks Highway # 386, 99654
(907) 376-7472; (800) 478-7472
fax: (907) 376-7470
E-mail: yukondon@alaska.net

When you're traveling in Alaska, or to and from Denali National Park, you don't want to miss staying at Yukon Don's B&B, "Alaska's most acclaimed bed and breakfast inn." Each spacious, comfortable guest room is decorated with authentic Alaskana. Stay in the Iditarod, Fishing, Denali, or Hunting Rooms, or select the Matanuska or Yukon executive suites. Our guests relax in the Alaska Room, complete with an Alaskan historic library, video library, pool table, cable TV, and gift bar. The all-glass-view room on the second floor offers a grand view in the Matanuska Valley, complete with fireplace, chairs, and observation deck. We provide phones in each room, Yukon Don's own expanded Continental breakfast bar, sauna, exercise room, and, according to Commissioner Glenn Olds (world traveler), "the grandest view ever seen from a home." Wasilla is home of the international Iditarod sled dog race.

Hosts: Yukon Don and Beverly
Rooms: 7 (3 PB; 4 SB) $79-125
Self-Serve Breakfast Bar
Credit Cards: A, B
Notes: 2, 5, 7, 10, 11, 12

NOTES: Credit cards accepted: A Master Card; B Visa; C American Express; D Discover; E Diners Club; F Other; 2 Personal checks accepted; 3 Lunch available; 4 Dinner available; 5 Open all year;

Arizona

FLAGSTAFF

Birch Tree Inn
Bed & Breakfast

824 W Birch Avenue, 86001-4420
(520) 774-1042; (888) 774-1042
fax: (520) 774-8462
E-mail: info@birchtreeinn.com
birchtreeinn.com

Situated in a cool Ponderosa Pine forest, this pristine white bungalow with blue shutters and trim is surrounded by an inviting wraparound veranda supported with Corinthian columns. The inn's guest rooms represent a variety of styles. A full breakfast and afternoon refreshments are served. Nearby are hiking trails and ski runs. Historic downtown Flagstaff is within walking distance for shops, restaurants, and entertainment. The Grand Canyon and Sedona are each an hour's drive away.

Hosts: Roder and Donna Pettinger;
  Sandy and Ed Zngtko
Rooms: 5 (3 PB; 2 SB) $69-119
Full Breakfast
Credit Cards: A, B, C, D
Notes: 5, 8, 10, 11, 12

Comfi Cottages
of Flagstaff

1612 North Aztec Street, 86001-1106
(928) 774-0731; (888) 774-0731
fax: (928) 773-7286
E-mail: pat@comficottages.com
www.comficottages.com

Perfect for a family vacation or a romantic weekend, Comfi Cottages are the "hub" of a relaxing getaway. The cottages are within walking distance of restaurants and shopping in historic downtown Flagstaff.

Hosts: Ed and Pat Wiebe
Rooms: 6 cottages (PB) $110-250
Full Breakfast
Credit Cards: A, B, D, F
Notes: 2, 5, 7, 8, 9, 10, 11, 12

Fall Inn to Nature

8080 North Colt Drive, 86004
phone/fax: (928) 714-0237; (888) 920-0237
E-mail: fallinn@infomagic.com
www.bbonline.com/az/fallinn/

The place with the personal touch— like visiting old friends! One-story cedar home sits on 2.5 acres with mountain views, pines, and the sounds of nature in a country setting. Small group tours to the Grand Canyon, in-house massage therapists. Winter special January-April. Hot tub, hiking, and horseback riding close by.

Hosts: Annette and Ron Fallaha
Rooms: 3 (2 PB; 1 SB) $65-95
Continental Breakfast
Credit Cards: A, B, C
Notes: 5, 7, 8, 10, 11, 12

---

6 Pets welcome; 7 Children welcome; 8 Tennis nearby; 9 Swimming nearby; 10 Golf nearby; 11 Skiing nearby; 12 May be booked through travel agent

ARIZONA

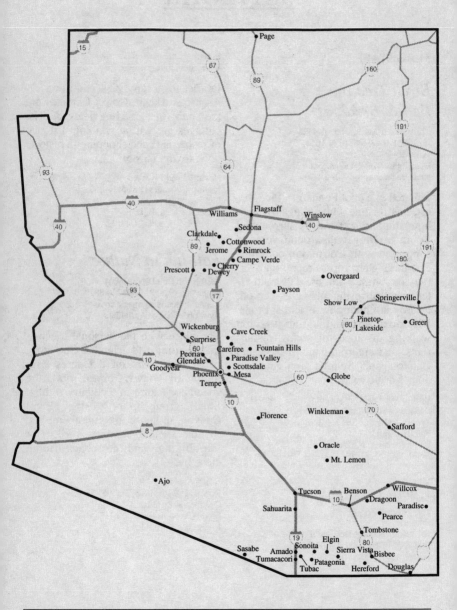

GREER

White Mountain Lodge

140 Main Street, P.O. Box 143, 85927-0143
(520) 735-7568; (800) 493-7568
fax: (520) 735-7498
E-mail: bast@cybertrails.com
www.wmlodge.com

White Mountain Lodge

This 1892 country home was remodeled in 1996. The common rooms reflect the home's Southwest heritage. Each bedroom is individually decorated with a king or queen bed and private bath. Overlooking a beautiful meadow and the Little Colorado River, and surrounded by pine and aspen-covered hills, the Lodge affords guests country hospitality, relaxation in the hot tub, and extraordinary, full breakfasts. The cabins are full housekeeping with fireplace and full kitchen. Some have whirlpool tubs.

Hosts: Charles and Mary Bast
Rooms: 13 (PB) $85-195
Full Breakfast
Credit Cards: A, B, C, D, E
Notes: 2, 3, 5, 7, 11, 12

SCOTTSDALE

La Paz in Desert Springs Bed & Breakfast

Scottsdale, AZ, 85254
(480) 922-0963; (888) 922-0963
fax: (480) 905-0085
E-mail: lapazindesertsprings@earthlink.net
www.lapazindesertsprings.com

Enjoy peace, comfort, and warm hospitality in this home B&B. Three guest accommodations are offered. The Arizona Suite with private entrance has a large master bedroom with king bed and private bath, living room with queen sleep sofa, an entertainment center with TV/VCR/cable, and a fully equipped kitchenette. The Desert Spring Room is furnished with a queen bed, and the Old West Room accommodates two in twin beds. These two rooms are located in the main part of the home and share a private hall bath. La Paz is ideally located in North Scottsdale within 20 minutes of downtown Phoenix and the airport. Continental-plus breakfast includes fruit, homemade breads, yogurt, and granola. Full breakfast on weekends with additional Southwestern dishes. Complimentary snacks of fruit, cookies, hot tea, and coffee. Reservations required. No smoking.

Hosts: Luis and Susan Cuevas
Rooms: 3 (1PB; 2SB) $65-175
Full Breakfast
Credit Cards: A, B, C
Notes: 2, 5, 7, 8, 9, 10, 11, 12

6 Pets welcome; 7 Children welcome; 8 Tennis nearby; 9 Swimming nearby; 10 Golf nearby; 11 Skiing nearby; 12 May be booked through travel agent

SEDONA

Boots & Saddles Bed & Breakfast

2900 Hopi Drive, 86336-3731
(928) 282-1944; (800) 201-1944
fax: (928) 204-2230
E-mail: oldwest@sedona.net
www.oldwestbb.com

Sedona's Western B&B in the shadow of Thunder Mountain and Chimney Rock offers rooms with Western elegance. Rooms include jetted tubs, fireplaces, unique Western décor, wonderful red rock views, full gourmet breakfast, and afternoon refreshments. Tour, horseback, and golf packages available.

Hosts: John and Linda Steele
Rooms: 4 (PB) $135-225
Full Breakfast
Credit Cards: A, B, C, D
Notes: 2, 5, 7, 8, 9, 10, 11, 12

The Lodge at Sedona

125 Kallof Place, 86336-5566
(928) 204-1942; (800) 619-4467
fax: (928) 204-2128
E-mail: lodge@sedona.net
www.lodgeatsedona.com

Originally home to Sedona's first doctor, later owned by Rev. Don Roberts, the lodge offers peaceful seclusion in the heart of Sedona. It's wooded acres include gardens, lawns, red rock views, sculptures, and an on-site labyrinth garden pathway. Beautifully appointed rooms include decks, fireplaces, and Jacuzzis. A full gourmet breakfast is served on a sunny porch with appetizers and desserts following later in the day.

Hosts: Barb and Mark Dinunzio
Rooms: 14 (PB) $130-260
Full Breakfast
Credit Cards: A, B, C, D, E
Notes: 2, 5, 7, 9, 10, 12

Territorial House: An Old West Bed & Breakfast

65 Piki Drive, 86336
(520) 204-2737
E-mail: oldwest@sedona.net
www.oldwestbb.com

Our large stone and cedar house has been tastefully decorated to depict Arizona's territorial era. Each room recalls different stages of Sedona's early history. Some rooms have a private balcony, Jacuzzi tub, or fireplace. An enormous stone fireplace graces the living room, and a covered veranda welcomes guests at the end of a day of sight-seeing. Relax in our outdoor hot tub. A full, hearty breakfast is served at the harvest table each morning. All of this is served with Western hospitality.

Hosts: John and Linda Steele
Rooms: 4 (PB) $115-185
Full Breakfast
Credit Cards: A, B, C, D
Notes: 2, 5, 7, 8, 9, 10, 11, 12

TEMPE

Valley o' the Sun Bed & Breakfast

P.O. Box 2214, Scottsdale, 85252
phone/fax: (480) 941-1281; (866) 941-1281
E-mail: bnb@valleyothesunbnb.com
www.valleyothesunbnb.com

NOTES: Credit cards accepted: A Master Card; B Visa; C American Express; D Discover; E Diners Club; F Other; 2 Personal checks accepted; 3 Lunch available; 4 Dinner available; 5 Open all year;

Established in 1983, "Arizona's only Irish B&B" is ideally located in the college area of Tempe, within walking distance of Arizona State University. Close to Phoenix and Scottsdale, and within minutes of golf, horseback riding, and more. Airport is only 15 minutes away.

Valley o' the Sun

Host: Kathleen K. Curtis
Rooms: 3 (1 PB; 2 SB) $45-60
Continental Breakfast
Credit Cards: C, D
Notes: 2, 5, 7, 8, 9, 10

TUCSON

Casa Alegre B & B

316 East Speedway Boulevard, 85705-7429
(520) 628-1800; (800) 628-5654
fax: (520) 792-1880
E-mail: alegre123.aol.com
www.casaalegreinn.com

Casa Alegre is a sprawling 1915 Arts and Crafts bungalow where your comfort is foremost and where you always feel welcome. Whether you want to be a part of lively conversation with other guests, or curl up with your favorite book, your wishes will be fulfilled. Our serene gardens, pool, and hot tub make "an oasis of comfort in central Tucson," just minutes from the University of Arizona. Looking forward to seeing you at Casa Alegre.

Host: Phyllis Florek
Rooms: 6 (PB) $80-135
Full Breakfast
Credit Cards: A, B, D
Notes: 2, 5, 8, 9, 10, 12

Copper-Bell Bed & Breakfast Inn

25 North Westmoreland Avenue, 85745
(520) 629-9229; fax: (520) 629-9229

Copper Bell B&B is a unique turn-of-the-century lava stone home which was built 1907 providing a unique blend of architectural styles. The owner relocated here from Germany (French border). He has created the inn by combining the Old World with the New. Four of the eight guest rooms have ground-level entry. Each has a private bath. A private honeymoon suite is available. Guests will enjoy the homemade German breakfast in the large and sunny dining room. Come celebrate the inn's 10th-year anniversary.

Host: Gertrude M Eich
Rooms: 8 (6 PB; 2 SB) $79-95
Full Breakfast
Credit Cards: None
Notes: 2, 5, 7, 8, 9, 10

El Presidio Bed & Breakfast Inn

297 North Main Avenue, 85701-8219
(520) 623-6151; (800) 349-6151
fax: (520) 349-6151
www.bbonline.com/az/elpresidio/

6 Pets welcome; 7 Children welcome; 8 Tennis nearby; 9 Swimming nearby; 10 Golf nearby; 11 Skiing nearby; 12 May be booked through travel agent

This luxury B&B in a historic Victorian adobe mansion circa 1880, is listed on the National Register in the El Presidio historic district with restaurants, shops, and museums

El Presidio

nearby. Lush garden courtyards with old-Mexico ambience surround three richly appointed suites. Gourmet breakfasts, complimentary beverages and snacks, private baths, TVs, phones, and antique décor. AAA three-star, Mobil three-diamond, awarded Best B&B in Southern Arizona, *Zagat Survey*—"one of best B&Bs in USA."

Host: Patti Toci
Rooms: 4 (PB) $95-125
Full Breakfast
Credit Cards: None
Notes: 2, 5, 8, 9, 10, 12

Hacienda
Bed & Breakfast

5704 East Grant Road, 85712-2235
(520) 290-2224; (888) 236-4421
fax: (520) 721-9066
E-mail: info@tucsonhacienda.com
www.tucsonhacienda.com

Disconnect from the world in this peaceful B&B. Enjoy quiet time in the patio, pool, spa, or large sitting rooms where you can sit and listen to music while you visit or read. Unwind in the exercise room. Make some memories while swimming in the pool and waiting for the stars to make their appearance. Relax a while before that important meeting. The central location provides easy access for any schedule.

Hosts: Barbara and Fred Shamseldin
Rooms: 6 (PB) $85-125
Full Breakfast
Credit Cards: A, B, C, D, E
Notes: 2, 5, 7, 8, 10, 11, 12

Jeremiah Inn
Bed & Breakfast, Ltd.

10921 East Snyder Road, 85749-9066
(520) 749-3072; (888) 750-3072
E-mail: jeremiahinn@juno.com
www.bbonline.com/az/jeremiah

"Oh, that I had in the desert a lodging place for travelers"—Jeremiah 9:29. This Santa Fe-style contemporary sits on 3.3 tranquil desert acres in the foothills of the Catalina Mountains. Spectacular mountain views, spacious accommodations, delightful breakfasts, inn-baked cookies, pool and spa will welcome you. Hike, bird, golf, or visit Kartchner Caverns and be refreshed.

Hosts: Robert and Beth Miner
Rooms: 5 (PB) $90-125
Full Breakfast
Credit Cards: A, B, C
Notes: 2, 5, 7, 8, 9, 10, 11, 12

Arkansas

BENTONVILLE

Tudor House at the Oak

806 N W, 72712
(501) 273-2200
E-mail: tudorhouse@nwa.quik.com
www.tudorplace.com

We pamper you! Feel the warmth of genuine friendship, savor specialty breakfasts, stroll thorugh flower gardens and woods. The Tudor House features guest bedrooms in a private wing, shared luxury bath, gathering room with a classic movie collection, and a quartz crystal fireplace in the elegant living room. Built in the early '20s, this recently remodeled stone home is full of international artifacts and antiques. In the area, visit the WalMart Museum and University of Arkansas, shop at craft fairs, choose from 21 golf courses, go fishing or horseback riding. A short drive brings you to Eureka Springs, Precious Moments in Carthage, Missouri, or Branson, Missouri.

Hosts: Leland and Linda Long
Rooms: 3 (1 PB; 2 SB) $50-75
Full Breakfast
Credit Cards: A, B
Notes: 2, 5, 8, 9, 10, 12

CALICO ROCK

Happy Lonesome Log Cabins

1444 Forest Home Lane, 72519-9102
(870) 297-8764 (phone/fax)
E-mail: hlcabins@centurytel.net
www.bbonline.com/ar/hlcabins

Unhosted, secluded comfort and charm, surrounded by Ozark National Forest. Cabins are provided with milk, juice, cereal, coffee, and homemade bread. Each cabin has a comfortable sleeping loft, bath, wood stove, air-conditioning, dishes, and linens. Outdoor grill, covered porch with swing or double rocker, and beautiful view of the White River Valley from the 200-foot bluff location. Handicapped-accessible cabin under construction.

Rooms: 4 (4 PB; 6 SB) $65-125
Continental Breakfast
Credit Cards: A, B, C, F
Notes: 2, 7, 8, 9, 10, 12

EUREKA SPRINGS

Beaver Lake Bed & Breakfast

1234 County Road 120, 72631-8958
(501) 235-9210; (888) 253-9210
E-mail: beaverbb@ipa.net
www.beaverlakebb.com

Secluded nine acres on pristine Beaver Lake in the Ozark Mountains. Fifteen minutes from the many attractions in historic Eureka Springs. Casual, comfortable country home decorated with unique antiques. Four guest rooms all with incredible lake views and private bathrooms. Full

ARKANSAS

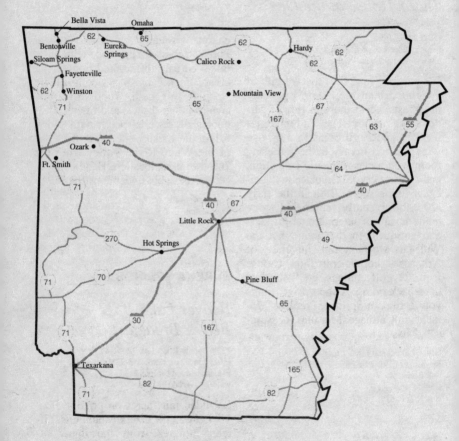

breakfast every morning. Private boat dock for fishing, swimming, and snorkeling. Abundant wildlife and nature trails. Knowledgeable, friendly innkeepers. Sorry, no smoking, children, or pets permitted.

Hosts: David and Elaine Reppel
Rooms: 4 (PB) $85-105
Full Breakfast
Credit Cards: A, B, D
Notes: 2, 9, 10

Bonnybrooke Farm Atop Misty Mountain

361 County Road 117, 72631-9544
(501) 253-6903
www.bonnybrooke.apexhosting.com

If your heart's in the country—or longs to be—we invite you to share the sweet quiet and serenity that await you in your place to come home to. We offer five cottages, each distinctly different in its tempting pleasures. Fireplace and Jacuzzi for two, full glass fronts and mountaintop views, shower under the stars, wicker porch swing in front of the fireplace. . . you're gonna love it! In order to preserve privacy the location is given to registered guests only. Bonnybrooke Farm was featured as the most ro-

mantic accommodation in Arkansas (*Country Heart Magazine*).

Hosts: Bonny and Josh
Rooms: 5 (PB) $125-185
Continental Breakfast
Credit Cards: None
Notes: 2, 5, 9, 12

1884 Bridgeford House Bed & Breakfast

263 Spring Street, 72632
(501) 253-7853; (888) 567-2422
fax (501) 253-5497
E-mail: henry@bridgefordhouse.com
www.bridgefordhouse.com

Where beauty and hospitality exceed expectations! Short relaxing stroll to shops, spas, restaurants, and galleries. Antiques, Jacuzzis, horse-drawn carriage/trolley route, queen/king beds, fireplaces, great packages, Southern-style breakfast, and romantic weddings. Our "Secret Garden" was recently honored with Garden of the Season. Southern hospitality combined with Victorian charm await you. Children over eight welcome.

Hosts: Linda and Henry Thornton
Rooms: 5 (PB) $95-150
Full Breakfast
Credit Cards: A, B, C, D
Notes: 5, 7, 9, 10, 12

11 Singleton House Bed & Breakfast

11 Singleton Street, 72632-3026
(501) 253-9111; (800) 833-3394
E-mail: info@singletonhouse.com
www.singletonhouse.com

This old-fashioned Victorian house is whimsically decorated and has an eclectic collection of treasures and antiques. All rooms include private baths, cable TV, and air-conditioning. Some suites have two beds. Breakfast is served on the balcony overlooking stony paths, fragrant wildflower gardens, and a lily-filled pond. Guests walk one block down a scenic wooded footpath to historic district shops and cafes. Passion Play and Holy Land tour reservations can be arranged. Ask about our Gardener's Cottage at a separate private location with its treetop porch, hammock, swing, Jacuzzi-for-two, and gas log fireplace. The 11 Singleton House has been featured in more than sixteen B&B guidebooks. We are currently celebrating our 19th year as a B&B in Eureka.

Gardner's Cottage

Play, the Gardener's Cottage features country décor, cathedral ceilings, skylight, full kitchen, gas-log fireplace, and a romantic Jacuzzi-for-two. The treetop porch with its hammock and swing is perfect for relaxing moments. Great for honeymooners or a long, peaceful stay. Ask about optional breakfast.

Host: Barbara Gavron
Rooms: 1 (PB) $125-145
Credit Cards: A, B, C, D, F
Notes: 2, 9, 10, 11

Heartstone Inn
Bed & Breakfast Cottages

35 Kingshighway, 72632-3534
(501) 253-8916; (800) 494-4921
fax: (501) 253-5361
E-mail: heartinn@ipa.net
www.heartstoneinn.com

11 Singleton House

Host: Barbara Gavron
Rooms: 5 (PB) $65-125
Full Breakfast
Credit Cards: A, B, C, D, F
Notes: 2, 9, 10, 11

Gardener's Cottage

11 Singleton Street, 72632-3026
(501) 253-9111; (800) 833-3394
E-mail: info@singletonhouse.com
www.singletonhouse.com

Tucked away in a wooded historic district valley close to the Passion

Heartstone Inn

NOTES: Credit cards accepted: A Master Card; B Visa; C American Express; D Discover; E Diners Club; F Other; 2 Personal checks accepted; 3 Lunch available; 4 Dinner available; 5 Open all year;

An award-winning inn with all private baths, private entrances, king and queen beds, and cable TV. Furnished with antiques galore, the inn offers a renowned gourmet breakfast, in-house massage therapy studio, and golf privileges. You'll find large decks and a gazebo under the trees—great for bird-watching. Recommended by the *New York Times, Country Home* magazine, *America's Wonderful Little Hotels and Inns, Recommended Inns of the South,* and many more. We are closed Christmas through January.

Hosts: Rick and Cheri Rojek
Rooms: 12 (PB) $75-134
Full Breakfast
Credit Cards: A, B, C, D
Notes: 2, 10, 12

1908 Ridgeway House Bed & Breakfast

28 Ridgeway Avenue, 72632
(479) 253-6618; (877) 501-2501
E-mail: rheureka@ipa.net
www.ridgewayhouse.com

Just the right combination of pampering and privacy. Historic district, luxurious rooms, antiques, wonderfully quiet street within walking distance of shops, incredible breakfasts, and desserts. Trolley just a block away, porches, decks, private Jacuzzi suites, and packages available. Will build custom package. Small weddings, complimentary cold and hot beverages. All of our guests are VIPs!

Hosts: Gayla and Keith Hubbard
Rooms: 5 (PB) $89-149
Full Breakfast
Credit Cards: A, B, D, F
Notes: 2, 5, 12

FAYETTEVILLE

Hill Avenue Bed & Breakfast

131 South Hill Avenue, 72701
(501) 444-0865

Hill Avenue

This century-old inn is located in a residential neighborhood near the University of Arkansas, Walton Art Center, and the Bud Walton Arena. The accommodations are smoke-free and feature king beds and private baths.

Hosts: Cecelia and Dale Thompson
Rooms: 3 (PB) $70
Continental Breakfast
Credit Cards: None
Notes: 2, 5

LITTLE ROCK

The Empress of Little Rock

2120 South Louisiana, 72206
(501) 374-7966; (877) 374-7966
fax: (501) 375-4537
E-mail: hostess@theempress.com
www.theempress.com

---

6 Pets welcome; 7 Children welcome; 8 Tennis nearby; 9 Swimming nearby; 10 Golf nearby; 11 Skiing nearby; 12 May be booked through travel agent

The Hornibrook Mansion, completed in 1888, has been described by the National Historic Register as the best example of ornate Gothic Victorian Queen Anne style in Arkansas and the surrounding region. It boasts a magnificent divided stairway, a three and a half story tower, eight-foot stained glass skylight, six original Eastlake fireplaces, and octagonal shaped rooms, all of which create a massive structure representing late-nineteenth-century architecture in its most flamboyant style. Step back in time, while taking a break from your everyday. Breakfast smells beckon you to a leisurely two-course breakfast served by candlelight where easy conversation epitomizes true Southern hospitality.

Hosts: Robert H Blair and Sharon Welch-Blair
Rooms: 5 (PB) $125-195
Full Breakfast
Credit Cards: A, B, C
Notes: 2, 5, 8, 9, 10, 12

OMAHA

Aunt Shirley's Sleeping Loft

7250 Shirley Lane North, 72662
(870) 426-5408; E-mail: shirleys@omahawcb.net
www.auntshirleysloft.com

Quiet, relaxed atmosphere. Rustic country setting with the convenience of home. Air-conditioning, private bath, clean. Beautiful view with walkways, patio. Gas grill, campfires available. Swings under the trees. Big country breakfast, lots of Southern hospitality. Children welcome. Located 10 miles north of Harrison, 24 miles south of Branson, Missouri. Near Eureka Springs, Buffalo River, Tablerock Lake, Bull Shoals Lake. Member of Harrison Chamber of Commerce.

Hosts: Buddy and Shirley Lebleu
Rooms: 3 (PB) $60
Full Breakfast
Credit Cards: A, B
Notes: 2, 5, 6, 7, 9, 10

SILOAM SPRINGS

Apple Crest Inn Bed & Breakfast

12758 South Highway 59, 72734
(501) 736-8201; (888) APPLE-US
fax: (501) 736-5742
E-mail: applecrestinn@tcainternet.com
www.bbonline.com/ar/applecrest

Apple Crest Inn

A Victorian home and carriage house nestled on five rural acres in a historical area the locals call "Sleepy Hollow." The home has six guest rooms, all spacious, with TV/VCRs, and private baths. King, queen, or twin bed suites all have sitting areas, and Jacuzzi or antique tubs and showers. Filled with stained glass and antiques, the Inn offers quiet relaxation with close proximity to canoeing, golf, hiking, antique shopping, craft festivals, John Brown University, the University of Arkansas, and the WalMart Headquarters. Apple Crest Inn is AAA rated three diamonds and featured in *Country Magazine*.

Hosts: Gary and Dianne Affolter
Rooms: 6 (PB) $100-150
Full Breakfast
Credit Cards: A, B, C, D
Notes: 2, 5, 6, 7, 10

6 Pets welcome; 7 Children welcome; 8 Tennis nearby; 9 Swimming nearby; 10 Golf nearby; 11 Skiing nearby; 12 May be booked through travel agent

CALIFORNIA

San Francisco Area

Los Angeles Area

Catalina Island

California

APTOS

Apple Lane Inn

6265 Soquel Drive, 95003
(831) 475-6868; (800) 649-8988;
fax: (831) 464-5790; E-mail: ali@cruzio.com
www.apolelaneinn.com

Apple Lane Inn is a historic Victorian farmhouse built in the 1870s with two and one half acres of fields, gardens and apple orchards. Just minutes south of Santa Cruz, the quiet country feeling has been crowned with a Victorian gazebo perched amid trim lawns and flowering gardens.

Host: Lori Hamilton
Rooms: 5 (PB) $120-200
Full Breakfast
Credit Cards: A, B, C, D
Notes: 2, 5, 6, 7, 8, 9, 10, 12

AUBURN

Power's Mansion Inn

164 Cleveland Avenue, 95603-4801
(530) 885-1166; fax: (530) 885-1386
E-mail: powerinn@westsierra.net
www.vfr.net/~powerinn/

An elegant B&B in the heart of the Gold Country. Built from a gold-mining fortune in 1898, and lovingly restored to its original Victorian grandeur by its owners, the landmark Power's Mansion offers visitors the hospitality of a country inn and the attentive service of a small, elegant European hotel.

Hosts: Arno and Jean Lejniers
Rooms: 13 (PB)
Full Breakfast
Credit Cards: A, B, C
Notes: 2, 5, 7, 8, 10, 11, 12

BEN LOMOND

Chateau Des Fleurs

7995 Highway 9, 95005-9715
(831) 336-8943; (800) 291-9966
E-mail: laura@chateaudesfleurs.com
www.chateaudesfleurs.com

Do you want Victorian elegance? Do you want a romantic hideaway? Do you want peace and serenity of the redwoods while still only minutes from Santa Cruz beaches? Come to Chateau des Fleurs. Our guest rooms have private baths and king- and queen-size beds with cozy down comforters. Air conditioning and fireplaces. Breakfast is full, fresh, and filling. Explore our quaint mountain community, hike in local state parks, play horse shoes at the Chateau. Come, let us pamper you.

Hosts: Lee and Laura Jonas
Rooms: 5 (PB)
Full Breakfast
Credit Cards: A, B, D
Notes: 2, 5, 7, 8, 9, 10

---

6 Pets welcome; 7 Children welcome; 8 Tennis nearby; 9 Swimming nearby; 10 Golf nearby; 11 Skiing nearby; 12 May be booked through travel agent

CALISTOGA

Foothill House

3037 Foothill Boulevard, 94515-1225
(707) 942-6933; (800) 942-6933
fax: (707) 942-5692
E-mail: gus@calicom.net
www.foothillhouse.com

"The romantic inn of the Napa Valley," according to the *Chicago Tribune* travel editor. Foothill House offers spacious suites individually decorated with antiques. All suites have private baths and entrances, fireplaces, small refrigerators, and air-conditioning. Some suites have Jacuzzis. A luxurious cottage is also available. A gourmet breakfast is served each morning; appetizers and refreshments each evening. Foothill House received the American Bed & Breakfast Association's highest award for 1997 and 1998 (four crowns—placing it in the top 5 percent in the U.S.). Spas, restaurants, and wineries are nearby.

Hosts: Doris and Gus Beckert
Rooms: 3 suites (PB); 1 cottage (PB) $175-325
Full Breakfast
Credit Cards: A, B, C, D
Notes: 2, 5, 8, 10, 12

Hillcrest Country Inn

3225 Lake County Highway, 94515-9738
(707) 942-6334; fax: (707) 942-3955
www.bnbweb.com/hillcrest

"Million Dollar view" secluded hilltop home overlooking lush wine country with swimming, hiking, and fishing on 40 acres. Rooms have fireplaces, Jacuzzi tubs for two, and TVs. House is decorated with heirlooms from family mansion which burned to the ground. Land family-owned since 1860. On-call masseur, trampoline, barbeque area, large pool, and fishing pond with canoe. Nearby wineries, spas, balloon rides, horseback riding, petrified forest, Old Faithful geyser, restaurants, shopping, and bike rentals.

Host: Debbie O' Gorman
Rooms: 6 (4 PB; 2 SB) $75-175
Continental Breakfast
Credit Cards: None
Notes: 2, 5, 6, 7, 8, 9, 10, 11, 12

Hillcrest Country Inn

Scarlett's Country Inn

3918 Silverado Trail, 94515
(707) 942-6669; fax: (707) 942-6669
E-mail: scarletts@aol.com
members.aol.com/scarletts

Three exquisitely appointed suites set in the quiet mood of green lawn and tall pines overlooking the famed Napa Valley vineyards. Seclusion, romance, queen beds, private baths, antiques, fireplace, air-conditioning, secluded woodland swimming pool. Phone and television available in rooms on request. Home-baked breakfast and afternoon refreshments served in rooms or under the apple trees by the pool.

Scarlett's Country Inn

Close to wineries and spas. Children welcome at no charge.

Host: Scarlett Dwyer
Rooms: 3 (PB; 70 SB) $135-205
Full Breakfast
Credit Cards: None
Notes: 2, 5, 7, 8, 9, 10, 12

CAMBRIA

The Pickford House Bed & Breakfast

2555 MacLeod Way, 93428
(805) 927-8619; (888) 270-8470

The Pickford House

fax: (805) 927-8016
www.thepickfordhouse.com

A romantic exquisite country inn, decorated in the style of 1920s, each room memorializing an early star of Hollywood films who visited the nearby Hearst Castle. Three rooms with fireplaces; fabulous saloon type dining room with 1860s bar reserved for guests only. This rustic Victorian mansion lends itself to a family, business, or church retreat; it will sleep 20. Non-smoking.

Rooms: 8 (PB) $125-165
Full Breakfast
Credit Cards: A, B, C, D
Notes: 2, 5, 7, 8, 9, 10, 12

CARMEL

Green Lantern Inn

Seventh and Casanova; P.O. Box 1114, 93921
(831) 624-4392; (888) 414-4392
fax: (831) 624-9591
E-mail: info@greenlanterninn.com
www.greenlanterninn.com

Charming historic property, a country garden inn by the sea with 18 guest rooms, all with private entrances and private baths. Easy five-minute walk to White Sand Beach; restaurants and shopping are also a five-minute walk. Delicious buffet-style breakfast and afternoon tea included.

Host: Sandy Moore
Rooms: 18 (PB)
Continental Breakfast
Credit Cards: None
Notes: 5, 7, 9, 10, 12

ESCONDIDO

The Parsonage Bed & Breakfast

239 South Maple Street, 92025-4120
(760) 741-9160; fax: (760) 741-2630
E-mail: parsonage5@juno.com

The Parsonage

Built in 1910 as the parsonage of the First Congregational Church, this home has been restored to its original glory. Relax in a claw-foot tub, sleep on queen beds (down comforters and feather beds are available upon request), and enjoy dessert every evening on the front porch. The Parsonage is within 30 minutes of all San Diego attractions, and within walking distance of the California Center for the Arts, fine restaurants, and antique stores. Children over 12 welcome.

Hosts: Robert and Ann McQuead
Rooms: 3 (1 PB; 2 SB) $95-105
Full Breakfast
Credit Cards: None
Notes: 2, 5, 7, 8, 9, 10

EUREKA

Abigail's "Elegant Victorian Mansion" Bed & Breakfast Lodging Accommodations

1406 C Street, 95501-1765
(707) 444-3144; fax (707) 442-3295
E-mail: info@eureka-california.com
www.eureka-california.com

An award-winning, 1888 National Historic landmark of opulence, grace, and grandeur featuring spectacular gingerbread exteriors, Victorian interiors, and antique furnishings. Available exclusively for the nonsmoking traveler, this is a "living history house-museum" for the discriminating connoisseur of authentic Victorian décor who also has a passion for quality, service, and the extraordinary. Indulge in four-star luxury. With complimentary exciting horseless carriage rides, bicycles, sauna, and laundry service, the inn is recommended by AAA, Mobil, Fodor's, and more. Arthur Frommer calls it "the very best that California has to offer—not to be missed."

Abigail's "Elegant Victorian Mansion"

NOTES: Credit cards accepted: A Master Card; B Visa; C American Express; D Discover; E Diners Club; F Other; 2 Personal checks accepted; 3 Lunch available; 4 Dinner available; 5 Open all year;

Hosts: Doug and Lily Vierra
Rooms: 3 (1 PB; 2 SB) $85-215
Full Breakfast
Credit Cards: A, B
Notes: 5, 8, 10, 12

FERNDALE

The Gingerbread Mansion Inn

400 Berding Street, P.O. Box 40, 95536-1380
(707) 786-4000; (800) 952-4136
fax: (707) 786-4381
E-mail: innkeeper@gingerbread-mansion.com
www.gingerbread-mansion.com

Nestled between giant redwoods and the rugged Pacific Coast is one of California's best-kept secrets: the Victorian village of Ferndale. A state historic landmark listed on the National Historic Register, Ferndale is a community frozen in time, with Victorian homes and shops relatively unchanged since their construction in the mid-to-late 1800s. One of Ferndale's best-known homes is the Gingerbread Mansion Inn. Decorated with antiques, the romantic guest rooms offer private baths, some with old-fashioned claw-foot tubs, and fireplaces. Also included is a full breakfast, high tea, four parlors, and formal English gardens. Rated four diamonds by AAA.

Host: Kenneth Torbert
Rooms: 11 (PB) $150-385
Full Breakfast
Credit Cards: A, B, C
Notes: 2, 5, 7, 10, 12

FORT BRAGG

Avalon House

561 Stewart Street, 95437
(707) 964-5555; (800) 964-5556
E-mail: anne@theavalonhouse.com
www.theavalonhouse.com

A 1905 Craftsman home in a quiet residential neighborhood, three blocks from the ocean and two blocks from the Skunk Train. Rooms with private baths, fireplaces, whirlpool tubs, down comforters, and ocean views. Enjoy all the romance of the Mendocino Coast, even if you never leave your room. No smoking allowed.

Avalon House

Host: Anne Sorrells
Rooms: 6 (PB) $85-155
Full Breakfast
Credit Cards: A, B, C, E
Notes: 2, 5, 7, 8, 10, 12

Grey Whale Inn

615 North Main Street, 95437-3240
(707) 964-0640; (800) 382-7244
fax: (707) 964-4408
E-mail: stay@greywhaleinn.com
www.greywhaleinn.com

Handsome, four-story, Mendocino Coast landmark since 1915. From

---

6 Pets welcome; 7 Children welcome; 8 Tennis nearby; 9 Swimming nearby; 10 Golf nearby; 11 Skiing nearby; 12 May be booked through travel agent

cozy to expansive, all rooms have private bath, phone, TV, and coffeemaker, and offer ocean, garden, hill or town views. Some rooms have fireplaces and VCRs; one with double Jacuzzi tub. Common areas include recreation area with pool table, library, TV/VCR room, fireside lounge, and 16-person conference room. Full buffet breakfast. Friendly, helpful staff. Located six blocks from the ocean and two blocks from shops, galleries, and Skunk Train.

Grey Whale Inn

Hosts: Colette and John Bailey
Rooms: 14 (PB) $100-200
Full Breakfast
Credit Cards: A, B, C, D
Notes: 2, 5, 8, 9, 10, 12

The Weller House

524 Stewart Street, 95437
(707) 964-4415; (877) 8WELLER
fax: (707) 964-4198
E-mail: innkeeper@wellerhouse.com
www.wellerhouse.com

In addition to the stunning Weller House ballroom and statue-filled English gardens, each guest room is individually special. Each of the eight guest rooms offer comfort and privacy. Hand-painted tiles, marble, and fireplaces, beautiful stained glass,

The Weller House

fluffy down comforters, and other thoughtful details result in a luxurious escape. Each and every guest enjoys a sumptuous breakfast in the Weller House ballroom.

Hosts: Eva and Ted Kidwell
Rooms: 8 (PB)
Full Breakfast
Credit Cards: A, B, C, D
Notes: 2, 5

GEORGETOWN
(GOLD COUNTRY)

American River Inn

Orleans and Main, P.O. Box 43, 95634-0043
(530) 333-4499; (800) 245-6566
fax: (530) 333-9253
E-mail: ariinnkeeper@aol.com
www.americanriverinn.com

American River Inn

The innkeepers carry on the century-old tradition of graciousness in a setting far removed from the fast pace of modern living. Cool off in a beautiful mountain pool or relax in the spa. Choose a day of bicycling amid the colorful, breathtaking daffodils, irises, and yellow-gold scotch broom; bicycles are provided. The historic Queen Anne inn specializes in ladies' and couples' retreats, and seminars and corporate meetings of fifteen to forty people. We will arrange white-water rafting and kyack trips.

Hosts: Will and Maria and Betty
Rooms: 15 (7 PB; 8 SB) $90-125
Full Breakfast
Credit Cards: A, B, C, D
Notes: 2, 5, 7, 8, 9, 10, 11, 12

Elam Biggs

GRASS VALLEY

Elam Biggs
Bed & Breakfast

220 Colfax Avenue, 95945
(530) 477-0906
www.virtualcities.com/ons/ca/g/cag1601.htm

This beautiful, 1892 Queen Anne Victorian is set amidst a large yard surrounded by grand shade trees and a rose-covered picket fence. It's just a short stroll from historic, downtown Grass Valley. In the morning, enjoy brewed coffee and a hearty breakfast served in the lovely dining room, or outside on the private porch.

Hosts: Barbara and Peter Franchino
Rooms: 5 (PB) $85-120
Full Breakfast
Credit Cards: A, B, C
Notes: 2, 5, 7, 8, 9, 10, 11, 12

GUALALA

North Coast Country Inn

34591 South Highway 1, 95445-9515
(707) 884-4537; (800) 959-4537
fax: (707) 884-1833; E-mail: ncci@mcn.org
www.northcoastcountryinn.com

On California's wild and beautiful North Coast, this cluster of redwood buildings, nestled into a forested hillside, is a haven to be returned to again and again. Guest rooms have king- or queen-size bed, fireplaces, dining areas, private bathrooms, and sitting areas, each elegantly appointed with antiques, art treasures, and memorabilia. Towering redwood and pine trees, a perfect setting for small wed-

North Coast Country Inn

dings, surround the gardens. Full gourmet breakfast. Hot tub. Golf, hiking, fishing, and beaches are nearby.

Hosts: Maureen and Bill Shupe
Rooms: 6 (PB) $175-195
Full Breakfast
Credit Cards: A, B, C
Notes: 2, 5, 8, 9, 10, 12

HALF MOON BAY

Old Thyme Inn

779 Main Street, 94019-1924
(650) 726-1616; (800) 720-4277
fax: (650) 726-6394
E-mail: innkeeper@oldthymeinn.com
www.oldthymeinn.com

You'll spend enchanted nights in our "Princess Anne" 1898 Victorian B&B. A lush and fragrant herb and flower garden provides a tranquil setting for romance, rest, and relaxation, or pleasant conversation beside gurgling fountains. The inn is furnished in antiques and the innkeepers' collection of fine art. We offer seven guest rooms, each with queen bed with featherbed and down comforter, cable TV/VCR, dataport, and private bath. Some rooms offer Jacuzzi and/or fireplace. Delectable full breakfast.

Hosts: Rick and Kathy Ellis
Rooms: 7 (PB) $130-290
Full Breakfast
Credit Cards: A, B, C, D, E
Notes: 2, 5, 9, 10, 12

JAMESTOWN

Palm Hotel
Bed & Breakfast

10382 Willow Street, 95327
(209) 984-3429; (888) 551-1852
fax: (209) 984-4929
E-mail: innkeeper@palmhotel.com
www.palmhotel.com

More home than hotel, this Gold Country Victorian offers eight guest rooms with private bath, lacy curtains, fresh flowers, claw-foot tubs, marble showers, and robes. Air-conditioning, in-room TV, and handicapped-accessibility. A full breakfast along with the Palm's special blend of coffee is served daily in the parlor. The Palm is located two and a half hours from San Francisco, about an hour from Yosemite Park's north entrance, and is within walking distance of Main Street shops, restaurants, and Railtown State Park. Guest comment from journal: "The simple elegance of our room and ambience of the Palm in general was a balm for our souls."

Hosts: Rick and Sandy Allen
Rooms: 8 (PB) $95-155
Full Breakfast
Credit Cards: A, B, C
Notes: 5, 7, 10, 11, 12

NOTES: Credit cards accepted: A Master Card; B Visa; C American Express; D Discover; E Diners Club; F Other; 2 Personal checks accepted; 3 Lunch available; 4 Dinner available; 5 Open all year;

JULIAN

Butterfield's Bed & Breakfast

2284 Sunset Drive, P.O. Box 1115, 92036-9447
(760) 765-2179; (800) 379-4262
fax: (760) 765-1229
E-mail: butterfield@abac.com
www.butterfieldbandb.com

Enjoy yourself and relax on our three-acre country garden sitting in the quiet hills of Julian. Rest under the oaks, walk among the dozens of roses and bonsai, and retreat to your unique room each night. Five rooms are offered; three with fireplaces or woodstove. Gourmet breakfast is served in the gazebo every morning during the warmth of summer, and by a crackling fireplace in winter.

Hosts: Ed and Dawn Glass
Rooms: 5 (PB) $130-180
Full Breakfast
Credit Cards: A, B, C
Notes: 2, 5, 7, 12

KERNVILLE

Kern River Inn Bed & Breakfast

119 Kern River Drive, P.O. Box 1725, 93238-1725
(760) 376-6750; (800) 986-4382
fax (760) 376-6643
E-mail: kernriverinn@lightspeed.net
www.virtualcities.com/ons/ca/s/cas3501.htm

A charming, classic country riverfront B&B located on the wild and scenic Kern River in the quaint little town of Kernville within the Sequoia National Forest in the southern Sierra Mountains. We specialize in romantic getaways. All guest rooms have private baths and feature river views; some have fireplaces and whirlpool tubs. A full breakfast is served. Within walking distance of restaurants, shops, parks, and the museum, and just a short drive to giant redwood trees. This is an all-year vacation area with white-water rafting, hiking, fishing, biking, skiing, and Lake Isabella water activities.

Hosts: Jack and Carita Prestwich
Rooms: 6 (PB) $99-109
Full Breakfast
Credit Cards: A, B, C, D
Notes: 2, 5, 7, 9, 10, 11, 12

Lavender Hill

683 South Barretta Street, Sonora, 95370
(209) 532-9024; (800) 446-1333, ext. 29
E-mail: lavender@sonnett.com
www.lavenderhill.com

Come home. . .to a 1900s Victorian home overlooking the historic gold rush town of Sonora. At sunset you can watch the world from a wraparound porch, enjoy a country walk through year-round flower gardens, and relax on a covered patio (ideal for a small wedding). In the morning, you wake to a home-cooked breakfast, listen and share experiences with others; perhaps plan a day of hiking in Yosemite, fishing, biking, river rafting, or even a scenic steam train ride. Afternoons and evenings may include a stroll to downtown antique shops and boutiques, fine dining, and a performance at one of the professional repertory theaters. We will be glad to plan a dinner-theater package for your stay. Gift certificates are available.

---

6 Pets welcome; 7 Children welcome; 8 Tennis nearby; 9 Swimming nearby; 10 Golf nearby; 11 Skiing nearby; 12 May be booked through travel agent

One visit will have you longing to return "home."

Hosts: Jean and Charlie Marinelli
Rooms: 4 (PB) $85-105
Full Breakfast
Credit Cards: A, B, C, D
Notes: 2, 5, 7, 8, 9, 10, 11, 12

LONG BEACH

Lord Mayor's Bed & Breakfast Inn

435 Cedar Avenue, 90802-2245
(562) 436-0324 (phone/fax)
E-mail: innkeepers@lordmayors.com
www.lordmayors.com

Lord Mayor's

Rest and relax in our 1904 award-winning historic landmark with meticulously restored rooms, private baths, and sundeck acces. Two recently restored 1906 cottages provide alternative space in the B&B Collection. You'll find warm hospitality enhanced by home-cooked specialty breakfasts. Within walking distance of shops and Convention Center, Aquarium of the Pacific and Tall Ships. Driving distance to Disneyland, Universal Studio, and Getty Museum. A

gateway to the Catalina Island by ferry.

Hosts: Laura and Reuben Brasser
Rooms: 12 (10 PB; 2 SB) $85-140
Full Breakfast
Credit Cards: A, B, C, D, E
Notes: 2, 5, 7, 9, 12

The Turret House Bed & Breakfast

556 Chestnut Avenue, 90802
(562) 983-9812; (888) 4TURRET
fax: (562) 437-4082
E-mail: innkeepers@turrethouse.com
turrethouse.com

Indulge in Victorian hospitality and antique finery in an elegant restored 1906 home in historic downtown residential Long Beach. Five romantic guest rooms with private baths, savory gourmet candlelit breakfasts, and relaxing afternoon tea and treats offer guests a peaceful retreat to a time when gracious hospitality and gentle manners were a way of life. Pleasant walk to ocean, aquarium, Convention Center, theaters, fine dining, and antique and specialty shops. Convenient to all Southern California attractions.

Hosts: Nina and Lee Agee
Rooms: 5 (PB) $110-150
Gourmet Breakfast
Credit Cards: A, B, C, D
Notes: 2, 5, 8, 9, 10, 12

MENDOCINO

Antioch Ranch

39451 Comptche Road, 95460
(707) 937-5570; fax: (707) 937-1757
E-mail: cbbd@antiochranch.com
www.antiochranch.com

A Christian atmosphere of peace, this is a place for refreshment and renewal. Located just five miles inland from the picturesque town of Mendocino, the ranch features four guest cottages on 20 acres of rolling hills, redwoods, and apple orchards. Each cottage has its own style and ambience. Rustic, yet comfortable, each features a woodstove, complete kitchen with microwave, two bedrooms, bath, and open living/dining room.

Hosts: Jerry and Pat Westfall
Rooms: 4 cottages (PB) $75-95
Credit Cards: None
Notes: 2, 5, 7, 8, 9, 10

DeHaven Valley Farm

39247 North Highway One, Westport, 95488
(707) 961-1660; (877) DEHAVEN
fax: (707) 961-1677
www.dehaven-valley-farm.com

This 1875 Victorian farmhouse sits amid twenty acres of meadows and hills, just a two-minute walk to the beach. The cozy parlor offers a crackling fire, piano, and VCR movies. The upstairs deck, perfect for reading or dozing, overlooks the ocean. A hot tub on the hill offers spectacular daytime views and evening stargazing. Entertainment is provided by the resident goats, donkey, horses, sheep, cat, and dog. Close to Mendocino Village, the Lost Coast, and giant Redwoods. The owner is a minister and will perform wedding ceremonies and other services if desired.

Host: Christa Stapp
Rooms: 8 (6 PB; 2 SB) $85-140
Full Breakfast
Credit Cards: A, B, C
Notes: 2, 4, 5, 7, 9, 10, 12

Elk Cove Inn

P.O. Box 367, 95459
(707) 877-3321; (800) 275-2967
fax: (707) 877-1808
E-mail: elkcove@mcn.org
www.elkcoveinn.com

A uniquely romantic B&B with dramatic ocean views, located in the town of Elk just an easy, five-minute walk from the sandy beach. All rooms are provided with complimentary port wine and chocolates, fluffy robes, coffeemakers, feather beds, and down comforters. Our suites have separate living and bedroom areas, fireplaces, large baths with spa tubs, and balconies.

Host: Elaine Bryant
Rooms: 14 (PB) $108-318
Full Breakfast
Credit Cards: A, B,C, D
Notes: 2, 5, 10, 12

MONTEREY

Grand View Inn

557 Ocean View Boulevard, Pacific Grove,
    93950-2653
(831) 372-4341
www.pginns.com

Built in 1910, the Grand View Inn is situated at the very edge of Monterey Bay overlooking the Pacific Ocean. Completely restored by the Flatley family, the Grand View Inn has unsurpassed views of Monterey Bay from each room. Guest rooms enjoy the comfort of beautiful antique furnishings, beautifully appointed marble bathrooms, patterned hardwood floors, and lovely grounds. Easily accessible to Monterey Aquarium, Can-

---

6 Pets welcome; 7 Children welcome; 8 Tennis nearby; 9 Swimming nearby; 10 Golf nearby; 11 Skiing nearby; 12 May be booked through travel agent

nery Row, 17-Mile Drive, Carmel, and Highway 1 to Big Sur. Children over 12 years old welcome.

Hosts: Susan and Ed Flatley
Rooms: 11 (PB) $175-385
Full Breakfast
Credit Cards: A, B, F
Notes: 5, 8, 9, 10, 12

Seven Gables Inn

555 Ocean View Boulevard, Pacific Grove, 93950-2934
(831) 372-4341
www.pginns.com

Crashing waves, rocky shorelines, sea otters, whales, and beautiful sunsets are the images seen from each guest room at the Victorian-style Seven Gables Inn. Such a romantic setting on the edge of Monterey Bay is enhanced by a dazzling display of fine European antiques, a sumptuous breakfast, afternoon tea, the comfort of all private baths, and excellent guest service. Nearby attractions include the Monterey Bay Aquarium, Pebble Beach, Carmel, and Highway 1 to Big Sur. Children over 12 years old welcome.

Hosts: Susan and Ed Flatley
Rooms: 14 (PB) $175-385
Full Breakfast
Credit Cards: A, B, F
Notes: 5, 8, 9, 10, 12

MOUNT SHASTA

Mount Shasta Ranch Bed & Breakfast

1008 W. A. Barr Road, 96067
(530) 926-3870; fax: (530) 926-6882

E-mail: alpinere@snowcrest.net
travelassist.com/reg/cal2s.html

The inn is situated in a rural setting with a majestic view of Mt. Shasta and features a main lodge, carriage house, and cottage. Group accommodations are available. Our breakfast room is ideally suited for seminars and retreats, with large seating capacity. The game room includes piano, Ping-Pong, pool table, and board games. Nearby recreational facilities include alpine and nordic skiing, fishing, hiking, mountain bike rentals, surrey rides, and museums. Call for pastors' discount.

Hosts: Bill and Mary Larsen
Rooms: 10 (5 PB; 5 SB) $55-115
Full Breakfast
Credit Cards: A, B, C, D
Notes: 2, 5, 7, 8, 9, 10, 11, 12

NAPA

Blue Violet Mansion

443 Brown Street, 94559-3349
(707) 253-2583; (800) 959-2583
fax: (707) 257-8205
E-mail: bviolet@napanet.net
www.bluevioletmansion.com

Blue Violet Mansion

Gold Award: Best B&B in North America, OHG '96. Elegant 1886 Queen Anne Mansion with gazebo, rose garden, heated swimming pool, and spa. Rooms with antiques, gas fireplaces, spas, and deluxe amenities. Private in-room candlelight dinners and massages for two. Camelot theme floor—all handpainted with murals, stained glass, and silver goblets. "Violette's at the Mansion" for a full breakfast and evening dining. A chef and minister on-site make this an ideal setting for weddings, receptions, and small corporate meetings. Balloon rides, limousine tours, and wine train can be arranged.

Hosts: Bob and Kathy Morris
Rooms: 17 (PB) $189-359
Full Breakfast
Credit Cards: A, B, C, D, E, F
Notes: 4, 5, 7, 8, 9, 12

The Napa Inn Bed & Breakfast

1137 Warren Street, 94559-2302
(707) 257-1444; (800) 435-1144
fax: (707) 257-0251
E-mail: info@napainn.com
www.napainn.com

Two Victorians, one, built in 1877, is on the National Historic Register, and the other, a stately Queen Anne, was built in 1899. Both adjacent homes are located on a tree-lined street in historic Napa, minutes from world-class wineries. Fourteen rooms in all, many have fireplaces and whirlpool tubs. A full, gourmet breakfast is served with dessert and liqueur in the evening. Relax in our gardens or walk to town for many nearby restaurants and shops

The Napa Inn

Hosts: Brooke and Jim Boyer
Rooms: 14 (PB) $140-300
Credit Cards: A, B, C, D, E
Notes: 2, 5, 6, 10, 12

The Old World Inn

1301 Jefferson Street, 94559-2412
(707) 257-0112; (800) 966-6624
fax: (707) 257-0112
E-mail: theoldworldinn@aol.com
www.oldworld

This 1906 home is an eclectic combination of architecture, detailed with wood shingles, shady porches, leaded and beveled glass. Each romantic room is adorned in bright welcoming colors and features canopy beds, clawfoot tubs, fireplaces, and Jacuzzis. You'll be pampered with an afternoon tea, early evening wine and cheese, and a chocolate lover's dessert buffet after dinner. In the morning, awaken to the aroma of freshly brewed coffee and a gourmet breakfast. Enjoy the outdoor spa under the stars. Romance spoken here.

Host: Sam Van Hoeve
Rooms: 9 (PB) $105-260
Full Breakfast
Credit Cards: A, B, C, D
Notes: 5, 8, 9, 10, 12

Rancho Caymus

1140 Rutherford Road, Rutherford, 94573
(707) 963-1777; (800) 845-1777
fax: (707) 963-5387
www.ranchocaymus.com

Rancho Caymus

Early California Hacienda-style inn. All 26 rooms encircle an award-winning garden courtyard. All rooms are nonsmoking and feature walnut-framed queen bed, air-conditioning, color TV, telephone, private bath, refrigerator, wet bar. Noted in the *New York Times* for "The central location, friendly service, and earthly rate."

Host: Komes Family
Rooms: 26 (PB) $195-345
Continental Breakfast
Credit Cards: A, B, C, E, F
Notes: 5, 8, 10, 12

NAPA VALLEY

Bartels Ranch & Bed & Breakfast Country Inn

1200 Conn Valley Road, Saint Helena, 94574
(707) 963-4001; fax: (707) 963-5100
E-mail: bartelsranch@webtv.net
www.bartelsranch.com

"Heaven in the Hills." Situated in the heart of the world-famous Napa Valley wine country is this secluded, romantic, elegant country estate overlooking a "hundred-acre valley with a ten thousand-acre view." Honeymoon "Heart of the Valley" suite has a sunken Jacuzzi, sauna, shower, stone fireplace, and private deck with vineyard view. Romantic, award-winning accommodations, expansive entertainment room, poolside lounging, personalized itineraries, afternoon refreshments, pool table, fireplace, library, and terraces overlooking the vineyard. Bicycle to nearby wineries, lake, golf, tennis, fishing, boating, mineral spas, and bird-watching. Come dream awhile!

Host: Jami Bartels
Rooms: 4 (PB) $225-455
Full Breakfast
Credit Cards: A, B, C, D, E, F
Notes: 2, 3, 4, 5, 7, 8, 9, 10, 11, 12

NEVADA CITY

Deer Creek Inn

116 Nevada Street, 95959-2604
(530) 265-0363; (800) 655-0363
fax: (530) 265-0980; E-mail: deercreek@gv.net
www.deercreek.com

Deer Creek Inn

NOTES: Credit cards accepted: A Master Card; B Visa; C American Express; D Discover; E Diners Club; F Other; 2 Personal checks accepted; 3 Lunch available; 4 Dinner available; 5 Open all year;

Romance and elegance abound as you wander through this lovely, Queen Anne Victorian home. She sits high above the gardens with the sound of Deer Creek to lull you to sleep each night. The guest rooms are appointed with period furniture, and several have private verandas or patios. A large gourmet breakfast is in store for you, and Nevada City is but a few steps away.

Hosts: Elaine and Chuck Matroni
Rooms: 5 (PB) $125-165
Full Breakfast
Credit Cards: A, B, C
Notes: 2, 5, 8, 9, 10, 11, 12

The Parsonage Bed & Breakfast Inn

427 Broad Street, 95959
(530) 265-9478; fax: (530) 265-8147

The Parsonage

History comes alive in this 125-year-old home in Nevada City's historic district. The cozy guest rooms, parlor, and dining and family rooms are lovingly furnished with the innkeeper's pioneer family antiques. Breakfast is served on the veranda or in the formal dining room each morning. You may enjoy lunch or dinner at one of the twenty-six restaurants within the four-block area.

Host: Deborah Dane
Rooms: 6 (PB) $75-140
Full Breakfast
Credit Cards: A, B, F
Notes: 2, 5, 7, 8, 9, 10, 11, 12

PACIFIC GROVE

Gatehouse Inn

Gatehouse Inn

225 Central Avenue, 93950
(831) 649-8436; (800) 753-1881
fax: (831) 648-8044
E-mail: lew@redshift
www.sueandlewinns.com

Built in 1884 as a summer retreat for Senator Langford, the inn features nine guest rooms, each with its own theme. Journey through the past in rooms such as the Steinbeck, Langford, or Victorian, all with Victorian elegance. For a different feel, try the Cannery Row, Turkish, or Italian rooms. Enjoy the sumptuous food, breathtaking views, and romantic elegance.

Host: Ruby Rustan
Rooms: 9 (PB) $125-195
Full Breakfast
Credit Cards: A, B, C, D
Notes: 2, 5, 7, 8, 9, 10

6 Pets welcome; 7 Children welcome; 8 Tennis nearby; 9 Swimming nearby; 10 Golf nearby; 11 Skiing nearby; 12 May be booked through travel agent

Old St. Angela Inn

321 Central Avenue, 93950
(831) 372-3246; (800) 748-6306
fax: (831) 372-8560
E-mail: lew@redshift.com
www.sueandlewinns.com

Built in 1910, this inn reminds you of a day on Cape Cod. Guest rooms are decorated in antiques, and provide ocean views, Jacuzzis, fireplaces, and cast-iron stoves. Add New England hospitality, a garden hot-tub spa, and a warm, homey feeling, and you have our inn. Bring your appetites!

Hosts: Lew, Sue, & Honey
Rooms: 9 (PB) $110-210
Full Breakfast
Credit Cards: A, B, D
Notes: 2, 5, 7, 8, 9, 10

Old St. Angela Inn

PALM DESERT

Tres Palmas
Bed & Breakfast

73135 Tumbleweed Lane, 92260-4207
(760) 773-9858; (800) 770-9858
fax: (760) 776-9159
www.innformation.com/ca/trespalmas

Tres Palmas

Tres Palmas is located just one block south of El Paseo, the "Rodeo Drive of the Desert," where you will find boutiques, art galleries, and many restaurants. Or you may choose to stay "home" and enjoy the desert sun in and around the pool and spa. The guest rooms feature queen- or king-size beds, climate controls, ceiling fans, and color cable televisions and are uniquely decorated in Southwestern style. Lemonade and iced tea are always available for guests. Snacks are served in the late afternoons. Tres Palmas is AAA three-diamond rated; Mobil three-star rated.

Hosts: Karen and Terry Bennett
Rooms: 4 (PB) $90-200
Continental Breakfast
Credit Cards: A, B, C
Notes: 2, 5, 8, 9, 10, 12

PALM SPRINGS

Casa Cody Country Inn

175 South Cahuilla Road, 92262-6331
(760) 320-9346; (800) 231-2639
fax: (760) 325-8610
E-mail: casacody@aol.com
www.palmsprings.com/hotels/casacody

NOTES: Credit cards accepted: A Master Card; B Visa; C American Express; D Discover; E Diners Club; F Other; 2 Personal checks accepted; 3 Lunch available; 4 Dinner available; 5 Open all year;

Romantic, historic hideaway nestled against the spectacular San Jacinto Mountains in the heart of Palm Springs village. One-story California adobe hacienda-style buildings surrounded by lovely gardens of bougainvillea and citrus. Completely redecorated in Santa Fe décor. Our 23 units include hotel rooms, studio suites, and one and two bedroom suites with private patios, fireplaces, and kitchens. Cable TV and private phones. Two pools and secluded, tree-shaded whirlpool spa.

Hosts: Frank Tysen and Therese Hayes
Rooms: 23 (PB) $89-349
Continental Breakfast
Credit Cards: A, B, C, D, E
Notes: 2, 5, 6, 7, 8, 9, 10, 11, 12

PALO ALTO

Adella Villa

P.O. Box 19528, 94309-4528
(650) 321-5195; E-mail: tricia@best.com
valleyviewinn.com/tricia

This 1920s Italian villa is in a park-like one-acre setting next to Silicon Valley. Corporate rates. Full breakfast. Internet access, sherry, robes, TV, CD player, hair dryers. Seasonal heated pool. Quiet with off-street parking and security gate. A half-mile from El Camino Real, and 30 minutes to San Francisco.

Host: Tricia Young
Rooms: 5 (PB) $165
Full Breakfast
Credit Cards: A, B, C, E
Notes: 2, 5, 8, 9, 10, 12

REDDING

Palisades Paradise Bed & Breakfast

1200 Palisades Avenue, 96003
(530) 223-5305; fax: (530) 223-1200
E-mail: bnbno1@jett.net
www.palisadesparadise.com

You will feel you are in Paradise when you watch the magnificent sunsets from a lovely contemporary

Palisades Paradise

home overlooking the Sacramento River. Enjoy a spectacular view of the city and the surrounding mountains, and awake to the music of singing birds. You are always made to feel "special" here. Travelers and business people alike seek out the comfort and relaxed atmosphere of Palisades Paradise in a quiet, residential neighborhood. All rooms are centrally heated, air-conditioned, and have cable television. Garden spa!

Host: Gail Goetz
Rooms: 2 (SB) $70-125
Continental Breakfast
Credit Cards: A, B, C
Notes: 2, 5, 6, 7, 8, 9, 10, 11, 12

---

6 Pets welcome; 7 Children welcome; 8 Tennis nearby; 9 Swimming nearby; 10 Golf nearby; 11 Skiing nearby; 12 May be booked through travel agent

REDONDO BEACH

Breeze Inn

122 South Juanita Avenue, 90277
(310) 316-5123

Located in a quiet, A-1 neighborhood, the Breeze Inn offers a large suite with private entrance, private bath with spa, California king bed, and oriental carpet. Breakfast area is complete with microwave, toaster oven, electric coffeemaker, and stocked refrigerator for Continental breakfast. Adjustable skylight, ceiling fan, cable TV. Brochure available with map. Located near Los Angeles, Lax Airport, Disneyland, Universal City, and more. Approximately five blocks from the pier and beach.

Host: Betty Binding
Rooms: 1 suite (PB) $55-60
Continental Breakfast
Credit Cards: None
Notes: 2, 5, 7, 8, 9, 10

RIDGECREST

Bevlen Haus Bed & Breakfast

809 North Sanders Street, 93555
(760) 375-1988; (800) 375-1989
fax: (760) 375-6871
E-mail: blh_b&b@iwvisp.com

"Once a guest, always a friend." Gracious, quiet, safe, and comfortable; your "secret high desert hideaway." Nearly 2,000 square feet, furnished with antiques, handmade quilts, and comforters in winter! Paved parking. Cooling air in summer. Old-fashioned kitchen has antique cast-iron cookstove and a hand-hammered copper sink. Year-round hot tub spa. In a full-service community close to Sierra Nevada, Death Valley, Naval Air Warfare Center, China Lake, ghost towns, movie sites, and ancient Indian cultural sites. Wildflowers in spring. No smoking.

Hosts: Bev and Len De Geus
Rooms: 3 (PB) $45-65
Full Breakfast
Credit Cards: A, B, C, D
Notes: 2, 5, 8, 9, 10, 12

SAINT HELENA

Bartels Ranch & Bed & Breakfast Country Inn

See description under Napa Valley, CA.

SAN ANDREAS

The Robin's Nest

247 West St. Charles Street, P.O. Box 1408,
    95249-1408
(209) 754-1076; (888) 214-9202
fax: (209) 754-3975
E-mail: info@robinest.com
www.robinest.com

A traditional, yet informal Victorian B&B country inn in the heart of the Gold Country. Eight hundred square feet of interior common space makes it ideal for group gatherings. The one and one-third acres of gardens and

---

NOTES: Credit cards accepted: A Master Card; B Visa; C American Express; D Discover; E Diners Club; F Other; 2 Personal checks accepted; 3 Lunch available; 4 Dinner available; 5 Open all year;

fruit orchards have several seating areas. Central heat and air-conditioning, hot spa, and five-course gourmet breakfast.

Hosts: Karen and William Konietzny
Rooms: 9 (PB) $90-125
Full Breakfast
Credit Cards: A, B, C, D
Notes: 5, 7, 8, 9, 10, 12

SAN DIEGO

Carole's Bed & Breakfast Inn

3227 Grim Avenue, 92104-4656
(619) 280-5258; (800) 975-5521

Built in 1904 by Mayor Frary, this historic site displays the handsome style and craftsmanship of its time. It has been restored by the present owners, who live on-site, giving it constant loving care. The décor is of its period, with antiques and comfort as the focus. Amenities include a spa, black-bottom pool, and rose garden. Carole's B&B is within walking distance of Balboa Park, an assortment of small shops, and restaurants.

Hosts: Carole Dugdale and Michael O'Brien
Rooms: 10 (4 PB; 6 SB) $79-179
Continental Breakfast
Credit Cards: A, B, C, D, E
Notes: 5, 7, 9, 10, 12

Heritage Park Bed & Breakfast Inn

2470 Heritage Park Row, 92110
(619) 299-6832; (800) 995-2470
fax: (619) 299-9465
E-mail: innkeeper@heritageparkinn.com
www.heritageparkinn.com

Heritage Park B&B Inn, unique lodging for discriminating travelers, is far from ordinary, yet central to everything in the area. Nestled in a quiet Victorian park lined with cobblestone walkways in the heart of historic Old Town, the award-winning Queen Anne mansion is only minutes from the San Diego Zoo, shops, beaches, and restaurants. Come for a glimpse of California's past. Stay and be pampered with feather beds, claw-foot tubs, Jacuzzi suites, full gourmet, candlelit breakfasts, and afternoon tea served on the veranda.

Hosts: Nancy and Charles Helsper
Rooms: 12 (PB) $120-250
Full Breakfast
Credit Cards: A, B, C, D, E
Notes: 2, 5, 7, 8, 9, 10, 12

SAN DIEGO (NORTH COAST)

Seabreeze Bed & Breakfast

121 North Vulcan Avenue, Encinitas, 92024
(760) 944-0318
www.seabreeze-inn.com

Seabreeze B&B Inn is a clean, comfortable, home away from home, and a private, romantic retreat. Five guest rooms all have their own entries and baths. All have cable TV; two with VCR and phone access. They are individually decorated with one-of-a-kind custom furnishings. Downstairs there is a common sitting room with a fireplace and kitchenette. The upstairs Penthouse Shangri-La, has a private, eight-foot hot tub on an ocean-view balcony. The private upstairs apartment has a fireplace, kitchen, double tub and shower bath, and ocean-view balcony.

Host: Kirsten Richter
Rooms: 5 (PB) $79-160
Continental Breakfast
Credit Cards: A, B
Notes: 5, 7, 8, 9, 10

SAN FRANCISCO

Garratt Mansion

900 Union Street, Alameda, 94501
(510) 521-4779
E-mail: garrattm@pacbell.net
www.garrattmansion.com

Garratt Mansion

Fifteen minutes from San Francisco, the quiet island of Alameda is convenient and unique. We can offer touring ideas or privacy to regroup. Whether you're on business or vacation, we love to anticipate and meet your needs with fresh flowers, down comforters, afternoon cookies, fresh orange juice, and direct-line phones. Twenty-four hour beverages and other amenities are provided.

Hosts: Royce and Betty Gladden
Rooms: 7 (5 PB; 2SB) $95-175
Full Breakfast
Credit Cards: A, B, C
Notes: 5, 8, 9, 10

The Monte Cristo

600 Presidio Avenue, 94115
(415) 931-1875; fax: (415) 931-6005
www.virtualcities.com

The Monte Cristo has been part of San Francisco since 1875, located two blocks from elegantly restored Victorian shops, restaurants, and antique stores on Sacramento Street. Convenient transportation to downtown San Francisco and to the financial district. Each room is elegantly furnished with authentic period pieces.

Host: George
Rooms: 14 (11 PB; 3 SB) $73-118
Continental Breakfast
Credit Cards: A, B, D
Notes: 5, 7

SAN LUIS OBISPO

Apple Farm Inn

2015 Monterey Street, 93401-2617
(805) 544-2040; (800) 374-3705
fax: (805) 546-9495
E-mail: reservations@applefarm.com
www.applefarm.com

Each room at the Apple Farm Inn and Trellis Court is individually decorated in a country Victorian style, and offers fireplaces, and canopy or brass beds. The four-diamond rated inn is understandably a favorite of guests traveling the California coast. Trellis Court guests enjoy a breakfast option at our Restaurant. An afternoon guest reception is offered daily. Visit our extensive gift shop and our working grist mill and millhouse. Stroll the beautiful gardens. We now offer hydrotheray soaking tubs in some of our rooms. On-site massage, spa treatment center, and meeting space available too.

Rooms: 104 (PB) $119-319
Continental Breakfast
Credit Cards: A, B, C, D
Notes: 2, 3, 4, 5, 7, 8, 9, 10, 12

SANTA BARBARA

The Bayberry Inn

111 West Valerio Street, 93101-2927
(805) 569-3398; fax: (805) 569-1120
E-mail: bayberryinn@aol.com
www.bayberryinnsantabarbara.com

Experience the charm and romance of Old Santa Barbara in one of its grand historic homes (c.1894). All rooms have queen canopy beds, and were decorated by the late Carlton Wagner, a world-renowned expert in the field of color theory. Some rooms have fireplaces and private decks. We serve a full gourmet breakfast, complimentary premium wines and cheese every afternoon, and a homemade dessert every evening.

The Bayberry Inn
SANTA BARBARA

Hosts: Jill and Kenneth Freeland
Rooms: 8 (PB) $149-229
Full Breakfast
Credit Cards: A, B, C, D
Notes: 2, 5, 8, 9, 10, 12

Prufrock's Garden Inn by the Beach

Prufrock's Garden Inn

600 Linden Avenue, Carpinteria, 93013-2040
(805) 566-9696; 8PR-UFR-OCKS
fax: (805) 566-9404
E-mail: innkeepers@prufrocks.com
www.prufrocks.com

A "Most Romantic Getaway" (*Santa Barbara Independent*); the "Best Beach in the West" (University Beach rating service); voted "Reader's Favorite" (*LA Times*); and photographed for Land's End Catalog. This B&B offers Jacuzzis, fireplaces, in-room fresh flowers, sunset hors d'oeuvres, bedtime chocolates. Best Santa Barbara B&B beach location; state beach one block away. Restaurants, boutiques, antique stores are nearby. The B&B is tucked between the ocean and the mountains in a community known for orchards and flower fields. AMTRAK, bicycles, beach amenities, wharf lunches are all nearby.

Hosts: Judy and Jim Halvorsen
Rooms: 7 (5 PB; 2 SB) $89-229
Full Breakfast
Credit Cards: A, B, D
Notes: 5, 7, 8, 9, 10, 11

---

6 Pets welcome; 7 Children welcome; 8 Tennis nearby; 9 Swimming nearby; 10 Golf nearby; 11 Skiing nearby; 12 May be booked through travel agent

Tiffany Country House

1323 De La Vina, 93101
(805) 963-2283; (800) 999-5672
fax: (805) 963-2825
E-mail: upham.hotel@verizon.net
www.tiffanycountryhouse.com

Circa 1898. This Victorian house features a steep front gable and balcony accentuating the entrance. Colonial diamond-paned bay windows and a front veranda welcome guests to an antique-filled inn. All seven rooms have private bathrooms with three rooms with spa tubs. Daily amenities include a full breakfast, afternoon fruit, wine and cheese, and cookies in the evening. Located in the heart of Santa Barbara, the Tiffany Country House is within walking distance of museums, restaurants, shops, and galleries.

Host: Jan Martin Winn
Rooms: 7 (PB) $150-300
Full Breakfast
Credit Cards: A, B, C, E, F
Notes: 5, 8, 9, 10, 12

The Upham Hotel & Garden Cottages

1404 De La Vina Street, 93101-3057
(805) 962-0058; (800) 727-0876
fax: (805) 963-2825
E-mail: upham.hotel@verizon.net
www.uphamhotel.com

Established in 1871, this beautifully restored hotel uniquely combines the quaint ambience of a B&B with the professionalism of a full-service hotel. Seven buildings surround an acre of lovely gardens, and house fifty guest rooms and suites, some with fireplaces, and private patios or porches.

Located in the heart of downtown within walking distance of museums, theaters, shopping, and restaurants.

Host: Jan Martin Winn
Rooms: 50 (PB) $160-410
Continental Breakfast
Credit Cards: A, B, C, E,
Notes: 3, 4, 5, 7, 8, 9, 10, 12

SANTA ROSA

The Gables Inn

4257 Petaluma Hill Road, 95404-9796
(707) 585-7777; (800) GABLES N
fax: (707) 584-5634
E-mail: innkeeper@thegablesinn.com
www.thegablesinn.com

This beautifully restored Victorian mansion sits on three and a half acres in the center of the Sonoma Wine Country. A separate creekside cottage features a whirlpool tub-for-two. A gourmet breakfast is served each morning, as well as freshly baked pastries, with coffee and tea service each afternoon. The Gables provides easy access to 200 premium wineries, the California redwoods, as well as the

The Gables Inn

craggy North coastline, and is just one hour north of San Francisco.

Hosts: Mike and Judy Ogne
Rooms: 8 (PB) $175-250
Full Breakfast
Credit Cards: A, B, C, D, E
Notes: 5, 8, 9, 10, 12

Pygmalion House Bed & Breakfast Inn

331 Orange Street, 95401
(707) 526-3407 (phone/fax)

Pygmalion House

Lovely 1880s Victorian, three stories, cozy rooms—each with its own bathroom. Victorian tub and shower. Tree-covered garden. Many antiques from Gypsy Rose Lee and other celebrities. Hot-air ballooning nearby. Three blocks from Railroad Square. Garden parking in the rear.

Host: Caroline E. Berry
Rooms: 6 (PB) $99-129
Full Breakfast
Credit Cards: A, B, D, E
Notes: 2, 10, 12

SEAL BEACH

The Seal Beach Inn & Gardens

The Seal Beach Inn and Gardens

212 Fifth Street, 90740
(562) 493-2416; (800) HIDEAWAY
fax: (562) 799-0483
E-mail: hideaway@sealbeachinn.com
www.sealbeachinn.com

Elegant, historic inn with lush, petite gardens cascading throughout the property. Beautiful fountains and private pool also help create a relaxing atmosphere. All of our rooms are decorated with antiques and fine furnishings. Our guests receive many complimentary amenities including lavish gourmet breakfast, fresh flowers, all-day coffee and tea bar, fresh fruit baskets, cookies, and evening tea and appetizers. Quaint seaside village directly west of Disneyland and south of Long Beach.

Hosts: Marjorie and Harty Schmaehl
Rooms: 23 (PB) $170-399
Full Breakfast
Credit Cards: A, B, C, D, E
Notes: 5, 8, 9, 10, 11, 12

6 Pets welcome; 7 Children welcome; 8 Tennis nearby; 9 Swimming nearby; 10 Golf nearby; 11 Skiing nearby; 12 May be booked through travel agent

SEQUOIA NATIONAL PARK

Plantation
Bed & Breakfast

33038 Sierra Highway #198;
Lemon Cove, 93244-1700
(559) 597-2555; (800) 240-1466
fax: (559) 597-2551
E-mail: relax@plantationbnb.com
www.plantationbnb.com

Nestled in the foothills of the Sierra Nevada Mountains among acres of orange groves, only 16 miles from Sequoia National Park. "Gone With the Wind" theme rooms; heated swimming pool in spring and fall; Jacuzzi hot tub located in orange groves for privacy—open 24 hours. A full gourmet breakfast is served, including orange juice made from oranges picked fresh each morning. Fireplaces, verandas, gazebos, fountains, and many gardens.

Hosts: Scott and Marie Munger
Rooms: 8 (6 PB; 2 SB) $69-189
Full Breakfast
Credit Cards: A, B, C, D, E
Notes: 2, 5, 9, 10, 11, 12

SONORA

Barretta Gardens Inn

700 South Barretta Street, 95370
(209) 532-6039; (800) 206-3333
fax: (209) 532-8257
E-mail: barrettagardens@hotmail.com
www.barrettagardens.com

Situated atop a terraced hillside, surrounded by an arce of landscaped gardens, this Victorian era inn is a ten-minute walk to the center of Sonora. Enjoy relaxing in two open-

Barretta Gardens Inn

air prches and three guest parlors. The five guest rooms, each with private bath, (two with whirlpool tubs) have been elegantly decorated in period antiques. A full breakfast is served (including fresh French pastries baked daily in the on-site bakery) in the formal dining room or screened breakfast porch.

Hosts: Bruno and Sally Trial
Rooms: 5 (PB) $95-235
Full Breakfast
Credit Cards: A, B, C, D
Notes: 2, 5, 9, 10, 11, 12

SUTTER CREEK

Sutter Creek Inn

75 Main Street, P.O. Box 385, 95685
(209) 267-5606; fax: (209) 267-9287
E-mail: info@suttercreekinn.com
www.suttercreekinn.com

The first B&B in California. Step back in time to enjoy the peace and tranquility of another era as depicted in Thomas Kinkade's painting of our inn, titled *The Village Inn*. Find year-round comfort in our secret gardens, or enjoy winter in front of your fireplace listening to the rain on the roof

---

NOTES: Credit cards accepted: A Master Card; B Visa; C American Express; D Discover; E Diners Club; F Other; 2 Personal checks accepted; 3 Lunch available; 4 Dinner available; 5 Open all year;

with a good book, snuggled close to your love. Walk to the antique and collectibles shops, theater, and restaurants. Our eighteen rooms all have private baths. Large country breakfast. Massage and handwriting analysis available by appointment.

Host: Jane Way
Rooms: 17 (PB) $65-175
Full Breakfast
Credit Cards: A, B
Notes: 2, 5, 8, 9, 10, 11, 12

TRINIDAD

The Lost Whale Bed & Breakfast Inn

3452 Patricks Point Drive, 95570-9782
(707) 677-3425; (800) 677-7859
fax: (707) 677-0284
E-mail: lmiller@lostwhaleinn.com
www.lostwhale.com

This beautiful inn is set on a bluff overlooking the rugged North Coast. The surrounding four acres have a private beach, tidepools, outdoor hot tub; a large gourmet breakfast and afternoon tea is offered. Families welcome."One of the top ten vacation spots in California. . .a divine place"—*San Francisco Chronicle*.

Rooms: 8 (PB) $132-192
Full Breakfast
Credit Cards: A, B, C, D
Notes: 2, 5, 7, 8, 12

UKIAH

Vichy Hot Springs Resort & Inn

2605 Vichy Springs Road, 95482
(707) 462-9515
E-mail: vichy@vichysprings.com
www.vichysprings.com

Vichy Springs is a delightful, two-hour drive north of San Francisco. Historic cottages and rooms await you with delightful vistas from all locations. Vichy Hot Springs features naturally sparkling, 90-degree mineral baths, a communal 104-degree pool, and an Olympic-sized pool. Guests can explore seven hundred private acres with trails and roads for hiking, jogging, picnicking, and mountain bicycling. Vichy's idyllic setting provides a quiet, healing environment for travelers. This is California State Landmark No. 980. AAA- and Mobil-rated three stars; a Historic Inns member.

Hosts: Gilbert and Marjorie Ashoff
Rooms: 22 (PB) $105-235
Full Breakfast
Credit Cards: A, B, C, D, E
Notes: 2, 5, 7, 8, 9, 10, 12

VARIOUS CITIES

Arizona Trails Bed & Breakfast Reservation Service

P.O. Box 18998, Fountain Hills, Arizona 85269
(480) 837-4284; (888)799-4284
fax: (480) 816-4224
E-mail: aztrails@arizonatrails.com
www.arizonatrails.com

Your free personal vacation-planning service. We cover the entire San Diego area and all of Arizona with inspected and approved lodging accommodations. Our host properties

---

6 Pets welcome; 7 Children welcome; 8 Tennis nearby; 9 Swimming nearby; 10 Golf nearby; 11 Skiing nearby; 12 May be booked through travel agent

include warm and cozy B&Bs, historic inns, boutique hotels, and world-class resorts. Arizona Trails is one-stop shopping for all your travel needs. Additional services include golf or romance packages, tours, day trips, and rental cars. Modest-to-luxury rates range from $75-$450 in season.

Hosts: Roxanne and Hank Boryczki
Rooms: $75-450
Credit Cards: A, B, C, D, E
Notes: 2, 4, 5, 6, 7, 8, 9, 10, 11, 12

VENTURA

La Mer Bed & Breakfast

411 Poli Street, 93001-2614
(805) 643-3600; fax: (805) 653-7329
E-mail: lamerbb@aol.com
www.lamerbnb.com

Nestled in a green hillside, this Cape Cod-style Victorian house overlooks the heart of historic Ventura and the spectacular California coastline. Each guest room has been individually furnished to capture a particular European country. A bottle of wine and a

sumptuous Bavarian breakfast is included.

Hosts: Gissela & Michael Baida
Rooms: 5 (PB) $95-185
Full Breakfast
Credit Cards: A, B, C, F
Notes: 2, 5, 7, 8, 9, 10, 12

The Victorian Rose Bed & Breakfast

896 East Main Street, 93001
(805) 641-1888; fax: (805) 643-1335
E-mail: victrose@pacbell.net
www.victorian-rose.com

This 112-year-old Gothic-Victorian church has a 96-foot steeple, and 26-foot stained-glass windows. All rooms have fireplaces and TVs; two have Jacuzzi tubs, rock waterfall shower, and much more.

Hosts: Richard and Nona Bogatch
Rooms: 5 (PB) $99-175
Full Breakfast
Credit Cards: A, B, C
Notes: 2, 5, 9, 10

WESTPORT

Howard Creek Ranch

40501 N. Highway One, P.O. Box 121, 95488
(707) 964-6725; fax: (707) 964-1603
www.howardcreekranch.com

Howard Creek Ranch is a historic, 4,000-acre, oceanfront farm dating to 1867, bordered by miles of beach and mountains in a wilderness area. Award-winning flower gardens, antiques, fireplaces, redwoods, a 75-foot swinging footbridge over Howard Creek, cabins, comfortable beds, hot tub, sauna, pool, nearby horseback

---

NOTES: Credit cards accepted: A Master Card; B Visa; C American Express; D Discover; E Diners Club; F Other; 2 Personal checks accepted; 3 Lunch available; 4 Dinner available; 5 Open all year;

Howard Creek Ranch

riding, and excellent restaurants are combined with hospitality and a full ranch breakfast. Termed "one of the most romantic places to stay on the planet" by the *San Francisco Examiner*. Inquire about pets.

Hosts: Charles and Sally Grigg
Rooms: 14 (12 PB; 2 SB) $75-160
Full Breakfast
Credit Cards: A, B, C, D
Notes: 2, 5, 6, 9

6 Pets welcome; 7 Children welcome; 8 Tennis nearby; 9 Swimming nearby; 10 Golf nearby; 11 Skiing nearby; 12 May be booked through travel agent

COLORADO

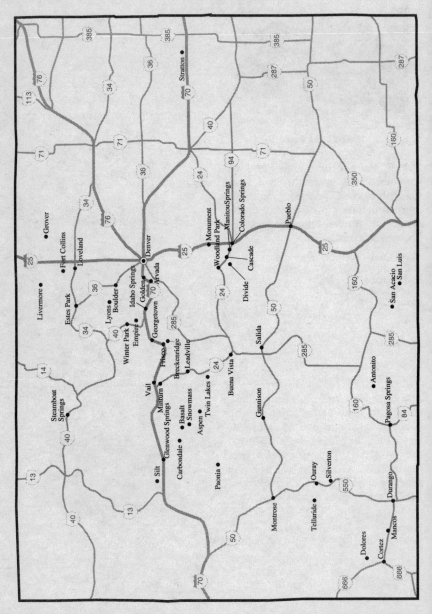

NOTES: Credit cards accepted: A Master Card; B Visa; C American Express; D Discover; E Diners
Club; F Other; 2 Personal checks accepted; 3 Lunch available; 4 Dinner available; 5 Open all year;

Colorado

BOULDER

Briar Rose
Bed & Breakfast Inn

Briar Rose

2151 Arapahoe Avenue, 80302
(303) 442-3007; fax: (303) 786-8440
E-mail: brbbx@aol.com
www.globalmall.com/brose

The Briar Rose is an English country cottage in light Victorian-style with nine elegant rooms and an extended-stay suite. New queen beds. Close to the university and Boulder's best restaurants. Afternoon and evening refreshments are served. Lovely gardens in the heart of town.

Hosts: Margaret and Bob Weisenbach
Rooms: 10 (PB) $119-189
Continental Breakfast
Credit Cards: A, B, C, E
Notes: 2, 5, 7, 8, 9, 10, 11, 12

COLORADO SPRINGS

Holden House—1902
Bed & Breakfast Inn

1102 West Pikes Peak Avenue, 80904-4347
(719) 471-3980; (888) 565-3980
fax (719) 471-4740
E-mail: mail@holdenhouse.com
www.holdenhouse.com

Discover a Pikes Peak treasure! These 1902 storybook Victorians are filled with antiques and family heirlooms. Each guest suite boasts feather pillows, period furnishings, queen bed, in-room fireplace, and oversized bubble bathtub-for-two. Centrally located in a residential area near historic Old Colorado City. You can enjoy shopping, restaurants, and attractions nearby. Experience "the romance of the past with the comforts of today." Inn cats "Mingtoy" and "Muffin" are in residence. AAA/Mobil Awards.

Holden House - 1902

Hosts: Sallie and Welling Clark
Rooms: 5 suites (PB) $130-150
Full Breakfast
Credit Cards: A, B, C, D, E
Notes: 5, 8, 9, 10, 12

6 Pets welcome; 7 Children welcome; 8 Tennis nearby; 9 Swimming nearby; 10 Golf nearby; 11 Skiing nearby; 12 May be booked through travel agent

The Painted Lady Bed & Breakfast Inn

1318 West Colorado Avenue, 80904
(719) 473-3165; (800) 370-3165
fax: (719) 635-1396
E-mail: innkeepers@paintedladyinn.com
www.paintedladyinn.com

The Painted Lady

This fanciful 1894 Victorian inn offers casual comfort for both the business or leisure traveler. Convenient to all Pikes Peak attractions, dining, shopping, and business districts. Pamper yourself in suites with oversized tubs, in-suite fireplaces, private outdoor hot tub, and sumptuous breakfasts. One suite with kitchenette is suitable for families or longer stays. Friendly resident cats, nonsmoking, air-conditioning, phones, TV/VCR, CD players, and refrigerators in all suites. Special packages all year. Off-season discounts.

Host: Valerie Maslowski
Rooms: 3 (PB) $90-160
Full Breakfast
Credit Cards: A, B, C, D, E
Notes: 2, 5, 7, 8, 9, 10, 12

DENVER

Capitol Hill Mansion Bed & Breakfast Inn

1207 Pennsylvania Street, 80203-2504
(303) 839-5221
E-mail: info@capitolhillmansion.com
www.capitolhillmansion.com

Walk to the convention center, museums, and restaurants from this nationally listed 1891 ruby sandstone mansion. Located in one of the most architecturally outstanding neighborhoods, it features high turrets, balconies, and soaring chimneys. Enjoy a full breakfast each morning and Colorado wine in the evening. Choose from eight distinct guest rooms, some with Jacuzzi tubs-for-two, fireplaces, or balconies. A fax/copy machine, modem-ready jacks, and telephones make business travel convenient. Business meetings and special events are welcome.

Capitol Hill Mansion

Hosts: Bill and Wendy Pearson
Rooms: 9 (PB) $90-175
Full Breakfast
Credit Cards: A, B, C, D, E
Notes: 2, 5, 7, 8, 9, 10, 11, 12

NOTES: Credit cards accepted: A Master Card; B Visa; C American Express; D Discover; E Diners Club; F Other; 2 Personal checks accepted; 3 Lunch available; 4 Dinner available; 5 Open all year;

Castle Marne—
A Luxury Urban Inn

1572 Race Street, 80206-1308
(303) 331-0621; (800) 92-Marne
fax: (303) 331-0623
E-mail: info@castlemarn.com
www.castlemarne.com

Chosen by *Country Inns* magazine as one of the "Top 12 Inns in North America." Fall under the spell of one of Denver's grandest historic mansions. Your stay here combines old-

Castle Marne

world elegance with modern convenience and comfort. Each guest room is a unique experience in pampered luxury. All rooms have private baths. Two suites have Jacuzzis-for-two. Three rooms have private balconies and hot tubs. Afternoon tea and a full gourmet breakfast are served in the cherry-paneled dining room. Castle Marne is a certified Denver Landmark and is on the National Register of Historic Structures.

Hosts: Diane Peiker, Owner/Innkeeper
Rooms: 9 (PB) $95-245
Full Breakfast
Credit Cards: A, B, C, D, E
Notes: 2, 3, 4, 5, 8, 9, 10, 11, 12

Queen Anne
Bed & Breakfast Inn

Queen Anne

2147 Tremont Place, 80205-3132
(303) 296-6666; (800) 432-4667
fax: (303) 296-2151
E-mail: travel@queenannebnb.com
www.queenannebnb.com

Facing quiet Benedict Fountain Park in downtown Denver are two side-by-side National Register Victorian homes with 14 guest rooms, including four gallery suites. Flowers, chamber music, phones, period antiques, and private baths are in all rooms. Seven rooms have special tubs; two have a fireplace. Air-conditioning, free parking. Located within walking distance of the capitol, 16th Street Pedestrian Mall, the Convention Center, Larimer Square, restaurants, shops, and museums. Among its many awards: Best 12 B&Bs Nationally, Ten Most Romantic, Best of Denver, and Best 105 in Great American Cities. Now in its 15th year, it is inspected and approved by major auto clubs, and *Distinctive Inns of Colorado*.

Hosts: The King Family
Rooms: 14 (PB) $75-175
Full Breakfast
Credit Cards: A, B, C, D, E
Notes: 2, 5, 8, 10, 11, 12

---

6 Pets welcome; 7 Children welcome; 8 Tennis nearby; 9 Swimming nearby; 10 Golf nearby; 11 Skiing nearby; 12 May be booked through travel agent

DIVIDE

Silverwood B&B

463 County Road 512, 80814-9731
(719) 687-6784; (800) 753-5592
E-mail: innkeeper@silverwoodinn.com
www.silverwood.com

At Silverwood B&B, you will find
plenty of mountain serenity and Western beauty; brilliant sunsets and starry
nights; world-class views of the Con-
tinential Divide mountains to the west
and Pikes Peak to the southeast; a
modern home with private baths and
quality comfort. Guests stay here for
the quietness, the superb breakfasts,
the views, and the hosts. Breakfast is
served next to the large windows of
the Great Room. Quiet country getaway only 45 minutes from downtown Colorado Springs. Hiking, fishing, sightseeing nearby.

Hosts: Bess and Lawrence Oliver
Rooms: 2 (PB) $62-95
Full Breakfast
Credit Cards: A, B, C, D
Notes: 2, 5, 7, 12

ESTES PARK

The Quilt House
Bed & Breakfast

P.O. Box 339, 80517
(970) 586-0427
E-mail: Hgraetzer@aol.com

A beautiful view can be enjoyed from
every window of this sturdy mountain
home. It is just a 15-minute walk from
downtown Estes Park and only four
miles from the entrance of Rocky
Mountain National Park. There are

three bedrooms upstairs, plus a lounge
where guests can read, look at the
mountains, and have a cup of coffee
or tea. A guest house beside the main
house has a kitchenette. The hosts
gladly help with information concern-
ing hiking trails, car drives, wildlife
viewing, shopping, etc. No smoking.

Hosts: Hans and Miriam Graetzer
Rooms: 4 (PB) $60-75
Full Breakfast
Credit Cards: None
Notes: 2, 5, 8, 9, 10, 11

GLENWOOD SPRINGS

Back in Time

927 Cooper Avenue, 81601-3629
(970) 945-6183; (888) 854-7733
fax: (970) 945-1324
E-mail: bitbnb@sprynet.com
www.backintimebb.com

Back in Time

Back in Time is a spacious Victorian
home built in 1903, filled with antiques, family quilts, and clocks. A
full breakfast is served in the dining
room including a hot dish accompanied by fresh hot muffins, fruit, and a
specialty of June's: mouth-watering
cinnamon rolls.

Hosts: June and Ron Robinson
Rooms: 3 (PB) $75-95
Full Breakfast
Credit Cards: A, B, C, D, E
Notes: 2, 5, 8, 9, 10, 11, 12

GUNNISON

Eagle's Nest

206 N Colorado Street, 81230-2104
(970) 641-4457

Wonderful accommodations for two people, or possibly three. Very large bedroom, bath, hallway, outside entrance, and sitting room—the entire upstairs of our house. Special breakfast after 9 A.M.; Continental before then. No smoking.

Hosts: Jane and Hugh Mcgee
Rooms: 1 (PB) $45
Continental or Full Breakfast
Notes: 2, 5, 10, 11

LEADVILLE

The Ice Palace Inn

813 Spruce Street, 80461-3555
(719) 486-8272; (800) 754-2840
fax: (719) 486-0345
E-mail: icepalace@bwn.net
http://icepalaceinn.com

This gracious Victorian inn was built at the turn of the century using lumber from the famous Leadville Ice Palace. Romantic guest rooms are elegantly decorated with antiques, feather beds, and quilts. Each has an exquisite private bath and is named after an original room of the Ice Palace. Begin your day with a delicious gourmet breakfast served at individual tables in this

The Ice Palace Inn

historic inn. Afternoon teas and goodies are available every day. Turndown service in the evening. Fireplaces and TV/VCRs. Hot tub.

Hosts: Giles and Kami Kolak
Rooms: 8 (PB) $89-149
Full Breakfast
Credit Cards: A, B, C, D, E
Notes: 2, 5, 7, 8, 9, 10, 11, 12

MANITOU SPRINGS

Spring Cottage Bed & Breakfast

113 Pawnee Avenue, 80829
(719) 685-9395; (888) 588-9395
fax: (719) 685-1248
E-mail: lancaster@springcottage.com
www.springcottage.com

"A time and a place to count as your own." Two private cottages. 1885 family-friendly Spring Cottage accommodates seven. Intimate "Spring Cottage, Too" accommodates two only for a personal holiday, honeymoon, anniversary, or retreat. Breakfast served privately in cottage. Fully equipped kitchens, TV, VCR, phone. One block to town center.

6 Pets welcome; 7 Children welcome; 8 Tennis nearby; 9 Swimming nearby; 10 Golf nearby; 11 Skiing nearby; 12 May be booked through travel agent

Hosts: Ron and Judy Lancaster
Rooms: 2 cottages (PB) $110
Full Breakfast
Credit Cards: A, B, F
Notes: 2, 5, 6, 7, 8, 9, 10, 11, 12

OURAY

Main Street Bed & Breakfast

334 Main Street, P.O. Box 641, 81427-0641
(970) 325-4871
E-mail: bates@netzone.com
http://colorado-bnb.com/mainst

A superbly renovated hundred-year-old residence which offers three suites and one room, plus a two-story cottage. All accommodations have private baths, queen beds, and satellite

Main Street

television. Two suites and the Mt. Abrams Room have decks with spectacular views of the San Juan Mountains. Three units have fully-equipped modern kitchens, and are provided with breakfast supplies for a hearty breakfast. Guests who stay in units without kitchens are served a full breakfast.

Hosts: Lee and Kathy Bates
Rooms: 5 (PB) $65-125
Full Breakfast
Credit Cards: A, B, C, F
Notes: 2, 5, 7, 8, 9, 10, 11

PAGOSA SPRINGS

Davidson's Country Inn

P.O. Box 87, 81147-0087
(970) 264-5863; fax: (970) 264-5492
E-mail: dcibb@aol.com

Davidson's, established in 1986, continues to be "home away from home" to our guests. We are located two miles east of town on Highway 160. Come enjoy our peaceful setting where you can view Pagosa Peak and wildlife from our porches. Inside you will find eight rooms tastefully decorated with antiques and heirlooms. Our two bedroom fully furnished cabin is very popular. Great country breakfasts keep our guests returning! Families and groups are welcome.

Hosts: Gilbert and Nancy Davidson
Rooms: 8 (4 PB; 4 SB) $75-95
Full Breakfast
Credit Cards: A, B, C, D
Notes: 2, 5, 7, 8, 9, 10, 11, 12

NOTES: Credit cards accepted: A Master Card; B Visa; C American Express; D Discover; E Diners Club; F Other; 2 Personal checks accepted; 3 Lunch available; 4 Dinner available; 5 Open all year;

PAONIA

Pitkin Mesa Bed & Breakfast

3954 P Road, 81428-9772
(970) 527-7576; (888) 245-0472

Pitkin Mesa B&B enjoys the mild climate of Paonia's fruit-growing area. Guests enjoy restful views of the North Fork Valley and nearby mountains. They can hike or bike to shops and restaurants. This is a newer home in a semi-rural area with an indoor, heated swimming pool and spa. From the porch swing on our spacious deck you can view Mt. Lamborn (Revelation 5:12). Close to Black Canyon National Park, scenic byways, and Grand Mesa's lakes. Tobacco- and alcohol-free. Children under 14 by special arrangement only.

Hosts: Dale and Barbara Soucek
Rooms: 3 (1 PB; 2 SB) $65-75
Full Breakfast
Credit Cards: A, B
Notes: 2, 5, 8, 9

SALIDA

The Tudor Rose Bed & Breakfast

P.O. Box 89, 81201
(719) 539-2002; (800) 379-0889
fax: (719) 530-0345
E-mail: tudorose@amigo.net
www.thetudorrose.com

Stately elegance and homelike comfort are combined tastefully at this majestic country manor. Nestled in the pines on 37 acres, and surrounded by three mountain ranges, the inn

commands views of the Rocky Mountains by day and starry skies by night. Overly large guestrooms, spacious common areas. Wildlife, native landscape, sunken hot tub, and a hiking trail enrich the surrounding grounds.

Hosts: Jon and Terre' Terrell
Rooms: 6 (PB) $65-150
Full Breakfast
Credit Cards: A, B, D
Notes: 2, 5, 7, 8, 9, 10, 11, 12

WOODLAND PARK

Woodland Inn Bed & Breakfast

159 Trull Road, 80863
(719) 687-8209; (800) 226-9565
fax: (719) 687-3112
E-mail: woodlandinn@aol.com
www.woodlandinn.com

Guests enjoy the relaxing, homelike atmosphere and fantastic views of Pikes Peak from this cozy country inn in the heart of the Rocky Mountains. Peacefully secluded on five private acres of woodlands, the Woodland Inn is 18 miles west of Colorado Springs. Guests enjoy our beautiful

6 Pets welcome; 7 Children welcome; 8 Tennis nearby; 9 Swimming nearby; 10 Golf nearby; 11 Skiing nearby; 12 May be booked through travel agent

hot tub nestled among the Aspen trees. Nearby attractions include Pikes Peak, Manitou Springs, hiking, biking, horseback riding, golf, cross-country skiing, and limited-stakes gambling in Cripple Creek. We welcome small retreats and seminars.

Hosts: Frank and Susan Gray
Rooms: 8 (6 PB; 2 SB) $89-99
Full Breakfast
Credit Cards: A, B, C, D
Notes: 2, 5, 7, 10, 12

Connecticut

GLASTONBURY

Butternut Farm

1654 Main Street, 06033-2962
(860) 633-7197; fax: (860) 659-1758
www.butternutfarmbandb.com

Butternut Farm

This 18th-century architectural jewel is furnished in period antiques. Prize-winning dairy goats, pigeons, and chickens roam in an estate setting with trees and herb gardens. Enjoy fresh eggs for breakfast. Ten minutes from Hartford by expressway; an hour and a half from any place in Connecticut. No pets, no smoking.

Host: Donald Reid
Rooms: 4 (PB) $85-105
Full Breakfast
Credit Cards: C
Notes: 2, 5, 7, 8, 9, 10, 11

MYSTIC

Antiques & Accommodations

32 Main Street, North Stonington, 06359-1709
(860) 535-1736; (800) 554-7829
fax: (860) 535-2613
E-mail: antaccbb; www.visitmystic.com/antiques

Stroll through our well-tended gardens filled with edible flowers and herbs. Relax on our porches and patios. Our country retreat is located two and a half miles from I-95, minutes from Mystic Seaport, Aquarium, and superb beaches. Gracious hospitality awaits you at our lovingly restored homes: antiques, canopy beds, fireplaces, private baths, air-conditioned rooms, and cable TV. Greet the day with our acclaimed, four-course candlelight breakfast. Always an abundance of flowers. We welcome children who appreciate antiques.

Hosts: Tom and Anne Gray
Rooms: 6 (PB) $99-229
Full Breakfast
Credit Cards: A, B
Notes: 2, 5, 7, 8, 9, 10, 12

Harbour Inne & Cottage

15 Edgemont Street, 06355-2853
(860) 572-9253
E-mail: harbourinne@earthlink.net
www. harbourinne-cottage.com

6 Pets welcome; 7 Children welcome; 8 Tennis nearby; 9 Swimming nearby; 10 Golf nearby; 11 Skiing nearby; 12 May be booked through travel agent

CONNECTICUT

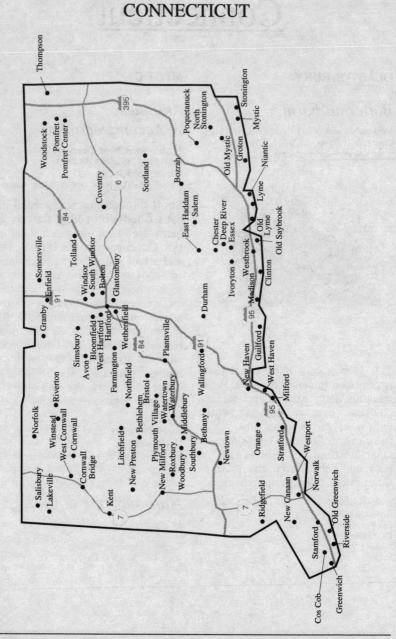

NOTES: Credit cards accepted: A Master Card; B Visa; C American Express; D Discover; E Diners Club; F Other; 2 Personal checks accepted; 3 Lunch available; 4 Dinner available; 5 Open all year;

Three-room cottage with a fireplace and two double beds in bedroom. Sleep sofa and cable color TV in living room with glider doors opening onto deck with hot tub spa. Shower/lavatory facilities, kitchen, and dining area. Guesthouse has five rooms, each with double bed, color TV, shower or bath, and air-conditioning. Equipped galley, dining area, and social area with fireplace and antique piano. Pets welcome.

Host: Charles Lecouras, Jr.
Rooms: 7 (PB) $55-300
Continental Breakfast
Credit Cards: None
Notes: 6, 7

NEW HAVEN

Bed & Breakfast, Ltd.

P.O. Box 216, 06513-0216
(203) 469-3260
E-mail: bandb@aol.com
www.bedandbreakfastltd.com

Bed and Breakfast, Ltd., now offers over 125 gracious and carefully selected B&B private homes and small inns throughout Connecticut. They range from elegantly simple. . .to simply elegant. A quick call after 4:00 p.m. daily or anytime weekends assures personalized service, descriptions, and up-to-the-minute availability. New listings nationwide invited to join our network.

Host: Jack M. Argenio
Rooms: 125 (85 PB; 40 SB) $75-175
Continental Breakfast
Credit Cards: A, B, C, F
Notes: 2, 5, 7, 8, 9, 10, 11

OLD SAYBROOK

The Deacon Timothy Pratt House

325 Main Street, 06475
(860) 395-1229
E-mail: shelley.nobile@snet.net
www.connecticut-bed-and-breakfast.com

The Deacon Timothy Pratt House

Step back in time and enjoy the splendor of this magnificent, circa 1746 center-chimney colonial, listed on the National Historic Register. Guest rooms are romantically furnished in period style with working fireplaces, four-poster and canopy beds, and Jacuzzis. A full breakfast is served in the elegant dining room on fine china by candlelight. Located in Old Saybrook where the Connecticut River meets Long Island Sound, the Pratt House is conveniently located in the historic and shopping district, on pretty, gaslit Main Street. Walk to shops, restaurants, theaters, town green, and Saybrook Point. The home is located near beaches, antique shops, museums, Mystic Seaport and Aquarium, Foxwoods and Mohegan

6 Pets welcome; 7 Children welcome; 8 Tennis nearby; 9 Swimming nearby; 10 Golf nearby; 11 Skiing nearby; 12 May be booked through travel agent

Sun Casinos, Goodspeed musicals, factory outlet malls, Essex Steam Train, Connecticut River and Long Island Sound cruises, Gillette Castle State Park, and lots more! Beach passes, maps, and advice provided. Picturesque grounds. Bicycle loop. Nonsmoking. Two-night minimum stay on weekends; three-night minimum on holiday weekends. Massage therapy on premises. Children over four welcome Sunday to Thursday.

Host: Shelley Nobile
Rooms: 4 (PB) $90-225
Full and Continental Breakfast
Credit Cards: A, B, C
Notes: 2, 5, 8, 9, 10, 11

PLYMOUTH

Shelton House Bed & Breakfast

663 Main Street, # 6, 06782-2212
(860) 283-4616 (phone/fax)
E-mail: sheltonhbb@prodigy.net

Shelton House

1825 Greek Revival nominated for the Historic Register, elegantly furnished with antiques and period furniture. Park-like grounds, perennial flower garden, and pineapple fountain. Spacious guest parlor with fireplace and TV. Full breakfast is served. Afternoon tea available. Convenient to I-84 and just one mile from Route 8, Exit 39. Twenty minutes to historic Litchfield; 30 minutes to State Capitol. Antique centers, restaurants, vineyards, nature preserves, museums, and skiing are all nearby.

Hosts: Pat and Bill Doherty
Rooms: 4 (2 PB; 2 SB) $80-95
Full Breakfast
Credit Cards: None
Notes: 2, 5, 9, 10, 11

WOODSTOCK

Bed & Breakfast at Taylor's Corner

880 Route 171, 06281
(860) 974-0490; (888) 503-9057
fax: (860) 974-0498
E-mail: peggy@bnbattaylorscorner.com
www.bnatttayolorscorner.com

In the quaint New England town of Woodstock in the "Quiet Corner" of Connecticut is a completely restored 18th-century country home with magnificent gardens offering three spacious, air-conditioned guest rooms with private baths, phones, individual thermostats, and fireplaces. In addition to our three guest rooms, we also have a first-floor two-room suite with private entrance, king-size bed, air-conditioning, TV, phone, cathedral ceiling, individual thermostat control, and sitting room with fireplace and a private bath with tub and shower. Suite is $155 per night with a two-night minimum. State parks, theatre, shopping, antiquing, and excellent restaurants close by. Old Sturbridge

---

NOTES: Credit cards accepted: A Master Card; B Visa; C American Express; D Discover; E Diners Club; F Other; 2 Personal checks accepted; 3 Lunch available; 4 Dinner available; 5 Open all year;

Village and Brimfield Antiques show 20 minutes away. Children 12 and older welcome. One guest commented: "We've found a jewel in the woods." Seventy-five minutes to Boston, MA; 50 minutes to Hartford, CT or Rhode Island; three hours to New York City. Ask about our New England tour.

Hosts: Peggy and Doug Tracy
Rooms: 3 (PB) $80-140
Continental Breakfast
Credit Cards: A, B, C, D, E, F
Notes: 2, 5, 7, 8, 9, 10, 12

DELAWARE

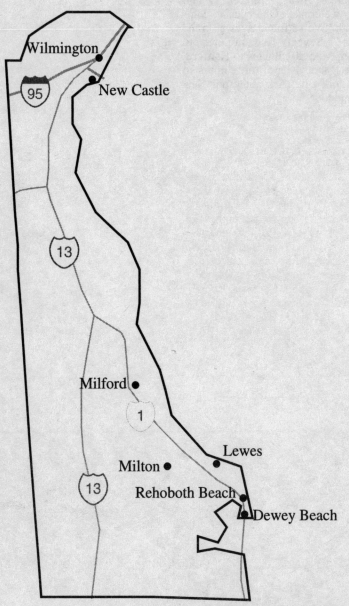

Delaware

Bed & Breakfast of Delaware

2701 Landon Drive, Suite 200, 19810-2211
(302) 479-9500; fax: (302) 478-1437
E-mail: bnbofde@juno.com

Bed & Breakfast of Delaware is a reservation service. We will make reservations for you in historic inns, farms, estates, private homes, mini efficiencies, and spacious manors in Delaware, Maryland, Pennsylvania, and Virginia. Credit cards accepted. We are ten minutes from Longwood Gardens, Winterthur, Nemours, Rockwood, the Brandywine Valley, ocean and parks, the University of Delaware, and Widner Las School.

Rooms: 3 (2 PB; 1 SB) $75-85
Full Breakfast
Credit Cards: A, B, C, D
Notes: 2, 5, 7, 8, 9, 10

DISTRICT OF COLUMBIA

District of Columbia

The Dupont at the Circle

1606 19th Street NW, 20009
(202) 332-5251; (888) 412-0100
fax: (202) 332-3244
E-mail: dupontatthecircle@erols.com
www.dupontatthecircle.com

The Dupont at the Circle is housed in two restored Victorian townhomes, built in 1885. Our eight guest rooms are luxuriously appointed with antique furniture and sumptuous linens with private baths. Tasteful decor and original features like gas lamps and ornate moldings give a cozy ambiance that belies our urban setting. Breakfast consists of fresh muffins and scones, seasonal fruits, homemade granola, and the best coffee around!

Hosts: Alan and Anexora Skvirsky
Rooms: 8 (PB) $140-300
Continental Breakfast
Credit Cards: A, B, C, D, E
Notes: 2, 5, 8, 9, 10, 12

Embassy Inn

1627 16th Street Northwest, 20009
(202) 234-7800; (800) 423-9111
fax: (202) 234-3309

The Embassy Inn is a lovely haven of European charm in the heart of Washington, D.C. Guests enjoy a warm, intimate, and relaxing atmosphere along with convenience and economical rates. All the guestrooms have a private bathroom, direct dial phone, digital alarm clock, cable television with complimentary HBO, and daily maid service. Begin each morning with an expanded Continental breakfast to get you going for the day's activities. The neighborhood includes the Dupont Circle and Adams Morgan areas with many diverse restaurants and shops to explore. The inn is easily accessible to Washington's business district, museums, monuments, and universities. The White House is only ten blocks south of the Inn, and the National Zoo is also nearby.

Host: Susan Stiles
Rooms: 38 (PB) $89-129
Continental Breakfast
Credit Cards: A, B, C, E
Notes: 5, 7, 8, 9, 10, 12

---

6 Pets welcome; 7 Children welcome; 8 Tennis nearby; 9 Swimming nearby; 10 Golf nearby; 11 Skiing nearby; 12 May be booked through travel agent

Swiss Inn

1204 Massachusetts Avenue NW, 20005-4501
(202) 371-1816; (800) 955-7947
fax: (202) 371-1138
E-mail: swissinndc@aol.com
www.theswissinn.com

The Swiss Inn is a charming turn-of-the-century Victorian townhouse located in Washington, D.C. Amenities include bay windows, high ceilings, and fully equipped kitchenettes. The small, family-owned and -operated inn is within walking distance of the White House, FBI, National Geographic, Chinatown, Convention Center, Smithsonian Museums, Ford's Theater, Women in the Arts Museum, subway, and many other attractions. We are also just two blocks from the main business district. Grocery stores are within walking distance, as are many noted churches, including St. Matthew's Cathedral.

Hosts: Kelley and Ralph
Rooms: 7 (PB)
Credit Cards: A, B, C, D, E
Notes: 5, 6, 7, 12

Windsor Inn

1842 16th Street Northwest, 20009
(202) 667-0300; (800) 423-9111
fax: (202) 667-4503

The Windsor Inn's main building features 36 guest rooms that vary from cozy twin bed singles to larger rooms with two double beds, ideal for families. An annex building adjacent to the inn offers suites with regular and sofa queen beds, a kitchenette, mini-suites with queen beds, and several extras, including mini-refrigerators in each room, bath amenities, oversized plush towels, and décor in different but elegant styles. Every room at the Windsor also has a private bath, direct dial phones with message lights, cable TV, and built-in hairdryers. Enjoy the inn's lovely, expanded Continental breakfast of croissants, muffins, sweet rolls, cereals, coffee, tea, and orange juice each morning.

Host: Susan Stiles
Rooms: 45 (PB) $89-179
Continental Breakfast
Credit Cards: A, B, C, E
Notes: 5, 7, 8, 9, 10, 12

NOTES: Credit cards accepted: A Master Card; B Visa; C American Express; D Discover; E Diners Club; F Other; 2 Personal checks accepted; 3 Lunch available; 4 Dinner available; 5 Open all year;

Florida

AMELIA ISLAND

Bailey House

28 South 7th Street, 32034-3960
(904) 261-5390; (800) 251-5390
fax: (904) 321-0103
E-mail: baileyhs@bellsouth.net
www.bailey-house.com

Bailey House

Bailey House is a picturesque Queen Anne style B&B with Victorian decor. Built in 1895, it is listed in the National Register. Features include a wraparound porch, turrets, gables, beautiful stained glass windows, a magnificent staircase, pocket doors, ten fireplaces, and much more. The house is located in the historic district of Fernandina Beach on Amelia Island. You will be able to walk to restaurants, shops, and historic facilities. A delicious full breakfast is included.

Hosts: Tom and Jenny Bishop
Rooms: 10 (PB) $129-189
Full Breakfast
Credit Cards: A, B, C, D
Notes: 2, 5, 8, 9, 10, 12

Elizabeth Pointe Lodge

98 South Fletcher Avenue, 32034
(904) 277-4851; (800) 772-3359
fax: (904) 277-6500
E-mail: info@elizabethpointelodge.com
www.elizabethpointelodge.com

Rated "One of the 12 Best Waterfront Inns" in America, the Pointe sits overlooking the Atlantic Ocean. Focusing on individualized attention, the inn is Nantucket "shingle-style" with oversized soaking tubs in each bath, fresh flowers, morning newspaper, full seaside breakfast, and a staff that wants to exceed your expectations. Horseback riding, tennis, golf, and sailing nearby. Only a short bike ride to the historic seaport of Fernandina.

Elizabeth Pointe Inn

Hosts: David and Susan Caples
Rooms: 25 (PB) $160-270
Full Breakfast
Credit Cards: A, B, C, D
Notes: 2, 3, 4, 5, 7, 8, 9, 10, 12

---

6 Pets welcome; 7 Children welcome; 8 Tennis nearby; 9 Swimming nearby; 10 Golf nearby; 11 Skiing nearby; 12 May be booked through travel agent

FLORIDA

ARCADIA

Historic Parker House

427 W Hickory Street, 34266-3703
(863) 494-2499; (800) 969-2499
E-mail: parkerhouse@desoto.net
www.historicparkerhouse.com

Step back in time at the Historic Parker House. This lovely two-story

Historic Parker House

1895 home is full of period antiques, old clocks, and bits of Florida history. Four elegantly appointed guest rooms are located on the second floor. Larger rooms feature private baths, cable TV, and in-room phones. Breakfast in the formal dining room is a real treat.

Hosts: Bob and Shelly Baumann
Rooms: 4 (3 PB; 2 SB) $69-85
Continental Breakfast
Credit Cards: A, B, C
Notes: 2, 5, 8, 10, 12

BIG PINE KEY

Deer Run Bed & Breakfast

Long Beach Road, P.O. Box 431, 33043
(305) 872-2015
E-mail: deerrunbb@aol.com

This oceanfront home offers a unique setting that includes a beach front spa and Key deer strolling along the beach. Antiques, wicker and rattan, along with Bahama fans and French doors enhance the tropical atmosphere. The inn's veranda overlooks the water and is the location of choice for breakfast.

Host: Sue Abbott
Rooms: 3 (PB) $95-165
Full Breakfast
Credit Cards: None
Notes: 2, 5

BRANDON

Behind the Fence Bed & Breakfast

1400 Viola Drive at Countryside, 33511
(813) 685-8201; (800) 448-2672

Retreat into the simplicity and tranquillity of a bygone era with the conveniences of today's world. Choose your accommodations, from a cottage by our pool, to a private room in our antique-filled New England saltbox house. Nearby parks, and river canoe-

Behind the Fence

6 Pets welcome; 7 Children welcome; 8 Tennis nearby; 9 Swimming nearby; 10 Golf nearby; 11 Skiing nearby; 12 May be booked through travel agent

ing offer lots of opportunities for family activities. Homemade Amish sweet rolls are featured, and "relaxing" is the word most guests use to refer to their stay "behind the fence." Country furniture is for sale. Tours are available upon request. AAA, three-star approved.

Hosts: Larry and Carolyn Yoss
Rooms: 5 (3 PB; 2 SB) $79-89
Continental Breakfast
Credit Cards: None
Notes: 2, 5, 6, 7, 8, 9, 10

CAPE CANAVERAL

Beachside Bed & Breakfast

629 Adams Avenue, 32920
(321) 799-4320
E-mail: saccarot@aol.com

See a space launch from the beach. The ocean is only a few yards from the guest suite which offers private entrance, bedroom with twin beds, one and one half private baths, and living room. Also includes a kitchen stocked for breakfast which guests may enjoy at their leisure. Port Canaveral and Kennedy Space Center are minutes away. Walt Disney World and Orlando are just an hour's drive. Orlando international airport (45 minutes) shuttle service available.

Hosts: Tony and Dorothy Dean Saccaro
Rooms: 1 suite (PB) $65
Continental Breakfast
Credit Cards: None
Notes: 2, 5, 8, 9, 10

FORT LAUDERDALE

Phoenix South Guest House

3609 Northeast 27th Street, 33308
(954) 733-7701 day; (954) 563-6665 evening
fax: (954) 739-0282
E-mail: info@beachguesthouse.com
www.beachguesthouse.com

World-class deep sea fishing, scuba diving on one of the many wrecks and reefs, sailing the Atlantic, or basking in the sun are just some of the activities available to complete the perfect stay at Phoenix Guest House. Nightlife and fine dining abound, all within walking distance. You can even take an early evening Water Taxi tour of the Intracoastal Waterway and stop off at the restaurant or nightclub of your choice.

Rooms: 5 (PB) $125-175
Credit Cards: None
Notes: 2, 5, 7, 9

KEY WEST

Whispers Bed & Breakfast

409 William Street, 33040-6853
(305) 294-5969; (800) 856-7444
fax: (305) 294-3899
E-mail: bbwhispers@aol.com
www.whispersbb.com

Whispers sits in the heart of Olde Town Key West, within view of the Gulf Harbor and surrounded by a 30-block historic district of distinctive 19th-century homes. Ceiling fans whirl above rooms filled with antique furnighings. Guests enjoy the cool porches and lush garden. Take advantage of our complimentary membership at the local state park beaches, pool, and full health club facilities. Enjoy our tropical fish, birds, and gourmet breakfast creations. Come to paradise. Come home to Whispers.

Host: John Marburg
Rooms: 7 (PB) $99-175
Full Breakfast
Credit Cards: A, B, C, D
Notes: 5, 6, 8, 9, 10, 12

LAKE WALES

Chalet Suzanne Inn & Restaurant

3800 Chalet Suzanne Drive, 33853
(863) 676-6011; (800) 433-6011
fax: (863) 676-1814
E-mail: info@chaletsuzanne.com
www.chaletsuzanne.com

Listed on the National Register of Historic Places, the "folkloric" village which is Chalet Suzanne lies on the shore of Lake Suzanne surrounded by fragrant Central Florida orange groves. Since 1931 the Hinshaw family has welcomed guests to the 30-room inn and five-star restaurant which serves breakfast, lunch, and dinner daily. Visit the gift shop, ceramic studio, Chapel Antiques, swim, tour the soup cannery, home of the soups that went to the moon.

Host: Vita Hinshaw
Rooms: 30 (PB) $169-229
Full Breakfast
Credit Cards: A, B, C, D, E, F
Notes: 2, 3, 4, 5, 7, 8, 9, 10, 12

The G.V. Tillman House Bed & Breakfast

301 East Sessoms Avenue, 33853
phone/fax: (863) 676-5499; (800) 488-3315
E-mail: tillmanbb@aol.com
www.tillmanbb.com

The G.V. Tillman House, built in 1914, was the original home of Mr. George Vernon Tillman. Guests are invited to a traditional tea which may be enjoyed on the veranda overlooking Crystal Lake. Delightful feather beds, a bountiful breakfast along with comfortable period antiques, and turndown service are just a few of the amenities available. This historic home provides a perfect backdrop for the small wedding, corporate retreat, or romantic getaway. Bass Fishing Packages are available on-site. Children over 12 are welcome.

Hosts: Jim and Kathy Dowling
Rooms: 5 (4 PB; 1 SB) $85-130
Continental Breakfast
Credit Cards: A, B, C
Notes: 2, 5, 7, 8, 9, 10, 11, 12

Chalet Suzanne

LAKE WORTH

Mango Inn
Bed & Breakfast

128 North Lakeside Drive, 33460
(561) 533-6900; (888) 626-4619
fax: (561) 533-6992
E-mail: info@mangoinn.com
www.mangoinn.com

Lake Worth's oldest B&B is just a short walk from the beautiful beaches of the Atlantic Ocean. Historic downtown Lake Worth with its antique stores, art galleries, museums, and sidewalk cafés is two blocks from the inn. Each of the eight guest rooms is decorated differently and has a private bath. Breakfast is served poolside and features a signature dish such as orange marmalade-stuffed French toast with orange-nutmeg syrup.

Hosts: Erin & Bo Allen
Rooms: 8 (PB) $70-225
Full Breakfast
Credit Cards: A, B, C, D
Notes: 5, 8, 9, 10, 12

MICANOPY

Shady Oak
Bed & Breakfast

201 Cholokka Boulevard, P.O. Box 327, 32667
(352) 466-3476; fax: (352) 466-9233
E-mail: goodtimes@shadyoak.com
www.shadyoak.com

The Shady Oak stands majestically in the center of historic downtown Micanopy. A marvelous canopy of live oaks, quiet streets, and many antique shops offers visitors a memorable connection to Florida's past. This three-story, nineteenth-century-style mansion features five beautiful spacious suites, private baths, porches, Jacuzzi, Florida room, and widow's walk. Three lovely, historic churches are within walking distance. Local activities include antiquing, bicycling, canoeing, bird-watching, and much more. "Playfully elegant accommodations where stained glass, antiques, and innkeeping go together as kindly as warm hugs with old friends."

Host: Frank James
Rooms: 8 (PB) $75-175
Full Breakfast
Credit Cards: A, B, C, D
Notes: 2, 4, 5, 7, 8, 9, 10, 12

ORLANDO

Courtyard at Lake Lucerne

211 North Lucerne Circle, 32801-3721
(407) 648-5188; (800) 444-5289
fax: (407) 246-1368
E-mail: info@orlandohistoricinn.com
www.orlandohistoricinn.com

Four different styles compromise this award-winning historic inn. The Normant-Parry Inn is Orlando's oldest house. The Wellborn, an Art-Deco-Modern building, offers one-bedroom

Courtyard at Lake Lucerne

NOTES: Credit cards accepted: A Master Card; B Visa; C American Express; D Discover; E Diners Club; F Other; 2 Personal checks accepted; 3 Lunch available; 4 Dinner available; 5 Open all year;

suites with kitchenettes. The I.W.
Phillips is an antebellum-style manor
house where breakfast is served on a
veranda overlooking gardens and
fountains. All buildings are authentically furnished. The Victorian Dr.
Phillips House, listed on the National
Register of Historic Places, has six
lovely and esquisitely furnished guest
suites, all of which include double
whirlpool tubs.

Rooms: 30 (PB) $89-225
Continental Breakfast
Credit Cards: A, B, C, E
Notes: 4, 5, 7, 8, 9, 10, 12

Meadow Marsh

Meadow Marsh Bed & Breakfast

940 Tildenville School Road, Winter Garden,
    34787
(407) 656-2064; (888) 656-2064
fax: (407) 654-0656
E-mail: cavelle5@aol.com
www.meadowmarshbnb.com

Peace and tranquility embrace you as
God's beauty unfolds in twelve acres
of ol' Florida. You'll enjoy the 1877
Victorian farmhouse where cozy fireplaces, hardwood floors, and lace curtains enhance the warmth and beauty
of this country estate. The spacious

lawn invites a romantic picnic or
hand-in-hand walk through the meadow to the adjacent rails-to-trails
path. Old-fashioned porch swings add
to the feeling of yesteryear. After a
busy day at Central Florida's many
attractions, relive the genteel era that
whispers faintly through Meadow
Marsh.

Hosts: Cavelle and John Pawlack
Rooms: 5 (PB) $109-229
Full Breakfast
Credit Cards: A, B
Notes: 5, 8, 9, 10, 12

PerriHouse Acres Estate Bed & Breakfast Inn

10417 Vista Oaks Court, 32836
(407) 876-4830; (800) 780-4830
fax: (407) 876-0241
E-mail: birds@perrihouse.com
www.perrihouse.com

PerriHouse is a quiet, country estate
inn secluded on 16 acres of land adjacent to the Walt Disney World Resort.
Surrounded by trees, grassy fields,
and orange groves, the PerriHouse
Estate is a natural bird sanctuary; bird
feeders and nature trails make bird-
watching a delightful pastime. Five
minutes to Disney, Pleasure Island,
and EPCOT Center. Upscale Continental breakfast buffet; pool and hot
tub on the patio. Eight guest rooms
with private bath and entrances. The
PerriHouse Acres Vacation Home is
available for extended stays, family
reunions, and corporate retreats.

Hosts: Nick and Angi Perretti
Rooms: 11 (PB) $99-129
Continental Breakfast
Credit Cards: A, B, C, D, E
Notes: 2, 5, 7, 8, 9, 10, 12

PALATKA

Ferncourt Bed & Breakfast

150 Central Avenue, San Mateo, 32187
(386) 329-9755
E-mail: ferncourt@gbso.net
www.ferncourt.com

Ferncourt

Ferncourt is a Victorian farmhouse built in 1889. Seventeen rooms, plus a large veranda allow lots of common area for guests. Hens on-site provide basis for many delightful breakfast entrees. St. Augustine is a short 25 miles through farm country. Drive a little, save a lot. Large comfortable rooms await you at the end of the day. Home is furnished in antiques and collectibles for your pleasure.

Hosts: Jack and Dee Dee Morgan
Rooms: 6 (5 PB; 1 SB) $65-85
Full Breakfast
Credit Cards: A, B
Notes: 2, 4, 5, 10

ST. AUGUSTINE

Carriage Way Bed & Breakfast

70 Cuna Street, 32084
(904) 829-2467; (800) 908-9832

fax: (904) 826-1461
E-mail: bjohnson@aug.com
www.carriageway.com

Built in 1833, this Victorian home is located in the heart of the historic district amid unique and charming shops, museums, and historic sites. The atmosphere is leisurely and casual, in keeping with the general attitude and feeling of Old St. Augustine. All guest rooms have a private bath with a claw-foot tub or shower. Rooms are furnished with antiques and reproductions including brass, canopy, or four-poster beds. A full home-baked breakfast is served.

Hosts: Bill and Larry Johnson
Rooms: 11 (PB) $69-175
Full Breakfast
Credit Cards: A, B, C, D
Notes: 2, 5, 7, 8, 9, 10, 12

Castle Garden Bed & Breakfast

15 Shenandoah Street, 32084
(904) 829-3839; fax: (904) 829-9049
E-mail: castleg@aug.com
www.castlegarden.com

Stay at a castle and be treated like royalty! Relax and enjoy the peace, quiet, and "royal treatment" at our newly restored, 100-year-old castle of Moorish Revival design. The only sounds you'll hear are the occasional roar of a cannon shot from the old fort 200 yards to the south, or the creak of solid wood floors. Awaken to the aroma of freshly baked goodies as we prepare a full, mouth-watering, country breakfast just like "Mom used to make." The unusual coquina stone exterior remains virtually untouched.

The interior of the former Castle Warden Carriage House boasts three beautiful bridal rooms, each complete with a soothing, in-room Jacuzzi and sunken bedroom! Our amenities include complimentary wine, chocolates, bikes, and private parking. Packages and gift baskets are available. We believe every guest is a gift from God.

Hosts: Bruce and Brian Kloeckner
Rooms: 7 (PB) $65-179
Full Breakfast
Credit Cards: A, B, C, D
Notes: 2, 5, 7, 8, 10, 12

The Cedar House Inn

79 Cedar Street, 32084
(904) 829-0079; (800) 233-2746
fax: (904) 825-0916
E-mail: cbb@cedarhouseinn.com
www.cedarhouseinn.com

The Cedar House Inn

Capture romantic moments at our 1893 Victorian home in the heart of the ancient city. Escape into your antique-filled bedroom with private whirlpool bath or claw-foot tub. Enjoy the comfortable parlor with its fireplace, player piano, and antique Victrola or sit on the shady veranda. Elegant full breakfast, evening snack, parking on premises, Jacuzzi spa, and bicycles. Walk to historical sites or bicycle to the beach. AAA-approved, three-diamond rated. Smoke-free home; mid-week discounts.

Hosts: Russ and Nina Thomas
Rooms: 6 (PB) $89-185
Full Breakfast
Credit Cards: A, B, C, D
Notes: 2, 3, 4, 5, 7, 8, 9, 10, 12

The Old Powder House Inn Bed & Breakfast

38 Cordova Street, 32084
(904) 824-4149; (800) 447-4149
fax: (904) 825-0143
E-mail: kalieta@aug.com
www.oldpowderhouse.com

Escape to a romantic getaway in this charming, turn-of-the-century Victorian inn. Lace curtains and hardwood floors adorn antique-filled rooms. Towering pecan and oak trees shade verandas. Sit in rockers, settees, or the porch swing and watch the horse-drawn carriages bring history to the present. At your leisure, enjoy complimentary morning coffee and specialty teas, afternoon lemonade, iced tea, fresh baked sweets, and evening wine and cordials. Enjoy our delicious hors d'oeuvres served Friday and Saturday.

Hosts: Katie and Kal Kalieta
Rooms: 9 (PB) $75-195
Full Breakfast
Credit Cards: A, B, C, D
Notes: 2, 5, 9, 10, 12

6 Pets welcome; 7 Children welcome; 8 Tennis nearby; 9 Swimming nearby; 10 Golf nearby; 11 Skiing nearby; 12 May be booked through travel agent

St. Francis Inn

279 Saint George Street, 32084
(904) 824-6068; (800) 824-6062
fax: (904) 810-5525
E-mail: innceasd@aug.com
www.stfrancisinn.com

Built in 1791, the St. Francis Inn is a beautiful Spanish Colonial building. The courtyard garden provides a peaceful setting for traditional hospitality. Our accommodations range from double rooms and suites to a five-room cottage, all with private bath, cable television, and central air/heat; many have fireplaces. The inn is centrally located in the historic district within easy walking distance of restaurants, shops, and sites.

Host: Joe Finnegan
Rooms: 17 (PB) $99-199
Full Breakfast
Credit Cards: A, B, C, D, F
Notes: 2, 5, 7, 8, 9, 10, 12

Victorian House
Bed & Breakfast

11 Cadiz Street, 32084
(904) 824-5214; (877) 703-0432
fax: (904) 824-7990

E-mail: kjc50@aol.com
www.victorianhouse-inn.com

The Victorian House, built in 1897, has been lovingly restored and furnished in period antiques. Enjoy canopy beds, quilts, stenciled walls, and heart pine floors. We are located in the historic district within walking distance of fine restaurants, the water front, shops, museums, and the plaza. Breakfast is served in the dining room from 8:30 until 10:00 A.M. and features homemade granola, sweet breads, muffins, fruit, juice, hot entrée, coffee, and tea.

Hosts: Ken and Marcia Cerotzke
Rooms: 8 (PB) $85-160
Full Breakfast
Credit Cards: A, B, C, D, F
Notes: 5, 7, 8, 9, 10, 12

ST. PETERSBURG

Island's End Resort

1 Pass A Grille Way, 33(706) 4326
(727) 360-5023; fax: (727) 367-7890
E-mail: jzgpag@aol.com
islandsend.com

Island's End, an oasis of real peace and quiet, where the crystal blue waters of the Gulf of Mexico meet the Intracoastal Waterway. Experience the brilliant sunrises while sipping freshly squeezed orange juice. Hunt for the shells along our private beach or stroll out to the end of our fishing dock and watch dolphins playfully swimming. Island's End features five well appointed one-bedroom cottages and a fantastic three-bedroom home with a private solar-heated pool. A

Continental breakfast is served three times a week in our gazebo.

Hosts: Jane and Millard Gamble
Rooms: 6 (PB) $87-215
Continental Breakfast
Credit Cards: A, B
Notes: 2, 5, 7, 8, 9, 12

Mansion House Bed & Breakfast & the Courtyard on Fifth

105 5th Avenue Northeast, 33701
(727) 821-9391; (800) 274-7520
fax: (727) 821-6906
E-mail: mansion1@ix.netcom.com
www.mansionbandb.com

Mansion House

This historic property, 1901-1912, features 13 rooms in two mansions and a carriage house surrounding a courtyard garden and swimming pool. Delicious breakfast, complimentary wine, soft drinks, and snacks, plus 10 common areas provide the ultimate inn experience for business and leisure travelers. "Preferred Hotel" Bank of America, InnPoint Travel Rewards; ABBA 3-Crowns for Excellence; AAA, Superior Small Lodging; FH/MA, PAII. Expect the unexpected! "Mansion House, The

Best!"—Michael & Kevin, Bacon Bros. Band.

Hosts: Robert and Rose Marie Ray
Rooms: 13 (PB) $149-220
Full Breakfast
Credit Cards: A, B, C, D, E
Notes: 2, 3, 5, 7, 8, 9, 10, 12

SANFORD

The Higgins House Victorian Bed & Breakfast

420 South Oak Avenue, 32771
(407) 324-9238; (800) 584-0014
fax: (407) 324-5060
E-mail: reservations@higginshouse.com
www.higginshouse.com

Enjoy the romance of a bygone era at this 107-year-old Queen Anne Victorian B&B. Three guest rooms and a cottage all have private baths. Enjoy the Victorian gardens and hot tub. The Higgins House B&B is located in historic Sanford near beautiful Lake Monroe and the St. Johns River. Antique shops are nearby.

The Higgins House

Hosts: Walter and Roberta Padgett
Rooms: 4 (PB) $100-135
Full Breakfast
Credit Cards: A, B, C, D
Notes: 2, 5, 8, 10, 12

---

6 Pets welcome; 7 Children welcome; 8 Tennis nearby; 9 Swimming nearby; 10 Golf nearby; 11 Skiing nearby; 12 May be booked through travel agent

SEBRING

Kenilworth Lodge

836 Southeast Lakeview Drive, 33870
(863) 385-0111; (800) 423-5939
fax: (863) 385-4686
E-mail: kenlodge@strato.net
www.kenilworthlodge.com

The Kenilworth Lodge is an historic hotel built in 1916 by the town's founder, George Sebring. Originally built as a retreat for well-to-do northerners, the Kenilworth retains its historic ambiance while adding modern amenities such as refrigerators in every guest room and satellite TV. The front veranda overlooks Lake Jackson, and guests gather each evening to watch the sun set over the lake. There is also an 80-foot heated

Kenilworth Lodge

pool, shuffleboard, billiards, and Ping Pong on the premises. Golf, tennis, fishing, and canoeing packages are available. Listed on the National Register of Historic Places, Kenilworth Lodge—where excellence is a tradition!

Hosts: Mark and Madge Stewart
Rooms: 106 (PB) $49-120
Continental Breakfast
Credit Cards: A, B, C, D, E, F
Notes: 5, 7, 8, 9, 10, 12

TARPON SPRINGS

East Lake Bed & Breakfast

421 Old East Lake Road, 34688
(727) 937-5487
E-mail: littleflower@prodigy.net
www.bbonline.com/fl/eastlake

East Lake B&B is a private home on two and a half acres situated on a quiet road along Lake Tarpon, close to the Gulf of Mexico. The hosts are retired businesspeople who enjoy new friends and are well-informed about the area. The room and adjoining bath are at the front of the house, away from the family quarters. The room has central air-conditioning, color TV, and telephone. Breakfast includes fresh fruit, juice, entrée, and homemade breads and jams. Located close to many Florida attractions. Smoking on porch/deck only.

Hosts: Dick and Marie Fiorito
Rooms: 1 (PB) $45
Full Breakfast
Credit Cards: None
Notes: 2, 5, 8, 9, 10

VERO BEACH

Redstone Manor Bed & Breakfast

806 43rd Avenue, 32960
(561) 562-8082

NOTES: Credit cards accepted: A Master Card; B Visa; C American Express; D Discover; E Diners Club; F Other; 2 Personal checks accepted; 3 Lunch available; 4 Dinner available; 5 Open all year;

Enjoy this Florida ranch-style home on two and a half acres of beautifully landscaped grounds. There are four tastefully decorated bedrooms with four private baths. The common areas consist of a great room, library, dining room, large screened porch, a large pool, and hot tub. A full breakfast and afternoon refreshments are served in gracious style. Just minutes from beaches, shopping mall, outlets, and many fine restaurants. Local activities include: Center for the Arts, Riverside Theater, Vero Beach Dodgers, Environmental Learning Center, Mel Fisher Treasure Museum, and Harbor Branch Oceanographic Institution. Nearby attractions include: Disney World, Wet and Wild in Orlando, and Cape Kennedy at Cocoa Beach.

Hosts: Butch and Joyce Redstone
Rooms: 4 (PB) $85-120
Full Breakfast
Credit Cards: None
Notes: 2, 5, 8, 9, 10

WELLBORN

1909 McLeran House Bed & Breakfast

12408 County Road 137, 32094
(386) 963-4603

A beautifully restored, two-story Victorian home on five landscaped acres features a lovely garden area with gazebo, garden swing, deck area, goldfish pond, and an abundance of trees and shrubs. Guests enjoy a large, comfortable room with mini-refrigerator and cable TV. The private bath downstairs features a claw-foot tub with shower. Enjoy the many antiques

1909 McLeran House

throughout the house, relax in the garden, stroll the grounds, or visit the "collectibles" shop in the old barn. Additional charge for extra people. Many local attractions are nearby, including the Stephen Foster Folk Culture Center. Canoeing and natural springs are nearby, as well as the Swannee River for fishing.

Hosts: Robert and Mary Ryals
Rooms: 2 (PB) $95
Full Breakfast
Credit Cards: None
Notes: 2, 5, 8, 9, 10

WHITE SPRINGS

White Springs Bed & Breakfast

P.O. Box 403, 32096
(386) 397-1665
E-mail: kgavronsky@aol.com
http://hometown.aol.com/kgavronsky/
    myhomepage/business.html

Charming 1905 boarding house located a short stroll to the romantic Suwannee River and the Stephen Fos-

---

6 Pets welcome; 7 Children welcome; 8 Tennis nearby; 9 Swimming nearby; 10 Golf nearby; 11 Skiing nearby; 12 May be booked through travel agent

ter Folk Center. Picturesque town with over 100 historic homes and buildings. Population 800—no traffic lights! Each guest will receive a complimentary bottle of wine or sparkling grape juice.

White Springs

Host: Kerry Gavronsky
Rooms: 4 (2 PB; 2 SB) $65-75
Full Breakfast
Credit Cards: A, B, F
Notes: 2, 3, 5, 6, 7, 9, 10

Georgia

ATHENS

Nicholson House Inn

6295 Jefferson Road, 30607
(706) 353-2200; fax: (706) 353-7799
E-mail: 1820@nicholhouseinn.com
www.nicholsonhouseinn.com

Slip back quietly in time to the splendor of the Old South in this elegant antebellum home. This historic 1820 inn is magnificently restored and decorated, set in a relaxing six-acre haven just five miles from downtown. It is splendidly appointed with antiques and fine prints. Join us on the veranda in the evening and gaze upon friendly fawn and deer feeding in the yard.

Nicholson House Inn

Hosts: Celeste and Harry Neely/owners
Rooms: 9 (PB) $99-119
Full Breakfast
Credit Cards: A, B, C, D
Notes: 2, 5, 10

ATLANTA

The Village Inn Bed & Breakfast

The Village Inn

992 Ridge Avenue, Stone Mountain, 30083
(770) 469-3459; (800) 214-8385
fax: (770) 469-1051
E-mail: reservations@villageinnbb.com
www.villageinnbb.com

Come experience Southern hospitality and classic antebellum charm. Built in the 1820s, restored in 1995, the Village Inn is Stone Mountain's ONLY historic B&B. Walk to over 60 unique shops and restaurants. Less than one mile from Georgia's Stone Mountain Park, and 15 minutes east of Atlanta. All rooms have private baths with oversized whirlpool tub, cable TV/VCR, telephone, and individual climate control. Several have verandas and gas fireplaces. Guests enjoy a

---

6 Pets welcome; 7 Children welcome; 8 Tennis nearby; 9 Swimming nearby; 10 Golf nearby; 11 Skiing nearby; 12 May be booked through travel agent

GEORGIA

NOTES: Credit cards accepted: A Master Card; B Visa; C American Express; D Discover; E Diners Club; F Other; 2 Personal checks accepted; 3 Lunch available; 4 Dinner available; 5 Open all year;

Southern breakfast and complimentary snacks and beverages.

Hosts: Earl and Christy Collins
Rooms: 6 (PB) $139-199
Full Breakfast
Credit Cards: A, B, C, D
Notes: 5, 7, 8, 9, 10, 12

CARROLLTON

Historic Banning Mills

205 Horsehoe Dam Road, Whitesburg, 30185
(770) 834-9149; (866) 447-8688
fax: (770) 214-3729
E-mail: info@historicbanningmills.com
www.historicbanningmills.com

The Historic Banning Mills is a secluded country inn and conference center on 88 wooded acres just 45 minutes west of Atlanta. Our mountain-like setting provides a quiet and serene site for church retreats, Bible study, and romantic escapes. Our inn has 14 beautifully decorated rooms. All of our rooms have Jacuzzi tubs, gas fireplaces, decks overlooking the Snake Creek, coffeemakers, and a full breakfast in the morning.

Hosts: Jim and Mary Fabian
Rooms: 14 (PB) $119-149
Full Breakfast
Credit Cards: A, B, C
Notes: 2, 3, 5, 7, 8, 9, 10, 12

HELEN

Chattahoochee Ridge Lodge

P.O. Box 175, 30545
(706) 878-3144

E-mail: rooms@alltel.net
www.alltel.net~rooms

Perched on a wooded ridge a mile from Alpine Helen, each new unit has cable TV, air-conditioning, refrigerator, coffee maker, free telephone, and large Jacuzzi. Some have a full kitchen, extra bedroom, and fireplace. There is also a gas grill on the back deck. Hosts are "earth friendly" with double insulation and back-up solar heating. Everything guests need is furnished and on the premises, including hosts who can fill guests in on the attractions. Enjoy the common family room, newly constructed for our guests' pleasure.

Hosts: Bob and Mary Swift
Rooms: 4 (PB) $50-70
Credit Cards: A, B, C, D
Notes: 2, 5, 7, 8, 9, 10

LITTLE ST. SIMONS ISLAND

The Lodge on Little St. Simons Island

P.O. Box 21078, 31522-0578
(912) 638-7472; (888) 733-5774
fax: (912) 634-1811
E-mail: lssi@mindspring.com
www.littlestsimonsisland.com

Nature prevails on this pristine island paradise where 10,000 acres and seven miles of secluded beaches are shared with no more than 30 overnight guests. Outdoor enthusiasts can enjoy endless recreational activities. Explore tidal creeks by boat; hike or bicycle on island trails; or enjoy swimming, shelling, and fishing. Creature comforts include 13 gracious

---

6 Pets welcome; 7 Children welcome; 8 Tennis nearby; 9 Swimming nearby; 10 Golf nearby; 11 Skiing nearby; 12 May be booked through travel agent

guest rooms and two suites (all with private baths) and gourmet cuisine. Rates include all activities, recreational equipment, and meals.

Hosts: Maureen Ahern and Bo Taylor
Rooms: 15 (PB) $375-550
Full Breakfast
Credit Cards: A, B, C, D
Notes: 2, 3, 4, 5, 7, 9, 12

MARIETTA

Sixty Polk Street, a Bed & Breakfast

60 Polk Street Northwest, 30064
(770) 419-1688; (800) 845-7266
E-mail: jmertes@aol.com
www.sixtypolstreet.com

Fully restored to its original glory, this French Regency Victorian home built in 1872 features warm, inviting bedrooms. Delight in exquisite period antiques as you peruse the library, relax in the parlor, or savor afternoon sweets in the dining room. Wake to early coffee followed by a sumptuous Southern breakfast before walking to the antique shops, restaurants, museums, or the theater on Marietta Square.

Hosts: Joe and Glenda Mertes
Rooms: 4 (PB) $95-150
Full Breakfast
Credit Cards: A, B, C
Notes: 2, 5, 8, 10, 12

QUITMAN

Malloy Manor Bed & Breakfast Inn, Inc.

401 West Screven Street, 31643
(229) 263-5704; (800) 239-5704
fax: (229) 263-6973
E-mail: malloy@surfsouth.com
www.malloymanor.com

Built in 1905, the Malloy Manor is located in historic Quitman, Georgia, on U.S. Highway 84, 15 minutes from Valdosta, Georgia, and I-75, exit 16. It is a white clapboard building with Doric columns. Warm-toned oak floors and paneling, as well as beauti-

Malloy Manor

ful leaded glass in sidelights and transoms, provide a turn-of-the-century welcome as guests enter. Original to he house, all staircases, wainscoting, and moldings have retained an authentic ornate splendor. Antiques and memorabilia add to the old-fashioned atmosphere of this Victorian home. Guestrooms are spacious with 14-foot high ceilings. Fireplaces and handmade quilts provide a warm touch to the rooms. The wraparound veranda is the perfect place to unwind and enjoy a favorite beverage. A full breakfast awaits guests each morning in the elegant dining room, on the wraparound porch, or, on request, in your room.

Hosts: Fred and Bobette Lamb
Rooms: 4 (2 PB; 2 SB) $55-85 plus tax
Full Breakfast
Credit Cards: A, B, C, D
Notes: 2, 5, 8, 10, 12

Host: Hamilton Schwartz
Rooms: 5 (PB) $84-95
Continental Breakfast
Credit Cards: A, B, C
Notes: 2, 4, 5, 7, 8, 9, 10

SAUTE NACOCHE

The Stovall House Country Inn & Restaurant

1526 Highway 255 North, 30571
(706) 878-3355
www.georgiamagazine.com/stovall

Our 1837 Victorian farmhouse, restored in 1983, is listed on the National Register of Historic Places. Located on 26 acres in the historic Sautee Valley, the inn has views of the mountains in all directions. The recipient of several awards for its attentive restorations, the inn is furnished with family antiques and decorated with hand-stenciling. The restaurant, open to the public, features regional cuisine prepared with a fresh

*Circa 1837
National Register
of Historic Places*

The Stovall House

difference, and served in an intimate yet informal setting. It's a country experience!

SAVANNAH

Joan's on Jones Bed & Breakfast

Joan's on Jones

17 West Jones Street, 31401
(912) 234-3863; (800) 407-3863
fax: (912) 234-1455
E-mail: joansonjones@aol.com
www.bbonline.com/ga/joans/

Privacy is the outstanding feature of this charming, 1883, privately-owned and run B&B. Each of the two garden-level, antique-filled suites features a private entrance, off-street parking, sitting room, queen bedroom, bath, and kitchen. Early reservations are a must!

Hosts: Joan and Gary Levy
Rooms: 2 suites (PB) $145-165
Continental Breakfast
Credit Cards: None
Notes: 2, 5, 6, 7, 8, 10

6 Pets welcome; 7 Children welcome; 8 Tennis nearby; 9 Swimming nearby; 10 Golf nearby; 11 Skiing nearby; 12 May be booked through travel agent

THOMASVILLE

Evans House
Bed & Breakfast

725 South Hansell Street, 31792
(229) 226-1343

A Victorian B&B located across the street from a 26-acre park, and just two blocks from Bysad Street, antique shopping, and restaurants. Enjoy the wraparound porch with rocking chairs. A full breakfast is served. Near one of the best hospitals in the U.S. Just a good Christian home away from home.

Host: Gladys B. Deese
Rooms: 6 (4 PB; 2 SB) $95-125
Full Breakfast
Credit Cards: None
Notes: 2, 5, 7, 8, 9, 10

TOCCOA

Simmons-Bond Inn
Bed & Breakfast

130 West Tugalo Street, 30577-2360
(706) 282-5183; (877) 658-0746
fax: (706) 282-7170
E-mail: simmons@bandb@juno.com

Simmons-Bond Inn

Built as an opulent private residence in 1903, this Queen Anne-Greek Revival mansion is carefully restored and decorated in the Victorian style. Listed on the National Register of Historic Places, dozens of oak columns decorate the entry and dining areas, along with beautiful windows of beveled, stained, and curved glass. Relax in front of the fire in our Victorian parlor. Enjoy our collection of old books and countless interesting antiques.

Hosts: Todd and Joy Cusato
Rooms: 4 (PB) $69-99
Full Breakfast
Credit Cards: A, B, C, D
Notes: 2, 5, 7, 8, 9, 10, 12

VILLA RICA

Twin Oaks Country Inn &
Bed & Breakfast Cottages

9565 East Liberty Road, 30180
(770) 459-4374; (770) 459-5156
E-mail: ecturner@bellsouth.net
www.bbonline.com/ga/twinoaks/

Located on 23 acres in the foothills of the northwest Georgia Mountains are three exquisite cottages perfect for honeymoons, anniversaries, birthdays, or just unwinding. Watch peacocks stroll through the beautiful gardens fanning their tails. Many other animals on the property for viewing. Up to one child welcome per family.

Hosts: Earl and Carol Turner
Rooms: 4 (PB) $105-175
Full Breakfast
Credit Cards: A, B, C
Notes: 3, 4, 5, 7, 10, 12

NOTES: Credit cards accepted: A Master Card; B Visa; C American Express; D Discover; E Diners Club; F Other; 2 Personal checks accepted; 3 Lunch available; 4 Dinner available; 5 Open all year;

WARM SPRINGS

Hotel Warm Springs Bed & Breakfast

P.O. Box 351, 31830
(706) 655-2114; (800) 366-7616
fax: (706) 655-2406
E-mail: hotelwarmsprings@alltel.net

Hotel Warm Springs

"Presidents, passion, and the past." Relive history and the Roosevelt era in our 1907 hotel, ice cream parlor, and gift shops. Authentically restored and beautifully decorated with Roosevelt furniture and family antiques. Featuring our cozy honeymoon suite with king bed, suspended canopy, Victorian antiques, red heart tub, gold fixtures, breakfast in bed, flowers, champagne, and chocolates. Our large living room and dining room with Queen Anne furniture, oriental rugs, and crystal teardrop chandelier are ideal for group meetings. Nestled in quaint Warm Springs Village—a shopper's paradise, home of FDR's Little White House, 14 miles from Callaway Gardens, and one hour from Atlanta. Award-winning cheese grits and homemade peach ice cream.

Rooms: 14 (PB) $45-170
Full Breakfast
Credit Cards: A, B, C, D
Notes: 2, 5, 7, 8, 9, 10, 12

---

6 Pets welcome; 7 Children welcome; 8 Tennis nearby; 9 Swimming nearby; 10 Golf nearby; 11 Skiing nearby; 12 May be booked through travel agent

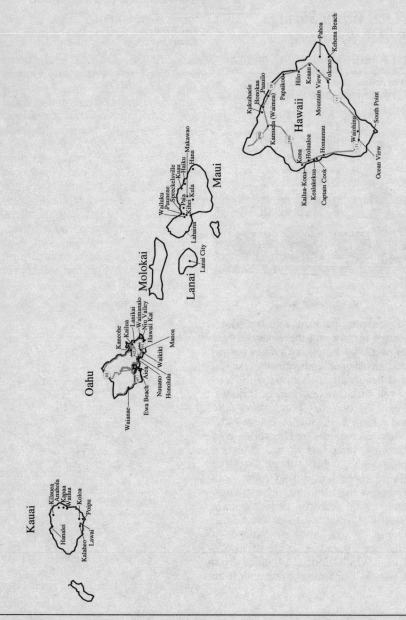

OAHU-KAILUA

Akialoa Hale
O Na Wailele

1478 Akialoa Place, Kailua, 96734
phone/fax: (808) 262-7466; (888) 489-9655
E-mail: vickeryd001@hawaii.rr.com
www.kailuavacation.com

Akialoa Hale O Na Wailele B&B offers you a truly Hawaiian experience with all of the amenities of your own private resort. You'll never want to leave! The breathtaking views, swimming pool with waterfalls, and private air-conditioned bedrooms make it the perfect Hawaiian getaway. If you do decide to venture away, you are just minutes from Honolulu and the most beautiful beach in the world, "Kailua Beach." In addition, you're just a five-minute drive from Kailua town and Olomana golf links, a public golf course.

Hosts: Donald and Nastia Vickery
Rooms: 2 (PB) $95
Continental Breakfast
Credit Cards: A, B
Notes: 2, 5, 7, 8, 9, 10

VOLCANO VILLAGE

The Chalet Kilauea
Collection

998 Wright Road, 96785
(808) 967-7786; (800) 937-7786
fax: (808) 967-8660
E-mail: reservations@volcano-hawaii.com
www.volcano-hawaii.com

These fine accommodations are situated in the native Hawaiian forest outside of Volcanoes National Park. Choose from deluxe boutique inns, modest lodges, and spacious vacation homes near Kilauea Volcano, the most active in the world, where you may hike or watch molten lava flow into the ocean. Twenty-six miles from Hilo Airport and five miles from Volcano Golf Course in the town of Volcano Village offering restaurants, shops, art galleries, botanical gardens, and a winery.

The Chalet Kilauea Collection

Hosts: Lisha and Brian Crawford
Rooms: 32 (26 PB; 6 SB) $45-395
Continental Breakfast
Credit Cards: A, B, C, D, E
Notes: 2, 5, 7, 10, 12

WAIKIKI

Aston Waikiki
Beachside Hotel

2452 Kalakaua Avenue, Honolulu, 96815
(808) 931-2100; (800) 922-7866
fax: (808) 931-2129
E-mail: resawb@aston-hotels.com
www.aston-hotels.com

6 Pets welcome; 7 Children welcome; 8 Tennis nearby; 9 Swimming nearby; 10 Golf nearby; 11 Skiing nearby; 12 May be booked through travel agent

This intimate, elegant boutique hotel overlooking the beach is Waikiki's answer to a gracious B&B, including complimentary Continental breakfast in all room rates. Named as one of the "Best Places to Kiss in Hawaii," the property is a re-creation of a late 1800s Hawaiian estate home, featuring antiques and artwork from around the world.

Rooms: 79 (PB) $190-395
Continental Breakfast
Credit Cards: A, B, C, D, E
Notes: 2, 5, 7, 8, 9, 10, 12

NOTES: Credit cards accepted: A Master Card; B Visa; C American Express; D Discover; E Diners Club; F Other; 2 Personal checks accepted; 3 Lunch available; 4 Dinner available; 5 Open all year;

Idaho

ATHOL

The Ponderosa

2579 East Brunner Road, 83801
(208) 683-2251; (888) 683-2251
fax: (208) 683-5112
E-mail: stay@theponderosa.net
www.theponderosa.net

The Ponderosa is a breathtaking log
home located on a 10-acre wooded estate just minutes north of Coeur d'A-
lene, near Silverwood Theme Park
offering queen log beds, private baths,
an enclosed spa, full breakfast, and
wine-tasting in our 2,000-bottle wine
cellar. Many sports activities are
nearby. Ask about children. Guests
receive free passes to Silverwood.

Hosts: Jack and Betty Bonzey
Rooms: 4 (PB) $99-149
Full Breakfast
Credit Cards: A, B
Notes: 2, 5, 7, 8, 9, 10, 11

COEUR D'ALENE

Gregory's McFarland House Bed & Breakfast

601 East Foster Avenue, 83814
(208) 667-1232; (800) 335-1232
www.bbhost.com/mcfarlandhouse

Surrender to the elegance of this
award-winning historical home, circa
1905. The full breakfast is gourmet to
the last crumb. Guests will be de-
lighted by an ideal blending of beauty,

Gregory's McFarland House

comfort, and clean surroundings.
Jerry Hulse, travel editor for the *Los
Angeles Times*, wrote, "Entering Gregory's McFarland House is like stepping back 100 years to an unhurried
time when four-posters were in fashion and lace curtains fluttered at the
windows." Our guest accommodations offer private baths and are air-
conditioned. This is a nonsmoking
house. If you're planning a wedding,
our resident minister and professional
photographer are available to make
your special day beautiful.

Hosts: Winifred, Carol, and Stephen Gregory
Rooms: 5 (PB) $90-175
Full Breakfast
Credit Cards: A, B, D
Notes: 2, 8, 9, 10, 11, 12

Katie's Wild Rose Inn

7974 East Coeur Dalene Lake Drive, 83814
(208) 765-9474; (800) 971-4345
fax: (208) 765-9474
E-mail: leek@dmi.net
www.katieswildroseinn.com

---

6 Pets welcome; 7 Children welcome; 8 Tennis nearby; 9 Swimming nearby; 10 Golf nearby; 11 Skiing
nearby; 12 May be booked through travel agent

IDAHO

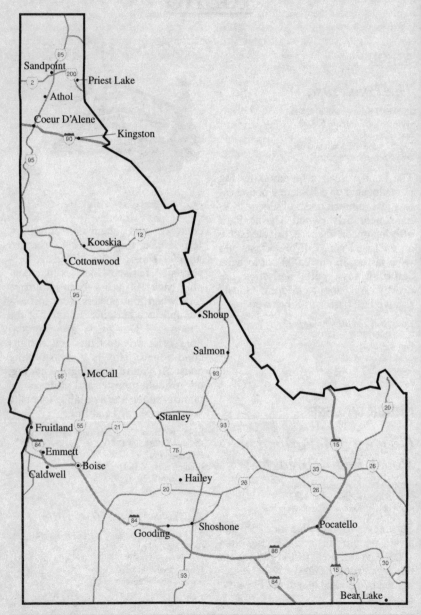

NOTES: Credit cards accepted: A Master Card; B Visa; C American Express; D Discover; E Diners Club; F Other; 2 Personal checks accepted; 3 Lunch available; 4 Dinner available; 5 Open all year;

This four-bedroom cozy cottage-style house with full wraparound decking overlooks beautiful Coeur d'Alene Lake, rated by *National Geographic* as one of the top five most beautiful lakes in the world. Play a game of pool or relax in front of the fireplace in the den/library. Hike or bike on the Centennial Trail located at your doorstep. Golf on the famous floating green two miles away. Fine dining, skiing, white water or float trips all nearby. Weddings, honeymoons, and anniversaries are our specialty.

Hosts: Karin and Gary Spence
Rooms: 4 (2 PB; 2 SB) $65-120
Full Breakfast
Credit Cards: A, B
Notes: 2, 5, 8, 9, 10, 11, 12

Since opening in 1987, Smith House has offered homestyle atmosphere with top service at affordable rates. The well-appointed rooms offer breathtaking views of the famous Selmon River. Enjoy the hot tub, orchard, float trips, library, and covered decks. Kitchen, laundry, complimentary beverage and snacks are available; the friendly hosts cater to your needs. Weekly rates. Ask about our Honeymoon/Anniversary Package. Open April 15th-October 20th.

Hosts: Aubrey and Marsha Smith
Rooms: 4 (2 PB; 2 SB) $55-65
Full Breakfast
Credit Cards: A, B
Notes: 2, 6, 7, 9, 11, 12

SHOUP

Smith House Bed & Breakfast

3175 Salmon River Road, 83469
(208) 394-2121; (800) 238-5915
fax: (208) 394-2121
E-mail: aesmith49@yahoo.com

Smith House

---

6 Pets welcome; 7 Children welcome; 8 Tennis nearby; 9 Swimming nearby; 10 Golf nearby; 11 Skiing nearby; 12 May be booked through travel agent

ILLINOIS

Illinois

ALGONQUIN

Victorian Rose Garden

314 Washington Street, 60102
(847) 854-9667; (888) 854-9667
E-mail: roses@mc.net
www.sleepandeat.com

Built in 1886, the Victorian Rose Garden invites guests to relax on its wraparound porch, read by the fireplace, play the baby grand piano, and enjoy the old-fashioned barber corner. Bedrooms are individually decorated with antiques and collectibles. A delicious breakfast is served formally in the dining room each morning. Nearby you will find golf courses, antiques, a bike trail, restaurants, and a dinner boat. Chicago is only an hour away. The Victorian Rose Garden is a nonsmoking, nonalcoholic, animal-free residence. Special guest packages are available. Come and let us pamper you! Children over 12 welcome.

Victorian Rose Garden

Hosts: The Brewers
Rooms: 4 (PB) $70-139
Full Breakfast
Credit Cards: A, B, C
Notes: 2, 5, 7, 8, 10

ARTHUR

Heart & Home

137 East Illinois Street, 61911
(217) 543-2910

Located in the heart of Illinois Amish country and constructed in 1906, Heart and Home is a Victorian B&B filled with the warmth of oak floors and stained-glass windows. A large front porch and second-story sun porch await guests for their relaxation. Choose from three nice guest rooms, one with a pull-out Murphy bed, ideal for an additional guest. All guestrooms are upstairs (not handicapped-accessible). Heart and Home is a smoke- and alcohol-free lodging. Situated only two blocks from downtown. We have central air-conditioning. Open everyday, April-October.

Hosts: Don and Amanda Miller
Rooms: 3 (PB) $60-65
Full Breakfast
Credit Cards: None
Notes: 2, 7, 10

---

6 Pets welcome; 7 Children welcome; 8 Tennis nearby; 9 Swimming nearby; 10 Golf nearby; 11 Skiing nearby; 12 May be booked through travel agent

BELLEVILLE

Swans Court
Bed & Breakfast

421 Court Street, 62220
(618) 233-0779; (800) 840-1058
fax: (618) 277-3150
E-mail: mdixon@isbe.accessus.net
www.bbonline.com/il/swanscourt

Swans Court, built in 1883 and restored in 1995, is located in a federal historic district. Furnished in period antiques, it reflects the gracious lifestyle of an earlier time without sacrificing modern amenities. Walk to shops, restaurants, and historic houses. Visit the many nearby attractions of southwestern Illinois; an easy 20-minute drive to downtown St. Louis.

Host: Monty Dixon
Rooms: 4 (2 PB; 2 SB) $65-90
Full Breakfast
Credit Cards: A, B, C, D
Notes: 2, 5, 8, 9, 10, 12

CAHOKIA

Jermone Place
Bed & Breakfast

827 Ester, 62206
(618) 337-1537

Enjoy historic Cahokia, located only 10 minutes away from the attractions of downtown St. Louis. Treat yourself to a getaway. Come relax; experience a warm down-home, comfortable feeling. Families as well as business travelers who want a change of pace are welcome. (Come as a guest; leave as a friend.)

Jerome Place

Host: Ruthanna Bryant
Rooms: 3 (PB) $45-69
Full Breakfast
Credit Cards: A, B, C, D
Notes: 2, 5, 7, 8, 9, 10

COLLINSVILLE

Maggie's Bed & Breakfast

2102 North Keebler Ave, 62234-4713
(618) 344-8283
E-mail: maggies-b-n-b@charter-il.com

Beautiful, quiet country setting just minutes from downtown St. Louis,

Maggie's

NOTES: Credit cards accepted: A Master Card; B Visa; C American Express; D Discover; E Diners Club; F Other; 2 Personal checks accepted; 3 Lunch available; 4 Dinner available; 5 Open all year;

near hospital, restaurants, shopping, golf courses, and sports. Maggie cooks with all natural ingredients. Antiques and art works collected in Maggie's world travels; cable TV, hot tub, mini kitchen. Terrycloth robes and house slippers are provided.

Host: Maggie Leyda
Rooms: 5 (4 PB; 1 SB) $45-100
Full Breakfast
Credit Cards: None
Notes: 2, 5, 6, 7, 8, 10

ELSAH

Maple Leaf Cottages Bed Inn Breakfast

12 Selma; P.O. Box 156, 62028
(618) 374-1684; (866) 323-5323
fax: (618) 374-1684

"I knew by the smoke that so gracefully curl'd above the green elms, that a cottage was near. And I said, If there's peace to be found in the world, a heart that was humble might hope for it here."—Thomas Moore. With over 50 years as a B&B, we offer the tradition of the past with today's quality hospitality. Fine food and lodging in a retreat garden setting. All accommodations have full private baths and bedroom and sitting areas. Your "somewhere INN time" is now. Children over 10 are welcome.

Host: Patricia Taetz
Rooms: 5 (PB) $80-100
Full Breakfast
Credit Cards: None
Notes: 2, 5, 7, 9, 10

EVANSTON

The Margarita European Inn

1566 Oak Avenue, 60201-4234
(847) 869-2273; fax: (847) 869-2353
E-mail: www.margaritainn.com

Housed in a stately vintage building the inn provides comfortable lodging and pleasing service.

Rooms: 41 (21 PB; 20 SB) $78-155
Continental Breakfast
Credit Cards: A, B, C, E
Notes: 4, 5, 7, 8, 9, 10, 12

GALENA

Belle Aire Mansion Guest House

11410 Route 20 West, 61036
(815) 777-0893
E-mail: belleair@galenalink.com
www.galena-bnb.com/belleaire

Belle Aire Mansion

Belle Aire Mansion Guest House is a pre-Civil War Federal home surrounded by 11 well-groomed acres that include extensive lawns, flowers, and a block-long, tree-lined driveway. Whirlpool and fireplace suites are available. We do our best to make guests feel like special friends.

Hosts: Jan and Lorraine Svec
Rooms: 5 (PB) $90-170
Full Breakfast
Credit Cards: A, B, D
Notes: 2, 7, 8, 10, 12

Brierwreath Manor Bed & Breakfast

216 North Bench Street, 61036
(815) 777-0608
E-mail: brierw@galinalink.com
www.brierwreath.com

Brierwreath Manor, circa 1884, is just one block from Galena's Main Street and has a dramatic, inviting wrap-around porch that beckons after a hard day. The house is furnished in an eclectic blend of antique and early American. You'll not only relax but feel right at home. Two suites offer gas log fireplaces; the third one has an extra twin-size bed. Central air-conditioning, ceiling fans, and cable TV add to your enjoyment.

Hosts: Mike and Lyn Cook
Rooms: 3 (PB) $95-120
Full Breakfast
Credit Cards: A, B, D
Notes: 2, 5, 8, 9, 10, 11

Captain Harris Guest House

Captain Harris Guest House

713 South Bench Street, 61036
(815) 777-4713; fax: (815) 777-4723
E-mail: inquiry@captainharris.com
www.captainharris.com

This circa 1836 home built by a riverboat captain, was lovingly restored in 1920 with leaded-glass windows and doors by an associate of Frank Lloyd Wright. Each of the five guest rooms offers a private bath and cable TV. A double whirlpool suite and detached honeymoon cottage are available. Full formal breakfast. One block from Main Street shops and restaurants.

Hosts: Judy Dixon and Ed Schmit
Rooms: 5 (PB) $90-190
Full Breakfast
Credit Cards: A, B, D
Notes: 2, 5, 10, 11

NOTES: Credit cards accepted: A Master Card; B Visa; C American Express; D Discover; E Diners Club; F Other; 2 Personal checks accepted; 3 Lunch available; 4 Dinner available; 5 Open all year;

Forget-Me-Not Bed & Breakfast

1467 North Elizabeth Scales Mound, Elizabeth, 61028
(815) 858-3744
E-mail: info@galena-illinois.net
www.galena-illinois.net

You won't forget the beautiful views of distant rolling hills that compliment this warm country home. Take a stroll down a nearby nature path. Three romantic, nonsmoking rooms with baths. Private patio entrances, scrumptious breakfast, large screened porch, spacious great room with fireplace. Gift certificates available. Children over 12 years old welcome

Hosts: Christa and Richard Grunert
Rooms: 3 (PB) $95-115
Full Breakfast
Credit Cards: A, B, D
Notes: 2, 5, 7, 8, 9, 10, 11

Hawk Valley Retreat

Hawk Valley Retreat

2752 West Cording Road, 61036
(815) 777-4100; (888) 777-6016
fax: (815) 777-1941
E-mail: hawkvaly@galenalink.com
www.hawkvalleyretreat.com

Luxurious home and cottages on 10 secluded acres with pond, walking trails, and gardens. Birdwatcher's paradise. Three guest rooms in main house (each with private entrance) and two cottages. Each unit has private bath, TV/VCR, king or queen bed. Each cottage also has a large double whirlpool tub, fireplace, air-conditioning, sitting area, phone, galley kitchen, covered porch. Main house has fireplace in living room, book/video library, covered porch with swing, and wraparound deck. Sumptuous full breakfast included. Children under 12 by special arrangement. Limited one-night stays. Off-season, midweek, and multiple-night specials. Packages and gift certificates available. IBBA inspected (highest rating in 2000 and 2001). No smoking, no pets; fully handicapped accessible.

Hosts: Fritz and Jane Fuchs
Rooms: 5 (PB) $75-235
Full Breakfast
Credit Cards: A, B, D
Notes: 2, 5, 7, 8, 9, 10, 11

Park Avenue Guest House

208 Park Avenue, 61036
(815) 777-1075; (800) 359-0743
fax: (815) 777-1097
E-mail: parkave@galenalink.com
www.galena.com/parkave

This is an 1893 Queen Anne "painted lady." Wraparound screened porch, gardens, and gazebo for summer. Fireplace and opulent Victorian Christmas in winter. One suite sleeps three, and there are three antique-filled guest rooms, all with queen beds and fireplaces. Located in a quiet residential area. Only a short walk to Grant Park or across a footbridge to Main Street shopping and restaurants.

Host: Sharon Fallbacher
Rooms: 4 (PB) $95-135
Full Breakfast
Credit Cards: A, B, D
Notes: 2, 5, 8, 9, 10, 11

Pine Hollow Inn

4700 North Council Hill Road, 61036
(815) 777-1071
E-mail: pinehollowinn@pinehollowinn.com
www.pinehollowinn.com

Located on acres of unspoiled beauty,
where blue heron fish in the stream
and dear and wild turkeys are common. You can enjoy sitting in front of
the fireplace in one of our guest rooms
or suites. In the spring, summer, or
fall you might want to sit on the wraparound porch and just daydream.
Amenities include large suites and
guest rooms, individual wood-burning
fireplaces, private baths and whirlpools, skylights, country kitchen, and
gardens.

Hosts: Larry and Sally Priske
Rooms: 5 (PB) $85-150
Continental Breakfast
Credit Cards: A, B, D
Notes: 2, 5, 8, 9, 10, 11

Pine Hollow Inn

JERSEYVILLE

The Homeridge Bed & Breakfast

The Homeridge

1470 North State Street, 62052
(618) 498-3442; fax: (618) 498-5662
E-mail: innkeeper@homeridge.com
www.homeridge.com

The Homeridge B&B is a beautiful,
warm, brick, 1867 Italianate Victorian
private home on 18 acres in an elegant
country atmosphere. Drive through
stately iron gates and a tree-lined
driveway to the 14-room historic estate of Senator Theodore Chapman.
Enter through an expansive, pillared
front porch and up the hand-carved,
curved stairway to the spacious guest
rooms. Large swimming pool. Central
air-conditioning. Located between St.
Louis, Missouri, and Springfield, Illinois.

Hosts: Sue and Howard Landon
Rooms: 4 (PB) $75-95
Full Breakfast
Credit Cards: A, B, C
Notes: 2, 5, 8, 9, 10

NOTES: Credit cards accepted: A Master Card; B Visa; C American Express; D Discover; E Diners
Club; F Other; 2 Personal checks accepted; 3 Lunch available; 4 Dinner available; 5 Open all year;

NAUVOO

Mississippi Memories Bed & Breakfast

1 Riverview Terrace, 62354
(217) 453-2771

Located on the banks of the Mississippi, this gracious home offers peaceful lodging and an elegantly served, all-homemade, full breakfast. Every room features fresh fruit, flowers, and robe. In a quiet, wooded setting, it's just two miles from historic Nauvoo, where you'll find 30 restored Mormon-era homes and shops. Two decks offer spectacular sunsets, dift-

ing barges, bald eagle-watching; the B&B also has two pianos, two fireplaces, and a library. Inspected by two motor clubs. No smoking, alcohol, or pets will interrupt your stay.

Hosts: Marge and Dean Starr
Rooms: 5 (3 PB; 2 SB) $59-95
Full Breakfast
Credit Cards: A, B
Notes: 2, 10

OAKLAND

Inn on the Square

3 Montgomery Street, 61943
(217) 346-2289; fax: (217) 346-2005
E-mail: innonsq@advant.net
www.bedandbreakfast.com/bbc/p210688.asp

Located 20 minutes from Eastern Illinois University, the inn specializes in fine food and friendly atmosphere. Best of all is the return of B&B tourism. Blending the old with the new, we offer warm hospitality and simple country pleasures, as well as historical sites, recreational activities, shopping, and plain old sittin' and rockin'. Three upstairs bedrooms are comfortably furnished for country living, each with a private bath. Dinner is available Fridays and Saturdays.

Hosts: Gary and Linda Miller
Rooms: 3 (PB) $55-60
Full Breakfast
Credit Cards: A, B
Notes: 2, 3, 4, 5, 7, 8, 9, 10, 12

ONARGA

Dairy on the Prairie

1437 North State Route 49, 60955
(815) 683-2774

Situated among miles of corn and soybean fields on God's prairie is this recently remodeled homestead that has been "in the family" since 1892. Three tall silos and Holstein cows await you at the modern dairy/grain family farm. Enjoy the piano, organ, or keyboard along with hearty food, "down on the farm" hospitality, and a Christian atmosphere.

Hosts: Kenneth and Martha Redeker
Rooms: 3 (2 PB; 1 SB) $50-60
Full Breakfast
Credit Cards: None
Notes: 2, 5, 7, 8, 9, 10

OTTAWA

Prairie Rivers Bed & Breakfast

121 East Prospect Avenue, 61350
(815) 434-3226; (888) 288-2659, ext. 5
E-mail: prairieriversbb@aol.com
prairieriversbandb.com

High on a bluff where the Fox and Illinois Rivers converge, this 1890 New England cottage offers folks a taste of 19th-century charm. Rooms are spacious and sunny, and three fireplaces add romantic glow to the evening. Private baths and downy beds cater to creature comforts. Breakfast is served in the period dining room or in the sunroom overlooking the rivers. This is a friendly place where you can come and go just as you would in your own home.

Hosts: Carole and Ed Mayer
Rooms: 4 (3 PB; 1 SB) $85-125
Full Breakfast
Credit Cards: A, B
Notes: 2, 5, 7, 8, 10

Prairie Rivers

PEORIA

Old Church House Inn Bed & Breakfast

Old Church House Inn

1416 East Mossville, Mossville, 61552
(309) 579-2300
E-mail: churchhouse@prodigy.net
www.bed andbreakfast.com/bbc/p210657.asp

Come take sanctuary from the cares of life in our lovingly restored, 1869 "country church." Enjoy afternoon tea curled up by a wood-burning fire, or on a bench among a riot of garden flowers. Experience 18-foot ceilings, a library loft, Victorian antiques, classical music, a crackling fire, pillow chocolates, featherbeds, flowers, and "made-from-scratch" breakfasts. Nearby. . .Rock Island Bike Trail, tearooms, antiquing, fine dining, scenic drives, and sweet memories. Children welcome by arrangement.

Hosts: Dean and Holly Ramseyer and family
Rooms: 2 (SB) $75-115
Continental Breakfast
Credit Cards: A, B, D
Notes: 2, 3, 5, 7, 8, 9, 10, 11, 12

NOTES: Credit cards accepted: A Master Card; B Visa; C American Express; D Discover; E Diners Club; F Other; 2 Personal checks accepted; 3 Lunch available; 4 Dinner available; 5 Open all year;

QUINCY

The Kaufmann House Bed & Breakfast

1641 Hampshire Street, 62301
(217) 223-2502

Nestled among majestic trees and lush gardens, our eclectic Queen Anne is in the heart of the historic district. It has been lovingly restored and is filled with an abundance of antiques. Your comfort and pleasure are of utmost importance to us. You'll delight in your breakfast of fresh pastries and fruit, and our special blend of piping-hot coffee. Relax and prepare to be pampered.

Hosts: Emery and Bettie Kaufmann
Rooms: 3 (PB) $75
Full Breakfast
Credit Cards: None
Notes: 2, 5, 7, 8, 9, 10

SPRINGFIELD

Country Dreams Bed & Breakfast

3410 Parks Lane, Rochester, 62563
(217) 498-9210
E-mail: host@countrydreams.com
www.countrydreams.com

This newly-built country hideaway on 16 acres is just 7 miles from Springfield and features a whirlpool, fireplaces, TV/VCR, evening snacks, and air-conditioning. Stroll outside and admire the swans and flowers. Why settle for city streets and city traffic when beauty and serenity in an immaculate setting are only a few minutes away?

Hosts: Ralph and Kay Muhs
Rooms: 4 (PB) $75-160
Full Breakfast
Credit Cards: A, B, C, D
Notes: 2, 5, 10

6 Pets welcome; 7 Children welcome; 8 Tennis nearby; 9 Swimming nearby; 10 Golf nearby; 11 Skiing nearby; 12 May be booked through travel agent

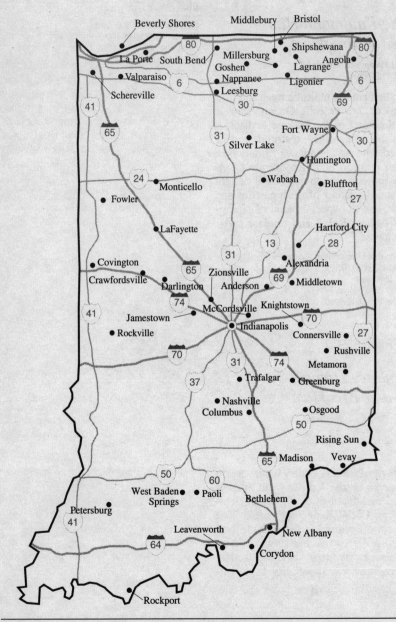

INDIANA

Indiana

ALEXANDRIA

Country Gazebo Inn

13867 North 100 West, 46001
(765) 754-8783; fax: (765) 754-8723
E-mail: ccunningham@iquest.net
www.innsites.com

This inn offers quiet country living, ground-level accommodations, indoor parking in winter, an outside swimming pool, and deck with built-in spa. Five bedrooms all have private baths. Handicapped-accessible. Pets extra charge. Children extra charge of $15.00 if sharing a room with parents. Rates include a full hot breakfast for two, and evening snack and beverage. Each room is different in size and beautifully decorated. Coffeemakers, phones, refrigerators, and satellite TV in all rooms. Fax and E-mail service are available.

Host: Carolyn Cunningham
Rooms: 5 (PB) $60-75
Full Breakfast
Credit Cards: None
Notes: 2, 5, 6, 7, 8, 9

CORYDON

The Kintner House Inn

101 South Capitol Avenue, 47112-1103
(812) 738-2020; fax: (812) 738-7181

This historic B&B was built in 1873, restored in 1986. Fifteen elegant guest rooms all have private baths and televisions; five have fireplaces, and eight have VCRs. Antique furnishings are in all the rooms. It is a nonsmoking facility. The home is open year-round. The first floor is handicapped accessible. Listed on the National Register of Historic Places and featured on two 1991 Hallmark Christmas cards. A hideaway for romantics, the inn is located in historic downtown Corydon, Indiana's first state capital.

Host: Dee Windell
Rooms: 15 (PB) $49-99 plus tax
Full Breakfast
Credit Cards: A, B, C, D
Notes: 2, 5, 7, 8, 9, 10, 11

GOSHEN

Indian Creek Bed & Breakfast

20300 County Road 18, 46528
(219) 875-6606; fax: (219) 875-8396
E-mail: indiancreekb&b@msn.com
www.bestinns.net/usa/in/indiancreek.html

Indian Creek

Come and enjoy our nine-year-old, Victorian-style home in the middle of Amish Country. Guests can enjoy the spacious dining, kitchen, and guestroom combination where they can relax, read a book, or visit. Watch for wildlife from a large deck while taking in the countryside. The B&B is 3-diamond AAA- and Mobil-approved. Handicapped-accessible.

Hosts: Jim and Jeanette Vellenga
Rooms: 4 (PB) $79
Full Breakfast
Credit Cards: A, B, C, D
Notes: 2, 5, 7, 10

Prairie Manor Bed & Breakfast

Prairie Manor

66398 U.S. Highway 33, 46526
(219) 642-4761; fax: (219) 642-4762
E-mail: jeston@npcc.net
www.prairiemanor.com

Prairie Manor, our historic, English country manor-style home, is situated on twelve acres. The living room replicates the builder's favorite painting of an English baronial hall. The house has many interesting architectural details such as arched doorways, wainscoting, window seats, and hidden compartments. Many activities are available including antiquing, the famous Shipshewana antique auction and flea market, and northern Indiana Amish country. Pool, TV, and Grandma's attic.

Hosts: Jean and Hesston Lauver
Rooms: 4 (PB) $69-95
Full Breakfast
Credit Cards: A, B, D
Notes: 2, 5, 7, 8, 9, 10

LA PORTE

Hidden Pond

5342 North Highway 35, 46350
(219) 879-8200; fax: (219) 879-1770
E-mail: edberent@adsnet.com
www.bbonline.com/in/hiddenpond/

Comfortable country home on 10 acres between Michigan City and La Porte. Gardens and trails to explore, a pond for fishing, swimming pool, hot tub, and luxurious rooms add to your relaxation experience. Full gourmet breakfast in the morning and snacks available during the day; close to outlet mall, antiquing, golf, Lake Michigan, casino, and Notre Dame. Families with children most welcome.

Rooms: 4 (3 PB; 1 SB) $89-149
Gourmet Breakfast
Credit Cards: A, B
Notes: 2, 3, 5, 7, 8, 9, 10, 11

LEESBURG

Prairie House Bed & Breakfast

495 East 900 North, 46538
(219) 658-9211
E-mail: marietom3@yahoo.com
www.prairiehouse.net

Come enjoy a peaceful farm atmosphere. Our B&B offers four tastefully decorated rooms with air-conditioning, TV/VCR, and fans are available. Close to Grace College, the Wagon Wheel Playhouse, Shipshewana Flea Market, Amish Acres, antique browsing, the Old Bag Factory at Goshen, swimming, skiing, boating, and golfing. Excellent dining in the area. Tours of the farm available. Prepare to be pampered!

Hosts: Everett and Marie Tom
Rooms: 4 (2 PB; 2 SB) $45-65
Full Breakfast
Credit Cards: A, B
Notes: 2, 5, 7, 8, 9, 10

LEAVENWORTH

The Leavenworth Inn

930 West State Road 62, 47137
(812) 739-2120; (888) 739-2120
fax: (812) 739-2012
E-mail: leavenworthinn@aol.com
www.leavenworthinn.com

The Leavenworth Inn, a country inn, consists of two beautifully renovated turn-of-the-century homes overlooking the Ohio River. Outside, enjoy our walking and biking paths, tennis

The Leavenworth Inn

court, and spacious gardens; inside, enjoy our exercise room, parlor games, and extensive video and reading library. Ask the innkeeper about our Jacuzzi or fireplace suite. The Inn is perfect for quiet getaways, romantic weddings, family reunions, business meetings, and church retreats. Enoy breakfast provided at our Overlook Restaurant.

Host: Bert Collins
Rooms: 11 (PB) $69-119
Full Breakfast
Credit Cards: A, B, C, D
Notes: 3, 4, 5, 7, 8, 9, 10, 11

MADISON

Schussler House Bed & Breakfast

514 Jefferson Street, 47250
(812) 273-2068; (800) 392-1931
E-mail: schussler@voyager.net
www.schusslerhouse.com

Experience the quiet elegance of a circa 1849 Federal/Greek Revival home tastefully combined with today's modern amenities. Located in Madison's historic district, where antique shops, historic sites, restaurants, and churches are within a pleasant walking distance. This gracious home offers spacious rooms decorated with antiques, reproductions, carefully selected fabrics, and wall coverings. A sumptuous breakfast in the sun-filled dining room begins your day.

Hosts: Bill and Judy Gilbert
Rooms: 3 (PB) $120
Full Breakfast
Credit Cards: A, B, D
Notes: 2, 5, 8, 9, 10, 12

6 Pets welcome; 7 Children welcome; 8 Tennis nearby; 9 Swimming nearby; 10 Golf nearby; 11 Skiing nearby; 12 May be booked through travel agent

METAMORA

The Thorpe House Country Inn

The Thorpe House

P.O. Box 36, 19049 Clayborne Street, 47030-0036
(765) 647-5425; (888) HAPPYDAY
fax: (765) 647-6729
E-mail: thorpe_house@hotmail.com
metmora.com/thorpehouse

Eatery. Sleepery. Shoppery. This peaceful, easy-feeling inn is a typical 1960s middle-class clapboard with "gingerbready" front porch. Located amid a quaint, historic canal town; convenient to Indianapolis and Cincinnati. No in-room telephone, television, radio, or alarm clock to interrupt your relaxation. Enjoy a heary breakfast before exploring nearly a hundred nearby shop or recreational diversions.

Hosts: Mike and Jean Owens
Rooms: 5 (PB) $70-125
Full Breakfast
Credit Cards: A, B, C, D
Notes: 2, 3, 6, 7, 8, 9, 10, 12

MIDDLEBURY

Bee Hive Bed & Breakfast

P.O. Box 1191, 46540
(219) 825-5023

Beee yourself at the Bee Hive B&B. Have a honey of a time relaxing with tea and honey. The Bee Hive is a two-story, open-floor plan with exposed, hand-sawn, red oak beams and a loft. Enjoy Herb's steam engines and antique tractors. Snuggle under handmade quilts and wake to the smell of a full country breakfast being prepared. Located on a farm in the Amish community. Four rooms and one cottage available.

Hosts: Herb and Treva Swarm
Rooms: 4 (SB); 1 cottage (PB) $60-80
Full Breakfast
Credit Cards: A, B
Notes: 2, 5, 9, 10, 11

Bontreger Guest Rooms Bed & Breakfast

10766 County Road 16, 46540
(219) 825-2647

Bontreger Guest Rooms

This B&B is located between Middleburg and Shipshewana on a county road in an Amish neighborhood. Relax in the pleasant atmosphere of the sun room where Continental breakfast is served, or retreat to your cozy, air-conditioned room and common room, away from family space. Private baths and private entrance.

Hosts: Tom and Ruby Bontreger
Rooms: 2 (PB) $59
Continental Breakfast
Credit Cards: None
Notes: 2, 5, 7, 8, 9, 10, 11

Rust Hollar
Bed & Breakfast

55238 County Road 31, Bristol, 46507
(219) 825-1111; (800) 313-7800
fax: (219) 825-4614
E-mail: tim@rusthollar.com
www.rusthollar.com

Rust Hollar B&B is a rustic log home on a peaceful country road in a wooded "hollar." You may enjoy bird-watching, a country walk, or just relaxing on our oak-covered grounds. A full, hot breakfast is served each morning. The B&B is located in Amish country. Shipshewana, Middlebury (Das Essenhaus), Goshen, Elkhart, South Bend, and Nappanee are within a half-hour's drive. AAA-approved. Clergy discounts available.

Hosts: Tim and Janine Rust
Rooms: 4 (PB) $71.10-79
Full Breakfast
Credit Cards: A, B, C, D
Notes: 2, 5, 7, 8, 10, 11

That Pretty Place
Bed & Breakfast Inn

212 U.S. 20, 46540
(219) 825-3021; (800) 418-9487
E-mail: inbasket@thatprettyplace.com
www.thatprettyplace.com

A long lane leads through the woods to our inn overlooking our private, stocked pond. You may feed the fish, take a quiet walk on the path through our woods, or sit on the deck that overlooks the pond. Choose from five rooms with private baths, including a honeymoon suite with a heart-shaped, whirlpool tub. A hot breakfast is served. We are located in the heart of Amish country, close to the Shipshewana Flea Market.

Hosts: Cary and Candy Hansen
Rooms: 5 (PB) $80-115
Full Breakfast
Credit Cards: A, B, D
Notes: 2, 5, 10

Tiffany Powell's

Tiffany Powell's
Bed & Breakfast

523 South Main Street, 46540
(219) 825-5951; fax: (219) 825-2992
E-mail: tiff@npcc.net
www.tiffanypowells.com

Tiffany's was built in 1914 and features oak woodwork and leaded glass in a warm Christian atmosphere. It is our goal to pass on the blessings God has given us. All rooms include full breakfast, TV, and air-conditioning. Children are welcome. This B&B was featured on Oprah's Angel Network. We do hope you will enjoy your stay with us. Let us pamper you.

Host: Judy Powell
Rooms: 3 (PB) $55-65
Full Breakfast
Credit Cards: None
Notes: 2, 5, 7, 8, 9, 10, 12

MIDDLETOWN

Country Rose Bed & Breakfast

Country Rose

5098 North Mechanicsburg Road, 47356
(765) 779-4501; (800) 395-6449

The Country Rose is a small-town B&B overlooking berry patches and a flower garden. Awake early or late to a delicious, full breakfast. Only 50 minutes from Indianapolis; 20 minutes from Anderson and Ball State Universities.

Hosts: Rose and Jack Lewis
Rooms: 2 (1 PB; 1 SB) $55-75
Full Breakfast
Credit Cards: None
Notes: 2, 5, 7, 8, 10

MONTICELLO

Quiet Water Bed & Breakfast

4794 East Harbour Court, 47960
(219) 583-6023
E-mail: quietwtrbb@aol.com
members.aol.com/quietbnb/index.html

Our four new guest rooms await your arrival: relax in the Ivy, Quilt, or Paisley Rooms, or the large Southwest Room with its own Jacuzzi tub. Cable TV and central air in each room. Enjoy breakfast on the spacious deck overlooking beautiful Lake Shafer. Visit the antique and specialty shops in town. Golf on one of the three local courses, and take pleasure in the fine or casual dining Monticello has to offer. Within walking distance of the famous Indiana Beach Amusement Park. The cookie jar is always open. All four rooms are handicapped accessible.

Host: Ola Bergdall
Rooms: 4 (PB) $50-80
Full Breakfast
Credit Cards: A, B, D
Notes: 2, 5, 7, 9, 10, 11

NAPPANEE

Christian S. Stahly Olde Buffalo Inn

1061 Parkwood Drive, 46550
(219) 773-2222; (888) 773-2223
fax: (219) 773-4275
E-mail: stay@olde-buffalo-b-b.com
www.olde-buffalo-b-b.com

Step back in time to an era that was peaceful and serene. The Olde Buffalo Inn has all of today's amenities and lots of 19th-century charm. The inn is surrounded by a white picket fence and a restored red barn, windmill, carriage house, brick sidewalk, and east patio. Situated on two and a half acres with a beautiful view of the golf course.

Hosts: Larry Lakins
Rooms: 7 (PB) $79-159
Full Breakfast
Credit Cards: A, B, D
Notes: 2, 5, 7, 8, 9, 10

The Homespun Country Inn

302 North Main Street, P.O. Box 369, 46550
(219) 773-2034; (800) 311-2996
fax: (219) 773-3456
E-mail: home@hoosierlink.net
www.homespuninn.com

Our Queen Anne-style inn was built in 1902. Our home is filled with antiques and family pieces we have enjoyed collecting. We are located within walking distance of seven antique and craft shops. Enjoy homespun hospitality and friendly conversation in the heart of Amish country.

Hosts: Dennis and Dianne Debelak
Rooms: 5 (PB) $59-79
Full Breakfast
Credit Cards: A, B, D
Notes: 2, 5, 7, 8, 9, 10

Victorian Guest House

302 East Market Street, 46550
(219) 773-4383
E-mail: vghouse@binn.net
www.victoriab-b.com

Antiques, stained-glass windows, and pocket doors highlight this 1887 Historical Register mansion nestled amongst the Amish countryside where antique shops abound. A warm welcome awaits as you return to gracious living with all the ambience of the 1800s. Everything has been designed to make your B&B stay a memorable one. Close to Notre Dame and Shipshewana. Two hours from Chicago. Complimentary evening tea and sweets. "Prepare for a memory."

Hosts: Bruce and Vickie Hunsberger
Rooms: 6 (PB) $59-149
Full Breakfast
Credit Cards: A, B, D
Notes: 2, 5, 8, 9, 10

NASHVILLE

Day Star Inn

87 East Main Street, P.O. Box 361, 47448
(812) 988-0430

A friendly, homey atmosphere awaits as you retreat to the heart of Nashville's unique downtown shopping area. Short drive to Brown County State Park, golf courses, and other recreational areas. Five clean rooms can accommodate up to twenty-two guests (including children, if well-supervised). Air-conditioning, cable television, private bath, and parking for guests. No smoking, alcohol, or pets, please.

Host: Edwin K Taggart
Rooms: 5 (PB) $88-104.50
Continental Breakfast
Credit Cards: A, B, D
Notes: 2, 5, 8, 9, 10, 11

SHIPSHEWANA

Morton Street
Bed & Breakfast

140 Morton Street, P.O. Box 775, 46565
(219) 768-4391; (800) 447-6475
fax: (219) 768-7468
E-mail: hostess@shipshewanalodging.com
www.shipshewanalodging.com

Located in the heart of Amish Country, our three turn-of-the-century homes provide an escape from the everyday bustle of life. Sit on the porch and watch the buggies go by, or walk to more than fifty shops, restaurants, and the famous Shipshewana Flea Market. We offer queen beds, wraparound front porch, gazebos,

Morton Street

fireplaces, Victorian garden, full hot breakfast, and more. Book your next church retreat, marriage encounter,

family reunion, or couples' getaway with us.

Hosts: Peggy Scherger and Kelly McConnell
  (mother and daughter)
Rooms: 8 (PB) $59-99
Full Breakfast
Credit Cards: A, B, C, D
Notes: 2, 5, 7, 10, 11, 12

SILVER LAKE

Rollin' Acres Holsteins
Bed & Breakfast

11434 South 100 West, 46982
(219) 352-2725; fax: (219) 352-0095
E-mail: rtmartin@kconline.com

Enjoy Hoosier hospitality on our working dairy farm located near Grace and North Manchester Colleges. After a day of antique shopping, you will enjoy relaxing in our flower-water garden sitting area and listen to nature's harmony singers. In the morning, begin your day with a farmer-style breakfast. Gift certificates available.

Hosts: Randy and Teresa Martin
Rooms: 2 (PB) $35-55
Full Breakfast
Credit Cards: None
Notes: 2, 5, 7, 8, 9, 10

SOUTH BEND

Oliver Inn
Bed & Breakfast

630 West Washington Street, 46601
(219) 232-4545; (888) 697-4466
fax: (219) 288-9788
E-mail: oliver@michiana.org

NOTES: Credit cards accepted: A Master Card; B Visa; C American Express; D Discover; E Diners Club; F Other; 2 Personal checks accepted; 3 Lunch available; 4 Dinner available; 5 Open all year;

Iowa

BURLINGTON

The Schramm House Bed & Breakfast

616 Columbia Street, 52601
(319) 754-0373
E-mail: visit@schramm.com
www.visit.schramm.com

Step into the past when you enter this restored 1870s Victorian in the heart of the Burlington historic district. Unique architecture and antique furnishings create the mood of an era past. Four guest rooms, all with private baths, offer queen or twin beds, quilts, and more. Experience Burlington hospitality while having lemonade on the porch or tea by the fire with your hosts. Walk to the Mississippi River, antique shops, and restaurants.

Hosts: Sandy and Bruce Morrison
Rooms: 4 (PB) $85-100
Full Breakfast
Credit Cards: A, B, C, D, E
Notes: 2, 5, 7, 8, 9, 10, 12

The Schramm House

CALMAR

Calmar Guesthouse Bed & Breakfast

103 West North Street, 52132
(319) 562-3851
E-mail: lbkruse@salamander.com
www.bestinns.net/atway/ia/calmar.html

This beautifully restored, antique-filled Victorian home is located in northeastern Iowa near Decorah, Luther College, N.I.C. College, Hand-Carved Bily Brother Clocks Museum, world's smallest church, the Little Brown Church, Niagara Cave, and Seed Sower Farm. Bike trails, canoeing, and trout fishing also nearby. IBBIA member. This B&B offers a memorable experience.

Host: Lucille B. Kruse
Rooms: 5 $45-49.95
Full Breakfast
Credit Cards: A, B
Notes: 2, 5, 7, 8, 9, 10, 11

CEDAR RAPIDS

Joy in the Morning Bed and Breakfast

1809 Second Avenue SE, 52403
(319) 363-9731; (800) 363-5093
fax: (319) 363-7548
E-mail: joyinmorng@aol.com
www.joyinthemorning.cjb.net

"Elegant yet peaceful and inviting" describes this 1915 colonial villa

6 Pets welcome; 7 Children welcome; 8 Tennis nearby; 9 Swimming nearby; 10 Golf nearby; 11 Skiing nearby; 12 May be booked through travel agent

IOWA

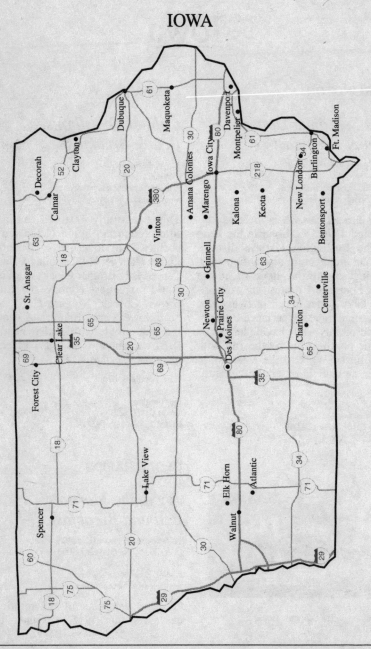

NOTES: Credit cards accepted: A Master Card; B Visa; C American Express; D Discover; E Diners Club; F Other; 2 Personal checks accepted; 3 Lunch available; 4 Dinner available; 5 Open all year;

Joy in the Morning

home that has been recently redecorated. It is characterized by the "Gone with the Wind" staircase in the entrance hall. Each room has a private bath; the romantic Garden Room has a whirlpool. King and queen beds; TV/VCR in each room. Enjoy the hot tub on the deck. Delicious full breakfast. Nestled amongst historic homes, it is conveniently located to shopping, theatres, restaurants, and colleges.

Hosts: Ron Cuchna and Joy Miller-Cuchna
Rooms: 3 (PB) $75-115
Full Breakfast
Credit Cards: A, B, C, D
Notes: 2, 5, 8, 9, 10

The Lion & the Lamb

913 2nd Avenue, Vinton, 52349
phone/fax: (319) 472-5086; (888) 390-5262
E-mail: lionlamb@lionlamb.com
www.lionlamb.com

Located along the Cedar River, this small town whispers of a time gone by when Victorian opulence was at its peak. Vinton boasts many turn-of-the-century homes. Experience elegant accommodations in this 1892 Queen Anne mansion. Each guest room fea-

tures a queen bed, TV, overhead fan, air-conditioning, and coffeemaker. Call for a free brochure and information. Murder mystery dinners are available, priced from $175-205 per couple.

Hosts: Richard and Rachel Waterbury
Rooms: 5 (2 PB; 3 SB) $75-105
Full Breakfast
Credit Cards: A, B, C, D
Notes: 2, 5, 7, 8, 9, 10, 11, 12

CENTERVILLE

One of a Kind

314 West State Street, 52544
(515) 437-4540

One of A Kind

One of a Kind is a stately, three-story brick home built in 1867. Situated in one of Iowa's delightful small communities, you'll be within walking distance of antique shops, the town square, city park with tennis courts, the swimming pool, and just 12 minutes to Lake Rathbun, Iowa's largest lake. Browse the gift shop filled with collectibles, original paintings, and more. Enjoy our special delicacies in the tearoom.

6 Pets welcome; 7 Children welcome; 8 Tennis nearby; 9 Swimming nearby; 10 Golf nearby; 11 Skiing nearby; 12 May be booked through travel agent

Hosts: Jack and Joyce Stufflebeem
Rooms: 5 (2 PB; 3 SB) $35-65
Full Breakfast
Credit Cards: A, B, C, D
Notes: 2, 3, 4, 5, 8, 9, 10, 11, 12

CLEAR LAKE

Blessing on Main Bed & Breakfast

1204 Main Avenue, 50428
(641) 357-0341; fax: (641) 357-5813
E-mail: blessing@netins.net
showcase.netins.net/web/

Upon arrival at Blessing on Main, you will receive a warm welcome, refreshments, and a "Blessing Basket." Discover a calm leisure in the charm of this restored, century-old Victorian home furnished with antiques and cherished family heirlooms. Guestrooms offer king, queen, and twin beds with private baths and air-conditioning. A bountiful breakfast is served. Our Main Avenue location is only four blocks from restored downtown and many attractions: casual/fine dining, antique/speciality shops,

Blessing on Main

and Lakeside City Park with its beautiful view of Clear Lake; try a "Lady of the Lake" evening cruise.

Hosts: Jim and Janet Allard
Rooms: 2 (PB) $80
Full Breakfast
Credit Cards: A, B
Notes: 2, 5, 8, 9, 10

Larch Pine Inn

Larch Pine Inn

401 North 3rd Street, 50428
(515) 357-7854; fax: (515) 357-7854
E-mail: larchinn@netins.net
www.clearlakeiowa.com

This 1875 Victorian on a wooded lot has a screened veranda; rooms furnished with queen or twin beds, handsome quilts, and antiques; private baths; guest parlor; and kitchenette. Walk to lake, city park, shopping, and fine dining. Evening refreshments and full breakfast.

Host: Elain La Pierre
Rooms: 3 (PB) $85
Full Breakfast
Credit Cards: A, B, C
Notes: 2, 5, 7, 8, 9, 10, 11, 12

NOTES: Credit cards accepted: A Master Card; B Visa; C American Express; D Discover; E Diners Club; F Other; 2 Personal checks accepted; 3 Lunch available; 4 Dinner available; 5 Open all year;

DUBUQUE

The Mandolin Inn

199 Loras Boulevard, 52001
(563) 556-0069; (800) 524-7996
fax: (563) 556-0587
www.mandolininn.com

The Mandolin Inn is an Edwardian B&B dedicated to sharing the elegance and comfort of an earlier era with a few discerning guests. It's a perfect place to kindle romance with its gourmet breakfasts, queen beds, and beautifully furnished rooms. Explore historic Dubuque, Galena, and other lovely towns nearby along the upper Mississippi River.

Host: Amy Boynton
Rooms: 8 (6 PB; 2 SB) $85-175
Full Breakfast
Credit Cards: A, B, C, D
Notes: 2, 5, 7, 8, 9, 10, 11

FOREST CITY

1897 Victorian House Bed & Breakfast

306 South Clark Street, 50436
(641) 585-3613; fax: (641) 585-1165
www.victorianhouse.net

As a guest in this turn-of-the-century Queen Anne Victorian home, you may choose from four beautifully decorated bedrooms, each with private bath. There is one luxurious carriage house suite with whirlpool bath. Beautiful, quiet, and very private. Breakfast, included in your rate, is served in our dining room, and we specialize in good, homemade food. A Victorian antique shop and tearoom

are two blocks away. Play our 1923 baby grand player piano, have a game of croquet, or relax in Forest City, a quiet yet progressive, rural, mid-western community.

Hosts: Richard and Doris Johnson
Rooms: 4 (PB) $80-130
Full Breakfast
Credit Cards: A, B
Notes: 2, 3, 10

FORT MADISON

Kingsley Inn

707 Avenue H, 52627
(319) 372-7074; (800) 441-2327
fax: (319) 372-7096
E-mail: kingsley@interl.net
www.kingsleyinn.com

Kingsley Inn

Experience the refined Victorian elegance of Kingsley Inn with sumptuous breakfasts, whirlpool, elevator, off-street parking, and spectacular Mississippi River view. Two-bedroom family suite also available. Restaurant and gift shop on the premises. Near historic Nauvoo, Illinois and other sites, golfing, tennis,

---

6 Pets welcome; 7 Children welcome; 8 Tennis nearby; 9 Swimming nearby; 10 Golf nearby; 11 Skiing nearby; 12 May be booked through travel agent

water sports, tennis, and antiquing. AAA and AARP discounts, as well as special discounts for clergy and church groups. Ask us about special packages. Visit our web site to view our lovely rooms.

Rooms: 15 (PB) $75-135
Full Breakfast
Credit Cards: A, B, C, D, E
Notes: 2, 3, 4, 5, 8, 10, 12

from Des Moines and Iowa City. Member of the Iowa Bed and Breakfast Guild and Iowa Lodging Association. State licensed and inspected. Gift certificates available.

Hosts: Ray and Dorothy Spriggs
Rooms: 5 (PB) $50-70
Full Breakfast
Credit Cards: A, B, C, D
Notes: 2, 5, 8, 9, 10, 11, 12

GRINNELL

Carriage House Bed & Breakfast

1133 Broad Street, 50112
(641) 236-7520; fax: (641) 236-5085
E-mail: irishbnb@iowatelecom.net
www.bedandbreakfast.com

Queen Anne-style Victorian. Relax in the wicker on the front porch or enjoy several fireplaces in winter. Lovely rooms with queen beds and private baths. Central air, stained-glass windows, and a hand-painted ceiling. Elegant breakfasts with Irish soda bread. Excellent restaurants nearby. One block from Grinnell college; one hour

Carriage House

IOWA CITY

Bella Vista Bed & Breakfast

2 Bella Vista Place, 52245
(319) 338-4129
www.virtualcities.com/ia/bellavista.htm

Daissy Owen has furnished her lovely, air-conditioned, 1920s home with antiques and artifacts she has acquired on her travels in Europe and Latin America. The home is conveniently located on the city's historic north side with a beautiful view of the Iowa River. The Hoover Library, the Amana Colonies, and the Amish center of Kalona are all nearby. A full breakfast, with Daissy's famous coffee, is served in the dining room's unique setting each morning. Daissy is fluent in Spanish and speaks some French. From I-80 take Dubuque Street, Exit 244, turn left on Brown Street, then take the first left on Linn Street; it is one block to #2 Bella Vista Place B&B.

Host: Daissy P. Owen
Rooms: 5 (3 PB; 2 SB) $70-130
Full Breakfast
Credit Cards: None
Notes: 2, 5, 8, 9, 10

NOTES: Credit cards accepted: A Master Card; B Visa; C American Express; D Discover; E Diners Club; F Other; 2 Personal checks accepted; 3 Lunch available; 4 Dinner available; 5 Open all year;

Haverkamps' Linn Street Homestay Bed & Breakfast

619 North Linn Street, 52245
(319) 337-4363; fax: (319) 354-7057
E-mail: havb-b@soli.inav.net
ww.bbhost.com/haverkampslinnstbb

Enjoy the warmth and hospitality of our 1908 Edwardian home filled with heirlooms and collectibles. Only a short walk to downtown Iowa City and the University of Iowa's main

Haverkamps'

campus; just a short drive to the Hoover Library in West Branch, the Amish in Kalona, and seven Amana Colonies.

Hosts: Clarence and Dorothy Haverkamp
Rooms: 3 (SB) $45-50
Full Breakfast
Credit Cards: None
Notes: 2, 5, 7, 8, 9, 10, 12

KALONA

The Carriage House

1140 Larch Avenue, 52247
(319) 656-3824; E-mail: chouse@kctc.net
www.carriagehousebb.net

Come and relax in the country. Watch the sun set and wake up to the sunrise. Stroll past neighboring Amish farms or sit on our porch swing. Visit Kalona's quilt, antique, craft, or gift shops. Swim in the local public pool or golf at Kalona's nearby course. Experience Kalona's charm. The Univerity of Iowa is 18 miles away, and Coral Ridge Mall, Tanger Outlet Mall, and Herbert Hoover Museum are all nearby.

Hosts: Dan and Edie Kemp
Rooms: 4 (PB) $63-75
Full Breakfast
Credit Cards: A, B
Notes: 2, 3, 4, 5, 7, 8, 9, 10

MAQUOKETA

Squiers Manor Bed & Breakfast

418 West Pleasant Street, 52060
(319) 652-6961; fax: (319) 652-5995
E-mail: innkeeper@squiersmanor.com
www.squiersmanor.com

---

6 Pets welcome; 7 Children welcome; 8 Tennis nearby; 9 Swimming nearby; 10 Golf nearby; 11 Skiing nearby; 12 May be booked through travel agent

Squiers Manor B&B is located in the West Pleasant Street historic district. This 1882 Queen Anne mansion features walnut, cherry, and butternut woods throughout. Enjoy period furnishings, queen beds, in-room phone and TV, and private baths, as well as single and double Jacuzzis. Come hungry and enjoy delicious, candlelight evening desserts and breakfasts (more like brunch) served in the elegant dining room. Virl's and Kathy's goal is to make your stay as pleasant and enjoyable as possible. Give us a call today!

Hosts: Virl and Kathy Banowetz
Rooms: 8 (PB) $80-195
Full Breakfast
Credit Cards: A, B, C, D
Notes: 2, 5, 8, 9, 10, 11, 12

MAVENGO

Loy's Bed & Breakfast

2077 Kk Avenue, 52301
(319) 642-7787
E-mail: lbw20771@zews.ia.net

Gracious contemporary country home on a working farm. Master homemaker offers a full gourmet breakfast. Enjoy a quiet respite in the Iowa countryside. Recreation equipment inside and outside. Take a ride on a tractor. Hauting, Anama Colonies, Tanger Outlet, Iowa University events, Cedar Rapids, and local lakes are all nearby.

Hosts: Loy and Robert Walker
Rooms: 3 (1 PB; 2 SB) $80 plus tax
Full Breakfast
Credit Cards: None
Notes: 2, 4, 5, 7, 8, 9, 10

PRAIRIE CITY

Country Connection Bed & Breakfast

9737 West 93rd Street South, 50228
(515) 994-2023

Country Connection

Guests can experience the friendly atmosphere of a working farm community surrounded by the tranquility of bountiful cropland away from the hustle and bustle of everyday life. This turn-of-the-century farm home is filled with period furnishings, treasures lovingly preserved from six generations, walnut woodwork, leaded glass, and lace, all blended with privacy, charm, and hospitality. Arise to the aroma of a hearty country breakfast served by candlelight on the sunporch or formal dining room. A complimentary bedtime snack of old-fashioned, homemade ice cream is served. Open April-November. Near Walnut Creek Wildlife Refuge, Pella Tulip Time, and twenty miles east of Des Moines. Member of and inspected by Iowa Bed and Breakfast Innkeepers' Association (IBBIA).

Hosts: Jim and Alice Foreman
Rooms: 2 (SB) $50-65
Full Breakfast
Credit Cards: A, B
Notes: 2, 7, 8, 9, 10

SAINT ANSGAR

The Blue Belle Inn

513 West 4th Street; P.O. Box 205, 50472
(641) 713-3113; (877) 713-3113
E-mail: innkeeper@bluebellinn.com
www.bluebelleinn.com

Rediscover the romance of the 1890s while enjoying all the modern comforts and convenience of the 21st century in one of the six distinctively decorated guest rooms at the Blue Belle Inn. This festive Victorian "painted lady" features air-conditioning, fireplaces, and Jacuzzis, as well as lofty tin ceilings, gleaming maple woodwork, stained glass, crystal chandeliers in bay windows, and curved window pockets which create a shimmering interplay of light and color. Enjoy gourmet dining by candlelight.

Host: Sherrie C. Hansen
Rooms: 6 (5 PB; 1 SB) $70-150
Full Breakfast
Credit Cards: A, B, C, D
Notes: 2, 3, 4, 5, 7, 9, 10

SPENCER

Hannah Marie Country Inn

4070 Highway 71, 51301
(712) 262-1286; fax: (712) 262-3294
hannahmarieinn.com

Hannah Marie

There's a warm welcome here. The 1910 parlor and fireside room have welcomed guests through the years since 1986. Queen feathered beds and in-room private whirlpools. Yummy breakfasts, butterfly gardens, a classical labyrinth, croquet, kites, central air-conditioning, bath bubbles, and softened water. Our Romance of Country theme inspired the trope l'oeil flour and wall paintings. Our veranda is for: reading, sipping tea, and playing marbles. Nearby are Iowa Great Lakes, antiquing, shopping. Come. . . grab a camera and pack lightly.

Host: Mary Nichols
Rooms: 6 (PB) $79-120
Full Breakfast
Credit Cards: A, B, C, D
Notes: 2, 5, 7, 8, 9, 10, 11, 12

WALNUT

Antique City Inn Bed & Breakfast

400 Antique City Drive, P.O. Box 584, 51577
(712) 784-3722
E-mail: sylvias@netins.net
www.netins.netshowcase/walnutia

---

6 Pets welcome; 7 Children welcome; 8 Tennis nearby; 9 Swimming nearby; 10 Golf nearby; 11 Skiing nearby; 12 May be booked through travel agent

This 1911 Victorian home has been restored and furnished to its original state. All rooms are air-conditioned and have private baths; the carriage house has a double whirlpool. The inn is located one block north of eight malls and stores with 250 antique dealers. The home boasts beautiful woodwork, a dumbwaiter icebox, French doors, and a wraparound porch.

Host: Sylvia Reddie
Rooms: 6 (5 PB; 1 SB) $53-63.60
Full Breakfast
Credit Cards: A, B, C, D
Notes: 2, 5, 8, 9, 10

Clark's Country Inn Bed & Breakfast

701 Walnut Street, P.O. Box 533, 51577
(712) 784-3010
pionet.net/~inns/clarks.html

Come visit Iowa's antique capital, just a mile south of I-80 between Omaha and Des Moines. The city of Walnut offers six malls, individual shops, and more than 200 dealers. Open all year, Clark's Country Inn is a 1912, two-story home with oak interior, antiques, newly remodeled guest rooms, private baths, king and queen beds, and central air-conditioning. Mastercard/Visa deposit required. No smoking.

Hosts: Mary Lou and Ron Clark
Rooms: 3 (PB) $58
Full Breakfast
Credit Cards: A, B
Notes: 2, 5, 8, 9, 10

NOTES: Credit cards accepted: A Master Card; B Visa; C American Express; D Discover; E Diners Club; F Other; 2 Personal checks accepted; 3 Lunch available; 4 Dinner available; 5 Open all year;

Kansas

GREAT BEND

Peaceful Acres Bed & Breakfast

R.R. 5, Box 153, 67530
(316) 793-7527

Enjoy a mini-farm and sprawling, tree-shaded old farmhouse furnished with some antiques. If you like peace and quiet, chickens, calves, guineas, kittens in the spring, and old-fashioned hospitality, you need to come and visit us. Breakfast will be fixed from homegrown products. We are near historical areas—Sante Fe Trail, Ft. Larned, Cheyenne Bottoms—and close to the zoo and tennis courts. A full country breakfast is served.

Hosts: Dale and Doris Nitzel
Rooms: 3 (1 PB; 2 SB) $35
Full Breakfast
Credit Cards: None
Notes: 2, 3, 4, 5, 7, 8, 9, 10, 12

NEWTON

Old Parsonage Bed & Breakfast

330 East 4th Street, 67114
(316) 283-6808

Located in Newton's oldest neighborhood, this charming home once served as the parsonage for the First Mennonite Church. It features a cozy yet spacious atmosphere filled with antiques and family heirlooms. The Old Parsonage is a short walk from the historical Warkentin House and Warkentin Mill, which are listed on the National Register of Historic Places. Two miles from Bethel College. Dine in one of Newton's fine ethnic eateries, or browse quaint antique and craft shops.

Hosts: Karl and Betty Friesen
Rooms: 3 (1 PB; 2 SB) $48
Continental Breakfast
Credit Cards: A, B
Notes: 2, 5, 7

SALINA

Trader's Lodge

1392 North 210th Road, Wells, 67467-5016
(785) 488-3930; (866) 360-1813
www.come.to/traderslodge

Join us for "a taste of the Wild West" and experience the history of the fur trade era in our lodge of fir and limestone, decorated with antiques, furs, and Indian artifacts. Choose from the Trapper's Room, Plains Indian Room, Southwest Room, or Renaissance Room, each with individual climate control and private bath. Fitness room and hot tub downstairs. Quiet country setting near a state lake. No alcohol or tobacco, please.

Hosts: Neal and Kathy Kindall
Rooms: 4 (PB) $65-85
Full Breakfast

6 Pets welcome; 7 Children welcome; 8 Tennis nearby; 9 Swimming nearby; 10 Golf nearby; 11 Skiing nearby; 12 May be booked through travel agent

KANSAS

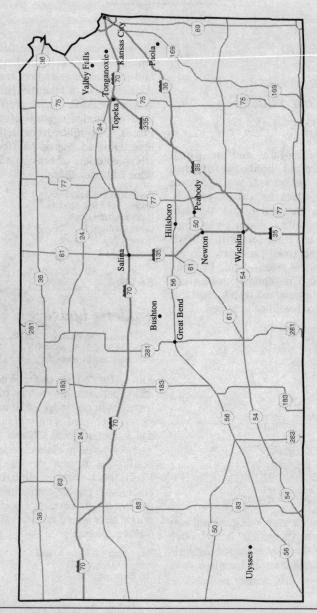

NOTES: Credit cards accepted: A Master Card; B Visa; C American Express; D Discover; E Diners
Club; F Other; 2 Personal checks accepted; 3 Lunch available; 4 Dinner available; 5 Open all year;

Credit Cards: A, B, C, D
Notes: 2, 3, 4, 5, 7, 10

VALLEY FALLS

The Barn Bed & Breakfast Inn

14910 Blue Mound Road, 66088-4030
(785) 945-3225; (800) 869-7717
fax: (785) 945-3432
E-mail: thebarn@thebarnbb.com
www.thebarnbb.com

Country living at its best in the rolling hills of northeast Kansas, this 108-year-old peg-barn has been converted into a B&B. Sitting high on a hill with a beautiful view, it has a large indoor heated pool, hot tub, fitness room, three large living rooms, and king-sized beds in all rooms. A home-cooked dinner is included with your room, as well as a full breakfast. The Barn has three large living rooms available.

Hosts: Tom and Marcella Ryan and Patricia
  Miller
Rooms: 20 (PB) $110-114
Full Breakfast
Credit Cards: A, B, C, D
Notes: 2, 3, 4, 5, 7, 8, 9, 10, 11, 12

WICHITA

The Castle Inn Riverside

1155 North River Boulevard, 67203
(316) 263-4998
E-mail: castle@gte.net
www.castleinnriverside.com

This luxurious inn is a stunning example of Richardsonian Romanesque architecture. The home includes 14 guest rooms, each individually appointed. Twelve of the guest rooms include fireplaces, and six have double whirlpool tubs. Guests are pampered with a gourmet breakfast, and later in the day, with a sampling of wine, cheeses, light hors d'oeuvres, gourmet coffees and teas, and homemade desserts. The inn offers many amenities for its business travelers, including rooms equipped with TVs, VCRs, telephones, and data ports. The inn is just a few minutes from downtown Wichita and near attractions like Old Town, Exploration Place, and the Wichita Art Museum.

Hosts: Dr. Terry and Paula Lowry
Rooms: 14 (PB) $125-275
Full Breakfast
Credit Cards: A, B, D, E
Notes: 2, 5, 7, 8, 9, 10, 12

The Castle Inn Riverside

KENTUCKY

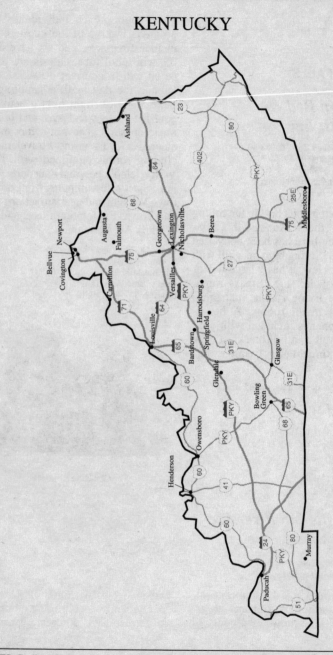

NOTES: Credit cards accepted: A Master Card; B Visa; C American Express; D Discover; E Diners Club; F Other; 2 Personal checks accepted; 3 Lunch available; 4 Dinner available; 5 Open all year;

Kentucky

ASHLAND

Gambill Mansion Bed & Breakfast

State Route 32 & 201 Intersection, Blaine, 41124
(606) 652-3120; (800) 485-3362
fax: (606) 652-3120
E-mail: gambill@foothills.net
www.bbonline.com/ky/gambill

Candlelight and lace and the rustic outdoors. . . This 18-room, three-story home was built in 1923. Spas, luncheons, wedding accommodations, and candlelight dinners are offered. The Barn Loft is perfect for private parties or overnight retreats. We are surrounded by mountains, lakes, parks, outdoor activities, and winding mountain roads, yet only 25 miles from I-64.

Hosts: Art and Ella Seals
Rooms: 4 (2 PB; 2 SB) $65-150
Full Breakfast
Credit Cards: A, B, C
Notes: 3, 4, 5, 7, 8, 9, 10, 11

BARDSTOWN

Beautiful Dreamer Bed & Breakfast

440 East Stephen Foster Avenue, 40004
(502) 348-4004; (800) 811-8312
www.geocities.com/bdreamerbb/

Antiques and cherry furniture complement this Federal-design home that overlooks historic "My Old Kentucky Home." The Beautiful Dreamer Room has a double Jacuzzi. The Captain's Room has a single Jacuzzi and fireplace. The Stephen Foster Room has a cherry four-poster bed and double Jacuzzi. All rooms are air-conditioned, have queen beds, and color TVs. A hearty breakfast is included. Located within walking distance of the Stephen Foster Story.

Hosts: Dan and Lynell Ginter
Rooms: 3 (PB) $109-139
Full Breakfast
Credit Cards: A, B, C, D
Notes: 2, 5, 7, 8, 9, 10, 12

Coffee Tree Cabin

980 McCubbins Lane, 40004
(502) 348-1151
www.bbonline.com/ky/bbak

Coffee Tree Cabin

This spacious log home on 41 acres offers abundant wild life, a quiet natural retreat, large porches, a glass ve-

---

6 Pets welcome; 7 Children welcome; 8 Tennis nearby; 9 Swimming nearby; 10 Golf nearby; 11 Skiing nearby; 12 May be booked through travel agent

randa, a mountain gazebo, evening desserts, a full breakfast, Southern hospitality with elegance, cathedral ceilings, large porches, and antiques. Located five and a half miles west of historic Bardstown, second oldest town west of the Allegany Mountains. Many attractions are nearby.

Hosts: J.L. and Joann Young Bland
Rooms: 3 (PB) $90-120
Full Breakfast
Credit Cards: None
Notes: 2, 5, 8, 9, 10

Jailer's Inn

111 West Stephen Foster Avenue, 40004
(502) 348-5551; (800) 948-5551
fax: (502) 349-1837
E-mail: cpaul@jailersinn.com
www.jailersinn.com

Windows covered with iron bars, 30-inch thick stone walls, and a heavy steel door slamming behind one may not sound like the typical tourist accommodation, and Jailer's Inn is anything but typical. The historic Jailer's Inn, circa 1819, offers a unique and luxurious way to "do time." Jailer's Inn is a place of wonderful, thought-provoking contrasts. Each of the six guest rooms is beautifully decorated with antiques and heirlooms, all in the renovated front jail. The back jail, built in 1874, is basically unchanged; guests will get a chilling and sobering look at what conditions were like in the old Nelson County jail that was in full operation as recently as 1987. Call for rates.

Host: C. Paul McCoy
Rooms: 6 (PB) $70-135
Full Breakfast
Credit Cards: A, B, C, D
Notes: 2, 7, 8, 9, 10, 12

A Rose MarkHaven

714 North 3rd Street, 40004
(502) 348-8218; (888) 420-9703
fax: (502) 348-8219
E-mail: arosemarkhaven@aol.com
arosemarkhaven.com

We invite you to experience Southern hospitality in our 1824 antebellum mansion, exquisitly decorated with four-poster king-sized beds and antiqes. You will enjoy the feelings of being pampered in a Haven. Chef Mark prepares a full gourmet breakfast for you to relax and start your day at a slower pace.

Hosts: Rosemary and Mark Southard
Rooms: 7 (PB) $110-150
Full Breakfast
Credit Cards: A, B, C, D
Notes: 4, 5, 10

BELLEVUE

Mary's Belle View Inn

444 Van Voast Avenue, 41073
(859) 581-8337; (888) 581-8875
www.bbonline.com/ky/belleview

This B&B features quiet, comfortable rooms, all with their own private baths. Each room has access to a large deck, offering a spectacular view of the Cincinnati skyline and surrounding areas. Full breakfast served. Ten minutes from Cincinnati. Children welcome, no pets.

NOTES: Credit cards accepted: A Master Card; B Visa; C American Express; D Discover; E Diners Club; F Other; 2 Personal checks accepted; 3 Lunch available; 4 Dinner available; 5 Open all year;

Host: Mary Bickers
Rooms: 3 (PB) $55-110
Full Breakfast
Credit Cards: A, B
Notes: 2, 5, 7

BEREA

Cabin Fever Bed & Breakfast

112 Adams Street, 40403
(859) 986-9075; fax: (859) 986-6045
E-mail: afredoescobar@hotmail.com
www.staycabinfever.com

See Kentucky's Folk Arts and Crafts Capital from the center of it all at Cabin Fever B&B. Choose from three lovely rooms, decorated artistically with family collections and the Escobars' own works of art. Enjoy all the modern conveniences while surrounded by all the Old World ambience of a log home and traditional Southern hospitality.

Hosts: Alfredo and Jennifer Rose Escobar
Rooms: 3 (1 PB; 2 SB) $75

Cabin Fever

Full Breakfast
Credit Cards: D
Notes: 2, 5, 6, 7, 8, 9, 10

BOWLING GREEN

Alpine Lodge

5310 Morgantown Road, 42101
(270) 843-4846; fax: (270) 843-4833
E-mail: alplodge@aol.com
www.christianB&B.com/ky/alpinelodge.htm

Alpine Lodge is a swiss chalet with 6,000 square feet located on 12 acres. There is a honeymoon suite, a family suite that sleeps five, and two other guest rooms. We have a pool and hot tub. A full breakfast is served.

Hosts: Dr. and Mrs David Livingston
Rooms: 5 (3 PB; 2 SB) $65 plus tax
Full Breakfast
Credit Cards: None
Notes: 2, 5, 6, 7, 9, 10, 12

CARROLLTON

General Butler

713 Highland Avenue, 41008
(502) 732-6154
E-mail: cwobbnb@aol.com
bbonline.com/ky/genbutler

This 1825 home of General William O. Butler has outstanding brick South Georgian architecture with gracious Palladin windows. Relax on the

General Butler

---

6 Pets welcome; 7 Children welcome; 8 Tennis nearby; 9 Swimming nearby; 10 Golf nearby; 11 Skiing nearby; 12 May be booked through travel agent

screen patio or curl up in front of the fireplace in the library. The Elijah Room has a queen bed, bath, and fireplace. The General's Hideaway is a cozy upstairs room with twin beds, baths, and a library motif. Enjoy our English and herb garden and garden railroad.

Hosts: Dick and Norman Firestone
Rooms: 2 (PB) $75-95
Full Breakfast
Credit Cards: A, B
Notes: 2, 5, 10

Ghent House
Bed & Breakfast

411 Main Street, U.S. 42, P.O. Box 478, 41045
(502) 347-5807
www.bbonline.com/ky/ghent/

Ghent House

A historic river home, Ghent House is a gracious reminder of the antebellum days of the old South. Walk back in time—visit this 1833 home. Relax in the whirlpool or by the fireplaces, walk in the English garden, view the Ohio River on your porch, or relax in the Rose Garden Cottage and gazebo. Come as a guest. . .leave as a friend.

Hosts: Wayne and Diane Young
Rooms: 4 (PB) $70-175
Full Breakfast
Credit Cards: A, B, C, D
Notes: 2, 5, 7, 10

COVINGTON

Christopher's
Bed & Breakfast

See description under Newport, KY.

The Licking-Riverside
Bed & Breakfast

516 Garrard Street, 41011
(859) 291-0191; (800) 483-7822
fax: (859) 291-0939
E-mail: freelyn@aol.com
www.lickingriversidebandb.com

This historic home along the Licking River offers accommodations including two all-inclusive suites with a river view. All units include queen beds, Jacuzzis-for-two, private baths, TVs, refrigerators, phones, and coffeemakers. A courtyard with decks overlooks a wooded area with river frontage. Just a short walk to many restaurants, the Newport Aquarium, Ohio River, and the local shuttle. Near Cincinnati, Ohio.

Host: Lynda Freeman
Rooms: 4 (PB) $129-169
Continental Breakfast
Credit Cards: A, B, D, E
Notes: 5, 7, 8, 9, 10, 11, 12

FALMOUTH

The Red Brick House

201 Chapel Street, 41040
(859) 654-4834

This 1890 Victorian Gothic house in historic downtown Falmouth is fur-

---

NOTES: Credit cards accepted: A Master Card; B Visa; C American Express; D Discover; E Diners Club; F Other; 2 Personal checks accepted; 3 Lunch available; 4 Dinner available; 5 Open all year;

The Red Brick House

nished with family antiques. Located 39 miles south of Cincinnati and four miles from Kincaid Lake State Park. Breakfast with fresh baked goods is served in our dining room for our guests. Member of Kentucky Bed & Breakfast Association. Please inquire about children.

Hosts: Gene and Joellen Kearns
Rooms: 4 (1 PB; 3 SB) $45-50
Continental Breakfast
Credit Cards: A, B, C, D
Notes: 2, 5, 7, 8, 9

GEORGETOWN

Blackridge Hall Bed & Breakfast

4055 Paris Pike, 40324
phone/fax: (502) 863-2069; (800) 768-9308
E-mail: jblack1310@aol.com
www.blackridgehall.com

Blackridge Hall is an upscale, luxurious, Southern Georgian-style mansion on five acres in Bluegrass horse country. There are six guest suites/rooms containing antique and reproduction furnishings. Two master suites have marble Jacuzzi tubs, while all baths are private. A full, gourmet candlelight breakfast is served in the dining room or on the veranda. A cozy guest kitchenette is available with snacks and soft drinks. Minutes to Lexington, Kentucky Horse Park, Keeneland and Red Mile racetracks, University of Kentucky, Toyota Motor Corporation tours, and historic Georgetown antique shops. Near I-64 and I-75.

Host: Jim D. Black
Rooms: 6 (PB) $89-199
Full Breakfast
Credit Cards: A, B, C, D
Notes: 2, 5, 8, 10, 12

Pineapple Inn Bed & Breakfast

645 South Broadway Street, 40324
(502) 868-5453

Located in beautiful, historic Georgetown, our inn—built in 1876—is on the Historic Register. Furnished with antiques and beautifully decorated. Three of the guest rooms are upstairs: the Country Room and Victorian Room, each with full bed, and the Americana Room, with two full beds and one twin bed. Our Derby Room is on the main floor with a queen canopy bed and hot tub in a private bath. A full breakfast is served each morning in our French country dining room. Relax in our large living room.

Hosts: Les and Muriel
Rooms: 4 (PB) $65-90
Full Breakfast
Credit Cards: A, B
Notes: 2, 5, 7, 8, 9, 10, 12

---

6 Pets welcome; 7 Children welcome; 8 Tennis nearby; 9 Swimming nearby; 10 Golf nearby; 11 Skiing nearby; 12 May be booked through travel agent

GLENDALE

Glendale Crossing Gate Bed &Breakfast Inn

883 West Glendale Hodgenville Road, P.O. Box
207, 42740
(270) 369-8327; (877) 357-GATE
fax: (270) 369-6588
E-mail: cgbb@msn.com
www.crossinggatebb.com

Experience a getaway out of the ordinary with extraordinatry theme room accommodations. This B&B is located in historic Glendale (many antique and gift shops), near the Whistle Stop and Depot restaraunts. We offer fully stocked fishing pond, horseshoes, meeting rooms. Enjoy a time of spiritual renewal and refreshment. Non-smoking facility (inside) and alcohol not allowed on grounds. Located a short drive from Churchill Downs, Coca Cola Museum, Fort Knox, National Corvette Museum, Mammoth Cave, and National Southern Gospel Quartet Convention. *By wisdom a house is built, and through understanding it is established; through knowledge its rooms are filled with rare and beautiful treasures.* (Prov. 24:3–4 NIV)

Glendale Crossing Gate

Hosts: Jim and Patti Stewart
Rooms: 6 (PB) $85-150
Full Breakfast
Credit Cards: A, B, C, D
Notes: 2, 5, 7, 8, 10

HARRODSBURG

Bauer Haus Bed & Breakfast

362 North College Street, 40330
(859) 734-6289; (877) 734-6289
www.bbonline.com/ky/bauer

Bauer Haus

Savor the craftsmanship of the past in this 1880s Victorian home listed on the National Register, and designated a Kentucky landmark. Nestle in the sitting room, sip tea or coffee in the dining room, repose in the parlor, or ascend the stairs to a private room for a relaxing visit. In Kentucky's oldest settlement, Bauer Haus is within walking distance of Old Fort Harrod State Park and historic Harrodsburg.

Hosts: Dick and Marian Bauer
Rooms: 5 (3 PB; 2 SB) $65-125
Full Breakfast
Credit Cards: A, B, C
Notes: 2, 5, 8, 10, 12

NOTES: Credit cards accepted: A Master Card; B Visa; C American Express; D Discover; E Diners Club; F Other; 2 Personal checks accepted; 3 Lunch available; 4 Dinner available; 5 Open all year;

Baxter House

Baxter House

1677 Lexington Road, 40330
(859) 734-4877; (888) 809-4457
E-mail: baxterhousebnb@juno.com
www.bbonline.com/ky/baxterhouse

Built in the 1840s, this log cabin is a unique American four-square that rests on seven pristine acres, surrounded by horse farms, on scenic byway 68. A great getaway, you'll enjoy rest and relaxation, privacy, and unforgettable views. Come and experience the beauty of the bluegrass and the hospitality of your hosts. In-room stocked refrigerator, microwave, coffee pot, telephone, sitting area, cafe set, snacks, and turndown service.

Hosts: Gaylynn Gardner and Donna Kirk
Rooms: 3 (PB) $79-109
Credit Cards: A, B, C, D, E
Notes: 2, 3, 4, 5, 7, 8, 9, 10

HENDERSON

L & N
Bed & Breakfast Ltd.

327 North Main Street, 42420
(270) 831-1100; fax: (270) 826-0075
E-mail: info@lnbbky.com
www.lnbbky.com

L & N is a two-story, Victorian home featuring oaken floors and woodwork, stained glass, antique furnishings, and a convenient location in the heart of downtown Henderson, next door to a railroad overpass. Four bedrooms are available, each with private bath, direct-dial telephone, and cable TV. The John James Audubon Park and Museum is only three and a half miles away and is open year-round. Your innkeepers reside next door.

L & N

Hosts: Mary Elizabeth and Norris Priest
Rooms: 4 (PB) $75
Continental Breakfast
Credit Cards: None
Notes: 2, 5, 7, 8, 10

LEXINGTON

Riverhill Bed & Breakfast

661 River Hill Drive, Richmond, 40475
(859) 624-3222; (800) 378-3877
fax: (859) 625-5439
E-mail: riverhill@riverhill.net
riverhill.net

The inn is conveniently located just three miles off of I-75, 15 minutes south of Lexington. We offer special packages for staff retreats, ladies' get-

---

6 Pets welcome; 7 Children welcome; 8 Tennis nearby; 9 Swimming nearby; 10 Golf nearby; 11 Skiing nearby; 12 May be booked through travel agent

away, or other small-group activities. Enjoy the peace and quiet. Elegant, country accommodations are roomy and comfortable. Numerous attractions and places of interest are immediately nearby or within a short drive.

Hosts: Glenda and Terry Fields
Rooms: 4 (PB) $78-145
Full Breakfast
Credit Cards: A, B, C
Notes: 2, 3, 4, 5, 7, 9, 10, 12

Sandusky House & O' Neal Log Cabin

Sandusky House

1626 Delaney Ferry Road, Nicholasville, 40356
phone/fax: (859) 223-4730
E-mail: llchumphrey@cs.com
www.100megsfree4.com/logcabin

A tree-lined drive to the Sandusky House is just a prelude to a wonderful visit to the bluegrass. A quiet, 10-acre country setting amid horse farms, yet close to Lexington, Horse Park, and Shakertown. The Greek Revival Sandusky House was built circa 1850 from bricks fired on the farm. A 1,000-acre land grant from Patrick Henry, governor of Virginia, was given in 1780 to soldiers who had

fought in the American Revolution. In addition to the Sandusky House, we have an 1820s reconstructed, two-story, two-bedroom log cabin with full kitchen and whirlpool bath. The cabin has a large stone fireplace and air-conditioning, and is located in a wooded area close to the main house. An ideal getaway for the entire family! Please call for a brochure.

Hosts: Jim and Linda Humphrey
Rooms: 3 (PB); 2 BR cabin (SB) $85-129
Full Breakfast
Credit Cards: A, B
Notes: 2, 5, 7

LOUISVILLE

The Inn at Woodhaven

401 South Hubbards Lane, 40207
(502) 895-1011; (888) 895-1011
E-mail: info@innatwoodhaven.com
www.innatwoodhaven.com

This circa 1853 Gothic Revival mansion is on the National Register. Rooms feature outstanding carved woodwork with crisscross windows, winding staircases, decorative mantels, and hardwood floors. Guest quarters are tastefully decorated with antiques suitable for their 13-foot ceilings. There are several common areas in the Main House and guests also take advantage of the porches and gardens and balconies. Other features include whirlpools, steam showers, fireplaces, and complimentary coffee stations.

Host: Marsha Burton
Rooms: 8 (PB) $75-225
Full Breakfast
Credit Cards: A, B, C, D
Notes: 2, 5, 6, 8, 9, 10, 12

NOTES: Credit cards accepted: A Master Card; B Visa; C American Express; D Discover; E Diners Club; F Other; 2 Personal checks accepted; 3 Lunch available; 4 Dinner available; 5 Open all year;

Pinecrest Cottage

2806 Newburg Road, 40205
(502) 454-3800; fax: (502) 452-9791
E-mail: allanm@prodigy.net
www.bbonline.com/ky/pinecrest

Situated on land deeded by forefather Patrick Henry, this century-old, fully-renovated, 1,400-square-foot cottage near the Louisville Zoo and Kentucky Kingdom features a six-and-a-half-acre wooded "yard," perennial beds, gazebo, tennis court, and pool. The guesthouse has a king bedroom, separate living room with two sofas (one folds out into a double bed), large bath, and sunporch. TV, VCR, phone, gas log fireplace, and kitchen stocked with breakfast and lunch goodies. Air-conditioned.

Hosts: Nancy and Allan Morris
Rooms: 1 (PB) $95-145
Continental Breakfast
Credit Cards: A, B, C
Notes: 2, 5, 7, 8, 9

The Rocking Horse Manor Bed & Breakfast

The Rocking Horse Manor

1022 South Third Street, 40203
(502) 583-0408; (888) 467-7322
fax: (502) 583-6077, ext. 129
E-mail: rockinghorsebb@webtv.net
rockinghorse-bb.com

Stay in a beautifully restored Victorian mansion in "old Louisville." All the ambiance of yesteryear with the amenities that today's traveler requires. All rooms have private attached baths, cable TVs, telephones, and individual temperature controls. We also provide for guests' convenience with robes, hair dryers, irons, and ironing boards. A two-course breakfast is served whenever you choose! Complimentary snacks and beverages available all day. Close to downtown, airport, and many attractions. "Business friendly!"

Host: Diana Jachimiak
Rooms: 6 (PB) $79-169
Full Breakfast
Credit Cards: A, B, C, D
Notes: 2, 5, 8, 9, 10, 12

MIDDLESBORO

The RidgeRunner Bed & Breakfast

208 Arthur Heights, 40965
(606) 248-4299; fax: (606) 248-8851
www.bbonline.com/ky/ridgerunner/

This 1891 Victorian home is furnished with authentic antiques and is nestled in the Cumberland Mountains. A picturesque view is enjoyed from the 60-foot front porch, welcoming guests with rocking chairs, swings, and hammocks. Guests are treated like special people, in a relaxed, peaceful atmosphere. Five minutes

---

6 Pets welcome; 7 Children welcome; 8 Tennis nearby; 9 Swimming nearby; 10 Golf nearby; 11 Skiing nearby; 12 May be booked through travel agent

RidgeRunner

from Cumberland Gap National Park, 12 minutes from Pine Mountain State Park, 50 miles from Knoxville, Tennessee. Interesting history and hosts await.

Hosts: Susan Richards and Irma Gall
Rooms: 4 (2 PB; 2 SB) $65-75
Full Breakfast
Credit Cards: None
Notes: 2, 5, 8, 9, 10, 12

NEWPORT

Christopher's
Bed & Breakfast

604 Poplar Street, Bellevue, 41073
(859) 491-9354; (888) 585-7085
fax: (513) 853-1360
E-mail: christbb@fuse.net
www.bbonline.com/ky/christophers/

This late 1800s church was transformed into Christopher's B&B in 1997. This unique establishment is located in Bellevue's historic district, Taylor's Daughters. Christopher's, named after the Patron Saint of Travelers, features two standard rooms and a suite. Guestrooms have stained-glass windows, and private baths with

whirlpool. One-half mile south of downtown Cincinnati. Easily accessible from I-71, I-75, I-275, and I-471.

Host: Brenda Guidugli
Rooms: 3 (PB) $79-159
Continental Breakfast
Credit Cards: A, B, C
Notes: 2, 5, 7, 10, 12

Cincinnati's Weller Haus
Bed & Breakfast

319 Poplar Street, 41073
(859) 431-6829; (800) 431-4287
fax: (859) 431-4332
E-mail: innkeepers@wellerhaus.com
www.wellerhaus.com

Enjoy a stay in our historic home. The Weller Haus is within walking distance of the downtown stadiums, Riverboat Row restaurants, and the Newport Aquarium. We specialize in pampering our guests with all the amenities they desire. Our double Jacuzzi is suited for the romantic at heart. Business travelers will find corporate rates, fax machine, in-room desks, meeting space, and other conveniences with them in mind. A full, candle-lit breakfast will start your day off right!

Hosts: Valerie and David Brown
Rooms: 5 (PB) $89-168
Full Breakfast
Credit Cards: A, B, C, D, E
Notes: 2, 5, 7, 10, 11, 12

OWENSBORO

Helton House
Bed & Breakfast

103 East 23rd Street, 42303
(270) 926-7117; fax: (270) 926-6621
E-mail: graceeconley@aol.com
www.bbonline/ky/helton

Our B&B was eatured in the *Louisville Courier-Journal* 2000. Neighborhood songbirds issue the first welcome to visitors as they climb the front steps to the open front porch of the circa 1910 Arts and Crafts home. The house sits on a corner lot in the tree-lined. Buena Vista neighborhood where streets are divided into boulevards by leafty medians. The second-floor sun porch offers a panaromac view. Each room is individually decorated with antiques, oriental carpets, and cherry and walnut handmade furniture. Almost as much attention has been given to the surrounding landscaping as to the decor and furnishing of the house. Guests from around the globe have enjoyed the comfort, peace, and love of the Helton House. Please inquire regarding private or shared baths.

Hosts: Don and Grace Conley
Rooms: 5 (PB or SB) $65-85
Full Breakfast

Helton House

Credit Cards: A, B, C
Notes: 2, 5, 8, 9, 10

PADUCAH

Trinity Hills Farm Bed & Breakfast Home— Stained Glass Studio

Trinity Hills Farm

10455 Old Lovelaceville Road, 42001
(270) 488-3999; (800) 488-3998
E-mail: info@trinityhills.com
www.trinityhills.com

Share the serenity of our 17-acre country retreat and guesthouse amidst beautiful gardens, hills, woods, and fishing lake. Features romantic whirlpools, stained glass, fireplaces, vaulted ceilings, and handicapped-accessibility. Children or pets are welcome in our first-floor apartment suite with prior notice. Let Trinity Hills Farm be your haven for pleasure or business. Request info about our "Dayroom" for meetings and social activities. We offer minister and missionary discounts.

---

6 Pets welcome; 7 Children welcome; 8 Tennis nearby; 9 Swimming nearby; 10 Golf nearby; 11 Skiing nearby; 12 May be booked through travel agent

Hosts: Mike and Ann Driver
Rooms: 5 (PB) $80-150
Full Breakfast
Credit Cards: A, B, C, D
Notes: 2, 5, 6, 7, 8, 9, 10, 12

ROCKPORT

Trail's End
Bed & Breakfast

2032 South County Road 200 West, 47635
(270) 771-5590; fax: (270) 771-4723
E-mail: jramey@mindspring.com
www.mindspring.com/~jramey/bedandbreak.html

Trail's End can truly be just that! Located adjacent to our riding stables, you can pet the horses across the fence after your arrival, go for a trail ride or lesson, or enjoy the "condo cottage." You enjoy complete privacy in the two-bedroom cottage beautifully appointed with antiques, full bath, laundry and kitchen, which offers you a choice of breakfast fixin's in the fridge to enjoy at your convenience. There is also a bunkroom for extras. Seven miles north of Owensboro, Kentucky.

Host: Joan G. Ramey
Rooms: 2 (PB) $75-85
Full Breakfast
Credit Cards: A, B, D
Notes: 2, 5, 6, 7, 8, 9, 10

Louisiana

METAIRIE

New Orleans Bed & Breakfast & Accommodations

671 Rosa Avenue Ste 208, 70005
(504) 838-0071; (888) 240-0070
fax: (504) 838-0140
E-mail: nobba@bellsouth.net
www.neworleansbandb.com

If you appreciate the beauty of crystal chandeliers, hardwood floors, antiques, oriental rugs, interesting architecture, or simple, traditional elegance, call us. Whatever your choice, you will find gracious hospitality and knowledgeable hosts who are concerned about your safety, comfort, and pleasure. We are also familiar with B&B plantations, homes, and cottages throughout Louisiana. Call us, too, for referrals to other states or England.

Host: Sara-Margaret Brown
Rooms: 200
Continental Breakfast
Credit Cards: A, B, C, D
Notes: 5

NATCHITOCHES

Levy-East House Bed & Breakfast

358 Jefferson Street, 71457
(318) 352-0662; (800) 840-0662
fax: (318) 352-9685
E-mail: judy@levyeasthouse.com
www.levyeasthouse.com

A most luxurious B&B located in the heart of the historic district. Listed on the National Register of Historic Places, the Greek Revival house (circa 1838) has been recently restored and tastefully renovated to capture the spirit of an earlier time and features fine antiques, queen beds, private whirlpool baths, a full gour-

Levy-East House

met breakfast, and romantic music piped into each guest room. Enjoy elegant rooms and luxurious leisure.

Hosts: Judy and Avery East
Rooms: 4 (PB) $105-200
Full Breakfast
Credit Cards: A, B, C
Notes: 2, 5, 8, 10, 12

---

6 Pets welcome; 7 Children welcome; 8 Tennis nearby; 9 Swimming nearby; 10 Golf nearby; 11 Skiing nearby; 12 May be booked through travel agent

LOUISIANA

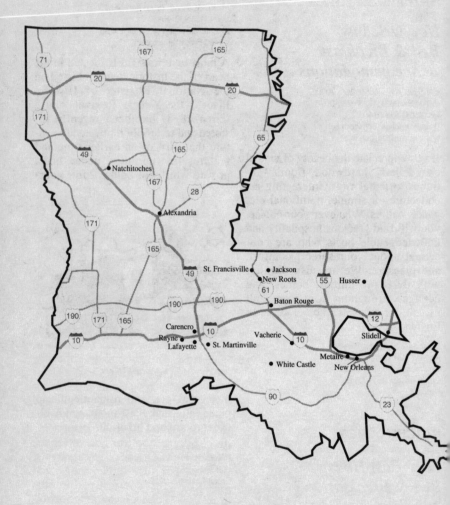

NOTES: Credit cards accepted: A Master Card; B Visa; C American Express; D Discover; E Diners Club; F Other; 2 Personal checks accepted; 3 Lunch available; 4 Dinner available; 5 Open all year;

NEW ORLEANS

Depot House at Mm. Julia's

748 Okeefe Avenue, 70113-1907
(504) 529-2952; fax: (504) 529-1908
E-mail: dhiltonlll@aol.com
mmejuliadepothouse.com

Unlike all the regular hotels around us, we have the most unique accommodations downtown. Located in an old railroad boardinghouse, which began operation around 1900, our rooms have queen-size beds, air-conditioning, carpet, antiques, and more. Conveniently located near the streetcar line and close to the convention center, aquarium, museums, art galleries, French Quarter, Superdome, Linerwalk, and some of the oldest churches in New Orleans! We also have free, gated parking.

Hosts: Joanne, Dennis, and Layne Hilton
Rooms: 15 (PB) $65-125
Continental Breakfast
Credit Cards: None
Note: 2

Essem's House of New Orleans

3660 Gentilly Boulevard, 70122
(504) 947-3401; (888) 240-0070
fax: (504) 838-0140
E-mail: nobba@bellsouth.net
www.neworleansbandb.com

Tree-shaded boulevards; direct transport to the French Quarter (15-20 minutes); safe, convenient area of stable family homes. This ten-room brick home, "New Orleans' First Bed and Breakfast," has three bedrooms—one king with private bath, and two doubles with a shared bath. Separate cottage efficiency (one king or two singles with private bath). Enjoy the solarium, living room, and back garden!

Host: Sarah Margaret Brown
Rooms: 3 (1 PB; 2 SB) $69-125
Continental Breakfast
Credit Cards: A, B, C, D
Notes: 5, 6, 8, 9, 10

St. Charles Guest House

1748 Prytania Street, 70130
(504) 523-6556
E-mail: dhiltonlll@aol.com
www.stcharlesguesthouse.com

St. Charles Guest House

Located in the historic Garden District, just minutes from the French Quarter, Superdome, Convention Center, Business District, museums, galleries, and shopping, either by trolly or on foot, the St. Charles Guest House has been welcoming guests for over 50 years. Rooms are simple and antique-cozy. Continental breakfast is served poolside. Hosts are helpful and full of suggestions for how to see the "Real New Orleans." Restaurants, from Emeril's to Burger Kings, and much in between, are steps from the front door. Perfect location for travelers with no need for a car. Best value downtown.

---

6 Pets welcome; 7 Children welcome; 8 Tennis nearby; 9 Swimming nearby; 10 Golf nearby; 11 Skiing nearby; 12 May be booked through travel agent

Hosts: Joanne and Dennis Hilton
Rooms: 38 (28 PB; 10 SB)
Continental Breakfast
Credit Cards: A, B, C
Notes: 2, 5, 9

ST. FRANCISVILLE

Lake Rosemound Inn

10473 Lindsey Lane, 70775
(225) 635-3176; fax: (225) 635-2224
www.lakerosemoundinn.com

Lake Rosemound is one of the most picturesque areas in the heart of plantation country, just minutes from historic St. Francisville. All four guest rooms have a view of the lake and king or queen beds, TV, air-conditioning, and paddle fans. The Rosemound and Feliciana suites have Jacuzzis-for-two. Start your day with a great country breakfast, then enjoy the hammocks, porch swings, canoe, paddleboat, and famous "help yourself" ice cream bar. The inn is handicapped-accessible. Hiking and horseback riding are nearby.

Hosts: Jon and Jeane Peters
Rooms: 4 (PB) $75-125
Full Breakfast
Credit Cards: A, B, C, D
Notes: 2, 5, 6, 7, 9, 10

WHITE CASTLE

Nottoway Plantation Restaurant & Inn

30970 Highway 405, P.O. Box 160, 70788
(225) 545-2730; fax: (225) 545-8632
E-mail: nottoway@att.net
www.nottoway.com

Named one of the "top 25 bed and banquets" by *Conde Nast Traveler*, Nottoway proves that excellence withstands the test of time. Experience 19th-century Southern living in the largest plantation home in the South, circa 1859. Accommodations are available in the mansion and overseer's cottage, all with private baths. Rates include a guided tour, wake-up breakfast, and full plantation breakfast. Daily guided tours from 9:00 A.M.-5:00 P.M. Restaurant serves Louisiana cuisine for both lunch and dinner. Gift shop. Pool.

Nottoway Plantation

Host: Cindy Hidalgo
Rooms: 13 (PB) $135-250
Full Breakfast
Credit Cards: A, B, C, D
Notes: 2, 3, 4, 5, 7, 8, 9, 10, 12

NOTES: Credit cards accepted: A Master Card; B Visa; C American Express; D Discover; E Diners Club; F Other; 2 Personal checks accepted; 3 Lunch available; 4 Dinner available; 5 Open all year;

Maine

BAILEY ISLAND

Captain York House Bed & Breakfast

P.O. Box 298, 04003
(207) 833-6224
E-mail: athorn7286@aol.com
www.iwws.com/captainyork

Stay at a restored sea captain's house on Bailey Island affording a spectacular view of the ocean and beautiful sunsets. Relax in a peaceful environment, yet close to Portland, Freeport, Brunswick, Bath, and Boothbay Harbor. Quiet island living in midcoast Maine. Quaint fishing villages nearby.

Hosts: Alan and Jean Thornton
Rooms: 5 (PB) $80-125
Full Breakfast
Credit Cards: A, B
Notes: 2, 5, 9, 10

BAR HARBOR

Black Friar Inn

10 Summer Street, 04609
(207) 288-5091; fax: (207) 288-4197
E-mail: blackfriar@blackfriar.com
www.blackfriar.com

Black Friar Inn is a completely rebuilt and restored inn incorporating beautiful woodwork, mantels, windows, and bookcases from old mansions and churches on Mount Desert Island. Gourmet breakfast may include

Black Friar

homemade breads, pastry, and muffins; fresh fruit; eggs du jour; and more. Afternoon refreshments are provided. All rooms have queen beds; the suite has a king bed. Within walking distance of the waterfront, restaurants, and shops, with ample parking available. A short drive to Acadia National Park.

Hosts: Perry and Sharon Risley, and Falke
Rooms: 7 (PB) $95-150
Full Breakfast
Credit Cards: A, B, D
Notes: 2, 7, 8, 9, 10, 11

Stratford House Inn

45 Mount Desert Street, 04609
(207) 288-5189; fax: (207) 288-4184
E-mail: info@stratfordinn.com
www.stratfordinn.com

Built in 1900 by the noted Boston publisher Lewis A. Roberts, the Stratford House Inn is styled with the romantic charm of an English Tudor manor. The Inn boasts ten beautifully

---

6 Pets welcome; 7 Children welcome; 8 Tennis nearby; 9 Swimming nearby; 10 Golf nearby; 11 Skiing nearby; 12 May be booked through travel agent

MAINE

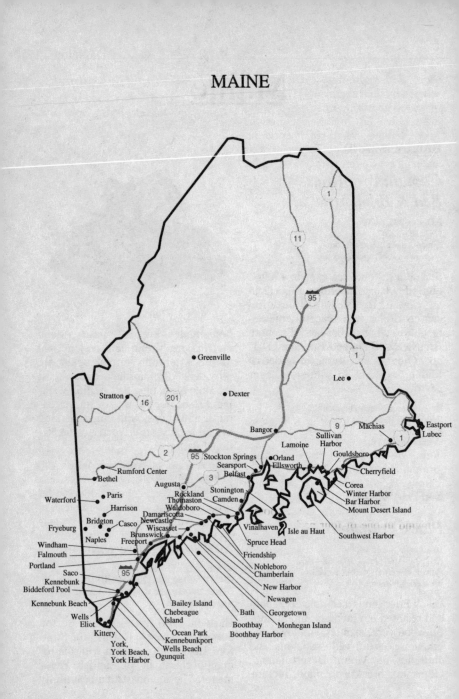

NOTES: Credit cards accepted: A Master Card; B Visa; C American Express; D Discover; E Diners Club; F Other; 2 Personal checks accepted; 3 Lunch available; 4 Dinner available; 5 Open all year;

decorated bedrooms, each with its own individual charm and style. In the morning guests are treated to a Continental breakfast in the elegant dining room, replete with original period furnishings. After the day's events, find evening relaxation with a book in the library, interesting conversation on our large veranda, or try your hand at the grand piano in the music room.

Hosts: Norman and Barbara Moulton
Rooms: 10 (8 PB; 2 SB) $75-150
Continental Breakfast
Credit Cards: A, B, D
Notes: 2, 7, 8, 9, 10

BELFAST

Belhaven Inn
Bed & Breakfast

14 John Street, 04915
(207) 338-5435
E-mail: stay@belhaveninn.com
www.belhaveninn.com

Stay with us in our circa 1851 Victorian home, a comfortable, family-oriented inn. A full, three-course country breakfast is served. A circular staircase leads up to four bright and charmingly decorated guest rooms. Unwind in one of four parlors or the veranda. A fully equipped efficiency guest suite with private entrance and sundeck is available for longer stays. Harbor shops and restaurants are just a short walk away.

Hosts: Paul and Anne Bartels
Rooms: 5 (3 PB; 2 SB) $65-105
Full Breakfast
Credit Cards: A, B
Notes: 2, 5, 6, 7, 8, 9, 10, 11

The Jeweled Turret Inn

40 Pearl Street, 04915
(207) 338-2304; (800) 696-2304
E-mail: jturret@gwi.net
www.jeweledturret.com

The Jeweled Turret Inn

This grand representative of the Victorian era, constructed circa 1898, offers unique architectural features, and is listed on the National Register of Historic Places. The inn is named for the grand staircase that winds up the turret which is lighted by both stained- and leaded-glass panels with jewel-like embellishments. Luxurious guest chambers: antiques, four-poster, iron and brass beds, fine linens, and rooms with turrets, fireplace, or marble bathroom with whirlpool tub await you. . .very romantic! A gourmet breakfast is served each morning. Shops, restaurants, and the waterfront are just a pleasant stroll away.

Hosts: Carl and Cathy Heffentrager
Rooms: 7 (PB) $90-145
Full Breakfast
Credit Cards: A, B
Notes: 2, 5, 8, 9, 10, 11, 12

---

6 Pets welcome; 7 Children welcome; 8 Tennis nearby; 9 Swimming nearby; 10 Golf nearby; 11 Skiing nearby; 12 May be booked through travel agent

BOOTHBAY HARBOR

Admiral's Quarters Inn

71 Commercial Street, 04538
(207) 633-2474; fax: (207) 633-5904
E-mail: loon@admiralsquartersinn.com
www.admiralsquartersinn.com

Admiral's Quarter's Inn

Private baths, decks/patios, entrances, color cable TV, phones, and central air-conditioning complete the ammenties offered at this inn. Linger over your full homemade breakfast on the wraparound porch or by the wood stove in the glass solarium gathering room. The inn overlooks the harbor and meticulously manicured gardens. Afternoon refreshments greet you upon arrival. "We don't claim to have the best views. . .our guests make that claim!"

Hosts: Les and Deb Hallstrom
Rooms: 6 (PB) $85-165
Full Breakfast
Credit Cards: A, B, D
Notes: 2, 5, 7, 8, 9, 10, 11, 12

Anchor Watch Bed & Breakfast

9 Eames Road, 04538
(207) 633-7565
E-mail: diane@lincoln.midcoast.com
www.anchorwatch.com

On the beautiful shores of the Anchor Watch, guests may watch boating activities from our pier, or lounge on the shorefront patio. Walk to the village for dining and shopping, or stay comfy under down comforters for an afternoon nap. Our five charmingly decorated rooms are light and airy; most have windows facing the lovely water views; all have private baths. Guests rave about the delicious breakfast served in the sunny seaside room where local lobsterman can often be seen hauling trips right near our dock. Your welcome begins on our front porch with the cool, sea breeze fresh from the shore. Inside, a warm ambience is created in the seaside room with its gas-fired fireplace, pine floor, and windows on the water.

Full Breakfast
Credit Cards: A, B, D
Notes: 2

Harbour Towne Inn on the Waterfront

71 Townsend Avenue, 04538-1843
(207) 633-4300; E-mail: gtme@gwi.net

"The finest B&B on the waterfront." Our refurbished Victorian inn retains turn-of-the-century ambience while providing all modern amenities. The colorful gardens and quiet, tree-shaded location slopes right to the edge of the beautiful New England

---

NOTES: Credit cards accepted: A Master Card; B Visa; C American Express; D Discover; E Diners Club; F Other; 2 Personal checks accepted; 3 Lunch available; 4 Dinner available; 5 Open all year;

harbor. Choose a room with outside deck for waterfront views. Two- to five-minute scenic walk to harbor. Our luxurious penthouse is a modern, spacious home that sleeps up to six in luxury and privacy. Stay just once and you will know why our guests return year after year. No smoking or pets.

Hosts: The Thomas Family
Rooms: 12 (PB) $69-299
Continental Breakfast
Credit Cards: A, B, C, D
Notes: 2, 8, 9, 10, 11, 12

BRIDGTON

Greenwood Manor Inn

52 Tolman Road; P.O. Box 551, Harrison, 04040
(207) 583-4445; (866) 583-4445
fax: (207) 583-2480
E-mail: info@greenwoodmanorinn.com
www.greenwoodmanorinn.com

Greenwood Manor Inn is located at the tip of Long Lake on 108 secluded acres of lawns, gardens, and woodlands. Nine uniquely decorate guest rooms, all with private baths, are yours to choose from. A full country breakfast is served on the covered deck overlooking the formal gardens. Canoes are available for use on nearby lakes. Greenwood Manor has facilities available for weddings and special occasions. Meeting room available for small (10-12 people) conferences.

Hosts: Patty Douthett and Mike Rosenbauer
Rooms: 9 (PB) $90-140
Full Breakfast
Credit Cards: A, B
Notes: 2, 5, 7, 8, 9, 10, 11, 12

DAMARISCOTTA

Brannon-Bunker Inn

349 State Route 129, Walpole, 04573
phone/fax: (207) 563-5941; (800) 563-5941
E-mail: brbnkinn@lincoln.midcoast.com

Brannon-Bunker Inn is an intimate and relaxed country B&B situated only minutes from a sandy beach, lighthouse, and historic fort in Maine's mid-coastal region. Located in a 1920s cape, converted barn, and carriage house, the guest rooms are furnished in themes that combine the charm of yesterday with the comforts of today. You'll find antique shops nearby.

Hosts: Joe and Jeanne Hovance
Rooms: 7 (5 PB; 2 SB) $70-80
Continental Breakfast
Credit Cards: A, B, C, D, E
Notes: 2, 7, 8, 9, 10

ELIOT

Farmstead Bed & Breakfast

379 Goodwin Road, 03903
(207) 748-3145; (888) 829-0332
fax: (207) 748-3659
E-mail: farmsteadb@aol.com
www.farmstead.qpg.com

This lovely country inn is situated on three acres. Its warm, friendly atmosphere exemplifies farm life of the late 1800s. Each Victorian-style guest room has a mini-refrigerator and microwave for snacks or special diets. Breakfast may include blueberry pancakes or French toast, homemade syrup, fruit, and juice. Limited

---

6 Pets welcome; 7 Children welcome; 8 Tennis nearby; 9 Swimming nearby; 10 Golf nearby; 11 Skiing nearby; 12 May be booked through travel agent

handicapped-accessibility. Minutes from Kittery Factory Outlets, York beaches, Portsmouth, and historic sites. One hour from Boston.

Hosts: Meb and John Lippincott
Rooms: 6 (PB) $62-72
Full Breakfast
Credit Cards: A, B, D
Notes: 2, 5, 6, 7, 10, 12

FREEPORT

Captain Josiah Mitchell House Bed & Breakfast

188 Main Street, 04032
(207) 865-3289
E-mail: bluesuf2@aol.com
www.captainjosiahhamitchellhouse.com

Captain Josiah Mitchell House

Two blocks from L.L. Bean, this house is a few minutes' walk past centuries-old sea captains' homes and shady trees to more than 120 factory discount shops. After exploring, relax on our beautiful, peaceful veranda with antique wicker furniture and swing. State-approved. Family-owned and -operated. AAA three-diamond.

Hosts: Alan and Loretta Bradley
Rooms: 7 (PB) $87-97
Full Breakfast
Credit Cards: A, B
Notes: 2, 5, 8, 9, 10, 11, 12

White Cedar Inn

178 Main Street, 04032
(207) 865-9099; (800) 853-1269
fax: (207) 865-6636
E-mail: capandphil@aol.com
www.whitecedarinn.com

The White Cedar Inn is a historic inn just two blocks north of L.L. Bean and most of Freeport's luxury outlets. Our seven air-conditioned bedrooms are spacious and furnished with antiques. We serve a full country breakfast each morning overlooking our beautifully landscaped grounds. A common room with a television and library is available to our guests. This is a nonsmoking inn. The White Cedar Inn has a AAA three-diamond rating.

Hosts: Gwen and Jim Sartoris
Rooms: 7 (PB) $80-145
Full Breakfast
Credit Cards: A, B, C, D
Notes: 2, 5, 7, 9, 10, 11

HARRISON

Harrison House Bed & Breakfast

R.R. 2, Box 2035, 04040-9529
(207) 583-6564
E-mail: hrsnbnb@megalink.net
megalink.net/~hrsnbnb

The Harrison House was built at the head of Long Lake in 1876 by John Woodsum Casewell; it is one of the most costly and elegant residences in the village. It has been restored to reflect the warmth and charm enjoyed by the first residents. After a restful night on your featherbed, come to the breakfast room and partake of the homemade muffins, breads, jams, jellies, fresh fruits, and one of our many specialties, such as Double Cinnamon French Toast, while watching the activities on the lake.

Hosts: Shelia Baxter and Catherine McMahon
Rooms: 5 (4 PB; 1 SB) $85-95
Full Breakfast
Credit Cards: A, B, C
Notes: 2, 5, 7, 9, 10, 11, 12

KENNEBUNKPORT

Captain Fairfield Inn

P.O. Box 2690, 8 Pleasant Street, 04046
(207) 967-4454; (800) 322-1928
fax: (207) 967-8537
E-mail: jrw@captainfairfield.com
www.captainfairfield.com

This gracious Federal mansion in the heart of Kennebunkport's picturesque historic district is surrounded by towering trees and beautiful gardens. The Inn offers antiques and period furnishings, fireplaces, four-poster and canopied beds, all with private bath and air-conditioning. Four-course gourmet breakfasts, with a choice of entrees all prepared to your order. The Inn is ideal for those who enjoy a location within walking distance to the ocean, restaurants, shops, and gal-

leries; yet seek a peaceful, quiet, and romantic retreat.

Hosts: Janet and Rick Wolf
Rooms: 9 (PB) $110-275
Full Breakfast
Credit Cards: A, B, C, D, E
Notes: 2, 5, 7, 8, 9, 10

The Captain Lord Mansion

P.O. Box 800, 04046
(207) 967-3141; fax: (207) 967-3172
E-mail: innkeeper@captainlord.com
www.captainlord.com

Enjoy an unforgettable romantic experience at the Captain Lord Mansion, where both your personal comfort and intimacy are assured by large, beautifully appointed guest rooms, luxurious amenities such as oversized four-poster beds, cozy gas fireplaces, heated marble/tile bathroom floors, several double Jacuzzis, as well as fresh flowers, full breakfasts, afternoon sweets, and personal attention. At the head of a sloping village green overlooking the Kennebunk River, the inn affords a picturesque, quiet, convenient location from which to explore historic Kennebunkport.

Hosts: Bev Davis and Rick Litchfield
Rooms: 16 (PB) $99-399
Full Breakfast
Credit Cards: A, B, D, E
Notes: 2, 5, 8, 9, 10, 12

King's Port Inn

Junction of Routes 9 & 35, P.O. Box 1070, 04046
(207) 967-4340; (800) 286-5767
fax: (207) 967-4810
E-mail: info@kingsportinn.com
www.kingsportinn.com

---

6 Pets welcome; 7 Children welcome; 8 Tennis nearby; 9 Swimming nearby; 10 Golf nearby; 11 Skiing nearby; 12 May be booked through travel agent

King's Port Inn offers affordable lodging, unique amenities, and convenience to Kennebunkport's Dock Square shopping, restaurants, beaches, and historical attractions. Tastefully decorated rooms offer two double beds or a single king bed, while more luxurious rooms offer king or queen beds, private Jacuzzis, and gas fireplaces. Additional amenities include a complimentary pantry sideboard breakfast buffet, a cozy fireside parlor, and a conference room that doubles as a surround-sound theater. Several off-season packages are available.

Maine Stay Inn

its perennial flower garden and spacious lawn. The white clapboard house, built in 1860 and listed on the National Historic Register, and the adjoining cottages sit grandly in Kennebunkport's historic district. The Maine Stay features a variety of delightful accommodations, all with private baths, color cable TV, and air-conditioning. Many of the rooms have fireplaces. A sumptuous full breakfast and afternoon tea are included. The inn is an easy walk from the harbor, shops, galleries, and restaurants. AAA three-diamond and Mobil three-star rated.

King's Port Inn

Hosts: Bill and Rosita Greer
Rooms: 32 (PB) $65-185
Continental Breakfast
Credit Cards: A, B, C, D
Notes: 2, 5, 7, 8, 9, 10, 12

Maine Stay Inn & Cottages

P.O. Box 500A, 04046
(207) 967-2117; (800) 950-2117
fax: (207) 967-8757
E-mail: innkeeper@mainestayinn.com
www.mainestayinn.com

A grand Victorian inn that exudes charm, from its wraparound porch to

Hosts: Lindsay and Carol Copeland
Rooms: 17 (PB) $95-250
Full Breakfast
Credit Cards: A, B, C
Notes: 2, 5, 7, 8, 9, 10

KITTERY

Enchanted Night Bed & Breakfast

Scenic Coastal Route 103, 29 Wentworth Street, 03904
(207) 439-1489
www.enchanted-nights-bandb.com

NOTES: Credit cards accepted: A Master Card; B Visa; C American Express; D Discover; E Diners Club; F Other; 2 Personal checks accepted; 3 Lunch available; 4 Dinner available; 5 Open all year;

The Enchanted Night B&B is a Victorian fantasy for the romantic at heart. Step back in time to experience romance and splendor in our 1890 Princess Anne Victorian with its French-country flare: whimsical and colorful, yet elegant French and Victorian décor, from sweetly tattered iron beds and hand-painted floral furnishings, to elegant hand-carved oak bed chamber sets. Indulge in a whirlpool tub-for-two room with fireplace, or a tiny but enchanting turret room, all with fanciful bedding. CATV and VCR.

Hosts: Nancy Bogerberger and Peter Lamandia
Rooms: 8 (6 PB; 2 SB) $40-250
Full Breakfast
Credit Cards: A, B, C, D, E
Notes: 2, 5, 6, 7, 8, 9, 10, 12

NAPLES

The Augustus Bove House

R.R. 1, Box 501, 04055-9801
(207) 693-6365; (888) 806-6249
E-mail: augbovehouse@pivot.net
www.naplesmaine.com

Guests are always welcome at the historic 1850 hotel. Originally known as Hotel Naples, it is restored for comfort and a relaxed atmosphere at affordable prices. Guest rooms have elegant yet homey furnishings, some with views of Long Lake. An easy walk to the water, shops, and recreation in a four-season area. Open all year, with off-season and midweek discounts. Telephones in each room. Air-conditioning, TVs, VCRs, and hot tubs. Coffee or tea anytime.

Hosts: Dave and Arlene Stetson
Rooms: 11 (7 PB; 4 SB) $69-175
Full Breakfast
Credit Cards: A, B, C, D, E
Notes: 2, 5, 9, 10, 11, 12

OGUNQUIT

The Terrace by the Sea

P.O. Box 831, 03907
(207) 646-3232
E-mail: innkeeper@terracebythesea.com
www.terracebythesea.com

The Terrace by the Sea blends the elegance of our colonial inn and our deluxe motel accommodations. Both offer spectacular ocean views in a peaceful, secluded setting across from the beach. All rooms have private baths, air-conditioning, telephones, color cable televisions, heat, refrigerators; some offer efficiency kitchens. There is a heated outdoor pool. The Terrace by the Sea is within easy walking distance of the beautiful sandy beach, Marginal Way, shops, restaurants, and a link to the trolleys. Come share the charm and hospitality of New England!

Hosts: John and Daryl Bullard
Rooms: 36 (PB) $59-215
Continental Breakfast
Credit Cards: None
Notes: 2, 8, 9, 10

PARIS

King's Hill Inn

56 King Hill Road, South Paris, 04281
(207) 744-0204; (877) 391-KING
fax: (207) 744-0204

6 Pets welcome; 7 Children welcome; 8 Tennis nearby; 9 Swimming nearby; 10 Golf nearby; 11 Skiing nearby; 12 May be booked through travel agent

E-mail: kingsinn@megalink.net
members.aol.com/kingsinn561/inn.htm

This Victorian inn is the birthplace of Horatio King, native son of Paris, Maine, who became postmaster general in 1861. The 25 acres of mountain views, gardens, trails, and sheer luxury offer any visitor a tranquil retreat. Open year round, serving a delicious breakfast of local blueberries and maple syrup. You'll be treated like a king and queen while visiting. The inn and the post-and-beam barn are filled with antiques, and all rooms offer queen or king beds and private baths.

Hosts: Janice and Glenn Davis
Rooms: 6 (5 PB; 1 SB) $75-135
Full Breakfast
Credit Cards: A, B, C, D
Notes: 2, 5, 7, 8, 9, 10, 11, 12

PORTLAND

Inn at St. John

939 Congress Street, 04102
(207) 773-6481; (800) 636-9127
fax: (207) 756-7629
E-mail: theinn@maine.rr.com
www.innatstjohn.com

The Inn at St. John is a most unique, 100-year-old inn noted for its European charm and quiet gentility. Centrally located in Portland, Maine, it's just a short walk to the Old Port, Waterfront, and arts district. Take pleasure in tastefully decorated rooms with traditional and antique furnishings. Enjoy complimentary Continental breakfast, free parking, and value rates. All rooms offer free local calls, cable, and HBO. Stay with us and learn why our guests return year after

year. An ideal inn for that off-season getaway! Children and pets welcome! Air-conditioned and nonsmoking rooms. All major credit cards accepted.

Rooms: 37 (22 PB; 15 SB) $38-190
Continental Breakfast
Credit Cards: A, B, D, E
Notes: 2, 5, 6, 7, 8, 9, 10, 12

SEARSPORT

Brass Lantern Inn

81 West Main Street, 04974
(207) 548-0150
E-mail: stay@brassblanternmaine.com
www.brasslanternmaine.com

Step back in time when you enter this beautiful circa 1850 sea captain's home. You will be treated to warm and casual hospitality in gracious surroundings. Ornate tin ceilings grace the dining room and one of the par-

Brass Lantern Inn

lors. Glorious sunrises, and glimpses of the bay can be seen from the windows, while the harbor, museum, shops, and restaurants are just a short walk away. Acadia National Park, Camden, Castine, and Stonington are all an easy drive away.

Hosts: Dick and Maggie Zieg
Rooms: 5 (PB) $85-105
Full Breakfast
Credit Cards: A, B, D
Notes: 2, 5, 7, 8, 9, 10, 11, 12

Old Glory Inn

89 West Main Street, P.O. Box 461, 04974-0461
(207) 548-6232

OLD GLORY INN - Route 1, Searsport, Maine

Colonial brick sea captain's home, circa 1830, offers your choice of the captains's suite with full sitting room, or either of two additional guest rooms, all with private baths. The Old Glory Inn allows you the peace, quiet, and hospitality only a small inn can provide. Antique shop on premises. Open May to December.

Hosts: Bruce and Rita Haddleston
Rooms: 3 (PB) $60-70
Continental Breakfast
Credit Cards: None
Notes: 2, 8, 9, 10

1794 Watchtide by the Sea!

1794 Watchtide by the Sea!

190 West Main Street, 04974
(207) 548-6575; (800) 698-6575
fax: (207) 548-0938
E-mail: stay@watchtide.com
www.watchtide.com

This 18th-century National Register of Historic Places seaside inn has served up scrumptuous breakfasts for over 80 years on the 60-foot sunporch overlooking the Penobscot Bay and our bird and wildlife sanctuary. Totally updated to include all en suite private baths and a special suite complete with double Jacuzzi and skylight. Walk to Moosepoint State Park beach. The perfect stay between Rockland and Acadia National Park. Angels to Antiques gift shop on premises affords guest discount. Come watch the tides; let us indulge you in life's little luxuries. We love to spoil our guests! Maine's abundance of wild lilacs makes our world beautiful and aromatic between May 15 and June 15. We offer a special 10 percent discount if you stay with us during Lilac Time in Maine (two-night minimum). Check our reservations and availability now.

Rooms: 4 (PB) $95-175
Full Breakfast
Credit Cards: A, B, D
Notes: 2, 5, 7, 8, 9, 10, 11, 12

6 Pets welcome; 7 Children welcome; 8 Tennis nearby; 9 Swimming nearby; 10 Golf nearby; 11 Skiing nearby; 12 May be booked through travel agent

SOUTHWEST HARBOR

The Island House

P.O. Box 1006, 04679-1006
(207) 244-5180
E-mail: islandab@acadia.net
www.acadia.net/island_house/

The Island House

The Island House was the first summer hotel on Mount Desert Island. It still retains the old-fashioned charm of that period. Furnishings from Ann's childhood years in Southeast Asia blend comfortably with this Maine seacoast home. A veranda and large garden and tasty, ample breakfasts all add to a homey and relaxed atomsphere. Ann and Charlie know the island well and take pleasure in helping their guests plan outings to nearby Acadia National Park.

Hosts: Ann and Charles Bradford
Rooms: 4 (PB) $75-120
Full Breakfast
Credit Cards: A, B
Notes: 2, 5, 7, 8, 9, 10, 11, 12

VARIOUS CITIES

Elaine's Bed & Breakfast Selections

4987 Kingston Road, Elbridge, NY 13060
(315) 689-2082

A reservation service that lists B&Bs in the following towns: Kennebunkport, Ocean Park, Tenants Harbor, and Waldoboro. Elaine Samuels, director.

WATERFORD

Kedarburn Inn

Route 35, Box 61, 04088
(207) 583-6182; fax: (207) 583-6424
E-mail: kedarburn@cybertours.com
members.aol.com/kedarol

Located in historic Waterford Village, the Kedarburn Inn is a place to step back in time while you enjoy the comforts of today. The charming bedrooms are decorated with warm country touches such as quilts, handmade by Margaret, adding pleasure to

Kedarburn Inn

NOTES: Credit cards accepted: A Master Card; B Visa; C American Express; D Discover; E Diners Club; F Other; 2 Personal checks accepted; 3 Lunch available; 4 Dinner available; 5 Open all year;

your visit. Each day will start with a hearty breakfast. In the evening, relax and enjoy the elegant dinner (served daily). Whether you come for outdoor activities or simply to enjoy the countryside, let us pamper you in our relaxed and friendly atmosphere.

Hosts: Margaret and Derek Gibson
Rooms: 7 (5 PB; 2 SB) $75-125
Full Breakfast
Credit Cards: A, B, C, D
Notes: 7, 9, 10, 11, 12

YORK BEACH

Homestead Inn Bed & Breakfast

Homestead Inn

P.O. Box 15, 8 South Main Street, Route 1A,
   03910-0015
(207) 363-8952; fax: (207) 363-8952
E-mail: homstedbb@aol.com
members.aol.com/homstedbb

This clean, quiet, adult bed & breakfast on Maine's southern coast is an easy walk to beaches, shops, restaurants, and Nubble Lighthouse. Visit historic York Village; 60 miles north of Boston, Massachusetts; 35 miles south of Portland, Maine. Experience sunsets, seafood, shorelines, serenity!

Hosts: Dan and Danielle Duffy
Rooms: 4 (SB) $69
Continental Breakfast
Credit Cards: None
Notes: 2, 8, 9, 10

YORK HARBOR

York Harbor Inn

Coastal Route 1A, P.O. Box 573, 03911
(207) 363-5119; (800) 343-3869
fax: (207) 363-7151
E-mail: info@yorkharborinn.com
www.yorkharborinn.com

York Harbor is a historic inn, nestled amid classic, oceanfront estates. Walk to a peaceful, protected swimming beach. Activities include a scenic cliff walk, golf, swimming, boating, fishing, and outlet shopping. Antiques, poster beds, private baths, fireplaces, ocean view decks, and Jacuzzi spas enhance your stay. An ocean-view dining room offers top-rated cuisine and fine wines. The Wine Cellar Pub features fireplaces and entertainment. Banquet and meeting facilities are available. AAA 3-diamond-rated. Reach Boston in an hour. As seen on "Great Country Inns of America."

Hosts: Garry and Nancy Dominguez
Rooms: 40 (PB) $89-269
Continental Breakfast
Credit Cards: A, B, C, E
Notes: 2, 3, 4, 5, 7, 8, 9, 10, 11, 12

---

6 Pets welcome; 7 Children welcome; 8 Tennis nearby; 9 Swimming nearby; 10 Golf nearby; 11 Skiing nearby; 12 May be booked through travel agent

MARYLAND

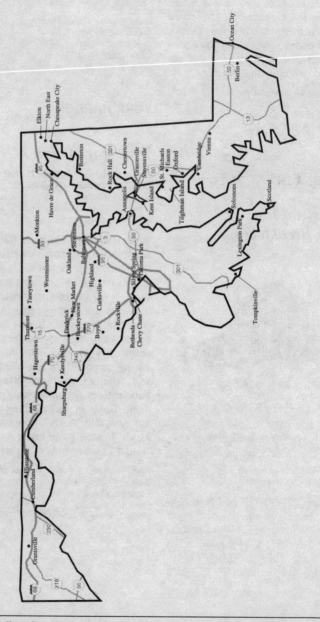

NOTES: Credit cards accepted: A Master Card; B Visa; C American Express; D Discover; E Diners Club; F Other; 2 Personal checks accepted; 3 Lunch available; 4 Dinner available; 5 Open all year;

Maryland

ANNAPOLIS

The Barn on Howard's Cove

The Barn on Howard's Cove

500 Wilson Road, 21401
(410) 266-6840; fax: (410) 266-7293
E-mail: mlgutsche5@aol.com
bnbweb.com/howards-cove.html

The Barn on Howard's Cove welcomes you with warm hospitality to a converted, 1850s horse barn overlooking a beautiful cove of the Severn River. You will be located just outside the hubbub of Annapolis, and convenient to both Baltimore and Washington, D.C. Begin the day with a choice of full breakfast served in the dining area, on a sunny deck, or in a solarium—all overlooking the river. Our guests enjoy the beautiful gardens, rural setting, antiques, quilts, oriental rugs, and the charming Noah's ark collection. Two guest bedrooms, each with a private bathroom, await you. One room has a sleeping loft and private deck on the river. Both guest rooms overlook the river. Docking in deep water is provided. Canoes and a kayak are available for guests to use.

Hosts: Graham and Libbie Gutsche
Rooms: 2 (PB) $100
Full Breakfast
Credit Cards: None
Notes: 2, 5, 7, 8, 9, 10, 12

Chez Amis Bed & Breakfast

85 East Street, 21401
(410) 263-6631; (888) 224-6455
fax: (410) 295-7889

Around 1900, Chez Amis "House of Friends" was a grocery store. Still evident are the original oak display cabinet, tin ceiling, and pine floors. One-half block from the capital, 1 block from the harbor, and minutes by foot from the Naval Academy. "European country" décor with antiques and quilts. Four guest rooms with private baths. King and queen brass beds, TVs, central air-conditioning, robes, coffee service, and down comforters in every room. Don is a retired army lawyer, Mickie a former tour guide. They welcome you with true "Southern" Christian hospitality!

Hosts: Don and Mickie Deline
Rooms: 4 (PB) $115-140
Full Breakfast
Credit Cards: A, B
Notes: 2, 5

---

6 Pets welcome; 7 Children welcome; 8 Tennis nearby; 9 Swimming nearby; 10 Golf nearby; 11 Skiing nearby; 12 May be booked through travel agent

Meadow Gardens
Bed & Breakfast

504 Wilson Road, 21401
(410) 224-2729; (410) 266-6840
fax: (410) 266-7293
E-mail: wendymays@aol.com
www.bnbweb.com/meadowgardens

Surrounded by six and a half acres of rolling meadow and woods, Meadow Gardens is a sanctuary of peacefulness. Flower and fruit gardens complete the scenery. Direct access to a private dock (11 feet deep at the end) allows boaters to moor for the night, or enjoy a canoe or kayak. The spacious interior allows for a large common room and charming bedrooms. Breakfast is served on a glassed-in porch with lovely view of the meadow, gardens, and woods. Guests have a choice of eight specialties of the hostess including eggs Benedict, French toast a l'orange, and Hungry Man's Western omelet. Wendy Mays is an artist and illustrator, as well as a professional cateress. She works out of her studio which is part of her house, and displays her works of art throughout the home.

Host: Wendy Mays
Rooms: 2 (1 PB; 1 SB) $85
Full Breakfast
Credit Cards: None
Notes: 2, 5, 6, 7, 9, 10, 12

BETTERTON

Lantern Inn

115 Ericsson Avenue, P.O. Box 29, 21610
(410) 348-5809; (800) 499-7265
fax: (410) 348-2323
E-mail: lanterninn@dmv.com

Lantern Inn

www.virtualcities.com/ons/md/s/mds5601.htm

Circa 1904, four-story Victorian inn with a two-story front porch, located one block from the nettle-free beach on the Chesapeake Bay. Comfortable rooms are furnished with individual themes and handmade quilts. The surrounding area offers wildlife preserves, excellent biking, antiquing, historical sites, boating, hunting, fishing, sporting clays, and tennis. Cycling maps are available for trips of 10-90 miles around Kent County. Holiday specials available.

Hosts: Ray and Sandi Sparks
Rooms: 14 (4 PB; 10 SB) $75-90
Continental Breakfast
Credit Cards: A, B, C
Notes: 2, 5, 8, 9

CAMBRIDGE

Lodgecliffe
Bed & Breakfast

103 Choptank Terrace, 21613
(401) 228-1760
E-mail: dawson_richardson@ml.com

NOTES: Credit cards accepted: A Master Card; B Visa; C American Express; D Discover; E Diners Club; F Other; 2 Personal checks accepted; 3 Lunch available; 4 Dinner available; 5 Open all year;

This beautiful three-story 100-year-old home is perched on the banks of the Choptank River. Bedrooms have expansive view of the river. Victorian furniture highlights three large rooms. Blackwater National Wildlife Refuge is 20 minutes away, a must for waterfowl enthusiasts. Wonderful restaurants and two 18-hole golf courses nearby.

Host: Sarah Richardson
Rooms: 3 (2 PB; 1 SB) $90
Continental Breakfast
Credit Cards: None
Notes: 2, 5, 6, 7, 8, 9, 10, 12

CUMBERLAND

The Inn at Walnut Bottom

120 Greene Street, 21502-2934
(301) 777-0003; (800) 286-9718
fax: (301) 777-8288
E-mail: iwb@iwbinfo.com
www.iwbinfo.com

Two historic residences comprise the Inn at Walnut Bottom—the 1820 Georgian Style Cowden House, and the 1890 Queen Anne Style Dent House. With its 12 delightfully decorated guest rooms, sumptuous breakfast, and excellent service, it is an ideal spot for a wonderful getaway, small family reunion, or corporate retreat. Bicycles are available at no extra charge, and the Inn also offers Scenic Train and golf packages. Short drive to Frank Lloyd Wright's Fallingwater. AAA three-diamond and Mobil three-star rated.

Hosts: Grant M. Irvin and Kirsten O. Hansen
Rooms: 12 (8 PB; 4 SB) $87-145
Full Breakfast
Credit Cards: A, B, C, D
Notes: 2, 5, 7, 8, 9, 10, 11, 12

ELKTON

Garden Cottage at Sinking Springs

234 Blair Shore Road, 21921-8025
(410) 398-5566; fax: (410) 392-2889
www.cecilcounty.com/sinkspring/

With an early plantation house, including a 400-year-old sycamore, the cottage nestles at the edge of a meadow flanked by herb gardens and a historic barn with a gift shop. Sitting room with fireplace, bedroom, bath, air-conditioning, electric heat. Freshly ground coffee and herbal teas are offered with breakfast. Longwood Gardens and Winterthur Museum are 50 minutes away. Chesapeake City is nearby (excellent restaurants!). Sleeps three in two rooms; third person pays only $25. Enter at Elk Forest Road.

Hosts: Bill and Ann Stubbs
Rooms: 1 (PB) $95
Full Breakfast
Credit Cards: A, B
Notes: 2, 5, 6, 7, 8, 10, 12

FLINTSTONE

Mt. Valley Farm

20500 Root Road, P.O. Box 87, 21530
(301) 478-2497
E-mail: mvfarm28@hereintown.net

Beautiful farm in western Maryland near the town of Flintstone. We offer two lovely rooms with a balcony view, and a third-floor efficiency apartment with a skylight. Well-stocked pond. Hiking and bike riding. Ice skating, swimming, and tree house for the children. Full country break-

---

6 Pets welcome; 7 Children welcome; 8 Tennis nearby; 9 Swimming nearby; 10 Golf nearby; 11 Skiing nearby; 12 May be booked through travel agent

fast with homemade bread. Nearby are Rocky Gap State Park, Rocky Gap Golf Course, historic Cumberland with Western Maryland Railroad, antiques, and craft stores.

Hosts: Ann and Donnie Swope
Rooms: 3 (1 PB; 2 SB) $60-85
Full Breakfast
Credit Cards: None
Notes: 2, 5, 7, 9, 10

FREDERICK

Hazelwood Heights

12101 Glissans Mill Road, Union Bridge, 21791
(301) 831-9220; (866) 444-4048
fax: (301) 631-0220
www.hazelwoodheights.com

You will make lasting memories with a taste of simplicity at "Grandma's Treasured Haven." The gentle relaxing atmosphere is ideal for a leisure retreat, the business traveler, a family vacation, or a couple's romantic getaway. A lovely three-bedroom single dwelling has privacy, comfort, and country charm. It's the perfect place to begin and end the day. Fully equipped kitchen, air-conditioning, cable, TV/VCR, washer, and dryer. Complimentary Continental breakfast; no smoking inside. We are centrally located with easy access to Washington, D.C., Baltimore's Inner Harbor, and the Civil War battlefields at Antietam, Gettysburg, Harpers Ferry, and the Monocacy. Historic Frederick, the C&O Canal and New Market, Maryland's Antique Capitol, are also nearby.

Hosts: Marion and Glenna Hazelwood
Rooms: 3 (0 PB; 2 SB) $65-95
Continental Breakfast

Credit Cards: A, B, C, D
Notes: 5, 7, 8, 9, 10, 11

Middle Plantation Inn

9549 Liberty Road, 21701
(301) 898-7128
E-mail: bandb@mpinn.com
www.mpinn.com

From this charming inn built of stone and log, you can drive through horse country to the village of Mt. Pleasant. The inn is located several miles east of Frederick on 26 acres. Each guestroom is furnished with antiques and has a private bath, television, and airconditioning. The keeping room, a common room, features stained glass and a stone fireplace. Nearby you can find antique shops, museums, and a number of historic attractions. Middle Plantation Inn is located within 40 minutes of such Civil War-era sites as Gettysburg, Antietam Battlefield, and Harper's Ferry.

Hosts: Shirley and Dwight Mullican
Rooms: 4 (PB) $90-110
Continental Breakfast
Credit Cards: A, B, C
Notes: 2, 5, 8, 9, 10, 12

HAGERSTOWN

Lewrene Farm Bed & Breakfast

9738 Downsville Pike, 21740
(301) 582-1735
E-mail: lewrenebedandbreakfst@juno.com
www.christianbedbreakfast.com

Enjoy our quiet, colonial country home on 125 acres near I-70 and I-81, a home away from home for tourists,

NOTES: Credit cards accepted: A Master Card; B Visa; C American Express; D Discover; E Diners Club; F Other; 2 Personal checks accepted; 3 Lunch available; 4 Dinner available; 5 Open all year;

Lewrene Farm

businesspeople, and families. We have ample room for family celebrations. Sit by the fireplace or enjoy the great outdoors. Antietam Battlefield and Harper's Ferry are nearby; Washington and Baltimore are an hour and a half away. Quilts for sale.

Hosts: Lewis and Irene Lehman
Rooms: 5 (2 PB; 3 SB) $62-110
Full Breakfast
Credit Cards: None
Notes: 2, 5, 8, 9, 10, 11

Sunday's Bed & Breakfast

39 Broadway, 21740
(301) 797-4331
E-mail: info@sundaysbnb.com
www.sundaysbnb.com

Sunday's

Elegant, 1893 Queen Anne Victorian home located in a historic area, tastefully furnished with period antiques. Suite with two-person whirlpool to soothe your spirits. Gourmet breakfast, afternoon tea and desserts in the wicker-filled TeaRoom, evening wine and cheese in the parlor with working fireplace, and late-night cordial and chocolates are included in the rates. Antietam and Gettysburg Battlefields, Harpers Ferry, the C&O canal, antiquing, skiing, and outlets are all nearby.

Host: Bob Ferrino
Rooms: 4 (PB) $79-159
Full Breakfast
Credit Cards: A, B, E
Notes: 2, 4, 5, 7, 8, 9, 10, 11, 12

NORTH EAST

Sandy Cove Ministries Hotel & Conference Center

60 Sandy Cove Road, 21901
(410) 287-5433; (800) 234-COVE
fax: (410) 287-3196
E-mail: info@sandycove.org
www.sandycove.org

Enjoy the cozy warmth of our beautiful rooms and suites on the headwaters of the Chesapeake Bay. Savor a full breakfast in our main dining room overlooking the Bay. Get away—take time after a conference, or come for a mid-week break and escape to peace and comfort.

Rooms: 153 (PB)
Full Breakfast
Credit Cards: A, B, D
Notes: 2, 4, 5, 7, 8, 9, 10

---

6 Pets welcome; 7 Children welcome; 8 Tennis nearby; 9 Swimming nearby; 10 Golf nearby; 11 Skiing nearby; 12 May be booked through travel agent

ST. MICHAELS

The Inn at Christmas Farm

8873 Tilghman Island Road, Whittman, 21676
(410) 745-5312; (800) 986-9784
fax: (410) 745-5618
www.innatchristmasfarm.com

Located just seven miles west of St. Michaels, our waterfront inn and farm (circa 1830) contain a unique collection of historic buildings, including St. James Chapel (1893), saved from destruction, moved to the farm, and restored as the Gabriel and Bell Tower suites. The inn is set back from Route 33 just past the general store in the small village of Wittman. The beauty of the Chesapeake and its wildlife bring visitors from afar. Enjoy the tranquility; sit by our spring-fed pond (or swim in warm weather!); walk along the shore. Bike into St. Michaels where the Chesapeake Bay Maritime Museum, antiques, seafood delicacies, and sights in the charming colonial town await. Visit nearby Tilghman Island, where the last sailing oyster fleet is harbored. A full gourmet breakfast features our signature Christmas Farm quiche; it's served on our enclosed farmhouse porch overlooking field, farm, and woods. You can observe our "toy" farm animals—peacocks, chickens, sheep, and miniature horses. Waterfowl are also part of our special animal world.

Hosts: Bea and David Lee
Rooms: 6 (PB) $145-195
Full Breakfast
Credit Cards: A, B
Notes: 2, 5, 6, 8, 9, 10

Kemp House Inn

412 Talbot Street, P.O. Box 638, 21663
(410) 745-2243
www.info@kemphouseinn.com

Kemp House Inn

Built in 1807 by Col. Joseph Kemp, this superbly crafted home is one of a small collection of Federal period brick structures in St. Michaels. Elegant Federal details are evident throughout the house. Each of the rooms is tastefully furnished with period décor. Cozy, antique four-poster beds with patchwork quilts, down pillows, wing-back sitting chairs, and Queen Anne tables grace each room. Old-fashioned nightshirts, low-light sconces, and working fireplaces create an ambience of the early 19th century.

Hosts: Diane and Steve Cooper
Rooms: 8 (PB) $90-130
Continental Breakfast
Credit Cards: A, B, D
Notes: 2, 5, 7, 10, 12

NOTES: Credit cards accepted: A Master Card; B Visa; C American Express; D Discover; E Diners Club; F Other; 2 Personal checks accepted; 3 Lunch available; 4 Dinner available; 5 Open all year;

Wades Point
Inn on the Bay

P.O. Box 7, 21663
(410) 745-2500; (888) 923-3466
fax: (410) 745-3443
E-mail: wadesinn@wadespoint.com
www.wadesinnpoint.com

For those seeking the serenity of the country and the splendor of the bay, we invite you to charming Wades Point Inn, just a few miles from St. Michaels. Complemented by the ever-changing view of boats, birds, and water lapping our shoreline, our 120 acres of fields and woodlands, with a mile of walking or jogging trail, provide a peaceful setting for relaxation and recreation on Maryland's eastern shore. Closed January through March.

Hosts: Betsy and John Feiler
Rooms: 23 (16 PB; 7 SB) $115-230
Continental Breakfast
Credit Cards: A, B
Notes: 2, 8, 9, 10

---

6 Pets welcome; 7 Children welcome; 8 Tennis nearby; 9 Swimming nearby; 10 Golf nearby; 11 Skiing nearby; 12 May be booked through travel agent

MASSACHUSETTS

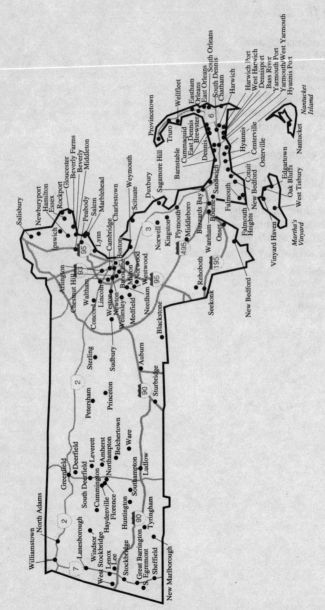

NOTES: Credit cards accepted: A Master Card; B Visa; C American Express; D Discover; E Diners Club; F Other; 2 Personal checks accepted; 3 Lunch available; 4 Dinner available; 5 Open all year;

Massachusetts

BOSTON

B & B Agency of Boston

47 Commercial Wharf, 02110-3804
(617) 720-3540; (800) 248-9262
fax: (617) 523-5761
E-mail: bosbnb@aol.com
www.boston-bnbagency.com

Downtown Boston's largest selection of guest rooms in historic bed and breakfast homes, including Federal and Victorian town houses and beautifully restored 1840s waterfront lofts. Available nightly, weekly, monthly. Or choose from the lovely selection of fully furnished, private studios, one- and two-bedroom condos, corporate suites, and lofts with all amenities, including fully furnished kitchens, private baths (some with Jacuzzis), TVs, and phones. Exclusive locations include waterfront, Faneuil Hall/Quincy Market, North End, Back Bay, Beacon Hill, Copley Square, and Cambridge.

Host: Ferne Mintz
Rooms: 150 (147 PB; 3 SB) $100-180
Continental Breakfast
Credit Cards: A, B, C
Notes: 5, 7, 12

Greater Boston Hospitality

P.O. Box 1142, Brookline, 02146-0009
(617) 277-5430; fax: (617) 277-7170
E-mail: kelly@bostonbedandbreakfast.com
www.bostonbedandbreakfast.com

Largest bed and breakfast professional reservation service in Boston. We offer inns, condos, and B&B accommodations throughout the greater Boston area. All include breakfast. Many hosts are native Bostonians and live on the premises. Parking included in many areas; many are close to the "Y," our excellent public transport system. Wide range of prices, amenities, and architectural styles. Visit Boston as a native.

Hosts: Lauren Walter and Kelly Simpson
Rooms: 200 (180 PB; 20 SB) $85-250
Full Breakfast
Credit Cards: A, B
Notes: 2, 5, 7, 8, 9, 10, 12

Joan's Bed & Breakfast

210R Lynn Street, Peabody, 01960
(978) 532-0191; fax: (978) 536-2726
E-mail: joansbandb@rcn.com

Joan's B&B is in a prime New England location, only 10 minutes from historic Salem, 25 minutes from Boston, and an hour from the many shopping outlets. Numerous great restaurants, theaters, and shopping malls are in the area. The 16-by-32-foot, in-ground pool is available for use by the guests. Make my home your home! Children 5 years and older are welcome.

Host: Joan Hetherington
Rooms: 3 (SB) $55-80
Full Breakfast
Credit Cards: None
Notes: 2, 5, 7, 9

---

6 Pets welcome; 7 Children welcome; 8 Tennis nearby; 9 Swimming nearby; 10 Golf nearby; 11 Skiing nearby; 12 May be booked through travel agent

BROOKLINE

The Beacon Inn

1087 & 1750 Beacon Street, 02445
(617) 566-0088; (888) 575-0088
fax: (617) 278-9736
E-mail: beacon1750@aol.com
www.beaconinn.com

The Beacon Inn

These late 19th-century brownstones have been fully restored into two of Brookline's most charming and inviting guesthouses. Large, comfortable, clean rooms provide pleasant accommodations at surprisingly affordable rates. Situated at 1087 and 1750 Beacon Street, the Beacon Inn is minutes away from downtown Boston. The area offers a wide variety of museums, theaters, restaurants, and other points of interest.

Hosts: Valerie Ferrier, Dave and Cora Long
Rooms: 25 (23 PB; 2 SB) $79-299
Credit Cards: A, B, C
Notes: 5, 7

CAPE COD/HARWICH PORT

Augustus Snow House

528 Main Street, 02646
(508) 430-0528; (800) 320-0528
fax: (508) 432-6638
E-mail: info@augustussnow.com
www.augustussnow.com

Chosen as "One of the Most Romantic Inns on Cape Cod. For the ultimate splurge the Augustus Snow House has few rivals in all of New England." This romantic, 1901 Victorian inn offers luxurious accommodations: exquisitely decorated bedrooms, queen or king beds, fireplaces, TVs, air-conditioning, telephones, elegant private baths (some with Jacuzzis). A wonderful gourmet breakfast is served each day. The private beach is just a three-minute stroll away. Walk to restaurants and shops. Every guest is promised a memorable and pampered visit.

Augustus Snow House

Hosts: Joyce and Steve Roth
Rooms: 5 (PB) $170-190
Full Breakfast
Credit Cards: A, B, C, D
Notes: 2, 5, 8, 9, 10, 12

NOTES: Credit cards accepted: A Master Card; B Visa; C American Express; D Discover; E Diners Club; F Other; 2 Personal checks accepted; 3 Lunch available; 4 Dinner available; 5 Open all year;

DENNISPORT

The Rose Petal Bed & Breakfast

152 Sea Street, 02639
(508) 398-8470
E-mail: info@rosepetalofdennis.com
www.rosepetalofdennis.com

Surrounded by a white picket fence and picturesque gardens, the Rose Petal is situated in the heart of Cape Cod, a short walk past century-old homes to the sandy beaches of Nantucket Sound. Home-baked pastries highlight a superb full breakfast. Three rooms all have spacious, bright, private baths, queen beds, and air-conditioning. Heirlooms and lace appoint a beautiful antique home built in 1872 for Almond Wixon, a seafaring Mayflower descendant. AAA three-diamond award.

Hosts: Dan and Gayle Kelly
Rooms: 3 (PB) $75-115
Full Breakfast
Credit Cards: A, B, C
Notes: 4, 7, 8, 9, 10, 12

DUXBURY

The Winsor House Inn

390 Washington Street, 02332
(781) 934-0991; fax: (781) 934-5955
E-mail: winsorhouse@dreamcom.net

Built in 1803 by sea captain Nathaniel Winsor, this charming, antique-filled country inn is located 35 miles south of Boston in the quaint seaside village of Duxbury. The four cozy, sunlit bedrooms are complete with canopy beds. Enjoy casual dining in the English-style pub, a gourmet dinner in the flower-filled carriage house, or a romantic evening in the candlelit dining room. Rates are subject to change. Single occupancy from $105; double occupancy from $130.

Hosts: David and Patricia O'Connell
Rooms: 4 (PB) $140-210
Full Breakfast
Credit Cards: A, B, C, D
Notes: 2, 4, 5, 7, 8, 9, 10, 12

EAST ORLEANS

The Farmhouse at Nauset Beach

163 Beach Road, Orleans, 02653
(508) 255-6654
www.virtualcapecod.com/thefarmhouse

"Be our guests." You'll get a good night's rest on our mattresses. Bright, airy rooms. Residential—no business deliveries and noise. Ninety feet from the road. Walk to Nauset Beach (Atlantic) and save parking fees. Open year-round. One and one-half acres; deck with picnic tables. Cedar tree sitting. Truly a B&B experience. Dot will help you find delicious food restaurants and fun things to do. Come and enjoy Cape Cod.

Host: Dot Standish
Rooms: 8 (PB) $75-135
Continental Breakfast
Credit Cards: A, B
Notes: 5, 7, 8, 9, 10

Nauset House Inn

P.O. Box 774; 143 Beach Road, 02643-
(508) 255-2195; fax: (508) 240-6276
E-mail: info@nausethouseinn.com
nausethouseinn.com

---

6 Pets welcome; 7 Children welcome; 8 Tennis nearby; 9 Swimming nearby; 10 Golf nearby; 11 Skiing nearby; 12 May be booked through travel agent

A real, old fashioned country inn farmhouse, circa 1810, is located on three acres with an apple orchard, one-half mile from Nauset Beach. A quiet, romantic getaway. Large commons room with fireplace, brick-floored breakfast room, and a beautiful 1907 glass conservatory filled with wicker furniture and blooming plants. Cozily furnished with eclectic antiques—a true fantasy.

Hosts: Diane and Al Johnson; Cindy and John Vessella
Rooms: 14 (8 PB; 6 SB) $75-150
Full Breakfast
Credit Cards: A, B, D
Notes: 2, 8, 9, 10

Ship's Knees Inn

186 Beach Road, P.O. Box 756, 02643
(508) 255-1312; fax: (508) 240-1351
E-mail: skinauset@aol.com
capecodtravel.com/shipskneesinn

This 170-year-old restored sea captain's home is a three-minute walk from beautiful, sand-duned Nauset Beach. Inside the warm, lantern-lit doorways are nineteen rooms individually appointed with special, colonial color schemes and authentic antiques. Some rooms feature authentic ship's knees, hand-painted trunks, old clipper ship models, braided rugs, and four-poster beds. Tennis and swimming are available on the premises. Three miles away, overlooking Orleans Cove, the Cove House offers three rooms, a one-bedroom efficiency, and two cottages.

Host: Donna Anderson
Rooms: 19 (8 PB; 11 SB) $45-140
Continental Breakfast
Credit Cards: A, B
Notes: 2, 5, 8, 9, 10, 12

ESSEX

George Fuller House

148 Main Street, 01929
(978) 768-7766; (800) 477-0148
fax: (978) 768-6178
E-mail: gfuller@ziplink.net
www.georgefullerhouse.com

This 1830 Federal-style house was built by Essex shipwrights with the same pride and craftmanship used to build the famous "Essexbuilt" schooners. It retains many of its fine architectural features, including folding Indian shutters, working fireplaces, original paneling and wood carving. Three porches and a balcony give access to the outside and a splendid view of the salt marsh and Essex River beyond. Each day begins with a full complimentary breakfast. Enjoy such specialties as Belgian waffles with fresh fruit, freshly baked breads, gingerbread pancakes and an inn favorite, praline French toast. There are over 50 antique shops in town. Boston is accessible by highway or public transportation. Close to Gordon College and Gordon Conwall seminary.

Host: Kathleen A. Tilden
Rooms: 7 (PB) $125-225
Full and Continental Breakfast
Credit Cards: A, B, C, D, E
Notes: 2, 5, 7, 8, 9, 10

FALMOUTH/CAPE COD

Captain Tom Lawrence House

75 Locust Street, Falmouth, 02540
(508) 540-1445; (800) 266-8139
fax: (508) 457-1790

NOTES: Credit cards accepted: A Master Card; B Visa; C American Express; D Discover; E Diners Club; F Other; 2 Personal checks accepted; 3 Lunch available; 4 Dinner available; 5 Open all year;

E-mail: capttomhouse@aol.com
www.sunsol.com/captaintom

Elegant and historic, this beautifully restored 1861 whaling captain's residence is now an intimate inn for those who appreciate warm hospitality, a peaceful atmosphere, and delicious, homecooked breakfasts. The rooms are fresh and romantic, with private baths, TV, refrigerator, and air-conditioning. The inn is close to the village green, beach bikeway, island ferries, and bus station. Walk to Falmouth Village Center. Near sea beaches, numerous golf courses, myriad restaurants, and ferries to Martha's Vineyard and Nantucket.

Grafton Inn

ing views of Martha's Vineyard. Rooms feature comfortable queen and king beds and period antiques. A sumptuous, full breakfast is served at individual tables overlooking Nantucket Sound. Air-conditioning/heat and CCTV. Thoughtful amenities including fresh flowers, homemade chocolates, evening wine and cheese, and beach chairs and towels. Eight-minute walk to island ferry. Dining a block away. AAA- and Mobil-rated three stars.

Host: Rudy Cvitan
Rooms: 10 (PB) $169-265
Full Breakfast
Credit Cards: A, B, C
Notes: 8, 9, 10

Captain Tom Lawrence House

Hosts: Anne Grebert and Jim Cotter
Rooms: 6 (PB) $90-175
Full Breakfast
Credit Cards: A, B, C
Notes: 2, 8, 9, 10

Grafton Inn

261 Grand Avenue South, 02540
(508) 540-8688; (888) 642-4069
fax: (508) 540-1861
www.graftoninn.com

This oceanfront Victorian is 30 steps to a sandy beach and offers breathtak-

Village Green Inn

40 Main Street, 02540
(508) 548-5621; (800) 237-1119
fax: (508) 547-5051; E-mail: VGF40@aol.com
www.villagegreeninn.com

This gracious, 1804, colonial-Victorian is ideally located on Falmouth's historic village green. Walk to fine shops and restaurants, or bike to beaches and picturesque Woods Hole along the Shining Sea Bike Path. Enjoy 19th-century charm and warm

---

6 Pets welcome; 7 Children welcome; 8 Tennis nearby; 9 Swimming nearby; 10 Golf nearby; 11 Skiing nearby; 12 May be booked through travel agent

hospitality amidst elegant surroundings. Four lovely guest rooms and one romantic suite all have private baths and unique fireplaces (two are working). A full gourmet breakfast features delicious house specialties. Many thoughtful amenities are included. Air-conditioned, CCTV.

Hosts: Diane and Don Crosby
Rooms: 5 (PB) $90-225
Credit Cards: A, B, C
Notes: 5, 8, 9, 10, 12

GREAT BARRINGTON

Thornewood Inn

453 Stockbridge Road, 01230-1287
(413) 528-3828; (800) 854-1008
fax: (413) 528-3307
E-mail: inn@thornewood.com
thornewood.com

Enjoy our antique-appointed guest rooms, some with fireplaces, views of the gardens, or canopy beds. Delight in the relaxing atmosphere of Spencer's Restaurant, relax by our outdoor pool, or treat yourself to a massage by our own massage therapist. Our sitting room offers quiet for a good book or family board game. Hiking, skiing, shopping, antiquing are all nearby.

Hosts: Terry and David Thorne
Rooms: 12 (PB) $95-275
Full Breakfast
Credit Cards: A, B, C, D
Notes: 2, 4, 5, 8, 9, 10, 11

IPSWICH

Town Hill
Bed & Breakfast

Town Hill

16 North Main Street, 01938
(978) 356-8000; (800) 457-7799
fax: (978) 356-8000
E-mail: reserve@townhill
www.townhill.com

This historic Greek Revival home was built in 1845 and features eleven individually decorated rooms. It's a short drive to beautiful Crane Beach and guests can walk to shops, restaurants, and the train to Boston. Nearby are whale-watching, antique hunting, canoeing, bird-watching, polo, and much more.

Hosts: Bob and Chere
Rooms: 11 (9 PB; 2 SB) $90-165
Full Breakfast
Credit Cards: A, B, C
Notes: 5, 7, 9, 10, 12

LYNN

Diamond District
Breakfast Inn

142 Ocean Street, 01902-2007
(781) 599-4470

NOTES: Credit cards accepted: A Master Card; B Visa; C American Express; D Discover; E Diners Club; F Other; 2 Personal checks accepted; 3 Lunch available; 4 Dinner available; 5 Open all year;

Architect-designed Georgian mansion in the historic "Diamond District," built in 1911. Gracious foyer and grand staircase, fireplace, living and dining room with ocean view, and French doors to veranda overlooking the gardens and ocean. Guest rooms offer antiques, air-conditioning, TVs, phones, down comforters, some fireplaces, whirlpools, decks, ocean views, and private baths. Deluxe king suites, outdoor heated spa, candlight breakfast. Three hundred feet off three-mile sandy beach for swimming, walking, jogging. Walk to restaurants. Home-cooked breakfast; vegetarian, lowfat available. Eight miles northeast of Boston.

Hosts: Sandra and Jerry Caron
Rooms: 11 (7 PB; 4 SB) $110-250
Full Breakfast
Credit Cards: A, B, C, D, E
Notes: 2, 5, 7, 9, 10, 12

MARBLEHEAD

Harborside House

23 Gregory Street, 01945
(781) 631-1032
E-mail: swliving@shore.net
www.shore.net/~swliving

Harborside House
Marblehead, Massachusetts

An 1850s home that overlooks Marblehead Harbor where guests enjoy water views from the fireplaced living room, period dining room, sunny breakfast porch, and third-story deck. A generous breakfast includes fresh fruit, home-baked goods, and cereals. Antique shops, gourmet restaurants, historic sites, and beaches are a pleasant stroll away. The owner is a professional dressmaker and nationally ranked competitive swimmer. Harborside House is a smoke-free B&B. Children over 8 welcome.

Host: Susan Livingston
Rooms: 2 (PB) $75-90
Continental Breakfast
Credit Cards: None
Notes: 2, 5, 7, 8, 9

NANTUCKET

House of the Seven Gables

32 Cliff Road, 02554
(508) 228-4701; (800) 905-5005
fax: (508) 228-2898
E-mail: walton@nantucket.net
www.houseofthesevengables.com

This quiet informal inn, built in the 1800s, is minutes from Main Street and beach. Large back yard and patio in back are available for guest enjoyment. Continental breakfast is served to room in the morning. Very relaxing.

Host: Sue Walton
Rooms: 10 (8 PB; 2 SB)
Continental Breakfast
Credit Cards: A, B, C
Notes: 2, 8, 9, 12

6 Pets welcome; 7 Children welcome; 8 Tennis nearby; 9 Swimming nearby; 10 Golf nearby; 11 Skiing nearby; 12 May be booked through travel agent

The Woodbox Inn
County Inn

29 Fair Street, 02554
(508) 228-0587; fax: (508) 228-7527
E-mail: woodbox@nantucket.net
woodboxinn.com

The Woodbox is Nantucket's oldest inn, built in 1709. Located a block and a half from the center of Nantucket, the inn serves "the best breakfast on the island" and offers gourmet dinners by candlelight, queen-size beds, and private baths. One- and two-bedroom suites have working fireplaces.

Host: Dexter Tutein
Rooms: 9 (PB) $175-205
Credit Cards: None
Notes: 2, 4, 7, 8, 9, 10, 12

NEW BEDFORD

1875 House
Bed & Breakfast

36 7th Street, 02740
(508) 997-6433; fax: (508) 991-5095
E-mail: bandb1875@cs.com

The 1875 House is a wooden house built in the early Victorian era. The home has undergone thoughtful restoration which is reflected throughout in the tasteful décor. We are located close to the newly designated Whaling National Historic Park, two blocks from the Rotch Jones Duff Museum in the historic area of New Bedford, and in a neighborhood which figured prominently in the "Underground Railroad." We are also conveniently located to Cape Cod, Newport, Providence, and Boston, all within an hour's drive.

Hosts: Steven Saint-Aubin and Cynthia Poyant
Rooms: 3 (PB) $65-75
Continental Breakfast
Credit Cards: None
Notes: 2, 5, 7, 9

NORWELL

1810 House
Bed & Breakfast

147 Old Oaken Bucket Road, 02061
phone/fax: (781) 659-1810; (888) 833-1810
E-mail: tuttle1810@aol.com
www.1810house.com

1810 House

A comfortable B&B, lovingly restored and enlarged. The antique half-Cape features original beamed ceilings, wide-pine floors, and stenciled walls. Three bright, cheery rooms share two full baths. Breakfast is served next to the fireplace in the country kitchen or, weather permitting, on the screened porch. The large, fireplaced family room with piano, TV, and VCR welcomes you to relax after a busy day. Oceanfront dining, interesting antique shops, and major highways are just minutes away.

NOTES: Credit cards accepted: A Master Card; B Visa; C American Express; D Discover; E Diners Club; F Other; 2 Personal checks accepted; 3 Lunch available; 4 Dinner available; 5 Open all year;

Hosts: Susanne and Harold Tuttle
Rooms: 3 (2 PB; 2 SB for families or two couples together) $75-95
Full Breakfast
Credit Cards: None
Notes: 2, 5, 9, 10

PLYMOUTH

Foxglove Cottage

101 Sandwich Road, 02360
(508) 747-6576; (800) 479-4746
fax: (508) 747-7622
E-mail: tranquility@foxglove-cottage.com
www.foxglove-cottage.com

Elegant and romantic lodging for the discerning traveler. Lovingly restored 1820 cape in a pastoral setting, away from the bustle of tourist traffic, yet close to Plantation and beaches. All our antique-furnished rooms have en suite private baths, air-conditioning/heat, a sitting area, and working fireplaces. Enjoy a full breakfast on our deck off the large common room. Foxglove Cottage is the perfect "hub" for day trips to Boston, the Islands, Newport, and Cape Cod. Listed in *Fodor's Best Bed and Breakfasts in America*.

Hosts: Mr. and Mrs. Charles K. Cowan
Rooms: 3 (PB) $95-115
Full Breakfast
Credit Cards: None
Notes: 2, 5, 9, 10

REHOBOTH

Gilbert's Tree Farm Bed & Breakfast

30 Spring Street, 02769
(508) 252-6416

E-mail: glbrtsbb@aol.com
members.aol.com/glbrtsbb

Gilbert's Tree Farm

Our 17-acre tree farm provides a quiet place to enjoy the beauty of nature and God's bountiful gifts. The body is nourished with hearty breakfasts, and refreshed with hikes through the woods and exercise in the in-ground swimming pool. Two rooms have fireplaces. Within an hour's drive of Boston, Newport, Mystic, and Plymouth; 15 minutes from Providence, Rhode Island.

Host: Jeanne Gilbert
Rooms: 5 (2 PB; 3 SB) $65-85
Full Breakfast
Credit Cards: None
Notes: 2, 5, 7, 8, 9, 10, 12

ROCKPORT

Tuck Inn

17 High Street, 01966
(978) 546-7260; (800) 789-7260
E-mail: tuckin@shore.net
www.thetuckinn.com

This welcoming, 1790 colonial home is located on a quiet secondary street

---

6 Pets welcome; 7 Children welcome; 8 Tennis nearby; 9 Swimming nearby; 10 Golf nearby; 11 Skiing nearby; 12 May be booked through travel agent

just one block from the village center. The nearby train station offers convenient access to Boston as well. Featuring antiques, colorful quilts, and local artwork throughout, the inn offers all private baths, CCTVs, air-conditioning, and an in-ground pool. Nonsmoking, pet-free environment. Breakfast each morning is a hearty, home-baked buffet. The Woods graciously invite you to "come and stay with us!"

Hosts: Liz and Scott Wood
Rooms: 11 (PB) $69-109
Continental Breakfast
Credit Cards: A, B
Notes: 2, 5, 7, 8, 9, 10

SALEM

Amelia Payson House

16 Winter Street, 01970
(978) 744-8304
E-mail: stay@ameliapaysonhouse.com
www.ameliapaysonhouse.com

Welcome to our home! Built in 1845 for Amelia and Edward Payson, 16 Winter Street is one of Salem's finest examples of Greek Revival Architecture. Elegantly restored and beautifully decorated, each room is furnished with period antiques and warmed by a personal touch. Comfort amenities include: private bath, air-conditioning, cable TV, radio, and hair dryer. Guests will not only enjoy the grace and charm that is tradition at a B&B host home, but will also appreciate our convenient historic district location just steps from all of Salem's limitless activities.

Hosts: Ada and Donald Roberts
Rooms: 4 (PB) $95-150
Continental Breakfast

Credit Cards: A, B, C, D
Notes: 8, 9, 10

The Salem Inn

7 Summer Street, 01970
(978) 741-0680; (800) 446-2995
fax: (978) 744-8924
E-mail: saleminn@earthlink.net
www.saleminnma.com

The Salem Inn which is comprised of the West House (c. 1834), the Curwen House (c. 1854) and the Peabody House (c. 1874), testifies to the glory that was 19th-century Salem. These impressive and historical buildings are centrally located just a short walk from Salem's museums, antique shops, and the waterfront. The Inn's individually decorated rooms and suites provide an array of modern amenities. Many feature kitchenettes, canopy beds, fireplaces, and oversized Jacuzzis. Antiques and tasteful furnishings grace all of the buildings.

Rooms: 42 (PB) $119-230
Continental Breakfast
Credit Cards: A, B, C, D, E
Notes: 5, 6, 7, 9, 12

SANDWICH

Captain Ezra Nye House

152 Main Street, 02563
(508) 888-6142; (800) 388-2278
fax: (508) 833-2897
E-mail: captnye@aol.com
www.captezranyehouse.com

Whether you come to enjoy summer on Cape Cod, a fall foliage trip, or a quiet winter vacation, the Captain Ezra Nye House is a great place to start. It is located only 60 miles from

---

NOTES: Credit cards accepted: A Master Card; B Visa; C American Express; D Discover; E Diners Club; F Other; 2 Personal checks accepted; 3 Lunch available; 4 Dinner available; 5 Open all year;

Boston, 20 miles from Hyannis, and within walking distance of many noteworthy attractions including the Heritage Plantation, Sandwich Glass Museum, and the Cape Cod Canal. Award-winning "Readers Choice"; named "Best Bed and Breakfast, Upper Cape," by *Cape Cod Life* magazine.

Hosts: Elaine and Harry Dickson
Rooms: 6 (PB) $85-125
Full Breakfast
Credit Cards: A, B, C, D
Notes: 2, 5, 7, 8, 9, 10, 12

SOUTH DEERFIELD

Deerfield's Yellow Gabled House

111 North Main Street, 01373
(413) 665-4922

Located on the site of the historic battle Bloody Brook Massacre of 1675, and a mile and a half from the crossroads of I-91, Route 116, and Route 5 and 10 is a picturesque house with gardens and three decorated bed chambers. Guests have access to a sitting room and library for reading and meeting fellow travelers. Enjoy early

morning coffee in the summer room. Located one mile from Yankee Candle and historic Deerfield. Featured on the cover page of the *Springfield Republican*.

Host: Edna Julia Stanelek
Rooms: 3 (1 PB; 2 SB) $75-140
Full Breakfast
Credit Cards: None
Notes: 2, 5, 8, 9, 10, 11, 12

SOUTH DENNIS

Captain Nickerson Inn

Captain Nickerson

333 Main Street, 02660
(508) 398-5966
E-mail: captnick@capecod.net

This delightful, Victorian sea captain's home is located on a bike path in the historic section of Dennis. This is the mid-Cape area, close to all points of interest. The comfortable front porch is lined with white wicker rockers. Guest rooms are decorated in period four-poster or white iron queen beds, and oriental or hand-woven rugs. Cozy terry robes and air-conditioning are available in all rooms. The fireplaced living room is comfortable,

---

6 Pets welcome; 7 Children welcome; 8 Tennis nearby; 9 Swimming nearby; 10 Golf nearby; 11 Skiing nearby; 12 May be booked through travel agent

yet lovely, and has cable TV, VCR, and stained-glass windows. The dining room also has a fireplace, parquet floors, and a stained-glass window. Walk to Indian Lands Trail and the Bass River. Bike to Cape Cod (20-plus-mile bike trail is only a mile from the inn) on complimentary bicycles. Championship golf courses, world-class beaches, paddleboats, horseback riding, ferry service, museums, Cape Playhouse, fishing, and craft and antique shops are all nearby. Children welcome! Smoking outside only. One suite available.

Hosts: Pat and Dave York
Rooms: 6 (4 PB; 2 SB) $95-14 7
Full Breakfast
Credit Cards: A, B, D
Notes: 2, 7, 8, 9, 10, 12

STOCKBRIDGE

Arbor Rose Bed & Breakfast

8 Yale Hill Road, 01262
(413) 298-4744; (877) 298-4744
E-mail: innkeeper@arborrose.com
www.arborrose.com

Cluster roses shroud the entrance way to this old farmhouse, inviting you onto the front porch and through the French doors. Fine antiques and china, new four-poster beds, lovely fabrics, and rural paintings decorate the rooms. Next door, the old sawmill has a more historic and country flare with its post and beam construction and sounds of the flowing stream. Extra beds and ski packages are available. We're a half mile from Stockbridge center.

Hosts: Christina Alsop and Family
Rooms: 6 (PB) $105-175
Full Breakfast
Credit Cards: A, B
Notes: 2, 5, 6, 7, 8, 9, 10, 11, 12

VARIOUS CITIES

Elaine's Bed & Breakfast Selections

4987 Kingston Road, 13060
(315) 689-2082

This reservation service lists B&Bs in the following towns: Chatham, Dennisport, Great Barrington, and West Stockbridge. Elaine Samuels, director.

WARE

Antique 1880 Bed & Breakfast

14 Pleasant Street, 01082
(413) 967-7847

Built in 1876, this colonial-style inn has pumpkin and maple hardwood floors, beamed ceilings, six fireplaces, and antique furnishings. Afternoon tea is served by the fireplace; breakfast is in the dining room or on the porch, weather permitting. It is a short, pretty country ride to historic Old Sturbridge Village and Old Deerfield Village. Hiking and fishing are nearby. We are midway between Boston and the Berkshires.

Host: Margaret Skutnik
Rooms: 5 (2 PB; 3 SB) $40-65
Full Breakfast
Credit Cards: None
Notes: 2, 5, 8, 9, 10, 11, 12

NOTES: Credit cards accepted: A Master Card; B Visa; C American Express; D Discover; E Diners Club; F Other; 2 Personal checks accepted; 3 Lunch available; 4 Dinner available; 5 Open all year;

WAREHAM

Mulberry
Bed & Breakfast

257 High Street, 02571
(508) 295-0684; fax: (508) 291-2909

Mulberry B&B sits on a half-acre lot shaded by a majestic, seven-trunk mulberry tree. This Cape Cod-style home, built in 1847 by a blacksmith, offers three cozy guest rooms with two shared baths and a hearty, home-made breakfast. Mulberry is a mile from I-195 and I-495. The historic, picturesque cities of Boston, Newport, New Bedford, and Plymouth are within an hour's drive.

Host: Frances Murphy
Rooms: 3 (SB) $55-75
Full Breakfast
Credit Cards: A, B, C, D
Notes: 2, 5, 7, 8, 9, 10, 11, 12

YARMOUTH PORT

Colonial House Inn

277 Main Street, 02675
(508) 362-4348; (800) 999-3416
fax: (508) 362-8034
E-mail: info@colonialhousecapecod.com
www.colonialhousecapecod.com

The Colonial House is a year-round, full-service country inn with a restaurant and lounge, in the center of the Cape on Historic Route 6A. An historic landmark with 21 rooms, it offers all private baths, TVs, telephones, data ports, air-conditioning, canopy beds, and antiques. Guests will also find a heated indoor pool and Jacuzzi, sun deck, beautiful garden sitting area, waterfall, and fountain. Available for receptions up to 150. Within walking distance are nature trails, golf, tennis, fresh and salt water beaches, and antique shops.

Hosts: Malcolm J.Perna and Tony Malcolm
Rooms: 21 (PB) $70-95
Continental Breakfast
Credit Cards: A, B, C, D
Notes: 2, 3, 4, 5, 6, 7, 8, 9, 10, 11, 12

---

6 Pets welcome; 7 Children welcome; 8 Tennis nearby; 9 Swimming nearby; 10 Golf nearby; 11 Skiing nearby; 12 May be booked through travel agent

MICHIGAN

NOTES: Credit cards accepted: A Master Card; B Visa; C American Express; D Discover; E Diners
Club; F Other; 2 Personal checks accepted; 3 Lunch available; 4 Dinner available; 5 Open all year;

Michigan

BLANEY PARK

Celibeth House

Route 1, Box 58A, 49836-9623
(906) 283-3409; fax: (906) 283-3537
E-mail: celibeth@up.net
www.celibethhouse.com

Celibeth House

Built in 1895, this Victorian home is situated on 71 acres overlooking a small lake. It became part of the Blaney Park Resort in 1929. The resort closed and the buildings were sold in 1985. At that time, the house and adjacent acreage was purchased as a B&B. In the spring of 2000, Mary French and Scott Barr became the new owners. This lovely country manor with adult atmosphere offers nine bedrooms with private baths. Each room is spacious and clean and tastefully furnished. All rooms accommodate a maximum of two persons, except one room that will accommodate four. Reservations guaranteed with one night's deposit. Cancellation policy: seven days' notice required for full refund. This home is located within an hour's drive of most of the scenic attractions in the upper Peninsula. A full gourmet breakfast is served. Visit the tearoom and gift shoppe.

Hosts: Mary French and Scott Barr
Rooms: 8 (PB) $85-100
Full Breakfast
Credit Cards: A, B, D
Notes: 2, 5, 7, 8, 9, 10, 11, 12

BROOKLYN

Buffalo Inn

10845 U.S. 12, 49230
phone/fax: (517) 467-6521
www.bbonline.com/mi/buffaloinn

Comfortable, inviting. . .a uniquely different B&B with a Southwestern charm. Enjoy your generous, home-cooked breakfast by our large stone fireplace. Play pinball in our game room. We have five themed bedrooms with private and shared baths, one with a fireplace. The Inn is along the road known as "Antique Alley." Our area also offers 54 lakes, numerous golf courses, fine dining and dancing, and many family attractions. We welcome you to the beautiful Irish Hills.

Host: Carol Zarr
Rooms: 5 (1 PB; 4 SB) $45-85
Full Breakfast
Credit Cards: A, B, D
Notes: 2, 5, 7, 9, 10

---

6 Pets welcome; 7 Children welcome; 8 Tennis nearby; 9 Swimming nearby; 10 Golf nearby; 11 Skiing nearby; 12 May be booked through travel agent

CANTON

Willow Brook Inn
Bed & Breakfast

44255 Warren Road, 48187-2147
(734) 454-0019; (888) 454-0019
E-mail: wbibnb@earthlink.net
www.willowbrookinn.com

Located between Ann Arbor and Detroit. Childhood memories and pampering pleasures are yours on a secluded wooded acre with a wandering brook, lovely perennial gardens, deck, and hot tub. Graceful antiques, unique collections, featherbeds, silky robes, air-conditioning, in-room TVs/VCRs, and CD system. Enjoy a candlelight breakfast, consisting of fresh fruit, beverages, and an entree. Local attractions: Greenfield Village, University of Michigan, Pheasant Run Golf Course. Detroit Metro Airport 10 minutes away; two miles from I-275.

Hosts: Michael and Bernadette
Rooms: 3 (PB) $110-125
Full Breakfast
Credit Cards: A, B, C
Notes: 2, 3, 4, 5, 6, 7, 8, 9, 10, 11

DIMONDALE

Bannick's
Bed & Breakfast

4608 Michigan Road, 48821
(517) 646-0224

This large, ranch-style home features a stained-glass entry, nautical-style basement, and a Mona Lisa bathroom. Accommodations include a large comfortable bedroom with TV, queen bed, and fresh hot coffee. Almost three rural acres offer a quiet escape from the fast pace of a working world. Located on a main highway (M99), Bannick's is five miles from Lansing, and Michigan State University is just eight miles away. Breakfast specialties are frittata's or Polish apple pancakes.

Hosts: Pat and Jim Bannick
Rooms: 1 (SB) $45
Full Breakfast
Credit Cards: None
Notes: 5, 9, 10

FLUSHING

Main Street Manor
Bed & Breakfast

516 East Main Street, 48433
(810) 487-1888; (877) 487-1888
E-mail: mainstreetmanor@att.net
www.bbonline.com/mi/mainstreet

Main Street Manor

Main Street Manor is an 1888 Victorian Painted Lady located in Flushing, four miles west of Flint off I-75. We feature two comfortable rooms with

---

NOTES: Credit cards accepted: A Master Card; B Visa; C American Express; D Discover; E Diners Club; F Other; 2 Personal checks accepted; 3 Lunch available; 4 Dinner available; 5 Open all year;

queen beds, luxury linens, fresh flowers, antiques, lace, and Jacuzzi, along with small town ambience. We serve evening refreshments, as well as a full breakfast. Whether you are visiting the area, are here for business or a romantic retreat, you will be pampered and refreshed by your stay.

Hosts: Tim and Sue Sodeman
Rooms: 2 (PB) $95-110
Full Breakfast
Credit Cards: A, B, C, D, E
Notes: 2, 5, 8, 10

FRANKENMUTH

Bavarian Town Bed & Breakfast

206 Beyerlein Street, 48734
(989) 652-8057
E-mail: btbedb@juno.com
www.laketolake.com/bavarian

Beautifully decorated Cape Cod dwelling with central air-conditioning in a peaceful, residential district of Michigan's most popular tourist town, just three blocks from Main Street. Bilingual hosts are descendants of original German settlers and will serve as tour guides of the area, including historic St. Lorenz Lutheran Church. Color television in each room. We share recipes and provide superb hospitality. Hot tub on deck and sauna in basement.

Hosts: Louie and Kathy Weiss
Rooms: 3 (2 PB; 1 SB) $80
Full Breakfast
Credit Cards: A, B
Notes: 2, 5, 7, 8, 10

GRAND HAVEN

Boyden House Bed & Breakfast

301 South 5th Street, 49417-1413
(616) 846-3538; fax: (616) 847-4030
E-mail: gkowalski@chartermi.net
www.bbonline.com/mi/boyden

Built in 1875, our Queen Ann style home with spacious rooms and a comfortable and eclectic decor is designed to afford privacy for our guests. We specialize in group gatherings that also include meals. Allow our expertise to creatively customize your stay and include events that make your stay memorable. We are located a within walking distance to downtown and the Lake Michigan shores, making for a relaxing, interesting stay.

Hosts: Tony and Gail Kowalski
Rooms: 7 (PB) $110-150
Full Breakfast
Credit Cards: A, B, C, D, E
Notes: 2, 5, 7, 9, 10, 11, 12

Seascape Bed & Breakfast

20009 Breton, Spring Lake, 49456
phone/fax: (616) 842-8409
www.bbonline.com/mi/seascape

Seascape B&B, located on private, sandy Lake Michigan Beach, offers scenic, relaxing, lakefront rooms. Enjoy the warm hospitality and "country living" ambience of our nautical lakeshore home. A full homemade breakfast is served in the gathering room with fieldstone fireplace, or on the large sun deck. Either provides a panoramic view of Grand Haven Har-

6 Pets welcome; 7 Children welcome; 8 Tennis nearby; 9 Swimming nearby; 10 Golf nearby; 11 Skiing nearby; 12 May be booked through travel agent

bor. Stroll or cross-country ski on dune land nature trails. Open all year, with a kaleidoscope of scenes reflecting the changing seasons. A separate Victorian cottage sleeps eight.

Host: Susan Meyer
Rooms: 4 (PB) $85-185
Full Breakfast
Credit Cards: A, B
Notes: 2, 5, 8, 9, 10, 11

Seascape

HILLSDALE

The Munro House

202 Maumee Street, Jonesville, 49250
(517) 849-9292; (800) 320-3792
fax: (517) 849-7685
E-mail: info@munrohouse.net
www.munrohouse.net

This spectacular 1840 Greek Revival mansion was once a station on the Underground Railroad. Seven guest rooms all have private baths, queen beds, telephones, cable TVs, and VCRs. Some have gas fireplaces or two-person Jacuzzis. Common area has big-screen TV, acoustic guitar, and grand piano. Rate includes soft drinks, cookies, and videos.

The Munro House

Hosts: Mike and Lori Venturini
Rooms: 7 (PB) $89-199
Full Breakfast
Credit Cards: A, B, C, D
Notes: 5, 10

HOLLAND

Dutch Colonial Inn

560 Central Avenue, 49423
(616) 396-3664; fax: (616) 396-0461
E-mail: dutchcolonialinn@juno.com
www.dutchcolonialinn.com

Relax and enjoy a gracious, 1928 Dutch colonial. Your hosts have elegantly decorated their home with family heirloom antiques and furnishings from the 1930s. Guests enjoy the cheery sunporch, honeymoon suites with fireplaces, and rooms with TVs

Dutch Colonial Inn

NOTES: Credit cards accepted: A Master Card; B Visa; C American Express; D Discover; E Diners Club; F Other; 2 Personal checks accepted; 3 Lunch available; 4 Dinner available; 5 Open all year;

and double whirlpool tubs. Nearby are Dutch attractions, charming downtown shops, Hope College, Michigan's finest beaches, bike paths, and cross-country ski trails, plus the Tulip Festival. Corporate rates are available for business travelers.

Hosts: Bob and Pat Elenbaas
Rooms: 4 (PB) $100-160
Full Breakfast
Credit Cards: A, B, C, D
Notes: 2, 5, 8, 9, 10, 11

Shaded Oaks Bed & Breakfast

Shaded Oaks

444 Oak Street, 49424
(616) 399-4194
E-mail: shadedoaks@chartermi.net
www.shadedoaks.com

Charming Cape Cod offers a wooded setting 75 feet off Lake Macatawa. Beautiful interior includes 700-square-foot suite with fireplace, double tub, and sunroom. Makes for a beautiful and romantic getaway. Charter a sunset or dinner cruise aboard Shaded Oaks' very own 32-foot Marinette yacht. Enjoy a gourmet

breakfast, then walk to the state park. Sorry, no smoking.

Hosts: Jack and Karen Zibell
Rooms: 2 (PB) $135-185
Full Breakfast
Credit Cards: A, B
Notes: 2, 5, 8, 9, 10

HOUGHTON

Charleston House Historic Inn

918 College Avenue, 49931
(906) 482-7790; (800) 482-7404
fax: (906) 482-8608
E-mail: inquiries@charlestonhouseinn.com
www.charlestonhouseinn.com

Turn-of-the-century Georgian house with double veranda, ceiling fans, and wicker furniture. The inn features ornate woodwork, leaded- and beveled-glass windows, a library with fireplace, and grand interior staircase. Comfortable period reproduction and antique furnishings with king canopy and twin beds. All private baths, air-

Charleston House

conditioning, cable color TV, and telephones. Full breakfast. Walk to university and downtown. Smoking limited to the garden. AAA-approved. Children 12 and older welcome.

---

6 Pets welcome; 7 Children welcome; 8 Tennis nearby; 9 Swimming nearby; 10 Golf nearby; 11 Skiing nearby; 12 May be booked through travel agent

Hosts: John and Helen Sullivan
Rooms: 6 (PB) $135-238
Full Breakfast
Credit Cards: A, B, C
Notes: 2, 5, 7, 8, 9, 10, 11, 12

HUDSON

Quigley's Log Home Bed & Breakfast

8450 Acker Highway, 49247
(517) 448-1057
E-mail: quigleybnb@tc3net.com

Entering the front door of this lovely log home located on 40 acres, you will feel the warm welcome of wood. Freshly baked cinnamon bread hints of the gourmet breakfasts. Choose bedrooms in the loft or family suite on walkout lower level. Air-conditioned rooms are beautifully decorated. Enjoy fabulous sunsets or walks around the wildlife pond. Visit many kinds of recreation. Leave refreshed and planning a return visit. Packages available. No tobacco or alcohol.

Hosts: Jack and Choyce Quigley
Rooms: 4 (2 PB; 2 SB) $65-95

QUIGLEY'S
Log Home Bed & Breakfast

Full Breakfast
Credit Cards: None
Notes: 2, 3, 4, 5, 9, 10, 12

IONIA

Union Hill Inn

306 Union Street, 48846
(616) 527-0955
uonhilbb@1serv.net
www.unionhillbb.com

Union Hill Inn

This elegant, 1868 Italianate-style home served as a station for the underground railroad. The inn is beautifully furnished with antiques. Enjoy the living area with its fireplace, piano, porcelain village, and dolls. The home is air-conditioned. Flower beds surround the home, which is noted for its expansive veranda and panoramic view overlooking the historic city. With all the beauty at Union Hill Inn, the greatest thing you will experience is God's love and peace that abide here.

Hosts: Tom and Mary Kay Moular
Rooms: 6 (1 PB; 5 SB) $50-95
Full Breakfast
Credit Cards: None
Notes: 2, 5, 7, 8, 9, 10, 12

JONESVILLE

Horse & Carriage Bed & Breakfast

7020 Brown Road, 49250
phone/fax: (517) 849-2732
E-mail: horsecarriagebb@yahoo.com

Coming from near or far, here's an oasis for the traveler looking for a relaxing, quiet country setting. Enjoy fireside hospitality and starry-night sleeping. After a delicious breakfast served on the sun-porch, step back in time with an old-fashioned carriage ride. There are stories of days-gone-by told behind the rhythmic clip-clop of Rosa, our Amish mare. No TV, smoking, or alcohol. Lots of nearby antiquing.

Hosts: Keith L. Brown and Family
Rooms: 3 (1 PB; 2 SB) $50-100
Full Breakfast
Credit Cards: None
Notes: 2, 5, 7, 9, 10

LAKE CITY

Bed & Breakfast in the Pines

1940 Schneider Park Road, 49651
(231) 839-4876

Pick your own raspberries and apples from our orchard when in season. Located 13 miles east of Cadillac. Enjoy downhill/cross-country skiing, fishing, swimming, hiking, biking, and boating. No alcohol, smoking, or pets. Handicap ramp. Two-week advance reservation with $50 deposit required. Check-in time 4:00-8:00 P.M. Check

Bed and Breakfast in the Pines

out time 10:00 A.M. May be booked with AAA of Livonia.

Host: Reggie Ray
Rooms: 1 (PB) $100
Full Breakfast
Credit Cards: None
Notes: 2, 5, 8, 9, 10, 11

LELAND

Manitou Manor

P.O. Box 864, 49654
(231) 256-7712; fax: (231) 256-7941
www.bbhost.com/manitoumanorbb

A spacious country estate that makes staying in Leelanau County a peaceful experience. Open year-round, the home features private baths and family-style breakfasts. Unique guest rooms all have inviting themes. A perfect place to celebrate the seasons.

Hosts: Sandy and Mike Lambdin
Rooms: 5 (PB) $95-140
Full Breakfast
Credit Cards: A, B, D
Notes: 2, 5, 7, 8, 9, 10, 11

6 Pets welcome; 7 Children welcome; 8 Tennis nearby; 9 Swimming nearby; 10 Golf nearby; 11 Skiing nearby; 12 May be booked through travel agent

McGee Homestead

LOWELL

McGee Homestead Bed & Breakfast

2534 Alden Nash Northeast, 49331
(616) 897-8142
E-mail: mcgeebb@iserv.net
www.iserv.net/~mcgeebb

Wake up to the rooster crowing! Our 1880s brick farmhouse is surrounded by orchards next to a golf course. We have a big ol' barn full of animals. Guest rooms are furnished in antiques and have private baths. Hot tub on the screen porch. Big country breakfast and full cookie jar.

Hosts: Bill and Ardie Barber
Rooms: 4 (PB) $55-75
Full Breakfast
Credit Cards: A, B, C, D
Notes: 2, 7, 8, 9, 10, 11

LUDINGTON

Bed & Breakfast at Ludington

2458 South Beaune Road, 49431
(231) 843-9768

E-mail: bedbkfst@carrinter.net
www.carrinter.net/bedbkfst

Picture quiet privacy, northern woods, creek, and walking trails, all just a five-minute drive from Lake Michigan beaches and a half mile from golf. Lazy place to "sleep in" if you want. Have the comfort of beds and amenities, but gather after sunset around our campfire for s'mores and star-gazing. In winter, use our 16 acres (next to state property) to cross-country ski, or

Bed and Breakfast at Ludington

make the short drive to groomed ski trails. Indoor Jacuzzi.

Hosts: Grace and Robert Schneider
Rooms: 3 (2 PB; 1 SB) $45-75
Full Breakfast
Credit Cards: None
Notes: 2, 5, 6, 7, 9, 10, 11

The Inn at Ludington

701 East Ludington Avenue, 49431
(231) 845-7055; (800) 845-9170
www.inn-ludington.com

Enjoy the charm of the past with the comforts of today. No stuffy, hands-off museum atmosphere here—our vintage furnishings invite you to relax

---

NOTES: Credit cards accepted: A Master Card; B Visa; C American Express; D Discover; E Diners Club; F Other; 2 Personal checks accepted; 3 Lunch available; 4 Dinner available; 5 Open all year;

The Inn at Ludington

and feel at home. The bountiful breakfast will sustain you for a day of beachcombing, biking, or antiquing. In winter, cross-country skiing awaits at Ludington State Park. Looking for something different? Murder mysteries are a specialty. Make this your headquarters for a Ludington/Lake Michigan adventure. Just look for the "Painted Lady" with the three-story turret. The Inn at Ludington is a non-smoking home.

Hosts: Diane and David Nemitz
Rooms: 6 (PB) $80-100
Full Breakfast
Credit Cards: A, B, C, D
Notes: 2, 5, 7, 8, 9, 10, 11, 12

Snyder's Shoreline Inn

903 West Ludington Avenue, P.O. Box 667, 49431
(231) 845-1261; fax: (231) 843-4441
E-mail: sharon@snydersshoreinn.com
www.snydersshoreinn.com

Snyder's Shoreline Inn offers a beautiful location on the edge of town, nestled at the harbor front. View the Ludington Lighthouse, sailboats, freighters, and sunsets from room pa-tios or private balconies. Sleep comfortably in pleasant guest rooms individually decorated with stenciled walls, pieced quilts, antiques, and reproductions. Honeymoon suites feature in-room whirlpools. A great, quiet retreat or romantic getaway. Luxury, barrier-free, handicapped-accessible rooms. Heated outdoor pool and spa. Smoke-free. No pets. AAA.

Rooms: 44 (PB) $65-289
Continental Breakfast
Credit Cards: A, B, C
Notes: 8, 9, 10

MACKINAC ISLAND

Haan's 1830 Inn

P.O. Box 123, 49757
(906) 847-6244
www.mackinac.com

Haan's 1830 Inn

The earliest Greek Revival home in the Northwest Territory, this completely restored inn is on the Michigan Historic Registry. It is located in a quiet neighborhood three blocks around Haldiman Bay from the bustling 1800s downtown and Old Fort MacKinac. Adjacent to St. Anne's Church and gardens. Rooms are furnished with antiques. Experience the 19th-century ambience of horse-drawn buggies and wagons. Closed late October-mid-May.

6 Pets welcome; 7 Children welcome; 8 Tennis nearby; 9 Swimming nearby; 10 Golf nearby; 11 Skiing nearby; 12 May be booked through travel agent

Hosts: Nick and Nancy Haan
Rooms: 8 (6 PB; 2 SB) $95-175
Continental Breakfast
Credit Cards: None
Notes: 2, 7, 8, 9, 10

MANISTIQUE

Royal Rose
Bed & Breakfast

230 Arbutus Avenue, 49854
(906) 341-4886; fax: (906) 341-4886
E-mail: gsablack@chartermi.net
www.manistique.com

Royal Rose

Experience the elegant but relaxed atmosphere of this newly remodeled 1903 home. Guest rooms have queen beds and are uniquely decorated. Enjoy the sunroom where you may read, socialize by the fireplace, or view the spectacular sights of Lake Michigan. Savor a full breakfast served in the formal dining room or out on the large deck. Within walking distance of shopping, dining, movies, the marina, and the boardwalk.

Hosts: Gilbert and Rosemary Sablack
Rooms: 4 (PB) $75-110
Full Breakfast
Credit Cards: A, B, D
Notes: 2, 8, 9, 10, 11

MIO

Teaspoon Bed & Breakfast

615 West Kneeland Road, 48647
(989) 826-3889
E-mail: stay@teaspoonbb.com
www.teaspoonbb.com

Have you been looking for that perfect place to take that special someone? A place that speaks of grandeur and elegance? That place is Teaspoon. Offering ultimate privacy, the Amish Fireplace Room and the Victorian Honeymoon Room have private hot tubs, fireplaces, baths, balconies, VCRs, and four course candlelight breakfasts. Without leaving the property, spend the day sitting on the balcony overlooking 30 acres of woods or wandering through our antique shop; or browse the Amish shops and take a lazy float on the AuSable River.

Hosts: Fred and Kathy Gottschalk
Rooms: 2 (PB) $99-125
Full Breakfast
Credit Cards: None
Notes: 2, 5, 8, 9, 10, 11

MUSKEGON

Port City Victorian Inn

1259 Lakeshore Drive, 49441
phone/fax: (231) 759-0205; (800) 274-3574
www.portcityinn.com

An 1877, romantic Victorian getaway on the bluffs of Muskegon Lake, minutes from Lake Michigan beaches, state parks, theaters, sports arena, and restaurants. Choose from five bedrooms with private baths. Two feature suites with lake views and private

---

NOTES: Credit cards accepted: A Master Card; B Visa; C American Express; D Discover; E Diners Club; F Other; 2 Personal checks accepted; 3 Lunch available; 4 Dinner available; 5 Open all year;

Port City Victorian Inn

double whirlpools. Enjoy the rooftop balcony and TV/VCR room with a view of the lake. The main floor is all common area for our guests' enjoyment including two parlors (one with a fireplace), a large dining room, sunroom, and music room with piano. All rooms have air-conditioning, cable TV, and phones. Fax and bicycles available. AAA-approved.

Host: Barbara Schossau
Rooms: 5 (3 PB; 2 SB) $80-150
Full Breakfast
Credit Cards: A, B, C, D, E
Notes: 2, 5, 7, 8, 9, 10, 11, 12

ONEKAMA

Lake Breeze House

5089 Main Street, Box 301, 49675
(231) 889-4969
www.manistee.com/lakebreeze.html

Our two-story frame house on Portage Lake is yours with a shared bath, living room, and breakfast room. Each room has its own special charm with family antiques. Come, relax, and enjoy our back porch and the sounds of

the babbling creek. By reservation only. Boating and charter service available.

Hosts: Bill and Donna Erickson
Rooms: 3 (1 PB; 2 SB) $55-65
Full Breakfast
Credit Cards: None
Notes: 7, 8, 9, 10, 11

OWOSSO

Rossman's R & R Ranch

308 East Hibbard Road, 48867
(517) 723-2553; fax: (517) 729-9064

A newly remodeled farmhouse from the 1900s, the ranch sits on 130 acres overlooking the Maple River Valley. A large, concrete circular drive with white board fences leads to stables of horses and cattle. Area wildlife includes deer, fox, rabbits, pheasant, quail, and songbirds. Observe and explore from the farm lane, river walk, or outside deck. Country-like accents adorn the farmhouse interior, and guests are welcome to use the family parlor, garden, game room, and fireplace. Central air-conditioning.

Hosts: Carl and Jeanne Rossman
Rooms: 3 (SB) $55-60
Full Breakfast
Credit Cards: None
Notes: 2, 5, 6, 7, 10

PENTWATER

Historic Nickerson Inn

P.O. Box 986; 262 Lowell Street, 49449-0986
(231) 869-6731; (800) 742-1288
fax: (231) 869-6151

6 Pets welcome; 7 Children welcome; 8 Tennis nearby; 9 Swimming nearby; 10 Golf nearby; 11 Skiing nearby; 12 May be booked through travel agent

E-mail: nickerson@voyager.net
www.nickersoninn.com

Pentwater is nestled between the white sand beach of Lake Michigan and the calm waters of Pentwater Lake. The Nickerson Inn sits high on a hill just two short blocks from the beach with views of both lakes. Our village will remind you of a small New England town. The Nickerson Inn, with its distinctive veranda, has been a Pentwater landmark since 1913. Extensively renovated from 1990 to the present, the traditional sense of grace and casual charm has been maintained. Featuring casual, fine dining in our candlelit dining room. Refresh your spirit; recapture fond memories!

Hosts: Gretchen and Harry Shiparski
Rooms: 13 (PB) $85-235
Full Breakfast
Credit Cards: A, B, D
Notes: 2, 4, 8, 9, 10, 12

PITTSFORD

The Rocking Horse Inn

8652 North Street, 49271
(517) 523-3826

The Rocking Horse Inn

Our guests love sitting on the wrap-around porch of this Italianate-style farmhouse while sipping lemonade and eating the "dessert of the evening." The morning brings wonderful smells of a full breakfast. Close to Hillsdale College, shopping, and golf. Twenty-five minutes to MIS Speedway for NASCAR and Indy races. Packages and corporate rates are available. Four rooms are air-conditioned with TVs/VCRs, private baths, and full and queen beds.

Hosts: Mary Ann and Phil Meredith
Rooms: 4 (PB) $50-80
Full Breakfast
Credit Cards: A, B
Notes: 2, 5, 8, 9, 10

PORT HOPE

Stafford House

4489 Main Street (M-25), P.O. Box 204, 48468
(989) 428-4554
E-mail: staffordhouse@centurytel.net
www.laketolake.com

Peace and rest await your stay in our 1886 country Victorian home featuring original woodwork, marble fireplace, full and queen beds, and air-conditioning and cable TV. Delight in a full breakfast and evening desserts. Bicycles, historic walking tours, and snowshoes are available. Visit nearby lighthouses. Ask about our dinner packages. One-third mile from Lake Huron.

Hosts: Greg and Kathy Gephart
Rooms: 4 (PB) $65-90
Full Breakfast
Credit Cards: A, B
Notes: 2, 4, 5, 7, 9, 10, 11, 12

NOTES: Credit cards accepted: A Master Card; B Visa; C American Express; D Discover; E Diners Club; F Other; 2 Personal checks accepted; 3 Lunch available; 4 Dinner available; 5 Open all year;

SAGINAW

East Tawas Junction Bed & Breakfast Inn

514 West Bay Street, 48730
(989) 362-8006
E-mail: info@east-tawas
www.east-tawas.com

Twin Gables Inn

This turn-of-the-century country Victorian is in park-like setting overlooking beautiful Tawas Bay. The five bedrooms have private baths and cable TVs. Public areas include parlor with fireplace, piano, cable TV, VCR; glass enclosed wraparound porch; library; dining room; game room; and two decks. Sumptuous full breakfast. Just a few steps to the beach and a short walk to shops, restaurants, and churches Tawas State Park, biking, hiking, canoeing, golfing, and scenic routes are all nearby with year-round activities.

Hosts: Leigh and Donald Mott
Rooms: 5 (PB) $89-149
Full Breakfast
Credit Cards: A, B, D
Notes: 2, 5, 7, 8, 9

lax on the porch and delight in the sunset over Lake Kalamazoo. Our fourteen rooms have private baths and central air-conditioning; several with fireplaces, plus three cottages with kitchens. Gourmet breakfasts are served in a spacious common room. Enjoy the hot tub, fireplace, gardens, and summer pool.

Hosts: Bob Lawrence and Susan Schwaderer
Rooms: 14 (PB); 3 cottages $75-210
Full Breakfast
Credit Cards: A, B, C, D, E
Notes: 2, 5, 7, 8, 9, 10, 11

SAUGATUCK

Twin Gables Inn

900 Lake Street, P.O. Box 1150, 49453
(616) 857-4346; (800) 231- 2185
fax: (616) 857-3482
E-mail: relax@twingablesinn.com
www.twingablesinn.com

Enjoy personalized service at this historic B&B. We're a pleasant, romantic inn, just a short walk to the village center, while still being in a country-like setting on 1.25 rolling acres. Re-

6 Pets welcome; 7 Children welcome; 8 Tennis nearby; 9 Swimming nearby; 10 Golf nearby; 11 Skiing nearby; 12 May be booked through travel agent

MINNESOTA

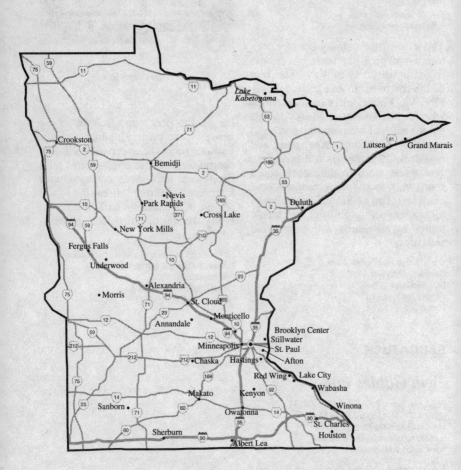

Minnesota

ALBERT LEA

Victorian Rose Inn

609 West Fountain Street, 56007
(507) 373-7602; (800) 252-6558
E-mail: inn@victorianrose.net
www.victorianrose.net

Queen Anne Victorian home (1898) in virtually original condition, with fine woodwork, antique light fixtures, stained glass, gingerbread, antique furnishings, and down comforters. Spacious rooms, one with fireplace. Air-conditioning. A full breakfast is served each day. Business/extended-stay rates and gift certificates offered. Children by arrangement; no pets; no smoking.

Hosts: Darrel and Linda Roemmich
Rooms: 4 (PB) $65-95
Full Breakfast
Credit Cards: A, B
Notes: 2, 5, 10, 12

ALEXANDRIA

Cedar Rose Inn
Bed & Breakfast

422 7th Avenue West, 56308
(320) 762-8430; (888) 203-5333
fax: (320) 762-8044
E-mail: cedarose@gctel.com
www.echopress.com/cedarose

From the wild blooming roses in the summer to the warm crackling fire in the winter, the Cedar Rose Inn offers year-round comfort for anyone away from home. Conveniently located within walking distance of downtown Alexandria, with its quaint shops and friendly people. The inn is located in the spectacular Minnesota lake country.

Hosts: Aggie and Florian Ledermann
Rooms: 4 (PB) $75-130
Full Breakfast
Credit Cards: A, B
Notes: 2, 5, 8, 9, 10, 11, 12

The Pillars
Bed & Breakfast

1004 Elm Street, 56308,
(320) 762-2700
E-mail: pillarbb@rea-alp.com
pillarsbandb.itgo.com

A turn-of-the-century home in the historic section of Alexandria and lake country, filled with antiques, collectibles, and charm of the era. Lovely gardens and sitting areas. Serene and comfortable. Close to shopping, eating, golf, and many lakes. Relax and allow us to pamper you.

Hosts: Jim and Anita Tollefson
Rooms: 5 (2 PB; 3 SB) $55-105
Full Breakfast
Credit Cards: A, B
Notes: 2, 5, 7, 8, 9, 10, 11

---

6 Pets welcome; 7 Children welcome; 8 Tennis nearby; 9 Swimming nearby; 10 Golf nearby; 11 Skiing nearby; 12 May be booked through travel agent

FERGUS FALLS

Bakketopp Hus
Bed & Breakfast

20571 Hillcrest Road, 56537
(218) 739-2915; (800) 739-2915
E-mail: ddn@prtel.com
www.bbonline.com/mn/bakketopp

Quiet, spacious lake home with vaulted ceilings, fireplaces, private spa, flower garden patio, and lakeside decks. Antique furnishings from family homestead; four-poster, draped, French canopy bed; and private baths. Here you can listen as loons call to each other across the lake in the still of dusk, witness the falling foliage splendor, relax by the crackling fire, or sink into the warmth of the spa after a day of hiking or skiing. Near antique shops and Maplewood State Park. Ten minutes off I-94. Gift certificates available. Reservation with deposit.

Hosts: Dennis and Judy Nims
Rooms: 3 (PB) $70-105
Full Breakfast
Credit Cards: A, B, D
Notes: 2, 5, 8, 9, 10, 11

HOUSTON

Addie's Attic
Bed & Breakfast

117 South Jackson, P.O. Box 677, 55943
(507) 896-3010; fax: (507) 896-4010

Beautiful, turn-of-the-century home, circa 1903. Cozy front parlor with curved-glass window. Games, TV, player piano. Rooms are decorated and furnished with "attic finds."

Addie's Attic

Hearty breakfast served in dining room. Near hiking, biking, cross-country ski trails, canoeing, and antique shops. Weekday rates.

Hosts: Fred and Marilyn Huhn
Rooms: 3 (SB) $40-50
Full Breakfast
Credit Cards: None
Notes: 2, 5, 8, 9, 10, 11

LUTSEN

Lindgren's
Bed & Breakfast
on Lake Superior

5552 County Road 35, P.O. Box 56, 55612
phone/fax: (218) 663-7450

This 1920s Northwoods, rustic lodge log home is in Superior National Forest on Lake Superior's walkable shoreline. This romantic, secluded hideaway on spacious, manicured grounds is like being on the ocean, surrounded by forest. Truly away from it all! Wildlife décor with Finnish sauna, fireplaces, whirlpool, baby grand piano, and TVs, VCRs, and CDs. In the center of an area known for skiing, fall colors, Superior

Hiking Trail, golf, state parks, rock collecting, fishing, mountain biking, horseback riding, alpine slide, Boundary Waters Canoe Area Wilderness, and art. One-half mile off scenic Highway 61 on the Lake Superior Circle Tour. Gift certificates. Three-diamond AAA-rated. Children over 12 welcome.

Host: Shirley Lindgren
Rooms: 4 (PB) $105-150
Continental Breakfast
Credit Cards: A, B
Notes: 2, 3, 5, 8, 9, 10, 11, 12

Lindgren's

MANKATO

Butler House Bed & Breakfast

704 South Broad Street, 56001
(507) 387-5055; fax: (507) 388-5462
E-mail: butlerhouse@bresnanlink.net
www.butlerhouse.com

This English-style (1905) mansion is elegantly furnished and includes a palatial porch, beautiful suites, canopy beds, whirlpool, fireplace, and private baths. Features include hand-painted murals, a Steinway grand pi-

Butler House

ano, window seats, and a large dining room. No smoking. Near the state trail, civic center, biking, skiing, golf, and antiquing. Come join us for an escape into a world of comfort and relaxation.

Hosts: Ron and Sharry Tschida
Rooms: 5 (PB) $55-115
Full Breakfast weekends; Continental Breakfast weekdays
Credit Cards: A, B, C
Notes: 2, 5, 8, 9, 10, 11, 12

OWATONNA

Northrop-Oftedahl House Bed & Breakfast

358 East Main Street, 55060
(507) 451-4040; fax: (507) 451-2755
E-mail: northoft@the bestbnb.com
northrop-oftedahl.com

This 1898 Victorian with stained glass is three blocks from downtown. One of 12 historical homes, it has original family furnishings, oak woodwork, and a six-foot footed bathtub. Home of the late Dr. Harson A. Northop (candidate for governor and the U.S. Senate) and Tessie Oftedahl

Northrop-Oftedahl House

Northop (humanitarian). The house is six miles from Cabela's Medford Outlet, 38 miles from the Mayo Clinic, 50 miles from Mall of America. Antiques and collectibles from the estate are on sale. Lunch or dinner is available with prior arrangement. See the Art Linkletter Room and the Dr. Joyce Brothers Rooms (celebrity guests of the B&B). Explore history with John Howard Northop (Nobel Prize winner), Jack Northop (Flying Wing/ Stealth bomber), and more.

Hosts: Jean and Darrell Stewart; Gregory Northop
Rooms: 7 (2 PB; 5 SB) $70-100
Full Breakfast
Credit Cards: None
Notes: 2, 3, 4, 5, 6, 7, 8, 9, 10, 11, 12

SAINT CHARLES

Thoreson's Carriage House Bed & Breakfast

606 Wabasha Avenue, 55972
(507) 932-3479

Located near beautiful Whitewater State Park with its swimming, trails, and demonstrations by the park naturalist. Horseback riding available nearby. We are in Amish territory, and just minutes from the world-famous Mayo Clinic. Piano and videos available. Write for brochure.

Host: Moneta Thoreson
Rooms: 2 (SB) $45-50
Full Breakfast
Credit Cards: None
Notes: 2, 5, 7, 8, 9, 10

SANBORN

Sod House Bed & Breakfast

12598 Magnolia Avenue, 56083
(507) 723-5138
E-mail: sodhouse@springfield-sanborn.net

This authentic replica of an 1880 sod house is surrounded by prairie grasses and wildflowers. Charming one-room house is fully furnished, lit by oil lamps, and heated by wood-burning stoves. Clothes to play "prairie dress-up" are provided. The Sod House is 20 miles east of Walnut Grove, childhood home of Laura Ingalls. Full breakfast served to you. Children wel-

Sod House

come; no pets please; smoking permitted.

Host: Virginia McCone
Rooms: 1 (PB) $100-150
Full Breakfast
Credit Cards: None
Notes: 2, 7

SHERBURN

Four Columns Inn

668 140th Street, 56171
(507) 764-8861

Enjoy Scandinavian hospitality in an antique-filled, lovingly remodeled, Greek Revival inn. Four antique-filled bedrooms, clawfoot tubs, and working fireplaces welcome guests. A library, circular stairway, living room with grand piano, and a solarium with Jacuzzi make a stay here memorable. A hideaway bridal suite, perfect for honeymooners or anniversary couples, has access to a roof deck with a super view of the countryside. A hearty breakfast is served in the formal dining room, on the balcony, in the gazebo, or in the kitchen by the fireplace. Near Iowa's Lake Okobogi, antiques, amusement park, and live, summer theater. Two miles north of I-90 between Chicago and the Black Hills. Call for brochure. No smoking. Children welcome by arrangement.

Hosts: Norman and Pennie Kittleson
Rooms: 5 (PB) $70-80
Full Breakfast
Credit Cards: None
Notes: 2, 5, 7, 8, 9, 10, 11, 12

STILLWATER

James Mulvey Residence Inn

622 West Churchill Street, 55082
(651) 430-8008; (800) 820-8008
fax: (651) 430-2801
E-mail: truettldem@aol.com
www.jamesmulveyinn.com

This is an enchanting place. Built in 1878 by lumberman James A. Mulvey, the Italianate residence and stone

James Mulvey Residence Inn

carriage house grace the most visited historic river town in the upper Mid West. Exclusively for you are the grand parlor, formal dining room, Victorian sunporch, and seven fabulously decorated guest rooms filled with exquisite art and antiques. The inn offers a four-course breakfast, double whirlpools, fireplaces, mountain bikes, and air-conditioning. You'll receive grace-filled service from innkeepers who care.

Hosts: Truett and Jill Lawson
Rooms: 7 (PB) $99-219
Full Breakfast
Credit Cards: A, B, C, D
Notes: 2, 5, 8, 9, 10, 11, 12

MISSISSIPPI

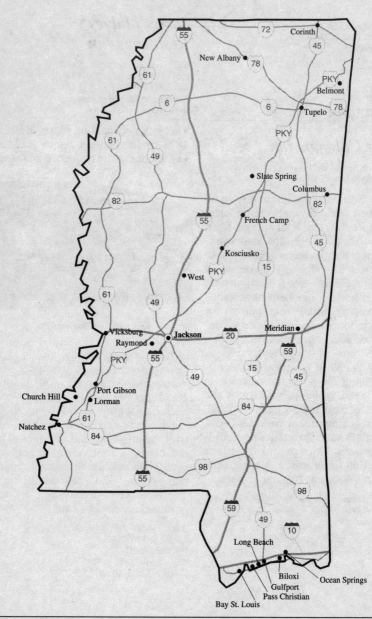

NOTES: Credit cards accepted: A Master Card; B Visa; C American Express; D Discover; E Diners Club; F Other; 2 Personal checks accepted; 3 Lunch available; 4 Dinner available; 5 Open all year;

Mississippi

BILOXI

The Old Santini House Bed & Breakfast

The Old Santini House

964 Beach Boulevard, 39530
(228) 436-4078; (800) 686-1146
fax: (228) 432-9193
E-mail: jad39530@cs.com
www.santinibnb.com

Enjoy the gulf view and breeze as you sit on the front gallery of our circa 1837 "American Cottage" featuring twelve-foot ceilings, expansive rooms with private baths, king beds, and cable TV. Each room has individual coffee/tea stations. The servants' quarters features a two-room suite, Jacuzzi tub, wet bar, refrigerator, and private porch. AAA-approved. Relive the quaint charm of the early 1800s in our 160 year-old B&B listed on the National Register of Historic Places. Located on over an acre of park-like grounds across from the beach, convenient to all attractions.

Hosts: James and Patricia Dunay
Rooms: 4 (PB) $80-175
Full Breakfast
Credit Cards: A, B, C, D
Notes: 5, 8, 9, 10, 11, 12

CORINTH

The Generals' Quarters Bed & Breakfast Inn

924 Fillmore Street, 38834
(662) 286-3325; (800) 664-1866
fax: (662) 287-8188
E-mail: genqtrs@tsixroads.com
www.tsixroads.com/~gengtrs

Two Victorian Homes (circa 1872 & 1909) connected by lovely gardens, are located in the historic district of an old Civil War town. Both homes have been recently remodeled and provide a taste of history combined with mod-

The Generals' Quarters

---

6 Pets welcome; 7 Children welcome; 8 Tennis nearby; 9 Swimming nearby; 10 Golf nearby; 11 Skiing nearby; 12 May be booked through travel agent

ern conveniences. All rooms have TV/VCR, fireplaces, telephones, data ports, antique furnishings, lovely views, and private baths. A wonderful breakfast is prepared each day by our chef. Early morning coffee and muffins are also available. Our inn is rated among the top 10 B&B's in the state, and has been featured on PBS, and in *Mississippi* magazine.

Hosts: Luke and Charlotte Doehner
Rooms: 10 (PB) $75-120
Full Breakfast
Credit Cards: A, B, D
Notes: 5, 7, 8, 9, 10, 12

FRENCH CAMP

French Camp Bed & Breakfast Inn

P.O. Box 120, 39745-0120
(662) 547-6835; fax: (662) 547-9591
E-mail: fcainfo@frenchcamp.org
www.frenchcamp.org

Welcome to the old-fashioned comfort of the only inn on the Natchez Trace-French Camp Academy's B&B Inn. Be our guest. Experience fresh sheets, clinked log walls, and air that is scented with the sweet smell of pine and cypress. Enjoy the spacious view of shaggy forest and unrestricted wildlife from the wide-eyed windows of this rustic inn made from two log cabins, each more than 100 years old. Awake and indulge in Southern cooking at its finest. A traditional countrystyle breakfast of homemade breads and muffins, creamy grits, fresh eggs, crispy bacon, and homemade jams and jellies won't taste any better than here. So, whenever you travel the Trace, stop and experience true hospitality French Camp style. Our B&B Inn and quaint log cottage have four comfortable bedrooms, each with a private bath. We can easily accommodate eight visitors with additional space for children. Leave a recorded message if no one is home or call the Development Office at French Camp Academy (662) 547-6482.

Hosts: Paul and Donna Perkins
Rooms: 5 (PB) $60-75
Full Breakfast
Credit Cards: None
Notes: 2, 3, 4, 5, 7, 8, 9

JACKSON

Fairview Inn

734 Fairview Street, 39202
(601) 948-3429; (888) 948-1908
fax: (601) 948-1203
E-mail: fairview@fairviewinn.com
www.fairviewinn.com

The Fairview Inn is a Colonial Revival mansion listed on the National Historic Register. Its elegant and comfortable ambience is accented by fine

Fairview Inn

NOTES: Credit cards accepted: A Master Card; B Visa; C American Express; D Discover; E Diners Club; F Other; 2 Personal checks accepted; 3 Lunch available; 4 Dinner available; 5 Open all year;

fabrics and antiques in a historic neighborhood. Near churches, shopping, two colleges, and major medical complexes. AAA award, four diamonds; "Top Inn of 1994" award by *Country Inns* magazine. "The Fairview Inn is southern hospitality at its best."—*Travel & Leisure*.

Hosts: Carol and Bill Simmons
Rooms: 18 (PB) $115-290
Full Breakfast
Credit Cards: A, B, C, D
Notes: 2, 4, 5, 8, 9, 10, 12

LONG BEACH

Red Creek Inn, Vineyard, & Racing Stable

Red Creek Inn

7416 Red Creek Road, 39560
(228) 452-3080; (800) 729-9670
fax: (228) 452-4450
E-mail: info@redcreekinn.com
www.redcreekinn.com

This raised French cottage was built in 1899 by a retired Italian sea captain to entice his young bride away from her parents' home in New Orleans. Red Creek Inn, Vineyard, and Racing Stable is situated on 11 acres with an-

cient live oaks and fragrant magnolias, and is a delight with its peaceful comforts. A 64-foot-long porch complete with porch swings provides relaxation for guests, and the inn is furnished in antiques for guests' enjoyment. A new marble Jacuzzi awaits in the Victorian Room. A ministerial discount of 10 percent is offered.

Hosts: Karl and Toni Mertz
Rooms: 7 (5 PB; 2 SB) $49-124
Continental Breakfast
Credit Cards: None
Notes: 2, 3, 4, 5, 7, 9, 10, 12

NATCHEZ

Monmouth Plantation

36 Melrose Avenue, 39120
(601) 442-5852; (800) 828-4531
fax: (601) 446-7762
E-mail: luxury@monmouthplantation.com
www.monmouthplantation.com

Built in 1818, Monmouth was once the home of General John A. Quitman, a Mexican war hero and early governor of Mississippi. Visitors to Monmouth can enjoy 26 acres of

Monmouth Plantation

---

6 Pets welcome; 7 Children welcome; 8 Tennis nearby; 9 Swimming nearby; 10 Golf nearby; 11 Skiing nearby; 12 May be booked through travel agent

beautifully landscaped gardens. All buildings are set amid pebble paths and brick sidewalks, magnolias and moss-draped oaks. With 30 beautifully appointed rooms, exquisite antiques, and an outstanding collection of carved four-poster and canopy beds, Monmouth awaits to enfold you in luxury and service.

Hosts: Ron and Lani Riches
Rooms: 30 (PB) $155-275
Full Breakfast
Credit Cards: A, B, C, D, E
Notes: 2, 4, 5, 8, 10, 12

NATCHEZ TRACE

Natchez Trace Bed & Breakfast Reservation Service

P.O. Box 193, Hampshire, TN, 38461
(913) 285-2777; (800) 377-2770
E-mail: natcheztrace@worldnet.att.net
www.bbonline.com/natcheztrace

This reservation service is unusual in that all the homes listed are close to the Natchez Trace, the delightful National Parkway running from Nashville, Tennessee, to Natchez, Mississippi. Kay Jones can help you plan your trip along the Trace, with homestays in interesting and historic homes along the way. Many locations of bed and breakfasts, including in the cities of Ashland City, Columbia, FairView, Franklin, Hohenwald, and Nashville, Tennessee; Florence and Cherokee, Alabama; and Church Hill, Corinth, French Camp, Kosciusko, Lorman, Natchez, New Albany, Tupelo, and Vicksburg, Mississippi. $60-125.

PORT GIBSON

Oak Square Plantation

1207 Church Street, 39150-2609
(601) 437-4350; (800) 729-0240
fax: (601) 437-5768
E-mail: oaksquare@cs.com

This restored antebellum mansion of the Old South is in the town General U. S. Grant said was "too beautiful to burn." On the National Register of Historic Places, it has family heirloom antiques and canopied beds and is air-conditioned. Your hostess's families have been in Mississippi 200 years. Christ is the Lord of this house. "But as for me and my house, we will serve the Lord" (Joshua 24:15). Located on U.S. Highway 61, adjacent to the Natchez Trace Parkway.

Hosts: Mr. and Mrs. William Lum
Rooms: 10 (PB) $95-135
Full Breakfast
Credit Cards: A, B, C, D
Notes: 2, 5, 7, 12

VICKSBURG

Annabelle Bed & Breakfast Inn

501 Speed Street, 39180
(601) 638-2000; (800) 791-2000
fax: (601) 636-5054
E-mail: annabelle@vicksburg.com
www.annabellebnb.com

At Annabelle, built circa 1868, you'll experience the grand feeling of a bygone era; an era of the genteel life. Relax in the beautifully furnished parlor or on a veranda by a trickling fountain. Stroll through the old courtyard shaded by giant Magnolia trees.

NOTES: Credit cards accepted: A Master Card; B Visa; C American Express; D Discover; E Diners Club; F Other; 2 Personal checks accepted; 3 Lunch available; 4 Dinner available; 5 Open all year;

Annabelle

Refresh yourself with a dip in the sparkling swimming pool and snuggle into a big, luxuriously comfortable bed. Listed in *Fodor's Best B&Bs of the South*. AAA 3 diamonds, Mobil Guides 3 stars.

Hosts: George and Carolyn Mayer
Rooms: 8 (PB) $93-125
Full Breakfast
Credit Cards: A, B, C, D
Notes: 2, 5, 8, 9, 10, 12

Cedar Grove Mansion Inn

2200 Oak Street, 39180
(601) 636-1000; (800) 862-1300
fax: (601) 636-6126
E-mail: info@cedargrove.com
www.cedargroveinn.com

Cedar Grove Mansion
Circa 1840

Capture "Gone with the Wind" elegance and romance in exquisite guest rooms/suites in the mansion or one of the historic cottages. Each room is lavishly decorated with period antiques combined with the conveniences of private bath, cable television, telephone, and air-conditioning. Bask in the luxury of an elegant time and let Cedar Groves dedicated staff spoil you.

Hosts: Ted Mackey and Pamela Netterville
Rooms: 30 (PB) $95-185
Continental Breakfast
Credit Cards: A, B, C, D
Notes: 4, 5, 7, 8, 9, 10, 12

---

6 Pets welcome; 7 Children welcome; 8 Tennis nearby; 9 Swimming nearby; 10 Golf nearby; 11 Skiing nearby; 12 May be booked through travel agent

MISSOURI

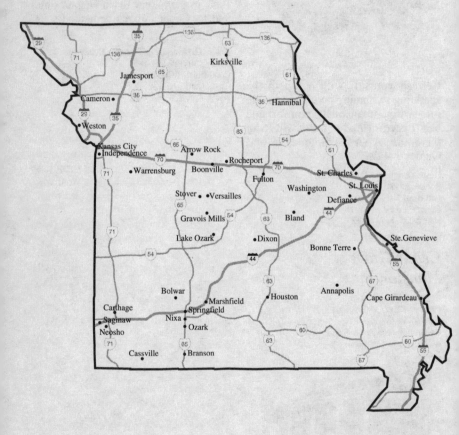

Missouri

ANNAPOLIS

Rachel's Bed & Breakfast

202 West Second Street, 63620
(573) 598-4656; (888) 245-7771
fax: (573) 598-3439
E-mail: info@rachelsbb.com
www.rachelsbb.com

The Old Bolch Mansion, built in 1920, is now home to Rachel's B&B, where the innkeepers make an effort to get to know every guest, and yet allow for privacy as desired. Rachel's is a Christ-centered home with private decks, entrances, and two-person Jacuzzis. The home is available for large or small groups; it hosts many church-related events annually. We count it an honor to serve the children of God.

Hosts: Joe and Sharon Cluck
Rooms: 7 (PB) $55-125
Full Breakfast
Credit Cards: A, B, C, D
Notes: 2, 4, 5, 7, 9, 10, 11, 12

Caverly Farm and Orchard

three bedrooms, all with private bath, a parlor and sunroom for visiting, and a spacious dining room. The farm has a stocked pond for fishing, a freshwater creek, and space to walk and play. Antique shopping, winery tours, country auctions, and country fairs are nearby. The guest rooms on the second floor are accessible with an electric stair chair; no steps on the first floor.

Hosts: David and Nancy Caverly
Rooms: 3 (PB) $60
Full Breakfast
Credit Cards: None
Notes: 2, 4, 5, 7

BLAND

Caverly Farm & Orchard Bed & Breakfast

100 Cedar Ridge Road, 65014
(573) 646-3732; fax: (573) 646-5274
E-mail: caverlydn@socket.net

Our remodeled 1860 farmhouse on 57 acres of Ozark Hill country features

BOLIVAR

Bavarian Bed & Breakfast

105 East Freeman, 65613
(417) 777-5964; (888) 296-7037

This is a beautifully restored 1914 Bavarian Craftsman home. The individually decorated rooms are both

---

6 Pets welcome; 7 Children welcome; 8 Tennis nearby; 9 Swimming nearby; 10 Golf nearby; 11 Skiing nearby; 12 May be booked through travel agent

comfortable and romantic. Gourmet breakfasts with an international flair are graciously served. Your hostess will also provide special treats and complimentary tea and coffee. Enjoy a stroll to the historic city square, museum, tea room, and specialty and antique shops. You will be 30 scenic minutes from Bass Pro Headquarters in Springfield and only 90 minutes from Branson, Missouri.

Rooms: 3 (1 PB; 2 SB) $55-65
Full Breakfast
Credit Cards: A, B, D
Notes: 5, 7, 10

BONNE TERRE

Victorian Veranda Bed & Breakfast

207 East School Street, 63628
(573) 358-1134; (800) 343-1134
E-mail: victoriaveranda@ldd.net
www.bbim.org/vicveranda

This elegant, 1880 Victorian mansion overlooks the town's Bicentennial Park. Choose from four romantic guest rooms, all with a private bath. Guests may relax in the parlor or cozy up to the fireplace in the gathering room. The aroma of freshly ground coffee and variety of home-baked goodies will guide the guest to the large dining room for a candlelight breakfast. Escape to a quiet getaway, and enjoy the porch swing on our large wraparound veranda.

Hosts: Galen and Karen Forney
Rooms: 4 (PB) $70-110
Full Breakfast
Credit Cards: A, B, D
Notes: 2, 5, 7, 8, 9, 10, 12

BRANSON

Cameron's Crag

P.O. Box 295, 65615
phone/fax: (417) 335-8134; (800) 933-8529
E-mail: mgcameron@aol.com
www.cameronscrag.com

Cameron's Crag is located high on a bluff overlooking Lake Taneycomo and the valley, three miles south of Branson. Guests enjoy a spectacular view from a new, spacious, detached private suite with private tub, whirlpool tub, kitchen, and living-and-bedroom area. Also available is a two-room suite with indoor hot tub and private bath. A third room has a great view of the lake and a private hot tub on the deck. All rooms have king beds, hot tubs, private entrances, TVs/VCRs, and a video library.

Hosts: Glen and Kay Cameron
Rooms: 3 (PB) $85-115
Full Breakfast
Credit Cards: A, B, D
Notes: 2, 5, 7, 8, 9, 10, 12

Grandpa's Farm Bed & Breakfast

4738 West State Highway 86, Lampe, 65681
(417) 779-5106
E-mail: keithpat@interlinc.net
www.grandpasfarmbandb.com

A real, old-time, 116-acre Ozark Mountain farm with plenty of friendly animal life. Choose from the luxurious Honeymoon Suite with spa, Red Bud Suite with large whirlpool tub, Dogwood Suite with kitchenette, and Mother Hen Room. Near Branson, Missouri, and Eureka Springs, Arkansas. A big country breakfast is

---

NOTES: Credit cards accepted: A Master Card; B Visa; C American Express; D Discover; E Diners Club; F Other; 2 Personal checks accepted; 3 Lunch available; 4 Dinner available; 5 Open all year;

served on a screened-in porch. There are secret hideout lofts for children.

Hosts: Keith and Pat Lamb
Rooms: 4 (PB) $65-95
Full Breakfast
Credit Cards: A, B, D
Notes: 2, 5, 7, 9, 12

Josie's Peaceful Getaway

508 Tablerock Circle, 65616
(417) 338-2978; (800) 289-4125
www.josiesbandb.com

Pristine, gorgeous lakefront scenery on Table Rock Lake where sunsets and moonlit nights lace the sky. The contemporary design features cathedral ceilings and stone fireplaces mingled with a Victorian flair. Cozy, wood-burning fireplaces, lavish Jacuzzi spas, candlelight, and fresh flowers abound. Dine in luxury as you enjoy breakfast served on china and crystal. Celebrate your honeymoon or anniversary in style. Eight miles from Branson and music shows; five minutes from Silver Dollar City/Marina. Smoke-free environment.

Hosts: Bill and Jo Anne Coats
Rooms: 2 (PB) $85-125
Continental Breakfast
Credit Cards: A, B, C, D
Notes: 2, 5, 7, 9, 10, 12

Lakeshore Bed & Breakfast

47 Elm Lane, 65616
phone/fax: (417) 338-2698; (800) 285-9739
www.lakeshorebandb.com

A peaceful place on beautiful Table Rock Lake, two miles from Silver Dollar City, this contemporary home offers boat docks, a paddle boat, and

Lakeshore

glide swing-for-four. All three units have queen beds, TV/VCR, coffee bar, refrigerator and microwave, and private bath. A family unit for six has a private entrance, a covered patio overlooking the lake, kitchen, and sitting area with sofa and chairs. The Honeymoon unit has a private deck, sofa and chair, and whirlpool tub. A nutritious, hearty breakfast is served in a smoke-free environment.

Host: Gladys Lemley
Rooms: 3 (PB) $55-90
Full Breakfast
Credit Cards: None
Notes: 2, 5, 7, 9, 10, 11, 12

Schrolls Lakefront Bed & Breakfast

418 North Sycamore Street, 65616
(417) 335-6759; (800) 285-8830
E-mail: patchworkquilt@msn.com

When you visit this lovely lakefront inn in Branson, you can fish for trout from the dock or a boat, or stroll three blocks into downtown to enjoy the many shops, restaurants, and other attractions. Silver Dollar City and music shows are nearby. All suites overlook the lake and have Jacuzzi tubs, full kitchens, and TVs. A full country breakfast is served in our

---

6 Pets welcome; 7 Children welcome; 8 Tennis nearby; 9 Swimming nearby; 10 Golf nearby; 11 Skiing nearby; 12 May be booked through travel agent

breakfast room overlooking the lake. Outdoor hot tub. Honeymoon specials available.

Hosts: Jeff and Mendy Schroll
Rooms: 3 (PB) $55-85
Full Breakfast
Credit Cards: A, B, D
Notes: 2, 5, 7, 8, 9, 10, 11, 12

CAMERON

Cook's Country Cottage Bed & Breakfast

7880 Northeast Bacon Road, 64429
(816) 632-1776

A perfect country hideaway to escape the fast pace of today's society. Relax in luxury and have your every whim catered to. Water gardens, lakes to fish, trails to walk, birds and wildlife to watch, and porches where you may rock are a few options to enjoy. Candlelight dinners and day tours to historical sites and Missouri's largest Amish community. "Coming home" was never better!

Hosts: Don and Loura Cook
Rooms: 2 (PB) $65-85
Full Breakfast
Credit Cards: None
Notes: 2, 3, 4, 5, 8, 9, 10, 11

CARTHAGE

The Leggett House Bed & Breakfast

1106 Grand Avenue, 64836
(417) 358-0683; fax: (417) 359-8999
E-mail: bjm0329@aol.com
www.leggetthouse.com

Innkeepers Michael and Bonnie Melvin extend a warm welcome and invite you to share their home. The Victorian Carthage Stone house built in 1901 has period decor, beveled and curved windows, and an open staircase with beautiful woodwork. The Solarium with its marble foun-tain is a perfect nook for reading. Enjoy the

The Leggett House

front porch swing and watch the world go by. Nearby attractions: historical Carthage Courthouse and square, Precious Moments, Civil War museum, Stone's Throw Theatre.

Hosts: Michael and Bonnie Melvin
Rooms: 5 (4 PB; 1 SB) $75-85
Full Breakfast
Credit Cards: A, B, C
Notes: 2, 5, 8, 9, 10

CASSVILLE

Allsburys' Bed & Breakfast

3 Dogwood Hills, 65625
(417) 847-2706
E-mail: sidall@mo-net.com
www.allsburys.com

NOTES: Credit cards accepted: A Master Card; B Visa; C American Express; D Discover; E Diners Club; F Other; 2 Personal checks accepted; 3 Lunch available; 4 Dinner available; 5 Open all year;

Allsburys' B&B is located in the beautiful Ozark Hills close to trout and lake fishing; an easy drive to Branson and Eureka Springs, AK. A woods-surrounded suite includes two bedrooms, a bathroom, and a great room featuring a fireplace, dining area, kitchenette, and private entrance. One mile from Roaring River State Park; five miles south of Cassville.

Hosts: Sid and Mary Allsbury
Rooms: 1 suite (PB) $85
Full Breakfast
Credit Cards: None
Notes: 2, 5, 9, 10

Parsons House

Hosts: Al and Carol Keyes
Rooms: 3 (PB) $95-110
Full Breakfast
Credit Cards: A, B, D
Notes: 2, 5, 7, 10

DEFIANCE

Parsons House Bed & Breakfast

211 Lee Street, 63341
(636) 798-2222; (800) 355-6878
fax: (636) 798-2220
E-mail: mkeyes@win.com
www.theparsonshouse.com

This stately, 1842 Federalist home overlooks the Missouri River Valley. Listed in the Historic Survey, it features an antique-furnished gathering room and guest rooms. On eight acres, the gardens feature fountains, a hammock, and spa. This antebellum home has fireplaces, a large library, and an enclosed porch where afternoon tea is served. Nearby are the Daniel Boone Home, wineries, and Katy Bicycle Trail, yet St. Louis is only 35 miles away. Amenities include central air-conditioning and private baths. Our huge, country breakfast is an "Event!"

FULTON

Loganberry Inn

310 West Seventh Street, 65251
(573) 642-9229; (888) 866-6661
E-mail: loganberry@socket.net
www.loganberryinn.com

The Loganberry Inn is a top-rated B&B in the heart of historic Fulton. The inn is conveniently located just

Loganberry Inn

6 Pets welcome; 7 Children welcome; 8 Tennis nearby; 9 Swimming nearby; 10 Golf nearby; 11 Skiing nearby; 12 May be booked through travel agent

off I-70 between St. Louis and Kansas City. This inviting 1899 Victorian hosted Margaret Thatcher and Scotland Yard in 1996. Enjoy elegant and gracious surroundings with marble fireplaces, wood floors, antiques, quilts, and stained glass. Stroll to restaurants, shops, and museums. Savor special pampering, like fresh-baked cookies, in-room tea service, Jacuzzi, and indulgent bed linens.

Hosts: Carl and Cathy McGeorge
Rooms: 4 (PB) $75-160
Full Breakfast
Credit Cards: A, B, C, D
Notes: 2, 5, 6, 7, 8, 10

Romancing the Past Victorian Inn

830 Court Street, 65251
(573) 592-1996
E-mail: innkeeper@socket.net
www.romancingthepast.com

A spacious lawn and serene gardens enfold this 1860s home in central Missouri in a graceful old neighborhood. The inn boasts a grand hall with magnificent arch and staircase, and elegantly appointed rooms with period adornments. Lavish antiques, fireplaces, bed drapings and florals can be found throughout, as well as six fireplaces, luxurious baths, indoor and outdoor spas, and aromatherapies. Enjoy excellent food; many amenities to pamper you. Walk to many fascinating amusements. Children over eight welcome.

Hosts: Jim and Renée Yeager
Rooms: 3 (PB) $100-170
Full Breakfast
Credit Cards: A, B, C, D
Notes: 2, 3, 4, 7, 8, 9, 10

GRAVOIS MILLS

Buck Creek Bed & Breakfast

32907 Buck Creek Acres Road, 65073
(573) 372-1212; fax: (573) 372-3737

Four guest rooms on the second floor; have your choice of king- or queen-size bed. Full breakfast served daily at 8 A.M. overlooking the beautiful Lake of the Ozarks. "A beautiful place to relax in a family atmosphere."

Hosts: Richard and June Hackathorn
Rooms: 4 (2 PB; 2 SB) $65-95
Full Breakfast
Credit Cards: None
Notes: 2, 5, 7, 9, 10

HANNIBAL

Fifth Street Mansion Bed & Breakfast Inn

213 South 5th Street, 63401
(573) 221-0445; (800) 878-5661
fax: (573) 221-3335
E-mail: fifthstbb@nemonet.com
hannibal.com/fifthstreetbedandbreakfast

Fifth Street Mansion

NOTES: Credit cards accepted: A Master Card; B Visa; C American Express; D Discover; E Diners Club; F Other; 2 Personal checks accepted; 3 Lunch available; 4 Dinner available; 5 Open all year;

This historic mansion built in 1858 brings a more gracious past alive with its antiques, period décor, original fireplaces, chandeliers, and stained glass. Perfect for a romantic getaway, convenient for both business travelers and sightseers, it is also ideal for a longer, refreshing vacation. Walk to the Mark Twain historic district, the riverfront, shops, and restaurants. Golf courses and lake area nearby. Family reunions, weddings, and retreats are accommodated. Hospitality is our hallmark.

Host: Donalene Andreotti
Rooms: 7 (PB) $85-105
Full Breakfast
Credit Cards: A, B, C, D
Notes: 2, 5, 7, 8, 9, 10, 12

Windstone House

ment with games, books, a TV, and a VCR.

Host: Barbara Kimes
Rooms: 3 (1 PB; 2 SB) $50-60
Full Breakfast
Credit Cards: None
Notes: 2, 5, 10

HOUSTON

Windstone House Bed & Breakfast

539 Cleveland Road, 65483
(417) 967-2008
E-mail: windstone@pcis.net

Windstone House is a large, two-story home with a spacious wraparound porch and balcony, sitting in the middle of more than 80 acres that provide a breathtaking view of the Ozark Mountains and countryside. The home has been tastefully furnished with a collection of antiques. In warm weather, breakfast is served on the balcony overlooking a spectacular panorama of meadows and woodland. If you are bent on unwinding, then this is the place for you. There is a special sitting room for your enjoy-

INDEPENDENCE

Woodstock Inn Bed & Breakfast

1212 West Lexington Avenue, 64050
(816) 833-2233; (800) 276-5202
www.independence-missouri.com

Nestled within Independence's famous historical district, the Woodstock Inn B&B, a-turn-of-the-century doll and quilt factory, has an ideal location. The Inn is just a short stroll from all the major sites of Independence, and any Kansas City destination is less than 30 minutes from the Inn. Today, the Woodstock Inn is a luxury B&B featuring a fenced-in courtyard and garden area, thermomassage spa tubs, fireplaces, TVs and VCRs, CD players and a wealth of fine collectibles, rare antiques, and priceless artwork from around the world. All eleven of the Inn's

6 Pets welcome; 7 Children welcome; 8 Tennis nearby; 9 Swimming nearby; 10 Golf nearby; 11 Skiing nearby; 12 May be booked through travel agent

uniquely and beautifully appointed guest rooms include a minibar refrigerator, hair dryer, extension make-up mirror, alarm clock radio, individual climate control, Sprint PCS phone, private bath and, of course, our full breakfast featuring our famous malted Belgian waffles. Be sure to ask about our special romance packages and remember, gift certificates make great presents!

Hosts: Todd and Patricia Justice
Rooms: 11 (PB) $75-207
Full Breakfast
Credit Cards: A, B, C, D
Notes: 2, 5, 12

KANSAS CITY

Mulberry Hill Bed & Breakfast

226 North Armstrong, 64080
(816) 540-3457
E-mail: mulberryhill@earthlink.net
mulberryhillbandb.com

Come relax and let us pamper you in our 1904 colonial-style home located in a quiet country town only 30-45 minutes from most Kansas City attractions. Locally, enjoy antiques, golf, swimming, country music shows, and relaxing. A delicious full breakfast is served daily featuring our melt-in-your-mouth Belgian waffles. Our spacious honeymoon suite has a Jacuzzi-for-two and is perfect for your wedding night, anniversary, or other special occasion.

Hosts: Roy and Patricia Keck
Rooms: 5 (PB) $60-100
Full Breakfast
Credit Cards: A, B, D
Notes: 2, 5, 9, 10, 12

KIRKSVILLE

Travelers Inn Christian Bed & Breakfast

301 West Washington Street, 63501
(660) 665-5191; (800) 320-5191
fax: (660) 665-0825
www.travelers-inn-bnb.com

Built in 1922, the Inn's 22 theme rooms with elegant decor still reflect a rich history from the days when Harry S. Truman walked its hallways. Lo-

Travelers Inn

cated just a short drive from Thousand Hills State Park and Lake, it provides the perfect setting for a getaway or overnight stay. You'll find a peaceful atmosphere with Christian hospitality and a hot breakfast every morning of your stay. The Inn has a restaurant, book store, chocolate and gift shop, and conference room onsite. Historical sites and shopping within walking distance. Every room air-conditioned with extra amenities. Single, double, and suites available.

Host: Janice Smith
Rooms: 22 (PB) $74.95-125
Full Breakfast
Credit Cards: A, B, C, D
Notes: 3, 5, 7, 8, 9, 10, 12

LAKE OF THE OZARKS

Castleview Bed & Breakfast

R.R. 1, Box 183M, Camdenton, 65020
(573) 346-9818; (877) 346-9818
fax: (573) 346-9818
E-mail: allers@usmo.com
www.lakelinks.com/castleview

Castleview is an elegant yet comfortable modern Victorian with a beautiful view of the Lake of the Ozarks. Nestled next to Ha Ha Tonka State Park with castle ruins and hiking trails, it is a nature lover's paradise. Golf, fish, boat, or shop at the 100+-store outlet mall. Or relax in our gazebo by the pond and let us pamper you with our Romance Packages. Perfect for small weddings, anniversaries, birthdays. Children welcome over 12.

Hosts: Rod and Kathleen Allers
Rooms: 4 (PB) $94-99
Gourmet Breakfast
Credit Cards: A, B
Notes: 2, 5, 7, 8, 9, 10

The Dickey House

décor, double Jacuzzi, fireplace, and cable TV. The inn and dining room are enhanced by a display of fine American and European art and antiques. A gourmet breakfast is served in Victorian style amid fine china, silver, and crystal. The B&B has a four-diamond AAA rating.

Hosts: Larry and Michalene Stevens
Rooms: 7 (PB) $65-145
Full Breakfast
Credit Cards: A, B, C, D
Notes: 2, 5, 8, 9, 10, 12

MARSHFIELD

The Dickey House Bed & Breakfast

331 South Clay Street, 65706
(417) 468-3000; (800) 450-7444
E-mail: info@dickeyhouse.com
www.dickeyhouse.com

This mansion situated on an acre of park-like grounds is one of Missouri's finest B&B inns. The Dickey House offers three antique-filled guest rooms with private baths, plus four spectacular suites with luxuriously appointed

NIXA

Wooden Horse Bed & Breakfast

1007 West Sterling Court, 65714
(417) 724-8756; (800) 724-8756
fax: (417) 725-3853
E-mail: bigoaktree@msn.com
www.bbonline.com/mo/woodenhorse/

Come create a memory at this quiet country setting, where you'll experience the warm atmosphere of the Rocking Horse Room, or the shimmering floral décor of the Carousel

Room. Enjoy the sprinkling of antiques, collections, and wood-burning stove in the living room with TV/VCR. Relaxing outside includes a deck, the spa, gardens, and a swing in the big oak. Indulge in the hearty, full breakfast. Between Springfield and Branson, the Wooden Horse is a member of Bed and Breakfast Inns of Missouri. Children over age 9 welcome.

Host: Valeta Hammar
Rooms: 2 (PB) $90
Full Breakfast
Credit Cards: None
Notes: 2, 5, 6, 7, 8, 9, 10, 12

OZARK

Dear's Rest
Bed & Breakfast

1408 Capp Hill Ranch Road, 65721
(417) 581-3839; (800) 588-2262
fax: (417) 581-3839
E-mail: stay@dearsrest.com
www.dearsrest.com

Luxury accommodations; Amish-built cabin surrounded by nature. Enjoy a hot tub under the stars or cozy up to a

Dear's Rest

stone, woodburning fireplace. Start your day with a plentiful breakfast; then enjoy hiking, exploring Bull Creek, or a shopping trip for antiques or at the many outlet malls. Entertainment abounds in Branson. We accommodate only one party at a time, providing our guests complete privacy. Isaiah 40:31.

Hosts: Linda and Allan Schilter
Rooms: 1 suite (PB) $125
Full Breakfast
Credit Cards: A, B, D
Notes: 2, 5, 6, 7, 9, 10, 12

SPRINGFIELD

Virginia Rose
Bed & Breakfast

317 East Glenwood Street, 65807
(417) 883-0693; (800) 345-1412
bbonline.com/mo/virginiarose

This two-story farmhouse, built in 1906, offers country hospitality right in town. Situated on a tree-covered acre, our home is furnished with early-1900s antiques, quilts on queen beds, and rockers on the porch. Relax in the parlor with a book, puzzle, or game, or watch a movie on the TV/VCR. We are located only minutes from BASS Pro Outdoor World, restaurants, shopping, antique shops, and miniature golf, and only 40 miles from Branson. Inspected and approved by the Bed and Breakfast Inns of Missouri.

Hosts: Jackie and Virginia Buck
Rooms: 5 (PB) $60-120
Full Breakfast
Credit Cards: A, B, C, D
Notes: 2, 5, 7, 9, 10, 12

NOTES: Credit cards accepted: A Master Card; B Visa; C American Express; D Discover; E Diners Club; F Other; 2 Personal checks accepted; 3 Lunch available; 4 Dinner available; 5 Open all year;

STOVER

The Nestle Down Inn

5157 Whispering Timbers Road, 65078
(573) 377-2670; (888) 284-9650
fax: (573) 377-4190
E-mail: williams1@access2k1.net

The Nestle Down Inn is an upscale retreat nestled in the woods on a private lake stocked with catfish, bluegill, and bass, with a covered dock and paddleboat available. The condo-style Inn is a single unit, accommodating four adults comfortably. It is greatroom style, with furnished kitchen, two large bedrooms, comfortable king-sized beds, one bath, covered patio, grill, and laundry room. A delicious pre-prepared breakfast allows you to sleep in. Clergy discount available.

Hosts: John and Nancy Williams
Rooms: 2 (SB) $79.95 per couple
Full Breakfast
Credit Cards: None
Notes: 2, 5

VARIOUS CITIES

Ozark Mountain Country Bed & Breakfast Service

P.O. Box 295, 65616
phone/fax: (417) 334-4720; (800) 695-1546
E-mail: mgcameron@aol.com

Ozark Mountain Country has been arranging accommodations for guests in southwestern Missouri and Northwestern Arkansas since 1982. Our services are free. In the current list of more than 100 homes and small inns, some locations offer private entrances, fantastic views, guest sitting areas, swimming pools, Jacuzzis, and/or fireplaces. Most locations are available all year. Personal checks accepted. Some homes welcome children, a few welcome pets (even horses). Write for complimentary host brochure describing the B&Bs available, listings, and discount coupons. Coordinator: Kay Cameron. $45-195. Major credit cards accepted.

VERSAILLES

The Hilty Inn Bed & Breakfast

206 East Jasper Street, 65084
(573) 378-2020; (800) 667-8093
www.bbim.org/hilty

The Hilty Inn

Come enjoy a relaxing atmosphere away from the rush. This is off the beaten path on your way to Branson, mid-way through Missouri. There is a Mennonite Community to visit, as well as the Lake of the Ozarks. We also have a community theatre group

6 Pets welcome; 7 Children welcome; 8 Tennis nearby; 9 Swimming nearby; 10 Golf nearby; 11 Skiing nearby; 12 May be booked through travel agent

that gives wonderful performances. Please check the schedule with me.

Host: Doris Hilty
Rooms: 4 (PB) $65-105
Full Breakfast
Credit Cards: A, B, C, D
Notes: 2, 3, 4, 5, 7, 10

WARRENSBURG

The Camel Crossing

210 East Gay Street, 64093
(660) 429-2973; fax: (660) 429-2722
E-mail: camelx@iland.net
www.bbim.org/camelx/index.html

Ride a magic carpet to this B&B that is homey in atmosphere, but museum-like in its décor. Brass, copper, hand-tied carpets, and furnishings from the Far East will captivate your imagination. An oasis for mind and body. Phillipians 4:8. If you come a stranger, you'll leave as a friend. Smoking permitted outside only.

Hosts: Ed and Joyce Barnes
Rooms: 4 (2 PB; 2 SB) $70-90
Full Breakfast
Credit Cards: A, B
Notes: 2, 5, 8, 9, 10

Good House Bed & Breakfast

707 North Holden, 64093
(660) 747-9563
E-mail: goodhouse@imail.net

Multiple sitting areas create a pastoral setting at this 1903 Victorian mansion, inside and out. The original stained-, leaded-, and cut-glass windows, and golden oak staircase, fireplace, and entry mirror let visitors revisit the past without loss of modern amenities. There is ample off-street parking. Come, relax, and enjoy our combined eras under majestic oaks.

Host: Nita Good
Rooms: 2 (PB) $75
Full Breakfast
Credit Cards: A, B, D
Notes: 2, 5, 7, 8, 9, 10

Old Drum Inn

315 East Gay Street, 64093
(660) 422-8334
E-mail: olddrum@iland.net
www.olddruminn.com

This 1910 Empire home is filled with antiques for a casual elegance. Watch the world go by from rocking chairs on the wide front porch. Enjoy the peace of the gurgling fountains and profusion of flowers on the patio garden. Sit out under the stars warmed by the patio fireplace. Books and box games in the library. Hammock under the tree. Romantic guest rooms. Cozy robes, thick towels. King and queen beds. Nice innkeepers!

Hosts: Heidi and Roger Gauert
Rooms: 3 (1 PB; 2 SB) $75-80
Full Breakfast
Credit Cards: A, B, C, D
Notes: 2, 5, 8, 9, 10, 12

Montana

BILLINGS

Josephine
Bed & Breakfast

514 North 29th Street, 59101-1128
(406) 248-5898; (800) 552-5898
E-mail: josephine@imt.net
www.thejosephine.com

A lovely, historic home within walking distance of downtown, minutes from airport, and one hour to skiing and Little Big Horn Battlefield. Comfortable, elegant, antique-filled rooms each with private bath, modem-friendly phone, cable TV, and air-conditioning. Two suites, one with romantic whirlpool tub. Yesteryear dining room, study, parlor, and porch. Full gourmet breakfast. AAA two-diamond rating.

Hosts: Doug and Becky Taylor
Rooms: 5 (PB) $75-160
Full Breakfast
Credit Cards: A, B, C, D
Notes: 2, 5, 8, 9, 10, 11, 12

BOZEMAN

The Lehrkind Mansion
Bed & Breakfast

719 North Wallace Avenue, 59715-3063
(406) 585-6932; (800) 992-6932
E-mail: lehrkindmansion@imt.net
www.bozemanbedandbreakfast.com

Featured on the cover of June 2001 Victorian Homes magazine, the mansion is listed in the National Register and was built in 1897. It offers one of Montana's finest examples of Victorian Queen Anne architecture. A spacious yard and gardens, porches, and the large corner tower are among this three-story mansion's spectacular features. Period antiques throughout. The music parlor features Victrolas and a rare 1897 Regina music box—seven feet tall! Queen beds, comforters, and overstuffed chairs. A large hot tub will soak away the aches of an active day. Seven blocks off the historic Main Street shopping district.

Hosts: Jon Gerster and Christopher Nixon
Rooms: 5 (3 PB; 2 SB) $79-159
Full Breakfast
Credit Cards: A, B, C, D
Notes: 2, 5, 7, 8, 9, 10, 11

EMIGRANT

Johnstad's Bed & Breakfast
& Log Cabin

03 Paradise Lane, P.O. Box 981, 59027
phone/fax: (406) 333-9003; (800) 340-4993
E-mail: rjohnstad@aol.com
www.wtp.net/go/johnstad

Johnstad's B&B and log cabin are strategically located in Paradise Valley, just 36 miles north of Yellowstone National Park. The newly built B&B was designed for the comfort of

---

6 Pets welcome; 7 Children welcome; 8 Tennis nearby; 9 Swimming nearby; 10 Golf nearby; 11 Skiing nearby; 12 May be booked through travel agent

MONTANA

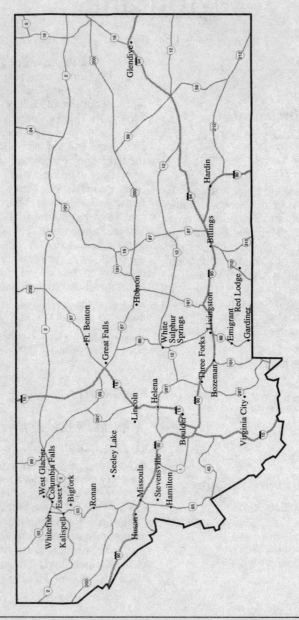

NOTES: Credit cards accepted: A Master Card; B Visa; C American Express; D Discover; E Diners Club; F Other; 2 Personal checks accepted; 3 Lunch available; 4 Dinner available; 5 Open all year;

Johnstad's

our guests and features spacious, beautifully decorated rooms, all with private baths and spectacular views of the valley. Each morning our guests enjoy a hearty breakfast served either in the dining room or on the deck. And just a few feet away you can enjoy fly fishing at its best in the Yellowstone River. Also available is our log cabin which features three bedrooms, two baths, a fully equipped kitchen, laundry facilities, and panoramic views of the Absaroka Mountain range. Come and enjoy classic Montana hospitality in the heart of Paradise Valley. Member of the Montana B&B Association.

Hosts: Ron and Mary Ellen Johnstad
Rooms: 3 (PB) $85-135
Full Breakfast
Credit Cards: A, B, D
Notes: 2, 5, 8, 9, 10, 11

FORT BENTON

Long's Landing Bed & Breakfast

1011 17th Street, P.O. Box 935, 59442
(406) 622-3461; fax: (406) 622-3455
E-mail: longsbnb@juno.com
www.longsbedandbreakfast.com

Experience Western hospitality at Long's Landing B&B in Fort Benton, Montana at 1011 17th Street and the corner of Washington. The downtown area is an easy walk of three blocks away. Open May 1st-November 1st. Come as a guest and leave as a friend.

Host: Amy Long
Rooms: 3 (1 PS; 2 SB) $50
Continental Breakfast
Credit Cards: None
Notes: 2, 8, 9, 10

GARDINER

Headwaters of the Yellowstone Bed & Breakfast

9 Olson Lane, P.O. Box 25, 59030
(406) 848-7073; fax: (406) 848-7420
E-mail: mervo@headwatersbandb.com
www.headwatersbandb.com

Our home on the pristine Yellowstone River, five minutes from the north entrance of Yellowstone Park, is a quiet place where you can enjoy the spectacular views of Yellowstone's high country and native wildlife, cast a line in the river, have a picnic in the shade, or just appreciate a respite after viewing the wonders of Yellowstone. Each guest room has a great view, a private bath, and a comfortable bed to provide a refreshing night's sleep. In the morning we will send you on your way after a hearty Montana breakfast.

Rated by and member of the Montana B&B Association.

Hosts: Joyce and Merv Olson
Rooms: 6 (PB) $85-125
Full Breakfast
Credit Cards: A, B
Notes: 2, 5, 7, 9, 11, 12

Paradise Gateway Bed & Breakfast & Log Cabins

P.O. Box 84, 59027
(406) 333-4063; (800) 541-4113
fax: (406) 333-4626
E-mail: paradise@gomontana.com
www.wtp.net/go/paradise

Paradise Gateway B&B, on 20 acres just minutes from Yellowstone National Park, offers quiet, charming, comfortable guest rooms in the shadow of the majestic Rocky Mountains. As day breaks, enjoy a country, gourmet breakfast by the banks of the Yellowstone River, a noted blue-ribbon trout stream. A "cowboy treat tray" is served in the afternoon.The Emigrant Peak Log Cabin is located on 28 acres of Yellowstone River frontage next to the B&B. Another modern, two-bedroom cabin on 20 acres offers laundry services and a complete kitchen. Decorated in country charm. Extremely private. Member of the Montana Bed and Breakfast Association. Pets welcome in kennels only.

Hosts: Pete and Carol Reed
Rooms: 4 (PB); 2 cabins $85-175
Full Breakfast
Credit Cards: A, B
Notes: 2, 5, 7, 8, 9, 10, 11, 12

GLENDIVE

The Hostetler House Bed & Breakfast

113 North Douglas Street, 59330
(406) 377-4505; (800) 965-8456
fax: (406) 377-8456
E-mail: hostetler@midrivers.com

Two blocks from downtown shopping and restaurants, the Hostetler House B&B is a charming, 1912 historic home with two comfortable guest rooms, a sitting room, sunporch, tandem bicycle, and hot tub. A full

The Hostetler House

gourmet breakfast is served on Grandma's china. Located on I-94 and the Yellowstone River, close to parks, swimming pool, tennis courts, golf course, antique shops, and churches. Craig and Dea invite you to "arrive as a guest and leave as a friend."

Hosts: Craig and Dea Hostetler
Rooms: 3 (1 PB; 2 SB) $50-65
Full Breakfast
Credit Cards: None
Notes: 2, 5, 8, 9, 10, 11

NOTES: Credit cards accepted: A Master Card; B Visa; C American Express; D Discover; E Diners Club; F Other; 2 Personal checks accepted; 3 Lunch available; 4 Dinner available; 5 Open all year;

Greystone Inn

LIVINGSTON

Greystone Inn
Bed & Breakfast & Cabins

122 South Yellowstone Street, 59047
phone/fax: (406) 222-8319

"Step back in time" at the Greystone Inn, with its turn-of-the-century charm. The inn is located two blocks from historic downtown Livingston, and four blocks from the Yellowstone River. Enjoy a made-from-scratch breakfast. We also have two cabins to choose from. One is a stone's throw to the Yellowstone River, great for fishermen and families. The other is in the mountains, located just this side of heaven.

Hosts: Lin and Gary Lee
Rooms: 3 (1 PB; 2 SB) $65-110
Full Breakfast
Credit Cards: None
Notes: 2, 5, 7, 8, 9, 10, 11, 12

RONAN

Zarephath Inn

2280 Leighton Road, 59864
(406) 676-3451
E-mail: zarephath@hotmail.com
www.angelfire.com/mt/zarephath

This English Tudor-style home is furnished in antiques and offers a beautiful view of a pond and the Mission Mountains. In a country setting, it is located two hours south of Glacier Park and a half hour from the National Bison Range. You'll find plenty of golfing, hiking, and skiing nearby. Flathead Lake with all its water sports is only 15 minutes away. Lunch and dinner are available upon request.

Hosts: Jim and Barbara Ball
Rooms: 3 (1 PB; 2SB) $65-75
Full Breakfast
Credit Cards: None
Notes: 2, 3, 4, 5, 8, 9, 10, 11, 12

SEELEY LAKE

Rocky Mountain Retreat

1535 Grandview, 59868
(406) 677-3023; (877) 378-7947
fax: (406) 677-2544
E-mail: bandb@rockymtnretreat
www.rockymtnretreat.com

The warm hospitality of the West awaits you at Rocky Mountain Retreat, located in a peaceful wooded area, overlooking a six-acre pond. Nestled in the mountains, it is far from the hustle and bustle of the world. A Montana Lumberjack breakfast is served in the cozy sunroom.

6 Pets welcome; 7 Children welcome; 8 Tennis nearby; 9 Swimming nearby; 10 Golf nearby; 11 Skiing nearby; 12 May be booked through travel agent

Here you can bird watch, see the ducks play on the pond, and view wildlife in the surrounding forest. Year round, the Spectacular Seeley Lake Valley has it all—lakes, streams, rivers, mountains, waterfalls, wildlife. Special vacation packages.

Stonehouse Inn

Rocky Mountain Retreat

Hosts: Will and Ilowee Owens
Rooms: 3 (PB) $50-70
Full Breakfast
Credit Cards: A, B, D
Notes: 2, 5, 7, 10, 11

VIRGINIA CITY

Stonehouse Inn Bed & Breakfast

P.O. Box 205, 59755-0205
(406) 843-5504

Located on a quiet street only blocks from the historic section of Virginia City, this Victorian stone home is listed on the National Register of Historic Places. Brass beds and antiques in every room give the inn a romantic touch. Five bedrooms share two baths.

Full breakfasts are served each morning, and smoking is allowed on our porches. Skiing, snowmobiling, golfing, hunting, and fly-fishing nearby.

Hosts: John and Linda Hamilton
Rooms: 5 (SB) $65
Full Breakfast
Credit Cards: A, B
Notes: 2, 5, 7, 8, 10, 12

WHITEFISH

Tucker's Inn & Guest Ranch

P.O. Box 220, 227 Magnesia Creek Road, Trego, 59934
(406) 882-4200; (800) 500-3541
fax:: (406) 882-4201
E-mail: tuckrinn@libby.org
www.tuckersinn.com

Nestled in the Glacier Outback, our ranch features a Jacuzzi suite or log-style cabins that sleep 10 to 12 people and offer fireplaces, a bath and a half, a fully equipped kitchen, and outdoor hot tub, basketball, horseshoes, volleyball, evening bonfires, and a breathtaking mountain setting. Summer activities: horseback riding, whitewater rafting, chuckwagon dinner, Glacier Park, canoeing, and swimming. Winter activities: snowmobiling, skiing, snowshoeing, and sledding. A wonderful family getaway. Where you come as a guest but leave as family!

Hosts: Jan and Charles Tucker
Rooms: 4 cabins (PB); 1 suite (PB) $125-175
Continental Breakfast
Credit Cards: A, B, C, D
Notes: 2, 3, 4, 5, 7, 9, 10, 11, 12

NEBRASKA

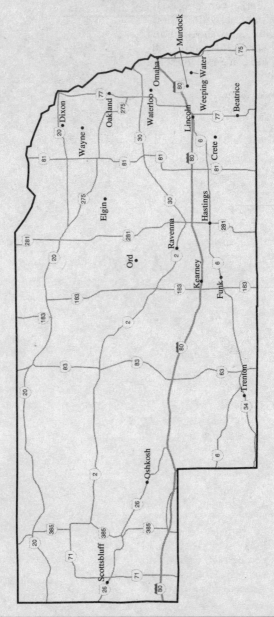

Nebraska

KEARNEY

Uncle Sam's Hilltop Lodge

74451 R. Road, Box 110, Funk, 68940
(308) 995-5568
E-mail: samslodge@hotmail.com

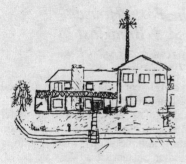

Uncle Sam's

Uncle Sam says "we want you to be our guest." Located five minutes from Interstate 80, close to Kearney, our spacious 1979 solar home is built into Nebraska's sandhills. All four levels are ground level with an indoor sand pile and game room. Two rooms are available: a brass queen bed with private bath, and an antique four-poster full bed with a shared bath and sunken tub-for-two. Relax by the fireplaces or tour the nearby Pioneer Village, Cabela's, Morris Cookbooks, Phelps County Museum and the Great Platte River Road Archway Monument; see the Sandhill Cranes. The rare white ones have been seen on our land. Start your day with a hearty country breakfast served in the formal dining room and end with a complimentary bedtime snack.

Hosts: Sam and Sharon
Rooms: 2 (1 PB; 1 SB) $50-60
Full Breakfast
Credit Cards: D
Notes: 2, 5, 6, 7, 8, 9, 10

LINCOLN

Atwood House

740 South 17th Street, 68508
(402) 438-4567; (800) 884-6554
fax: (402) 477-8314
E-mail: larry@atwoodhouse.com
www.atwoodhouse.com

"Experience the elegance" of a suite in this 7,500-plus square-foot, 1894 neoclassical Georgian Revival mansion. Suites have queen/king beds, private sitting areas with TV/VCR,

Atwood House

---

6 Pets welcome; 7 Children welcome; 8 Tennis nearby; 9 Swimming nearby; 10 Golf nearby; 11 Skiing nearby; 12 May be booked through travel agent

and private bath (three with two-person whirlpools). The Atwood Suite is Lincoln's most elegant bridal suite. It provides more than 800 square feet of ambience. Breakfast is served as late as 11 A.M. on bone china with sterling flatware, Waterford crystal, and linens. Great for the business traveler as well as for that special occasion.

Hosts: Ruth and Larry Stoll
Rooms: 4 (PB) $85-179
Full Breakfast
Credit Cards: A, B, C, D
Notes: 2, 5, 8, 9, 10

OAKLAND

Benson Bed & Breakfast

402 North Oakland Avenue, 68045
(402) 685-6051
E-mail: sanderson@genesisnet.net
www.bbonline.com/ne/benson/

Located in the center of a small town, Benson B&B is beautifully decorated and offers a breakfast you won't soon forget served in the dining room with all its finery. Features include a large collection of soft-drink collectibles, a library full of books, a beautiful gar-

THE BENSON BUILDING
Oakland, Nebraska

den room to relax in, and a large whirlpool tub with color TV on the wall. All rooms are on the second level. Three blocks west of Highway 77. No smoking.

Hosts: Stan and Norma Anderson
Rooms: 3 (SB) $55-60
Full Breakfast
Credit Cards: D
Notes: 2, 5, 8, 9, 10, 12

OMAHA

The Farm House Bed & Breakfast

32617 Church Road, Murdock, 68407
(402) 867-2062

This 100-year-old home is on a paved road in the country. It offers handmade quilts, antiques, and an angel collection. Near aircraft museum, Zoo Safari, antique shops, malls, summer theather, restaurants, two state parks, and two auto race tracks. Quiet, relaxed, and affordable; only 30 minutes from Lincoln or Omaha. Hiking and biking trails, porch swing, horseshoe pits, croquet set, games, videos, private parlor, and air-conditioning.

Hosts: Mike and Pat Meierhenry
Rooms: 4 (2 PB; 2 SB) $40-55
Full Breakfast
Credit Cards: None
Notes: 2, 5, 7, 8, 9, 10

The Jones'

1617 South 90th Street, 68124
(402) 397-0721

Large, private residence with large deck and gazebo in the back. Fresh cinnamon rolls are served for breakfast. Your hosts' interests include golf, travel, needlework, and meeting other people. Located 5 minutes from I-80.

Hosts: Theo and Don Jones
Rooms: 3 (1 PB; 2 SB) $35
Continental Breakfast
Credit Cards: None
Notes: 2, 5, 6, 7, 8

ORD

The Shepherds' Inn Bed & Breakfast

Route 3, Box 108A, 68862
(308) 728-3306; (800) 901-8649
E-mail: ddvshep@cornhusker.net
www.bbonline.com/ne/shepherd

Treat yourself to a quiet escape in the heart of the country. Watch the sunrise, walk along a country road, or spend a lazy afternoon on our lawn swing. Spend an evening reading in the parlor or gaze at the star-studded skies while relaxing in the outdoor hot tub. This charming early 1900s farmhouse is furnished with exquisite antiques in Victorian décor. A full

country breakfast is served. Innkeepers live a shout away.

Hosts: Doris and Don Vancura
Rooms: 3 (PB) $65
Full Breakfast
Credit Cards: A, B
Notes: 2, 5, 7, 8, 9, 10, 11

OSHKOSH

The Locust Tree Bed & Breakfast

400 West 5th Street, 69154
(308) 772-3530
E-mail: pregier@lakemac.net
www.rimstarintl.com/loc00001.htm

Enjoy small-town hospitality in a contemporary family home. The large brick home is graced with majestic spruce and locust trees. Gracious guest rooms with baths. Continental breakfast. Access to free summer swimming, spa, Pony Express route, Ash Hollow State Park and Museum.

Hosts: Pete and Ardena Regier
Rooms: 2 (1 PB; 1 SB) $45-75
Continental Breakfast
Credit Cards: None
Notes: 2, 5, 7, 9, 10

RAVENNA

Aunt Betty's Bed & Breakfast

804 Grand Avenue, 68869
(308) 452-3739; (800) 632-9114

Enjoy the peace of a small town while staying at Aunt Betty's three-story Victorian B&B. Four bedrooms are furnished with antiques and decorated

---

6 Pets welcome; 7 Children welcome; 8 Tennis nearby; 9 Swimming nearby; 10 Golf nearby; 11 Skiing nearby; 12 May be booked through travel agent

with attention to detail. Relax in the sitting room while awaiting a delicious, full breakfast that includes Aunt Betty's "sticky buns" and homemade goodies. Stroll the flower garden with fishpond for relaxation. Accommodations for hunters in the hunter's loft. An antique shop is part of the B&B. Golf and tennis nearby. Only a half hour from I-80. Dinner available by appointment.

Hosts: Harvey and Betty Shrader
Rooms: 6 (3 PB; 3 SB) $55-65
Full Breakfast
Credit Cards: A, B
Notes: 2, 3, 4, 5, 7, 8, 9, 10

SCOTTSBLUFF

Barn Anew
Bed & Breakfast

170549 County Road L, Mitchell, 69357
(308) 632-8647; fax: (308) 632-5518
E-mail: barnanew@alltel.net
prairieweb.com/barnanew

Enjoy a country formal setting in this "reborn" 100-year-old barn located just minutes west of Scottsbluff in the shadow of Scotts Bluff National Monument and Museum. Very close to the historic Oregon Trail. Guest rooms furnished in Victorian antique furniture and appointments. Leisure room and sunroom available for guests' enjoyment. The formal dining room is surrounded by a mural of the farm in 1910. Breakfast by candlelight and browse through mini-museum and antique shop. Peace and quiet guaranteed. Double occupancy for husbands and wives.

Hosts: Dick and Jane Snell
Rooms: 4 (PB) $85-90
Full Breakfast
Credit Cards: A, B, C, D, E
Notes: 2, 5, 8, 9, 10

WAYNE

Swanson's
Bed & Breakfast

86334 Highway 15, 68787
(402) 584-2277

Come home to real country living in our hundred-year home, remodeled for comfort. Beautiful flowers, hot tub, and delicious home-cooked breakfast. Quiet country living with delicious, home-cooked breakfast and charming Mid-West hospitality, perfect for honeymooners, vacationers, business travelers, and hunters.

Hosts: Ernie and Lyla Swanson
Rooms: 3 (1 PB; 1 SB) $40-55
Full Breakfast
Credit Cards: None
Notes: 2, 5, 6, 7. 9, 10

WEEPING WATER

Lauritzen's Blue Heron
Bed & Breakfast

5102 Highway 50, 68463
(402) 267-3295
E-mail: blueheron@alltel.net
www.bbonline.com/ne/lauritzens/index.html

Country pleasures will be yours at Ken and Alice's comfortable farm. Specializing in romantic getaways. Linger over dinner, relax in the hot

---

NOTES: Credit cards accepted: A Master Card; B Visa; C American Express; D Discover; E Diners Club; F Other; 2 Personal checks accepted; 3 Lunch available; 4 Dinner available; 5 Open all year;

Lauritzen's Blue Heron

tub and enjoy a full home-cooked breakfast.

Hosts: Ken and Alice Lauritzen
Rooms: 2 (PB) $65-75
Full Breakfast
Credit Cards: A, B
Notes: 2, 4, 5, 9, 10

NEVADA

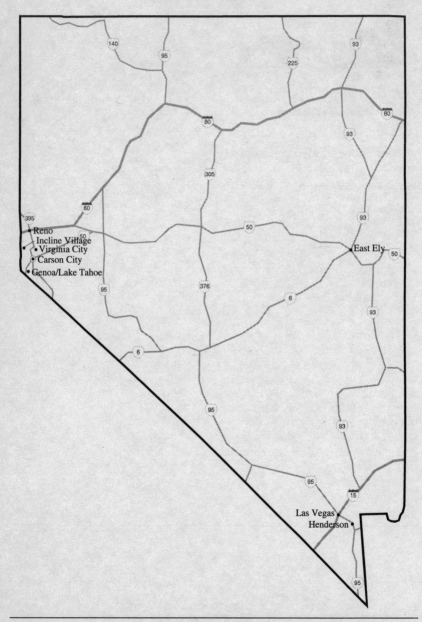

NOTES: Credit cards accepted: A Master Card; B Visa; C American Express; D Discover; E Diners Club; F Other; 2 Personal checks accepted; 3 Lunch available; 4 Dinner available; 5 Open all year;

Nevada

LAKE TAHOE

Genoa House Inn

180 Nixon Street, P.O. Box 141, 89411
(775) 782-7075
E-mail: genoahouseinn@pyramid.net
www.genoahouseinn.com

Genoa House Inn

Tucked against the mountain, Genoa, Nevada's first settlement is located in the green Carson Valley. The Genoa House was built in 1872 and it captures the spirit of an earlier time. Children 8 and over are welcome. Dogs welcome on approval.

Hosts: Bob and Linda Sanfilippo
Rooms: 3 (PB) $110-165
Full Breakfast
Credit Cards: A, B, D
Notes: 2, 5, 6, 7, 8, 9, 10, 11, 12

---

6 Pets welcome; 7 Children welcome; 8 Tennis nearby; 9 Swimming nearby; 10 Golf nearby; 11 Skiing nearby; 12 May be booked through travel agent

NEW HAMPSHIRE

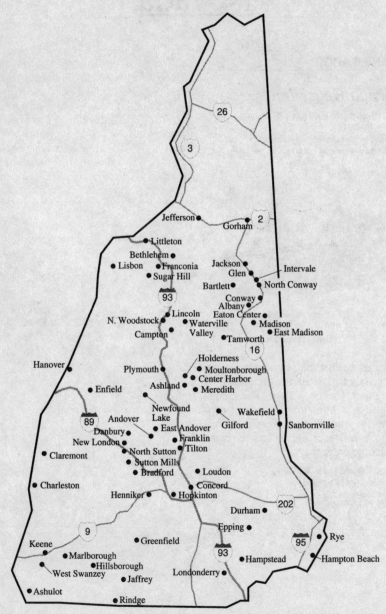

NOTES: Credit cards accepted: A Master Card; B Visa; C American Express; D Discover; E Diners Club; F Other; 2 Personal checks accepted; 3 Lunch available; 4 Dinner available; 5 Open all year;

New Hampshire

ASHLAND

Glynn House Inn
Bed & Breakfast

59 Highland Street, 03217-9714
(603) 968-3775; (800) 637-9599
fax: (603) 968-9415
E-mail: glynnhse@lr.nett
glynnhouse.com

Romantic escape in New Hampshire's majestic White Mountains and pristine Lakes Squam and Winnepesaukee. Honeymoon suites feature whirlpool for two, fireplace, and queen canopy bed. All rooms have TVs/VCRs and air-conditioning, and are smoke-free. Mobil- and AAA-rated. Less than two hours from Boston, one hour from Manchester airport. Directions: I-93 to exit 24.

Hosts: Karol and Betsy Paterman
Rooms: 11 (PB) $99-199
Full Breakfast
Credit Cards: A, B
Notes: 2, 5, 7, 8, 9, 10, 11

BETHLEHEM

The Mulburn Inn
at Bethlehem

2370 Main Street, 03574
(603) 869-3389; (800) 457-9440
E-mail: info@mulburninn.com
www.mulburninn.com

Step into a gracious age of elegance when you visit this historic inn originally built in 1908 as a Woolworth family summer estate. This beautiful Inn boasts wraparound porches, hardwood floors, stained glass, and three fireplaces. Relax in the cozy atmosphere where legends such as Cary Grant and Barbara Hutton once stayed. The Mulburn Inn is located in the heart of New Hampshire's White Mountains where hiking, golfing, skiing, and all of nature's splendors abound.

Hosts: Christina Ferraro and Alecia Loveless
Rooms: 7 (PB) $80-145
Full Breakfast
Credit Cards: A, B
Notes: 2, 5, 7, 8, 9, 10, 11, 12

BRADFORD

Candlelite Inn
Bed & Breakfast

5 Greenhouse Lane, 03221
(603) 938-5571; (888) 812-5571
fax: (603) 938-2564
E-mail: candlelite@conknet.com
www.virtualcitites.com/nh/candlelite.htm

CANDLELITE INN

---

6 Pets welcome; 7 Children welcome; 8 Tennis nearby; 9 Swimming nearby; 10 Golf nearby; 11 Skiing nearby; 12 May be booked through travel agent

Voted as the 2001 Inn of the Year, this 1897 country Victorian inn has all the grace and charm you'll want for that perfect getaway. We serve a full breakfast, right down to the dessert, in the Sun Room overlooking the pond. Relax on the gazebo porch, sipping lemonade on a lazy summer day, or curl up in the parlor in front of a crackling fire with a cup of warm cranberry cider. Come and experience the relaxed atmosphere and the quiet elegance of this all-seasons inn.

Hosts: Marilyn and Les Gordon
Rooms: 6 (PB) $80-110
Full Breakfast
Credit Cards: A, B, C, D, E
Notes: 2, 5, 8, 9, 10, 11, 12

CAMPTON

Mountain-Fare Inn

P.O. Box 553, 03223
(603) 726-4283

Lovely 1840s village home with the antiques, fabric, and feel of country cottage living. Gardens in summer, foliage in fall, and a true skier's lodge in winter. Accessible, peaceful, warm, friendly, and affordable. Unspoiled beauty from Franconia Notch to Squam Lake. Four-season sports, soccer field, tennis, championship golf course, music, theatre. Perfect for hiking vacations and family reunions.

Hosts: Susan and Nick Preston
Rooms: 10 (9 PB; 1 SB) $60-105
Full Breakfast
Credit Cards: None
Notes: 2, 3, 4, 5, 6, 7, 8, 9, 10, 11, 12

CHARLESTOWN

MapleHedge Bed & Breakfast Inn

355 Main Street, Route 12, P.O. Box 638, 03603
(603) 826-5237; (800) 9-MAPLE-9
E-mail: debrine@fmis.net
www.maplehedge.com

Rather than just touring homes two and a half centuries old, make one your "home away from home" while visiting western New Hampshire or eastern Vermont. MapleHedge offers distinctly different bedrooms with antiques that complement the individual décor. It has very tastefully added all modern-day amenities such as central air-conditioning, a fire sprinkler system, and queen beds. Enjoy a gourmet breakfast in the grand dining room of this magnificent home that is on the National Register and situated among 200-year-old maples and lovely gardens. Day trips show local attractions. Brochure sent on request. Highly rated by Mobil and ABBA. Closed January-March.

Hosts: Joan and Dick DeBrine
Rooms: 5 (PB) $90-105
Full Breakfast
Credit Cards: A, B
Notes: 9, 10, 11, 12

MapleHedge

CLAREMONT

Goddard Mansion Bed & Breakfast

25 Hillstead Road, 03743
(603) 543-0603
E-mail: deb@goddardmansion.com
www.goddardmansion.com

Goddard Mansion

Circa 1905, this mansion with adjacent garden tea house is set amid acres of lawns and gardens with panoramic mountain views. The beautifully restored, English manor-style, eighteen-room mansion has expansive porches and ten uniquely decorated guest rooms. The living room has a fireplace and window seats for cuddling up with a good book; enjoy the vintage baby grand piano. A 1939 Wurlitzer jukebox lights up a corner of the walnut-paneled dining room where a full, natural breakfast awaits guests each morning. Four-season activities, historic sites, cultural events, fun, and "fine" dining are nearby. The area is an antique buff's adventureland! Brochure available. Families welcome.

Host: Debbie Albee
Rooms: 10 (3 PB; 7 SB) $75-125
Full Breakfast
Credit Cards: A, B, C, D
Notes: 2, 5, 7, 8, 9, 10, 11

CONWAY

Darby Field Inn

185 Chase Hill Road, Albany, 03818
(603) 447-2181; (800) 426-4147
fax: (603) 447-5726
E-mail: marc@darbyfield.com
www.darbyfield.com

The Darby Field Country Inn and Restaurant, situated near New Hampshire's scenic Kancamagus Highway, is a perfect setting for weekend getaways or extended vacations. Nearby North Conway has great shopping and antiquing. The White Mountain National Forest abutting the inn offers nordic and alpine skiing, snowshoeing, hiking, mountain biking, and fishing. Return to the inn and enjoy swimming in our sparkling pool, soaking in our outdoor hot tub, quiet relaxation, fine dining, and friendly hospitality.

Hosts: Marc and Maria Donaldson
Rooms: 14 (PB) $120-240
Full Breakfast
Credit Cards: A, B, C
Notes: 2, 4, 5, 8, 9, 10, 11, 12
Full Breakfast

FRANCONIA

Franconia Inn

1300 Easton Road, 03580
(603) 823-5542; (800) 473-5299
fax: (603) 823-8078
E-mail: info@franconiainn.com
franconiainn.com

On a winding country road, just past Robert Frost's summer cottage, the Franconia Inn has been welcoming guests since 1886. Elegant American

---

Franconia Inn

cuisine highlights the Inn's quiet country sophistication. Year-round fun at the Inn includes hiking to secluded waterfalls, riding horseback through wooded streams, horsedrawn sleigh rides, cross-country skiing on groomed trails, tennis on clay courts, and poolside "New England Clam Bakes." Children are welcome! Rated three stars by AAA.

Hosts: Morris Family
Rooms: 35 (PB) $130-190
Full Breakfast
Credit Cards: A, B, C
Notes: 4, 5, 7, 8, 9, 10, 11, 12

FRANKLIN

Maria W. Atwood Inn

71 Hill Road, Route 3A, 03235-9803
(603) 934-3666
E-mail: info@atwoodinn.com
www.atwoodinn.com

Nestled in the heart of the Lakes Region, the Inn is convenient for all tourist attractions, restaurants, seasonal sports, and activities. Candles in the window welcome you to this 1830 brick Federal home that was restored in 2000. Spacious rooms, four with working fireplaces, all with private baths and comfortable beds. Hosts offer old-fashioned hospitality, scrumptuous breakfasts, and complimentary snacks. A unique experience you will want to enjoy again and again!

Maria W. Atwood

Hosts: Fred and Sandi Hoffmeister
Rooms: 7 (PB) $80-90
Full Breakfast
Credit Cards: A, B, C, D
Notes: 2, 5, 7, 8, 9, 10, 11

HAMPTON

D.W.'s Oceanside Inn

365 Ocean Boulevard, 03842
(603) 926-3542; fax: (603) 926-3549
E-mail: info@oceansideinn.com
www.oceansideinn.com

The Oceanside overlooks the Atlantic Ocean and its beautiful sandy beaches. The interior has been completely renovated and is immaculately maintained. All common areas, as well as the guest bedrooms reflect the owner's special attention to detail. Each of the ten rooms is tastefully and individually decorated, many with period antiques and all with private, modern baths. Lofty ceilings, oriental

NOTES: Credit cards accepted: A Master Card; B Visa; C American Express; D Discover; E Diners Club; F Other; 2 Personal checks accepted; 3 Lunch available; 4 Dinner available; 5 Open all year;

carpets, braided rugs, hand-screened wallpapers, and an eclectic mix of fine furnishings, paintings, and prints add to the intimacy and ambience.

Hosts: Skip and Debbie Windemiller
Rooms: 9 (PB) $120-185
Full Breakfast
Credit Cards: A, B, C, D
Notes: 9, 10

HANOVER

Shaker Farm Bed & Breakfast

597 NH Route 4-A, Enfield, 03748
(603) 632-7664; (800) 613-7664
fax: (603) 632-9290
E-mail: charlotte.toms@valley.net
www.shakerfarm.com

Historic Shaker property, circa 1794. The B&B offers lovely guest rooms with king beds, air-conditioning, TV, period décor, a legendary breakfast, warm country atmosphere, lake and mountain views, hiking trails, boating, swimming, and fishing. We pamper our guests. Dartmouth College is 10 miles away.

Hosts: Hal and Charlotte Toms
Rooms: 6 (4 PB; 2 SB) $75-135
Full Breakfast
Credit Cards: A, B
Notes: 2, 9, 10, 11

HOLDERNESS

The Inn on Golden Pond

Route 3, P.O. Box 680, 03245
(603) 968-7269; fax: (603) 968-9226
E-mail: innongp@lr.net
www.innongoldenpond.com

This 1879 colonial home is nestled on 50 wooded acres, offering guests a traditional New England setting. A short distance away is Squam Lake, setting for the classic film *On Golden Pond*. Guest rooms are individually decorated in traditional country style. A hearty, home-cooked breakfast each morning features farm-fresh eggs, homemade muffins, breads, and delicious house specialties.

Hosts: Bill and Bonnie Webb
Rooms: 8 (PB) $130-165
Full Breakfast
Credit Cards: A, B, C, D
Notes: 2, 5, 8, 9, 10, 11, 12

The Inn on Golden Pond

JACKSON

Ellis River House

Route 16, Box 656, 03846
(603) 383-9339; (800) 233-8309
fax: (603) 383-4142
E-mail: innkeeper@erhinn.com
www.erhinn.com

Sample true New England hospitality at this enchanting, small hotel/country inn within a short stroll of the village. The house has comfortable king and queen guest rooms decorated with

Ellis River House

Laura Ashley prints, some with fireplaces and two-person Jacuzzis, cable TV, scenic balconies, and period antiques; all with individually controlled heat and air-conditioning. Also available are two-room and family suites, a riverfront cottage, hot tub, sauna, heated pool, sitting and game rooms, and a sundeck overlooking the pristine Ellis River. Enjoy a breakfast with homemade breads or a delicious trout dinner. Relax with libations and billiards in the pub.

Hosts: Monica and Jim Lee
Rooms: 20 (PB) $95-295
Full Breakfast
Credit Cards: A, B, C, D, E
Notes: 2, 4, 5, 8, 9, 10, 11, 12

Nestlenook Farm Resort

P.O. Box Q, 03846
(603) 383-9443; (800) 659-9443
fax: (603) 383-4515
E-mail: mshaw@luxurymountaingetaways.com
www.nestlenook.com

Nestlenook Farm on the River. . .experience the romance of Victorian elegance on our 65-acre estate. Our smoke-free inn offers seven guest rooms, each with a private, two-person Jacuzzi bathroom, period antiques, and either parlor stove or fireplace. Full country breakfast and

afternoon hospitality hour daily! In winter enjoy views, horse-drawn sleigh rides, ice-skating, and snowshoeing. In summer enjoy daily horse-drawn champagne carriage ride, hiking, biking, row boating, and fly-fishing. Amenities include a year-round outdoor heated swimming pool, chapel, fireplaced lakeside gazebo, award-winning gardens, and much more! Our newest addition, Victorian Village, provides luxurious private accommodations with suites, penthouses, and two bedroom villas. Perched on a knoll overlooking the estate, these truly defy description!

Nestlenook Farm Resort

Host: Robert Cyr
Rooms: 21 (PB) $125-520
Full Breakfast
Credit Cards: A, B, D
Notes: 5, 7, 8, 9, 10, 11, 12

Whitney's Inn

Route 16B, P.O. Box 822, 03846
(603) 383-8916; (800) 677-5737
fax: (603) 383-6886
E-mail: whitneys@ncia.net
www.whitneysinn.com

Located in the heart of the White Mountains at the base of Black Moun-

---

NOTES: Credit cards accepted: A Master Card; B Visa; C American Express; D Discover; E Diners Club; F Other; 2 Personal checks accepted; 3 Lunch available; 4 Dinner available; 5 Open all year;

Whitney's Inn

tain, Whitney's Inn offers families and couples a great setting as a base for outdoor recreation. We have hiking, lawn games, a heated outdoor pool, mountain pond, and in winter, cross-country and downhill skiing at our doorstep, as well as skating and sledding. Nearby activities include golf, picnicking, and tax-free shopping. Come and relax with us.

Host: Bob Bowman
Rooms: 30 (PB) $70-155
Full Breakfast
Credit Cards: A, B, C, D, E
Notes: 2, 4, 5, 6, 7, 8, 9, 10, 11, 12

JEFFERSON

The Jefferson Inn

Route 2, 03583
(603) 586-7998; (800) 729-7908
fax: (603) 586-7808
E-mail: jeffinn@ncia.net
www.jeffersoninn.com

A warm, romantic 1896 renovated Victorian home nestled in the Northern White Mountains. There are mountain views in all directions. Each of the nine unique rooms and two family suites has a private bath and distinctive decor. Wake up each morning to a full breakfast. Spend the day hiking, cycling, or swimming in the summer; and skiing, ice skating, or snow-mobiling in the winter. The outdoor opportunities and attractions abound. Afternoon tea and homemade baked goods are served at the end of the day before you return to the comfort of your well-appointed room for another restful night.

Hosts: Mark and Cindy Robert and Bette Bovio
Rooms: 11 (PB) $85-175
Full Breakfast
Credit Cards: A, B, C, D
Notes: 2, 7, 8, 9, 10, 11, 12

KEENE

Carriage Barn Guest House Bed & Breakfast

358 Main Street, 03431
(603) 357-3812
E-mail: carriagebarn@webryders.net
www.carriagebarn.com

We have comfortable, peaceful, friendly accommodations in a country setting in the heart of a wonderful city. We are part of a historic gateway with museums, restaurants (acclaimed International Eating Center of New England), entertainment, shopping, and colleges all within walking distance, as well as bike trails and most sports. Mount Monadnick is the second most hiked mountain in the world and Keene hosts many events. Covered bridges, antiques, candles, and butterflies are all near.

Hosts: Dave and Marilee Rouillard
Rooms: 4 (PB) $75-125
Continental Breakfast
Credit Cards: A, B, C, D
Note: 5

6 Pets welcome; 7 Children welcome; 8 Tennis nearby; 9 Swimming nearby; 10 Golf nearby; 11 Skiing nearby; 12 May be booked through travel agent

MANCHESTER

The Greenfield Bed & Breakfast Inn

Box 400, Forest Road, Greenfield, 03047
(603) 547-6327; (800) 678-4144
fax: (603) 547-2418
E-mail: grenfieldinn@earthlink.net
www.greenfieldinn.com

Renovations in 1999 include whirl-pool tubs, Jacuzzis, and fireplaces. We can sleep six in the hayloft suite, two in the honeymoon hideaway suite, or six in the carriage house. The B&B features canopied beds, Victorian splendor, air-conditioning, TV/VCR, phone system, and hot tub. Children welcome. Multiday discounts, low weekly and monthly rates.

Hosts: Barbara and Vic Mangini
Rooms: 12 (9 PB; 3 SB) $49-79
Credit Cards: B
Notes: 2, 5, 7, 8, 9, 10, 11, 12

Stillmeadow Bed & Breakfast at Hampstead

545 Main Street,
    P.O. Box 565, Hampstead, 03841
(603) 329-8381; fax: (603) 329-0137
E-mail: stillmeadowb@yahoo.com
stillmeadowbandb.com

Historic 1850 home with five chimneys, three staircases, hardwood floors, oriental rugs, and woodstoves. Set on rolling meadows adjacent to conservation trails. Single, doubles, and suites, all with private baths. Families are welcome, with amenities such as a fenced-in play yard and children's playroom. Easy commute to Manchester and Boston. Complimentary refreshments—the cookie jar is always full! Formal dining/living rooms.

Host: Lori Offord
Rooms: 4 (PB) $60-90
Continental Breakfast
Credit Cards: A, B, C, D
Notes: 2, 5, 7, 8, 9, 10, 11

NEW LONDON

Inn at Pleasant Lake

P.O. Box 1030, 125 Pleasant Street, 03257-1030
(603) 526-6271; (800) 626-4907
fax: (603) 526-4111
E-mail: bmackenz@kear.tds.net
www.innatpleasantlake.com

Descending 500 feet from Main Street, visitors will find the inn situated on the shore of Pleasant Lake with Mt. Kearsarge as its backdrop. All ten well-appointed guest rooms have private baths and are furnished with antiques. Mornings start with a bountiful Continental or hot breakfast. Upon checking in, guests are invited to afternoon tea. A five-course dinner is served. Reservations required. Hiking, boating, swimming, skiing, biking, and cozy accommodations make this inn a destination, not just a place to stay.

Hosts: Brian and Linda Mackenzie
Rooms: 10 (PB) $110-175
Full Breakfast
Credit Cards: A, B, D
Notes: 2, 4, 5, 7, 8, 9, 10, 11, 12

NOTES: Credit cards accepted: A Master Card; B Visa; C American Express; D Discover; E Diners Club; F Other; 2 Personal checks accepted; 3 Lunch available; 4 Dinner available; 5 Open all year;

NORTH CONWAY

The Buttonwood Inn

The Buttonwood Inn

P.O. Box 1817, Mt. Surprise Road, 03860
(603) 356-2625; (800) 258-2625
fax: (603) 356-3140
E-mail: innkeeper@buttonwoodinn.com
www.buttonwoodinn.com

The Buttonwood Inn is nationally recognized for superior innkeeping. Visit our 1820s farmhouse on 17 secluded acres, two miles from the village of North Conway. Enjoy a peaceful, rural setting, with the convenience of being close to everything. Decorated with Shaker furniture, stenciling, and antiques. Breakfasts are second to none. Award-winning perennial gardens surround the inn. You can hike or cross-country ski from the back door. Individually prepared, daily itineraries are available. A memorable blend of hospitality, laughter, and kindness.

Hosts: Claudia and Peter Needham
Rooms: 10 (PB) $95-225
Full Breakfast
Credit Cards: A, B, C, D
Notes: 8, 9, 10, 11, 12

Eastman Inn

Route 16, P.O. Box 882, 03860
(603) 356-6707; (800) 626-5855
fax: (603) 356-7708
E-mail: stay@eastmaninn.com
www.eastmaninn.com

We offer New England hospitality with a Southern flair! Our 14 immaculately maintained guest rooms have private baths, color cable televisions, in-room telephones for making limited free local calls. Walk to the village of North Conway.

Hosts: Lea Greenwood and Tom Carter
Rooms: 14 (PB) $80-240
Full Breakfast
Credit Cards: A, B, C, D
Notes: 2, 8, 9, 10, 11

The 1785 Inn

3582 White Mountain Highway, P.O. Box 1785, 03860
(603) 356-9025; (800) 421-1785
fax: (603) 356-6081
E-mail: the1785inn@aol.com
www.the1785inn.com

A relaxing place to vacation any time of year. The inn is famous for its views and food. Located at the Scenic Vista, popularized by the White

The 1785 Inn

Mountain School of Art, its famous scene of Mt. Washington is virtually unchanged from when the inn was built more than two centuries ago. The homey atmosphere will make you feel right at home, and the food and service will make you eager to stay with us again.

Hosts: Becky and Charlie Mallar
Rooms: 17 (12 PB; 5 SB) $69-199
Full Breakfast
Credit Cards: A, B, C, D, E
Notes: 2, 4, 5, 7, 8, 9, 10, 11, 12

PLYMOUTH

Colonel Spencer Inn

3 Colonel Spencer Road, Campton, 03264
(603) 536-3438
www.colonelspencerinn.com

A 1764 center-chimney colonial with antique furnishings, wide pine floorboards, hand-hewn beams, and Indian shutters. Seven antique-appointed bedrooms with private baths welcome guests. A full country breakfast is served in a fireplaced dining room. The inn is convenient to both lake and

mountain attractions, at Exit 27 off I-93, a half mile south on Route 3.

Hosts: Carolyn and Alan Hill
Rooms: 7 (PB) $45-75
Full Breakfast
Credit Cards: None
Notes: 2, 5, 7, 8, 9, 10, 11, 12

SUGAR HILL/FRANCONIA

Sunset Hill House— A Grand Inn

231 Sunset Hill Road, 03585
(603) 823-5522; (800) SUN HILL
fax: (603) 823-5738
E-mail: innkeeper@sunsethillhouse.com
www.sunsethillhouse.com

Sunset Hill House

This full-service, luxury inn is perched on an 1800-foot ridge between the White and Green Mountains. A completely renovated historic property, every room has mountain views, a private bath, and phone; some with Jacuzzis, fireplaces, decks, and suites. Visit the fireplaced living rooms for afternoon cookies. Gourmet dining overlooks the mountains; guests will find lighter fare in the tavern. Golf (green fees included), heated mountainside pool, decks, gardens, trails, snowshoeing, and cross-country skiing are on-site. Spectacular downhill skiing and mountain climbing are within 5 miles.

Hosts: Lon and Nancy Henderson
Rooms: 28 (PB) $100-350
Full Breakfast
Credit Cards: A, B, C, D, E
Notes: 2, 3, 4, 5, 7, 8, 9, 10, 11, 12

TAMWORTH

Whispering Pines Bed & Breakfast

9 Hemenway Road, 03886
(603) 323-7337; fax: (603) 323-7337
E-mail: erickson@landmarknet.net
www.choice1.com/whisperingpines.htm

Escape to the foothills—to the quaint village of Tamworth minutes south of Conway. Its location between the White Mountains and the Winnipesaukee Lakes Region makes it a perfect location. Set in a woodland setting offering sheltering pines, sparkling starlight, and a wonderful, relaxing quiet. Rooms have view of woods and gardens—Springtime,

Whispering Pines

Rosegarden, Memories, and Woodlands. Enjoy our guest sitting room/porch. Genuine New England hospitality at it's best!

Hosts: Karen and Kim Erickson
Rooms: 4 (2 PB; 2 SB) $75-120
Full Breakfast
Credit Cards: A, B, C, D
Notes: 2, 5, 8, 9, 10, 11

VARIOUS CITIES

Elaine's Bed & Breakfast Selections

4987 Kingston Road, Elbridge, NY 13060-9773
(315) 689-2082

A reservation service that lists B&Bs in the following towns: Ashland, Ashuelot, Hopkinton, Intervale, Loudon, Madison, Meredith, North Conway, and Wakefield. Elaine Samuels, director.

WATERVILLE VALLEY

The Valley Inn & Red Fox Tavern

P.O. Box 1, Tecumseh Road, 03215
(603) 236-8336; (800) 343-0969
fax: (603) 236-4294
E-mail: info@valleyinn.com
www.valleyinn.com

Waterville Valley's only full-service inn. Heated year-round.

Host: Lynn T. McArdle
Rooms: 50 (PB) $68-98
Continental Breakfast
Credit Cards: A, B, C, D, E
Notes: 4, 5, 7, 8, 10, 11, 12

6 Pets welcome; 7 Children welcome; 8 Tennis nearby; 9 Swimming nearby; 10 Golf nearby; 11 Skiing nearby; 12 May be booked through travel agent

NEW JERSEY

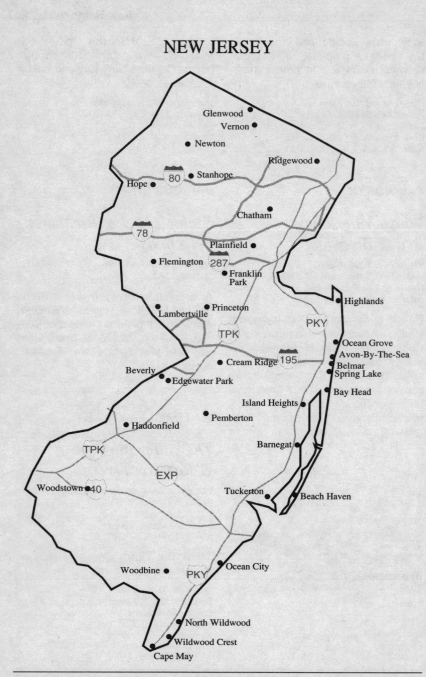

NOTES: Credit cards accepted: A Master Card; B Visa; C American Express; D Discover; E Diners Club; F Other; 2 Personal checks accepted; 3 Lunch available; 4 Dinner available; 5 Open all year;

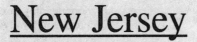

New Jersey

AVON-BY-THE-SEA

Cashelmara Inn

22 Lakeside Avenue, 07717
(732) 776-8727; (800) 821-2976
fax: (732) 988-5819
E-mail: cashelmara@monmouth.com
www.cashelmara.com

A tastefully restored turn-of-the-century inn rests on the bank of a swan lake and the Atlantic Ocean. This desirable setting offers a unique opportunity to smell the fresh salt air, to feel the ocean breeze, and to hear the sounds of the surf and the sea gulls from the privacy of your seaside room. Hearty breakfasts are a tradition on the Cashelmara Inn.

Host: Mary Wiernasz
Rooms: 14 (PB) $83-295
Full Breakfast
Credit Cards: A, B, D
Notes: 2, 5, 7

BELMAR

The Inn at the Shore

301 Fourth Avenue, 07719
(732) 681-3762; fax: (732) 280-1914
E-mail: tomvolker@aol.com
www.theinnattheshore.com

Beaches and boardwalk, just steps away from serene Silver Lake, and home to the first flock of swans bred in America. Guests will enjoy the casual, Victorian-style ambience on our expansive wraparound porch, where

The Inn at the Shore

relaxing in a rocking chair takes you back to the seashore of days gone by. Visitors make themselves comfortable in our spacious common areas, including the café-style brick patio ready for barbecues or refreshing beverages after a day of reflection, our large living room with its lovely stone fireplace and state-of-the-art entertainment center, and the grand dining room and library which are perfect for quiet moments of reading, writing, or just unwinding by our tranquil aquarium. We serve a bountiful, extended continental breakfast consisting of home-baked muffins, croissants, fresh fruits, cereals, juices, etc. Bikes, beach badges, and air-conditioning available. The guest pantry has a refrigerator, microwave, and dishes available for family reunions, retreats, and weddings. Sixty miles from Atlantic City, New York City, and Philadelphia; 20 miles from Six Flags Great Adventure Theme Park. Fifty percent off on the third night in our low season. We are child friendly.

6 Pets welcome; 7 Children welcome; 8 Tennis nearby; 9 Swimming nearby; 10 Golf nearby; 11 Skiing nearby; 12 May be booked through travel agent

Hosts: Tom and Rosemary Volker
Rooms: 10 (4 PB; 6 SB) $105-180
Full Breakfast
Credit Cards: A B C
Notes: 2, 5, 7, 8, 9, 10, 12

CAPE MAY

The Albert Stevens Inn

127 Myrtle Avenue, 08204-1237
(609) 884-4717; (800) 890-2287
fax: (609) 884-8320
E-mail: albertstevensinn@hotmail.com
www.beachcomber.com/capemay/Bbs/
    stevens.html

Built by Dr. Albert Stevens around 1898, this Queen Anne Free Classic house was both his home and office. The floating staircase and tower guide you to ten spacious bedrooms and suites with king-, queen-, and full-size beds, all with private baths, ceiling fans, and air-conditioning. Full breakfasts are served, as well as afternoon tea and refreshments. Relax on the inviting veranda or enjoy our heated sunroom. An outside hot tub and free on-site parking with the beach and

The Albert Stevens Inn

shopping only three blocks away. Epicurean and family restaurants are only a half block away. Beach towels and beach chairs available to our guests. Children over 12 are welcomed.

Hosts: Jim and Lenanne Labusciano
Rooms: 10 (PB) $90-230
Full Breakfast
Credit Cards: A, B
Notes: 2, 5, 7, 8, 9, 10

Bedford Inn

Bedford Inn

805 Stockton Avenue, 08204
(609) 884-4158; fax: (609) 884-6320
E-mail: info@bedfordinn.com
www.bedfordinn.com

This fully restored Victorian B&B is romantic and elegant. All rooms and "honeymoon" suites are furnished with authentic antiques and have a private bath, television, and air-conditioning; most with queen beds. We also have two suites with king beds available. Rates include gourmet breakfast and afternoon tea and treats, beach passes, beach chairs, and on-site parking. Great location—very close to the beach and town center. Parlor fireplace and two-story porch.

Hosts: James and Cindy Schmucker
Rooms: 11 (PB) $90-235
Full Breakfast
Credit Cards: A, B, C, D
Notes: 2, 8, 9, 10

Buttonwood Manor

115 North Broadway, 08204
(609) 884-4070
E-mail: ring@dandy.net
www.buttonwoodmanorbb.com

Buttonwood Manor is an elegant Colonial Revival house built in 1908. It is just four short blocks from the beach. Cape May is known for its lovely beaches, outstanding restaurants, quaint shops, antique stores, birding activities, lighthouse, and fishing. The home showcases many antique furnishings, including American Brilliant Cut Glass. All rooms have queen- or king-sized beds, private baths, ceiling fans, and air-conditioning. A full breakfast is served, with refreshments in the afternoon. There is off-street parking for all guests; children 12 and

Buttonwood Manor

over are welcome. Your hosts Diane and Roger invite you to join them in front of the cozy parlor fireplace or on the shady terrace to relax and "find rest for your soul." Open all year.

Hosts: Diane and Roger Ring
Rooms: 7 (PB) $95-190
Full Breakfast
Credit Cards: A, B
Notes: 2, 5, 7, 8, 9, 10

Duke of Windsor Inn

817 Washington Street, 08204
(609) 884-1355; (800) 826-8973
fax: (609) 884-1887
E-mail: innkeeper@dukeofwindsorinn.com
www.dukeofwindsorinn.com

Sense the romance of a classic Victorian, Queen Anne B&B inn. The Duke of Windsor Inn, built in 1896 with a 45-foot tower, has a large, central foyer with a three-story, carved oak staircase and Tiffany stained-glass windows. The parlor with a corner fireplace, two formal dining rooms, and ten guest rooms decorated with lovely antique furnishings extend a feeling of warmth and elegance. Gourmet breakfasts, afternoon tea and treats, on-site parking, and air-conditioned rooms await our guests. Open year-round.

Host: Patricia Joyce
Rooms: 10 (PB) $85-200
Full Breakfast
Credit Cards: A, B
Notes: 2, 5, 8, 9, 10

Jeremiah Hand House

814 Washington Street, 08204
(609) 884-1135; (800) 532-6559
E-mail: innkeeper@jeremiahhandhouse.com
www.jeremiahhandhouse.com

6 Pets welcome; 7 Children welcome; 8 Tennis nearby; 9 Swimming nearby; 10 Golf nearby; 11 Skiing nearby; 12 May be booked through travel agent

The Jeremiah Hand House was built as a parsonage for the Presbyterian church. The inn has four beautifully decorated bedrooms, a relaxing parlor, front and side porches, and a patio to enjoy. The walking mall is two blocks away while the beach is about four blocks away. Breakfast is served in the beautiful toile-papered dining room at individual tables. Afternoon sweets are served at 4 P.M. Come and enjoy beautiful Victorian Cape May. Children over 7 are welcome.

Hosts: Barbara Downs and Bill Fisher
Rooms: 4 (PB) $90-200
Full Breakfast
Credit Cards: A, B
Notes: 2, 5, 7, 8, 9, 10

John Wesley Inn

30 Gurney Street, 08204
(609) 884-1012
www.capemay.com

Step back in time to Victorian days in a romantic, peaceful setting. Parking, air-conditioning; all a half block from the beach.

Hosts: John and Rita Tice
Rooms: 8 (6 PB; 2 SB); 2 apartments $105-180
Continental Breakfast
Credit Cards: None
Notes: 2, 7, 8, 9, 10

The Queen Victoria® Bed & Breakfast

102 Ocean Street, 08204
(609) 884-8702
www.queenvictoria.com

The Queen Victoria

The Queen Victoria offers 21 antique-furnished rooms and suites in two faithfully restored homes located in the center of the historic district, just one block to the Atlantic Ocean and shops. All rooms have a private bath, mini-refrigerator, and air-conditioning. Luxury suites have a whirlpool tub and television. A hearty buffet breakfast is served each morning and a proper tea is enjoyed each afternoon. Complimentary bicycles, beach chairs, beach towels, and beverages are available. Open all year.

Hosts: Joan and Dane Wells
Rooms: 21 (PB) $90-295
Full Breakfast
Credit Cards: A, B
Notes: 2, 5, 7, 8, 9, 10

NOTES: Credit cards accepted: A Master Card; B Visa; C American Express; D Discover; E Diners Club; F Other; 2 Personal checks accepted; 3 Lunch available; 4 Dinner available; 5 Open all year;

Windward House

Windward House

24 Jackson Street, 08204
(609) 884-3368; fax: (609) 884-1575
www.windwardhouseinn.com

This elegant, Edwardian seaside inn has an entryway and staircase that are perhaps the prettiest in town. Spacious guest rooms filled with fine antiques have king and queen beds, mini-refrigerators, air-conditioning, and TV/VCR. Three sun and shade porches, cozy parlor fireplace, Christmas finery. In an unbeatable location in the historic district, a half block from the beach, shopping mall, and wonderful restaurants. Homemade breakfast, afternoon refreshments, and beach passes. Midweek discounts during the off-season. Children 8 and over are welcome.

Hosts: Sandy and Owen Miller
Rooms: 8 (PB) $100-205
Full Breakfast
Credit Cards: A, B
Notes: 2, 7, 8, 9, 10, 12

EDGEWATER PARK

Historic Whitebriar Bed & Breakfast

1029 Cooper Street, Beverly, 08010
(609) 871-3859

Historic Whitebriar is a German salt-box-style home that has been added on to many times since it was the home of John Fitch, steam ship inventor of 1787. The latest addition is an English conservatory built in Beverly, England, from a two-hundred-year-old design and shipped to Beverly just a few years ago. Breakfast is served in the conservatory overlooking the seasonal pool and spa. Whitebriar is a living history farm with animals to be tended. Guests are welcome to collect the eggs, brush the ponies, and pick the raspberries. Located thirty minutes from historic Philadelphia, three hours from Washington, and an hour amd a half from the Big Apple, just off interstates. Monthly executive rates are $400-525.

Hosts: Carole and Bill
Rooms: 4 (2 PB; 2 SB) $50-125
Full Breakfast
Credit Cards: None
Notes: 2, 3, 4, 5, 6, 7, 8, 9

NEWTON

The Wooden Duck Bed & Breakfast

140 Goodale Road, 07860-2788
(973) 300-0395; fax: (973) 300-0395
www.woodenduckinn.com

---

6 Pets welcome; 7 Children welcome; 8 Tennis nearby; 9 Swimming nearby; 10 Golf nearby; 11 Skiing nearby; 12 May be booked through travel agent

The Wooden Duck is a secluded, 17-acre mini-estate about an hour's drive from New York City. Located on a country road in rural Sussex County, it is close to antiques, golf, the Delaware Water Gap, Waterloo Village, and winter sports. The rooms are spacious with private bath, televisions, VCRs, phones, and desks. Features include central air-conditioning, an in-ground pool, game room, and living room with see-through fireplaces. The home features antique furnishings and reproductions. Biking and hiking are at the doorstep, with a 1,000-acre state park across the street and a "Rails to Trails" (abandoned railway maintained for hiking and biking) running behind the property. Wildlife abounds in the area.

Hosts: Bob and Barbara Hadden
Rooms: 7 (PB) $110-190
Full Breakfast
Credit Cards: A, B, C, D
Notes: 2, 5, 7, 8, 9, 10, 11

Castle by the Sea

service with delicious bedside chocolates, and many other delightful amenities. Enjoy enchanting guest rooms with private baths, televisions, VCRs, bedside clocks, and elegant bed linens and toiletries. We even have a whimsical "Jacuzzi-for-two" room and two romantic fireplace rooms.

Rooms: 9 (PB) $109-229
Full Breakfast
Credit Cards: A, B, C, D
Notes: 5, 8, 9, 10, 12

OCEAN CITY

Castle by the Sea. . .A Romantic Bed & Breakfast

701 Ocean Avenue, 08226-3728
(609) 398-3555; (800) 622-4894
fax: (609) 398-8742
E-mail: castle701@aol.com
castlebythesea.com

Discover the storybook magic of this very special English-Country B&B. Nestled in the historic district of lovely Ocean City, New Jersey, you will be treated with a gourmet three-course breakfast, afternoon tea with sumptuous sweets, nightly turndown

Delancey Manor

869 Delancey Place, 08226
(609) 398-6147

Delancey Manor is a turn-of-the-century summer house situated just 100 yards from a great beach and our 2.5-mile boardwalk. Summer fun is available for families and friends at "America's greatest family resort." We have two breezy porches with ocean views. Guests can walk to nearby restaurants, boardwalk fun, and the Tabernacle with its renowned speakers. The inn is located in a residential neighborhood in a dry town. Larger family rooms are available.

Advance reservations are recommended. Two-night minimum applies.

Hosts: Stewart and Pam Heisler
Rooms: 6 (3 PB; 3 SB) $65-95
Credit Cards: None
Notes: 2, 7, 8, 9, 10

The Ebbie

820 East 6th Street, 08226-3837
(609) 399-4744
E-mail: ebbienj@hotmail.com
www.ebbie.com

The Ebbie

Circa 1920, this family-owned and -operated seashore house includes both rooms and apartments. There is a two-bedroom apartment with a living area and kitchen, as well as two studio apartments. Both of the studio apartments include kitchens. Guest quarters and common areas are decorated in a comfortable, relaxed, country style. The home is only a half block from the beach and boardwalk and 11 miles south of Atlantic City.

Hosts: The Warringtons
Rooms: 7 (5 PB; 2 SB) $50-100
Continental Breakfast
Credit Cards: A, B
Notes: 7, 8, 9, 10

Scarborough Inn

720 Ocean Avenue, 08226
(609) 399-1558; (800) 258-1558
fax: (609) 399-4472
E-mail: cgbruno@earthlink.net
www.scarboroughinn.com

The Scarborough Inn, invitingly adorned in Wedgwood, rose, and soft cream, lends its special character to the neighborhood where it stands, just one and a half short blocks from the beach and boardwalk of this island town. The Scarborough is reminiscent of a European-style inn—small enough to be intimate, yet large enough for privacy. Scrumptious gourmet breakfast, afternoon refreshments, and bountiful amenities. Featured in *Country Inns* magazine.

Rooms: 24 (PB) $90-190
Full Breakfast
Credit Cards: A, B, C, D
Notes: 7, 8, 9, 10, 12

Serendipity Bed & Breakfast

Serendipity

---

6 Pets welcome; 7 Children welcome; 8 Tennis nearby; 9 Swimming nearby; 10 Golf nearby; 11 Skiing nearby; 12 May be booked through travel agent

712 Ninth Street, 08226
(609) 399-1554; (800) 842-8544
fax: (609) 399-1527
E-mail: info@serendipitynj.com
www.serendipitynj.com

Serendipity is a Mobil-approved, fully air-conditioned, and beautifully renovated 1912 inn. Rooms of wicker and pastels feature private baths with hair dryers and cable TV. A full breakfast of your choice is served in the spacious dining room or on the garden veranda. Vegetarian, heart-healthy, and macrobiotic diets are accommodated. Serendipity is just a half block to the beaches and boardwalk, and minutes to Atlantic City's shows/casinos, and Victorian Cape May.

Hosts: Clara and Bill Plowfield
Rooms: 6 (4 PB; 2 SB) $80-159
Full Breakfast
Credit Cards: A, B, C, D
Notes: 2, 4, 5, 7, 8, 9, 10, 12

OCEAN GROVE

The Carriage House Bed & Breakfast

18 Heck Avenue, 07756
(732) 988-3232; fax: (732) 988-9441
E-mail: carriagehouseog@aol.com
www.carriagehousenj.com

Ocean Grove's newest! Innkeepers Kathi and Phil will greet the 21st century with a 19th-century Ocean Grove treasure. The Carriage House is a gem of elegance, a block from the ocean and a block from town, in the heart of Ocean Grove's charming historic section. Enjoy newly renovated, spacious, air-conditioned suites with TVs, queen beds, private baths, fire-

The Carriage House

places, and ocean view porches. We are open all seasons to pamper you.

Hosts: Kathi and Phil Franco
Rooms: 8 (PB) $120-150
Continental Breakfast
Credit Cards: A, B
Notes: 2, 5, 8, 9, 10, 12

House by the Sea

14 Ocean Avenue, 07756
(732) 775-2847; fax: (732) 502-0403
E-mail: housebysea@monmouth.com
www.travelguides.com/bb/house_by_the_sea

Ocean Grove is a Victorian seaside community founded in 1869 featuring a large auditorium for Christian worship. The House by the Sea is an oceanfront B&B with 18 rooms and three large porches facing the Atlantic Ocean. Centrally located within walking distance of all activities, shops, and restaurants. Your innkeepers live here year-round and share their home from Memorial Day weekend to Labor Day.

Hosts: Sally and Alyn Heim
Rooms: 18 (10 PB; 8 SB) $70-120
Continental Breakfast
Credit Cards: A, B
Notes: 8, 9, 10

NOTES: Credit cards accepted: A Master Card; B Visa; C American Express; D Discover; E Diners Club; F Other; 2 Personal checks accepted; 3 Lunch available; 4 Dinner available; 5 Open all year;

The Lillagaard

5 Abbott Avenue, 07756
(732) 988-1216; fax: (732) 988-8381
E-mail: lillagaard@aol.com
www.lillagaard.com

The Lillagaard is a 25-room Victorian inn. We are steps from the beach providing ocean-view rooms. Each unique room is decorated in a different theme. Relax on our expansive porches with rocking chairs and antique wicker, and enjoy the panoramic view of the Atlantic Ocean and refreshing ocean breezes. Your stay will be filled with all the pleasures that Ocean Grove offers. Our tearoom is open 12 P.M. to 4 P.M.; public welcome. Beach badges discounted. All rooms have air-conditioning, fans, and guest phones.

The Lillagaard

Hosts: Dick and Jane Wehr
Rooms: 25 (21 PB; 4 SB) $75-140
Continental Breakfast
Credit Cards: A, B, D
Notes: 2, 5, 8, 9, 10, 12

Pine Tree Inn

10 Main Avenue, 07756
(732) 775-3264; fax: (732) 775-2939
E-mail: angelofog@aol.com
www.pinetreeinn.com

A small Victorian inn (a half-block from the beach) offering a quiet interlude for visitors to the Jersey Shore. It is truly a B&B adhering to the charm of an earlier time. Enjoy a complimentary Continental-plus breakfast each morning amidst ocean breezes on our front porch or sunny side yard. The Pine Tree Inn is accessible by all major forms of transportation. We are only an hour from New York City and Newark International Airport, and an hour and a half from Atlantic City and Philadelphia. Train and bus stations are minutes away, and taxi services are also available. Children over 10 are welcome.

Host: Karen Mason
Rooms: 12 (5 PB; 7 SB) $70-130
Continental Breakfast
Credit Cards: A, B, C
Notes: 2, 5, 7, 8, 9, 10

PLAINFIELD

The Pillars of Plainfield Bed & Breakfast

922 Central Avenue, 07060
(908) 753-7448; (888) 745-5277
fax: (603) 719-2177
E-mail: pillars2@juno.com
www.pillars2.com

Luxurious, private bath suites in a restored Victorian mansion. Close to New York, I-95, I-78, I-287. Full Swedish breakfast, private phone/voice mail, data ports, HBO, evening sherry, soda, chocolates, and cookies. Close to New York, Newark, Sandy Hook, and New Hope. Wood-burning fireplaces, stained-glass windows, secluded grounds with trees and gar-

The Pillars of Plainfield

dens. Nonsmoking. Ideal for business or vacation travelers. Will accept dogs, but no cats. We have a Cairn Terrier, "Mac."

Hosts: Tom and Chuck Hale
Rooms: 7 (PB) $114-225
Full Breakfast
Credit Cards: A, B, C, D
Notes: 2, 5, 6, 7, 8, 9, 10, 11, 12

SPRING LAKE

The Hewitt-Wellington Hotel

200 Monmouth Avenue, 07762
(732) 974-1212; fax: (732) 974-2338
E-mail: reservations@hewittwellington.com
www.hewittwellington.com

Three-diamond award winner. Twelve beautifully appointed single rooms and 17 two-room suites on the lake overlooking the ocean have private balconies, wraparound porches, air-conditioning, ceiling fans, private marble baths, remote cable TVs, and phones. Heated pool and free beach passes. Refined dining in our intimate restaurant. Children 12 and over welcome. Call for brochure.

Rooms: 29 (PB) $95-290
Continental Breakfast
Credit Cards: A, B, C, D, E
Notes: 2, 5

Sea Crest by the Sea

19 Tuttle Avenue, 07762-1533
(732) 449-9031; (800) 803-9031
fax: (732) 974-0403
E-mail: capt@seacrestbythesea.com
www.seacrestbythesea.com

Your romantic fantasy escape, this Spring Lake B&B inn is just for the two of you. Lovingly restored 1885 Queen Anne Victorian for adults on holiday. Only 1.25 hours from New York City and Philadelphia. Ocean views, open fireplaces, luxurious linens, feather beds, Jacuzzis for two, antique-filled rooms, sumptuous breakfasts and afternoon teas, bicycles, beach bedges and chairs. *Victoria Magazine* call it "a perfect ocean refuge." Your innkeepers welcome you with old-fashioned hospitality to an atmosphere that will soothe your weary body and soul.

Sea Crest by the Sea

NOTES: Credit cards accepted: A Master Card; B Visa; C American Express; D Discover; E Diners Club; F Other; 2 Personal checks accepted; 3 Lunch available; 4 Dinner available; 5 Open all year;

Hosts: Barbara and Fred Vogel
Rooms: 11 (PB) $195-305
Full Breakfast
Credit Cards: A, B, C
Notes: 2, 5, 8, 9, 10, 12

Spring Lake Inn

104 Salem Avenue, 07762
(732) 449-2010; fax: (732) 449-4020
E-mail: sprnglkinn@aol.com
www.springlakeinn.com

Spring Lake Inn

We invite you to come to our inn and relax in a warm, informal atmosphere. Built in 1888, the Inn is nestled on a quiet street surrounded by fascinating history. Take a refreshing jog on the boardwalk, a barefoot stroll on a beach that goes on for miles, or just let the ocean breeze renew your spirit on our 80-foot Victorian porch lined with rockers. The town center, within walking distance, has over 60 unique shops to explore. The Spring Lake Inn is a private place for one, or a romantic inn for two. . .so plan your relaxing vacation, reunion, conference, or intimate wedding at the Spring Lake Inn. . .the best kept secret in Spring Lake.

Hosts: Jim and Pat Gatens
Rooms: 15 (PB) $135-225
Full Breakfast
Credit Cards: A, B, C
Notes: 2, 5, 8, 9, 10

White Lilac Inn

414 Central Avenue, 07762-1020
(732) 449-0211; fax: (732) 974-0568
E-mail: mari@whitelilac.com
www.whitelilac.com

The White Lilac Inn, circa 1880, is located in a peaceful corner of Spring Lake, just a stone's throw from Wreck Pond and four and a half blocks from the ocean. Guests can enjoy swimming, boating, cycling, antiquing, golf and tennis, or give up the hectic pace for quiet moments on the old porch. Built with a Southern accent, the White Lilac Inn has triple-tiered porches and comfortable common rooms. It is decorated in eclectic Victorian style. Sit by the fireplace and enjoy friendly hosptiality. Enjoy a leisurely breakfast at tables for two in our garden room or on our enclosed porch. The Inn's nine air-conditioned guest rooms, inluding several with fireplaces, are all decorated with Victorian cottage charm. All have private baths.

White Lilac Inn

Host: Mari Kennelly Slocum
Rooms: 10 (PB) $125-225
Full Breakfast
Credit Cards: A, B, C, D
Notes: 2, 5, 8, 9, 10, 12

---

6 Pets welcome; 7 Children welcome; 8 Tennis nearby; 9 Swimming nearby; 10 Golf nearby; 11 Skiing nearby; 12 May be booked through travel agent

NEW MEXICO

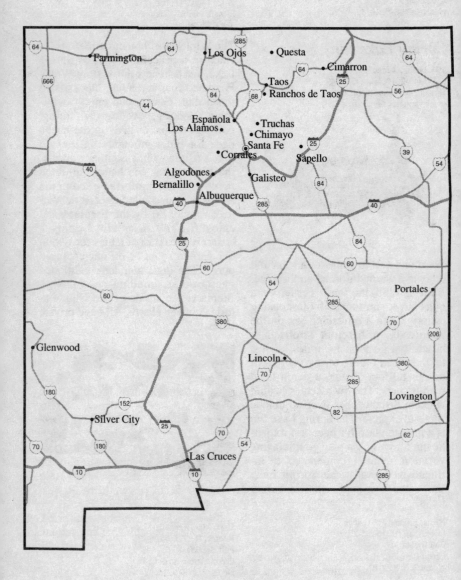

NOTES: Credit cards accepted: A Master Card; B Visa; C American Express; D Discover; E Diners Club; F Other; 2 Personal checks accepted; 3 Lunch available; 4 Dinner available; 5 Open all year;

New Mexico

ALBUQUERQUE

Enchanted Vista
Bed & Breakfast

10700 Del Rey Avenue Northeast, 87122-3516
(505) 823-1301

Enchanted Vista offers the best of both worlds—its on the edge of the city yet offers peaceful and spectacular views of Sandia mountains and city lights by night. Minutes from airport and old town. All suites have private entrances and private baths. Very spacious with refrigerator-microwave-TV breakfast bar and telephone. Continental breakfast at your pleasure. Beautiful gardens and verandas are all for your enjoyment!

Rooms: 3 (PB) $62-84
Continental Breakfast
Credit Cards: None
Notes: 2, 5, 6, 7, 8, 9, 10, 11, 12

CIMARRON

Casa del Gavilan
Historic Inn

Highway 21 South, P.O. Box 518, 87714
(505) 376-2246; (800) GAVILAN
fax: (505) 376-2247
www.casadelgavilan.com

Nestled in the majestic foothills of the Sangre de Christo Mountains, the Casa del Gavilan is a place of spirit, where hawk and eagle soar. It is a secluded, turn-of-the-century adobe villa. Enjoy elegant hospitality and breathtaking views in a historic setting. Four guest rooms plus a two-room suite. Join us and experience the uncommon tranquillity of Casa del Gavilan.

Host: Isabel Lloyd
Rooms: 5 (PB) $75-130
Full Breakfast
Credit Cards: A, B, C, D
Notes: 4, 5, 7, 11

LAS CRUCES

Hilltop Hacienda
Bed & Breakfast

2600 Westmoreland Street, 88012-7357
(505) 382-3556; fax: (505) 382-3556
E-mail: hilltop@zianet.com
www.zianet.com/hilltop

Secluded romantic retreat with breathtaking sunrises, sunsets, and star-filled nights atop 18 acres. Spectacular views of Las Cruces, the Rio Grande Valley, and the Organ Mountains. Unique two-story arched adobe brick dwelling of Spanish Moors architecture with spacious verandas and patios. Guest rooms beautifully decorated. Spacious private baths. Romantic walks through lovely rose and desert gardens. Gourmet full breakfast. Lots of amenities. Only minutes to downtown Las Cruces and Old Mesilla.

---

6 Pets welcome; 7 Children welcome; 8 Tennis nearby; 9 Swimming nearby; 10 Golf nearby; 11 Skiing nearby; 12 May be booked through travel agent

Hosts: Bob and Teddi Peters
Rooms: 3 (PB) $75-95
Full Breakfast
Credit Cards: A, B, C, D
Notes: 2, 5, 8, 9, 10, 12

LOVINGTON

Pyburn House Bed & Breakfast

203 North 4th Street, 88260
(505) 396-3460

This folklore two-story house, built in 1935 by John Pyburn, is listed on the State and National Registers of Historic Places. A very comfortable and romantic atmosphere, where each guest room has a special ambience and is furnished with lovely antiques, luxury linens, thick towels, and plush bathrobes. Described as a "special place" and "oasis in the desert." Amenities include cable TVs/VCRs, full, queen, and king beds, Jacuzzi, fireplace, and a bicycle-built-for-two. Smoking is permitted outside.

Hosts: Don and Sharon Ritchey
Rooms: 4 (PB) $55-125
Continental Breakfast
Credit Cards: A, B, D
Notes: 2, 5, 8, 9, 10

SANTA FE

Hacienda Vargas Bed & Breakfast Inn

P.O. Box 307, Algodones, 87001
(505) 867-9115; (800) 261-0006
fax: (505) 867-0640
E-mail: stay@haciendavargas.com
www.haciendavargas.com

Hacienda Vargas

Hacienda Vargas offers the sights, sounds, and scents of New Mexico! Conveniently located between Albuquerque and Santa Fe, on the historic El Camino Real, the site has been a stagecoach stop, a train depot, and an Indian trading post. All our guest rooms and suites offer private bathrooms and entrances. Our suites have fireplaces and private double Jacuzzis. A bountiful breakfast is served in the dining room each morning. Ask about our Romance Packages!

Rooms: 7 (PB) $79-149
Full Breakfast
Credit Cards: A, B
Notes: 5, 10, 11, 12

The Madeleine Bed & Breakfast Inn

106 Faithway Street, 87501
(505) 982-3465; (888) 877-7622
fax: (505) 982-8572
E-mail: madeleineinn@aol.com
www.madeleineinn.com

An elegant 1886 Queen Anne Victorian in a quiet and secluded garden setting near the Plaza. Stained-glass

---

NOTES: Credit cards accepted: A Master Card; B Visa; C American Express; D Discover; E Diners Club; F Other; 2 Personal checks accepted; 3 Lunch available; 4 Dinner available; 5 Open all year;

windows, ornate fireplaces, antiques, and hot tub. Full breakfasts of pancakes, frittatas and enchiladas, along with fresh fruit, yogurt, granola, whole grain breads, and more. Superb homemade baked goodies throughout the day. Decorated with your utmost comfort in mind. Incredible personal service and attention to detail. Hot tub, phones, cable TV, and health club privileges. Pets welcome.

Hosts: Carolyn Lee/George Padilla
Rooms: 8 (6 PB; 2 SB) $70-165
Full Breakfast
Credit Cards: A, B, D
Notes: 2, 5, 8, 9, 10, 11, 12

TAOS

Hacienda del Sol

P.O. Box 177, 87571-0177
(505) 758-0287; fax: (505) 758-5895
E-mail: sunhouse@newmex.com
www.taoshaciendadelsol.com

Selected by *USA Today* as "one of the 10 most romantic inns in America." The original 197-year-old adobe building once belonged to Mabel Dodge Luhan and her husband Tony. Adjoining 95,000 acres of Taos Pueblo land, the 11-room inn offers country ambiance just a mile and a half from the plaza. You'll find gourmet breakfasts, Jacuzzis, outdoor hot tub, steamrooms, handcrafted furnishings, luxury linens, and attention to detail.

Hosts: Dennis Sheehan and Elton L. Moy
Rooms: 11 (PB) $95-195
Full Breakfast
Credit Cards: A, B, C, D
Note: 5

The Willows Inn Bed & Breakfast

Box 6560 NDCBU or 412 Kit Carson Road, 87571
(505) 758-2558; (800) 525-8267
fax: (505) 758-5445
E-mail: willows@newmex.com
www.willows-taos.com

The Willows Inn is a five-guest room B&B that is listed on the National and State Registers of Historic Places. It was the adobe estate (home and art studio) of E. Martin Hennings, member of the famous 1920s Taos Society of Artists. The property features an acre of gardens with lily ponds, courtyards, fountains, and two of America's largest willow trees (30 feet in circumference; registered in the 1970s). Many delectable items are prepared from the Willows Inn gardens and orchard for the full, family-style breakfast and lavish afternoon hospitality time. All rooms are authentic adobe and have courtyard entrances, private baths with hand-painted Mexican tiles, kiva wood-

The Willows Inn

---

6 Pets welcome; 7 Children welcome; 8 Tennis nearby; 9 Swimming nearby; 10 Golf nearby; 11 Skiing nearby; 12 May be booked through travel agent

burning fireplaces, and queen beds. Each room is uniquely decorated to celebrate a different culture of the Taos area. Guests can stay in the sutdio where Hennings actually painted during the last 20 years of his life.

Hosts: Doug and Janet Camp
Rooms: 5 (PB)
Credit Cards: A, B, D
Notes: 2, 5, 7, 8, 9, 10, 11, 12

VARIOUS CITIES

Advance Reservations Inn/Arizona/ Mi Casa Su Casa

P.O. Box 950, Tempe, AZ, 85280
(480) 990-0682; (800) 456-0682
fax: (480) 990-3390
E-mail: micasa@primenet.com
www.azres.com

Since 1981, we have listed inspected, clean, comfortable host-homes, inns, cottages, and ranches in the Southwestern U.S. We list about 200 modest-to-luxurious, historic-to-contemporary B&Bs. New Mexico listings include: Albuquerque, Algodones, Bernalillo, Chimayo, Espanola, Las Crucis, Lincoln, Los Ojos (near Chama), Santa Fe, Taos. We also represent two luxury villas, one in Puerto Vallarto, Mexico, and the second in the Costa Brava area of Spain. Most rooms have private baths and range from $75-$275, based on double occupancy. Continental to gourmet breakfasts. All major credit cards accepted. Ruth Young, coordinator.

New York

ALBION

Friendship Manor

349 South Main Street, 14411
(716) 589-2983; fax: (716) 589-1162
E-mail: baker@iinc.com

Friendship Manor

This historical house dating back to 1880, is surrounded by lovely roses, perennial and herb gardens, and lots of shade trees. A swimming pool and tennis court are provided for your pleasure. The intimate interior is an artful blend of Victorian-style furnishings with antiques throughout. Enjoy a breakfast of muffins, breads, fruit, juice, and coffee or tea in the formal dining room. Friendship Manor is central to Niagara Falls, Buffalo, and Rochester. A great place if traveling through, or for just a weekend getaway.

Hosts: John and Marylin Baker
Rooms: 3 (1 PB; 2 SB) $65
Continental Breakfast
Credit Cards: A, B, D
Notes: 2, 5, 7, 8, 9, 10, 12

ALEXANDRIA BAY

Hart House Inn

21979 Club Road, Wellesley Island, 13640
(315) 482-5683; (888) 481-5683
fax: (315) 482-5683
E-mail: info@harthouseinn.com
www.harthouseinn.com

In the heart of the Thousand Islands our grand gentleman's cottage is a true destination for your special occasion. Adjacent to a golf course with a fine St. Lawrence River view we're just minutes from major boat cruises. Wellesley Island is accessible by car, located just five minutes from I-81 and 10 minutes from the Canadian border. Thousand Islands is an all-season getaway-with a difference! We offer luxury accommodations: canopied beds with decorator sheeting, cozy fireplaces, and private whirlpool baths featuring Italian ceramic tile. All of this plus the stunning Grace Wedding Chapel which seats 50.

---

6 Pets welcome; 7 Children welcome; 8 Tennis nearby; 9 Swimming nearby; 10 Golf nearby; 11 Skiing nearby; 12 May be booked through travel agent

NEW YORK

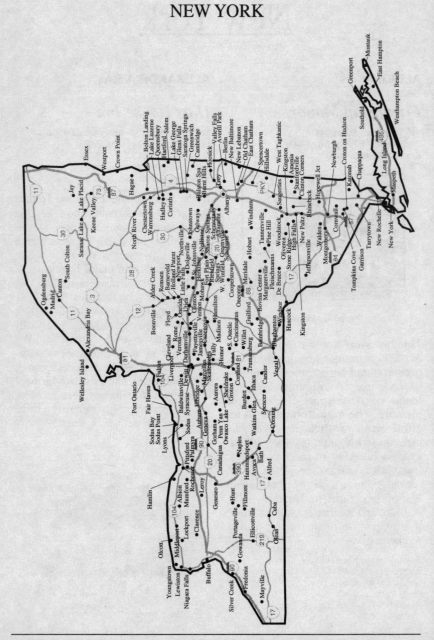

NOTES: Credit cards accepted: A Master Card; B Visa; C American Express; D Discover; E Diners
Club; F Other; 2 Personal checks accepted; 3 Lunch available; 4 Dinner available; 5 Open all year;

Hosts: Rev. Dudley and Kathy Danielson
Rooms: 8 (7 PB; 1 SB) $135-295
Full Breakfast
Credit Cards: A, B
Notes: 2, 4, 5, 7, 8, 9, 10, 11, 12

Hosts: Jean Fowler and Cecilio Rios
Rooms: 5 (2 PB; 3 SB) $75-125
Full Breakfast
Credit Cards: A, B, C
Notes: 2, 5, 7, 8, 9, 10, 11, 12

BAINBRIDGE

Berry Hill Gardens Bed & Breakfast

242 Ward Loomis Road, 13733
(607) 967-8745; (800) 497-8745
fax: (607) 967-2227
E-mail: info@berryhillgardens.com
www.berryhillgardens.com

This restored 1820s farmhouse on a hilltop is surrounded by extensive flower and herb gardens, and 200 acres where you can hike, swim, fish, bird-watch, cross-country ski, or sit on the wraparound porch and watch the nature parade. Our rooms are furnished with comfortable antiques. A 10-minute drive takes you to restaurants, golf, auctions, and antique centers. You can buy plants, dried flowers, and wreaths grown and handcrafted on the farm. Cooperstown and most local colleges are only 45 minutes away. Three hours from New York City. Weekly rental of a private, two-bedroom riverside cottage is also available.

Berry Hill Gardens

BATH

Patchwork Peace Bed & Breakfast

4279 Waterbury Hill Road, Avoca, 14809
(607) 566-2443
E-mail: patchworkpeace@infoblvd.net
www.patchworkpeace.com

Patchwork Peace

Come enjoy the patchwork of quilts throughout the house, the patchwork of scenery out your window, and the quiet to contemplate the patchwork of your life. We think you'll like our 1925 farmhouse in the middle of farm country. We raise dairy heifers, corn, oats, and hay. A full breakfast is served. Finger Lakes area, near Corning, Alfred, and Watkins Glen.

Hosts: Bill and Betty Mitchell
Rooms: 4 (1 PB; 3 SB) $55-75
Full Breakfast
Credit Cards: None
Notes: 2, 7, 9, 10

---

6 Pets welcome; 7 Children welcome; 8 Tennis nearby; 9 Swimming nearby; 10 Golf nearby; 11 Skiing nearby; 12 May be booked through travel agent

BINGHAMTON

Angels in the Bell Tower Retreat

242 Ward Loomis Road, Bainbridge, 13733
(607) 967-8745; (800) 497-8745
fax: (607) 967-2227
E-mail: angelsretreat@berryhillgardens.com
www.angelsinthebelltower.com

This charming, 1898 country church is now available for short retreats. It is situated in a small hamlet along the Tioughnioga River, 12 miles north of Binghamton, N.Y., and contains a full kitchen, two bedrooms, a large, open living room with original cathedral ceiling, and stained-glass windows. Country craft and antique shops are nearby. Great location when visiting Binghamton University. Short drive to wineries, Ithaca College, and Cornell University. Sleeps four to six people.

Rooms: 2 (SB) $500-800 weekly
Continental Breakfast
Credit Cards: A, B, C
Notes: 2, 5, 8, 9, 10, 11

Angels in the Bell Tower Retreat

CANDOR

The Edge of Thyme, A Bed & Breakfast Inn

6 Main Street, P.O. Box 48, 13743
(607) 659-5155
www.edgeofthyme.com

Featured in *Historic Inns of the Northeast*. Located in this quiet rural village is a large, gracious Georgian home. Leaded glass, windowed

The Edge of Thyme

porch, marble fireplaces, period sitting rooms, gardens, and pergola. Epicurean breakfast served in a genteel manner. The location is central to Cornell, Ithaca College, Corning, Elmira, Watkins Glen, and wineries. Gift shoppe. High tea is served by appointment.

Hosts: Eva Mae and Frank Musgrave
Rooms: 5 (3 PB; 2 SB) $75-135
Full Breakfast
Credit Cards: A, B, C
Notes: 2, 5, 7, 8, 9, 10, 11, 12

NOTES: Credit cards accepted: A Master Card; B Visa; C American Express; D Discover; E Diners Club; F Other; 2 Personal checks accepted; 3 Lunch available; 4 Dinner available; 5 Open all year;

CANTON

Ostrander's Bed & Breakfast

1675 State Highway 68, 13617
(315) 386-2126; (877) 707-2126
fax: (315) 386-3843
E-mail: ostbbinn@northnet.org
www.ostranders.com

A 22-acre country estate surrounded by board and stone fences and farm pastures. Two spacious guest rooms in our 1996 Cape Cod home are decorated with antiques. Two guest cottages with kitchens overlook an acre pond. Queen beds, cable TV, air-conditioning, in-room phones, clock radios, ceiling fans, and private baths. Awaken to the aroma of baked-apple French toast and muffins to be served in the large country kitchen, or on the front porch or rear deck. Within 10 minutes of St. Lawrence and Clarkson universities, SUNY Canton, and Potsdam, three eighteen-hole golf courses, ultramodern and family farms, antique shopping, cycling, canoeing, and hiking trails. We are a working sheep farm; we raise border collie dogs and have a sheepskin shop. We offer extended-stay discounts.

Hosts: Rita and Alan Ostrander
Rooms: 4 (PB) $55-75
Full Breakfast
Credit Cards: A, B, C
Notes: 2, 5, 8, 9, 10, 11, 12

CLARENCE/BUFFALO

Asa Ransom House

10529 Main Street, 14031
(716) 759-2315; fax: (716) 759-2791

E-mail: innfo@asaransom.com
www.asaransom.com

Asa Ransom House

The Asa Ransom House, an intimate village inn located in historic Clarence Hollow, is minutes from downtown Buffalo and only 28 miles from Niagara Falls. The inn features nine beautifully appointed guest rooms, all with private baths and most with fireplaces, porch, or balcony. Voted "#1 Bed and Breakfast" by a recent *Buffalo News* reader survey. The Asa Ransom House was awarded grand prize for the "Waverly Room of the Year," and our gourmet cuisine has been featured in *Bon Appetit* and *Gourmet*. Clarence Hollow is known throughout the East for its treasured antique shops.

Hosts: Robert Lenz and Abigail Lenz
Rooms: 9 (PB) $95-150
Full Breakfast
Credit Cards: A, B, D
Notes: 2, 4, 5, 7, 8, 9, 10, 12

CORNING

1865 White Birch Bed & Breakfast

69 East First Street, 14830
(607) 962-6355; www.corningny.com/whitebirch

---

6 Pets welcome; 7 Children welcome; 8 Tennis nearby; 9 Swimming nearby; 10 Golf nearby; 11 Skiing nearby; 12 May be booked through travel agent

The White Birch, Victorian in structure but decorated in country, has been refurbished to show off its winding staircase, hardwood floors, and wall window in the dining room that overlooks the backyard. We are located in a residential area, two blocks from restored historic Market Street, and six blocks from the Corning Museum. Our large common room welcomes guests where TV and great conversation are available. A full, home-baked gourmet breakfast is served each morning.

Hosts: Kathy and Joe Donahue
Rooms: 4 (2 PB; 2 SB) $75-90
Full Breakfast
Credit Cards: A, B, C
Notes: 2, 5, 7, 8, 9, 10, 11

CUBA

Helen's Tourist Home

7 Maple Street, 14727
(716) 968-2200

Your hostess has been welcoming tourists to her comfortable, turn-of-the-century home for 47 years. Located on a quiet residential street. Guests have the run of the house, including the large living room with TV. Coffee, a toaster, and a refrigerator are always available. Visit Cuba Lake, the Cuba Cheese Shop, and Seneca Oil Springs—first oil discovered in America. A restaurant is just around the corner; a small shopping center is nearby.

Host: Dora W. Wittmann
Rooms: 5 (1 PB; 4 SB) $35-45
Credit Cards: None
Notes: 5, 7, 9, 10

DELHI/ONEONTA

The Old Stageline Stop Bed & Breakfast

P.O. Box 125, Meridale, 13806
(607) 746-6856
E-mail: stagebb@catskill.net
www.catskill.net/stagebb

This early 1900s farmhouse, once part of a dairy fam, is high on a hill overlooking the peaceful countryside. Comfortable rooms are tastefully decorated with country furnishings. Guests enjoy a variety of attractions, relaxing on the porch, and taking walks to absorb the beautiful views. A full breakfast and afternoon treats are served with pleasure. Delhi, Oneonta, and Hartwick Colleges are nearby. We are within a short drive of Cooperstown and many other attractions-antiques, fairs, auctions, and historical sites such as Hanford Mills. Well behaved children welcome.

Hosts: Rose Rosino
Rooms: 4 (1 PB; 3 SB) $60-75
Full Breakfast
Credit Cards: A, B
Notes: 2, 5, 7, 8, 10, 11

FILLMORE

Just a (Plane) Bed & Breakfast

11152 Route 19A, 14735
(716) 567-8338

Enjoy a relaxing, peaceful stay at Just a "Plane." Situated on the banks of the historic Genesee Valley Canal, the three-story, Dutch Colonial home was

---

NOTES: Credit cards accepted: A Master Card; B Visa; C American Express; D Discover; E Diners Club; F Other; 2 Personal checks accepted; 3 Lunch available; 4 Dinner available; 5 Open all year;

constructed in 1926. Renovated in 1995, it has four guest rooms, each with a private bath. The "Plane" in the name refers to the scenic airplane rides, offered for an additional fee. Your host Craig, a licensed commercial pilot, flies a Piper PA-22, which is hangared on the farm. In the morning, enjoy a full country breakfast in the dining room or sunroom.

Hosts: Audrey and Craig Smith
Rooms: 4 (PB) $65.00
Full Breakfast
Credit Cards: A, B, C
Notes: 2, 5, 7, 8, 10, 11

Battle Island Inn

dens. The Inn overlooks the golf course and the Oswego River. The Honeymoon Suite features a canopy bed, full bath, and private Jacuzzi.

Hosts: Richard and Joyce Rice
Rooms: 5 (PB)
Full Breakfast
Credit Cards: A, B, C, D
Notes: 2, 5, 7, 9, 10

Just a (Plane) B&B

FULTON

Battle Island Inn

2167 State Route 48 North, 13069
(315) 593-3699
E-mail: jkrice@usadatanet.net
battle-island-inn.com

A pre-Civil War farm estate, restored and furnished with period antiques. There are three antique-filled parlors. Guest accommodations are furnished in a variety of styles, including Victorian and Renaissance Revival. Guests are often found relaxing on one of the porches, or strolling through the gar-

GLENS FALLS

Crislip's Bed & Breakfast

693 Ridge Road, Queensbury, 12804
(518) 793-6869

Located in the Adirondack area just minutes from Saratoga Springs and Lake George, this landmark Federal home provides spacious accommodations with period antiques, four-poster beds, and down comforters. The country breakfast menu features such items as buttermilk pancakes, scrambled eggs, and sausages. Your hosts invite you to relax on their porches and enjoy the beautiful mountains of Vermont.

Crislip's

Hosts: Ned and Joyce Crislip
Rooms: 3 (PB) $65-85
Full Breakfast
Credit Cards: A, B, D
Notes: 2, 5, 6, 8, 9, 10, 11

GOWANDA

The Teepee

14396 Four Mile Level Road, Route 438, 14070
(716) 532-2168
E-mail: play7635@aol.com

This B&B is operated by Seneca Indians on the Cattaraugus Indian Reservation near Gowanda. Tours of the

The Teepee

reservation and the Amish community nearby are available.

Hosts: Phyllis & Max Lay
Rooms: 4 (1 PB; 3 SB) $50
Full Breakfast
Credit Cards: None
Notes: 2, 5, 7, 8, 9, 10, 11

HAMMONDSPORT

The Amity Rose Bed & Breakfast

8264 Main Street, 14840
(607) 569-3408; (800) 928-8818
fax: (607) 569-3483
E-mail: bbam@infoblud.net
www.amityroseinn.com

"Country Inn the Village," a quaint Finger Lakes Historic Village, where guests can find antiques, shops, restaurants, or just relax. Eight wineries surround the area. Swim or boat on the lake nearby. The Corning Glass Museum and Watkins Glen Raceway are just 30 minutes away. Niagara Falls just a couple of hours away. All rooms have Queen beds and air-conditioning. Two have whirlpool soaking tubs. Enjoy the spacious guest parlor with fireplace and soft music. A scrumptious breakfast is served. Join us for a delightful stay!

Rooms: 4 (PB) $95-135
Full Breakfast
Credit Cards: None
Notes: 2, 8, 9, 10

Gone with the Wind Bed & Breakfast

453 West Lake Road, Branchport, 14418
(607) 868-4603; fax: (607) 868-0388
www.yatesny.com

NOTES: Credit cards accepted: A Master Card; B Visa; C American Express; D Discover; E Diners Club; F Other; 2 Personal checks accepted; 3 Lunch available; 4 Dinner available; 5 Open all year;

The name paints the picture—an 1887 stone Victorian on 14 acres overlooking our quiet lake cove (adorned by an inviting picnic gazebo). Feel the magic of total relaxation and peace of mind soaking in the solarium hot tub or walking on our pleasant nature trails. Fireplaces, delectable breakfasts, private beach, and dock. Reserve our log lodge for small retreats and friendly gatherings. Located just an hour and a half south of Rochester, N.Y., and 45 minutes from Corning; on Keuka Lake in the Finger Lakes wine country. Come see us soon.

Hosts: Linda and Robert Lewis
Rooms: 10 (4 PB; 6 SB) $80-130
Full Breakfast
Credit Cards: None
Notes: 2, 5, 8, 9, 10, 11

ITHACA

Rose Inn

Route 34 North, Box 6576, 14851
(607) 533-7905; fax: (607) 533-7908
E-mail: info@roseinn.com
www.roseinn.com

An elegant country inn in the heart of the Finger Lakes. Twelve suites with Jacuzzis (seven with fireplaces). Breakfast and dinners served in restored 1850s carriage house. Live jazz Friday and Saturday nights (April through November).

Hosts: Charles and Sherry Rosemann
Rooms: 20 (PB) $125-320
Full Breakfast
Credit Cards: A, B, C
Notes: 2, 4, 5, 8, 9, 10, 11, 12

LAKE GEORGE

Hilltop Cottage Bed & Breakfast

P.O. Box 186, Lakeshore Drive, Bolton Landing, 12814
(518) 644-2492
www.hilltopcottage.com

Homestay B&B in summer resort area of Lake George and eastern Adirondacks. Clean, comfortable, reasonable, and usually quiet.

Hosts: Anita and Charlie Richards
Rooms: 3 (PB) $65-85
Full Breakfast
Credit Cards: None
Note: 2

LEROY

Oatka Creek Bed & Breakfast

71 East Main Street, 14482
(716) 768-6990; (877) 768-6990
E-mail: ocbb@eznet.net

Enjoy warm hospitality and comfortable accommodations at Oatka Creek Bed and Breakfast located in the beautiful, historic village of LeRoy, N.Y.—the birthplace of Jello. Air-conditioned guest rooms feature antique and reproduction furnishings, some with queen beds. A full breakfast and afternoon refreshments are served. Located just five minutes off Exit 47 of I-90. Walk to shops and dining. The perfect overnight hub for exploring Rochester, Buffalo/Niagara Falls, Finger Lakes, museums, colleges, antiquing, and Letchworth State Park.

Hosts: Craig and Lynn Bateman
Rooms: 4 (PB) $70-85
Full Breakfast
Credit Cards: A, B, C
Notes: 2, 5, 7, 8, 10, 12

MADRID

Brandy-View Bed & Breakfast

24 Walker Road, 13660
(315) 322-4429; fax: (315) 322-4678
E-mail: hargrove@northnet.org
home.att.net/~llandi/

Enjoy true country hospitality in a country brick home built in 1849 by Jim's great-grandfather. Located in St. Lawrence County, bordering the U.S.-Canada border. The home is furnished with family heirlooms. Snuggle under homemade quilts and relax in the claw-foot tub. This is a chance to see a modern dairy farm in action; guests are encouraged to tour the milking facility, help feed the many baby calves, meander through the meadows, woods, or along the bab-

**BRANDY-VIEW
BED & BREAKFAST**

bling Brandy Brook. Nearby are the Adirondack Mountains, the St. Lawrence Seaway, the 1,000 Islands, and many Canadian landmarks and attractions, including Ottawa, the Capitol.

Hosts: Grace and James Hargrave
Rooms: 4 (SB) $60
Full Breakfast
Credit Cards: D
Notes: 2, 5, 7, 9, 10, 11, 12

Chipman Acres Guest House

CHIPMAN ACRES GUEST HOUSE

207 Brandy Brook Road, 13660
(315) 322-5588
E-mail: kpacres@northnet.org

A charming and spacious new home adjacent to the family farm communicates warmth and distinctive character with a solarium and five guest rooms. Convenient to area colleges and the majestic St. Lawrence River. Depending on the seasonal whims of the weather, there may be good cross-country skiing, fishing, skating, sailing, and swimming. All rooms are air-conditioned.

Host: Marion Acres
Rooms: 5 (3 PB; 2 SB) $60-75
Full Breakfast
Credit Cards: None
Notes: 2, 5, 7, 8, 9, 10, 11

MARCELLUS

Blakeslee House

3708 South State Road, 13108
(315) 673-2881
E-mail: antiki@twcny.rr.com
cnylodging.com/blakeslee

The Blakeslee House is nestled among the rolling hills of charming and historic Marcellus, New York. Located five minutes from Skaneatles, 20 minutes from Syracuse, and 50 minutes from wine country. You'll be greeted by your hosts Bev and Dave, and at first glance you'll feel right at home. The dwelling built in 1990 is a one of a kind. The interior is accompanied by antiques and four poster beds.

Hosts: Bev and Dave Blakeslee
Rooms: 3 (1 PB; 2 SB) $85-130
Full Breakfast
Credit Cards: A, B
Notes: 2, 7, 8, 9, 10, 11

MUMFORD

The Genesee Country Inn, Circa 1833

948 George Street, 14511
(716) 538-2500; (800) 697-8297
fax: (716) 538-4565
E-mail: room2escapeinn@aol.com
www.geneseecountryinn.com

Don't visit us unless you bring someone you want to like you very much! This historic romantic old mill minutes from downtown Rochester, is just three hours from Toronto. Relax, fly fish, walk our unique eight acres, visit the Genesee Country Museum Nature Center (third largest in U.S.), or take day trips to, Niagara Falls, Letchworth State Park, Rochester, New York, wineries. All rooms have private baths, TVs, air-conditioning, tea, gourmet breakfast. Giftshop. Select Registry, AAA, Mobil.

Hosts: Glenda Barcklow and Kim Rasmussen
Rooms: 9 (PB) $95-160
Full Breakfast
Credit Cards: B, D
Notes: 2, 5, 7, 8, 10

NEW YORK CITY

Holy Family Bed & Breakfast

10-11 49th Avenue, Long Isand City, 11101-5612
(718) 392-7597; fax: (718) 786-3640
E-mail: holyfamilybnb@mindspring.com
www.holyfamilybedandbreakfast.com

Close to the core of the Big Apple, the B&B is just a three-minute subway train ride to Midtown Manhattan, from where guests can walk to Manhattan's interesting spots: The Empire State Building, Fifth Avenue, Rockefeller Center, Times Square, and a host of favorite tourist places. Full breakfast, fully-equipped guests' kitchen, library, organ/piano, telephones, TVs/VCRs. Guests are given free tips on how to get around Manhattan. Nearby are restaurants, diners, stores, and the Gantry Plaza State Park, offering a panoramic view of the Manhattan Skyline. The B&B is two-blocks away from the East River, across from the United Nations. On a starry night, the B&B guests can bask in the glorious sight of the Empire State Building. Saint Mary's Catholic

---

6 Pets welcome; 7 Children welcome; 8 Tennis nearby; 9 Swimming nearby; 10 Golf nearby; 11 Skiing nearby; 12 May be booked through travel agent

Church, across the street, looms tall over the B&B.

Hosts: Tom and Sonia Salerni
Rooms: 4 (2 PB; 3 SB) $75-180
Full Breakfast
Credit Cards: A, B, C, E
Notes: 5, 7, 8

NIAGARA FALLS

The Cameo Inn

4710 Lower River Road, Route 18-F, Lewiston, 14092
(716) 745-3034; E-mail: cameoinn@adelphia.net
www.cameoinn.com

Imagine the ambience of our gracious Queen Anne Victorian authentically furnished with family heirlooms and period antiques, all with a breathtaking view of the Niagara River. Situated on an 80-foot bluff, the inn offers the tranquility of days past with the comforts of today. Three lovely guest rooms with shared or private baths are available, as well as our romantic "Riverview Suite." Breakfast is served at Cameo Manor (our other location) each morning. Smoke-free. No pets, please. Come and enjoy.

Hosts: Greg and Carolyn Fisher
Rooms: 4 (2 PB; 2 SB) $65-115
Full Breakfast
Credit Cards: A, B, D
Notes: 5, 7, 8, 9, 10, 11, 12

The Cameo Manor North

3881 Lower River Road, Route 18-F, Youngstown, 14174
(716) 745-3034
E-mail: cameoinn@adelphia.net
www.cameoinn.com

Located just seven miles north of Niagara Falls, our English manor house is the perfect spot for that quiet getaway you have been dreaming about. Situated on three secluded acres, Cameo Manor North offers a great room with fireplaces, solarium, library, and an outdoor terrace for your enjoyment. Our beautifully appointed guest rooms include suites with private sunrooms and cable television. A breakfast buffet is served daily.

Hosts: Greg and Carolyn Fisher
Rooms: 5 (3 PB; 2 SB) $65-130
Full Breakfast
Credit Cards: A, B, D
Notes: 5, 7, 8, 9, 10, 11, 12

The Country Club Inn

5170 Lewiston Road, Lewiston, 14092
(716) 285-4869; fax: (716) 285-5614
E-mail: ctyclubinn@pcom.net
www.countryclubinn.com

Located just minutes from Niagara Falls, the Country Club Inn is a non-smoking B&B. Three large and beautifully decorated guest rooms each have a private bath, queen bed, and cable TV. A great room with a wood-burning fireplace and pool table leads to a covered patio overlooking the golf course. A full breakfast is served at guests' convenience in our elegant dining room. Convenient to the NYS thruway and bridges to Canada.

Hosts: Barbara Ann and Norman Oliver
Rooms: 3 (PB) $90-115
Full Breakfast
Credit Cards: None
Notes: 2, 5, 7, 9, 10

NOTES: Credit cards accepted: A Master Card; B Visa; C American Express; D Discover; E Diners Club; F Other; 2 Personal checks accepted; 3 Lunch available; 4 Dinner available; 5 Open all year;

Manchester House

653 Main Street, 14301-1701
(716) 285-5717; (800) 489-3009
fax: (716) 282-2144
E-mail: carl@manchesterhouse.com
www.manchesterhouse.com

This brick-and-shingle residence was built in 1903 and used as a doctor's residence and office for many years. After extensive renovation, Manchester House opened as a B&B in 1991. Carl and Lis received a Niagara Falls beautification award for their work. Manchester House is within easy walking distance of the falls, aquarium, and geological museum. Off-street parking.

Hosts: Lis and Carl Slenk
Rooms: 3 (PB) $60-100
Full Breakfast
Credit Cards: A, B, D
Notes: 2, 5, 10, 12

OLIVEREA

Slide Mountain Forest House

805 Oliverea Road, 12410-5317
(845) 254-5365; fax: (845) 254-6107
E-mail: slide_mtn@yahoo.com
slidemountain-inn.com

Nestled in the Catskill Mountains State Park our inn offers the flavor and charm of the old country. A 1900s farmstead with views of apple orchard lawns, towering evergreens, and gentle mountains. Come enjoy our beautiful country setting, superb lodging, fine dining, and chalet rentals. Family-run for 65 years, we strive to give you a pleasant and enjoyable stay.

Hiking, fishing, tennis, pool and lawn sports available on site.

Hosts: Ralph and Ursula Combe
Rooms: 19 (15 PB; 4 SB) $50-120
Full Breakfast
Credit Cards: A, B, D
Notes: 2, 3, 4, 5, 7, 8, 9, 10, 11

ONEONTA

The Murphy House

33 Walnut Street, 13820
(607) 432-1367 (phone/fax)
E-mail: mmurphy@dmcom.net
www.community-mine.com/murphy

Gracious accommodations in the historic district of Oneonta, a small rural city nestled among the hills of upstate New York. This 1920 B&B home features delightful breakfasts, and is within walking distance of Main Street. Nearby attractions include the National Soccer and Baseball Halls of Fame, the beauty of God's four seasons, and cultural events ranging from opera to dancing under the stars. Thirty minutes from Cooperstown, three and a half hours from New York City.

Hosts: Nancy and Mike Murphy
Rooms: 2 (PB) $85-95
Full Breakfast
Credit Cards: None
Notes: 2, 5, 7

PIFFARD

The Silver Tendril

3054 Main Street, Route 36, Piffard, 14533
(716) 243-3912

---

6 Pets welcome; 7 Children welcome; 8 Tennis nearby; 9 Swimming nearby; 10 Golf nearby; 11 Skiing nearby; 12 May be booked through travel agent

E-mail: silvertendril@juno.com
website.mciworld.com/~silvertendril
@mciworld.com

Our easy-to-find, 1827 Federal-style home is located in the western Finger Lakes area, south of Rochester near spectacular Letchworth State Park and the Abbey of the Genesee. Stroll through Gary's 150-vine vineyard, enjoy Shirley's beautiful flower gardens, or relax on the swinging bench near the spring-fed pond. A full breakfast features homemade specialities. Reserve the Monet room or the Shaker Room; each is very attractive and has a private bath. Children 13 and over welcome.

Hosts: Gary and Shirley Cox
Rooms: 2 (PB) $85
Full Breakfast
Credit Cards: None
Notes: 2, 5, 7, 9, 10

PORTAGEVILLE

Broman's Genesee Falls Inn

Main & Hamilton Streets, P.O. Box 238, 14536
(716) 493-2484; fax: (716) 468-5654

An 1870 inn with a beautiful Victorian dining room and guest rooms. Chef-owned and family-operated. Fine food and wine selections with a large appetizer list. Varied menu includes steaks, seafood, chicken, and prime rib. Delicious dinners-for-two. Homemade soups, dressing, breads, and desserts. One-half mile from the south entrance to Letchworth State Park. The history and old-world charm will bring you here; the friendly atmosphere and fine food will bring you back.

Hosts: John (JB) Broman & Lynne
Rooms: 13 (11 PB; 2 SB) $62-140
Full Breakfast
Credit Cards: A, B
Notes: 2, 3, 4, 5, 7, 9, 10, 11

SILVER CREEK

Pinewoods Cottage Bed & Breakfast

11634 York Road, 14136
(716) 934-4173; fax: (716) 934-2415
E-mail: estelle@crinopinewoodscottage.com
www.crinopinewoodscottage.com

Pinewoods Cottage B&B, surrounded by 20 acres of woodlands, offers an eclectic atmosphere and décor in a private home-away-from-home. The centrally air-conditioned cottage has three guest rooms with private baths. Enjoy a full, candlelight breakfast in the formal dining room or sunroom; partake of afternoon tea and snacks in the family room. Relax on the covered front porch, sunroom, or back deck. Watch TV, play the piano, organ, chess, cards, or Scrabble. Walk through the woods. Enjoy a relaxing visit in a nonsmoking B&B.

Host: Estelle M. Crino
Rooms: 3 (PB) $65-85
Full Breakfast
Credit Cards: A, B
Notes: 2, 9, 10, 11

SYRACUSE AREA

Elaine's Bed & Breakfast Selections

4987 Kingston Road, Elbridge, NY 13060-9773
(315) 689-2082

Elaine's Bed & Breakfast Selections is a reservation service that lists B&Bs in New York State in the following towns: Auburn, Aurora, Baldwinsville, Canastota, Chittenango, Cincinnatus, Cleveland, Clinton, Cortland, DeWitt, Durhanville, Elbridge, Fair Haven, Fayetteville, Geneva, Glen Haven, Gorham, Groton, Hague, High Falls, Homer, Jamesville, Johnstown, Kingston, Lafayette, Lyons, Marcellus, Margaretville, Marathon, New Lebanon, Northville, Ovid, Oneida Castle, Owasco Lake, Palmyra, Port Ontario, Preble, Richfield Springs, Rome, Rock Stream, Sheldrake-on-Cayuga, Sherrill, Skaneateles, South Otselic, Spencer, Syracuse, Tully, Vernon, Vesper, and Westport. Elaine N. Samuels, director.

Braeside

SOUTH COLTON

Braeside Bed & Breakfast

20A Cold Brook Drive, 13687
(315) 262-2553; fax: (208) 247-2077
E-mail: braesidebb@webtv.net
www.braesidebb.com

Braeside, a modified Cape Cod riverfront home with a wraparound deck and two docks, is situated on a hill on the Raquet River, nestled in the northern foothills of the Adirondacks. Featuring antique furnishings and collections, the B&B offers four cozy, comfortable country guest rooms. Nature beckons you to hike, bike, canoe, bird-watch, fish, kayak, cross-country ski, or just relax. Rowboat and canoe available. Golf, museums, antiquing, and colleges are nearby. Freshly prepared, full breakfast at riverside, in dinette, or gazebo. Package deals. Air-conditioning.

Host: Joann E. Ferris
Rooms: 4 (SB) $60-85
Full Breakfast
Credit Cards: None
Notes: 2, 5, 7, 8, 9, 10, 11, 12

SOUTHOLD

Seahouse

12910 Main Road, P.O. Box 13, East Marion,
11939
(631) 477-0472
E-mail: millerseahouse@webtv
www.northfork.com/seahouse

Enjoy waterviews from 22-foot living room window—lighthouse, Shelter Island, Orient State Park. Three steps down and you begin shell collecting or swimming in crystal clear Bay. Chaise lounges on furnished patio await. Full breakfast served under new awning overlooking the beach. Bike, golf, play golf or tennis nearby. Shopping mall, antiques, and many vineyards. Two bedrooms share skylighted bath.

Host: Norma Miller
Rooms: 2 (SB) $125.00 plus tax
Full Breakfast
Credit Cards: None
Notes: 2, 8, 9, 10

TOMKINS COVE

Cove House

Cove House

P.O. Box 81, 10986
(845) 429-9695
E-mail dpscis@aol.com
www.pojonews.com/covehouse

The Cove House B&B is a modern but rustic home with a majestic view of the Hudson River. Enjoy coffee and pastries in the sunny, intimate solarium on the large, airy deck. History buffs can tour Stony Point Battlefield

and the U.S. Military Academy at West Point. Nature lovers can hike for miles through the scenic woods of Bear Mountain and Harriman State Parks. Weekend foragers will find the village of Nyack perfect for antiquing and lunch. All just minutes away.

Hosts: Pat and Dan Sciscente
Rooms: 3 (1 PB; 2 SB) $75-100
Full Breakfast
Credit Cards: None
Notes: 2, 8, 10

UTICA

The Iris Stonehouse Bed & Breakfast

16 Derbyshire Place, 13501
(315) 732-6720; (800) 446-1456
fax: (315) 797-5134
E-mail: irisbnb@borg.com
innsmart.com/newyork/central/smartlistings/

Located in a quiet residential neighborhood convenient to all Utica area attractions, the Iris Stonehouse B&B offers hospitality and charm within. A 1930 English Tudor Historic Register house with leaded-glass windows and iris motifs throughout, it has been out-

The Iris Stonehouse

fitted with central air-conditioning to quietly cool your sleep on those hot nights of summer, and a sitting room fireplace to warm conversations on those snowy days of winter. The hospitality starts with a warm welcome from hosts, and it is sustained with an appetizing full breakfast offered daily. Four eclectically furnished bedrooms, two of them with private baths, offer rest and relaxation for up to eight guests. One of the most popular rooms is the Queen Bedroom, with a private bath. This room feature a unique shower with six side sprays and the overhead shower. Often guests call and request "The Room with the Great Shower."

Hosts: Jim and Nellie Chanatry
Rooms: 4 (2 PB; 2 SB) $59-89
Full Breakfast
Credit Cards: A, B, D
Notes: 2, 5, 7, 8, 10, 11

What Cheer Hall Bed & Breakfast

7482 Main Street, P.O. Box 417, Newport, 13416
(315) 845-8312
E-mail: jimmer@borg.com
www.borg.com/~jimmer

What Cheer Hall was built in 1812 for Benjamin Bowen, pioneer, miller, distiller, of the Kuyahoora Valley. The stone home is of Georgian Federal foursquare architecture, comfortably furnished with antiques, some of which may be purchased. The house was listed on the New York State and National Registers of Historic Places in 1998. Area attractions include a premier golf course, fishing in the renowned West Canada Creek, an-

tique shopping, skiing, hiking, biking, restaurants, and theater.

Hosts: Phyllis and Jim Fisher
Rooms: 2 (PB) $55-65
Full Breakfast
Credit Cards: A, B, C
Notes: 2, 5, 8, 10, 11

WARRENSBURG

White House Lodge

3760 Main Street, 12885
(518) 623-3640

An 1847 Victorian home in the heart of the queen village of the Adirondacks, an antiquer's paradise. The home is furnished with many Victorian antiques which sends you back in time. Five minutes to Lake George, Fort William Henry, and Great Escape. Walk to restaurants. Enjoy air-conditioned TV lounge for guests only, window and Casablanca fans. Children over 7 welcome.

Hosts: Jim and Ruth Gibson
Rooms: 3 (SB) $85
Continental Breakfast
Credit Cards: A, B
Notes: 5, 7, 8, 9, 10, 11

WATKINS GLEN

South Glenora Tree Farm Bed & Breakfast

546 South Glenora Road, Dundee, 14837
(607) 243-7414
www.fingerlakes.net/treefarm

Just seven miles above Watkins Glen, situated on a 60-acre tree farm, this 1850 converted barn has five queen

---

6 Pets welcome; 7 Children welcome; 8 Tennis nearby; 9 Swimming nearby; 10 Golf nearby; 11 Skiing nearby; 12 May be booked through travel agent

South Glenora Tree Farm

bedrooms with private baths. The barn has central air-conditioning, an extra furnished great room, and a guest kitchen. Three fireplaces. Enjoy the wraparound front porch, picnic pavilion, and hiking trails. Bring your camera and appetite.

Host: Steve Ebert , D. Min.
Rooms: 5 (PB) $75-139
Full Breakfast
Credit Cards: A, B, D
Notes: 5, 7, 9, 10

WEST HAMPTON BEACH

1880 House
Bed & Breakfast

2 Seafield Lane, P.O. Box 648, 11978

1880 House

(631) 288-1559; (800) 346-3290
fax: (631) 288-7696
E-mail: bb1880house@worldnet.att.net
www.1880-house.com

The Seafield House is a hidden, 100-year-old country retreat perfect for a romantic hideaway, a weekend of privacy, or just a change of pace from city life. Located only 90 minutes from Manhattan, Seafield House is ideally situated on Westhampton Beach's exclusive Seafield Lane. The estate includes a swimming pool and tennis court, and is a short, brisk walk from the ocean beach. The area offers outstanding restaurants, shops, and opportunities for antique hunting. Indoor tennis, Guerney's International Health Spa, and Montauk Point are nearby.

Host: Elsie Pardee Collins
Rooms: 3 suites (PB) $125-225
Full Breakfast
Credit Cards: A, B
Notes: 5, 8, 9, 10, 12

WINDHAM

Country Suite
Bed & Breakfast

P.O. Box 700, 12496
phone/fax: (518) 734-4079; (888) 883-0444
E-mail: ctrysuite@aol.com

"First you notice the level of taste, the fit and finish. Then you see the gracious rooms, the sprawling grounds, the perfectly placed gazebo. Here, you'll discover exquisite country elegance with a distinctly urban flair."— *Inn Review*. This beautifully restored 1865 farmhouse is located just 2 miles from Ski Windham. Nestled deep in

---

the heart of Greene County's Catskill Mountains, this retreat invites you to take a deep breath, relax and indulge yourself. It offers five guest rooms, each with its own private bath, and king or queen beds. Country Suite is a favorite for those interested in quiet romantic stays. All visits include a full gourmet breakfast. Nearby, you'll find excellent dining, quaint shops, historic sites, golfing, biking, swimming, boating, tennis, hiking, skiing, horseback riding, and a wealth of antiques. Experience the magic of the Catskills and the beauty of the New York countryside at Country Suite, "a noteworthy bed & breakfast." You will certainly find your stay enjoyable.

Hosts: Sondra Clark and Lorraine Seidel

66 Garrett Road, 13865
(607) 655-1204
E-mail: cntryhaven@aol.com

Country Haven is a "haven" for today's weary travelers, as well as a weekend hideaway where warm hospitality awaits you. We offer guest rooms in a restored 1800s family farmhouse and a new log home, all in a quiet country setting on 350 acres. Browse through our gift shop. We are located a mile from Interstate 17, Exit 78; 12 miles east of Binghamton; and seven miles from Interstate 81.

Host: Rita Saunders
Rooms: 6 (PB) $45-65
Full Breakfast
Credit Cards: A, B, D
Notes: 2, 5, 7, 9, 10

Rooms: 5 (PB) $99-129
Full Breakfast
Credit Cards: A, B, C, D, E
Notes: 2, 5, 8, 9, 10, 11, 12

WINDSOR

Country Haven
Bed & Breakfast

NORTH CAROLINA

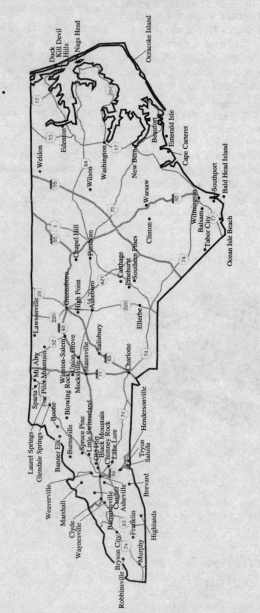

Duck
Kill Devil Hills
Nags Head
Ocracoke Island
17
19
Edenton
Weldon
64
Wilson
Washington
17
New Bern
Beaufort
Emerald Isle
Cape Carteret
Southport
Bald Head Island
Ocean Isle Beach
Warsaw
40
Wilmington
Tabor City
Balsam
17
Clinton
70
74
Chapel Hill
1
85
Pittsboro
Carthage
Southern Pines
Pinehurst
421
Ellerbe
220
Lawsonville
29
Greensboro
High Point
Asheboro
Salisbury
85
Charlotte
74
220
40
Union Grove
Winston-Salem
Statesville
52
Mocksville
Sparta
Mt. Airy
Pilot Mountain
77
Boone
Blowing Rock
Hendersonville
74
Laurel Springs
Glendale Springs
Banner Elk
Burnsville
Spruce Pine
Little Switzerland
Old Fort
Black Mountain
Chimney Rock
Lake Lure
85
Tryon
Saluda
Weaverville
Marshall
Clyde
Waynesville
Asheville
Candler
Barnardsville
23
Franklin
Brevard
Highlands
74
Bryson City
Murphy
Robbinsville

29

95

17

NOTES: Credit cards accepted: A Master Card; B Visa; C American Express; D Discover; E Diners
Club; F Other; 2 Personal checks accepted; 3 Lunch available; 4 Dinner available; 5 Open all year;

North Carolina

ASHEVILLE

Albemarle Inn

86 Edgemont Road, 28801
(828) 255-0027; (800) 621-7435
fax: (828) 236-3397
E-mail: info@albemarleinn.com
www.albemarleinn.com

This elegant Greek Revival mansion, listed on the National Register of Historic Places and located in the beautiful residential Grove Park section of Asheville, features an exquisite carved oak staircase with unique balcony, and a 60-foot stone veranda overlooking three-quarters of an acre of landscaped grounds. Exceptionally specious period rooms offer private baths with clawfoot tubs, fine linens, robes, and queen- or king-sized beds.

Hosts: Cathy and Larry Sklar
Rooms: 11 (PB) $125-285
Full Breakfast
Credit Cards: A, B, C, D
Notes: 2, 5, 8, 10, 12

Cedar Crest Victorian Inn

674 Biltmore Avenue, 28803
(828) 252-1389; (800) 252-0310
fax: (828) 253-7667
E-mail: stay@cedarcrestvictorianinn.com
www.cedarcrestvictorianinn.com

This 1890 Queen Anne mansion is listed on the National Register of Historic Places. One of the largest and most opulent residences surviving Asheville's 1890s boom period, it boasts a captain's walk, projecting turrets, lavish interior woodwork, stained glass, and expansive veranda to welcome guests. Rooms are furnished with antiques, and all the Victorian trappings of satin and lace. Children over 10 welcome.

Hosts: Jack and Barbara McEwan
Rooms: 11 (PB) $145-210
Full Breakfast
Credit Cards: A, B, C, D
Notes: 2, 5, 8, 10, 12

Chestnut Street Inn

176 East Chestnut Street, 28801
(828) 285-0705; (800) 894-2955
www.chestnutstreetinn.com

Located in the Chestnut Hill historic district, just a five-minute walk from downtown Asheville's antique shops, art galleries and restaurants, this lovely, antique-filled Colonial Revival home, circa 1905, offers a delightful "visit to Grandma's house." Enjoy full gourmet breakfasts, afternoon tea, rocking on the beautiful porches, or petting the canine butler, Mr. Bentley. Five rooms/one suite, all have private baths and air-conditioning, some with working fireplaces and whirlpool. Includes a full breakfast and afternoon tea.

Hosts: Paulette and Gene Dugger
Rooms: 5 (PB); 1 suite (PB) $120-265
Full Breakfast
Credit Cards: A, B, C, D
Notes: 2, 5, 8, 9, 10, 11, 12

---

6 Pets welcome; 7 Children welcome; 8 Tennis nearby; 9 Swimming nearby; 10 Golf nearby; 11 Skiing nearby; 12 May be booked through travel agent

Dry Ridge Inn

26 Brown Street, Weaverville, 28787
(828) 658-3899; (800) 839-3899
fax: (828) 658-9533
E-mail: innkeeper@dryridgeinn.com
www.dryridgeinn.com

Our charming three-story home has eight rooms with private baths, some with fireplaces and some can be combined to make suites for large families. You will find our home comfortable, food delicious, and our spacious grounds inviting and relaxing. Enjoy a book on the porch swing or gaze into our water garden and let the waterfall soothe you.

Hosts: Howard and Kristen Dusenberg
Rooms: 8 (PB) $95-155
Full Breakfast
Credit Cards: A, B, C, D
Notes: 2, 5, 7, 10, 11

The Old Reynolds Mansion

100 Reynolds Heights, 28804
(828) 254-0496; (800) 709-0496
www.oldreynoldsmansion.com

An antebellum mansion in a country setting, this elegant, restored inn has

The Old Reynolds Mansion

mountain views from all rooms, huge verandas, wood-burning fireplaces, a swimming pool, and air-conditioning. A Continental breakfast and evening beverage are served. Located just minutes from area attractions, but far enough away from the inner city to experience what coming to the mountains is all about.

Hosts: Fred and Helen Faber/ Lance and Meta
 Faber
Rooms: 11 (PB) $85-150
Full Breakfast
Credit Cards: None
Notes: 2, 5, 8, 9, 10, 11

BALD HEAD ISLAND

Theodosia's Bed & Breakfast Inn

P.O. Box 3130, 28461
(910) 457-6563; (800) 656-1812
fax: (910) 457-6055
E-mail: garrett.albertson@worldnet.att.net
www.theodosias.com

Theodosia means "gift of God." Dr. and Mrs. Albertson have spent 35 years in ministry and now seek to share this wonderful place where guests may be reminded again of who they are and whose they are. A place to recapture your heart and rekindle your life. A "new Victorian" seaside inn on an unspoiled island.

Hosts: Donna and Garrett Albertson
Rooms: 13 (PB) $175-265
Full Breakfast
Credit Cards: A, B, D
Notes: 2, 5, 8, 9, 10, 12

NOTES: Credit cards accepted: A Master Card; B Visa; C American Express; D Discover; E Diners Club; F Other; 2 Personal checks accepted; 3 Lunch available; 4 Dinner available; 5 Open all year;

BALSAM

Balsam Mountain Inn

P.O. Box 40, 68 Seven Springs Drive, 28707
(828) 456-9498; (800) 224-9498
fax: (828) 456-9298
E-mail: balsaminn@earthlink.net
www.balsaminn.com

Nestled among lofty peaks in the Great Smoky Mountains just off the Blue Ridge Parkway, this historic inn was built in 1908, restored in 1991, and now offers 50 cheerful rooms, two 100-foot porches with rockers and a view, a 2,000-volume library, and gracious dining. Plump pillows and soft comforters will inspire pleasant dreams, while the friendly staff attend to your every need.

Hosts: Merrily Teasley, Forest Ray
Rooms: 50 (PB) $90-150
Full Breakfast
Credit Cards: A, B, D
Notes: 2, 4, 5, 7, 8, 9, 10, 12

BANNER ELK

The Old-Turnpike House

317 Old Turnpike Road, 28604
phone/fax: (828) 898-5611; (888) 802-4487
E-mail: otph@skybest.com
www.oldturnpikehouse.com

This delightful, restored farmhouse offers guests a refreshing retreat and is reminiscent of a bygone era. The turn-of-the-century farmhouse is located at the foot of Beech Mountain in the picturesque town of Banner Elk, just twenty minutes from the Blue Ridge Parkway (exit State Route 221), and Grandfather Mountain. After a hearty breakfast enjoy a day in the mountains: downhill skiing at Sugar and Beech Mountains, white water rafting, fishing, hiking, horseback riding, or just browsing through the many shops in Banner Elk and nearby Blowing Rock. Families welcome.

Hosts: Ernest and Rebecca Du Ross
Rooms: 5 (PB) $85-119
Full Breakfast
Credit Cards: A, B, C
Notes: 2, 5, 8, 9, 10, 11, 12

BLACK MOUNTAIN

Friendship Lodge

P.O. Box 877, 28711
(828) 669-9294 (mid-May–mid-Nov.)
(727) 895-4964 (Dec.–mid-May)
(888) 669-6066

A cozy haven on Old 70 East in Ridgecrest, two miles east of Black Mountain. We have ten nicely decorated rooms, most with two double beds, two with king beds. A delicious breakfast is included. Groups and reunions are welcome. We can accommodate up to 24 people. It's like going to Grandma's house. We are a half mile from the Ridgecrest Conference Center and minutes away from

---

6 Pets welcome; 7 Children welcome; 8 Tennis nearby; 9 Swimming nearby; 10 Golf nearby; 11 Skiing nearby; 12 May be booked through travel agent

Montreat, Blue Ridge Assembly, and Christmont.

Hosts: Bob and Sarah La Brant
Rooms: 10 (8 PB; 2 SB) $55
Full Breakfast
Credit Cards: None
Notes: 2, 7, 8, 9, 10

BOONE

Gragg House
Bed & Breakfast

Kalmia Acres, 210 Ridge Point Drive, 28607
(828) 264-7289
E-mail: gragghouse@boone.net
www.gragghousebandb.com

Nestled on a densely wooded ridge, the Gragg House is ten minutes from the Blue Ridge Parkway, and only one mile from downtown Boone and Appalachian State University. Every portal opens to a lush landscape of native wildflowers and perennial gardens. This secluded, restful haven is best described as an atmosphere of interior design elegance offered with true Southern hospitality. Immaculate,

Gragg House

spacious, private rooms and a silver-service, full breakfast ensure a truly wonderful B&B stay. Children 12 and over welcome.

Hosts: Judy and Robert Gragg
Rooms: 3 (1 PB; 2 SB) $89-99
Full Breakfast
Credit Cards: None
Notes: 2, 5, 7, 8, 9, 10, 11

BURNSVILLE

A Little Bit of Heaven
Bed & Breakfast

937 Bear Wallow Road, 28714-6539
(828) 675-5379
E-mail: heavenbb@m-y.net
bbonline.com/nc/heaven

North Carolina's best kept secret! Very private, yet very convenient to town. Large home on top of mountain with breathtaking views. Unique stone structure with circular stone wall and fireplace in great room. All guest rooms have private baths. Traditionally decorated. We specialize in hospitality and great food!

Hosts: Shelley and John Johnson
Rooms: 4 (PB) $70-80
Full Breakfast
Credit Cards: A, B
Notes: 2, 5, 7, 8, 9, 10, 11

CAPE CARTERET

Harborlight
Guest House
Bed & Breakfast

332 Live Oak Drive, 28584
(252) 393-6868; (800) 624-VIEW

NOTES: Credit cards accepted: A Master Card; B Visa; C American Express; D Discover; E Diners Club; F Other; 2 Personal checks accepted; 3 Lunch available; 4 Dinner available; 5 Open all year;

fax: (252) 393-6868
www.bbhost.com/harborlightgh

The Harborlight is a romantic, secluded inn situated on a peninsula with a waterview on three sides! All suites feature two-person Jacuzzis, and/or fireplaces, and stunning waterviews. A gourmet breakfast is served in suite or deckside. Favorite guest activities include barrier island excursions for shelling and pristine beaches, horseback riding on the beach, or shopping in the waterfront villages of Beaufort and Swansboro. Visit our website for photos/descriptions of all suites.

Hosts: Bobby and Anita Gill
Rooms: 7 (PB) $140-250
Full Breakfast
Credit Cards: A, B, C
Notes: 5, 8, 9, 10

EDENTON

Albemarle House Bed & Breakfast

204 West Queen Street, 27932
(252) 482-8204
E-mail: albemarlehouse@inteliport.com
www.bbonline.com/nc/albemarle/

Enjoy welcoming refreshments on the gingerbread porch or in the parlor of our circa 1900 country Victorian home. Located in Edenton's historic district, we are just two blocks from the Albemarle Sound and downtown. Our air-conditioned home is furnished with antiques and reproductions, stenciling, quilts, collections, and the innkeeper's artwork. Three spacious guest rooms are complete with queen beds, TVs, and private baths. A fam-

Albemarle House

ily suite is available. Coffee and sweet breads await outside your door each morning. An elegant full breakfast is served by candlelight. Bicycles and sailing cruises are offered to guests. Children over 10 welcome.

Hosts: Marijane and Reuel Schappel
Rooms: 3 (PB) $80
Full Breakfast
Credit Cards: A, B, C
Notes: 2, 5, 7, 8, 9, 10

Captain's Quarters Inn

202 West Queen Street, 27932-1840
(252) 482-8945; (800) 482-8945
E-mail: captqtrinn@coastalnet.com
www.captainsquartersinn.com

"The South's prettiest town" is awaiting your visit to the Captain's Quarters Inn in the heart of the historic district, two blocks form the Albemarle Sound. This 1907 Colonial Revival Inn, an elegant B&B with each guest room featuring sailing captain themes, offers private, modern baths (one Jacuzzi), TVs, and phones in each room. Welcome refreshments, a Continental breakfast brought to your door, a served three-course breakfast

---

6 Pets welcome; 7 Children welcome; 8 Tennis nearby; 9 Swimming nearby; 10 Golf nearby; 11 Skiing nearby; 12 May be booked through travel agent

Captain's Quarters Inn

Monday through Saturday, and a breakfast buffet on Sunday are features you won't want to miss. A guided historic walking tour, three-hour sail with Captain Bill, four-course gourmet dinner, welcome hors d'oeuvres, and gourmet breakfasts are included in your night sailing package for two people April-October at $299-$319 per couple. Mystery weekends are offered October through March at $279-$299 per couple. Guided trolley tours through the first capital of the Carolinas, biking, fishing, antiquing, art galleries, and nearby plantations are additional attractions.

Hosts: Bill and Phyllis Pepper
Rooms: 8 (PB) $85-100
Full Breakfast
Credit Cards: A, B
Notes: 2, 5, 7, 8, 9, 10

EMERALD ISLE

Emerald Isle Inn & Bed & Breakfast by the Sea

502 Ocean Drive, 28594
(252) 354-3222

Located on the ocean, this jewel of a Crystal Coast inn is truly a treasure to be discovered. It's a peaceful haven to all who seek a quiet, restful, sun-filled getaway. Your stay includes a full Continental breakfast with freshly ground coffee and other tempting samplings. Suites include Victorian, French country, tropical, new luxury suite, and a new king suite with ocean views and a porch swing. All suites have private entrances and bathrooms. With direct beach access, you are only steps away from discovering the gentle shoreline treasures. We are minutes from antiquing, fine restaurants, historic sites, and the outdoor drama passion play *Worthy is the Lamb.* Come to your home away from home for a visit you'll always remember! AAA-rated.

Hosts: Al and Marilyn Detwiller
Rooms: 4 (PB) $75-150
Continental Breakfast
Credit Cards: A, B, D
Notes: 5, 7, 8, 9, 10, 12

FRANKLIN

Franklin Terrace

159 Harrison Avenue, 28734-2913
(828) 524-7907; (800) 633-2431
E-mail: stay@franklinterrace.com
www.franklinterrace.com

The Franklin Terrace, built as a school in 1887, is listed on the National Register of Historic Places. The Terrace is a lovely two-story B&B that offers nostalgic charm and comfortable accommodations. Its wide porches and large guest rooms filled with period antiques will carry you to a time gone

NOTES: Credit cards accepted: A Master Card; B Visa; C American Express; D Discover; E Diners Club; F Other; 2 Personal checks accepted; 3 Lunch available; 4 Dinner available; 5 Open all year;

by when Southern hospitality was at its best. The Terrace offers a casual shopping experience where you can browse through the antiques, crafts, and gifts for sale on the main floor. You also will be within walking distance of Franklin's famous gem shops, clothing boutiques, and fine restaurants.

Hosts: Ed and Helen Henson
Rooms: 9 (PB) $59-69
Full Breakfast
Credit Cards: A, B, C, D
Notes: 2, 7, 8, 9, 10, 12

Heritage Inn Bed & Breakfast

43 Heritage Hollow Drive, 28734
(828) 524-4150; (888) 524-4150
E-mail: heritage@smnet.net
www.heritageinnbb.com

Five cozy, comfortable rooms with private shower baths and private entrances with porches/balconies. Kitchenettes and apartment available. Gathering room for reading, cable TV, and videos, with complimentary snacks and beverages available during the day. Large veranda with rockers. In downtown Franklin, walk to shops, antiques, and restaurants. Short drives to rafting, hiking, golf, gem mines, and most area attractions. Children over 12 welcome.

Rooms: 6 (PB) $75-105
Full Breakfast
Credit Cards: A, B, C, E
Notes: 2, 5, 7, 8, 9, 10, 11, 12

HENDERSONVLLE

Apple Inn: A Bed & Breakfast

1005 White Pine Drive, 28739
(828) 693-0107; (800) 615-6611
fax: (828) 693-0173
www.appleinn.com

There's no place like home—unless it's Apple Inn! Only two miles from downtown Hendersonville, the inn is situated on three acres and features charmingly comfortable rooms, each with a modern, private bath that awaits your arrival. Delicious, home-cooked breakfast, fresh flowers, and antiques compliment the ambience of this turn-of-the-century home. Enjoy billiards, tennis, swimming, hiking, antiquing, bird-watching, or just relaxing.

Rooms: 5 (PB) $75-125
Full Breakfast
Credit Cards: A, B
Notes: 2, 5, 7, 8, 9, 10, 11, 12

The Waverly Inn

783 North Main Street, 28792-3622
(828) 693-9193; (800) 537-8195
fax: (828) 692-1010
E-mail: waverlyinn@ioa.com
weaverlyinn.com

Personal service helps to set us apart and being in the mountains helps to keep us there. Special touches like 300-count sheets, Egyptian cotton towels, robes, data-ports, VCRs, and cable televisions make our rates well worth it. The Waverly Inn is listed on the National Register of Historic Places and is Hendersonville's oldest inn. The inn has been cited in national

---

6 Pets welcome; 7 Children welcome; 8 Tennis nearby; 9 Swimming nearby; 10 Golf nearby; 11 Skiing nearby; 12 May be booked through travel agent

publications such as *The New York Times, Southern Living*, and *Vogue Magazine*.

Hosts: John and Diane Sheiry, Darla Olmstead
Rooms: 14 (PB) $109-195
Full Breakfast
Credit Cards: A, B, C, D, E
Notes: 5, 7, 8, 9, 10, 12

HIGHLANDS

Long House
Bed & Breakfast

P.O. Box 2078, 28741-2078
(828) 526-4394; (877) 841-9222
fax: (828) 526-4394
E-mail: lylong@aol.com

Long House B&B is located at the 4,000-foot level in the Blue Ridge Mountains of Western North Carolina. Our community is surrounded by the Nantahala National Forest with lots of hiking trails, water falls, and scenic areas as well as some unique shopping and dining experiences.

Long House

Hosts: Lynn and Valerie Long
Rooms: 4 (PB) $75-150
Full Breakfast
Credit Cards: A, B
Notes: 2, 5, 7, 8, 9, 10

HIGH POINT

The Bouldin House
Bed & Breakfast

4332 Archdale Road, 27263
(336) 431-4909; (800) 739-1816
fax: (336) 431-4914
E-mail: relax@bouldinhouse.com
www.bouldinhouse.com

The Bouldin House

Enjoy fine lodging and hospitality amidst America's finest home furnishings showrooms! Our finely crafted, historic B&B sits on three acres of a former tobacco farm. Quiet, country atmosphere; casual and relaxed, yet elegant. Warmly decorated rooms combine old and new, each with spacious, modern, private baths. Awaken to an early morning coffee/tea service. Follow the aroma of our chef's choice, gourmet breakfast, to the oak-paneled dining room. Come; indulge.

Hosts: Ann and Larry Miller
Rooms: 4 (PB) $90-120
Full Breakfast
Credit Cards: A, B, C, D
Notes: 2, 5, 8, 10, 12

NOTES: Credit cards accepted: A Master Card; B Visa; C American Express; D Discover; E Diners Club; F Other; 2 Personal checks accepted; 3 Lunch available; 4 Dinner available; 5 Open all year;

KILL DEVIL HILLS

Cypress House
Bed & Breakfast

500 North Virginia Dare Trail, 27948
(252) 441-6127; (800) 554-2764
fax: (252) 441-2009
E-mail: cypresshse@aol.com
www.cypresshouseinn.com

Cypress House B&B, a romantic seaside inn, is ideally located only 200
yards from the Atlantic Ocean in Kill
Devil Hills. Originally built in the
1940s as a private, Outer Banks hunting and fishing lodge, the interior is
noted for its soft cypress tongue-and-
groove paneled walls and ceilings.
The six guest rooms offer private
shower baths, ceiling fans, central air-
conditioning, and color cable television. A hearty, home-baked breakfast
is served each morning, as well as afternoon tea.

Hosts: Karen and Leon Faso
Rooms: 6 (PB) $75-140
Full Breakfast
Credit Cards: A, B, C, D
Notes: 2, 5, 8, 9, 10

The White Egret
Bed & Breakfast

1057 Colington Road, Ocean Bay Boulevard,
    27948
(252) 441-7719; (888) 387-7719
fax: (252) 480-1931
E-mail: jparsons@pinn.net
www.whiteegret.com

A central location on North Carolina's Outer Banks gives access to
historical areas such as the Wright
Brothers Memorial, the Lost Colony,
Elizabeth II sailing ship, and much

more. Our spacious rooms are furnished with king beds, private baths
with Jacuzzis, central air, ceiling fans,
TV/VCR, room phones, antiques, and
fireplaces. Beautifully decorated,
each room has a relaxing view of the
bay. Amenities include: full breakfast,
bicycles (bike trails), kayak and canoe, beach chairs, and a common
lounge with kitchenette. Children 14
and over welcome.

Hosts: Jo Ann Parsons and daughter-in-law Judy
Rooms: 3 (PB) $75-150
Full Breakfast
Credit Cards: A, B, C, D
Notes: 2, 5, 8, 9, 10

LAWSONVILLE

Southwyck Farm
Bed & Breakfast

R.R. 1, Box 456, 27022-9768
(336) 593-8006; fax: (336) 593-9180
E-mail: southwyckfarm@mindspring.com
www.southwyckfarm.com

Southwyck Farm is in the foothills of
the Blue Ridge Mountains in Law-

Southwyck Farm

sonville, North Carolina, near Hanging Rock State Park and the Dan River. The hosts have created the ambience of a New England gentleman's farm with two houses. We have whirlpool baths, king-size beds, and fireplaces. There are walking trails, both easy and difficult, with views of the mountains and the meadows. We have a bass pond and dock for fishing. We offer three-course gourmet meals at an extra charge. Please let us know if you want dinner at the time of reservations. Southwyck Farm was built by Captain Robert Carl, a Sandy Hook pilot, to be a haven for friends and family. His wife and son have continued this tradition. There is canoeing available on the Dan River and Kibler Valley.

Hosts: Diana Carl and David Hoskins
Rooms: 6 (4 PB; 2 SB) $90-125
Full Breakfast
Credit Cards: A, B
Notes: 2, 3, 4, 5, 7, 10, 12

MARSHALL

Marshall House
Bed & Breakfast

100 Hill Street, 28753
(828) 649-9205; fax: (828) 649-2784
E-mail: ruthmarshallhouse@prodigy.net

Built in 1903, the inn overlooks the peaceful town of Marshall and the French Broad River. This country inn, listed on the National Historic Register, is decorated with fancy chandeliers, antiques, and pictures, and boasts four fireplaces, a formal dining room, parlor, and upstairs TV/reading room. Enjoy storytelling about the

house, the town, the people, and the history. Our loving house pets will gladly welcome your pets also. The toot of a train and good service make your visit a unique experience. Smoking permitted.

Hosts: Ruth and Jim Boylan
Rooms: 9 (2 PB; 7 SB) $40-75
Continental Breakfast
Credit Cards: A, B, C, D, E
Notes: 5, 6, 7, 9, 10, 11, 12

MT. AIRY

Briar Patch
Bed & Breakfast

150 Wild Rose Trail, Dobson, 27017
(336) 352-4177; fax: (336) 352-4177
E-mail: philneel@surry.net
www.briarpatchbedandbreakfast.com

Briar Patch

Beautiful log home surrounded by 48 acres of wooded land in the foothills of northwestern North Carolina. Within a short driving distance of the Blue Ridge Parkway, Western Virginia, and several historic sites. A great place to spend a quiet week, weekend, or to just relax. No traffic or noises except for the woods and its wildlife.

NOTES: Credit cards accepted: A Master Card; B Visa; C American Express; D Discover; E Diners Club; F Other; 2 Personal checks accepted; 3 Lunch available; 4 Dinner available; 5 Open all year;

Hosts: Phil and Sharon Neel
Rooms: 4 (SB) $70-75
Full Breakfast
Credit Cards: None
Notes: 2, 5, 10, 11

MURPHY

A Gathering of Angels Mountain Retreat Inn

P.O. Box 404, 28906
(828) 837-3202; fax: (828) 835-9269
E-mail: agoa@dnet.net
www.a-gathering-of-angles.com

A Gathering of Angels Inn offers 12 rooms with private baths in a secluded mountain retreat. Come and enjoy this restful getaway for couples, weddings, family gatherings, and groups. Enjoy 50 wooded acres with hiking trails, a fish pond, and a mountain stream with 45-foot natural cascading waterfalls. The grounds also boast several tranquil flower gardens, one with a 21-foot waterfall. Guest may use the Gathering Room which has a fireplace, refrigerator, pay phone, TV with a VCR, and grill; and the kitchen is available for group rentals. An evening campfire is great fun! Party-themed events are also available for groups; See the website for more information. A Gathering of Angles Inn is a peaceful mountain retreat to heal the mind, body, and spirit.

Hosts: Steven Williams, Michael Lanning
Rooms: 12 (PB) $40-65
Full Breakfast
Credit Cards: A, B
Notes: 2, 5, 8, 9, 10

Huntington Hall Bed & Breakfast Inn

272 Valley River Avenue, 28906
(828) 837-9567; (800) 824-6189
fax: (828) 837-2527
E-mail: huntington@grove.net

Each of the five spacious guest rooms, one of which is a separate cottage, has a personality of its own with period furnishings. Individual heating and air-conditioning unit, color TV, and private bath are part of each room. A full breakfast, afternoon refreshments, and nightly turn-down services are part of a guest's stay. Huntington Hall is charming, relaxing, and inviting: an escape from hurry and worry. A place to be pampered.

Hosts: Nancy and Curt Harris
Rooms: 5 (PB) $65-125
Full Breakfast
Credit Cards: A, B, C, D
Notes: 2, 5, 8, 10, 12

Park Place Bed & Breakfast

54 Hill Street, 28906
(828) 837-8842
www.virtualcities.com/nc/parkplace.htm

Welcome to your home away from home! For your comfort, Park Place—a two-story clapboard/brick house, circa 1900—offers three, well-appointed, climate-controlled guest-rooms, each with private bath. A full gourmet breakfast is served each morning. The hosts greatly enjoy sharing with guests the home's congenial atmosphere and its eclectic décor of family treasures, antiques, collectibles, and hand-knotted Oriental

6 Pets welcome; 7 Children welcome; 8 Tennis nearby; 9 Swimming nearby; 10 Golf nearby; 11 Skiing nearby; 12 May be booked through travel agent

Park Place

rugs. While relaxing on the screened, treetop-level porch, guests love shooting the breeze or just rocking the time away. *Willkommen—wir sprechen Deutsch!*

Hosts: Rikki and Neil Wocell
Rooms: 3 (PB) $70-$90
Full Breakfast
Credit Cards: None
Notes: 2, 5, 8, 10, 12

NEW BERN

Harmony House Inn

215 Pollock Street, 28560
(252) 636-3810; (800) 636-3113
fax: (252) 636-3810
E-mail: harmony@cconnect.net
www.harmonyhouseinn.com

Comfortable, yet elegant historic inn in the heart of New Bern, a quaint relaxing town located at the confluence of the Neuse and Trent Rivers. Seven rooms and three suites (two with heart-shaped Jacuzzis). Walk to Tryon Palace, antique and specialty shops, Fireman's Museum, Trolley Tours, restaurants, river front, and Union Point Park. Full homemade breakfast. Private bathrooms. Relaxing front porch with swings and rocking chairs. Each room personally decorated by the innkeepers. Many "extras."

Hosts: Ed and Sooki Kirkpatrick
Rooms: 10 (PB) $109-150
Full Breakfast
Credit Cards: A, B, D
Notes: 2, 5, 7, 8, 9, 10, 12

Howard House Victorian Bed & Breakfast

Howard House Victorian

207 Pollock Street, 28560
(252) 514-6709; (800) 705-5261
fax: (252) 514-6710
E-mail: info@howardhouse.com
www.howardhouseandb.com

Step back in time to a gracious, elegant era by staying in this 1890, Victorian-style B&B. Located in the downtown historic district of New Bern, the Howard House is within walking distance of the riverfront, a variety of restaurants, historic homes, and sites like Tryon Place and spe-

---

NOTES: Credit cards accepted: A Master Card; B Visa; C American Express; D Discover; E Diners Club; F Other; 2 Personal checks accepted; 3 Lunch available; 4 Dinner available; 5 Open all year;

cialty shops. The Wynns offer desserts, refreshments, and good conversation on the front porch, or in the parlor as you return from a busy day around town. A bountiful breakfast is served each morning in the formal dining room. We await your arrival.

Hosts: Steven and Kimberly Wynn
Rooms: 4 (PB) $89-109
Full Breakfast
Credit Cards: A, B, C, D
Notes: 2, 5, 9, 10

SALISBURY

Rowan Oak House

208 South Fulton Street, 28144
(704) 633-2086; (800) 786-0437
fax: (704) 633-2084
www.rowanoakbb.com

An elegant, high Victorian located in the historic district. Stained and leaded glass, seven fireplaces, wraparound porch, and gardens adorn this 100-year-old mansion. Each of the four guest rooms is lavishly furnished with antiques, a sitting area, desk, phone, duvet with down comforter, reading lights, fruit, and flowers. Pri-

Rowan Oak House

vate baths (one room has a double Jacuzzi). Central air-conditioning and heat. Color TV, books, magazines, and board games are in the upstairs parlor. Smoking limited. Full gourmet breakfast is served. Close to furniture shopping and Charlotte Motor Speedway. Within walking distance of downtown churches, antique shopping, historic buildings, and fine restaurants. Children over 10 welcome.

Hosts: Barbara and Les Coombs
Rooms: 4 (PB) $115-140
Full Breakfast
Credit Cards: A, B, D
Notes: 2, 5, 7, 8, 9, 10, 12

SOUTHERN PINES

Knollwood House

1495 West Connecticut Avenue, 28387
(910) 692-9390; fax: (910) 692-0609
E-mail: knollwood@pinehurst.net
www.knollwoodhouse.com

This English manor house stands among five acres of longleaf pines, dogwoods, azaleas, towering holly trees, and 40-foot magnolias. From a terrace where Glenn Miller's orchestra once gave a concert, Knollwood's lawns roll down to the fifteenth fairway of a famous golf course. Furnished with late 18th-century/early 19th-century antiques, both suites and guest rooms are available. Special golf package rates available.

Hosts: Dick and Mimi Beatty
Rooms: 6 (PB) $115-160
Full Breakfast
Credit Cards: A, B
Notes: 2, 5, 7, 8, 9, 10, 12

6 Pets welcome; 7 Children welcome; 8 Tennis nearby; 9 Swimming nearby; 10 Golf nearby; 11 Skiing nearby; 12 May be booked through travel agent

STATESVILLE

The Kerr House Bed & Breakfast

519 Davie Avenue, 28677
(704) 881-0957; (877) 308-0353
fax: (704) 878-6380
E-mail: thekerrhouse@abts.net
www.statesville-nc-lodging.com

Come and experience Southern hospitality at the Kerr House, a lovely Queen Anne Victorian located within walking distance of downtown Statesville. The Kerr House features 4 impeccably maintained guest rooms, all with private baths. A gourmet breakfast is served in the family dining room. Much attention has been paid to detail for your comfort and pleasure. Please come and experience our moto "There is no place like home. . .except the Kerr House!"

Hosts: John and Mary Ann Kerr
Rooms: 4 (PB) $75-125
Full Breakfast
Credit Cards: A, B, C, E
Notes: 2, 5, 8, 9, 10, 12

Madelyn's in the Grove

1836 West Memorial Highway, P.O. Box 249, Union Grove, 28689
(704) 539-4151; (800) 948-4473
fax: (704) 539-4080
E-mail: innkeeper@madelyns.com
www.madelyns.com

Listen to the birds and unwind. We have moved our B&B to Union Grove, only 15 minutes north of Statesville and I-40, and just two minutes from I-77, Exit 65. There are many things to see and do. After a fun-filled day, come back and have cheese and crackers and a glass of lemonade. Sit on one of the porches or in the gazebo; watch the stars and be glad you are at Madelyn's in the Grove. Personal checks preferred.

Hosts: Madelyn Hill
Rooms: 5 (PB) $75-155
Full Breakfast
Credit Cards: A, B, C, D
Notes: 2, 5, 10, 12

TRYON

The Foxtrot Inn

P.O. Box 1561, 28782
(828) 859-9706; (888) 676-8050
E-mail: wim@foxtrotinn.com
www.foxtrotinn.com

This lovingly restored residence, circa 1915, is situated on six wooded acres within the city limits of Tryon. It is convenient to everything, yet secluded with a quietly elegant atmosphere. Guests are treated to a full gourmet breakfast, heated swimming pool, and fully furnished guest house with two bedrooms, a kitchen, living room, fireplace, deck, and outstanding mountain views. Two of the guest rooms have sitting rooms. Both the inn and guest house are fully air-conditioned.

Host: Wim Woody
Rooms: 4 (PB) $90-140
Full Breakfast
Credit Cards: None
Notes: 2, 5, 6, 7, 8, 9, 10, 12

WILMINGTON

Curran House

312 South Third Street, 28401
(910) 763-6603; (800) 763-6603

NOTES: Credit cards accepted: A Master Card; B Visa; C American Express; D Discover; E Diners Club; F Other; 2 Personal checks accepted; 3 Lunch available; 4 Dinner available; 5 Open all year;

Curran House

fax: (910) 763-5116
www.bbonline.com/nc/curran/

In historic downtown Wilmington, this three-diamond AAA-rated B&B is three blocks from the Cape Fear River and 15 minutes from Atlantic Beaches. Choose from three unique bedrooms with king and queen beds, guest robes, cable TV/VCR, telephones, and private baths. Central air-conditioning and ceiling fans in each room. Fresh ground coffee before a full breakfast. Walk to superb dining, carriage and riverboat rides, museums, and galleries. Children over 12 welcome.

Hosts: Greg and Vickie Stringer
Rooms: 3 (PB) $75-119
Full Breakfast
Credit Cards: A, B, C
Notes: 2, 5, 7, 8, 9, 10, 12

C. W. Worth House Bed & Breakfast

412 South 3rd Street, 28401
(910) 762-8562; (800) 340-8559
fax: (910) 763-2173
E-mail: relax@worthhouse.com
www.worthhouse.com

Let us pamper you in our circa 1893, Queen Anne Victorian home. After a restful night, enjoy a sumptuous breakfast in the formal dining room. Walk to unique shops, fine dining, and attractions. Beaches are 20 minutes away.

Hosts: Margi and Doug Erickson
Rooms: 7 (PB) $115-150
Full Breakfast
Credit Cards: A, B, C, D
Notes: 2, 5, 7, 8, 9, 10, 12

Taylor House Inn

14 North Seventh Street, 28401
(910) 763-7581; (800) 382-9982
E-mail: taylorhousebb@aol.com
www.taylorhousebb.com

Taylor House Inn

You'll find this haven of warm Southern hospitality and thoughtfulness in the downtown historic district, just blocks from the Cape Fear River. The five bedrooms are filled with period antiques, fresh flowers, and beautiful linens. A full gourmet breakfast is served in the formal dining room by candlelight. A slice of heaven—allow yourself to be pampered and enjoy all that the Cape Fear area has to offer.

6 Pets welcome; 7 Children welcome; 8 Tennis nearby; 9 Swimming nearby; 10 Golf nearby; 11 Skiing nearby; 12 May be booked through travel agent

Hosts: Karen and Scott Clark
Rooms: 5 (PB) $75-125
Full Breakfast
Credit Cards: A, B, C
Notes: 2, 5, 7, 8, 9, 10, 12

WILSON

Miss Betty's Bed & Breakfast Inn

600 West Nash Street, 27893
phone/fax: (252) 243-4447; (800) 258-2058
E-mail: missbettysbnbinn@coastalnet.com
www.missbettysbnbinn.com

Selected as one of the "best places to stay in the South," Miss Betty's is ideally located midway between Maine and Florida along the main north-south route, I-95. Comprised of four beautifully restored structures in the downtown historic section, the Nationally Registered Davis-Whitehead-Harriss House (circa 1858), the Riley House (circa 1900), Rosebud (circa 1942), and the Queen Anne (circa 1911) have recaptured the elegance and style of quiet Victorian charm, but with modern conveniences. Guests can browse for antiques in the inn or visit numerous shops that give

Miss Betty's

Wilson the title "Antique Capital of North Carolina." A quiet town famous for its barbecue, Wilson has four beautiful golf courses and many tennis courts. Rooms include three king suites.

Hosts: Betty and Fred Spitz
Rooms: 14 (PB) $60-85
Full Breakfast
Credit Cards: A, B, C, D, E
Notes: 2, 5, 8, 9, 10

WINSTON-SALEM

Lady Anne's Victorian Bed & Breakfast

612 Summit Street, 27101
(336) 724-1074
E-mail: ladyannes1@bellsouth.net
www.bbonline.com/nc/ladyannes/

Warm, Southern hospitality surrounds you in this 1890 Victorian home, listed on the National Register of Historic Places. An aura of romance touches each suite or room. All are individually decorated with period antiques, treasures, and modern luxuries. Some rooms have two-person whirlpools, cable TVs, HBO, stereos, telephones, coffee, refrigerators, private entrances, and balconies. An evening dessert and full breakfast are served. Lady Anne's is ideally located near downtown attractions, performances, restaurants, shops, and Old Salem Historic Village. Smoking permitted on the porch only please! Children over 12 welcome.

Rooms: 4 (PB) $60-185
Full Breakfast
Credit Cards: A, B, C, D
Notes: 5, 7, 8, 9, 10, 12

NOTES: Credit cards accepted: A Master Card; B Visa; C American Express; D Discover; E Diners Club; F Other; 2 Personal checks accepted; 3 Lunch available; 4 Dinner available; 5 Open all year;

North Dakota

MCCLUSKY

Midstate Bed & Breakfast

980 Highway 200 Northeast, 58463
phone/fax: (701) 363-2520; (888) 434-2520
E-mail: midstatebb@webtv.net
www.bbonline.com/nd/midstate/

In central North Dakota, this country home is very easy to locate: Mile Marker 232 on ND 200. Built in 1980. The guest entrance takes you to a complete and private lower level containing your bedroom and bath, plus a large TV lounge with fireplace and kitchenette. Additional bedrooms are on the upper level. Air-conditioning. Breakfast is served in the formal dining room or the plant-filled atrium. In an area of great hunting; guests are allowed hunting privileges on more than 4,000 acres. Good fishing nearby. Very close to the Lewis and Clark Trail through North Dakota, and the Lewis and Clark Interpretive Center at Washburn, ND. Outstanding bird-watching on premises. Nearby areas are noted for great birding experiences.

Host: Grace Faul
Rooms: 4 (1 PB; 3 SB) $40
Full Breakfast
Credit Cards: None
Notes: 2, 3, 4, 5, 6, 7, 8, 9

---

6 Pets welcome; 7 Children welcome; 8 Tennis nearby; 9 Swimming nearby; 10 Golf nearby; 11 Skiing nearby; 12 May be booked through travel agent

NORTH DAKOTA

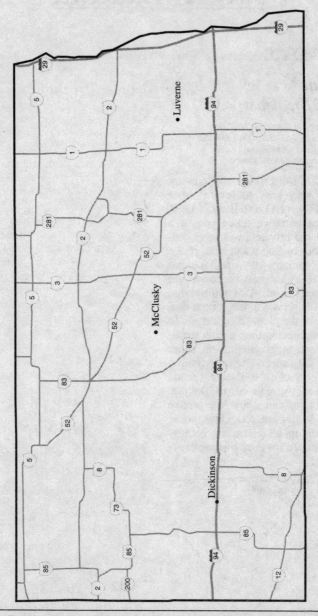

NOTES: Credit cards accepted: A Master Card; B Visa; C American Express; D Discover; E Diners Club; F Other; 2 Personal checks accepted; 3 Lunch available; 4 Dinner available; 5 Open all year;

Ohio

Back in Tyme
Private Inn Lodging

P.O. Box 231, 400 Massilon State U.S. 62,
   Wilmot, 44689
(330) 359-4080; (800) 520-0091
E-mail: backntyme@usa.net
www.backntyme.com

Back in Tyme offers lodging for up to
eight persons. Available to only one
party at a time; couple, family, or
group will share complete private
home. Full kitchen, living room, first
floor bathroom, tub/shower; two king
and two twin bedrooms are on second
floor. Private yard, gas grill, air-conditioning, cable TV, VCR. Children
under 15 stay free; $15.00 per extra
adult. Luxury Suite-Romantic Getaway offers king bed and two-person
heartshaped Jacuzzi, four-foot shower
with seats, and fireplace. The perfect
getaway with all the ambiance for romance. Special packages for anniver-
sies, Sweetest Day, Valentines Day,
birthdays. Price for packages: $99-
129. Special packages include breakfast at local restaurant.

Rooms: 5 (SB) $79-109
Full Breakfast
Credit Cards: A, B, D
Notes: 2, 5, 7, 9

Coblentz Country Cabin

5130 T.R. 359, Sommerset Road, 44610
(330) 893-1300; (877) 99-SLEEP
E-mail: ecoblentz@valkyrie.net
www.amishcountrylodging.com

Beautiful, peaceful, and romantic log
cabin nestled on a wooded hillside in
the heart of Ohio's Amish Country.
Experience the serenity and quiet
beauty of the rolling countryside.
Conveniently located near dozens of
shops and restaurants. Enjoy the perfect tranquility from your hickory
rocker on our front porch or balcony
overlooking a quiet pond. Each room
has a private entrance and bath, fireplace, Jacuzzi, kitchenette, and balcony or front porch. Perfect for
honeymoons, anniversaries, or families. No breakfast.

Host: Elvin Coblentz
Rooms: 4 (PB) $55-169
Credit Cards: A, B, D
Notes: 2, 5, 7, 10

Donna's Premier Lodging
Bed & Breakfast

P.O. Box 307, 307 East Street, 44610
(330) 893-3068; (800) 320-3338
E-mail: info@donnasb-b.com
www.donnasb-b.com

At Donna's we offer a variety of elegant accommodations where couples

---

6 Pets welcome; 7 Children welcome; 8 Tennis nearby; 9 Swimming nearby; 10 Golf nearby; 11 Skiing
nearby; 12 May be booked through travel agent

OHIO

can share their hopes and dreams. Charming and relaxing cottages, bridal suites, and villas are within walking distance of the quaint village of Berlin. Nature lovers will enjoy the steep, winding paved driveway that leads to our original log cabin, as well as our chalets and cedar log cabins. One of these is our luxurious "Romancing the Stone" Cabin, where you can unwind in the light rose, heart-shaped Jacuzzi in a log alcove that faces a magnificent rock waterfall. Please ask about our breakfast.

Hosts: Johannes and Donna Marie Schlabach
Rooms: 19 (PB) $55-369
Continental Breakfast
Credit Cards: A, B, D
Notes: 2, 5, 7, 8, 9, 10

Gilead's Balm Manor

8690 County Road 201, Fredericksburg, 44627
(330) 695-3881; (888) 612-3436
E-mail: gileadbalmmanor@valkyrie.net
www.gileadbalm.com

Gilead's Balm Manor is nestled among the Amish Farms of Holmes County, seven miles north of Berlin, Ohio. You will find European elegance in Amish country with five luxurious rooms 12-foot ceilings, waterfall Jacuzzis, fireplaces, kitchenettes, air-conditioning, satellite TV, VCR, and CD player. On two-and-a-half-acre lake with a gazebo and paddleboat.

Hosts: John and Ilene Hess
Rooms: 5 (PB) $100-165
Full Breakfast
Credit Cards: A, B, C, D
Notes: 2, 5, 7, 9, 10, 12

BOLIVAR

Enchanted Pine Bed & Breakfast and Gifts

1862 Old Trail Road Northeast, 44612
(330) 874-3197; fax: (330) 874-2405
E-mail: linda@wilkshire.net
enchantedpines.com

Enchanted Pines B&B and Gift Shop is nestled on six wooded acres in cen-

Enchanted Pine

tral Ohio. Being just two miles from I-77, 15 miles from Canton Football Hall of Fame, and 20 miles from the largest Amish settlement in the world, makes our B&B very accessible. Our English Ivy Suite includes two large rooms that sleep four and a bath. Other uniquely decorated rooms available. Amenities include a pool, hot tub, and spacious decks.

Hosts: Linda and Earl Menges
Rooms: 3 (2 PB; 1 SB) $75-150
Full Breakfast
Credit Cards: A, B
Notes: 3, 5, 9, 10

---

6 Pets welcome; 7 Children welcome; 8 Tennis nearby; 9 Swimming nearby; 10 Golf nearby; 11 Skiing nearby; 12 May be booked through travel agent

BLUE ROCK

McNutt Farm II/ Outdoorsman Lodge

6120 Cutler Lake Road, 43720
(740) 674-4555

Country B&B in rustic quarters on a working farm in the quiet of the Blue Rock hill country. Only 11 miles from I-70, 35 miles from I-77, and 60 miles from I-71. Guests enjoy their own private kitchen, living room with fireplace or wood-burner, private bath, porch with swing, and beautiful view with forests and pastured livestock. Choose the log cabin or the carriage house. For those who want more than an overnight stay, please ask about our log cabin by the week or weekend. A cellar house cabin (somewhat primitive) is also available. Sleep to the sounds of whippoorwills and tree frogs. Awaken to the crowing rooster and the wild turkey calling; sometimes the bleating of a newborn fawn can be heard. We welcome you by reservation and deposit.

Hosts: Don R. and Patty L. McNutt
Rooms: 3 (PB) $80 and up
Continental Breakfast
Credit Cards: None
Notes: 2, 5, 6, 7, 9, 10

BUCYRUS

Hide Away Bed & Breakfast

1601 State Route # 4, 44820-9587
(419) 562-3013; (800) 570-8233
fax: (419) 562-3003

E-mail: innkeeper@hideawayinn.com
www.hideawayinn.com

We are central to Cleveland, Columbus, and Toledo. Enjoy Ohio's north coast, antique shopping, or Amish country. Escape stress—pamper your senses in one of our 11 exquisite rooms, most with Jacuzzis and working fireplaces.

Host: Debbie Miller
Rooms: 11 (PB) $87-257
Full Breakfast
Credit Cards: A, B, D
Notes: 2, 3, 4, 5, 7, 8, 9, 10, 11, 12

CALDWELL

The Harkins House Inn

715 West Street, 43724
(740) 732-7347
E-mail: harkinsinn@cs.com
www.bbonline.com/oh/harkins/

Come spend an enchanted evening in this immaculately restored home. Built in 1905 by an influential family of the Caldwell area (ancestors of the proprietors), the inn features bountiful original woodwork with oak and heart pine flooring and a stately library with fireplace and French doors. Enjoy your stay in one of our rooms with air-conditioning and cable television. Then savor breakfast in the formal dining room. Caldwell is only 25 minutes between Cambridge and Marietta.

Hosts: Jeff and Stacey Lucas
Rooms: 2 (PB) $53-75
Full Breakfast
Credit Cards: A, B, C
Notes: 2, 5, 7, 8, 9, 10

NOTES: Credit cards accepted: A Master Card; B Visa; C American Express; D Discover; E Diners Club; F Other; 2 Personal checks accepted; 3 Lunch available; 4 Dinner available; 5 Open all year;

CAMBRIDGE

The Colonel Taylor Inn Bed & Breakfast

633 Upland Road, 43725
(740) 432-7802; fax: (740) 432-3152
E-mail: coltaylor@peoplepc.com
www.coltaylorinnbb.com

The historic Victorian Taylor Mansion built in 1878 is now a romantically elegant inn. There are four guest rooms with private baths, queen four-poster beds, gas fireplaces, and ceiling fans. White robes and slippers and other amenities are furnished. Central air-conditioning. Afternoon snacks and gourmet breakfasts are served. For business or pleasure, you will find the inn to be exceptional year-round lodging.

Hosts: Jim and Patricia Irvin
Rooms: 4 (PB) $105-175
Full Breakfast
Credit Cards: A, B, D
Notes: 5, 7, 9, 10, 12

CENTERVILLE

Yesterday Bed & Breakfast

39 South Main Street, 45458
(937) 433-0785; (800) 225-0485
E-mail: yesterdaybandb@webtv.net

Yesterday is located in the Centerville Historic District, 10 miles south of downtown Dayton, adjoining a group of fine antique shops. The house was built in 1882 and furnished with antiques and uniques. Walking distance to restaurants and two museums. Easy drive to U.S. Air Force Museum, King Island theme park, historic Way-

Yesterday

nesville and Lebanon, both major antique centers. The University of Dayton and Wright State University are 15 to 20 minutes away. Children over 12 are welcome.

Hosts: Judy and Chuck Haun
Rooms: 3 (PB) $75-95
Full Breakfast
Credit Cards: None
Notes: 2, 5, 7, 8, 9, 10

CINCINNATI

Christopher's Bed & Breakfast

See description under Newport, KY.

COLUMBUS

Shamrock Bed &Breakfast

5657 Sunbury Road, 43230-1147
(614) 337-9849; fax: (614) 337-9439
E-mail: shamrockbb@juno.com

Shamrock

Half mile from I-270, close to the airport, 15 minutes from downtown and major attractions. All guest rooms are on the first floor. More than an acre of landscaped gardens, patio, arbor, and pond. Bedrooms with queen beds, quiet ambience of antiques and art. Very restful. Guests have complete use of the first floor (living room, TV and music room, large solarium). Close to Polaris, New Easton Shoppes, gardens, movies, galleries. Air-conditioned.

Host: Tom McLaughlin
Rooms: 3 (2 PB; 1 SB) $60-75
Full Breakfast
Credit Cards: A, B, D
Notes: 2, 3, 5, 7, 8, 9, 10

DAYTON

Candlewick Bed & Breakfast

4991 Bath Road, 45424
(937) 233-9297
E-mail: gethompson@compuserve.com
www.bedandbreakfast.com

This tranquil Dutch Colonial home sits atop a hill on five rolling acres.

Your hosts, George, a retired engineer, and Nancy, a retired teacher, invite you to spend a peaceful night in comfortable rooms containing a blend of antiques and colonial and country furnishings. Full breakfast includes fresh fruit and juice, homemade pastries, and one of Nancy's special hot dishes. Weather permitting, enjoy breakfast on the screened porch overlooking a large pond often visited by wild ducks and geese. Convenient to the Air Force Museum and major universities, Candlewick is a perfect retreat for either business or pleasure. Member of Ohio B&B Association. Children 12 and over welcome.

Hosts: Nancy and George Thompson
Rooms: 2 (SB) $60-65
Full Breakfast
Credit Cards: None
Notes: 2, 5, 8, 9, 10

DE GRAFF

Rollicking Hills' Bed & Breakfast

#1 Rollicking Hills, 43318
(937) 585-5161
E-mail: llamas@logan.net

Here, nestled in the scenic hills of West Central Ohio, visitors share memorable experiences with the Smithers family on their six-generation family farm. The 160 acres contain 30 acres of woods and miles of nature trails that can be explored on foot, on a hayride, or during a llama trek. (Rollicking Hills is one of the area's leaders in raising these wonderful, exotic animals). A taste of farm life can be experienced in caring for the farm animals (llamas, chickens, goats, horses, cats, dogs, and a rabbit). Once you drive down the lane to Rollicking Hills, you will know you have come home again.

Hosts: Bob and Susie Smithers
Rooms: 2 (SB) $65
Full Breakfast
Credit Cards: None
Notes: 2, 3, 5, 7, 9, 10, 11

DELLROY

Candleglow Bed & Breakfast

4247 Roswell Road S.W., 44620
(330) 735-2407
www.carrollcountyohio.com/candleglow/

Today's comfort in yesterday's Victorian atmosphere with romantic, casual elegance. Three spacious guest rooms with private baths. King or queen beds, whirlpool or clawfoot tubs. Full breakfast, choice of entree, served at your convenience. Atwood Lake Resort area. Swimming, boating, hiking, horseback riding, tennis, golf, antique shops close by.

Host: Audrey Genova
Rooms: 3 (PB) $90
Full Breakfast
Credit Cards: None
Notes: 2, 5, 8, 9, 10

DOVER

The Olde World Bed & Breakfast & Tea Room

2982 State Route 516 N.W., 44622
(330) 343-1333; (800) 447-1273
E-mail: owbb@tusco.net
www.oldeworldbb.com

My childhood dream of restoring this Victorian home is truly a fairy tale I would love to share with you. Old-world tradition is reflected in our uniquely appointed suite, including Victorian, Oriental, Parisian, Mediterranean, and Alpine influences. An antiquer's delight, our entire home is open to our guests, including the parlor, veranda, and dining room. Your stay is complete with a soak in our private, two-person hot tub. Centrally located near Amish Country and other historical sites.

The Olde World

Host: Jonna Cronebaugh
Rooms: 5 (PB) $70-110
Full Breakfast
Credit Cards: A, B, D
Notes: 2, 3, 5, 8, 9, 10

FAYETTE

Red Brick Inn

206 West Main Street, 43521
(419) 237-2276

---

6 Pets welcome; 7 Children welcome; 8 Tennis nearby; 9 Swimming nearby; 10 Golf nearby; 11 Skiing nearby; 12 May be booked through travel agent

Guests will enjoy a visit to our 130-year-old Victorian home filled with antique furnishings, including many family heirlooms. Four bedrooms are available, each with private bath. Three rooms have a private porch and one is handicapped-accessible. We are located in North West Ohio near Harrison Lake State Park and Fayette's Historic Opera House at the corner of Routes 66 and 20.

Hosts: Don and Jane Stiriz
Rooms: 4 (PB) $55
Full Breakfast
Credit Cards: None
Notes: 2, 5, 8, 9, 10

FREEPORT

Rila's Rocks and Rills

28490 Birmingham Road, 43973
(740) 658-3360

Want to get away from the fast-paced world into yesterday's world of peace and quiet? Enjoy real country living in a restored 1800s farmhouse on 85 acres of Ohio woods, rocks, and rills. Six recreational lakes are within a 30-minute drive, and Amish country is an hour's drive away. For an overnight stopover going east, it's a comfortable day's drive to D.C. Rates include full usage of farmhouse with three bedrooms, bath, family/kitchen room, utility room with washer/dryer, and bunkhouse which sleeps four.

Hosts: Jim and Anna
Rooms: 3 (SB) $30-50
Credit Cards: None
Notes: 2, 5, 6, 7

GERMANTOWN (DAYTON/MIDDLETOWN)

Gunckel Heritage Bed & Breakfast & Antiques

33 West Market Street, 45327
(937) 855-3508; (877) 855-3508
E-mail: gunckelheritage@aol.com
www.bbonline.com/oh/gunckel/

Gunckel Heritage

Located in the heart of the Gunckel historic district, our B&B is a Federal-style brick home with Victorian influences. It features a front-to-back foyer with a grand staircase. The six fireplaces, beautiful woodwork, and original interior shutters add to the ambience. Enjoy a full breakfast by candlelight in our elegant dining room, on the covered balcony, or on the porch furnished in wicker, weather permitting. We like to spoil guests with complimentary refreshments and access to our ice cream sundae bar. Rooms are decorated in period antiques, with romantically furnished bedchambers. Antiquing, museums, parks, covered bridges, bike trails, and a nature center are all nearby. Ten-

---

percent dinner coupon at the famous Florentine Hotel, two doors east.

Host: Bonnie Gunckel Koogle
Rooms: 4 (PB) $85-125
Full Breakfast
Credit Cards: A, B, D
Notes: 2, 5, 7, 8, 9, 10, 11

GRAND RAPIDS

The Mill House Bed & Breakfast

P.O. Box 102, 24070 Front Street, 43522
(419) 832-6455
E-mail: innkeeper@millhouse.com
www.themillhouse.com

The Mill House is fully air-conditioned. Each room has a private bath. (Jetted tub in the Garden Room.) All rooms are on the first floor. Corporate rates available for frequent business stays. Discounts: winter rates; two nights or more; full-house rental. Room rates include all taxes. The Common Room is located at the rear of the residence, with its own guest

The Mill House

balcony overlooking the gardens. A library, cable television, and VCR are available in the Common Room.

Hosts: Jim and Karen Herzberg
Rooms: 3 (PB) $80-120
Full Breakfast
Credit Cards: A, B, C, D
Notes: 2, 5, 10, 12

LAURELVILLE (HOCKING COUNTY)

Painted Valley Farm

17232 Curtis Road, 43135
(740) 887-4446; (888) 887-4446
www.hockinghills.com/paintedvalley

Enjoy a real horse breeding farm and stay in our ten-year-old log home. We are close to all state parks in the beautiful Hocking Hills, plus we are near the famous outdoor drama *Tecumseh*, in Chillicothe. We love to pamper our guest with candlelight breakfasts, relaxing in our hot tub, turn-down service, and homemade cookies in their rooms. The cookie jar is always full of Luanne's famous oatmeal cookies and most of the breakfasts feature Larry's real maple syrup. God has loaned us this valley to share with others. Resident pets for petting.

Hosts: Larry and Luanne Guffey
Rooms: 2 (PB) $80
Full Breakfast
Credit Cards: None
Notes: 2, 5, 7, 9, 10, 11

---

6 Pets welcome; 7 Children welcome; 8 Tennis nearby; 9 Swimming nearby; 10 Golf nearby; 11 Skiing nearby; 12 May be booked through travel agent

LIMA

Bailey's Bed & Breakfast

1128 State Street, 45805
phone/fax: (419) 228-8172

Built in 1919, Bailey's is located in one of Lima's most beautiful and oldest neighborhoods. Central air-conditioning, private bath, cable television, and telephone are just some of the amenities offered in each of our three guest rooms. After a hearty breakfast, enjoy a good book by the fireplace, a leisurely swing on the front porch, or a quiet walk around the neighborhood. Whatever reason brings you to Lima, we have a room ready for you! Member of Ohio Bed & Breakfast Association.

Host: Diane Bailey
Rooms: 3 (PB) $55-65
Full Breakfast
Credit Cards: A, B, C
Notes: 5, 7, 10

MAGNOLIA

Elson Inn Bed & Breakfast

225 North Main Street, Route 183, 44643
(330) 866-9242; fax: (330) 866-3398
E-mail: jelson@neo.rr.com
www.elsoninn.com

This 1879 Victorian Italianate's common rooms include a parlor, library, sitting room, dining room, large wraparound porch with swings, rockers and an outdoor garden room. Close to Amish country, Football Hall of Fame, historical sites, fishing, hiking

Elson Inn

the Sandy-Beaver Canal, tennis, Atwood Lake golf courses, and fine dining. King, queen, and a dorm room with two double beds, private shower/baths, all individually controlled heating and air-conditioning. Original family antiques abound; visited by President William McKinley. Listed on the National Register of Historical Places. Located in a quaint canal village. Come relax with us; 24-hour reservations required but one-week preferred.

Hosts: JoLane and Gus Elson
Rooms: 4 (PB) $100-120
Full Breakfast
Credit Cards: A, B, D
Notes: 2, 5, 8, 9, 10

MILAN

Gastier Farm Bed & Breakfast

1902 Strecker Road West, 44846-9583
(419) 499-2985

NOTES: Credit cards accepted: A Master Card; B Visa; C American Express; D Discover; E Diners Club; F Other; 2 Personal checks accepted; 3 Lunch available; 4 Dinner available; 5 Open all year;

Located two miles west of Ohio Turn-pike Exit 7 next to the Norfolk Southern Railroad on Strecker Road in Milan, Ohio. The farm homestead has been in the family for over 100 years. Farm commodities have ranged from grains to cattle, from greenhouse plants to produce and pick-your-own vegetables. Now the farm home is available for sharing with travelers. Adults and children are welcome. Sorry, no pets or smoking permitted. Open year round.

Hosts: Ted and Donna Gastier
Rooms: 3 (PB) $50 plus tax
Continental Breakfast
Credit Cards: A, B
Notes: 2, 5, 7, 8, 9, 10

MOUNT VERNON

Red Fox Country Inn

26367 Danville-Amity Road, Danville, 43014
phone/fax: (740) 599-7369; (877) 600-7310
E-mail: sudsimp@aol.com
www.redfoxcountryinn.com

This circa 1830 inn, located on 15 acres, is nestled in the rolling hills of central Ohio near Amish country and Mohican State Park. It was originally built to house travelers. In 1994 the farm home was renovated into a country-style B&B. We have four guest rooms, all with private baths and showers. We also serve a full-course country breakfast.

Hosts: Sue and Denny Simpkins
Rooms: 4 (PB) $65-85
Full Breakfast
Credit Cards: A, B, D
Notes: 2, 4, 5, 6, 7, 8, 9, 10, 11, 12

NAPOLEON

The Augusta Rose Bed & Breakfast

345 West Main Street, 43545
(419) 592-5852; (877) 590-1960
E-mail: augrose@bright.net
www.augrose@bright.net

Restored Queen Anne-style Victorian located approximately three blocks from downtown Napoleon. The second floor is dedicated completely to our guests and includes air-conditioning and two sitting rooms, one with a TV. The neighborhood is beautiful, quiet, and architecturally interesting. Antique shops are located in Napoleon and all surrounding communities, along with many historic attractions and fun festivals.

The Augusta Rose

Hosts: Ed and Mary Hoeffel
Rooms: 4 (PB) $65-85
Full Breakfast
Credit Cards: A, B, C
Notes: 2, 5, 7, 8, 9, 10, 11, 12

6 Pets welcome; 7 Children welcome; 8 Tennis nearby; 9 Swimming nearby; 10 Golf nearby; 11 Skiing nearby; 12 May be booked through travel agent

OXFORD

The Duck Pond Bed & Breakfast LLC

6391 Morning Sun Road, P.O. Box 407, 45056
(513) 523-8914
E-mail: duck.pond@juno.com
www.duckpondbb.com

The Duck Pond

An 1863 farmhouse situated three miles north of Miami University and uptown Oxford, two miles south of Hueston Woods State Park, which has an eighteen-hole golf course, nature trails, boating, swimming, and fishing. Antiquing awaits 15 miles away. Come and enjoy the quaintness that only a B&B can offer. Be our guest and enjoy our famous Hawaiian French toast. Reservations are required, so please call in advance. The Duck Pond is a member of the Ohio B&B Association and has met OBBA inspection standards.

Host: Marge Pendleton
Rooms: 4 (2 PB; 2 SB) $65-80
Full Breakfast
Credit Cards: None
Notes: 2, 5, 7, 8, 9, 10

PAINESVILLE

Rider's 1812 Inn

792 Mentor Avenue, 44077-2516
(440) 354-8200; fax: (440) 350-9385
E-mail: ridersinn@ncweb.com
www.ridersinn.com

Rider's Inn, originally built as a stop for stagecoaches and travelers, has today been restored to its former grandeur in the traditional Western Reserve style. There are 11 charming rooms filled with furniture of the period, most with private baths, TVs, and telephones. A full breakfast is served in the morning in bed, if you wish, or outside on the patio or in front of the fire.

Hosts: Elaine Crane, Judge G.W. Herman
Rooms: 10 (9 PB; 1 SB) $80-101
Full Breakfast
Credit Cards: None
Notes: 2, 3, 4, 5, 6, 7, 9, 10, 11, 12

PLAIN CITY

Yoder's Bed & Breakfast

8144 Cemetery Pike, 43064
(614) 873-4489

Located on a 107-acre farm northwest of Columbus. Big Darby Creek runs along the front yard. Excellent birdwatching. Within minutes of Amish restaurants, gift shops, cheese house, Amish furniture store, bookstores, and antique shops. King and queen beds, air-conditioning. No smoking or pets.

Hosts: Loyd and Claribel Yoder
Rooms: 4 (1 PB; 3 SB) $55-68
Full Breakfast

NOTES: Credit cards accepted: A Master Card; B Visa; C American Express; D Discover; E Diners Club; F Other; 2 Personal checks accepted; 3 Lunch available; 4 Dinner available; 5 Open all year;

Credit Cards: None
Notes: 2, 5, 9, 10

SPRINGFIELD

Houstonia Bed & Breakfast

25 East Mound Street, Box 363, South Charleston, 45368
(937) 462-8855; (800) 462-8855
fax: (937) 462-8855
E-mail: houstoniabb@aol.com
houstonia.net

A Prairie-Victorian, the Houstonia B&B is situated in the charming village of South Charleston, in southwestern Ohio. Beautifully restored with original woodwork, spectacular staircase, and inviting wrap-around veranda, the Houstonia welcomes guests to four bedrooms and baths or a two-room suite. Each bedroom, complete with a romantic fireplace and cozy reading nook, is perfect for a couples' retreat, weekend getaway, or business overnight. Weekend guests enjoy a full course breakfast and week-day lodgers appreciate a quick-and-out-the-door extended Continental breakfast.

Hosts: Sherry and Jim Wahl
Rooms: 4 (2 PB; 2 SB) $60-99
Full Breakfast
Credit Cards: A, B, C
Notes: 5, 7, 10

SUGARCREEK

Breitenbach Bed & Breakfast

307 Dover Road, 44681
(330) 343-3603; (800) THE WINE
fax: (330) 343-8290
www.breitenbachwine.com

Splendid accommodations in a quaint Swiss village in the heart of Amish country. This home is artistically furnished with a mixture of antiques, ethnic treasures, and local arts and crafts.We can provide you with an itinerary and maps for places that might pique your interest. Nearby Amish restaurants, cheese houses, flea markets, antique malls, and quilt and craft shops. Evening refreshments and a full gourmet breakfast. All rooms are individually decorated and have air-conditioning and private baths.

Breitenbach

Host: Deanna Bear
Rooms: 4 (PB) $75-85
Full Breakfast
Credit Cards: A, B
Notes: 2, 5, 10

Marbeyo Bed & Breakfast

2370 County Road 144, 44681
(330) 852-4533; fax: (330) 852-3605
E-mail: marbeyo1@juno.com

---

6 Pets welcome; 7 Children welcome; 8 Tennis nearby; 9 Swimming nearby; 10 Golf nearby; 11 Skiing nearby; 12 May be booked through travel agent

Hosted by an Amish/Mennonite family, nestled in the heart of the Amish country in eastern Holmes County. Three bedrooms, private baths, air-conditioning. Relax in the quiet country; take leisurely walks on the farm; see the animals. Enjoy a delicious breakfast at your convenience.

Hosts: Mark and Betty Yoder
Rooms: 3 (PB) $55-75
Full Breakfast
Credit Cards: A, B
Notes: 2, 5, 7, 10

SUGAR GROVE

Hickory Bend Bed & Breakfast

Hickory Bend

7541 Dupler Road S.E., 43155
(740) 746-8381; E-mail: ppeery@ohiohills.com
www.users.ohiohills.com

Nestled in the Hocking Hills of southeastern Ohio on 10 wooded acres. "So peaceful, we go out to watch the car go by on Sunday afternoon," says Pat. Patty is a spinner and weaver. The cozy, private room is outside the home in the midst of dogwood, poplar, and oak trees. Guests come for full breakfast and conversation. Heated on the cold days, cooled on the hot days. Call, write, or e-mail for brochure.

Hosts: Pat and Patty Peery
Room: 1 (PB) $50
Full Breakfast
Credit Cards: None
Notes: 2, 8, 10

WAKEMAN

Melrose Farm Bed & Breakfast

727 Vesta Road, 44889
(419) 929-1867; (877) 929-1867
E-mail: melrose@accnorwalk.com
www.accnorwalk.com/~melrose

Melrose Farm is a peaceful country retreat halfway between Oberlin and Ashland. Each of the three lovely guest rooms in the 125-year-old brick house has a private bath. Guests enjoy the tennis court, stocked pond, peren-

Melrose Farm

NOTES: Credit cards accepted: A Master Card; B Visa; C American Express; D Discover; E Diners Club; F Other; 2 Personal checks accepted; 3 Lunch available; 4 Dinner available; 5 Open all year;

nial gardens, and quiet, rural setting. Thirty miles from Cedar Point, an hour's drive from Cleveland or Toledo, two hours from Columbus. Air-conditioned comfort with old-fashioned, relaxed hospitality. Special Monday-Thursday rates for a multi-night stay.

Hosts: Abe and Eleanor Klassen
Rooms: 3 (PB) $50-85
Full Breakfast
Credit Cards: A, B, C, D
Notes: 2, 3, 4, 5, 7, 8, 9, 10

Indiantree Farm

WALNUT CREEK

Indiantree Farm Bed & Breakfast

5488 State Route #515, Millersburg, 44654
(330) 893-2497; (888) 267-5607
E-mail: indiantree@valkyrie.net

Peaceful lodging in a guesthouse on a picturesque hilltop farm in the heart of Amish country, a mile from Walnut Creek. Large front porch, farming with horses, hiking trails. Apartments with kitchen and bath for the price of a room. An oasis where time slows and the mood is conversation, not television.

Hosts: Larry and Nola Miller
Rooms: 3 (PB) $75-90

Continental Breakfast
Credit Cards: None
Notes: 10

WILLSHIRE

Hillside Bed & Breakfast

2751 Van Wert Mercer County Line Road, 45898
(419) 495-2845; E-mail: dmgamble@webtv.net

Relax in a tranquil country setting overlooking the fields on a working grain farm. Watch the birds, squirrels, and rabbits, or enjoy the nature trails, antiques, and Oliver Tractor collection. Hot tub, central air, bikes, pool table, foosball table, satellite TV, or surf the web for your entertainment. Can also accommodate groups. Easy access off of US 33 and State Route 49. Restaurants and antique shops nearby.

Host: Dean Gamble
Rooms: 3 (1 PB; 2 SB) $55-60; whole house $200
Continental Breakfast
Credit Cards: None
Notes: 2, 5, 7 (supervised), 9, 10

WILMINGTON/WAYNESVILLE

The Lark's Nest Bed 'n' Breakfast at Caesar's Creek

619 Ward Road, Wilmington, 45177
(937) 382-4788; E-mail: larksnest@voyager.com
www.ohiobba.com/larksnest.htm

The Lark's Nest is a new log cabin home located on a country road. It is surrounded by the woods of Caesar's Creek State Park in Waynesville-Harveysburg Ohio. There are mountain

the LARK'S NEST BED 'n' BREAKFAST

bike trails, boating, and antique shopping all nearby. Each guest room is individually theme-decorated, with king beds. (Futons on request.) Enjoy a backyard bonfire or grill out on our deck. Close to Blue Jacket, Ohio Renaissance Festival, and Kings Island.

Hosts: Carla and Colin Stimpert
Rooms: 3 (PB) $85-105
Continental Breakfast
Credit Cards: A, B
Notes: 2, 5, 7, 9, 10, 11

YOUNGSTOWN

Inn at the Green

500 South Main Street, Poland, 44514
(330) 757-4688
www.acountryvillage.com/innatgreen

An 1876 classic Victorian town house sharing the village green with a Presbyterian church founded in 1802. The inn retains 12-foot ceilings, large moldings, five working Italian marble fireplaces, interior window shutters, and poplar floors. The inn is decorated with antiques, American art, and Oriental rugs. Poland is a preserved Western Reserve village in which President William McKinley grew up.

Hosts: Ginny and Steve Meloy
Rooms: 4 (PB) $60
Continental Breakfast
Credit Cards: A, B, D
Notes: 2, 7, 8, 9, 10, 12

ZOAR

The Cider Mill Bed & Breakfast

198 East 2nd St., P.O. Box 438, 44697
(330) 874-3240

The Cider Mill was built in 1863. It was and is the nation's most successful communal settlement. The Cider Mill served as a steam-operated mill and as the village cabinet shop. It was converted to living quarters in 1972. Rooms feature exposed ceiling beams and tastefully selected antiques. Clean and beautiful bathrooms provide modern comfort. Our three-story spiral staircase connects each level of the house. The fireplace with stone hearth in the gathering room is a perfect place to relax. To start your day, you'll be served a full breakfast from our country kitchen.

Hosts: Vernon and Dorothy Furbay
Rooms: 3 (1 PB; 2 SB) $60-75
Full Breakfast
Credit Cards: None
Notes: 2, 5, 8, 9, 10, 11

Oklahoma

ALINE

Heritage Manor

33 Heritage Road, 73716
phone/fax: (580) 463-2563; (800) 295-2563
E-mail: heritage@pldi.net
www.aj.org

Enjoy the vintage décor and ambience of a Victorian or country guest room. Roam the peaceful gardens, wander 80 acres of watchable wildlife habitat, or read in the 5,000-volume library! Browse for hours viewing the museum-like collections within Heritage Manor. Enjoy a breakfast of your choosing in one of the parlors, gazebo, courtyard, gardens, or on a treetop level deck at the time you wish to eat your Heritage "Good Morning" breakfast!

Hosts: A.J. and Carolyn
Rooms: 4 (3 PB; 1 SB) $75-150
Full Breakfast
Credit Cards: None
Notes: 2, 3, 4, 5, 6, 7, 8, 9, 10

CHICKASHA

Campbell-Richison House Bed & Breakfast

1428 Kansas Avenue, 73018
(405) 222-1754; fax: (405) 222-1754
E-mail: innkeeper@campbellrichison.com
www.campbellrichison.com

The Campbell-Richison house, built in 1909, recaptures the charm and hospitality of a past era. The house shares the history of three families who were all Grady County pioneers in their own way. At the present time the family-run B&B hosts three guest rooms, which have been restored and warmly decorated for your visit. Whether business or pleasure, come and enjoy this restored three-story red brick home.

Hosts: David and Kami Ratcliff
Rooms: 3 (PB) $50-70
Full Breakfast
Credit Cards: A, B
Notes: 2, 5, 7, 8, 9, 10

Jordan's River Cottage

Route 4, Box 96, 73018
(405) 222-3096; fax: (405) 222-1067
E-mail: jrcbb98@aol.com
www.bbonline.com/ok/jrcbb/

Jordan's River Cottage

This European farm house is located on River Bend Golf Course northeast of Chickasha. Three spacious rooms, each done in a different theme, are available. Our guests can enjoy the eight-and-a-half-foot pro pool table

OKLAHOMA

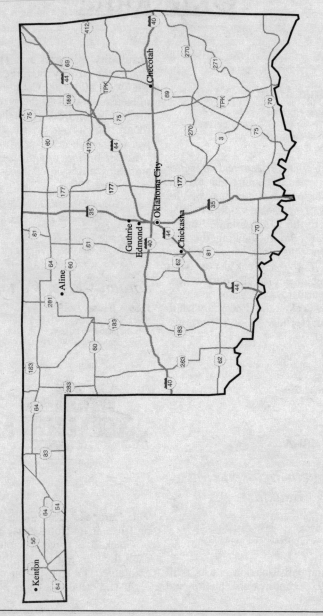

and a variety of games in our game room. Relax those tired muscles in the hot tub located in the sunroom. Enjoy up to 27 holes of golf, since green fees are free. Take in the beautiful view and peacefulness of the Oklahoma Frontier Country.

Hosts: David and Denice Riley
Rooms: 3 (PB) $75-95
Full Breakfast
Credit Cards: A, B
Notes: 2, 5, 8, 9, 10

EDMOND

The Arcadian Inn Bed & Breakfast

328 East 1st Street, 73034-4543
(405) 348-6347; (800) 299-6347
E-mail: arcadianinn@juno.com
www.bbonline.com/ok/arcadian

We invite you to "come away" from your everyday. Relax and enjoy one another. Take time to savor the small pleasures of life offered at the Arcadian Inn. . .a long soak in a deep whirlpool for two, a delicious cookie, an evening of cuddling in front of the

The Arcadian Inn

fire, yards of canopy over your bed, your favorite movie, or a lazy morning with a private candlelit breakfast. Rooms feature cable TVs and VCRs, stereos with CD players, telephones, free local calls, robes, candles, and bath salts. Corporate rates are available.

Hosts: Gary and Martha Hall
Rooms: 8 (PB) $99-209
Full Breakfast
Credit Cards: A, B, C, D
Notes: 2, 4, 5, 8, 9, 10

Victorian Rose

GUTHRIE

Victorian Rose Bed & Breakfast

415 East Cleveland Avenue, 73044
(405) 282-3928

The 100-year-old Queen Anne home, built in 1894, mixes the charm of the past with the comforts of the present. Located on a brick street, it features a wraparound porch with gingerbread accents, a porch swing, and garden area. Lovely restoration with quality workmanship: beautiful oak floors; exquisite, original beveled windows; gleaming brass light fixtures; and antiques. Three blocks from historic downtown (the largest urban historic district in the U.S.). Three beautiful Victorian guest rooms offer queen beds and private baths. Full, complimentary gourmet breakfast.

Hosts: Linda and Foy Shahan
Rooms: 3 (PB) $79-99
Full Breakfast
Credit Cards: A, B, D
Notes: 2, 5, 8, 9, 10, 12

KENTON

Black Mesa Bed and Breakfast

P.O. Box 81, 73946
(580) 261-7443; (800) 866-3009
E-mail: bmbb1@juno.com
www.ccccok.or/bmbb.html

Located two miles north of Kenton at the foot of the Black Mesa, this 1910 rock ranch house boasts the best in country hospitality. Accommodations include a ground-floor double-occupancy room with bath, a second-story family suite that sleeps eight with bath and a two-bedroom guest cottage with bath house. We offer days of adventure, spectacular sunsets, and down-home hospitality.

Hosts: Vicki and Monty Joe Roberts
Rooms: 4 (2 PB; 2 SB) $60-80
Full Breakfast
Credit Cards: A, B, D
Notes: 2, 3, 4, 5, 6, 7, 10

OKLAHOMA CITY

The Grandison at Maney Park

1200 North Shartel Avenue, 73103
(405) 232-8778; (800) 240-4667
fax: (405) 232-5039;
E-mail: grandison@juno.com
ww.bbonline.com/ok/grandison

Nine bedrooms feature antique furnishings, queen and king beds, private baths with double Jacuzzi and shower, and gas fireplaces. Built in 1904 and moved to its present location in 1909, the home features carved mahogany woodwork, a massive entry with curved staircase, original stained-glass and brass fixtures-charming details at every turn. We offer romantic getaways and executive services. Television and phone are available in rooms (take out on request). Refreshment bar and gift shop.

Hosts: Bob and Claudia Wright
Rooms: 9 (PB) $95-145
Continental Breakfast
Credit Cards: A, B, C, D
Notes: 2, 4, 5, 7, 8, 10, 12

NOTES: Credit cards accepted: A Master Card; B Visa; C American Express; D Discover; E Diners Club; F Other; 2 Personal checks accepted; 3 Lunch available; 4 Dinner available; 5 Open all year;

<u>Oregon</u>

ASHLAND

Cowslip's Belle
Bed & Breakfast

159 North Main Street, 97520
phone/fax: (541) 488-2901; (800) 888-6819
E-mail: stay@cowslip.com
www.cowslip.com

Teddy bears, chocolate truffles, cozy down comforters, and scrumptious breakfasts. A romantic luxury inn and nationally acclaimed award-winner featured in *McCall's* as one of the "most charming inns in America"; *Country Accents* says it's "a garden of many splendored delights"; and *Northwest Best Places* rates it as one of the Best Places to Kiss in the Northwest. Also listed in *Weekends for Two in the Pacific Northwest: 50 Romantic Getaways*.

Hosts: Jon and Carmen Reinhardt
Rooms: 5 (PB) $115-175
Full Breakfast
Credit Cards: None
Notes: 8, 9, 10, 11

ASTORIA

Benjamin Young Inn

3652 Duane Street, 97103
(503) 325-6172; (800) 201-1286
E-mail: benjamin@benjaminyounginn.com
www.benjaminyounginn.com

This Queen Anne Victorian built in 1888 by salmon packer Benjamin Young is ideal for romantic getaways. Enjoy the newly decorated Honeymoon Suite with cupola and antique furnishings, or the Fireplace Suite with two-person whirlpool tub. Feast at our legendary breakfast table. Watch the ships go by on the Columbia River. Private baths, riverviews, weddings, and catering.

Hosts: Carolyn and Rev. Ken Hammer
Rooms: 5 (PB) $85-145
Full Breakfast
Credit Cards: A, B, C, D
Notes: 2, 7, 8, 9, 12

Columbia River Inn
Bed & Breakfast

1681 Franklin Avenue, 97103
(503) 325-5044; (800) 953-5044
www.moriah.com/columbia

Columbia River Inn is charming in every way. Built in 1870, this beautiful "painted lady" Victorian has a gazebo for weddings and parties in the beautifully landscaped garden. Come see the "stairway to the stars," a unique terraced garden view of the celebrated Columbia River. Brand new aquatic center and seafood lab nearby. A new seven-screen theater close by; also close to museums. The inn offers four elegantly furnished rooms, one with a working fireplace and Jacuzzi. Beautiful side garden added with cobblestone sidewalk. The innkeeper's specialty is hospitality-"Home is where the heart is." Guests

---

6 Pets welcome; 7 Children welcome; 8 Tennis nearby; 9 Swimming nearby; 10 Golf nearby; 11 Skiing nearby; 12 May be booked through travel agent

OREGON

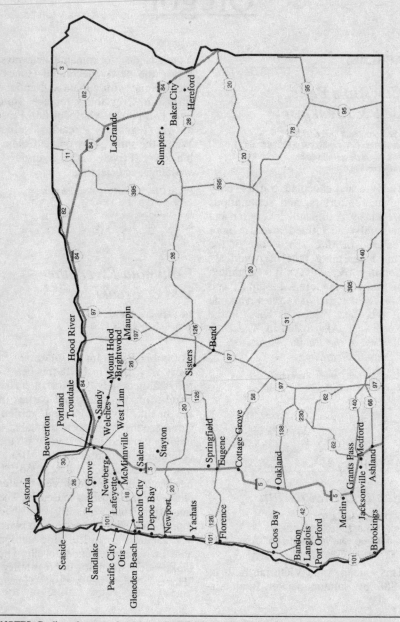

may use off-street parking. Gift certificates available.

Host: Karen N. Nelson
Rooms: 4 (PB) $75-125
Full Breakfast
Credit Cards: A, B, C, D
Notes: 2, 5, 7, 9

Franklin Street Station Bed & Breakfast

1140 Franklin Street, 97103
(503) 325-4314; (800) 448-1098
fax: (801) 681-5641
E-mail: franklinststationsbb@yahoo.com
www.franklin-st-station-bb.com

Centrally located above historic Astoria, Oregon, this classical turn-of-the-century home with its ornate craftsmanship reflects the early years of Astoria. It opened with three rooms, but has since been restored to offer six guest rooms, five with private baths. All of our rooms have queen beds. The Starlight Suite, with fireplace, TV, and telescope, offers a panoramic view of the Columbia River and beyond. The Sweet Tranquility Room has views of evening sunsets from its balcony. A full breakfast is served in the formal dining room.

Hosts: Sharon and Becky
Rooms: 6 (5 PB; 1 SB) $75-135
Full Breakfast
Credit Cards: A, B, C, D
Notes: 2, 5, 7, 8, 9, 10

Grandview

Franklin Street

Grandview Bed and Breakfast

1574 Grand Avenue, 97103
(503) 325-5555; (800) 488-3250
E-mail: grandviewbedandbreakfast@usa.net
www.pacifier.com/~grndview

Features of this home include a bullet turret, inset balconies, open staircase, bay windows, and a tower. Once owned by Eben Tallant, the first officer of a clipper ship, the house is now owned by the Maxwells. The Tallant's original home has been divided into eight apartments for over 40 years. Watch ships sailing on the river; walk the historic home tour or to restaurants, four museums, and the college campus; ride the old-fashioned trolley; swim in the new city pool; or jump in your car and visit umpteen beaches, two forts, the elk refuge, and the golf course a few miles away.

Host: Charleen Maxwell
Rooms: 9 (7 PB; 2 SB) $47-100
Full Breakfast
Credit Cards: A, B, D
Notes: 5, 7, 8, 9, 10

BAKER CITY

Baer House
Bed & Breakfast

2333 Main Street, 97814
(541) 524-1812
E-mail: innkeeper@baerhouse.com
www.baerhouse.com

Rendezvous with history. Experience luxury on the Oregon Trail. Enjoy an 1882 Victorian Italianate listed on the National Register, with Christian hosts. Two rooms share a new bath, and the large, two-room suite has a private bath with claw-foot tub and pedestal sink. Laundry and kitchenette are provided. Convenient Main Street location. Year-round recreational opportunities, including skiing and the National Oregon Trail Interpretive Center.

Hosts: Judy and Nick Greear
Rooms: 3 (1 PB; 2 SB) $70-85
Full Breakfast
Credit Cards: A, B, C, D, E
Notes: 2, 5, 9, 10, 11

BROOKINGS

Chetco River Inn
Lavender Bee Farm

21202 High Prairie Road, 97415
(541) 670-1645; (800) 327-2688
www.chetcoriverinn.com

Pristine river and modern inn awaits you a short distance from the coast. Big country breakfast, huge beds with down and handmade quilts, large indoor fireplace, common room, and covered porch with rocking chairs for your comfort. To do: trails, fishing, star gazing, swimming, mushrooming, birding, and gardens (flower and herb). New addition: Lavendar Farm.

Rooms: 6 (PB) $125-145
Full Breakfast
Credit Cards: A, B
Notes: 2, 4, 5, 7, 9, 10, 12

COTTAGE GROVE

Apple Inn
Bed & Breakfast

30697 Kenady Lane, 97424
(541) 942-2393
E-mail: appleinn@pond.net
www.moriah.com/appleinn

Lovely country home snuggled in our 190-acre forest and tree farm. Close to I-5 and Cottage Grove with covered bridges, antiques, golf, and lakes. Two rooms with private baths charmingly decorated in country and antiques with comfortable beds, views, TV/VCRs, phones, and luxury hot tubs. Featured in the Sunday *Oregonian* travel section. Homemade breakfast plus snacks. Smoking out-

---

NOTES: Credit cards accepted: A Master Card; B Visa; C American Express; D Discover; E Diners Club; F Other; 2 Personal checks accepted; 3 Lunch available; 4 Dinner available; 5 Open all year;

Apple Inn

side; children by arrangement. Cook-book available. Privacy and pampering. Be our guests!

Hosts: Harry and Katheryn McIntire
Rooms: 2 (PB) $80-110
Full Breakfast
Credit Cards: A, B, D
Notes: 2, 5, 7, 8, 9, 10

FOREST GROVE

Oak Tree
Bed & Breakfast

2300 N.W. Thatcher Road, 97116
(503) 357-6939; fax: (503) 357-3297
E-mail: oaktreebnb@aol.com
www.moriah.com/oaktree

Our home is less than a mile from the quiet, rural, yet progressive community of Forest Grove. Forest Grove lies between the mountains and the ocean, 35 minutes to Portland and 90 minutes to the Pacific. Our comfortable accommodations include an acre of well tended gardens, a view of rolling farmland from our guest living room, laundry facilities, robes, and slippers; fax and data port available. Sorry, no smoking or pets.

Hosts: Bob and Donna McIntosh
Rooms: 2 (PB) $60-65
Full Breakfast
Credit Cards: A, B
Notes: 2, 5, 7

GRANTS PASS

Flery Manor

2000 Jumpoff Joe Creek Road, 97526
(541) 476-3591; fax: (541) 471-2303
E-mail: flery@flerymanor.com
www.flerymanor.com

"Get away from the hurried world. . . retreat to the comfort and hospitality of Flery Manor." Elegant, romantic, secluded. On seven mountain-view acres near the Rouge River. Elegantly decorated bedrooms. Suites have king beds, fireplaces, Jacuzzi tubs, and private balconies. Ponds, paths, waterfall, streams, and gazebo. Library, parlor with piano, two-story high living room, huge balcony, and formal dining room. Three-course gourmet breakfast. Access to private health

Flery Manor

---

6 Pets welcome; 7 Children welcome; 8 Tennis nearby; 9 Swimming nearby; 10 Golf nearby; 11 Skiing nearby; 12 May be booked through travel agent

club/pool. Easy I-5 access. Open year-round. Featured in *Chef* magazine.

Hosts: John and Marla Vidrinskas
Rooms: 5 (4 PB; 1 SB) $85-150
Full Breakfast
Credit Cards: A, B
Notes: 2, 4, 5, 8, 9, 10, 11, 12

HEREFORD

Fort Reading Bed & Breakfast

Fort Reading

20588 Highway 245, 97837
(541) 446-3478; (800) 573-4285
fax: (541) 446-3478
E-mail: ftreading@ortelco.net
bedandbreakfast.com

Come, enjoy a stay in the secluded, beautiful Burnt River Valley in southeast Oregon. We're a working cattle ranch with stables available and trails to ride. Relax in our two-bedroom country-style cottage away from telephones and TV; there's a fully equipped kitchen to use or breakfast with us in the ranch house. Lake and stream fishing close by, historic cemeteries, mining town of Sumpter, and the Oregon Trail Interpretive Center in Baker City, all within an hours' drive.

Hosts: Daryl and Barbara Hawes
Rooms: 2 (SB) $55-85
Full Breakfast
Credit Cards: None
Notes: 2, 3, 6, 7

HOOD RIVER

Columbia Gorge Hotel

4000 Westcliff Drive, 97031
(541) 386-5566; (800) 345-1921
fax: (541) 387-5414
E-mail: cghotel@gorge.net
www.columbiagorgehotel.com

The Columbia Gorge Hotel, Oregon's finest country inn, offers comfort and service in an atmosphere of friendly elegance. Stroll in the creekside gardens, have a massage, linger over the five-course "World-Famous Farm Breakfast." Share a special dinner overlooking the Columbia River. In the heart of the Columbia Gorge National Scenic Area, the inn is surrounded by some of the most awesomely beautiful landscape in the world, including its own 208-foot waterfall. Enjoy!

Columbia Gorge Hotel

Host: Chavalla Lopez
Rooms: 39 (PB) $159-275
Full Breakfast
Credit Cards: A, B, C, D, E, F
Notes: 2, 3, 4, 5, 6, 9, 10, 11, 12

NOTES: Credit cards accepted: A Master Card; B Visa; C American Express; D Discover; E Diners Club; F Other; 2 Personal checks accepted; 3 Lunch available; 4 Dinner available; 5 Open all year;

JACKSONVILLE

The Touvelle House

455 North Oregon, P.O. Box 1891, 97530
(541) 899-8938; (800) 846-8422
fax: (541) 899-3992
E-mail: touvelle@wave.net
www.touvellehouse.com

The Touvelle House

Elegant 1916 three-story craftsman mansion located on over an acre of gardens and park-like grounds. The six rooms all have private baths and air-conditioning. Seasonal pool on-site; walking distance to town and minutes from the city of Ashford. Step back in time and enjoy our lovely home.

Rooms: 6 (PB) $135-160
Full Breakfast
Credit Cards: A, B, C, D
Notes: 5, 7, 8, 9, 10, 11, 12

LAGRANDE

Stang Manor

1612 Walnut Street, 97850
(541) 963-2400; (888) 286-9463
E-mail: innkeeper@stangmanor.com
stangmanor.com

Stang Manor is am impressive 1925 lumber baron's Georgian Colonial mansion. It features extraordinary architectural detail, including a basement ballroom and stage. The Manor sits on spacious grounds with a rose garden and magnificent trees. Guest rooms have queen beds and private baths. One room has a balcony overlooking the rose garden; the suite features a sitting room with fireplace. Full breakfast in the formal dining room sparkles with silver and crystal.

Hosts: Margie and Patrick McClure
Rooms: 4 (PB) $85-98
Full Breakfast
Credit Cards: A, B
Notes: 2, 5, 9, 10, 11, 12

LINCOLN CITY

Pacific Rest
Bed & Breakfast
& Cottages

1611 N.E. 11th Street, 97367
(541) 994-2337; (888) 405-7378
E-mail: jwaetjen@wcn.net
pacificrestbb.hypermart.net/

Pacific Rest is a newer home built with the B&B guest in mind. . .a spe-

Pacific Rest
Bed 'N' Breakfast

---

cial place where you'll find respite for the spirit as well as for the body. Located on a hillside within walking distance of shops, restaurants, lake and the ocean, you'll find two spacious suites with private baths and decks . . .ideal for a romantic getaway or family retreat. Also available: two- and three-bedroom, two-bath, fully furnished, oceanview cottages with hot tubs, TVs, and VCRs. Ideal for small retreats and family reunions. Gracious hospitality and personal service abound. We serve a full candlelight breakfast and gourmet coffee, teas, and snacks.

Hosts: Ray and Judy Waetjen
Rooms: 4 (PB) $90-125
Full Breakfast
Credit Cards: None
Notes: 2, 5, 7, 9, 10, 12

MOUNT HOOD AREA

Falcon's Crest Inn

87287 Government Camp Loop Highway,
    P.O. Box 185, Government Camp, 97028
(503) 272-3403; (800) 624-7384
fax: (503) 272-3454

Falcon's Crest Inn

E-mail: info@falconscrest.com
www.falconscrest.com

Falcon's Crest Inn is a beautiful mountain lodge/chalet-style house, architecturally designed to fit into the quiet natural forest and majestic setting of Oregon's Cascade Mountains. The inn is within walking distance of Ski Bowl, a year-round playground featuring downhill skiing in the winter and the Alpine Slide in the summer! Five suites, all with private baths. Each guest room is individually decorated with interesting and unique collectibles and offers beautiful views of mountains and forests. Phones are available in each suite. Smoking restricted. A fine-dining restaurant is on the premises. Ski packages and special event specialists! Children six and older welcome.

Hosts: B.J. and Melody Johnson
Rooms: 5 (PB) $125-179
Full Breakfast
Credit Cards: A, B, C, D
Notes: 2, 4, 5, 8, 9, 10, 11, 12

Old Welches Inn Bed & Breakfast

26401 East Welches Road, Welches, 97067
(503) 622-3754; fax: (503) 622-5370
E-mail: innmthood@cs.com
www.lodging.mthood.com

Memories are made in this 19th-century riverside retreat on two acres of lush mountain greenery. This quiet oasis will restore your mind and spirits. Cozy beds, designer robes, and the warm ambience will convince you you're visiting old friends. Experience wonderful breakfasts, and relaxation in great Adirondack chairs overlooking the river. In winter, enjoy the fire-

---

NOTES: Credit cards accepted: A Master Card; B Visa; C American Express; D Discover; E Diners Club; F Other; 2 Personal checks accepted; 3 Lunch available; 4 Dinner available; 5 Open all year;

Old Welches Inn

place, and in summer, sit under a million stars and share your secrets with someone special. We like to spoil our guests with homemade treats. So. . .come, let us pamper you!

Hosts: Judith & Ted Mondun
Rooms: 5 (3 PB; 2 SB) $106.50-162.50
Full Breakfast
Credit Cards: A, B, C, D
Notes: 2, 5, 6, 7, 8, 9, 10, 11, 12

PORTLAND

Hostess House
Bed and Breakfast

5758 N.E. Emerson Street, 97218
(503) 282-7892; (877) 860-2100
fax: (503) 282-7892
E-mail: hostess@hostesshouse.com
www.hostesshouse.com

Tranquil, affordable getaway which is city-close and country-quiet. Tastefully and simply refurbished contemporary inn is in a modest, residential neighborhood. Near bus, light rail, airport. Within 10-15 minutes of Convention Center, Rose Garden Arena, Coliseum, and downtown. Comfy

bathrobes provided. Guests served delectable breakfast in a dining room overlooking a deep terraced backyard. Special menus by request. "Rest your head. . .rest your heart." Make Hostess House your "home" away from home while traveling.

Host: Milli Laughlin
Rooms: 2 (SB) $60
Full Breakfast
Credit Cards: A, B, C, D
Notes: 2, 5, 7, 8, 9, 10, 11, 12

Hostess House

SALEM

A Creekside Inn,
The Marquee House

333 Wyatt Court N.E., 97301
(503) 391-0837; (800) 949-0837
fax: (503) 391-1713
E-mail: rickiemh@open.org
www.marqueehouse.com

Stunning garden setting on historic Mill Creek provides tranquility in the city. This 1930s Mt. Vernon colonial has antiques, fireplaces, and a truly relaxing atmosphere served up with sumptuous breakfasts. Within walking distance of the capitol, Willamette University, historic districts; convenient for wine country tours. Data ports available for business use.

6 Pets welcome; 7 Children welcome; 8 Tennis nearby; 9 Swimming nearby; 10 Golf nearby; 11 Skiing nearby; 12 May be booked through travel agent

Nightly film showing with "bottom-less" popcorn bowl; Murder Mystery Weekends available.

Host: Rickie Hart
Rooms: 5 (3 PB; 2 SB) $65-95
Full Breakfast
Credit Cards: A, B, D, E
Notes: 2, 5, 7, 8, 9, 10, 11, 12

SEASIDE

10th Avenue Inn
Bed & Breakfast

125 10th Avenue, 97138
(503) 738-0643; (800) 745-BEST (2378)
fax: (503) 738-0172
E-mail: 10aveinn@seasurf.net
www.10aveinn.com

Light cascades into this 1908 home, once belonging to a circuit court judge. Panoramic windows provide views of the ocean, Seaside's famous Promonade, beach homes, and the coast mountain range. Casual elegance greets you in the parlor, complete with breathtaking views, cozy fireplace, and a baby grand piano. Join us for evening snacks, lively conversation, and a magnificent ocean sunset. The morning brings breakfasts described as a feast for the eye as well as the palate. Children over 12 welcome. Please, no smoking or pets.

Hosts: Lesle and Jack Palmeri
Rooms: 3 (PB) $89-129
Full Breakfast
Credit Cards: A, B, C, D, E
Notes: 5, 9, 10, 12

SISTERS

Australian Outback
Country Lodge
Bed & Breakfast

68733 Junipine Lane, 97759
(541) 549-4312; (800) 930-0055
fax: (541) 549-4312
E-mail: squawcreek@sisterslodging.com
www.sisterslodging.com

Squaw Creek B&B in Sisters, Oregon, offers a big country breakfast and cozy beds in a wooded setting perfect for retreats, weddings, honeymoons, and getaways close to Mt. Bachelor, skiing, golfing, hiking, rafting, and fishing. Travel to Sisters, Oregon, and vacation in a comfortable, country B&B. Relax on our pine swing, feed our many deer friends, or take a walk along Squaw Creek. Our outdoor Jacuzzi is sure to delight even the weariest traveler; you'll be pampered as you relax next to the fire and unwind in the serene setting of our high desert B&B inn.

Hosts: Richard and Margaret Mason
Rooms: 5 (PB) $99-129
Full Breakfast
Credit Cards: A, B
Notes: 2, 5, 6, 7, 8, 9, 10, 11

Conklin's Guest House

69013 Camp Polk Road, 97759
(541) 549-0123; (800) 549-4262
fax: (541) 549-4481
www.conklinsguesthouse.com

Conklin's Guest House is surrounded by a sprawling meadow with a panoramic backdrop of snow capped peaks. Rich in history, near-century-old homesite gives evidence that early settlers chose the most beautiful sites first! Modern conveniences and attention to detail ensure a comfortable and restful stay. A truly peaceful environment within walking distance of Sisters' bustling shops and restaurants. Guests may use the barbecue, swimming pool, and laundry facilities, and otherwise be at home! The ponds are stocked with trout for catch-and-release fishing. The Sisters area has something for everyone, from rafting and rock climbing to dining and shopping and much more. Children 12 and over welcome.

Conklin's Guest House

Hosts: Marie and Frank Conklin
Rooms: 5 (PB) $90-150
Full Breakfast
Credit Cards: None
Notes: 2, 5, 8, 9, 10, 11, 12

STAYTON

Gardner House Bed & Breakfast

633 North 3rd Avenue, 97383
(503) 769-5748

Stately old home built in 1899 and refurbished in 1972 by your host who is a florist and owner of Stayton Flowers & Gifts on the premises. Two rooms with private baths, queen beds, TVs, and VCRs; two with kitchen. Breakfast is served at the Gardner House. Fifteen minutes from Salem, near Silver Falls State Park, skiing, and hiking. Great breakfast!

Host: Richard Jungwirth
Rooms: 2 (PB) $65-75 plus tax
Full Breakfast
Credit Cards: A, B, C, D
Notes: 2, 3, 4, 5, 6, 7, 8, 9, 10

SUMPTER

Sumpter Bed & Breakfast

344 Northeast Columbia, P.O. Box 40, 97877
(541) 894-0048; (877) 378-5322
fax: (541) 894-0048
E-mail: sumpbb@eoni.com

This 1900 hospital building is rich in history in an old gold mining town. Enjoy Victorian era furnishings and full breakfasts. Glimpse wildlife from the balcony. Ride the historic Sumpter Valley Railroad, tour a gold dredge, or shop the local antique stores. Close to the Oregon Trail Interpretive Cen-

Sumpter B&B

6 Pets welcome; 7 Children welcome; 8 Tennis nearby; 9 Swimming nearby; 10 Golf nearby; 11 Skiing nearby; 12 May be booked through travel agent

ter. Snowmobile groomed trails out
the back door.

Hosts: Jay and Barb Phillips
Rooms: 6 (SB) $70
Full Breakfast
Credit Cards: None
Notes: 2, 5, 7, 9, 10, 11

Pennsylvania

ADAMSTOWN

Adamstown Inn

62 West Main Street, 19501
(717) 484-0800; (800) 594-4808
fax: (717) 484-1384
E-mail: info@adamstown.com
www.adamstown.com

Experience the simple elegance of the
Adamstown Inn, a Victorian B&B resplendent with leaded-glass doors,
magnificent chestnut woodwork, and
oriental rugs, located in a small town
brimming with thousands of antique
dealers and minutes away from outlet
shopping. Several rooms feature two-
person Jacuzzis. Highly recommended!

Hosts: Tom & Wanda Berman
Rooms: 4 (PB) $69-149
Continental Breakfast
Credit Cards: A, B, C
Notes: 2, 5, 8, 9, 10, 11, 12

Brownstone Colonial Inn

590 Galen Hall Road, Reinholds, 17569
(717) 484-4460; (877) 464-9862
E-mail: info@brownstonecolonialinn.com
brownstonecolonialinn.com

This brownstone colonial inn is a 210-
year-old sandstone farmhouse built by
German Mennonite settlers. We offer
three beautifully furnished rooms featuring locally handcrafted authentic
furniture, plank floors, lofty win-
dowsills, and private bathrooms. Dine
by the fire in the summer kitchen with
a scruptious home-cooked country
breakfast. Enjoy a leisurely walk by
our flower and water gardens. Take a
step back in time and let us pamper
you soon!

Hosts: Brenda and Mark Miller
Rooms: 3 (PB) $85-115
Full Breakfast
Credit Cards: None
Notes: 2, 5, 7, 9, 10, 11

ALEXANDRIA

Hearthwood House Bed & Breakfast

Box #372, 16611
(814) 669-4386; (800) 699-4386
fax: (800) 699-4386 *51

Located seven miles west of Hunting-
don, Pennsylvania, on Route 22 and
only 30 minutes from State College.
The Lower Rail-Trail is a five-minute
walk away. This lovely ranch home
sits high on a hill surrounded by trees
and wildlife. Enjoy panoramic sunsets
from a front-porch rocking chair, or
relax by the fireplace in the cooler
months or on the patio in summer.
Two spacious bedrooms, plus a full
breakfast of your choice. You will
feel most welcome in this home setting.

Host: Jeanne L. Whittaker
Rooms: 2 (SB) $48
Full Breakfast
Credit Cards: None
Notes: 2, 7, 9, 12

---

6 Pets welcome; 7 Children welcome; 8 Tennis nearby; 9 Swimming nearby; 10 Golf nearby; 11 Skiing
nearby; 12 May be booked through travel agent

PENNSYLVANIA

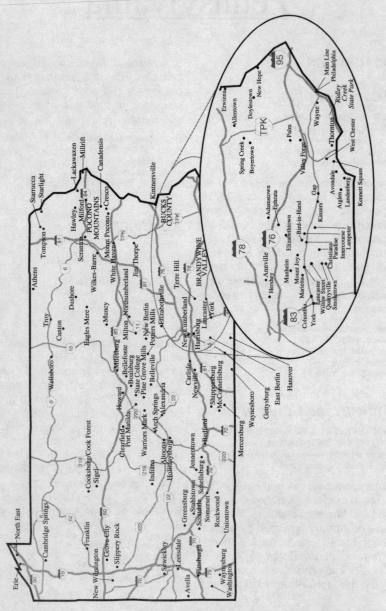

ALLENTOWN

Brennans
Bed & Breakfast

3827 West Linden Street, 18104
(610) 395-0869

A split-level ranch home, located in the outskirts of Allentown. Located near all major highways. Nearby are historic sites as well as an amusement park (Dorney). Malls are within a mile, and two local colleges are nearby. Churches of all denominations are within a mile.

Hosts: Lois and Edward Brennan
Rooms: 2 (1 PB; 1 SB) $45
Full Breakfast
Credit Cards: None
Notes: 2, 7, 9, 10

ANNVILLE

Swatara Creek Inn

10463 Jonestown Road, 17003
(717) 865-3259
www.swataracreekinn.com

Swatara Creek Inn

This charming 1860s Victorian mansion on 4.5 peaceful country acres, lovingly restored, has become not only our home, but a warm, graceful, and quiet retreat away from your home. Furnished in a comfortable style, all rooms feature quilted queen canopy beds, private baths, and air-conditioning. Awake to a homemade breakfast. Located near Lebanon Valley College, Fort Indiantown Gap, Appalachian Trail, Hershey, Harrisburg, Reading, and Lancaster. Wheelchair accessible. Smoking outside home. AAA three-diamond approved.

Hosts: Dick and Susan Hess
Rooms: 6 (PB) $60-80
Full Breakfast
Credit Cards: A, B, D
Notes: 2, 5, 7

BELLEVILLE

Twin Oaks
Bed & Breakfast

73 South Dryhouse Road, 17004
(717) 935-2026

In the heart of the Kishacoquillas Valley, only 30 minutes from Penn State. Norman and Sarah Glick welcome their guests to a new facility with clean, spacious rooms. In a quiet country setting with a panoramic view of Stone and Jacks Mountain. Full breakfast is served. Children are welcome. Open all year.

Hosts: Norman and Sarah Glick
Rooms: 4 (1 PB; 3 SB) $50-70
Full Breakfast
Credit Cards: None
Notes: 2, 5, 7, 10, 12

---

6 Pets welcome; 7 Children welcome; 8 Tennis nearby; 9 Swimming nearby; 10 Golf nearby; 11 Skiing nearby; 12 May be booked through travel agent

BOYERTOWN

Enchanted Cottage

Enchanted Cottage

22 Deer Run Road, 19512
(610) 845-8845
www.choice-guide.com/pa/enchanted/

Peace, quiet, and complete privacy await you in this romantic and secluded Cotswold-like cottage nestled in acres of woods. Double bed in air-conditioned bedroom adjoining Laura Ashley bathroom. Gourmet breakfast served in main house. Complimentary beverages and cheese. Fresh flowers, antiques. Near historic sites, cultural activities, reading outlets, Amish Country, churches. You—our only guests—will find our lifestyle informal but gracious.

Hosts: Peg and Richard Groff
Rooms: 1 (PB) $85-90
Full Breakfast
Credit Cards: None
Notes: 2, 5, 8, 10, 11, 12

CAMBRIDGE SPRINGS

Bethany Guest House

325 South Main, 16403
(814) 398-2046; (800) 777-2046

Curl up with a book in cozy wicker furniture as you enjoy gentle breezes through the huge maples. Savor a "made-to-order" breakfast in the ornate Greek Revival dining room. Soak in the double-wide whirlpool tub or play board games in the drawing room to your heart's content. Explore nearby Lake Erie, wildlife refuges, dinner theater, bicycle trails, amusement parks, or antique shops. Enjoy the luxury of a restored, 1876 Italianate National Register home built in a Victorian resort community by the town banker. However you choose to enjoy your getaway, it is our goal to make it a distinct pleasure.

Rooms: 4 (PB) $35-65
Full Breakfast
Credit Cards: A, B
Notes: 2, 5, 7, 8, 9, 10, 11

CANTON

M-Mm Good Bed & Breakfast

R.D. 1 # 71, 17724
(570) 673-8153

Located along Route 414, three miles east of Canton in the quiet country center of the Endless Mountains. Clean, comfortable rooms and a breakfast including our homemade muffins or sticky buns. Picnic tables under maple trees. Hiking, fishing.

Hosts: Melvin and Irene Good
Rooms: 4 (1 PB; 3 SB) $27.50-50.00
Full Breakfast
Credit Cards: None
Notes: 2, 5, 7

NOTES: Credit cards accepted: A Master Card; B Visa; C American Express; D Discover; E Diners Club; F Other; 2 Personal checks accepted; 3 Lunch available; 4 Dinner available; 5 Open all year;

CARLISLE

Line Limousin Farm House

2070 Ritner Highway, 17013
(717) 243-1281; fax: (717) 249-5537
E-mail: bline@planetcable.net
www.pafarmstay.com/line/index.html

Step back in time and stay with us in our 1864 brick and stone farmhouse which has always been owned by the Line family. French Limousin cattle are raised on our 100-acre farm. Cross over our stone fences to spot wildlife and a large variety of birds. After a large breakfast, join us for worship at our historic First Presbyterian Church. Two rooms have comfortable king beds, private baths, air-conditioning, and TV. Nonsmoking. Two-night minimum stay. Children over eight welcome.

Line Limousin Farm House

Hosts: Bob and Joan Line
Rooms: 3 (3 PB) $80-95
Full Breakfast
Credit Cards: None
Notes: 2, 5, 10

Pheasant Field Bed & Breakfast

150 Hickorytown Road, 17013
phone/fax: (717) 258-0717; (877) 258-0717
E-mail: stay@pheasantfield.com
www.pheasantfield.com

Stay in this lovely old brick farmhouse set in quiet country surroundings. Wake up to a full country breakfast including fresh bread or muffins, fresh fruit, a hot entrée, and plenty of hot coffee. After a game of tennis or a hike on the Appalachian Trail, relax in the family room or living room and help yourself to a homemade cookie (or two). Feel free to bring your horse—we offer overnight boarding, when space is available. Collector car shows, antiquing, and fly-fishing are nearby. Smoking is permitted outside. AAA three-diamond rating. "Come home to the country." Two-night minimum stay.

Host: Dee Fegan
Rooms: 5 (PB) $85-120
Full Breakfast
Credit Cards: A, B, C
Notes: 2, 5, 6, 8, 10, 12

CARLISLE/MECHANICSBURG

Homestay Farm Bed & Breakfast

1022 Park Place, Mechanicsburg, 17055
(717) 697-1864; fax: (717) 697-7335
E-mail: info@homestayfarm.com
www.homestayfarm.com

An 1841 Pennsylvania Dutch farmhouse filled with family antiques and located on a 113-acre flower and vegetable farm, bordered by the Yellow

Homestay Farm

Breeches Creek, a famous eastern trout stream. Each room has its own air-conditioning plus a floor fan. There is a comfortable TV room for guests, a screened flower porch to socialize, and a sitting room for reading.

Host: Barbara Marbain
Rooms: 4 (2 PB; 2 SB) $60-80
Full Breakfast
Credit Cards: A, B
Notes: 2, 9, 10

CHRISTIANA

Georgetown Bed &Breakfast

1222 Georgetown Road, 17509
(717) 786-4570

Once a miller's home, the original structure was converted to a B&B for the enjoyment of guests in a relaxing home away from home. Entrance to the house is by a brick walkway. A herb garden lets guests smell the lavender and mint, just two of the herbs used to garnish morning breakfasts. There is a choice of three bedrooms decorated with antiques and collectibles. Lancaster County Amish, a unique group of people who travel in horse-drawn carriages, pass in front of the Georgetown. Visit the local Strasburg Railroad and Train Museum.

Host: Doris W. Woerth
Rooms: 3 (1 PB; 2 SB) $50-60
Full Breakfast
Credit Cards: None
Notes: 2, 5, 9, 10

Spruce Edge Guest House

1586 Georgetown Road, 17509
(717) 529-3979

Relax and enjoy this charming 19th-century rustic B&B cottage situated on a working dairy farm. Originally a summer kitchen, Spruce Edge Guest House has been meticulously restored, down to the original paint. The original two rooms feature a downstairs living room and an upstairs bedroom. The living room contains a walk-in fireplace and dining area. Four beds are tucked upstairs, including one king-sized and one antique rope bed with feather ticking. The added bath allows you to shower in an old fashioned claw-foot tub. Spruce Edge Guest House is minutes from local attractions, and is quietly and quaintly nestled among beautiful Lancaster County farms. Your stay includes breakfast with the Harnishes or a private breakfast in the Guest House. Whether you stay for a night or for a week, Spruce Edge Guest House creates the perfect atmosphere for an enchanting stay.

Hosts: Ed and Arlene Harnish
Rooms: 1 guesthouse (PB) $50-60
Credit Cards: None
Notes: 2, 7, 10

NOTES: Credit cards accepted: A Master Card; B Visa; C American Express; D Discover; E Diners Club; F Other; 2 Personal checks accepted; 3 Lunch available; 4 Dinner available; 5 Open all year;

CLEARFIELD

Christopher Kratzer House

101 East Cherry Street, 16830
(814) 765-5024; (888) 252-2632
E-mail: bbaggett@uplink.net
www.virtualcities.com/pa/kratzerhouse.htm

Graceful circa 1840 Classic Revival mansion in Old Town historic district pre-dates Victorian era, and features antiques and objects d'art. Lovely views of river and park; children's playground. Three guest rooms; two air-conditioned suites with private baths. Wood-burning fireplace in common room. Gourmet breakfasts, afternoon tea, Sunday night candle-light suppers on request. Entertainment, art gallery, "attic flea market" on premises. State parks and Rails to Trails nearby. Just three miles off I-80.

Hosts: Bruce and Ginny Baggett
Rooms: 3 (2 PB; 1 SB) $65-80
Full Breakfast
Credit Cards: A, B, D
Notes: 2, 5, 7, 8, 9, 10, 12

Victorian Loft Bed & Breakfast

216 South Front Street, 16830
(814) 765-4805; (800) 798-0456
fax: (814) 765-9596
E-mail:pdurant@csrlink.net
www.virtualcities.com/pa/victorianloft.html

Elegant 1894 riverfront Victorian in the historic district. Air-conditioned rooms with balcony or skylights. Suite has private kitchenette-dining area, living room with entertainment center, and whirlpool bath. Family

movies provided. Fiber studio. Hosts are Bible college graduates. Perfect stop on PA I-80, three miles off Exit 19. Also, completely equipped, three-bedroom cabin on eight forested acres, located two miles from Parker Dam and Elliot State Parks. Or try our new "Second Street Suite" primarily

Victorian Loft

designed and especially nice for longer stays.

Hosts: Tim and Peggy Durant
Rooms: 6 (4 PB; 2 SB) $60-125
Full Breakfast
Credit Cards: A, B, C, D
Notes: 2, 5, 6, 7, 8, 9, 10, 11, 12

COCHRANVILLE

Elver Valley Bed & Breakfast

432 Sawmill Road, 19330
(717) 529-2803; (877) TO ELVER
fax: (717) 529-2803
E-mail: evrohrer@webtv.net
www.pafarmstay/elvervalley

Quiet, country woodlands overlook water gardens and wildlife. Ranch home offers queen beds, private baths, air-conditioning, full breakfast,

---

6 Pets welcome; 7 Children welcome; 8 Tennis nearby; 9 Swimming nearby; 10 Golf nearby; 11 Skiing nearby; 12 May be booked through travel agent

no stairs, dish TV. Four-seat swing gazebo, children's swings, and petting pasture. Pond for boating and fishing. Families our speciality. Farmland tour information. Midway between Lancaster County and Brandywine Valley; visit Longwood Gardens, Brandywine River Museum, Amish wood crafts, Herr Foods, outlet shopping, and antiques.

Hosts: Elvin and Vera Rohrer
Rooms: 2 (PB) $55
Full Breakfast
Credit Cards: None
Notes: 2, 5, 7, 10

CRESCO

La Anna Guest House

LA ANNA GUEST HOUSE

R.R. 2, Box 2801, 18326
phone/fax: (570) 676-4225

The 122-year-old Victorian home is furnished with Victorian and Empire antiques. It has spacious guest rooms, quiet surroundings, and a trout pond. You can walk to waterfalls and mountain views; deer and other wildlife are often seen nearby.

Host: Kay Swingle
Rooms: 4 (2 PB; 2 SB) $45
Continental Breakfast
Credit Cards: None
Notes: 2, 5, 7, 8, 9, 10, 11

DENVER

Cocalico Creek Bed & Breakfast

224 South 4th Street, 17517
(717) 336-0271; (888) 208-7334
E-mail: cocalicocrk@desupernet.net
www.cocalicocrk.com

Casual elegance in a country setting overlooking pastures, ponds, and Cocalico Creek. Four tastefully decorated rooms with queen beds, private baths; one room offers a private balcony. Air-conditioning for summer comfort; heated beds with down comforters for winter chills. Explore the history, culture, and rural scenic beauty. Minutes from antiquing, outlet shopping, golf, farmers' markets, and fine dining. This "at home atmosphere" will make it hard to leave. AAA-rated.

Cocalico Creek

NOTES: Credit cards accepted: A Master Card; B Visa; C American Express; D Discover; E Diners Club; F Other; 2 Personal checks accepted; 3 Lunch available; 4 Dinner available; 5 Open all year;

Host: Charlene Sweeney
Rooms: 4 (PB) $92-110
Full Breakfast
Credit Cards: A, B, C, D, E
Notes: 2, 5, 7, 8, 9, 10

EAGLES MERE

Crestmont Inn

Crestmont Inn

P.O. Box 371, Crestmont Drive, 17731
(570) 525-3519; (800) 522-8767
fax: (570) 525-3534
E-mail: crestmnt@epix.net
www.crestmont-inn.com

Crestmont Inn, your personal retreat of romance and nature at its very best! This romantic inn sits on the highest point in Eagles Mere, a picturesque Victorian village; surrounded by state parks, breathtaking vistas, and one of nature's wonders—Eagles Mere Lake. Crestmont is widely known for gracious hospitality and beautifully decorated rooms and suites. Our suites include air-conditioning, sitting area with TVs, and whirlpool tubs for two.

Hosts: The Oliver Family
Rooms: 13 (PB) $99-178
Full Breakfast
Credit Cards: A, B
Notes: 2, 7, 8, 9, 10, 12

ELIZABETHVILLE

The Inn at Elizabethville

P.O. Box 236, 30 West Main Street, 17023
(717) 362-3476; fax: (717) 362-1444

Built in 1883, this comfortable two-story house was owned by a Civil War veteran who was also the founder of a local wagon company. The Confederate Room features an unusual fireplace with cabinets and painted decorations. A breezy comfortable porch invites guests to relax, drink lemonade, eat homemade cookies, and watch the world go by. Country auctions, antiques, local craft fairs, and outdoor activities entice guests.

Host: Heidi Milbrand
Rooms: 7 (PB) $49-65
Full Breakfast
Credit Cards: A, B
Notes: 2, 5, 8, 9, 10

EPHRATA

The Inns at Doneckers

318-324 North State Street, 17522
(717) 738-9502; fax: (717) 738-9554
E-mail: donecker@doneckers.com
www.doneckers.com

Early American inns in the heart of Pennsylvania Dutch Country, historic Lancaster County. Stay in one of our elegantly appointed rooms or suites with fireplace and Jacuzzi, and enjoy the Doneckers Community: fine dining at our French/American Restaurant; fine furniture galleries; and local artists' studios at the Artworks; distinctive styles for women, men, children and the home in our upscale

---

6 Pets welcome; 7 Children welcome; 8 Tennis nearby; 9 Swimming nearby; 10 Golf nearby; 11 Skiing nearby; 12 May be booked through travel agent

fashion Store; and nearby antique/collectible markets. Anniversary, birthday, and corporation getaway packages. View each room online.

Hosts: Mr. & Mrs. H. William Donecker
Rooms: 40 (38 PB; 2 SB) $69-210
Continental Breakfast
Credit Cards: A, B, C, D
Notes: 2, 5, 7, 10

Meadow Valley Farm Guest Home

221 Meadow Valley Road, 17522
(717) 733-8390; (877) 562-4530
fax: (717) 733-9068
E-mail: walterhurst@juno.com

Visit our restored summer home in the heart of Lancaster County's beautiful farmland. Bring the family. We offer three cozy antique bedrooms. Original summer house offers three bedrooms with private and semi-private baths. Crib/cots available; fully furnished antique kitchen; air-conditioning; working farm. Milk cows, gather eggs, and enjoy local produce, flea markets, Green Dragon-Cloisters farm, pond boating, picnicking, biking, and play area. Families welcome!

Meadow Valley Farm

Host: Marlene Hurst
Rooms: 3 (1 PB; 2 SB) $35-45
Full Breakfast
Credit Cards: None
Notes: 2, 5, 7, 9, 10

GETTYSBURG

Baltimore Street Bed & Breakfast

449 Baltimore Street, 17325-2623
(717) 334-2454; (888) 667-8266
fax: (717) 334-6890
E-mail: tannery@cvn.net
www.baltimorestreetbandb.com

Baltimore Street

This 1868 Victorian is located in the heart of Gettysburg within walking distance to battlefields, museums, shops, restaurants. Library with over 650 books on the Civil War available for guest use.

Hosts: Jan and George Newton
Rooms: 9 (PB) $95-160
Full Breakfast
Credit Cards: A, B
Notes: 2, 5, 7, 10, 11

NOTES: Credit cards accepted: A Master Card; B Visa; C American Express; D Discover; E Diners Club; F Other; 2 Personal checks accepted; 3 Lunch available; 4 Dinner available; 5 Open all year;

The Doubleday Inn

104 Doubleday Avenue, 17325
(717) 334-9119; fax: (717) 334-7907
E-mail: doubledayinn@blazenet.net
www.bbonline.com/pa/doubleday

Located directly on the Gettysburg battlefield, this beautifully restored colonial country inn enjoys splendid views of historic Gettysburg and the battlefield. Guests enjoy candlelit country breakfasts, afternoon refreshments, and the cozy comfort of a centrally air-conditioned inn surrounded by lovely antiques and Civil War memorabilia. Free presentations by battlefield historians on selected evenings. Children over eight welcome.

Hosts: Ruth Anne and Charles Wilcox
Rooms: 10 (8 PB; 2 SB) $94-119
Full Breakfast
Credit Cards: A, B, D
Notes: 2, 5, 8, 9, 10, 11, 12

Hickory Bridge Farm

96 Hickory Bridge Road, Orrtanna, 17353
(717) 642-5261
E-mail: hickory@mail.cvn.net
www.hickorybridgefarm.com

Only eight miles west of historic Gettysburg. Unique country dining and B&B. Cozy cottages with woodstoves and private baths are located in secluded, wooded settings along a stream. Lovely rooms are available in the farmhouse with antiques, private baths, and whirlpool tubs. Full, farm breakfast served at the farmhouse, which was built in the late 1700s. Country dining offered on Fridays, Saturdays, and Sundays in a 130-year-old barn with many antiques. Family-owned/operated for more than twenty years.

Hosts: Robert and Mary Lynn Martin
Rooms: 9 (PB) $85-145
Full Breakfast
Credit Cards: A, B, D
Notes: 2, 4 (weekends), 5, 8, 9, 10, 11

Keystone Inn Bed & Breakfast

231 Hanover Street, 17325
(717) 337-3888
www.virtualcities.com/ons/pa/pag6601.htm

The Keystone Inn is a large, brick Victorian home built in 1913. The rooms' high ceilings are decorated with lace and flowers, and a handsome chestnut staircase rises to the third floor. The guest rooms are bright, cheerful, and air-conditioned. Each has a reading nook and writing desk. Choose your own breakfast from our full breakfast menu. One suite available.

Hosts: Wilmer and Doris Martin
Rooms: 5 (PB) $79-119
Full Breakfast
Credit Cards: A, B, D
Notes: 2, 5, 7, 8, 9, 10, 11

GROVE CITY

Snow Goose Inn

112 East Main Street, 16127
(724) 458-4644; (800) 317-4644
fax: (724) 458-1686
www.bbonline.com/pa/snowgoose/

The Snow Goose Inn is a large house, circa 1895, formerly a doctor's home. It has a large, wraparound front porch with an old-fashioned porch swing. Comfortable, air-conditioned guestrooms have private baths. Each is decorated with antiques and touches of

---

6 Pets welcome; 7 Children welcome; 8 Tennis nearby; 9 Swimming nearby; 10 Golf nearby; 11 Skiing nearby; 12 May be booked through travel agent

country. A full breakfast is served, along with homemade muffins, home-baked breakfast rolls, etc.

Hosts: Orvil and Dorothy McMillen
Rooms: 4 (PB) $65
Full Breakfast
Credit Cards: A, B, C
Notes: 2, 5, 8, 9, 10, 11

HERSHEY

Mottern's Bed & Breakfast

28 East Main Street, Hummelstown, 17036
(717) 566-3840; fax: (717) 566-3780
E-mail: motternsbb@hotmail.com
home.earthlink.net/~jmottern/lodging/title.html

Enjoy small-town hospitality five minutes from Hershey Park. B&B is a private apartment (sleeps a family of five) on the 1st floor of our restored 1860s limestone home. Living room, dining room, kitchen, bedroom, bath, central air, cable TV. A pergola covered patio (with gas grill) overlooks our walled garden. Private off-street parking. Located at the town center close to churches, shops, restaurants, and the local park. Discount Hershey Park tickets, complimentary Hershey tour, close to Lancaster, Gettysburg, and Harrisburg. No charge for children; internet discounts.

Hosts: Susan and Jeffrey Mottern
Rooms: 1 (PB) $145
Continental Breakfast
Credit Cards: A, B
Notes: 2, 5, 7, 8, 9, 10, 11

Nancy's Guesthouse

Nancy's Guesthouse

235 Hershey Road, Hummelstown, 17036
(717) 566-9844
E-mail: marnan@paonline.com

Comfort, homeyness, and privacy are what you find at our guesthouse where you are our only guests. Located two miles from Hershey Park, our second-floor, one-unit, nonsmoking apartment has a private entrance and a large deck. There are two bedrooms, a living room, a kitchen, and a bath with laundry. Color television and air-conditioning add to the comfort. Eat in or go out, choosing from fast food or fine dining. Travelers' checks or cash are accepted; checks limited. A ten-percent discount for five nights or more. Located three and a half miles from I-81 on Route 39.

Hosts: Marlin and Nancy Geesaman
Rooms: 2 (PB) $40-65 (winter);
    $65-85 (May-Sept.)
Credit Cards: None
Notes: 7, 8, 9, 10, 11

Shepherd's Acres Bed & Breakfast

Road 3, Box 370, Bell Road, Palmyra, 17078
(717) 838-3899; www.shepherdacres.com

NOTES: Credit cards accepted: A Master Card; B Visa; C American Express; D Discover; E Diners Club; F Other; 2 Personal checks accepted; 3 Lunch available; 4 Dinner available; 5 Open all year;

Welcome to the Hershey-Lancaster area! Join us in "our home away from home." Quiet country setting; eat-in porch area; sheep in the pasture; handmade quilt and wall hangings; TV and air-conditioning. Friendships for a lifetime; five minutes from Hershey.

Hosts: Jerry and Margy Allebach
Rooms: 3 (1 PB; 2 SB) $55-65
Full Breakfast
Credit Cards: None
Notes: 2, 5, 8, 9, 10, 11

INTERCOURSE

Intercourse Village Bed & Breakfast Suites

Route 340, Main Street, P.O. Box 340, 17534
(717) 768-2626; (800) 664-0949
E-mail: ivbbs@aol.com
www.amishcountryinns.com

AAA four-diamond rated. Enjoy these new romantic B&B suites for couples. Located in the heart of Amish country. See our fully restored 1909 Victo-

Intercourse Village

rian-style home. Then take a walk down the brick pathway to our new country homestead suites. All rooms have private baths, fireplaces, and include a gourmet candlelit breakfast. Come stay with us in this quaint Amish country village.

Host: Ruthann Thomas
Rooms: 8 (PB) $89-199
Full Breakfast
Credit Cards: A, B, C
Notes: 5, 10

JENNERSTOWN

Thee Olde Stage Coach Bed & Breakfast

P.O. Box 337, 1760 Lincoln Highway, 15547
(814) 629-7440
E-mail: carol@oldestagecoachbandb
www.oldestagecoachbandb.com

The Olde Stagecoach B&B is a renovated, 200-year-old farmhouse that during the 1700s and 1800s was a stagecoach rest stop. It now has four lovely bedrooms decorated with antiques, adding country charm, each with its own private bath. Guests relax in the Victorian-style common room. It is a place to stay in all four seasons, located on the historical Lincoln Highway. Nearby are the oldest professional summer theater, antique shops, golfing, outlet shopping, skiing, and cross-country skiing.

Hosts: Carol and George Neuhof
Rooms: 4 (PB) $75-85
Full Breakfast
Credit Cards: A, B
Notes: 2, 5, 8, 9, 10, 11

---

6 Pets welcome; 7 Children welcome; 8 Tennis nearby; 9 Swimming nearby; 10 Golf nearby; 11 Skiing nearby; 12 May be booked through travel agent

JIM THORPE

The Inn at Jim Thorpe

24 Broadway, 18229
(570) 325-2599; (800) 329-2599
fax: (570) 325-9145
E-mail: innjt@ptd.net
www.innjt.com

Nestled in the heart of a truly unique and historic village, the Inn combines Victorian elegance with 21st-century comforts. Our grand hotel features charming guest rooms and world-class suites with whirlpools and fire-places, classic cuisine, and a genuine Irish pub! Discover our rich history through tours of national historic landmarks and award-winning museums. Visit quaint shops and art galleries. For the adventurous there's top-rated mountain biking and white water rafting. You'll find all this and more in the enchanted village of Jim Thorpe.

Host: David Drury
Rooms: 36 (PB) $89-279
Continental Breakfast
Credit Cards: A, B, C, D, E
Notes: 3, 4, 5, 7, 10, 11, 12

KINZERS

Sycamore Haven Farm

35 South Kinzer Road, 17535
(717) 442-4901

We have approximately forty milking cows and many young cattle and cats for children to enjoy. Our farmhouse has three guest rooms, all with double beds and one single. Cots and playpen available. Fifteen miles east of Lancaster city. Route 30 to Kinzer Road; turn right at the first farm on the left.

Hosts: Charles and Janet Groff
Rooms: 3 (SB) $35-45
Continental Breakfast
Credit Cards: None
Notes: 2, 5, 6, 7, 8, 9, 10

LANCASTER

Alden House Bed & Breakfast

62 East Main Street, Lititz, 17543-1947
(717) 627-3363; (800) 584-0753
fax: (717) 627-5428
E-mail: inn@aldenhouse.com
www.aldenhouse.com

Step out our front door and into the quaint town of Lititz where art galleries, antique shops, country stores, and soda fountain shops line the street. The Alden House, an 1850s brick colonial home elegantly restored and beautifully decorated, is nestled in the historic district. With lovely rooms and spacious suites, private baths, queen beds, and cable TV, we offer a blend of Old World charm and New World comfort.

Hosts: Tom and Lillian Vazquez
Rooms: 5 (PB) $90-120
Full Breakfast
Credit Cards: A, B
Notes: 2, 5, 7, 8, 10

Australian Walkabout Inn Bed & Breakfast

837 Village Road; P.O. Box 294, Lampeter, 17537
(717) 464-0707; fax: (717) 464-2501
www.walkaboutinn.com

NOTES: Credit cards accepted: A Master Card; B Visa; C American Express; D Discover; E Diners Club; F Other; 2 Personal checks accepted; 3 Lunch available; 4 Dinner available; 5 Open all year;

The Walkabout is a 1925 brick, Mennonite farmhouse featuring large wraparound porches, balconies, and English gardens with goldfish pools and fountains. The inn itself is filled with antiques and each room has a private bath, cable TV, and fireplace; all rooms have queen canopies, whirlpools, or hot tubs. An elegant candlelight breakfast is served. The honeymoon and anniversary suites are beautiful and the fantasy cottage is fabulous! AAA 3 diamonds. Winter getaway packages available December through May.

Hosts: Jay and Val Petersheim
Rooms: 6 (PB) $99-289
Full Breakfast
Credit Cards: A, B, C
Notes: 2, 5, 8, 9, 10, 12

Ben Mar Farm Bed & Breakfast .

5721 Old Philadelphia Pike, Gap, 17527
(717) 768-3309; www.pamall.net/benmar

Come stay on our working dairy farm. We are located in the heart of the famous Amish country. Experience quiet country life while staying in the large, beautifully decorated rooms of our 200-year-old farmhouse. Our efficiency apartment is a favorite; it includes a full kitchen and queen and double beds with private bath. Enjoy a fresh Continental breakfast brought to your room. Air-conditioned.

Hosts: Herb and Melanie Benner
Rooms: 2 (PB) $65-75
Full Breakfast
Credit Cards: None
Notes: 2, 5, 7, 8, 9

Cedar Hill Farm

305 Longenecker Road, Mount Joy, 17552
(717) 653-4655; fax: (717) 653-9242
E-mail: cedarhill@supernet.com
www.cedarhillfarm.com

This 1817 stone farmhouse overlooks a peaceful stream and was the birthplace of the host. Stroll the acreage or relax on wicker rockers on the large front porch. Enjoy the singing of the birds and serene countryside. A winding staircase leads to the comfortable rooms, each with a private bath, one with a whirlpool tub. Central air-conditioning. A room for honeymooners offers a private balcony. Continental-plus breakfast is served beside a fireplace. Midway between the Lancaster and Hershey areas, where farmers' markets, antique shops, and good restaurants abound. Dinners arranged with Amish.

Hosts: Russel and Gladys Swarr
Rooms: 5 (PB) $75-95
Continental Breakfast
Credit Cards: A, B, C, D
Notes: 2, 5, 7, 8, 10, 12

The Columbian

360 Chestnut Street, Columbia, 17512
(717) 684-5869; (800) 422-5869
E-mail: inn@columbianinn.com
www.columbianinn.com

This circa 1897 inn is centrally located in the small historic river town of Columbia. The Colonial Revival mansion features an ornate stained-glass window and magnificent tiered staircase. Our large, air-conditioned rooms offer queen/king beds, private baths, and cable TV. Suite with balcony and/or fireplaces available. Come relax and unwind in our lovely

The Columbian

home and browse through the antique shops, art galleries, outlets, and museums only a brief stroll away. Getaway packages and gift certificates available.

Hosts: Chris and Becky Will
Rooms:5 (PB) $75-135
Full Breakfast
Credit Cards: A, B, D
Notes: 2, 5, 8, 9, 10, 11

Country Farmhouse Bed & Breakfast

1780 Donegal Springs Road, Mt. Joy, 17552
(717) 653-0935; fax: (717) 653-0935
E-mail: brguest@wideworld.net

Circa 1834 homestead surrounded by cornfields and pastures. Antique-filled rooms with modern amenities; candlelight gourmet breakfasts, afternoon tea. Come relax, watch our beautiful sunsets beyond the silos, walk by a trout stream, and renew your spirit. Antique shops, Hershey Park/Gardens/Spa, Lancaster/Hershey retail outlets, Renaissance Faire, Mt. Hope/Nissley Winery/concerts, farmers markets, and the National Civil War Museum within 20 minutes. Be

comfortable while here and refreshed when you leave.

Hosts: Terry and Barb Stephens
Rooms: 3 (PB) $75-125
Full Breakfast
Credit Cards: A, B
Notes: 2, 5, 10

Country Living Inn

2406 Old Philadelphia Pike, 17602
(717) 295-7295; fax: (717) 295-0994
www.countrylivinginn.com

Just like "home!" Warm, inviting hospitality. Country décor with quilts on full, queen, or king beds. New Shaker furniture, glider rockers, or sofas in the deluxe suite or queen rooms. Romantic suite with a whirlpool-for-two. Amish farms on the north and west sides. Coffee, tea, and hot chocolate served daily. Pastries served weekends (May-October) on the porch. The front porches have rockers and benches for visiting, relaxing, or watching Amish buggies go by.

Hosts: Bill and Judy Harnish
Rooms: 34 (PB) $54-135
Continental Breakfast
Credit Cards: A, B
Notes: 5, 8, 9, 10, 12

Eby's Farm Bed & Breakfast

345 Belmont Road, Gordonville, 17529
(717) 768-3615
E-mail: ebyfarm7@juno.com
www.ebyfarm.n3.net

In the heart of the Amish country between Intercourse and Paradise you'll find this 1814, seventh generation family dairy farm, where you can milk a cow or feed a calf. Efficiency

---

NOTES: Credit cards accepted: A Master Card; B Visa; C American Express; D Discover; E Diners Club; F Other; 2 Personal checks accepted; 3 Lunch available; 4 Dinner available; 5 Open all year;

apartment, patio, playground and tramp-oline, private baths, two-person Jacuzzi, fishing, canoeing, covered bridge, and water garden are all available for your enjoyment. Have dinner with an Amish neighbor. Watch a farm tour and video of the different seasons and birth of a calf. Wood carver shop next door. Open all year; air-conditioned. We've enjoyed entertaining guests for 30 years. Christian retreat groups welcome.

Hosts: Mel, Joyce, Mike, and Lynette
Rooms: 8 (5 PB; 3 SB) $60-95
Full Breakfast
Credit Cards: None
Notes: 2, 3, 4, 5, 6, 7, 8, 9, 10, 11

Flowers & Thyme Bed & Breakfast

238 Strasburg Pike, 17602
(717) 393-1460; fax: (717) 399-1986
E-mail: padutchbnb@aol.com
members.aol.com/padutchbnb

Flowers and Thyme

Our brick B&B is located in a country setting, overlooking a picturesque working farm and surrounded by English cottage gardens. You'll find tastefully created interiors, genuine hospitality, and clean comfortable rooms with queen beds. Your choice of room with canopy bed, fireplace, or Jacuzzi. Bountiful country breakfasts are served in the spacious gathering room. Dinner with an Amish family can be arranged. Nonsmoking.

Hosts: Don and Ruth Harnish
Rooms: 3 (PB) $85-120
Full Breakfast
Credit Cards: A, B
Notes: 2, 5, 8, 9, 10, 12

Gardens of Eden Bed & Breakfast

1894 Eden Road, 17601-4105
(717) 393-5179; fax: (717) 393-7722
E-mail: info@gardens-of-eden.com
www.gardens-of-eden.com

Victorian ironmaster's home built circa 1860 on the banks of the Conestoga River, three miles northeast of Lancaster. Antiques and family collections of quilts and coverlets fill the three guest rooms, all with private baths. The adjoining guest cottage (restored summer kitchen) features a fireplace, dining room, bedroom, and bath on the second floor. Marilyn's floral designs are featured and are for sale. Three acres of gardens feature herbs, perennials, and wildflowers among the woodsy trails. Local attractions are personalized by a tour guide service and dinner in an Amish couple's home. A canoe and rowboat are available. Two bike trails pass the house.

Hosts: Bill and Marilyn Ebel
Rooms: 4 (PB) $100-150
Full Breakfast
Credit Cards: A, B
Notes: 2, 5, 7 (in cottage), 9, 10, 12

---

6 Pets welcome; 7 Children welcome; 8 Tennis nearby; 9 Swimming nearby; 10 Golf nearby; 11 Skiing nearby; 12 May be booked through travel agent

Homestead Lodging

Homestead Lodging

184 Eastbrook Road, Smoketown, 17576
(717) 393-6927; fax: (717) 393-1424
E-mail: lkepiro@juno.com
www.bbonline.com/pa/homestead/

Come to our beautiful Lancaster County setting where you can hear the clippety-clop of horse-drawn Amish buggies and experience the sights and sounds of their unique culture. . .while you enjoy the freshness of well-kept farmlands. Enjoy a walk down the lane to the Amish farm adjacent to us, or enjoy a quiet evening on the porch. Clean country rooms with cable TV, refrigerator, queen and double beds, individually controlled heat and air-conditioning. Microwave available.

Hosts: Robert and Lori Kepiro
Rooms: 5 (PB) $42-69
Continental Breakfast
Credit Cards: A, B, C, D
Notes: 2, 5, 7, 8, 9, 10, 12

The Jakob Getz House

P.O. Box 216, 31-33 East Church Street, Reamstown, 17567
(717) 335-3510

Located right off the "Antique Mile," this classic 1884 Victorian B&B features woodwork milled by Lancaster County craftsmen, 10-foot ceilings, Pennsylvania pine floors, and tasteful stenciling throughout the house. Close to outlet shopping and farmers' markets. Listen for the "clippity clop" of the buggies driven by Amish and Mennonite families who still farm the area with horses. Awake to a delicious homemade breakfast served wi`th genuine warmth and hospitality.

Hosts: Bob and Loretta Miller
Rooms: 2 (PB) $65
Full Breakfast
Credit Cards: None
Notes: 2, 5, 8, 9, 10

The Jakob Getz House

The King's Cottage, A Bed & Breakfast Inn

1049 East King Street, 17602
(717) 397-1017; (800) 747-8717
fax: (717) 397-3447
E-mail: info@kingscottage.com
www.kingscottagebb.com

Escape to romantic elegance at an award-winning Spanish-style mansion near historic Lancaster City and Amish farmland. Shop for antiques, enjoy farmers' markets and outlets, golf, and then enjoy tea and cordials in front of our fireplace. Pamper yourself with our warm hospitality, comfortable king and queen beds, private

---

NOTES: Credit cards accepted: A Master Card; B Visa; C American Express; D Discover; E Diners Club; F Other; 2 Personal checks accepted; 3 Lunch available; 4 Dinner available; 5 Open all year;

baths, whirlpool tubs, fireplaces, and sumptuous gourmet breakfasts. Our Carriage House and the Baroness Suite offer breakfast delivered to your door. Listed on the National Register, AAA 3-diamond, Mobil Excellent, Select Registry!

Rooms: 8 (PB) $145-240
Full Breakfast
Credit Cards: A, B, D
Notes: 2, 5, 10, 12

Maytown Manor Bed & Breakfast

25 West High Street, P.O. Box 275, Maytown, 17550
(717) 426-2116; (866) 426-2116
fax: (717) 426-2116
E-mail: innkeepers@maytownmanorbandb.com
www.maytownmanorbandb.com

Built in 1880, this federal-style brick house is located in Maytown, Lancaster County, Pennsylvania. Awaken to the smells of freshly brewed coffee and homebaked muffins. After enjoying your hearty breakfast in the formal dining room, explore nearby Amish country, visit historical Gettysburg, or take a ride on the wild side at Hersheypark. In the late afternoon, relax in our parlor while sipping a soothing cup of tea. Upon returning from dinner, read a favorite book from the library, enjoy a snack from the guest pantry, and then retire to your thoughtfully appointed guest room.

Hosts: Jeffrey and Julie Clouser
Rooms: 3 (PB) $80-90
Full Breakfast
Credit Cards: A, B
Notes: 2, 5, 8, 10, 11

Meadowview Guest House

2169 New Holland Pike, 17601
(717) 299-4017

This Dutch Colonial home is located in the heart of the Pennsylvania Dutch Amish area. Three guest rooms and kitchen on the second floor. There is a stove, refrigerator, sink, and dishes. A breakfast tray is put in the kitchen in the morning for each guest room. Close to many historic sites and to farmers' and antique markets. Excellent restaurants and many attractions help guests enjoy the beautiful country. Personalized maps are provided. Children over 6 welcome.

Hosts: Edward and Sheila Christie
Rooms: 3 (1 PB; 2 SB) $35-50
Continental Breakfast
Credit Cards: None
Notes: 2 (deposits), 5, 8, 9, 10, 12

New Life Homestead Bed & Breakfast

1400 East King Street, 17602
(717) 396-8928; (888) 503-2987
fax: (717) 396-0461
E-mail: wgiersch@redrose.net
www.newlifebnb.com

New Life Homestead

Located in the heart of Amish country, close to all attractions. If you ever wanted to know about the Amish and Mennonite people, this is where to learn. The home features antiques and heirlooms. Full breakfasts and evening refreshments are served. Your hosts are a Mennonite family with traditional family values. Private baths, air-conditioning.

Hosts: Carol and Bill Giersch
Rooms: 3 (1 PB; 2 SB) $65-85
Full Breakfast
Credit Cards: None
Notes: 2, 5, 7, 8, 9, 10, 12

Penn's Valley
Farm & Guest House

6182 Metzler Road, Manheim, 17545
(717) 898-7386; fax: (717) 898-8489
E-mail: pennsvbandb@cs.com

Guest house and one pink Victorian room available for guests. Located on 64 acres of farmland. Full breakfast available and optional. Animals include pigs and cats. Guesthouse sleeps seven people. Decorative, clean, air-conditioned. Located halfway between Hershey Park and Amish community close to a town named East Petersburg on the map.

Hosts: Melvin and Gladys Metzler
Rooms: 2 (PB) $55-70
Full Breakfast
Credit Cards: A, B, C
Notes: 2, 5, 7, 10

The Village Inn
of Bird-in-Hand

2695 Old Philadelphia Pike, P.O. Box 253, Bird-in-Hand, 17505
(717) 293-8369; (800) 914-2473

fax: (717) 768-1117
E-mail: lodging@bird-in-hand.com
www.bird-in-hand.com/villageinn

Listed on the National Historic Register, our inn is located on Route 340, five miles east of Lancaster in the heart of Pennsylvania Dutch Country. Each room features its own private bath and includes a Continental-plus breakfast. Free use of indoor and outdoor pools and tennis courts located within walking distance, and a complimentary two-hour tour of the surrounding Amish farmlands. Reservations suggested. Packages available.

The Village Inn

Rooms: 11 (PB) $79-165
Continental Breakfast
Credit Cards: A, B, C, D
Notes: 2, 5, 8, 9, 10

Vogt Farm
Bed & Breakfast

1225 Colebrook Road, Marietta, 17547
(717) 653-4810; (800) 854-0399
fax: (717) 653-5288
E-mail: cbb@vogtfarm.com
www.vogtfarmbnb.com

NOTES: Credit cards accepted: A Master Card; B Visa; C American Express; D Discover; E Diners Club; F Other; 2 Personal checks accepted; 3 Lunch available; 4 Dinner available; 5 Open all year;

Here on the farm you can enjoy the countryside and starlit nights. Our rooms are supplied with the amenities adults expect at the finest lodging. We give you a delicious breakfast and Kathy is your personal concierge. Our rooms have cable TV, air-conditioning, and fine furnishings. Our guests leave with a rested spirit, having had a wonderful time.

Hosts: Keith and Kathy Vogt
Rooms: 3 (PB) $85-145
Full Breakfast
Credit Cards: A, B, C, D
Notes: 2, 5, 7, 8, 9, 10, 12

LANCASTER COUNTY

Amethyst Inn

144 West Main Street, P.O. Box 938, Adamstown
    19501
(717) 484-0800; (800) 594-4808
fax: (717) 484-1384
E-mail: info@adamstown.com
www.amethystinn.com

Situated high on a hill with a magnificent view of historic Main Street, the Amethyst Inn is a Victorian "Painted Lady" home built in the 1830s. Architectural elements have been painstakingly clad in seven colors—shades of amethyst, gold, lavender, and forest green. A magnificent nine-foot intricately carved front door welcomes guests into Victorian splendor and warm hospitality. Guest rooms feature period antique furnishings, queen beds, captivating two-person Jacuzzis, and charming gas log fireplaces; one room features a relaxing sauna.

Hosts: Tom and Wanda Berman
Rooms: 4 (PB) $125-165
Continental Breakfast
Credit Cards: A, B, C
Notes: 2, 5, 8, 9, 10, 12

The Artist's Inn & Gallery

117 East Main Street, P.O. Box 26,
    Terre Hill, 17581
(717) 445-0219; (888) 999-4479
E-mail: info@artistinn.com
www.artistinn.com

Spend the night in an art gallery! Antique-filled inn in the small town of Terre Hill, nestled among Amish farms, features colored pencil pictures of the innkeeper. Feel like you've escaped to a simpler time as horse-drawn buggies pass the house and chimes play from a nearby church. Three rooms available, each with private bath, one with Jacuzzi whirlpool bath-for-one and fireplace. Ten minutes from the Antiques Capital of the USA, Adamstown. Tennis, golf, hiking, and cross-country skiing nearby. Outlet shopping in Reading and Lancaster City. Small specialty shops, farm markets, auctions, and quilt shops abound.

Hosts: Jan and Bruce Garrabrandt
Rooms: 3 (PB) $75-179
Full Breakfast
Credit Cards: A, B, C, D
Notes: 2, 5, 8, 10, 11, 12

6 Pets welcome; 7 Children welcome; 8 Tennis nearby; 9 Swimming nearby; 10 Golf nearby; 11 Skiing nearby; 12 May be booked through travel agent

Carriage Corner Bed & Breakfast

3705 East Newport Road, P.O. Box 371,
Intercourse, 17534
(717) 768-3059; (800) 209-3059
fax: (717) 768-0691
E-mail: gschuit@supernet.com
www.bbonline.com/pa/carriagecorner/

Central, peaceful, and comfortable. Carriage Corner offers traditional Christian hospitality amid the Amish farmland where the rest of the world falls away. Within walking distance of a village from yesteryear with a myriad of local shops, where Amish buggies converge. Wake up and let the aroma of freshly brewed coffee lure you to the dining room where a hearty breakfast awaits you. Catering to couples or small families who desire to fully explore the Pennsylvania Dutch Country. Amish dinners ar-ranged.

Hosts: Mr. and Mrs. Gordon Schuit
Rooms: 5 (PB) $65-85
Full Breakfast
Credit Cards: A, B
Notes: 2, 5, 7, 12

Crosskeys Countryside

158 Colonial Road, Gordonville, 17529
(717) 768-7677
E-mail: rickers@supernet.com

Nestled in a cluster of trees in the middle of Lancaster County farmland, you will enjoy a slower pace as you rest and observe the pasture across the way. Your private suite of hand-stenciled rooms will allow you to get away from the pressures of the world and enable God to minister restoration to you. If you feel like touring local shops, we are just three blocks outside of Intercourse, PA.

Hosts: Glenn and Christina Ricker
Rooms: 1 (PB) $65
Continental Breakfast
Credit Cards: None
Notes: 2, 5

Inn-Between

177 Riverview Road, Peach Bottom, 17563
(717) 548-2141
E-mail: dempsey@epix.net
inn-between-bnb.com

Our century-old farmhouse sits serenely in the rolling hills of Lancaster County. Pleasant lawns and gardens provide a great area for relaxation. Inside there are three bright airy bedrooms furnished with simple antiques and family pieces. One room features a queen-sized canopy bed and has an adjoining enclosed porch. All rooms are air-conditioned. A full breakfast is provided, including specially prepared dishes along with homemade breads and pastries.

Hosts: Bob and Miriam Dempsey
Rooms: 3 (1 PB; 2 SB) $50-60
Full Breakfast
Credit Cards: None
Notes: 2, 5, 7, 10

Rock-A-Bye Bed & Breakfast/ Antique Shop

138 West Frederick Street, Millersville, 17551
(717) 872-5990; (877) 872-5990
E-mail: rockabyein@aol.com
www.rock-a-bye-bnb.com

A delightful three-story brick Victorian home situated in a small college town on the outskirts of Amish farm-

---

NOTES: Credit cards accepted: A Master Card; B Visa; C American Express; D Discover; E Diners Club; F Other; 2 Personal checks accepted; 3 Lunch available; 4 Dinner available; 5 Open all year;

land and craftworks. We love families and have a canopy crib with our family suite. Restaurants and activities are within walking distance; college activities are close at hand and provide many summer activities that are challenging both mentally and physically (i.e., Elderhostel and sport camps).

Hosts: Ann and Bill Marks
Rooms: 4 (3 PB; 1 SB) $75-85
Full Breakfast
Credit Cards: A, B
Notes: 2, 5, 7, 8, 9, 10

MANHEIM

Wengers Bed & Breakfast

571 Hossler Road, 17545
(717) 665-3862

Relax and enjoy your stay in the quiet countryside of Lancaster County. Our ranch-style house is within walking distance of our son's 100-acre dairy farm. The spacious rooms will accommodate families. Take a guided tour through the Amish farmland. Hershey, Pennsylvania's state capital at Harrisburg, and the Gettysburg Battlefield are within an hour's drive.

Hosts: Arthur and Mary Wenger
Rooms: 2 (PB) $60-65
Full Breakfast
Credit Cards: None
Notes: 2, 5, 7

MARIETTA

Lavender Patch Bed & Breakfast

190 Longenecker Avenue, 17547
(717) 426-4533; fax: (717) 426-0124

E-mail: lavpatch@desupernet.net
www.lavenderpatch.com

Our B&B lends itself to gardens with a Victorian flair. We bring the outside English gardens to the inside. We have walls and antique furniture hand-painted with flowers and herbs. We do afternoon teas and garden tours of local gardens. We provide tours for Amish Country. Check our website, call, or E-mail for more information.

Hosts: Marian and Chet Miller
Rooms: 3 (PB) $90-95
Full Breakfast
Credit Cards: A, B
Notes: 2, 5, 7, 9, 10, 12

MILFORD

The Black Walnut Country Inn Bed & Breakfast

179 Firetower Road, 18337
(570) 296-6332; fax: (570) 296-7696
E-mail: steward@theblackwalnutinn.com
www.theblackwalnutinn.com

It's hard to imagine that this circa 1897, English Tudor-style inn, located on 162 wooded acres, is less than two hours away from New York City and three hours from Philadelphia. Enjoy woods, catch-and-release fishing on the four-acre pond, berrypicking, paddle-boating, the petting zoo, and outdoor hot tub. Guests begin their day with a hearty full breakfast: eggs, French toast, lox, cream cheese, assorted breads, and fresh fruit salad. Nearby antique shopping, flea markets, museums, restaurants, canoeing, and rafting. Queen, full, and twin beds are available; some

---

6 Pets welcome; 7 Children welcome; 8 Tennis nearby; 9 Swimming nearby; 10 Golf nearby; 11 Skiing nearby; 12 May be booked through travel agent

rooms have air-conditioning. Two-night minimum stay on weekends. AAA ten percent discounts; gift certificates available.

Host: Awilda Torres
Rooms: 12 + cabin (4 PB; 8 SB) $60-175
Full Breakfast
Credit Cards: A, B, C, D
Notes: 5, 7, 9, 10, 11, 12

Cliff Park Inn & Golf Course

155 Cliff Park Road, 18337-9708
(570) 296-6491; (800) 225-6535
fax: (570) 296-3982
E-mail: info@cliffparkinn.com
www.cliffparkinn.com

This historic country inn is on a secluded 600-acre estate. It offers spacious rooms with private baths, phones, and climate control. Furnishings are Victorian-style. Fireplaces; golf at the door on one of America's oldest golf courses (1913). Cross-country ski or hike on seven miles of marked trails. Golf and ski equipment rentals; golf school. Full-service restaurant rated three stars by Mobil. Map or B&B plans available. Specialists in business conferences and country weddings.

Hosts: The Buchanan Family
Rooms: 18 (PB) $110-170
Full Breakfast
Credit Cards: A, B, C, D
Notes: 3, 4, 5, 7, 9, 10

MILTON

Pau-Lyn's Country Bed & Breakfast

Pau-Lyn's Country B&B

Broadway Road, 17847
(570) 742-4110; E-mail: paulyns@mail.uplink.net
www.welcome.to/paulyns

The beautiful Susquehanna Valley of central Pennsylvania is unique. Varied, pleasant experiences await those who want to be in touch with God's handiwork. Observe agriculture, scenic mountains, rivers, and valleys. Recreation abounds—underground railroad stops and much more. The innkeepers provide nostalgic memories throughout the antique-furnished, 1850 Victorian brick house, two miles from I-80, four miles from Route 15. Air-conditioned. "A restful haven."

Hosts: Paul and Evelyn Landis
Rooms: 7 (4 PB; 3 SB) $60-70
Full Breakfast
Credit Cards: None
Notes: 2, 5, 7, 8, 9, 10, 11

MUNCY

The Bodine House

307 South Main Street, 17756
(570) 546-8949; fax: (570) 546-0607
E-mail: bodine@pcspower.net
www.bodinehouse.com

NOTES: Credit cards accepted: A Master Card; B Visa; C American Express; D Discover; E Diners Club; F Other; 2 Personal checks accepted; 3 Lunch available; 4 Dinner available; 5 Open all year;

The Bodine House is located on a tree-lined street in historic Muncy, PA in the Susquehanna River valley one mile from Interstate 180. Built circa 1805, it has been restored to its original architecture and is listed on the National Register of Historic Places. It is the area's oldest B&B (established in 1983), and has been featured in several national publications. All guest rooms have private baths and individual heat and air-conditioning. Telephone, fax, and E-mail service are available upon request.

The Bodine House

Hosts: David and Marie Louise Smith
Rooms: 4 (PB) $65-125
Full Breakfast
Credit Cards: A, B, C, D, E
Notes: 2, 5, 7, 8, 9, 10, 11, 12

NEW WILMINGTON

Beechwood Inn

175 Beechwood Road, 16142
(724) 946-2342; E-mail: janet4147@aol.com

Welcome to our Civil War-era home which is filled with family antiques. All rooms enjoy private baths, queen beds, door keys, central air, and in-room conversation area. A common parlor is on the second floor that has cable TV, VCR, couch, table and chairs, coffeepot, teapot, refrigerator, and dishes. Across the front is a large covered balcony that looks down into our village park. About eight miles to Routes 79, 80, 60, and the Turnpike; close to outlets, Volant, antiques, Amish, and good restaurants. Relax amid yesterday's lifestyle.

Hosts: Tom and Janet Hartwell
Rooms: 3 (PB) $65
Full Breakfast
Credit Cards: A, B
Notes: 2, 5, 8, 9, 10, 11

Behm's Bed & Breakfast

166 Waugh Avenue, 16142
(724) 946-8641; (800) 932-3315

Located one block from Westminster College campus, Behm's 100-year-old B&B is comfortably furnished with family, primitive, and collected antiques. Located within walking distance of shops and restaurants, Behm's is surrounded by rural, Old Order Amish. Nationally recognized watercolorist Nancy Behm's

Behm's

---

6 Pets welcome; 7 Children welcome; 8 Tennis nearby; 9 Swimming nearby; 10 Golf nearby; 11 Skiing nearby; 12 May be booked through travel agent

gallery is on-site. Lighted, off-street parking is available for guests. The homemade breakfast varies daily and is served in our dining room.

Hosts: Bob and Nancy Behm
Rooms: 4 (2 PB; 2 SB) $50-65
Full Breakfast
Credit Cards: A, B
Notes: 2, 5, 7, 8, 9, 10

NORTH EAST

Vineyard Bed & Breakfast

10757 Sidehill Road, 16428
(814) 725-5307; (888) 725-8998
E-mail: vinyrdbb@erie.net
www.lakeside.net/vineyardbb

Your hosts welcome you to the "Heart of Grape Country" on the shores of Lake Erie, surrounded by vineyards and orchards. Our turn-of-the-century home is quiet and peaceful with rooms furnished with queen or king beds and tastefully decorated to complement the area.

Hosts: Clyde and Judy Burnham
Rooms: 5 (PB) $65-75
Full Breakfast
Credit Cards: A, B, C, D
Notes: 2, 5, 6, 7, 8, 9, 10, 11

NORTHUMBERLAND

Campbell's Bed & Breakfast

707 Duke Street, 17857
(570) 473-3276; www.pa-bedandbreakfast.com

Campbell's Bed & Breakfast is a country inn built in 1859. Three large bedrooms with queen beds await your occupancy. Enjoy a refreshing swim in the large, heated, in-ground pool surrounded by the rose garden, or relax beside the fireplace in the home's spacious living room during the cool months.

Hosts: Bob and Millie Campbell
Rooms: 3 (2 PB; 1 SB) $60-70
Full Breakfast
Credit Cards: A, B
Notes: 2, 5, 7, 8, 9, 10, 12

PARADISE

Hershey Farm Home Lodging

73 Oak Hill Drive, 17562
(717) 687-6037

Country life awaits you in our historic 1825 brick farmhouse. Experience the family-operated dairy farm. Quiet off-the-road setting, but close to attractions and restaurants, just minutes from everything. Close to Strasburg Railroad and Amish farm neighbors. Relax on the porch or lawn and listen to the birds sing; watch kittens play or children swinging. Warm hospitality.

Hosts: Nevin and Ruth Hershey
Rooms: 3 (1 PB; 2 SB) $34-46
Continental Breakfast
Credit Cards: None
Notes: 2, 5, 7, 8, 10

Maple Lane Farm Bed & Breakfast

505 Paradise Lane, 17562
(717) 687-7479

This 200-acre, family-owned dairy farm is situated in the heart of Amish

---

NOTES: Credit cards accepted: A Master Card; B Visa; C American Express; D Discover; E Diners Club; F Other; 2 Personal checks accepted; 3 Lunch available; 4 Dinner available; 5 Open all year;

country with nearby quilt and craft shops, museums, farmers' markets, antique shops, outlets, and auctions. The large front porch overlooks a spacious lawn, green meadows, and rolling hills with no busy highways. Pleasantly furnished rooms have quilts, crafts, canopy and poster beds, TVs, and air-conditioning. Victorian parlor for guest use. Breakfast served daily. Featured in several national magazines.

Hosts: Edwin and Marion Rohrer
Rooms: 4 (2 PB; 2 SB) $45-60
Full Breakfast
Credit Cards: A
Notes: 2, 5, 7

PHILADELPHIA

Haddonfield Inn

44 West End Avenue, Haddonfield, NJ 08033
(856) 428-2195; (800) 269-0014
fax: (856) 354-1273
E-mail: innkeeper@haddonfieldinn.com
haddonfieldinn.com

This recently remodeled Victorian features elegant rooms and suites, all with fireplaces and many with whirlpools. All rooms include private baths, cable television, telephones with voicemail, and internet access. Gourmet breakfast included, as well as complimentary snacks and beverages. Within walking distance to over 200 shops and restaurants in a lovely picturesque village. Short walk to the train for fast transportation to Rutgers University, the New Jersey Aquarium, Delaware waterfront, and downtown Philadelphia. Catered affairs and business conferences welcome. Offer-

ing Sunday afternoon tea service by reservation.

Hosts: Fred and Nancy Chorpita
Rooms: 9 (PB) $130-215
Full Breakfast
Credit Cards: A, B, C, D
Notes: 2, 5, 6, 7, 8, 9, 10, 12

PITTSBURGH

Inn at Oakmont

300 Route, P.O. Box 28, Oakmont, 15139
(412) 828-0410; fax: (412) 828-1358
www.pittsburghbnb.com

A meticulously designed B&B built in 1994 whose service and charm reflect a more gracious era. Eight luxurious rooms with private baths, two with fireplaces and whirlpool tubs; full gourmet breakfast. Five minutes from the Pennsylvania turnpike and twenty minutes from downtown Pittsburgh

Hosts: Shelley and Paul Cammisa
Rooms: 8 (PB) $135-155
Full Breakfast
Credit Cards: A, B, C, D
Notes: 2, 5, 10

QUARRYVILLE

Runnymede Farm Guest House Bed & Breakfast

1030 Robert Fulton Highway (Rt. 222), 17566
(717) 786-3625

Enjoy scenic southern Lancaster County. Vacation in our farm home. Clean, comfortable rooms. Lounge, country breakfast. Close to attractions

---

6 Pets welcome; 7 Children welcome; 8 Tennis nearby; 9 Swimming nearby; 10 Golf nearby; 11 Skiing nearby; 12 May be booked through travel agent

but not in mainstream. Pleasant porch. Air-conditioning; TV, PC.

Hosts: Herb and Sara Hess
Rooms: 3 (SB) $40-50
Full Breakfast
Credit Cards: None
Notes: 2, 5, 7, 8, 9, 10

in Scottdale. See Fallingwater and Ohiopyle.

Hosts: June and Paul Schrock
Rooms: 2 (PB) $75-85
Full Breakfast
Credit Cards: A, B, D
Notes: 2, 5, 8, 10, 11

SCOTTDALE

Inn the Woods

14 Park Avenue, 15683
(724) 887-4762
E-mail: info@innthewoodsbnb.com
www.innthewoodsbnb.com

Inn the Woods

An in-town, secluded, woodsy, New England-style home in Pennsylvania's Laurel Highlands, located just an hour from Pittsburg. Our friendly home is decorated with antiques, quilts, family heirlooms, and reproduction furniture. Full breakfast served on antique china. Pastries and beverages served on arrival. Relax on the back deck or if you're more ambitious, there are tennis courts and a golf course nearby, or enjoy a walking tour of Scottdale's historic Victorian homes; restaurants

SCRANTON

The Weeping Willow Inn

308 North Eaton Road, Tunkhannock, 18657
(570) 836-7257
E-mail: weepingwillow@emcs.net

Our charming colonial home has been lovingly restored and we cordially invite you to experience its warmth and rich history. All rooms are furnished in antiques. A full breakfast by candlelight is offered each morning. Beautiful mountains and the nearby roads of the Endless Mountains Region of northeastern Pennsylvania offer many antique shops and craft stores. A relaxing bed and breakfast experience awaits you at the Weeping Willow Inn!

The Weeping Willow Inn

Hosts: Patty and Randy Ehrenzeller
Rooms: 3 (PB) $60-80
Full Breakfast
Credit Cards: A, B, C
Notes: 2, 7, 8, 9, 10, 11, 12

SEWICKLEY

Whistlestop Bed and Breakfast

195 Broad Street, Leetsdale, 15056
(724) 251-0852

A quaint brick Victorian home built in 1888 by the Harmonist Society, a Christian communal group similar to the Shakers. Four guest units, two with private baths, and two with shared baths. Kids stay free with parents. Your hostess is well-known for her country cooking, specializing in breads, muffins, pastries, and jams. Leetsdale is located on the Ohio River, 12 miles west of Pittsburgh (the airport is 20 minutes away) and close to the classic American village of Sewickley, where fine examples of historic architecture are well-maintained. The home is smoke-free.

Hosts: Steve and Joyce Smith
Rooms: 4 (2 PB; 2 SB) $60-70
Full Breakfast
Credit Cards: A, B, C, D
Notes: 2, 5, 7

SHIPPENSBURG

Field & Pine Bed & Breakfast

2155 Ritner Highway, 17257
(717) 776-7179; fax: (717) 776-0076
E-mail: fieldpine@aol.com
www.virtualcities.com

Surrounded by stately pine trees, Field and Pine is a family-owned B&B with the charm of an Early American stone house on an 80-acre gentleman's farm. Built in 1790, the house has seven working fireplaces, original wide-pine floors, and stenciled walls. Bedrooms are furnished with antiques, quilts, and comforters. A gourmet breakfast is served in the formal dining room. Three miles from I-81, between Carlisle and Shippensburg.

Hosts: Allan and Mary Ellen Williams
Rooms: 3 (1 PB; 2 SB) $70-85
Full Breakfast
Credit Cards: A, B
Notes: 2, 5, 8, 9, 10, 12

SMOKETOWN

Smoketown Motor Lodge & Carriage House

190 East Brook Road, 17576
(717) 397-6944

Nestled on three beautiful acres of an original Amish homestead in the heart of Lancaster County. The grounds are inviting, with two shaded patios and a gazebo. Relax in the shade of a small wooded area between the main lodge and the Carriage House. The saying

---

6 Pets welcome; 7 Children welcome; 8 Tennis nearby; 9 Swimming nearby; 10 Golf nearby; 11 Skiing nearby; 12 May be booked through travel agent

"cleanliness is next to godliness" may not be found in the Bible, but you will find both at our lodge: clean rooms with a Bible.

Hosts: Mike and Linda Martin
Rooms: 17 (PB) $42-81
Continental Breakfast
Credit Cards: A, B, C, D
Notes: 2, 5, 7, 8, 9, 10, 12

SOMERSET

Bayberry Inn
Bed & Breakfast

611 North Center Avenue, 15501
(814) 445-8471

A romantic, friendly, comfortable inn that pays attention to detail. Homemade baked goods served at a lovely table for two. Eleven guest rooms, each with private bath (shower). The entire inn is nonsmoking. Located in the Laurel Highlands near Seven Springs and Hidden Valley Resorts with downhill and cross-country skiing. Near Fallingwater and Kentuck Knob, homes designed by Frank Lloyd Wright. Close to Ohiopyle State Park with whitewater rafting. Mountain Playhouse is also nearby.

Hosts: Marilyn and Robert Lohr
Rooms: 11 (PB) $55-65
Continental Breakfast
Credit Cards: A, B, C, D
Notes: 2, 5, 10, 11, 12

Quill Haven Country Inn

1519 North Center Avenue, 15501
(814) 443-4514; fax: (814) 445-1376
E-mail: quill@quillhaven.com
www.quillhaven.com

A 1918 "gentleman's farmhouse" furnished with antiques and reproductions. Four uniquely decorated guest rooms with private baths, air-conditioning, and cable TV and VCRs. Common room with fireplace and mini-kitchenette; breakfast is served in the sunroom; private deck with hot tub. AAA-rated, three diamonds. Our inn is near these attractions: Hidden Valley and Seven Springs ski resorts; Frank Lloyd Wright's Fallingwater; Youghiogheny Reservoir; Ohiopyle for hiking, biking, and white-water sports; outlet mall; golf courses; and antique shops. Located 1.2 miles from the Pennsylvania Turnpike, Exit 10.

Quill Haven

Hosts: Carol and Rowland Miller
Rooms: 4 (PB) $85-110
Full Breakfast
Credit Cards: A, B, C, D
Notes: 2, 5, 7, 8, 9, 10, 11, 12

SOMERSET COUNTY

Laurel Echo Farm
Vacation Bed & Breakfast

174 Crossroad, Rockwood, 15557
(814) 926-2760; (888) 655-5335
www.bbonline.com/pa/echofarm

We are a century-old family farm raising beef and dairy calves on 100 acres. Since the children are gone, I pursued my dream of opening a B&B in our two-story farmhouse. We are in the Laurel Highlands of Somerset Co. with beautiful mountains and farmland. There are two ski resorts nearby, two state parks, and the popular Frank Lloyd Wright homes, Falling Water and Kentucky Knob. We have two smaller rooms for kids, plus an extra kitchen for your use.

Hosts: Paul and Carol Pyle
Rooms: 2 (PB) $55-65
Full Breakfast
Credit Cards: None
Notes: 2, 5, 6, 7, 9, 10, 11

SPRUCE CREEK

The Marshall House Bed & Breakfast

HC-01, Box 10, Route 45, 16683
(814) 632-8319; E-mail: smdll@psu.edu

Our country home is located near the village of Spruce Creek. Spend time on the front porch listening to the creek, reading, or just resting. Family activities available at Old Bedford Village, Raystown Lake, Horse Shoe Curve, Bland's Park, Lincoln and Indian Caverns, and Penn State University. Fishermen and hunters welcome.

Hosts: Sharon and Jim Dell
Rooms: 2 (SB) $45-55
Full Breakfast
Credit Cards: None
Notes: 2, 5, 7, 10, 11

STAHLSTOWN

Thorn's Cottage Bed & Breakfast

R.D. 1, Box 254, 15687
(724) 593-6429

Located in the historic Ligonier Valley area of the Laurel Mountains, seven miles from the Pennsylvania Turnpike, 50 miles east of Pittsburgh, the cottage offers homey, woodland privacy. Relax on the sunporch or in the herb garden with its swing. Near Fallingwater, white-water rafting, biking and hiking trails, and the quaint town of Ligonier with shops, dining, amusement park. Breakfast includes home-baked muffins and scones. Full kitchen.

Hosts: Larry and Beth Thorn
Rooms: 1 (PB) $85
Full Breakfast
Credit Cards: None
Notes: 2, 5, 7, 9, 10, 11

STARRUCCA

Nethercott Inn

6 Starrucca Creek Road, 18462
(570) 727-2211; fax: (570) 727-3811
E-mail: netheinn@nep.net
www.nethercottinn.com

This lovely 1893 Victorian home is nestled in a small village in the Endless Mountains and furnished with country and antiques. All rooms have queen beds and private baths. Only three and a half hours from New York City and Philadelphia, eight hours from Toronto. Our "Winter Loft"

---

6 Pets welcome; 7 Children welcome; 8 Tennis nearby; 9 Swimming nearby; 10 Golf nearby; 11 Skiing nearby; 12 May be booked through travel agent

sleeps eight and has a full kitchen and two baths. Available for ski rentals, family reunions, etc.

Nethercott Inn

Hosts: Charlotte and John Keyser
Rooms: 7 (PB) $80-125
Full Breakfast
Credit Cards: A, B, C, D
Notes: 2, 5, 7, 9, 10, 11, 12

STATE COLLEGE

Cedar Hill
at Spruce Creek

Route 45, Box 26, Spruce Creek, 16683
(888) 764-9790; fax: (814) 632-6458
E-mail: cedarhill2@aol.com
cedarhill-sprucecreek.com

The Vance family offers warm welcome to their 1820 tastefully renovated stone farmhouse, located within easy access to Pennsylvania State University, Raystown Recreational Area, antique centers, caves, and world-class fly-fishing. Long-time cyclists, the Vances provide hiking and bicycling maps and lots of local information about your interests. Ameni-

ties include private baths, a family suite, cozy fireplaces, mountain views, 42-acre working farm. Reunions, weddings, and seminars can be arranged. Family suite ideal for vacations. Inquire about pets.

Hosts: Barry and Linda Vance
Rooms: 5 (PB) $90-117
Full Breakfast
Credit Cards: A, B, D
Notes: 2, 5, 7, 9, 10, 11, 12

WAKEFIELD

Pleasant Grove Farm
Bed & Breakfast

368 Pilottown Road, Peach Bottom, 17563
(717) 548-3100; E-mail: labtindall@juno.com
www.pleasantgrovefarm.com

Located in beautiful, historic Lancaster County, this 160-acre dairy farm has been a family-run operation for 110 years, earning the title of Century Farm by the Pennsylvania Department of Agriculture. As a working farm, it lets guests experience daily life in a rural setting. Built in 1814, 1818, and 1820, the house once served as a country store and post office. In the heart of Amish farmland with Amish friends nearby. We also have entertained teacher-and-class and Girl Scout groups. For a romantic getaway just for two as well. Antique beds and furniture in all rooms. A full country breakfast is served by candlelight.

Hosts: Charles and Labertha Tindall
Rooms: 4 (1 PB; 3 SB) $55-75
Full Breakfast
Credit Cards: None
Notes: 2, 5, 7, 9, 10

WASHINGTON

Rush House Bed & Breakfast

810 East Maiden Street, 15301
(724) 223-1890; (877) 671-9413
E-mail: jwheeler@cobweb.net

Hundred-year-old brick and stone Victorian, built over Catfish Creek. All-nonsmoking. Decorated with antiques from the Victorian era, and the owner's collection of antique clocks. Enjoy the serene atmosphere, minutes from I-70 and I-79 on historic National Pike (Route 40). Completely air-conditioned. Eight blocks from Washington and Jefferson College and historic downtown Washington. Tons of shopping and restaurants nearby.

Hosts: Jim and Judy Wheeler
Rooms: 4 (PB) $75-110
Full Breakfast
Credit Cards: A, B
Notes: 2, 5, 8, 9, 10

Weatherbury Farm Vacation

1061 Sugar Run Road, Avella, 15312
(724) 587-3763; fax: (724) 587-0125
E-mail: info@weatheburyfarm.com
www.weatherburyfarm.com

Far from the madding crowd, but just 45 minutes southwest of Pittsburgh. Weatherbury Farm offers lodging in a cluster of historic farm buildings, lov-ingly furnished with old-fashioned country charm. Meadows and gardens, fields and valleys, cows and sheep combine to create a perfect setting of tranquil relaxtion. There are many activities for the guest who wants to be busy, and those who so desire can be busy doing nothing at all. Guests may relax on the porches or enjoy the swimming pool on a summer day. Make some down-home-on-the-farm memories! Bring the kids.

Hosts: Dale, Marcy, and Nigel Tudor
Rooms: 7 (PB) $70-125
Full Breakfast
Credit Cards: A, B
Notes: 2, 5, 7, 8, 9, 10, 12

WAYNESBORO

The Shepherd & Ewe Bed & Breakfast

11205 Country Club Road, 17268
phone/fax: (717) 762-8525; (888) 937-4393

Renowned for its rich shepherding heritage, the Shepherd and Ewe extends that same nurturing tradition to

---

6 Pets welcome; 7 Children welcome; 8 Tennis nearby; 9 Swimming nearby; 10 Golf nearby; 11 Skiing nearby; 12 May be booked through travel agent

its guests, who are invited to unwind in one of four guest rooms or the spacious master suite. Four of the five rooms have private baths; three have baths within your private room. Hot country breakfasts include many of Twila's favorite recipes garnished with fruits, homemade pastries, and other down-home delights. Fine restaurants, state parks, trails, and antique shops await you.

Hosts: Twila and Robert Risser
Rooms: 5 (3 PB; 2 SB) $75-95
Full Breakfast
Credit Cards: A, B, C, D
Notes: 2, 5, 7, 8, 9, 10, 11

WELLSBORO

Kaltenbach's
Bed & Breakfast

Stony Fork Road, R.D. 6, Box 106A, 16901
(570) 724-4954; (800) 722-4954
www.kaltenbachsinn.com

Kaltenbach's

This sprawling, country home with room for 32 guests offers comfortable lodging, home-style breakfasts, and warm hospitality. Set on a 72-acre farm, Kaltenbach's provides opportunities for walks through meadows, pastures, and forests; picnicking; and watching the sheep, pigs, rabbits, and wildlife. All-you-can-eat country breakfasts. Honeymoon suites have tubs or Jacuzzis-for-two. Hunting and golf packages are available. Pennsylvania Grand Canyon nearby. Enjoy hiking and biking on Pine Creek's all-new "Rail Trails," built on the old Conrail bed. Kaltenbach's was awarded a two-star rating in the *Mobil Travel Guide* for its accommodations and hospitality. Professional Association of Innkeepers International inn member.

Host: Lee Kaltenbach
Rooms: 11 (PB) $70-150
Full Breakfast
Credit Cards: A, B, D
Notes: 2, 3, 4, 5, 7, 8, 9, 10, 11, 12

WEST CHESTER

The Crooked Windsor

409 South Church Street, 19382-3502
(610) 692-4896

Charming Victorian home centrally located in West Chester, completely furnished with fine antiques. Full breakfast served; tea time or refreshments for those who so desire. Pool and garden in season.

Host: Winifred Rupp
Rooms: 4 (2 PB; 2 SB) $75-90
Full Breakfast
Credit Cards: None
Notes: 2, 5, 9

NOTES: Credit cards accepted: A Master Card; B Visa; C American Express; D Discover; E Diners Club; F Other; 2 Personal checks accepted; 3 Lunch available; 4 Dinner available; 5 Open all year;

YORK

Friendship House Bed & Breakfast

728 East Philadelphia Street, 17403
(717) 843-8299
E-mail: friendshiphome@juno.com

An 1890s vintage town house located close to markets, shopping, and recreation. Spacious bedrooms with queen beds. Property has a beautiful private yard with quaint gardens. Also has a three-car garage. A country breakfast is served most mornings. New in 1999—gas log fireplace in living room.

Hosts: Becky Detwiler and Karen Maust
Rooms: 3 (2 PB; 1 SB) $55-65
Full Breakfast
Credit Cards: None
Notes: 2, 5, 7, 8, 9, 10, 11

RHODE ISLAND

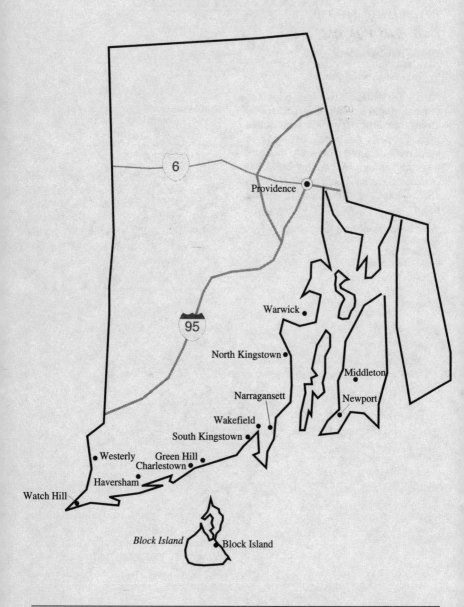

6

Providence

95

Warwick

North Kingstown

Middleton

Narragansett

Newport

Wakefield

South Kingstown

Westerly   Green Hill
Charlestown

Haversham

Watch Hill

Block Island   Block Island

NOTES: Credit cards accepted: A Master Card; B Visa; C American Express; D Discover; E Diners
Club; F Other; 2 Personal checks accepted; 3 Lunch available; 4 Dinner available; 5 Open all year;

Rhode Island

BLOCK ISLAND

The Rose Farm Inn

Box E, Roslyn Road, 02807
(401) 466-2034; fax: (401) 466-2053
E-mail: rosefarm@riconnect.com
www.blockisland.com/rosefarm

The Rose Farm Inn

Nestled in a sea and country setting, the Rose Farm Inn is situated on a hill a short walk from the town and the island's beaches. This historic 20-acre farm offers two buildings, the Farm House and the Captain Rose House. All rooms are furnished with antiques, some with king canopy beds. All have ocean or country views; some have single or double whirlpool tubs and separate decks. Bicycle rentals are available.

Host: Judith B. Rose
Rooms: 19 (17 PB; 2 SB) $99-250
Continental Breakfast
Credit Cards: A, B, C, D
Notes: 2, 8, 12

MIDDLETOWN

Inn at Shadow Lawn

120 Miantonomi Avenue, 02842
(401) 847-0902; (800) 352-3750
fax: (401) 848-6529
E-mail: randy@shadowlawn.com
www.shadowlawn.com

Shadow Lawn is a 142-year-old Victorian mansion. Eight rooms, private baths, TV with cable and VCR, telephones, air-conditioning, fireplaces, refrigerator, and complimentary wine. Also available for weddings, meetings, retreats, etc.

Hosts: Randy and Selma Fabricant
Rooms: 8 8 (PB) $99-225
Full Breakfast
Credit Cards: A, B, C, D, E
Notes: 5, 7, 8, 9, 10, 12

NEWPORT

Halidon Hill Guest House

25 Halidon Avenue, 02840
(401) 847-8318; (800) 448-5131

Modern spacious rooms with ample on-site parking and an inground pool-deck area (swim at your own risk). Ten-minute walk to Hammersmith Farm; minutes to the beach. Also convenient to shopping areas, local restaurants, and mansions.

Hosts: Helen and Paul Burke
Rooms: 4 (2 PB; 2 SB) $75-200

---

6 Pets welcome; 7 Children welcome; 8 Tennis nearby; 9 Swimming nearby; 10 Golf nearby; 11 Skiing nearby; 12 May be booked through travel agent

Full Breakfast
Credit Cards: C, D, E
Notes: 2, 7, 8, 9, 10, 12

Samuel Durfee House

352 Spring Street, 02840
(401) 847-1652; (877) 696-2374
E-mail: samueldurfeeinn@mindspring.com
www.samueldurfeehouse.com

The Samuel Durfee House is an elegant 1803 Federal Period Inn. Located in Newport's Yachting Village, we are just a block away from the restaurants and shops on Thames Street and the mansions on Bellevue Avenue. Enjoy a delicious, gourmet full breakfast each morning in the sitting room

Samuel Durfee House

or patio. All of our rooms have been uniquely decorated and have private bathrooms. Afternoon refreshments, air-conditioning, and private off-street parking are provided.

Hosts: Michael and Heather De Pinho
Rooms: 5 (PB) $85-195
Full Breakfast
Credit Cards: A, B
Notes: 2, 5, 8, 9, 10, 12

Stella Maris Inn

91 Washington Street, 02840-1531
(401) 849-2862
www.stellamarisinn.com

Early Newport mansion, 1861, red-stone exterior, extensive gardens on two acres, on-site parking, wrap-around porch. Some waterview rooms, fireplaces, elevator, antique furnishings, French Victorian style, former convent converted to B&B in 1990. Fresh home-cooked muffins and breads daily.

Hosts: Dorothy and Ed Madden
Rooms: 9 (PB) $95-225
Continental Breakfast
Credit Cards: None
Notes: 2, 5, 8, 9, 10

Wayside Guest House

406 Bellevue Avenue, 02840
(401) 847-0302; (800) 653-7678
fax: (401) 848-9374
E-mail: wayside406@earthlink.net

This lovely Georgian-style "summer cottage" sits among the famed mansions on Bellevue Avenue, in the very heart of historic Newport. Be our guest, and enjoy the comfort and the splendor of Newport's Gilded Age. . . in a warm, welcoming, and intimate way. Open year-round. Our summer season runs May 1-October 31st. Off-season rates are available November 1 to April 30th. Begin your morning with a wholesome Continental breakfast, then spend the day touring the city's many lovely attractions, returning home to enjoy a refreshing swim in our heated pool. Then, relax, read, or bird-watch on lawn chairs in a quiet garden spot or take a stroll along his-

---

NOTES: Credit cards accepted: A Master Card; B Visa; C American Express; D Discover; E Diners Club; F Other; 2 Personal checks accepted; 3 Lunch available; 4 Dinner available; 5 Open all year;

Wayside Guest House

toric Cliffwalk, safe above the crashing surf.

Host: Donnie Post
Rooms: 10 (PB) $135-175
Continental Breakfast
Credit Cards: None
Notes: 2, 5, 7, 8, 9, 10

Willows of Newport Romantic Inn & Garden

8 Willow Street, Historic Point, 02840
(401) 846-5486; fax: (401) 849-8215
E-mail: thewillowsofnewport@home.com
thewillowsofnewport.com

Historic 1700s inn exemplifies pre-Revolutionary charm and elegance.

Willows of Newport

Be pampered in turned-down hand-crafted canopy beds by Leonards N.E. laden with 310-count Charisma linens, fresh flowers, pillow mints, and poetry. Breakfast in bed! Only three blocks from the downtown/waterfront. Secret Garden featured on "Home & Garden" TV, Mobil three-star award, *Yankee Magazine* editors' pick 2001, listed Best Places to Kiss, Best Garden Awards!

Host: Pattie Murphy
Rooms: 5 (PB) $188-278
Continental Breakfast
Credit Cards: A, B
Notes: 2, 5, 8, 9, 10, 12

PROVIDENCE

Old Court Bed & Breakfast

144 Benefit Street, 02903
(401) 454-4074; fax: (401) 274-4830
E-mail: reserve@oldcourt.com
www.oldcourt.com

The Old Court B&B is filled with antique furniture, chandeliers, and memorabilia from the 19th century, with each room designed to reflect period tastes. The antique, Victorian beds are comfortable and spacious. Just a three-minute walk from the center of downtown Providence, near Brown University and Rhode Island School of Design.

Host: David M. Dolbashian ("Dolby")
Rooms: 10 (PB) $145-165
Full Breakfast
Credit Cards: A, B, C, D
Notes: 2, 5, 12

---

6 Pets welcome; 7 Children welcome; 8 Tennis nearby; 9 Swimming nearby; 10 Golf nearby; 11 Skiing nearby; 12 May be booked through travel agent

Perryville Inn

157 Perryville Road, Rehoboth, MA 02769
(508) 252-9239; (800) 439-9239
fax: (508) 252-9054
E-mail: pvinn@hotmail.com
perryvilleinn.com

This 19th-century restored Victorian (listed on the National Register of Historic Places) is located on four and a half wooded acres, featuring a quiet brook, millpond, stone walls, and shaded paths. Bicycles are available, including a tandem to explore the unspoiled countryside. The inn overlooks an 18-hole public golf course. All rooms are furnished with antiques and accented with colorful handmade quilts. Nearby you will find antique shops, museums, fine seafood restaurants, and even an old-fashioned New England clambake—or arrange for a horse-drawn hayride or a hot-air balloon ride. Located within a one-hour drive of Boston, Plymouth, Newport, and Mystic.

Hosts: Tom and Betsy Charnecki
Rooms: 4 (PB) $75-105
Continental Breakfast
Credit Cards: A, B, C, D
Notes: 2, 7, 10

State House Inn

43 Jewett Street, 02908-4904
(401) 351-6111; fax: (401) 351-4261
E-mail: statehouseinn@edgenet.net
www.providence-inn.com

Conveniently located minutes from downtown in a quiet and quaint neighborhood, the State House Inn offers business and vacation travelers privacy and personal service. Each guest room has a private bath and is decorated in Shaker or colonial furnishings. A hearty and healthy breakfast is served in our dining room.

Hosts: Frank and Monica Hopton
Rooms: 10 (PB) $99-149
Full Breakfast
Credit Cards: A, B, C, D
Notes: 5, 7, 8, 10, 12

WESTERLY

Woody Hill Bed & Breakfast

149 South Woody Hill Road, 02891
(401) 322-0452
E-mail: woodyhill@riconnect.com
www.woodyhill.com

This colonial reproduction is set on a hill overlooking 20 acres of informal gardens, woods, and fields. Antiques, wide-board floors, handmade quilts, and fireplaces create an Early American atmosphere. Guests enjoy a full breakfast and the use of a secluded, 40-foot in-ground pool.

Host: Ellen L Madison
Rooms: 4 (PB) $79-135
Full Breakfast
Credit Cards: None
Notes: 2, 5, 7, 8, 9, 10

NOTES: Credit cards accepted: A Master Card; B Visa; C American Express; D Discover; E Diners Club; F Other; 2 Personal checks accepted; 3 Lunch available; 4 Dinner available; 5 Open all year;

South Carolina

BEAUFORT

The Rhett House Inn

1009 Craven Street, 29902-5577
(843) 524-9030; (888) 480-9530
fax: (843) 524-1310
E-mail: rhetthse@hargray.com
www.rhetthouseinn.com

Located in historic Beaufort by the Bay, the Rhett House Inn is a beautifully restored 1820 plantation house, furnished with English and American antiques, oriental rugs, fresh flowers, fireplaces, and spacious verandas. Lush gardens provide the perfect setting for wedding and parties. Relax in the hammock on the second-floor veranda or spend the afternoon reading in the fountain garden. The Rhett House Inn is located within the historic district and is within walking distance of most tours, shops, and restaurants. The Rhett House Inn has been awarded the prestigious four-diamond AAA award and the four-star Mobil rating.

Hosts: Steve and Marianne Harrison
Rooms: 17 (PB) $150-300
Full Breakfast
Credit Cards: A, B, C, D
Notes: 2, 3, 5, 10

Two Suns Inn
Bed & Breakfast

1705 Bay Street, 29902
(843) 522-1122 (phone/fax); (800) 532-4244
E-mail: twosuns@isle.net
www.twosunsinn.com

Enjoy the charm of a small, resident-host B&B in a remarkably beautiful, nationally landmarked historic district about midway between Charleston and Savannah—complete with a panoramic bay-view veranda, individually appointed king or queen guest rooms, an informal afternoon "tea and toddy hour," and sumptuous breakfasts. The setting is idyllic; the atmosphere is casually elegant. The inn is a restored 1917 grand home with modern baths and amenities, accented throughout with many collectibles and wonderful antiques.

Hosts: Carrol and Ron Kay
Rooms: 6 (PB) $105-151
Full Breakfast
Credit Cards: A, B, C, D, E
Notes: 2, 5, 8, 9, 10, 12

CAMDEN

Candlelight Inn

1904 Broad Street, 29020
(803) 424-1057
E-mail: candlelightinncamden@yahoo.com

Two acres of gardens with native Southern plantings surround this candlelit Cape Cod-style inn. The décor is a delightful, tasteful mix of country, with quilts, hand-crafted samplers, poster beds, family antiques, and traditional furnishings. Enjoy a unique, hearty breakfast on the sunporch; the menu and place setting change daily. Or how about breakfast in the garden?

---

6 Pets welcome; 7 Children welcome; 8 Tennis nearby; 9 Swimming nearby; 10 Golf nearby; 11 Skiing nearby; 12 May be booked through travel agent

SOUTH CAROLINA

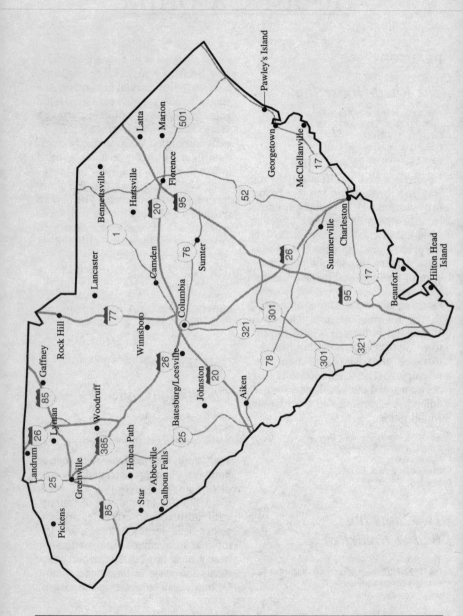

NOTES: Credit cards accepted: A Master Card; B Visa; C American Express; D Discover; E Diners Club; F Other; 2 Personal checks accepted; 3 Lunch available; 4 Dinner available; 5 Open all year;

Hosts: Jo Ann and George Celani
Rooms: 3 (PB) $90-105
Full Breakfast
Credit Cards: A, B, C, D
Notes: 2, 5, 8, 10, 12

CHARLESTON

Ashley Inn Bed & Breakfast

201 Ashley Avenue, 29403
(803) 723-8572; (800) 235-8039
fax: (843) 723-8007
E-mail: cannonboroinn@aol.com
www.charleston-sc-inns.com

Stay in a stately, historic, circa 1835 home. So warm and hospitable, the Ashley Inn offers seven intimate bedrooms featuring canopy beds, private baths, fireplaces, and air-conditioning. Delicious breakfasts are served on a grand columned piazza overlooking a beautiful Charleston garden or in the formal dining room. Relax with tea and cookies after touring nearby historic sites or enjoying the complimentary touring bicycles. The Ashley Inn offers simple elegance in a warm, friendly home noted for true Southern hospitality.

Hosts: Sally and Bud Allen
Rooms: 8 (PB) $89-250
Full Breakfast
Credit Cards: A, B, C, D
Notes: 2, 5

Belvedere Bed & Breakfast

40 Rutledge Avenue, 29401
(843) 722-0973; (800) 816-1664
www.belvedereinn.com

Belvedere

A Colonial Revival mansion built in 1900 with an exquisite Adamesque interior taken from the circa 1800 Belvedere Plantation house. In downtown historic district on Colonial Lake, walking distance from historical points of interest, restaurants, and shopping. Guests may use the public areas and piazzas in this romantic, beautifully restored mansion. Children over 8 welcome.

Host: David Spell, owner/innkeeper
Rooms: 3 (PB) $110-175
Continental Breakfast
Credit Cards: None
Notes: 2, 5, 7, 8, 9, 10, 12

Cannonboro Inn Bed & Breakfast

184 Ashley Avenue, 29403
(843) 723-8572; (800) 235-8039
fax: (843) 723-8007
E-mail: cannonboroinn@aolcom
www.charleston-sc-inns.com

This 1853 home offers beautifully decorated bedrooms with antique four-poster and canopied beds. Cannonboro Inn is a place to be pam-

---

6 Pets welcome; 7 Children welcome; 8 Tennis nearby; 9 Swimming nearby; 10 Golf nearby; 11 Skiing nearby; 12 May be booked through travel agent

pered. You may sleep in until the aroma of sizzling sausage and home-baked biscuits lures you to a full breakfast on the columned piazza overlooking a Low Country garden and fountain. After breakfast, tour nearby historic sites on complimentary bicycles; then enjoy some more pampering with afternoon sherry, tea, and sumptuous home-baked goods. Our private baths, off-street parking, color TV, and air-conditioning, along with that very special Southern hospitality, demonstrate this is what Charleston is all about! Children over 10 welcome.

Hosts: Sally and Bud Allen
Rooms: 6 (PB) $80-210
Full Breakfast
Credit Cards: A, B, C
Notes: 2, 5, 8, 9, 10

Country Victorian Bed & Breakfast

105 Tradd Street, 29401
(843) 577-0682

Come relive the charm of the past. Relax in a rocker on the piazza of this historic home and watch the carriages go by. Walk to antique shops, churches, restaurants, art galleries, museums, and all historic points of interest. The house, built in 1820, is located in the historic district south of Broad. Rooms have private entrances and contain antique

iron and brass beds, old quilts, antique oak and wicker furniture, and braided rugs over heart-of-pine floors. Homemade cookies will be waiting. Many extras! Featured in *Country Quilts* magazine. Children over 10 welcome.

Host: Diane Deardurff Weed
Rooms: 2 (PB) $95-185
Continental Breakfast
Credit Cards: None
Notes: 2, 5, 8, 9, 10

1837 B&B

1837 Bed & Breakfast

126 Wentworth Street, 29401
(843) 723-7166; (877) 723-1837
fax: (843) 722-7179
www.1837bb.com

Enjoy accommodations in a wealthy cotton planter's home and brick carriage house centrally located in Charleston's historic district. Canopied, poster, rice beds. Walk to boat tours, the old market, antique shops, restaurants, and main attractions. Near the Charleston Place (convention center) and College of Charleston. Gourmet breakfast is served in the formal din-

NOTES: Credit cards accepted: A Master Card; B Visa; C American Express; D Discover; E Diners Club; F Other; 2 Personal checks accepted; 3 Lunch available; 4 Dinner available; 5 Open all year;

ing room and includes sausage-and-grits casserole, raspberry French toast, ham frittata with Mornay sauce, and home-baked breads. The 1837 Tea Room serves afternoon tea to guests and public. Off-street parking available. Special winter rates.

Hosts: Sherri Weaver and Richard Dunn
Rooms: 9 (PB) $69-165
Full Breakfast
Credit Cards: A, B, C
Notes: 2, 5, 7, 8, 9, 10, 12

King George IV Inn

32 George Street, 29401
(843) 723-9339; (888) 723-1667
fax: (843) 723-7749
E-mail: info@kinggeorgeiv.com
www.kingorgeiv.com

A 200-year-old house in the heart of the historic district. The Federal-style inn has three levels of Charleston side porches. The house has 10- to 12-foot ceilings with decorative plaster moldings, wide-planked hardwood floors, old furnishings, and antiques. Private baths, off-street parking, air-conditioning, TVs. One-minute walk to King Street, five minutes to the market.

Hosts: Debra, Terry, and Debbie
Rooms: 10 (8 PB; 2 SB) $89-179
Continental Breakfast
Credit Cards: A, B, C
Notes: 2, 5, 8, 9, 10, 12

The Kitchen House (Circa 1732)

126 Tradd Street, 29401
(843) 577-6362; fax: (843) 965-5615
E-mail: loisevans@worldnet.att.net
www.cityofcharleston.com/kitchen.htm

The Kitchen House

Nestled in the heart of the historic district, the Kitchen House is a totally restored 18th-century dwelling. Dr. Peter Fayssaex, surgeon general to the Continental Army, called it home. You'll enjoy the Southern hospitality, absolute privacy, fireplaces, and antiques, as well as the private patio, colonial herb garden, fish pond, and fountain. Concierge service. This illustrious house has been featured in *Colonial Times* magazine, the *New York Times*, and *Best Places to Stay in the South*. Honeymoon packages are available.

Host: Lois Evans
Rooms: 3 (PB) $150-300
Full Breakfast
Credit Cards: A, B
Notes: 2, 5, 7, 8, 9, 10, 12

Laurel Hill Plantation Bed & Breakfast

8913 North Highway 17;
P.O. Box 190, McClellanville, 29458
(843) 887-3708; (888) 877-3708
fax: (843) 887-3878
E-mail: laurelhill@prodigy.net
www.bbonline.com/sc/laurelhill/

6 Pets welcome; 7 Children welcome; 8 Tennis nearby; 9 Swimming nearby; 10 Golf nearby; 11 Skiing nearby; 12 May be booked through travel agent

Nestled in a nook by a picturesque tidal creek, this spacious reconstruction of an 1850s plantation house has been designed to retain the romance of the past while affording the convenience of the contemporary. Wraparound porches overlook a sweeping panorama of Cape Romain's salt marshes, islands, and waterways. A nature lover's delight; rock on the porch, sit on the dock, soak in the serenity afforded by spectacular scenery and a leisurely lifestyle.

Hosts: Jackie and Lee Morrison
Rooms: 4 (PB) $125-150
Full Breakfast
Credit Cards: None
Notes: 2, 5, 9, 10, 12

The Magnolia Inn

103 South Magnolia Street, Summerville, 29483
(843) 873-8134
E-mail: magnoliab@awod.com
www.pride-net.com/magnolia

Circa 1880 Victorian inn located one block from historic Summersville's village green. Thirty minutes to Charleston and the beaches. The Rose Shell Room has king Rice bed and private bath. The Laura Beth Suite has queen brass bed and the bath is private or may be shared with the Charity Joe Room. All rooms have a day bed and fireplace. Surrounding piazzas are perfect for rocking and enjoying Becky's homemade goodies. Inquire about pets and children.

Hosts: Becky and Joe Bruton
Rooms: 3 (1 PB; 2 SB) $75-95
Full Breakfast
Credit Cards: None
Notes: 2, 5, 8, 10

Villa de La Fontaine

Villa de La Fontaine

138 Wentworth Street, 29401
(843) 577-7709
www.charleston.cityinformation.com/villa/

Villa de La Fontaine is a columned Greek Revival mansion in the heart of the historic district. It was built in 1838 and boasts a half-acre garden with fountain and terraces. Restored to impeccable condition, the mansion is furnished with museum-quality furniture and accessories. The hosts are retired ASID interior designers and have decorated the rooms with 18th-century American antiques. Several of the rooms feature canopy beds. Breakfast is prepared by a master chef who prides himself on serving a different menu every day. Parking on the property, with seven-foot brick wall and iron gates! It is in the safest part of Charleston, near the College of Charleston. Minimum-stay requirements for weekends and holidays. We have been featured in the *New York Times* travel section, *Best Places to Stay in the South*, *Southern Living*, and *Feinschmecker Magazine*.

Hosts: Bill Fontaine and Audrey Hancock
Rooms: 6 (PB) $125-200
Full Breakfast
Credit Cards: None
Notes: 2, 5, 8, 9, 10

FLORENCE

The Breeden Inn, Carriage House & Garden Cottage

404 East Main Street, Bennettsville, 29512
(843) 479-3665; (888) 335-2996
fax: (843) 479-7998
E-mail: breedeninn@att.net
www.bbonline.com/sc/breeden/

This romantic 1886 Southern mansion and the two before-the-turn-of-the-century guesthouses provide a haven for Christian travelers desiring to experience a true B&B stay or church retreat. Ten beautiful guest rooms, including four suites, one with sunken whirlpool, offer plush comfort, TVs, phones, many interesting architectural details, antiques, collectibles, and artwork. Enjoy four porches, an inground pool, period koi pond, bicycles, antique shops, nature trails, museums, and historic tours. Begin

The Breeden Inn

your day with a full, elegant breakfast. Located in the historic district, the inn is listed on the National Register of Historic Places and designated as a Backyard Wildlife Habitat. Come, allow us to impart gracious Southern hospitality to your memory making.

Hosts: Wesley and Bonnie Park
Rooms: 10 (PB) $85-135
Full Breakfast
Credit Cards: A, B, C
Notes: 2, 5, 7, 8, 9, 10, 12

GEORGETOWN

The Shaw House

613 Cypress Court, 29440
(843) 546-9663

The Shaw House is a spacious, two-story colonial home in a natural setting with a beautiful view overlooking miles of marshland—perfect for birdwatchers. Within walking distance of downtown and great restaurants on the waterfront. Rooms are large, with many antiques and private baths. Breakfast is served at our guests' convenience. Also included are nighttime chocolates on each pillow, turnbacks, and some loving extras. Guests leave with a little gift—prayers, recipes, and/or jellies. Approved by AAA, Mobil, and ABBA.

Hosts: Mary and Joe Shaw
Rooms: 3 (PB) $50-75
Full Breakfast
Credit Cards: None
Notes: 2, 5, 7, 8, 9, 10

---

6 Pets welcome; 7 Children welcome; 8 Tennis nearby; 9 Swimming nearby; 10 Golf nearby; 11 Skiing nearby; 12 May be booked through travel agent

Ship Wrights Bed & Breakfast

609 Cypress Court, 29440
(803) 527-4475

Three thousand-plus square feet of beautiful, quiet, clean home is yours to use when you stay. It's nautically attired and tastefully laced with family heirlooms. Guests say they feel like they just stayed at their best friend's home. The bedrooms and baths are beautiful and very comfortable. You'll never get "Grandma Eicker's Pancakes" anywhere else. (The inn is famous for them; there's a great story behind the pancakes!) The

Ship Wrights

view from the large porch is breathtaking, perfect for bird-watching. Five minutes from Ocean Beach. AAA-approved.

Host: Leatrice M. Wright
Rooms: 2 (PB) $60
Full Breakfast
Credit Cards: None
Notes: 2, 5, 7, 8, 9, 10

LANCASTER

Wade-Beckham House

3385 Great Falls Highway, 29720
(803) 285-1105; www.wwduke@infoave.net

Wade-Beckham House

Surrounded by 450 acres of rolling hills and farmland, this 1800s plantation home offers serenity, spacious porches, heirloom antiques, and historical artifacts in a pastoral setting. Guests may choose the Rose Room, Wade Hampton Room, Summer House Room or the quaint ambience and charm of the Guest House, a rehabilitated 100-year-old wooden country store. Horses, cows, and chickens on property. Listed on National Register.

Host: Jan Duke
Rooms: 3 (2 PB; 1 SB) + guesthouse $85
Full Breakfast
Credit Cards: None
Notes: 2, 5, 10

NOTES: Credit cards accepted: A Master Card; B Visa; C American Express; D Discover; E Diners Club; F Other; 2 Personal checks accepted; 3 Lunch available; 4 Dinner available; 5 Open all year;

LANDRUM

The Red Horse Inn

310 North Campbell Road, Ladrum, 29356
phone/fax: (864) 895-4968
E-mail: theredhorseinn@aol.com
www.theredhorseinn.com

Located on 190 acres in the foothills of the Blue Ridge Mountains, these five Victorian cottages are luxuriously appointed. Each offers a kitchen, bathroom, bedroom, living room with fireplace, deck or patio, color television, and air-conditioning. Three have Jacuzzis and sleeping lofts. The sweeping mountain views, hiking trails, and peaceful countryside offer spiritual renewal. Massage available.

Hosts: Mary and Roger Wolters
Rooms: 9 (PB) $95-175
Continental Breakfast
Credit Cards: A, B, D
Notes: 2, 5, 6, 7, 8, 9, 10, 12

MARION

Montgomery's Grove

408 Harlee Street, 29571
(843) 423-5220; (877) 646-7721
www.bbonline.com/sc/montgomery

Nestled amid five acres of century-old trees and gardens, this 1893 Victorian mansion features dramatic archways, elaborate woodwork, five bedrooms, and wraparound porches. Listed on the National Historic Register, this manor house is a two-block walk under Spanish moss to quaint historic Marion shops. Minutes off I-95 and near Myrtle Beach, we are the perfect

midway stopping point between the Northeast and Florida.

Hosts: Coreen and Rick Roberts
Rooms: 4 (PB) $80-110
Full Breakfast
Credit Cards: None
Notes: 2, 3, 4, 5, 7, 8, 9, 10, 12

SUMMERVILLE

Linwood Historic Home and Gardens Bed & Breakfast

200 South Palmetto Street, Summerville, 29483
(843) 871-2620; fax: (843) 875-2515
E-mail: linwoodbb@aol.com
www.bbonline.com/sc/linwood

Once the home of a 19th-century plantation owner. Gracious hospitality abounds at Linwood, a beautifully restored Victorian home featuring high ceilings, chandeliers, period antiques, and wide porches. Surrounded by two acres of lush gardens, Linwood is in the center of the charming village of

Linwood Historic Home and Gardens

---

6 Pets welcome; 7 Children welcome; 8 Tennis nearby; 9 Swimming nearby; 10 Golf nearby; 11 Skiing nearby; 12 May be booked through travel agent

Summerville, near shops and restaurants. Linwood has a lovely, large in-ground pool. Famous plantations, golf courses, beaches, and historic Charleston are nearby. Recreation or retreat—we are here to serve you.

Hosts: Peter and Linda Shelbourne
Rooms: 4 (PB) $85-150
Continental Breakfast
Credit Cards: A, B
Notes: 2, 5, 8, 9, 10, 12

Tastefully decorated guest rooms have many amenities and, according to several guests, "the most comfortable bed in the world." Murder Mystery weekends and more (see web site).

Host: Susan Yenner
Rooms: 5 (PB) $65-110
Full Breakfast
Credit Cards: A, B, C, D
Notes: 2, 4, 5, 8, 9, 10

WINNSBORO

Songbird Manor

116 North Zion Street, 29180
(803) 365-6963; (888) 636-7698
fax: (803) 635-6963
E-mail: songbirdmanor@msn.com
www.bbonline.com/sc/songbird

Songbird Manor

Experience a fine example of America's "Golden Age," when wealthy self-made men of the early 20th century built lavish homes to reflect their success. Songbird Manor is a showcase of expert craftsmanship from the regal molded plaster ceilings to the extensive oak woodwork. Beautfiully furnished, accented with antiques.

NOTES: Credit cards accepted: A Master Card; B Visa; C American Express; D Discover; E Diners Club; F Other; 2 Personal checks accepted; 3 Lunch available; 4 Dinner available; 5 Open all year;

South Dakota

CHAMBERLAIN

Cable's Riverview Ridge

24383 SD Highway 50, 57325-9519
(605) 734-6084
www.bbonline.com/sd/riverviewridge/

Contemporary home on a bluff over-looking a Missouri River bend. Lo-cated on the Lewis and Clark Trail. King and queen beds, full breakfast, and secluded country peace. Three and one-half miles from downtown Chamberlain on Highway 50. Enjoy outdoor recreation; visit museums, In-dian reservations, and casinos; or re-lax and make our home your home.

Hosts: Frank and Alta Cable
Rooms: 3 (1 PB; 2 SB) $65-80
Full Breakfast
Credit Cards: A, B
Notes: 2, 5, 7, 9, 10

DE SMET

The Prairie House Manor

209 Highway 25 South, 57231-9428
(605) 854-9131; (800) 297-2416
fax: (605) 854-9001
E-mail: phconnie@aol.com
www.bbonline.com/sd/prairie/

Author Laura Ingalls Wilder wrote six books based on De Smet, South Dakota. Families and couples are wel-come at our B&B. Spend time touring our charming town and then relax on our Victorian front porch. You will enjoy the relaxing environment of our

The Prairie House Manor

six rooms decorated with antiques. All the luxuries of the present com-bined with the gracious living of the past.

Hosts: Larry and Connie Cheney
Rooms: 6 (PB) $69-99
Full Breakfast
Credit Cards: A, B, D
Notes: 2, 7, 8, 9, 10, 12

HOT SPRINGS

The "B & J" Bed & Breakfast

HCR 52, Box 101-B, 57747
(605) 745-4243

Nestled in the southern Black Hills, this charming 1890 log cabin, deco-rated with antiques, provides guests with a unique pioneer setting. Enjoy peaceful mountain scenery while lis-tening to the Fall River that never freezes. Early mornings, deer and

---

6 Pets welcome; 7 Children welcome; 8 Tennis nearby; 9 Swimming nearby; 10 Golf nearby; 11 Skiing nearby; 12 May be booked through travel agent

SOUTH DAKOTA

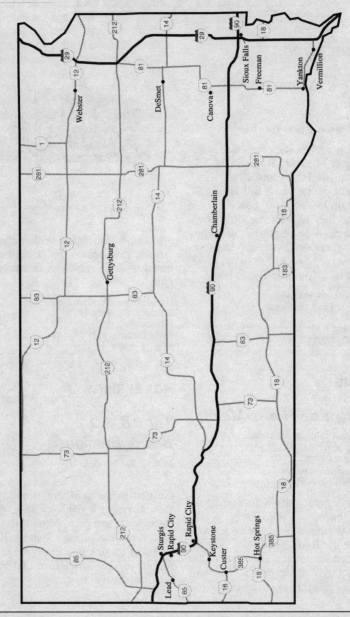

NOTES: Credit cards accepted: A Master Card; B Visa; C American Express; D Discover; E Diners Club; F Other; 2 Personal checks accepted; 3 Lunch available; 4 Dinner available; 5 Open all year;

The "B&J"

wild turkey may be seen. True Western hospitality and a home-cooked breakfast are waiting in Jeananne and Bill's kitchen. Down the entrance road, enjoy horseback riding. The "B and J" is located one mile south of Hot Springs on U.S. 385/18. In Hot Springs, swim at the historic Evans Plunge, where the water is always 87 degrees. Visit the world's largest find of Columbian Mammoth bones. Golf at one of the Midwest's most challenging and beautiful nine-hole courses. Minutes from Angostura Lake, Wind Cave National Park, and Custer State Park, where buffalo, antelope, elk, and prairie dogs roam.

Hosts: Bill and Jeananne Wintz
Rooms: 1 cabin (PB) $100-125
Full Breakfast
Credit Cards: None
Notes: 2, 7, 8, 9, 10, 11

The ultimate in charm and Old-World hospitality. We have been family-owned and -operated since 1985, and we are the area's first B&B establishment. Our spacious suites and cottages are furnished with comfortable European antiques. All feature a private entrance, private bath, patio, hot tub, and full Black Hills-style breakfast. Each suite provides a setting that quiets your heart. Our country home, the Cranbury House, has two suites. If the past intrigues you, the Old Powerhouse is for you. Das Abend Haus Cottage (the Evening House) is a restful, creekside hideaway, tucked into a mountainside; its two suites are designed after a German cottage in the Black Forest. The individual log cottages are also reminiscent of Germany. Soak in your private hot tub and watch Rapid Creek flow along.

Hosts: Hank and Audrey Kuhnhauser
Rooms: 10 (PB) $95-175
Full Breakfast
Credit Cards: None
Notes: 2, 8, 9, 10, 11

RAPID CITY

Abend Haus Cottages & Audrie's Bed & Breakfast

23029 Thunderhead Falls Road, 57702
(605) 342-7788
www.audriesbb.com

6 Pets welcome; 7 Children welcome; 8 Tennis nearby; 9 Swimming nearby; 10 Golf nearby; 11 Skiing nearby; 12 May be booked through travel agent

TENNESSEE

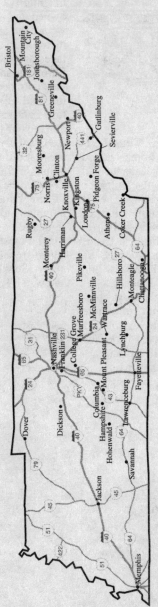

Tennessee

BOONE

Prospect Hill
Bed & Breakfast Inn

See description under Mountain City, TN.

BRISTOL

New Hope
Bed & Breakfast

822 Georgia Avenue, 37620
(423) 989-3343; (888) 989-3343
fax: (423) 989-3422
E-mail: newhope@preferred.com
www.newhopebandb.com

Late Victorian (dated 1892) in the foothills of Blue Ridge Mountains. Located in an historic neighborhood for leisurely strolls or just stay put and enjoy the front porch swing! Murder Mystery Weekends are available.

Hosts: Tom and Tonda Fluke
Rooms: 4 (PB) $100-225
Full Breakfast
Credit Cards: A, B, C
Notes: 2, 5, 12

CHATTANOOGA

Adams Hilborne Mansion

801 Vine Street, 37403
(423) 265-5000; (888) I-INNJOY

fax: (423) 265-5555
E-mail: innjoy@worldnet.att.net
www.innjoy.com

Cornerstone to Chattanooga's Fort Wood historic district; mayor's mansion in 1889. Rare Victorian Romanesque design with original coffered ceilings, hand-carved oak stairway, beveled-glass windows, and ceramic tile embellishments. Old-world charm and hospitality in a tree-shaded setting rich with Civil War history and turn-of-the-century architecture. Small, European-style hotel accommodations in ten tastefully restored, exquisitely decorated guest rooms. Awarded National Trust Home Beautiful, 1997. Private baths, fireplaces, and complimentary breakfast for guests. Fine dining nightly at the restaurant; wine and liquors available. Ballroom, meeting and reception areas, private dining, and catering available to the public by arrange-

Adams Hilborne Mansion

---

6 Pets welcome; 7 Children welcome; 8 Tennis nearby; 9 Swimming nearby; 10 Golf nearby; 11 Skiing nearby; 12 May be booked through travel agent

ment. Minutes from Chattanooga museums, fine shops and restaurants, the aquarium, UTC arena, and other cultural attractions. Off-street parking.

Hosts: Wendy and David Adams
Rooms: 11 (PB) $150
Full Breakfast
Credit Cards: A, B, C, E
Notes: 2, 3, 4, 5, 7, 8, 9, 10, 12

Alford House

5515 Alford Hill Drive, 37419
phone/fax: (423) 821-7625

A taste of Chattanooga past and present surround you in a Christian atmosphere in this 17-room home. Wooded on three sides with a valley-mountain view. Trains, carousel horses, and Coca Cola items fill three rooms. Century-old books scattered throughout. Many items for sale. Enjoy early coffee and breakfast in our dining room or on upper deck surrounded by towering trees. Relax in the gazebo, hike a mountain trail, or sit by a fire on a cool night. Only minutes from Tennessee Aquarium, Coolidge Park, Civil War Battlefield, museums, America's only carousel carving school, and all major attractions.

Host: Rhoda Alford Eaton
Rooms: 4 (PB) $65-155
Continental Breakfast
Credit Cards: None
Notes: 2, 5, 8, 9, 10, 11

COKER CREEK

Mountain Garden Inn

P.O. Box 153, 37314
(423) 261-2689

Enjoy luxurious, romantic suites and cozy bedrooms, all with private baths and air-conditioning. A stately cypress log inn with wraparound porches and rockers galore. A family-style B&B specializing in reunions—special group rates. Very peaceful setting with a panoramic, three-state view overlooking the Cherokee National Forests of North Carolina, Georgia, and Tennessee. Adjacent to the historic "Trail of Tears," waterfall hiking, gold panning, and horseback riding. Discounts to Christian groups.

Hosts: Stephen Wentworth
Rooms: 4 (PB) $45-85
Full Breakfast
Credit Cards: None
Notes: 2, 5, 7

DICKSON

East Hills Bed & Breakfast

100 East Hill Terrace (on Hwy. 70), 37055
(615) 441-9428; fax: (615) 446-2181
E-mail: jaluther@dickson.net
www.easthillsbb.com

A perfect place to relax, reflect, and strengthen body and soul; renew relationships; celebrate anniversairies or special events with friends; gather for church or social functions; or do business with Internet connections and phones. Built in the late 40s, restored in the early 90s, the Inn has four bedrooms and two cottages, all with private baths and cable TV, furnished throughout with period antiques. There are rocking chairs and swings on the porches. Located on Highway 70 near Luther Lake and Greystone

East Hills

Golf Course, six miles from Montgomery Bell State Park, convenient to the Renaissance Center, shopping, restaurants, downtown areas, historic Charlotte, and Cumberland Furnace. Rates include afternoon or evening refreshments and a full breakfast in the morning. No smoking, no alcohol.

Hosts: John and Anita Luther
Rooms: 7 (PB) $75-135
Full Breakfast
Credit Cards: A, B, C, D
Notes: 2, 5, 8, 9, 10, 12

FRANKLIN

Magnolia House Bed & Breakfast

1317 Columbia Avenue, 37064
(615) 794-8178; fax: (615) 794-1334
E-mail: magtenn@cs.com
www.bbonline.com/tn/magnolia

Craftsman-style home built circa 1905. Magnolia House is located in the historic district of Franklin, and it is also on the site of the famous Battle of Franklin. Shaded by a huge magnolia tree, Magnolia House is within walking distance of beautiful downtown Franklin. There are four guest rooms furnished with antiques and fine linens for a comfortable night's sleep. All four rooms surround a spacious gathering room.

Hosts: Jimmy and Robbie Smithson
Rooms: 4 (PB) $85-100
Full Breakfast
Credit Cards: A, B, C, D
Notes: 2, 5, 7. 8, 10

Namaste Acres Barn Bed & Breakfast

5436 Leipers Creek Road, 37064-9208
(615) 791-0333; fax: (615) 591-0665
E-mail: namaste@aol.com
www.bbonline.com/tn/namaste

Quiet valley setting. Poolside deck and hot tub, hiking, horseback trails. Country inn offers four theme suites, including the Loft, Bunkhouse, Cabin, and Franklin. In-room coffee, phone, and refrigerator; TV/VCR (movies). Private entrance and bath. Featured in Southern Living Magazine, Horse Illustrated, and Western Horseman. One mile from Natchez Trace Parkway, 11 miles from historic Franklin, and 23 miles from Nashville. Established 1993. Reservation requested. AAA three-diamond rating. Guided trail rides are available.

Hosts: Bill, Lisa, and Lindsay Winters
Rooms: 4 (PB) $75-85
Continental Breakfast
Credit Cards: A, B, C, D, E
Notes: 2, 5, 7, 9, 10, 12

GATLINBURG

Berry Springs Lodge

2149 Seaton Springs Road, Sevierville, 37862
(865) 908-7935; (888) 760-8297
fax: (865) 428-2814; E-mail: pseisert@aol.com
www.berrysprings.com

---

6 Pets welcome; 7 Children welcome; 8 Tennis nearby; 9 Swimming nearby; 10 Golf nearby; 11 Skiing nearby; 12 May be booked through travel agent

In our newly built lodge you can expect relaxing luxury and first-class service. We constructed and opened the Lodge in the summer of 2000. We are the closest lodge to Dollywood and only minutes to hiking trails and shopping. The Lodge offers 12 guest rooms, two large living room areas, a large dining room, spacious decks, and a view that will take your breath away. Imagine a quiet tranquil mountain top place where you can enjoy your vacation.

Hosts: Patrick and Susan Eisert
Rooms: 12 (PB) $109-189
Full Breakfast
Credit Cards: A, B, C
Notes: 5, 8, 9, 10, 11, 12

Cornerstone Inn

Cornerstone Inn Bed & Breakfast

P.O. Box 1600, 3966 Regal Way, 37738
(865) 430-5065; (877) 877-5045
fax: (865) 430-5064
E-mail: cornerstonesmkm@aol.com
www.bbon.com/tncornerstone

A delightful country inn with a 50-foot front porch, surrounded by a panoramic mountain view. The inn is located within five miles of the Great Smoky Mount National Park, the arts and crafts community, and very near Dollywood. Ideal for church groups, family reunions, anniversaries and wedding parties. The inn offers full kitchen facilities, private baths, and a great room with woodburning fireplace. A warm, serene, comfortable atmosphere.

Hosts: Kay and Don Cooper
Rooms: 4 (PB) $85-95
Full Breakfast
Credit Cards: A, B, C, D
Notes: 2, 5, 7, 9, 10, 11, 12

Eight Gables Inn

219 North Mountain Trail, 37738
(865) 430-3344 (phone/fax *51); (800) 279-5716
E-mail: 8gables@eightgables.com
www.eightgables.com

Nestled at the foot of the Great Smoky Mountains, Eight Gables is the perfect B&B with a four-diamond rating from AAA. Conveniently located near all area attractions. Luxurious bedrooms, full sit-down breakfast, and dessert and coffee bar in the evening. Be sure to make reservations for the four-course candlelight dinner on Saturday night.

Hosts: Don and Kim Cason
Rooms: 12 (PB) $89-199
Full Breakfast
Credit Cards: A, B, C, D, E
Notes: 2, 3, 4, 5, 7, 8, 10, 11, 12

Olde English Tudor Inn Bed & Breakfast

135 West Holly Ridge Road, 37738-3414
(865) 436-7760; (800) 541-3798
fax: (865) 430-7308
E-mail: tudorinn@oldeenglishtudorinn.com
www.oldeenglishtudorinn.com

NOTES: Credit cards accepted: A Master Card; B Visa; C American Express; D Discover; E Diners Club; F Other; 2 Personal checks accepted; 3 Lunch available; 4 Dinner available; 5 Open all year;

Romantic B&B in downtown Gatlinburg set on a quiet hillside one block and a half mile from the Parkway. Featuring eight guest rooms with private baths. Outside cottages with Jacuzzi tubs and fireplaces. Guests can walk to the shops or drive minutes to the National Park for hiking, fishing, or tubing. Walking distance to the Aquarium and all restaurants.

Hosts: Linda and Steve Pickel
Rooms: 13 (PB) $85-135
Full Breakfast
Credit Cards: A, B, C, D
Notes: 2, 5, 7, 8, 9, 10, 11, 12

GREENEVILLE

Hilltop House
Bed & Breakfast

6 Sanford Circle, 37743-4022
(423) 639-8202
E-mail: ashworth@greene.xtn.net
imagebyte.com/hilltop

Denise serves a full breakfast in the formal dining room; she has a different menu for every day of the month, featuring eggs cooked in a variety of

Hilltop House

ways, pancakes, crepes stuffed with apples, French toast, and other delectables. Many guests are outdoors types who enjoy hiking, fishing, mountain biking, and white-water rafting at the nearby Appalachian Trail, Nolichucky River, and several lakes. Hiking, trout fishing, horseback riding, river rafting, and scenic/historic tours available. Canoe rental available.

Host: Denise Ashworth
Rooms: 3 (PB) $80
Full Breakfast
Credit Cards: A, B, C
Notes: 2, 3, 4, 5, 7, 10, 12

HILLSBORO

Lord's Landing
Bed & Breakfast

375 Lords Landing Lane, 37342
(931) 467-3830; fax: (931) 467-3032
E-mail: lordslanding@blomand.net
www.lordslanding.com

Central Tennessee's 50-acre paradise awaits guests from near and far. You may drive in for a relaxing retreat or fly into our 2,400x80-foot turf airstrip for a quiet getaway. Located near the base of the Cumberland Plateau, the main house has breathtaking views from every window. A leisurely stroll takes guests to the eight-bedroom, seven-bath country cottage, beautifully decorated with antiques and fine furnishings. Fireplaces and Jacuzzi tubs in most rooms. Outdoor pool. Inquire about retreat packages.

---

6 Pets welcome; 7 Children welcome; 8 Tennis nearby; 9 Swimming nearby; 10 Golf nearby; 11 Skiing nearby; 12 May be booked through travel agent

Lord's Landing

Hosts: Denny and Pam Neilson
Rooms: 7 (PB) $95-150
Full Breakfast
Credit Cards: A, B, D
Notes: 2, 5, 7, 9, 10

KINGSTON

Woodland Cove Bed & Breakfast

P.O. Box 791, 37763
(865) 717-3719; (877) 700-2683
E-mail: woodlandcove@earthlink.net
www.woodlandcovebb.com

Come visit romantic, secluded Woodland Cove B&B on beautiful Watts

Woodland Cove

Bar Lake in Kingston, Tennessee. Amenities include three guest rooms with private baths, piped in music, and cable television provided in a smoke-free enviroment. Snacks and drinks in the Butler's Pantry are available 24 hours a day, plus a full gourmet breakfast. Canoes and paddle boats are provided for our guests on the lake. Fishing, swimming, and bird watching are available for our visitors as well. Experience a totally relaxing getaway!

Hosts: Bruce and Della Marshall
Rooms: 3 (PB) $95-125
Full Breakfast
Credit Cards: A, B, D
Notes: 2, 5, 7, 9, 10, 12

KNOXVILLE

Maplehurst Inn Bed & Breakfast

800 West Hill Avenue, 37920
(865) 523-7773; (800) 451-1562
E-mail: sonny@maplehurstinn.com
maplehurstinn.com

This lovely 84-year-old mansion is located right in downtown Knoxville in historic Maplehurst Park. Comfortable walking distance to over 30 restaurants, three museums, convention center, historic properties, etc. Our unique European style B&B on the hill overlooking the Tennessee River blends 18th-century charm with modern amenities.

Hosts: Sonny and Becky Harben
Rooms: 11 (PB) $69-149
Full Breakfast
Credit Cards: A, B
Notes: 2, 5, 6, 7, 8, 12

NOTES: Credit cards accepted: A Master Card; B Visa; C American Express; D Discover; E Diners Club; F Other; 2 Personal checks accepted; 3 Lunch available; 4 Dinner available; 5 Open all year;

Whitestone Farm

1200 Paint Rock Road, Kingston, 37763
(865) 376-0113; (888) 247-2464
fax: (865) 376-4454
E-mail: moreinfo@whitestones.com
www.whitestones.com

A luxurious, AAA four-diamond, secluded 360-acre country estate on the shores of Watts Bar Lake provides a perfect escape for your next getaway. Surrounded by a wildlife and waterfowl refuge, Whitestone Inn brings you close to all East Tennessee attractions, but far enough away to find sanctuary and relaxation in the tranquility of God's creation. Great location for retreats and weddings. Discount to ministers.

Hosts: Paul and Jean Cowell
Rooms: 20 (PB) $130-250
Full Breakfast
Credit Cards: A, B, C, D
Notes: 2, 3, 4, 5, 7, 8, 9, 10, 12

LOUDON/KNOXVILLE

The Mason Place

600 Commerce Street, 37774
(865) 458-3921
E-mail: thempbb@aol.com
www.themasonplace.com

Specializing in "stress-free weddings" and "a candlelight breakfast to die for!" Wonderful queen feather beds. Grecian swimming pool. Come to our honeymoon hideaway in a 135-year-old smokehouse or visit our award-winning antebellum plantation home where you will be surrounded by period-quality antiques. Three acres of beautiful grounds, large shade trees, pool, porches, swings, and hammock await your arrival. Ideally located in small-town America near Knoxville and the Smoky Mountains. "A wonderful opportunity to wander back in time without sacrificing the conveniences of today!"

Hosts: Bob and Donna Siewert
Rooms: 5 (PB) $96-135
Full Breakfast
Credit Cards: None
Notes: 2, 5, 8, 9, 10, 11

The Mason Place

LYNCHBURG

Cedar Lane
Bed & Breakfast

57 Cedar Lane, 37352
(931) 759-6891

Located on the outskirts of historic Lynchburg (home of Jack Daniel's Distillery). This newly built farmhouse offers comfort and relaxation. You can spend your time antiquing in nearby shops or reading a book in the sunroom. The rooms are beautifully decorated in rose, blue, peach, and green with queen and twin beds.

Hosts: Chuck and Elaine Quinn
Rooms: 4 (PB) $70
Continental Breakfast
Credit Cards: A, B, C
Notes: 2, 5, 7, 9, 10

6 Pets welcome; 7 Children welcome; 8 Tennis nearby; 9 Swimming nearby; 10 Golf nearby; 11 Skiing nearby; 12 May be booked through travel agent

Lynchburg Bed & Breakfast

P.O. Box 34, 37352
(931) 759-7158
E-mail: lynchburgbb@cafes.net
www.bbonline.com/tn/lynchburg/

Lynchburg

Lynchburg's first B&B, open since 1985, is within walking distance of Jack Daniel's Distillery and shopping area. The quaint atmosphere of this two-story home (circa 1877), provides relaxation and enjoyment in a small town. Each room is decorated with antiques. Big front porch for a quiet afternoon view of the beautiful hills.

Host: Virginia Tipps
Rooms: 3 (PB) $68-75
Continental Breakfast
Credit Cards: A, B
Notes: 2, 5, 7, 9, 10

MONTEAGLE

Adams Edgeworth Inn

Monteagle Assembly, 37403
(931) 924-4000; 87-RELAXINN
fax: (931) 924-3236

E-mail: innjoy@blomand.com
www.relaxinn.com

Circa 1896, the Adams Edgeworth Inn celebrates a century of fine lodging and still is a leader in elegance and quality. Recently refurbished in country chintz décor, the inn is a comfortable refuge of fine antiques, original paintings, and quaint atmosphere. Stroll through the 96-acre private Victorian village that surrounds the inn, or drive six miles to the Gothic campus of Sewanee, University of the South. Cultural activities year-round. Nearby are 150 miles of hiking trails, scenic vistas, and waterfalls, as well as tennis, swimming, golf, and riding. Fine candlelight dining. "One of the best inns I've ever visited anywhere" (Sara Pitzer, recommended by "Country Inns" in *Country Inns Magazine*). Top 54 Inns of America—*National Geographic Traveler*.

Adams Edgeworth

Rooms: 12 (PB) $125-195
Full Breakfast
Credit Cards: A, B, C
Notes: 2, 4, 5, 7, 8, 9, 10, 12

NOTES: Credit cards accepted: A Master Card; B Visa; C American Express; D Discover; E Diners Club; F Other; 2 Personal checks accepted; 3 Lunch available; 4 Dinner available; 5 Open all year;

MONTEREY

Muddy Pond Inn

129 Coal Lane, 38574
(931) 445-7853
E-mail: jnjwilson@twlakes.net
www.muddypondonline.com

Two-bedroom house with yard;
board-fenced area to accommodate
horses. Rural community. Innkeepers
have separate dwelling; guests enjoy
complete privacy! No TV, no telephone. (Unless you bring your own!)

Hosts: Judy and Jerry Wilson
Rooms: 2 (PB) $45-75
Full Breakfast
Credit Cards: None
Notes: 2, 5, 7, 9, 10

The Home Place

Host: Priscilla Rogers
Rooms: 4 (2 PB; 2 SB) $45-65
Full Breakfast
Credit Cards: A, B, C, D, E
Notes: 2, 5, 7, 10, 12

MOORESBURG

The Home Place
Bed & Breakfast

132 Church Lane, 37811-2208
(423) 921-8424; (800) 521-8424
fax: (423) 921-8003
E-mail: prisrogers@charter.net
homeplacebb.com

"Like going to Grandma's house," is
how guests describe this B&B near
Cherokee Lake in rural Tennessee.
Built in the early 1800s by the host's
ancestors, the house is furnished with
family heirlooms but also has modern
conveniences. All four guest rooms
have a TV/VCR and a telephone. One
suite features a Jacuzzi tub. A refrigerator and microwave are availabe for
guest use. Children are welcome. The
first floor is accessible for guests with
disabilities.

MOUNTAIN CITY

Doe Mountain Inn

412 K & R Road, Butler, 37640
(423) 727-2726
E-mail: doemtinn@preferred.com
www.mountaincityonline.com/doemtninn/

Doe Mountain Inn is the perfect, quiet
getaway with warm hospitality and
comfortable accommodations. Our
deluxe suites offer privacy with a
spectacular view of the mountains.
We are within minutes of Watauga
Lake, Roan Valley Golf Estates, and
many area antique and craft shops in
Boone, North Carolina. Hot tub suite
available with wood-burning fireplaces. Group packages available for
family reunions, church retreats, conferences, weddings, and any other social event. No smoking; no pets.

---

6 Pets welcome; 7 Children welcome; 8 Tennis nearby; 9 Swimming nearby; 10 Golf nearby; 11 Skiing
nearby; 12 May be booked through travel agent

Hosts: Jerry and Teresa Calhoun
Rooms: 2 (PB) $85-150
Full Breakfast
Credit Cards: A, B
Notes: 2, 4, 5, 7, 9, 10, 11

Iron Mountain Inn Bed & Breakfast & Creekside Chalet

P.O. Box 30, Butler, 37640
(423) 768-2446; (888) 781-2399
E-mail: ironmtn@preferred.com
www.ironmountaininn.com

Luxury mountaintop B&B or secluded creekside chalet. Both offer
guests a chance to relax and get away
from everyday troubles. Families and
friends share a natural vacation in the
cabin. Romance blooms anew atop the
mountain above the clouds at the Inn,
or reserve both facilities for a group
retreat. Whirlpools-spa under the
stars. Children and pets are welcome
in the chalet. A full breakfast is included in the Inn.

Host: Vikki Woods
Rooms: 5 (PB) $125-250
Full Breakfast
Credit Cards: A, B, C, D
Notes: 2, 3, 4, 5, 6, 7, 9, 10, 11, 12

NASHVILLE

Applebrook Bed, Breakfast & Barn

9127 Highway 100, 37221
(615) 646-5082; (877) 646-5082

Enjoy rural Nashville in an elegant
turn-of-the-century farmhouse circa
1896. All private baths. Full, delicious
country breakfast, swimming pool (in
season). Nestled on five panoramic
acres. Minutes from historic Second
Avenue or historic Franklin; only 2.5
miles from Natchez Trace Parkway. If
you enjoy history, antiques, lovely
rolling hills, and nature walks, Apple-
brook B&B is the place for you to stay
in Nashville. Open year-round. Please
call for reservations.

Hosts: Don and Cynthia Van Ryen
Rooms: 4 (PB) $95-120
Full Breakfast
Credit Cards: A, B, D, E
Notes: 2, 5, 10, 12

Crocker Springs Bed & Breakfast

2382 Crocker Springs Rd; , Goodlettsvlle, 37072
(615) 876-8502

Truly a haven that offers peace and
tranquility yet hidden only 14 miles
from the center of downtown
Nashville. Guests stay in 1880 farmhouse complete with high ceilings, restored wood floors, and antique
furnishings. Relax and enjoy our
beautiful country location (four miles
off I-24 and Old Hickory Boulevard,
northwest of downtown), still within
Nashville city limits. Southern hospitality abounds along with desserts and
mint tea. Guest rooms have private
baths, heat/air-conditioning, and
beautiful views. Please inquire about
children and pets.

Hosts: Jack and Bev Spangler
Rooms: 3 (PB) $110-165
Full Breakfast
Credit Cards: C, D
Notes: 2, 5, 6, 7, 8, 9, 10, 12

NOTES: Credit cards accepted: A Master Card; B Visa; C American Express; D Discover; E Diners
Club; F Other; 2 Personal checks accepted; 3 Lunch available; 4 Dinner available; 5 Open all year;

Rockhaven Cottage

147 Mires Road, Mount Juliet, 37122-4210
(615) 449-5227; (866) 500-3802
E-mail: rockhavencabin@aol.com

Near Nashville, brand new secluded cottage nestled among the trees on 10 private acres just off I-40 East. This one-bedroom one-bath cottage has a whirlpool tub, queen bed, fully equipped kitchen, cable TV, porch swing, and a beautiful fishpond. Continental breakfast provided. Grocery service available. Near lake, walking trails, restaurants, and shopping. Five minutes from 18-hole golf course. Open all year.

Hosts: Rhonda and Nate Powell
Rooms: 1 (PB) $75
Continental Breakfast
Credit Cards: A, B
Notes: 2, 5, 9, 10, 12

PIGEON FORGE

Huckleberry Inn

1754 Sandstone Way, Sevierville, 37876
(865) 428-2475; (800) 704-3278
E-mail: hberryinn@aol.com
www.bbonline.com/tn/huckleberry

Authentic hand-built log inn nestled in the heart of the Great Smoky Mountains, offering whirlpool baths, in-room fireplaces, and peace and quiet. Enjoy seclusion, tranquility, and screened porches for listening to the sounds of nature. Come, let us help you relax the body, refresh the soul, and rejuvenate the spirit!

Host: Karan Bailey
Rooms: 3 (PB) $89-109
Full Breakfast

Credit Cards: A, B
Notes: 2, 5, 10, 11

PIKEVILLE

Fall Creek Falls Bed & Breakfast Inn

R.R. 3, Box 298B, 37367
(423) 881-5494; fax: (423) 881-5040
E-mail: fcfbandb@bledsoe.net
www.fallcreekfalls.com

Fall Creek Falls

Elegant mountain inn featured in the August '94 *Tennessee* magazine and August '96 *Country* magazine. Seven guest rooms and one suite, all with private baths and air-conditioning. Some rooms have heart-shaped whirlpools and fireplaces. Victorian or country décor. One mile from nationally acclaimed Fall Creek Falls State Resort Park. Beautiful mountains, waterfalls, golfing, boating, fishing, tennis, hiking, horseback riding, and biking trails. AAA-rated. No smoking. Full breakfast. Romantic, scenic, and quiet.

Hosts: Doug and Rita Pruett
Rooms: 8 (PB) $79-143
Full Breakfast
Credit Cards: A, B, C, D
Notes: 2, 8, 9, 10, 12

---

6 Pets welcome; 7 Children welcome; 8 Tennis nearby; 9 Swimming nearby; 10 Golf nearby; 11 Skiing nearby; 12 May be booked through travel agent

SAVANNAH

White Elephant Bed & Breakfast Inn

200 Church Street, 38372
(731) 925-6410
E-mail: inn@whiteelephantbb.com
www. whiteelephantbb.com

Stately 1901 Queen Anne Victorian home on one and a half shady acres in the historic district. Within walking distance of the Tennessee River, downtown shopping, restaurants, and churches. Nearby are golf courses and Civil War attractions; 10 miles from Shiloh National Military Park (the innkeeper offers batttlefield tours); 12 miles from Pickwick Dam and Lake. Three individually decorated rooms feature antiques, queen beds. Two parlors, central heat and air-conditioning, wraparound porches, croquet. No smoking or pets. Children over 10 welcome. See the elephant!

Hosts: Ken and Sharon Hansgen
Rooms: 3 (PB) $100-120
Full Breakfast
Credit Cards: None
Notes: 2, 5, 8, 10, 12

SEVIERVILLE

Bonny Brook Bed and Breakfast

2301 Wears Valley Road, 37862
phone/fax: (865) 908-4745
E-mail: bonnybrookbb@msn.com
www.bonnybrook.net

"Rest and Be Thankful" at Bonny Brook B&B, a cozy inn tucked into the woods beside a cascading stream in the Smoky Mountains. Bonny Brook highlights the Scotch-Irish heritage of the area, as well as its natural beauty. Its peaceful location gives you privacy, yet is highly convenient to the Great Smoky Mountains National Park, Gatlinbur, Pigeon Forge, Townsend, and Dollywood.

Host: A.C. Thomason
Rooms: 2 (PB) $125-135
Full Breakfast
Credit Cards: A, B
Notes: 2, 5, 10

Calico Inn

757 Ranch Way, 37862
(865) 428-3833; (800) 235-1054
E-mail: calicoinn@aol.com
www.calico-inn.com

Voted "Inn of the Year." The Calico Inn is located in the Smoky Mountains near Gatlinburg and Dollywood. It is an authentic log inn with touches of elegance. Decorated with antiques, collectibles, and country charm. Enjoy the spectacular mountain view, surrounded by 25 acres of peace and tranquility. Minutes from fine dining,

Calico Inn

live entertainment shows, shopping, hiking, fishing, golf, horseback riding,

---

NOTES: Credit cards accepted: A Master Card; B Visa; C American Express; D Discover; E Diners Club; F Other; 2 Personal checks accepted; 3 Lunch available; 4 Dinner available; 5 Open all year;

and all other attractions the area has to offer, yet completely secluded.

Hosts: Lill and Jim Katzbeck
Rooms: 3 (PB) $99-109
Credit Cards: A, B
Notes: 2, 5, 7, 8, 9, 10, 11, 12

Little Greenbrier Lodge

3685 Lyon Springs Road, 37862
(865) 429-2500; (800) 277-8100
E-mail: littlegreenbrier@worldnet.att.net
www.bbonline.com/tn/lgl

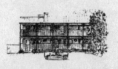 Borders national park entrance. Historic lodge on mountainside overlooks beautiful Wears Valley in the Great Smoky Mountains. Antique décor, very secluded and peaceful. Great hiking. The aroma of hot pecan pull-apart bread is mouthwatering. Just 150 yards from hiking trails. Or rock on the porch with lemonade and a great book.

Hosts: Susan and Charles Lebon
Rooms: 9 (PB) $100-115
Full Breakfast
Credit Cards: A, B, D
Notes: 2, 3, 5, 9, 10, 11, 12

Persephone's Farm Retreat

2279 Hodges Ferry Road, 37876
(865) 428-3904; fax: (865) 453-7089
E-mail: vnichols@smokymtnmall.com
www.smokymtnmall.com

Persephone's retreat, on the banks of the French Broad River, offers a peaceful escape within easy driving distance of all the major tourist attractions of the great Smoky Mountains, including Dollywood, factory outlet malls, golf courses, music theaters, and other Sevier and Knox County attractions. Elegant rooms offer private baths, large porches, spacious grounds, picturesque barn, miniature horses, farm animals (collect your own hen eggs), fruit trees, country road for walks, bonfire areas, and yard games. Directions: from I-40 Exit 407, take Highway 66 about four miles to Boyd's Creek Road. Turn right at AMOCO store, go 2.3 miles, and turn right on Hodges Ferry Road. Persephone's is the fourth house on the left.

Host: Bob Gonia and Victoria Nicholson
Rooms: 2 (PB) $95
Full Breakfast
Credit Cards: A, B, C, D
Notes: 2, 7, 8, 9, 10, 11, 12

VARIOUS CITIES

Natchez Trace Bed & Breakfast Reservation Service

P.O. Box 193, Hampshire, TN 38461
(931) 285-2777; (800) 377-2770
E-mail: natcheztrace@worldnet.att.net
www.bbonline.com/natcheztrace

This reservation service is unusual in that all the homes listed are close to the Natchez Trace, the delightful National Parkway running from Nashville, Tennessee, to Natchez, Mississippi. Kay Jones can help you plan your trip along the Trace, with homestays in interesting and historic homes along the way. Locations of bed and breakfasts include the cities

6 Pets welcome; 7 Children welcome; 8 Tennis nearby; 9 Swimming nearby; 10 Golf nearby; 11 Skiing nearby; 12 May be booked through travel agent

of Ashland City, Columbia, FairView,
Franklin, Hohenwald, and Nashville,
Tennessee; Florence and Cherokee,
Alabama; and Church Hill, Corinth,
French Camp, Kosciusko, Lorman,
Natchez, New Albany, Tupelo, and
Vicksburg, Mississippi, and Abedeen.
$60-125.

Texas

AUSTIN

Austin's Governors' Inn

611 West 22nd Street, 78705
(512) 477-0711; (800) 871-8908
fax: (512) 476-4769
E-mail: governorsinn@earthlink.net
governorsinnaustin.com

Relive Texas's colorful history at the Governors' Inn. Built in 1897, this Neoclassical Victorian was restored to its former glory in 1993. Each guest room, named for a Texas governor, is furnished with beautiful and tasteful antiques. You'll luxuriate in comfort and charm in this well-appointed mansion. Soak in a clawfoot tub in your private bath. Relax in the parlor or on the wraparound porch. Large trees shade the porches, which are complete with Victorian rockers and porch swings. Every morning breakfast will satisfy your appetite for fine food and good taste. Only a few blocks from the University of Texas, the State Capitol grounds, and all Austin has to offer, Governors' Inn is perfect for business or pleasure. Awarded 1997 and 1998 Best Bed & Breakfast in Austin by the Austin Chronicle, the Governors' Inn was chosen as one of only three B&Bs in Texas to be featured on the Travel Channel's "Romantic Inns of America."

Host: Lisa Wiedemann
Rooms: 10 (PB) $59-129
Full Breakfast
Credit Cards: A, B, C, D, E
Notes: 2, 5, 7, 8, 9, 10

Lake Travis Bed & Breakfast

4446 Eck Lane, 78734
phone/fax: (512) 266-9490; (888) 764-LTBB
E-mail: ltbinnb@aol.com
www.laketravisbb.com

Lake Travis B&B, a unique waterfront retreat, is a two-minute scenic drive from downtown Austin. A cliff, crystal water, hills, and expansive view create the setting for your luxurious getaway. The natural beauty of the surroundings is reflected in the hill country home. Each room has a king bed, private bath, and deck with a panoramic view of the lake. "Intimate resort" best describes the amenities: private boat dock, pool, hot tub, fitness center, massage and spa services, and sailing/boat charters. Inside is a stone fireplace, game room, pool table, and library/theater. Nearby are boat and jet ski rentals, golf, tennis, horseback riding, bicycling, hiking, a steam train, and wineries to tour.

Hosts: Judy and Vic Dwyer
Rooms: 4 (PB) $165-230
Full Breakfast
Credit Cards: A, B
Notes: 2, 5, 8, 9, 10, 12

---

6 Pets welcome; 7 Children welcome; 8 Tennis nearby; 9 Swimming nearby; 10 Golf nearby; 11 Skiing nearby; 12 May be booked through travel agent

TEXAS

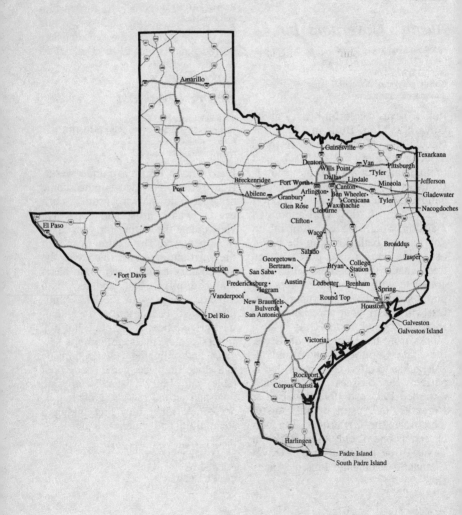

Amarillo

Gainesville
Denton· ·Van Texarkana
Wills Point ·Pittsburgh
Breckenridge· ·Fort Worth ·Tyler Jefferson
Post Arlington· Canton· Lindale Mineola
Abilene· Ben Wheeler· Gladewater
Granbury· Corsicana Tyler Nacogdoches
Glen Rose Waxahachie
Cleburne
Clifton·
Waco·
El Paso Broaddus
Salado
Georgetown Jasper
Bertram· Bryan· College
San Saba· Station
Fort Davis Junction Brenham
Fredericksburg· Austin Ledbetter Spring
Vanderpool ·Ingram Round Top
New Braunfels Houston
Bulverde·
Del Rio San Antonio Galveston
Galveston Island

Victoria·

Rockport
Corpus Christi

Harlingen
Padre Island
South Padre Island

NOTES: Credit cards accepted: A Master Card; B Visa; C American Express; D Discover; E Diners
Club; F Other; 2 Personal checks accepted; 3 Lunch available; 4 Dinner available; 5 Open all year;

CANTON

Texas Star
Bed & Breakfast

1434 V.Z.C.R. 3103, Edgewood, 75117
(903) 896-4277; fax: (903) 896-7061
E-mail: ohohm@aol.com
members.aol.com/starbnb/page/index.htm

The east Texas countryside with large oak and cedar trees is the setting for our guesthouse and private cottage. Four bedrooms with private baths/private patios and two additional rooms with a shared bath are in the main house. Each room reflects a different phase of Texas history and/or culture. Enjoy an exhilarating game of volleyball, horseshoes, croquet, or relax on the porch. Homemade bread and jams are featured in our family-style country breakfast (and dinner and lunch with advance request). A few miles from the world-famous Trade Days (flea market) of Canton.

Hosts: David and Marie Stoltzfus
Rooms: 8 (6 PB; 2 SB) $65-135
Full Breakfast
Credit Cards: None
Notes: 2, 4, 5, 7, 8, 10

DALLAS

St. Botolph Inn
Bed & Breakfast

808 South Lamar Street, Weatherford, 76086
(817) 594-1455; (800) 868-6520
fax: (817) 599-3257
E-mail: info@stbotolphinn.com
www.stbotolphinn.com

A beautifully restored, 1897 Queen Anne-style Victorian mansion set on a five-acre hilltop in a historic residential area. Five guest rooms and a carriage house suite all have baths; some have whirlpool tubs and spas/hot tubs. Afternoon tea is served on the veranda; a full gourmet breakfast is served in your room, the formal dining room, on the veranda, or around the pool. Weatherford was established in 1856 and is part of the Dallas/Fort Worth metroplex.

Hosts: Dan and Shay Buttolph
Rooms: 6 (PB) $85-180
Full Breakfast
Credit Cards: A, B, C, D
Notes: 2, 5, 7, 8, 9, 10

DENTON

The Heritage Inns

815 North Locust Street, 76201
(940) 565-6414; (888) 565-6414
fax: (940) 565-6515
E-mail: redbudbb@gte.net
www.theheritageinns.com

Originally the Redbud Inn, the Heritage B&B cluster group consists of three restored Victorian houses. The Magnolia House has Giuseppe's Italian Restaurant on the first floor, while the B&B suites complete the second floor. The Pecan House has a wheelchair-accessible suite, two honeymoon suites (with whirlpool tubs), and a long-term stay room and kitchen privileges.

Hosts: John and Donna Morris
Rooms: 11 (PB) $65-135
Full Breakfast
Credit Cards: A, B, C, D
Notes: 2, 3, 4, 5, 7, 9, 10, 12

---

6 Pets welcome; 7 Children welcome; 8 Tennis nearby; 9 Swimming nearby; 10 Golf nearby; 11 Skiing nearby; 12 May be booked through travel agent

FORT WORTH

Dabney House
Bed & Breakfast

106 South Jones Street, Granbury, 76048
(817) 579-1260; (800) 566-1260
E-mail: safe-dabney@flash.net
www.flash.net/~safe-dabney

Craftsman-style, one-story home built in 1907 by a local banker and furnished with antiques. It features hardwood floors and original woodwork. Long-term business rates available per request; romance dinner by reservation only. We offer custom, special-occasion baskets in the room upon arrival, by advance order only. Book the whole house for family occasions, staff retreats, or Bible retreats at discount rates. Hot tub available for all registered guests.

Hosts: John and Gwen Hurley
Rooms: 4 (PB) $65-110
Full Breakfast
Credit Cards: A, B, C
Notes: 2, 4, 5, 8, 9, 10, 12

FREDERICKSBURG

Keidel Gasthaus
Bed & Breakfast

231 East Main Street, 78624
(830) 997-5612; fax: (830) 997-8282
www.fbg.lodging.com

This charming, early 1900s Victorian two-story cottage is in a country setting a half block from the Admiral Nimitz Museum in the historic district. Within short walking distance of shops and restaurants, it sleeps four; king bed upstairs and queen sleeper sofa in the living room. Decorated with family antiques, with unique stencilling in the bathrooms, kitchen, and closet. Enjoy private parking, patio, goldfish pond; or watching squirrels, rabbits, and birds. Featured in the Historical Society' Christmas Candlelight Tour of Homes in 1999 and *Modern Bride Magazine* May 2000. Children five and over welcome.

Hosts: Robert & Barbara Heinen
Rooms: 1 (PB) $98
Continental Breakfast
Credit Cards: A, B, C, D
Notes: 5, 7, 8, 9, 10

Magnolia House

101 East Hackberry Street, 78624
(830) 997-0306; (800) 880-4374
fax: (830) 997-0766
E-mail: magnolia@hetc.net
www.magnolia-house.com

Built circa 1923, restored in 1991. Enjoy Southern hospitality in a grand and gracious manner. Outside are lovely magnolias and a bubbling fishpond. Inside, a beautiful living room and formal dining room provide areas for guests to mingle. There are two romantic suites with fireplaces and three rooms—all appointed with your com-

Magnolia House

---

fort in mind. You'll find a relaxing patio and porches. The beautiful, bountiful breakfast makes this a truly memorable experience.

Hosts: Dee and David Lawford
Rooms: 5 (PB) $95-140
Full Breakfast
Credit Cards: A, B, C, D
Notes: 2, 5, 8, 9, 10

Schmidt Barn
Bed & Breakfast

231 West Main Street, c/o Reservation Service, 78624
(830) 997-5612; fax: (830) 997-8484
E-mail: schmidtbarn@fbg.net
www.b-and-b-schmidt-barn.com

Schmidt Barn

Schmidt Barn is located a mile and a half outside historic Fredericksburg. The 1860s limestone structure has been turned into a charming guesthouse with a loft bedroom, living room, bath, and kitchen. Decorated with antiques. Hosts live next door. German-style breakfast is left in the guesthouse for you. The Barn has been featured in *Country Living*, *Travel* and *Leisure*, and *Country Accents* (cover story May-June 2000). A member of Historic and Hospitality

Accommodations of Texas. A B&B since 1980!

Hosts: Charles and Loretta Schmidt
Rooms: 1 house (PB) $95
Continental Breakfast
Credit Cards: A, B, D, F
Notes: 2, 5, 6, 7, 8, 9, 10, 12

Way of the Wolf

458 Wolf Way, 78624
(830) 997-0711; (888) 929-9653
E-mail: wawolf@ktc.com
www.wayofthewolf.com

This B&B retreat on 61 acres in the hill country offers a pool, space for picnics and hikes, wildlife, and scenic views. The four bedrooms and common living area with fireplace are furnished with antiques. A reconstructed Civil War-era cabin is also available. This destination B&B is peaceful and secluded, but only 15 minutes from shopping, golf, and churches in Kerrville or Fredericksburg. Assistance in preparing personal or group retreats is available.

Hosts: Ron and Karen Poidevin
Rooms: 5 (3 PB; 2 SB) $85-135
Full Breakfast
Credit Cards: None
Notes: 2, 5, 9, 10, 12

GAINESVILLE
(WHITESBORO AREA)

Alexander
Bed & Breakfast Acres, Inc.

3692 County Road 201, 76240
phone/fax: (903) 564-7440; (800) 887-8794
E-mail: abba@texoma.net
www.alexanderbnb.com

This three-story Queen Anne home and guesthouse are nestled peacefully on 65 acres of woods and meadows just south of Whitesboro between Lakes Texoma and Ray Roberts, near antiques, large outlet mall, ranches, farms, and a zoo. A full breakfast is included for Main House guests, where different themes decorate each bedroom; dinners are available by arrangement. Relax on large porches, the gazebo, the back deck with swimming pool and hot tub; or walk our wooded trails. A third-floor suite can be a bedroom, conference area, or extra lodging for groups, and includes a bar sink, dorm-fridge, and microwave. Two-story guesthouse offers three bedrooms sharing a bath and a half, complete kitchen and laundry, living area, and large screened porch. Children are welcome in guest house. Both houses are available for small retreats.

Hosts: Jim and Pamela Alexander
Rooms: 8 (5 PB; 3 SB) $60-125
Full Breakfast
Credit Cards: A, B, C, D
Notes: 2, 4, 5, 7, 9, 10, 11, 12

GALVESTON

Coppersmith Inn
Bed & Breakfast

1914 Avenue M, 77550
(409) 763-7004; (800) 515-7444
E-mail: coppersmithinn@att.net
www.coppersmithinn.com

Queen Anne-style home built in 1887, with five rooms and private baths. Three are located in the house; one in a separate cottage and one in the carriage house. The Inn boasts gingerbread trim, a double veranda, turret tower, spectacular winding staircase of teak, walnut and curly pine highlighted by stained glass and ornate newel post, large windows with original glass, exquisite heirloom antiques, Victorian decorations with romantic themes, and interesting faux painting. Also two fireplaces, a claw-foot porcelain tub, an antique tin tub used in a Kenny Rogers movie with three shower heads, whirlpool tub, lovely landscaped gardens, large wooden deck and brick sidewalks, and a full country breakfast served family-style in our dining room.

Coppersmith Inn

Hosts: Karen and Patrick Geary
Rooms: 5 (PB) $94-170
Full Breakfast
Credit Cards: A, B, D
Notes: 2, 5, 7, 8, 9, 10, 12

GLEN ROSE

Bussey's
Something Special
Bed & Breakfast

202 Hereford, P.O. Box 1425, 76043
(254) 897-4843; (877) 426-2233

fax: (254) 897-9881
E-mail: msbussey@busseys.net
www.busseys.net

The cozy Victorian cottage has a king bed, jet tub/shower, and kitchenette. The country arts and crafts cottage has king and full beds, a full kitchen, living room, and bath with shower. In the new Texas Garden Bunkhouse you'll find a queen willow bed, rustic garden/wood furniture, a shower and kitchen. All nestled in the heart of Glen Rose. Relax in the porch swing; take a leisurely stroll to the historic town square for shopping and lunch. Historic buildings and museums are close by. Walk to the river or explore the countryside to experience the heart of Texas. Free fossil hunts for guests! Note: Hosts not on the premises.

Hosts: Susan and Morris Bussey
Rooms: 3 (PB) $80-125
Continental Breakfast
Credit Cards: A, B, C, D
Notes: 2, 5, 7, 8, 9, 10, 12

Paluxy Glen Bed & Breakfast

405 Summit Ridge Drive, 76043
(254) 897-2994
E-mail: teresaun@hcnews.com

Your private river cottage awaits! It offers 122 feet of river frontage with deck and steps. Full bath with large clawfoot tub. Sleeps up to six guests. Kitchen is stocked with easily prepared breakfast items. Hostess not on premises. Children welcome. No smoking/no pets. Located a quarter mile northeast from the courthouse square.

Paluxy Glen

Host: Teresa Underwood
Rooms: 2 (PB) $100-160 plus tax
Continental Breakfast
Credit Cards: A, B, D
Notes: 2, 5, 7, 9, 10

HARLINGEN

Vieh's Bed & Breakfast

18413 Landrum Park Road, San Benito, 78586
(956) 425-4651
E-mail: viehbb@aol
www.vieh.com

Vieh's B&B is your home away from home. Ours is a south Texas, ranch-style home with a Mexican flavor in a five-acre palm grove. There is approximately a mile of bird-watching trail around a large lake at the back of the property. The landscaping includes two large butterfly gardens, along with a collection of exotic palm trees. Let us help make your south Texas visit enjoyable. *Mi casa es su casa.*

Hosts: Charles and Lana Vieh
Rooms: 4 (1 PB; 3 SB) $75
Full Breakfast
Credit Cards: None
Notes: 2, 5, 6, 7, 10

---

6 Pets welcome; 7 Children welcome; 8 Tennis nearby; 9 Swimming nearby; 10 Golf nearby; 11 Skiing nearby; 12 May be booked through travel agent

JASPER

The Swann Hotel

250 North Main Street, 75951
(409) 489-9224
www.swannhotel.com

Recently renovated this elegant turn-of-the-century B&B offers eight comfortable rooms, tastefully decorated with period furnishings. The on-site restaurant offers lunch to the public 11:00-2:00 Tuesday through Friday. We invite you to enjoy the fine Southern hospitality offered by this jewel of East Texas.

Hosts: Mary and Jerry Silmon
Rooms: 8 (5 PB; 3 SB) $55-99
Full Breakfast
Credit Cards: A, B, C, D
Notes: 2, 3, 4, 5, 7, 8, 9, 10

JEFFERSON

McKay House Bed & Breakfast Inn

306 East Delta Street, 75657
(903) 665-7322; (800) 468-2627
fax: (903) 665-8551
E-mail: mckayhouse@aol.com
www.mckayhouse.com

Timeless values. . .and Christian hospitality. When you cross the threshold, you will both feel and see the difference. Come to relax. . .to let your soul catch up with you. . .to be nurtured. . .not to rush around and get tired. Jefferson is a small historic village, little changed for over 100 years. Jefferson is the hometown of Lady Bird Johnson, our guest many times. Enjoy our classic "Gentleman's

Breakfast". . .and the Victorian nightgowns laid out in your bedchamber. Welcome!

Host: Lisa Cantrell
Rooms: 7 (PB) $89-169
Full Breakfast
Credit Cards: A, B, C
Notes: 2, 5, 7, 10, 12

Old Mulberry Inn Bed & Breakfast

209 Jefferson Street, 75657
(903) 665-1945; (800) 263-5319
fax: (903) 665-9123
E-mail: mulberry@jeffersontx.com
www.jeffersontx.com/oldmulberryinn

A gracious new inn built in the style of Jefferson's fine antebellum homes offers guests the best of the old and

Old Mulberry Inn

NOTES: Credit cards accepted: A Master Card; B Visa; C American Express; D Discover; E Diners Club; F Other; 2 Personal checks accepted; 3 Lunch available; 4 Dinner available; 5 Open all year;

the new. Adding to the charm are antique heartpine floors, tastefully eclectic furnishings, and designer touches throughout. Soak in a footed tub, relax by the fireplace in the library, or swing on the spacious porch. The inn offers five unique rooms with private baths, cable TV, gourmet breakfast, and 24-hour refreshments. Walk to shopping, museums, and home tours. Three-diamond rating from AAA.

Hosts: Donald and Gloria Degn
Rooms: 5 (PB) $70-139
Full Breakfast
Credit Cards: A, B, C, D
Notes: 5, 9, 10, 12

Urquhart House of Eleven Gables

301 East Walker Street, 75657-1741
(903) 665-8442; (888) 922-8442
E-mail: joycejacks@aol.com
urquharthouse.com

The Urquhart House of Eleven Gables B&B is an experience of luxury and historical elegance. Turn-of-the-century quality of life comes alive with period decor and antiques. Further creating the yesteryear ambience are equestrian carriages and wagons clip-clopping the street that fronts the wraparound porch of this expansive 1890 Queen Anne house located in Jefferson, the "Most Visited Small Town in Texas." Relax with in-room TV, VCR, and a wide selection of vintage and late-release videos.

Host: Joyce Jackson
Rooms: 2 (PB) $75-130
Continental Breakfast
Credit Cards: A, B, D, E
Notes: 2, 5, 7, 10, 12

JUNCTION

Shady Rest at the Junction Bed & Breakfast Inn

101 North 11th Street, 76849
(915) 446-4067; (888) 892-8292
E-mail: texasbnb@ctesc.net

Junction's one and only Victorian-style B&B offers guests an experience with "unforgettable cordial ambience." This turn-of-the-century home has been massively refurbished both

Shady Rest

inside and out. Relax on the beautiful wraparound front porch and enjoy the picturesque setting nestled between the North and South Llano Rivers. You will be within walking distance of the river, downtown area, and several local eateries. There are activities to participate in such as kayaking, canoeing, fishing, golf, and much more. Guests will be treated to a "full gourmet breakfast."

Hosts: Bill and Debbie Bayer
Rooms: 1 (PB) $85
Full Breakfast
Credit Cards: None
Notes: 2, 3, 4, 5, 10

---

6 Pets welcome; 7 Children welcome; 8 Tennis nearby; 9 Swimming nearby; 10 Golf nearby; 11 Skiing nearby; 12 May be booked through travel agent

LEDBETTER

Ledbetter Bed & Breakfast

P.O. Box 212, 100 Highway 290, 78946
(979) 249-3066; (800) 240-3066
fax: (979) 249-3330
E-mail: jjervis@fais.net
www.ledbetter-tx.com

Ledbetter B&B, established in 1988, is a collection of multigeneration, family, 1800-1900s homes within walking distance of the remaining 1870s downtown businesses. A full country breakfast buffet can serve up to 60 guests daily. Enjoy walks, fishing, bird-watching, cookouts, games, indoor pool, VCR/TV. A phone can be made available upon advance request.

Hosts: Chris and Jay Jervis
Rooms: 17 (15 PB; 2 SB) $75-105
Full Breakfast
Credit Cards: A, B, C
Notes: 2, 3, 4, 5, 7, 8, 9, 10, 11, 12

MINEOLA

Munzesheimer Manor

202 North Newsom, 75773
(903) 569-6634; (888) 569-6634
fax: (903) 569-9940
E-mail: innkeeper@munzesheimer.com
www.munzesheimer.com

Munzesheimer Manor, circa 1898, has provided a comfortable home for several prominent families and boasts of large rooms with high ceilings, seven fireplaces with antique mantles, bay windows, and a large wraparound porch which accentuates the setting for complete rest and reflection. Victorian nightgowns and nightshirts, a gourmet breakfast, and special "one of the family" pampering make any stay a memorable experience. It has been featured in national magazines, numerous newspaper articles, and on the "Best Twelve B&Bs in Texas."

Munzesheimer Manor

Hosts: Bob and Sherry Murray
Rooms: 7 (PB) $85-95
Full Breakfast
Credit Cards: A, B, C, D
Notes: 2, 5, 7, 8, 10, 12

NACOGDOCHES

Anderson Point Bed & Breakfast

29 East Lake Estates, 75964
(936) 569-7445
E-mail: anderpt@txucom.net
www.virtualcities.com

You won't want to leave this lovely, two-story, French-style home surrounded by 300 feet of lake frontage. Enjoy sweeping views of the water from every room and a double veranda for dining and dozing. You can

---

Anderson Point

stroll around the beautiful grounds or go fishing off the pier. Don't miss the glorious sunsets as you gather in the fireplace sitting room for coffee and conversation. A full breakfast is served every morning inside or out on the veranda. A private boat launch is available (excellent fishing). Enjoy a weekend on golden pond.

Host: Rachel Anderson
Rooms: 3 (1 PB; 2 SB) $75-85
Full Breakfast
Credit Cards: A, B
Notes: 2, 5, 6, 7, 9

PITTSBURG

Carson House Inn and Grille and Mrs. B's Cottage

302 Mount Pleasant Street, 75686-1335
(903) 856-2468; (888) 302-1878
fax: (903) 856-0709
E-mail: mailus@carsonhouse.com
carsonhouse.com

Nestled in the piney woods of east Texas, this luxurious six-room Victorian inn built in 1878 takes you back in time while providing modern

amenities and private baths. The grille located in the main house has been acclaimed "one of East Texas's finest casually elegant restaurants." Visitors to the Inn enjoy a slower pace, friendly staff, gourmet restaurant, two hot tubs, and a small-town atmosphere that revives the busiest people. Relaxation is assured!

Hosts: Eileen and Clark Jesmore
Rooms: 8 (6 PB; 2 SB) $75-85
Full Breakfast
Credit Cards: A, B, C, D, E
Notes: 2, 3, 4, 5, 7, 9, 10

Carson House Inn and Grille

POST

Hotel Garza Bed & Breakfast

302 East Main Street, 79356
(806) 495-3962
www.bbhost.com/hotelgarza

When you check into Hotel Garza, you'll experience the ambience of a 1915 Western inn. More than 80 years later, with modern conveniences, this fine establishment offers overnight accommodations, wonderful home cooking, and Texas hospitality. Post

6 Pets welcome; 7 Children welcome; 8 Tennis nearby; 9 Swimming nearby; 10 Golf nearby; 11 Skiing nearby; 12 May be booked through travel agent

is a Texas Main Street city founded by cereal king C.W. Post. Within walking distance of Hotel Garza you'll find theaters, museums, fine gift shops, boutiques, and Old Mill Trade Days. A new guest cottage is now available. Come enjoy the waterfall garden.

Hosts: Jim and Janice Plummer
Rooms: 4 (PB) $85-125
Full Breakfast
Credit Cards: A, B
Notes: 2, 5, 7, 8, 9, 10, 12

SALADO

Inn at Salado

7 North Main Street, P.O. Box 320, 76571
(254) 947-0027; (800) 724-0027
fax: (254) 947-3144
E-mail: rooms@inn-at-salado.com
www.inn-at-salado.com

Salado's first B&B is located in the heart of the historic district. Restored to its original 1872 splendor, the inn displays both a Texas historical marker and a National Register listing. The inn's ambience is enhanced by its antique furniture, porch swings, and live oak trees, all on two beautifully landscaped acres. A wedding chapel, meeting rooms, and catering complete the amenities offered by the inn.

Hosts: Rob and Suzanne Petro
Rooms: 8 (PB) $70-160
Full Breakfast
Credit Cards: A, B, C, D
Notes: 2, 5, 9, 10

SAN ANTONIO

Adams House Bed & Breakfast

231 Adams Street, 78210
(210) 224-4791; (800) 666-4810
fax: (210) 223-5125
E-mail: nora@adams-house.com
www.adams-house.com

Enjoy gracious Southern hospitality at the Adams House B&B, located in the King William historic district of downtown San Antonio. The Riverwalk, the Alamo Mission, and River Center shopping are within easy walking distance. The two-story home has

Adam's House

been lovingly restored to its original 1902 splendor. Full-width verandas grace both floors, front and back. All rooms are furnished with period antiques, Oriental rugs, and handmade reproductions. AAA and *Mobil Travel Guide* ratings.

Hosts: Nora Peterson and Richard Green
Rooms: 4 (PB) $99-179
Full Breakfast
Credit Cards: A, B, C, D, E
Notes: 2, 5, 7, 10, 12

NOTES: Credit cards accepted: A Master Card; B Visa; C American Express; D Discover; E Diners Club; F Other; 2 Personal checks accepted; 3 Lunch available; 4 Dinner available; 5 Open all year;

A Beckmann Inn & Carriage House Bed & Breakfast

222 East Guenther Street, 78204
(210) 229-1449; (800) 945-1449
fax: (210) 229-1061
E-mail: beckinn@swbell.net
www.beckmanninn.com

A wonderful Victorian house (1886) located in the King William historic district, across the street from the start of the Riverwalk. Beautifully landscaped, it will take you on a leisurely stroll to the Alamo, downtown shops, and restaurants. You can also take the trolley which stops at the corner, and within minutes you're there in style. The beautiful wraparound porch welcomes you to the main house and warm, gracious, Victorian hospitality. The large guest rooms feature antique, ornately carved, Victorian queen beds, private baths, ceiling fans, TVs, phones, refrigerators, desks, and robes. A gourmet breakfast, with breakfast dessert, is served in the dining room with china, crystal, and silver. Warm, gracious hospitality at its best. AAA three-diamonds, IIA rated excellent, and Mobil three stars.

Hosts: Betty Jo and Don Schwartz
Rooms: 5 (PB) $110-150
Full Breakfast
Credit Cards: A, B, C, D, E, F
Notes: 2, 5, 8, 9, 10

Brackenridge House Bed & Breakfast

230 Madison, 78204-1320
(210) 271-3442; (800) 221-1412
fax: (210) 226-3139

E-mail: benniesueb@aol.com
www.brackenridgehouse.com

Do you want a small, intimate (five-room) B&B, serving a delicious four-course breakfast, furnished with family quilts and antiques, just steps from the River Walk in historic King William? Then come to the Brackenridge House. Native Texan owners and innkeepers will attend to your every need.

Hosts: Bennie and Sue Blansett
Rooms: 6 (PB) $95-200
Full Breakfast
Credit Cards: A, B, D, E
Notes: 2, 5, 6, 7, 9, 10, 11, 12

A Victorian Lady Inn

421 Howard Street, 78212
(210) 224-2524; (800) 879-7116
fax: (210) 224-5123
E-mail: info@viclady.com
www.viclady.com

Elegant 1898 historic mansion offers some of the most spacious guest rooms in San Antonio! Well appointed rooms include period an-

A Victorian Lady

tiques, highback beds, sitting areas, porches, fireplaces, Jacuzzis, garden tubs, and wet bars. Full breakfast

---

6 Pets welcome; 7 Children welcome; 8 Tennis nearby; 9 Swimming nearby; 10 Golf nearby; 11 Skiing nearby; 12 May be booked through travel agent

served daily in the grand dining room. Relax in the crystal blue pool surrounded by tropical plants. The Riverwalk, Alamo, Convention Center, and trolley are just blocks away. Free parking, free local calls, and complimentary trolley passes.

Hosts: Joe and Kate Bowski
Rooms: 10 (PB) $89-135
Full Breakfast
Credit Cards: A, B, C, D
Notes: 2, 5, 8, 9, 10

SAN SABA

Sonshine Bed & Breakfast

1403 West Storey, 76877
(915) 372-4488; fax: (915) 372-6048

Sonshine B&B

This beautiful two-story home was built in 1910 by Mr. & Mrs. J.M. Kuykendall. Mr. Kuykendall was a retired wealthy cattleman in San Saba who employed an architect from New York to design and build the house, which was completed at a cost of $10,000. The home contains four beautiful fireplaces, each uniquely and elegantly crafted of wood and tile. The downstairs displays rare hide-a-way doors, while each room has 12-foot ceilings and exceptional woodwork and trim. A traditional Southern-style porch wraps the front of the home, which comes complete with a swing that makes the evenings seem timeless. Children welcome 13 years and older.

Hosts: Deryl and Tersa Hoyt
Rooms: 4 (0 PB; 3 SB) $80-100
Full Breakfast
Credit Cards: A, B, C, D
Notes: 2, 5, 7, 8, 10

SOUTH PADRE ISLAND

Brown Pelican Inn

207 West Aries, P.O. Box 2667, 78597
(956) 761-2722; fax: (956) 761-8683
E-mail: innkeeper@brownpelican.com
www.brownpelican.com

The Brown Pelican Inn, a bayside B&B located on the famed South Padre Island, offers immaculate accommodations in this subtropical vacation paradise. The inn's covered porches provide the perfect vantage point to watch spectacular sunsets over the bay, as well as a special setting for delicious breakfasts as Mother Nature entertains. Eight guest rooms are elegantly furnished with antiques, and each room has a private bath. The homey atmosphere encourages relaxation, but guests can stay quite busy if they choose. The pristine Gulf beaches are a four-minute walk away. Shopping, movie theaters, and great restaurants are nearby; other attractions are within easy driving distance.

Hosts: Chris and Yves de Diesbach
Rooms: 8 (PB) $75-150
Continental Breakfast
Credit Cards: A, B, C, D, F
Notes: 2, 5, 8, 9, 10

NOTES: Credit cards accepted: A Master Card; B Visa; C American Express; D Discover; E Diners Club; F Other; 2 Personal checks accepted; 3 Lunch available; 4 Dinner available; 5 Open all year;

SPRING

McLachlan Farm Bed & Breakfast

P.O. Box 538, 24907 Hardy Road, 77383
(281) 350-2400; (800) 382-3988
fax: (281) 288-1011
E-mail: stay@macfarm.com
www.macfarm.com

Beautiful 1911 farmhouse with porches and swings, nestled among 50 acres of shade trees and walking trails. Three guest rooms in main house with queen beds, sitting area, TV/VCR, private bath, and country gourmet breakfast. Separate cottage with two large private suites with queen beds, queen sleeper sofa, fireplace, TV/VCR, and stereo. Large bath with Jacuzzi tub and shower. Near Old Town Spring, with over 200 shops.

Hosts: Jim and Joycelyn Clairmonte
Rooms: 5 (4 PB; 2 SB) $89-165
Full Breakfast
Credit Cards: A, B, C, D
Notes: 2, 5, 10, 12

TEXARKANA

Mansion on Main Bed & Breakfast Inn

802 Main Street, 75501
(903) 792-1835; fax: (903) 793-0878
E-mail: mansiononmain@aol.com
www.bbonline.com/tx/mansion/

"Twice as nice" is the motto of Texarkana, a border city extending into both Arkansas and Texas. But for us "twice as nice" is a way of life. The recently restored inn's extravagant veranda is surrounded by 14 columns 22 feet tall. It makes quite a statement as the social center of downtown. Guests enjoy Christian pampering with that special "at-home" hospitality. Our classic "Gentleman's Break-

Mansion on Main

fast" is served in the parquet dining room. Corporate rates are available. Welcome!

Host: Laura Gentry
Rooms: 5 (PB) $65-109
Full Breakfast
Credit Cards: A, B, C
Notes: 2, 5, 7, 10

TYLER

Rosevine Inn Bed & Breakfast

415 South Vine Avenue, 75702
(903) 592-2221; fax: (903) 592-5522
E-mail: rosevine@iamerica.net
bedandbreakfast.com/bbc/p211717asp

Rosevine Inn is a quaint, two-story home complete with a white picket fence, located in the Brick Street district of Tyler. The inn offers many amenities, including a covered, outdoor hot tub, and a courtyard with both a fountain and a fireplace. In the lodge-style game room, you may enjoy billiards, lots of board-type games, cards, darts, and horseshoes, as well as volleyball and badminton. Outdoor fires are a common nightly occurrence. A full, formal breakfast

---

6 Pets welcome; 7 Children welcome; 8 Tennis nearby; 9 Swimming nearby; 10 Golf nearby; 11 Skiing nearby; 12 May be booked through travel agent

includes omelets or quiches, coffee cakes, muffins, fresh fruit, coffee, teas-more than you can eat! The hosts can direct you to great restaurants, antique shops, museums, lakes, the zoo, the rose garden, and sites in Tyler and the surrounding area.

Hosts: Bert and Rebecca Powell
Rooms: 6 (PB) $85-150
Full Breakfast
Credit Cards: A, B, C, D, E
Notes: 2, 5, 8, 9, 10, 12

VARIOUS CITIES

Reservation Service: Bed & Breakfast Texas Style

701 Honeysuckle Lane, College Station, 77845
(979) 696-9222; (800) 899-4538
fax: (979) 696-9444
E-mail: bnbtxstyle@aol.com
www.bnbtexasstyle.com

A reservation service for the state of Texas, we have been in business since 1982. You'll find nearly 100 listings, including Victorian mansions, private guest houses, cottages in the woods, and historic inns. Areas include Denton, Dallas, Waco, Bryan/College Station, Kemah Rockport, Hill Country, Tyler, Jefferson, and Marshall. All personally inspected.

Rooms: 100; $55-250
Full Breakfast
Credit Cards: A, B, C, D
Notes: 2, 5, 7, 9, 10

WACO

The Lighthouse Bed & Breakfast

421 South Harrison Street, McGregor, 76657
(254) 840-2589; (877) 496-4425
fax: (254) 840-2346
E-mail: stay@thelighthousebandb.com
www.thelighthousebandb.com

The Lighthouse B&B, perfect for romantic getaways, features atmosphere and hospitality that reminds you of going home to Grandma's. Evident throughout this three-story, Queen Anne Victorian home built in 1894, are Scriptures, Christian art work, and encouragement of the marriage relationship. Located midway between Dallas, Fort Worth, and Austin in a quiet suburb of Waco in the heart of central Texas. Each bedroom features a private bath, antiques, and family pieces from past generations.

Hosts: Jerry and Jan Walters
Rooms: 7 (PB) $48.75-85
Full Breakfast
Credit Cards: A, B, C, D, E
Notes: 2, 5, 7, 8, 9, 10, 12

NOTES: Credit cards accepted: A Master Card; B Visa; C American Express; D Discover; E Diners Club; F Other; 2 Personal checks accepted; 3 Lunch available; 4 Dinner available; 5 Open all year;

Utah

BLANDING

Grayson Country Inn

118 East 300 South, 84511
(435) 678-2388; (800) 365-0868
E-mail: graysoninn@hotmail.com
www.bbhost.com/graysoninn

Grayson Country Inn sits in the heart of San Juan County, known for Lake Powell, Monument Valley, Canyon Lands, Arches, Rainbow Bridge, and Natural Bridges. The inn is off Main Street near a pottery factory and gift shops. Private bath and cable TV in each of our six guest rooms. Couples, singles, and families welcome.

Hosts: Cliff and Diane Kerbs
Rooms: 6 (PB) $54-64
Full Breakfast
Credit Cards: A, B, C
Notes: 2, 5, 7, 12

MORGAN

Hubbard House Bed & Breakfast

5648 West Old Highway Road, 84050-9753
(801) 876-2005; www.hubbardhouse.com

Built in the 1920s, the Hubbard House B&B Inn has the warmth and charm of days gone by, with hardwood floors and stained-glass windows. It has awesome views of God's majestic mountains. Three ski resorts are in the area, as are fishing, boating, hiking, and golfing. Piano in dining room. Outdoor whirlpool spa. Additional rooms planned. Can accommodate horses. About one mile east from Exit 92 off I-84.

Hosts: Donald and Gloria Hubbard
Rooms: 6 (4 PB; 2 SB) $60-100
Full Breakfast
Credit Cards: A, B, C
Notes: 2, 4, 5, 7, 9, 10, 11

SAINT GEORGE

Quicksand and Cactus

346 North Main Street, 84770
phone/fax: (435) 674-1739; (800) 381-1654
E-mail: quicksand@infowest.com
www.infowest.com/quicksand/

Walk into the past with this historic home while enjoying the modern conveniences of today, with private baths, shaded porches, and complimentary gourmet breakfasts. The home is centrally located in a quiet, residential neighborhood just two blocks from St. George's historic district, with restaurants, art galleries, shops, antiques, and a restored 1927 movie theater.

Host: Carla Fox
Rooms: 3 (PB) $55-85
Gourmet Breakfast
Credit Cards: A, B,D
Notes: 2, 5, 7, 8, 9, 10, 12

---

6 Pets welcome; 7 Children welcome; 8 Tennis nearby; 9 Swimming nearby; 10 Golf nearby; 11 Skiing nearby; 12 May be booked through travel agent

UTAH

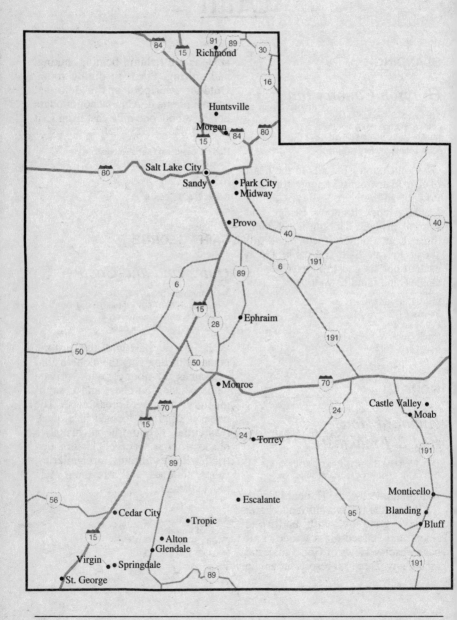

SALT LAKE CITY

Saltair Bed & Breakfast

164 South 900 East, 84102
(801) 533-8184; (800) 733-8184
fax: (801) 595-0332
E-mail: saltair@saltlakebandb.com
www.saltlakebandb.com

Feel right at home in centrally located Saltair B&B. Antiques and charm complement queen brass beds, Amish quilts, and period lamps. Amenities include full breakfast, evening snacks, air-conditioning, hot tub, and goose down comforters. For extended stays, choose Alpine Cottages, built around 1870 next door to the B&B. Cottages sleep four and include a fireplace, cable TV, full kitchen, sitting room, private bathroom, private phone line, and private entrance. Near Temple Square, the University of Utah, skiing, and canyons.

Hosts: Jan Bartlett and Nancy Saxton
Rooms: 5 (2 PB; 3 SB) $79-109
Full Breakfast
Credit Cards: A, B, C, D, E
Notes: 2, 5, 8, 9, 10, 11, 12

VERMONT

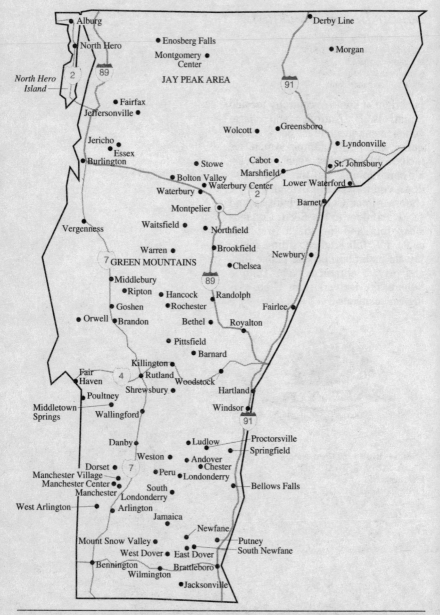

NOTES: Credit cards accepted: A Master Card; B Visa; C American Express; D Discover; E Diners
Club; F Other; 2 Personal checks accepted; 3 Lunch available; 4 Dinner available; 5 Open all year;

Vermont

ARLINGTON

Arlington Manor House
Bed & Breakfast

Buck Hill Road & Salter Hill Road, 05250
(802) 375-6784; Fax: (802) 375-2764
E-mail: kitandal@arlingtonmanorhouse.com
www.arlingtonmanorhouse.com

The Arlington Manor House is a charming, unusual Dutch Colonial home built in 1905 as a summer estate. Through the years it has been owned by several different families. In 1987, Al and Kit McAllister purchased the home. In August 1991, it was converted into a B&B with the added feature of many beautiful antiques, for sale. Nutmeg, our golden retriever, is known for her friendly greeting, as well as a sad face when guests leave. Frazier our cat is Nutmeg's good friend. Bring your camcorder for a B&B's "funniest home movies." We have 101 things to do; send for booklet.

Hosts: Al and Kit McAllister
Rooms: 4 (PB) $85-145
Full Breakfast
Credit Cards: A, B, C
Notes: 2, 8, 9, 10, 11, 12

Country Willows
Bed & Breakfast Inn
c. 1850

332 East Arlington Road, 05250
(802) 375-0019; (800) 796-2585

fax: (802) 375-8054
E-mail: cw@sover.net
countrywillows.com

Circa 1850 gracious Queen Anne Victorian, listed on the National Register of Historic Places. This boutique inn and village retreat in Arlington's historic district offers bountiful breakfasts, elegantly presented, spacious bedchambers with ensuite baths, antiques, queen beds, fireplaces, in-room cable TV, coffee/tea service, and air-conditioning. A wraparound porch invites relaxation among spacious lawns and gardens with mountain views. Minutes to Manchester, designer outlets, antiquing, Battenkill River, restaurants, theatre, and skiing. Summer and winter activities are nearby.

Country Willows

Hosts: Anne and Ron Weber
Rooms: 5 (PB) $95-145
Full Breakfast
Credit Cards: A, B, C, F
Notes: 2, 5, 7, 8, 9, 10, 11, 12

---

6 Pets welcome; 7 Children welcome; 8 Tennis nearby; 9 Swimming nearby; 10 Golf nearby; 11 Skiing nearby; 12 May be booked through travel agent

Hill Farm Inn

458 Hill Farm Road, Box 2015, 05250
(802) 375-2269; (800) 882-2545
fax: (802) 375-9918
E-mail: hillfarm@vermontel.com
www.hillfarminn.com

Hill Farm Inn is one of Vermont's original farmsteads granted from King George III in 1775. It has been an inn since 1905, and still retains the character of an old farm vacation inn on 50 beautiful acres between the Taconic and Green Mountains, with a mile of frontage on the Battenkill River. We specialize in warm, country hospitality. Outside, relax and enjoy the magnificent views from our porches. Inside, savor the aromas of homemade bread, fresh from the oven. Hiking, biking, canoeing, fishing, skiing, and shopping are all nearby. Families are welcome.

Hosts: Craig and Kathleen Yanez
Rooms: 15 (PB) $65 -150
Full Breakfast
Credit Cards: A, B, D
Notes: 2, 5, 7, 8, 9, 10, 11

Shenandoah Farm Bed & Breakfast

4862 Route 313 West, 05250
(802) 372-6372

Guests can enjoy quiet country lodging amid the gloious beauty of Vermont. This lovely 1820 colonial is furnished with beautiful antiques and colonial furniture. It maintains the "at home" atmosphere that was its hallmark when it was a roadhouse in 1930. The nearby Battenkill offers fishing, canoeing, tubing, and swimming. Many museums, recreational attractions, fine restaurants, and delightful craft shops are only minutes away.

Hosts: Woody and Donna Masterson
Rooms: 5 (1 PB; 4 SB) $70-80
Full Breakfast
Credit Cards: A, B
Notes: 2, 5, 7, 8, 9, 10, 11

Shenandoah Farm

BARNARD

The Maple Leaf Inn

P.O. Box 273, 05031
(802) 234-5342; (800) 51-MAPLE
www.mapleleafinn.com

The Maple Leaf is an elegant, Victorian-style inn resplendent with gables, dormers, wraparound porch, gazebo, gingerbread trim, and soaring chimneys, nestled within 16 acres of maple and birch trees. All of our guest rooms have a king bed, sitting area, TV/VCR, telephone, and private bath-most with whirlpool tubs. Woodburning fireplaces grace most of our guest rooms, as well. Stenciling, stitchery, and handmade quilts blend with antique and reproduction furnishings to give each guest room a warm and welcoming individuality.

NOTES: Credit cards accepted: A Master Card; B Visa; C American Express; D Discover; E Diners Club; F Other; 2 Personal checks accepted; 3 Lunch available; 4 Dinner available; 5 Open all year;

The Maple Leaf Inn

The aroma of our gourmet breakfast will entice you to our dining room, where your candlelit table awaits. The Maple Leaf Inn has been honored with the AAA four-diamond award.

Hosts: Gary and Janet Robison
Rooms: 7 (PB) $125-230
Full Breakfast
Credit Cards: A, B, C, D, E
Notes: 2, 5, 8, 9, 10, 11, 12

BARNET

The Old Homestead

1573 U.S. Route 5 South, P.O. Box 150, 05821
(802) 633-4016; (877) 653-4663
fax: (802) 633-4924
E-mail: reserve@theoldhomestead.com
www.theoldhomestead.com

The Old Homestead

This warm, friendly, colonial home in the Conneticut River Valley blends 1850 elegance with 2001 amenities. Enjoy antiques, treasure and collectibles, a cozy fire, warm sunporch, and clear Vermont night sky. Full breakfast and afternoon tea. Space available for conferences, family gatherings, and chamber music rehearsal retreats. Take Exit 18 off I-91 on U.S. Route 5 in the quiet village of Barnet.

Host: Gail Warnaar
Rooms: 5 (3 PB; 2 SB) $65-115
Full Breakfast
Credit Cards: A, B, D
Notes: 2, 5, 7, 8, 9, 10, 11, 12

BRATTLEBORO

1868 Crosby House

1868 Crosby House

175 Western Avenue, 05301
phone/fax: (802) 257-4914; (800) 528-1868
E-mail: lynn@crosbyhouse.com
www.crosbyhouse.com

Built in 1868, this restored Italianate Victorian beckons with historic archi-

---

6 Pets welcome; 7 Children welcome; 8 Tennis nearby; 9 Swimming nearby; 10 Golf nearby; 11 Skiing nearby; 12 May be booked through travel agent

tecture and a beguiling opportunity to step back in time. Bedrooms offer fireplaces, whirlpools, air-conditioning, TVs/VCRs, private line phones, gourmet breakfasts, and other luxury amenities. Two beautifully decorated suites with cathedral ceilings and garden views or skylights are fully equipped and furnished for self-catering stays. Private, landscaped gardens offer the perfect setting for quiet afternoons or elegant celebrations.

Rooms: 5 (PB) $115-165
Full Breakfast
Credit Cards: A, B, D
Notes: 2, 5, 7, 8, 9, 10, 11, 12

CABOT

Country Cottage Bed & Breakfast

P.O. Box 187, 05647
(802) 563-2819

"Come to Me, all you who labor and are heavy laden, and I will give you rest" (Matt. 11:28). We have two rooms, each with a private bath and overlooking Peachem Pond from a lovely hillside view of surrounding mountains. Enjoy full breakfasts in the warmth of the wood cookstove in winter with maple syrup from our sugarbush. . .or come during the rest of the year to hike, bike, or swim in Groton Forest.

Rooms: 2 (PB) $75-85
Full Breakfast
Credit Cards: None
Notes: 2, 4, 5, 7, 9, 10

DANBY

The Quail's Nest

P.O. Box 221, 81 South Main Street, 05739
(802) 293-5099; (800) 599-6444
fax: (802) 293-6300
E-mail: quailsnest@quailsnestbandb.com
www.quailsnestbandb.com

We're just off Route 7 in the village of Danby, a quiet and picturesque town where houses and farms look quite the same as they might have one hundred years ago. The Quail's Nest is a circa 1835 country inn. Its six air-conditioned guest rooms are wrapped in the warmth and comfort of handmade quilts. A four-course, home-cooked breakfast is lovingly prepared, then served by Nancy in period clothing. Whether you're gathered around the piano singing, curled up by the fire, or swinging in the hammock, you will enjoy your stay at the Quail's Nest!

Hosts: Gregory and Nancy Diaz
Rooms: 6 (PB) $70-115
Full Breakfast
Credit Cards: A, B, C, D, F
Notes: 2, 5, 8, 9, 10, 11, 12

EAST DOVER

Cooper Hill Inn

Cooper Hill Road, P.O. Box 146, 05341
(802) 348-6333; (800) 783-3229
E-mail: cooperhill@juno.com
www.cooperhillinn.com

Set high on a hill in southern Vermont's Green Mountains, Cooper Hill Inn commands a view to the east proclaimed by the *Boston Globe* as "one of the most spectacular mountain

Cooper Hill Inn

panoramas in all New England." A small portion of the inn was a farmhouse built in 1797. The inn offers ten rooms, all with private baths. The atmosphere is always homey and informal. Families are welcome. 2001 "Editor's Pick" for *Yankee Magazine*'s Travel Guide to New England.

Hosts: Pat and Marilyn Hunt
Rooms: 10 (PB) $84-130
Full Breakfast
Credit Cards: A, B, D
Notes: 2, 5, 7, 8, 9, 10, 11, 12

FAIR HAVEN

Maplewood Inn

Route 22A, 05743
(802) 265-8039; (800) 253-7729
fax: (802) 265-8210
E-mail: maplewd@sover.net
www.sover.net/~maplewd

Elegant accommodations with romantic charm in a historic, 1843 Greek Revival. Lovely rooms and suites boast antiques, fireplaces, air-conditioning, TVs, all with private baths. Relax and enjoy the sitting room or parlor, with a complimentary cordial. Near lakes, skiing, and many of Vermont's treasures and pleasures. Rec-

ommended by more than 30 guidebooks. A Four-Season Inn.

Hosts: Lisa and Don Osborne
Rooms: 5 (PB) $89-150
Full Breakfast
Credit Cards: A, B, C
Notes: 5, 6, 7, 8, 9, 10, 11, 12

FAIRLEE

Silver Maple Lodge & Cottages

520 U.S. Route 5 South, 05045
(802) 333-4326; (800) 666-1946
E-mail: scott@silvermaplelodge.com
www.silvermaplelodge.com

Silver Maple Lodge & Cottages

A historic B&B country inn located in a four-season recreational area. Enjoy canoeing, fishing, golf, tennis, and skiing within a few miles of the lodge. Visit nearby flea markets and country auctions. Choose a newly renovated room in our antique farmhouse or a handsome, pine-paneled cottage room. Three cottages with working fireplaces. Many fine restaurants nearby; Dartmouth College 17 miles away. Hot-air balloon packages, inn-

---

6 Pets welcome; 7 Children welcome; 8 Tennis nearby; 9 Swimming nearby; 10 Golf nearby; 11 Skiing nearby; 12 May be booked through travel agent

to-inn bicycling, canoeing, and walking tours. Brochures available.

Hosts: Scott and Sharon Wright
Rooms: 16 (14 PB; 2 SB) $59-95
Continental Breakfast
Credit Cards: A, B, C, D
Notes: 2, 5, 6, 7, 8, 9, 10, 11, 12

IRASBURG

Brick House Bed & Breakfast

4862 Route 14, 05845
(802) 754-2108; fax: (802) 754-2108
E-mail: vtlre@together.net
www.explorevermont.com

Brick House

This 1870s brick Victorian home is in the historic town of Irasburg, just off the village common in the beautiful Northeast Kingdom. Private bath bedroom with king or twin beds. Queen bed with lace-topped canopy and full-sized, antique brass bedroom share a bath. A full breakfast is served country-style, and is meant to spoil our guests. In business since 1988. Guest comment: "Everything was wonderful. Every need and more was taken care of."

Hosts: Roger and Jo Sweatt
Rooms: 3 (1 PB; 2 SB) $50-70
Full Breakfast
Credit Cards: None
Notes: 2, 5, 7, 8, 9, 10, 11

KILLINGTON

Cortina Inn & Resort

103 U.S. Route 4, 05751
(802) 773-3333; (800) 451-6108
fax: (802) 775-6948
E-mail: cortinaI@aol.com
www.cortinainn.com

Cortina Inn and Resort is located in the heart of the Green Mountains of central Vermont, near world-famous Killington Ski Resort, and is situated on 32 manicured acres with extensive gardens, woods, a pond, and 8 tennis courts. Conference and banquet facilities will accommodate up to 250. The beautiful gardens and landscaped grounds are perfect for outdoor weddings, receptions, and family reunions.

Hosts: Bob and Breda Harnish
Rooms: 96 (PB) $198-319
Full Breakfast
Credit Cards: A, B, C, D, E
Notes: 4, 5, 6, 7, 8, 9, 10, 11

The Peak Chalet

184 South View Path, P.O. Box 511, 05751
(802) 422-4278
E-mail: home@thepeakchalet.com
www.thepeakchalet.com

A four-room B&B located within the beautiful Green Mountains. The exterior is authentically European Alpine. The interior is furnished with a fine country inn flavor, and reflects high quality with attention to detail. It of-

---

NOTES: Credit cards accepted: A Master Card; B Visa; C American Express; D Discover; E Diners Club; F Other; 2 Personal checks accepted; 3 Lunch available; 4 Dinner available; 5 Open all year;

fers panoramic mountain views with a cozy stone fireplace to unwind by. All rooms have queen beds. Centrally located within Killington Ski Resort, this is a truly relaxing experience. AAA three-diamond- and Mobil-rated.

Hosts: Diane and Greg Becker
Rooms: 4 (PB) $64-127
Continental Breakfast
Credit Cards: A, B, C, E
Notes: 2, 5, 7, 8, 9, 10, 11, 12

LONDONDERRY

Blue Gentian Lodge

Magic Mountain Road, 05148
(802) 824-5908; (800) 456-2405
fax: (802) 824-3531
E-mail: kenalberti@csi.com
www.bluegentian.com

A special place to stay, nestled at the foot of Magic Mountain. All rooms have private baths and cable color TV, and include a full breakfast in the dining room. Enjoy seasonal activities on the grounds, the heated swimming pool, and walking trails. The recreation room offers Ping-Pong, bumper pool, board games, and library. Golf, tennis, fishing, outlet shopping, antiquing, horseback riding, and skiing (downhill and cross-country) are nearby.

Hosts: The Alberti Family
Rooms: 13 (PB) $50-95
Full Breakfast
Credit Cards: A, B
Notes: 2, 4, 5, 7, 8, 9, 10, 11

LOWER WATERFORD

Rabbit Hill Inn

48 Lower Waterford Road, 05848
(802) 748-5168; (800) 76-BUNNY
fax: (802) 748-8342
E-mail: info@rabbithillinn.com
www.rabbithillinn.com

Nestled between a river and the mountains, in a village untouched by time, sits the historic Rabbit Hill Inn. Escape to this tranquil place and experience the gentle comforts of enchanting guest rooms and suites, a Jacuzzi by candlelight, memorable gourmet dining, and pampering service. Enjoy a variety of activities or simply relax. We await you with truly heartfelt hospitality unlike any you've experienced. Meals included. Award-winning, nationally acclaimed inn, rated four stars by Mobil and four diamonds by AAA.

Hosts: Brian and Leslie Mulcahy
Rooms: 19 (PB) $260-410
Full Breakfast
Credit Cards: A, B, C
Notes: 2, 4, 5, 8, 9, 10, 11

LUDLOW

Golden Stage Inn

399 Depot Street, Proctorsville, 05153
(802) 226-7744; (800) 253-8226
E-mail: goldenstageinn@tds.net
www.goldenstageinn.com

Relaxed elegance in an historic antique-filled country inn. This 18th-century stagecoach stop was later home to Otis Skinner, famous theatre performer, and his daughter, writer Cornelius Otis Skinner. Enjoy full breakfast and candlelight dinners in the solarium. Full-size pool, air-conditioning, wheelchair accessible. An-

---

6 Pets welcome; 7 Children welcome; 8 Tennis nearby; 9 Swimming nearby; 10 Golf nearby; 11 Skiing nearby; 12 May be booked through travel agent

tique, golf, bike, attend summer theatre, ski at Okemo.

Hosts: Sandy and Peter Gregg
Rooms: 10 (8 PB; 2 SB) $79-225
Full Breakfast
Credit Cards: A, B, C
Notes: 2, 4, 5, 7, 10, 11, 12

Hound's Folly

9 Dawley Road, Mount Holly, 05758
(802) 259-2718
E-mail: durr2ofhf@aol.com

This 1810 colonial farmhouse is situated on 20 acres of beautiful open
meadowland. Here you will find
sheep grazing. The three guest rooms
are individually decorated. Our dogs
are an integral part of the setting.
Hearty breakfasts. If you love animals, this is the place for you.

Hosts: Luise and Elise Durr
Rooms: 3 (SB) $65-70
Full Breakfast
Credit Cards: A, B
Notes: 2, 7, 8, 9, 10, 11

LYNDONVILLE

Wildflower Inn

2059 Darling Hill Road, 05851
(802) 626-8310; (800) 627-8310
fax: (802) 626-3039
E-mail: wfiinfo@aol.com
www.wildflowerinn.com

The Wildflower Inn is situated on
over 500 acres atop a ridge overlooking the valley of Vermont's Northeast
Kingdom; the near 360-degree views
will take your breath away. You're
sure to enjoy roaming over the inn's
property, discovering the many
amenities the Wildflower Inn has to

Wildflower Inn

offer the single traveler, family, or
group. No matter what brings you
here, your stay will be renewing. For a
full tour of our inn, visit our website.

Hosts: Jim and Mary O' Reilly
Rooms: 21 (PB) $95-280
Full Breakfast
Credit Cards: A, B
Notes: 2, 3, 4, 5, 7, 8, 9, 10, 11

MANCHESTER

River Meadow Farm

P.O. Box 822, Manchester Center, 05255-0822
(802) 362-1602

The oldest portion of the New England farmhouse was built in the late
18th century. During one part of its
history, the home served as the Manchester Poor Farm. It is located at the
end of a country lane with beautiful
mountain views and is bordered on
one side by the Battenhill River. All
of the house and 90 acres are open for
guests to enjoy. Five bedrooms share
two and a half baths.

Host: Patricia J. Dupree
Rooms: 5 (SB) $60
Full Breakfast
Credit Cards: None
Notes: 2, 5, 7, 8, 9, 10, 11

NOTES: Credit cards accepted: A Master Card; B Visa; C American Express; D Discover; E Diners
Club; F Other; 2 Personal checks accepted; 3 Lunch available; 4 Dinner available; 5 Open all year;

MIDDLEBURY

The Middlebury Inn

14 Courthouse Square, 05753
(802) 388-4961; (800) 842-4666
fax: (802) 388-4563
E-mail: midinnvt@sover.net
middleburyinn.com

Welcoming travelers since 1827, the Inn is located in a lovely lively college town enchanced by a legion of historical, cultural, and entertaining attractions. Forty-five elegantly restored rooms in the main house, 10 in Porter House Mansion, and 20 contemporary motel rooms. Cable color TVs, blow dryers, telephones, and air conditioners/heaters in all rooms. The Inn offers breakfast, lunch, dinner, seasonal porch dining, afternoon tea, and Sunday brunch. Recommended by AAA: Member of Historic Hotels of America.

Hosts: The Emanuel Family
Rooms: 75 (PB) $88-365
Continental Breakfast
Credit Cards: A, B, C, D, E
Notes: 2, 3, 4, 5, 6, 7, 8, 9, 10, 11, 12

MONTGOMERY CENTER

The Inn on Trout River

241 Main Street, P.O. Box 76, 05471-0076
(802) 326-4391; (800) 338-7049
fax: (802) 326-3194
E-mail: info@troutinn.com
www.troutinn.com

AAA-rated historic country inn and restaurant in Montgomery Center, the Covered Bridge Town of the Green Mountains, ideally located for exploring the Jay Peak region. Guest rooms include a family suite and honeymoon suite, and feature queen beds, private baths, down quilts, and feather pillows. Recreation: downhill and cross-country skiing, snowmobiling, hiking, biking, golfing, fishing. Activities: nature photography, museums, shopping, foliage and cultural heritage driving tours.

Hosts: Michael and Lee Forman
Rooms: 10 (PB) $86-125
Full Breakfast
Credit Cards: A, B, C, D
Notes: 4, 5, 7, 8, 9, 10, 11, 12

The Inn on Trout Creek

NEWBURY

Peach Brook Inn

P.O. Box 122, 05051
(802) 866-3389

Our B&B is just off Vermont Route 5 which follows the Connecticut River. It is on a country lane with small farms and a variety of farm animals, plus a great farm stand. The house, colonial-style with a carriage house and barn, is on a bluff, giving us a panoramic view of the river, mountains, a village, and farmland. Built in the 1780s, the house gives you a feeling of bygone years with its beams, fireplaces, and antiques. Guests describe the Inn as "beautiful," "peaceful," and "home."

Host: Joyce Emery
Rooms: 3 (1 PB; 2 SB) $55-75
Full Breakfast
Credit Cards: None
Notes: 2, 5, 7, 8, 9, 10, 11

NORTH HERO
(CHAMPLAIN ISLANDS)

The North Hero House Inn & Restaurant

The North Hero House

Route 2, P.O. Box 207, 05474
(802) 372-4732; (888) 525-3644
fax: (802) 372-3218
E-mail: nhhlake@aol.com
www.northherohouse.com

Whether you're drawn to the Lake Champlain Islands of Northern Vermont by the wide-open vistas, or the lulling sound of water lapping at shore's edge, the North Hero House will warmly welcome you into the heart of the nation's "Sixth Great Lake." The Main Inn, built in 1891, first provided a retreat for guests arriving by steamship. You'll be enchanted with the beautifully restored buildings, antiques and collectibles, yet equally pleased to find all the modern conveniences you expect while traveling. The area's quiet rural charm, waterside farms, orchards, and sandy beaches are complemented by festivals, craft fairs, historical day trips, and plenty of outdoor activities to keep you busy exploring the string of islands.

Host: Walter Blasberg, Owner
Rooms: 26 (PB) $89-249
Full Breakfast
Credit Cards: A, B, C
Notes: 2, 4, 5, 6, 7, 8, 9, 10, 12

PITTSFIELD

Swiss Farm Inn

Route 100, P.O. Box 510, 05762
(802) 746-8341; (800) 245-5126
fax: (802) 746-8908
E-mail: info@swissfarminn.com
www.swissfarminn.com

A family tradition for fifty years now. Roger and Joyce Stevens will make you feel at home from the minute you arrive. Breakfast and dinner are prepared and served by your hosts, and promise to be a true homemade country delight. We are 12 miles from Killington Ski Resort, biking, hiking, snowmobiling, horseback riding, golf, tennis, and great swimming. Children are always welcome. Having lived in the Caribbean for some time, the Stevens family create a warm blend of Caribbean and country life.

Hosts: Roger and Joyce Stevens
Rooms: 17 (14 PB; 3 SB) $30-50

NOTES: Credit cards accepted: A Master Card; B Visa; C American Express; D Discover; E Diners Club; F Other; 2 Personal checks accepted; 3 Lunch available; 4 Dinner available; 5 Open all year;

Full Breakfast
Credit Cards: A, B, C
Notes: 2, 4, 5, 7, 8, 9, 10, 11, 12

PROCTORSVILLE

Whitney Brook Bed & Breakfast

Whitney Brook

2423 Twenty Mile Stream Road, 05153
(802) 226-7460
E-mail: whitney_brook@yahoo.com
www.wbrook.cjb.net

Whitney Brook B&B is located in an 1870 Vermont farmhouse on a private and quiet ten acres with stone walls, streams, meadows, and woods. The house has been renovated to provide a comfortable home atmosphere, while maintaining the old farmhouse charm. A large living room with fireplace and an upstairs sitting area with a selection of games are available for guests. Nearby are antique and specialty shops such as the well-known Vermont Country Store. For the sports-minded our area provides downhill (Okemo) and cross-country skiing within 10 minutes, and great hiking,

biking, golf, fishing, and horseback riding. Our picnic table and adirondack chairs are always ready for a pleasant afternoon of reading.

Rooms: 4 (2 PB; 2 SB) $55-95
Full Breakfast
Credit Cards: A, B, C, D
Notes: 2, 5, 8, 9, 10, 11

RANDOLPH

Sweetserenity Bed & Breakfast

40 Randolph Avenue, 05060
(802) 728-9590; (888) 491-9590
fax: 775-414-9487
E-mail: reserveb@sover.net
www.sweet-serenity.com

In the geographic center of Vermont, an 1870 Victorian three-bedroom B&B is waiting for you. Enjoy good conversation, a comfortable bed, and a hearty breakfast. Our library has many quality books. Walk to the Montague Golf Course in a wee two

Sweetserenity

---

6 Pets welcome; 7 Children welcome; 8 Tennis nearby; 9 Swimming nearby; 10 Golf nearby; 11 Skiing nearby; 12 May be booked through travel agent

minutes. The village center with the Chandler Music Hall is only a five-minute walk. May the Lord bless you as you consider your vacation or brief getaway time for relaxation and refreshment.

Hosts: Don and Evelyn Sweetser
Rooms: 3 (1 PB; 2 SB) $75-110
Full Breakfast
Credit Cards: A, B, C
Notes: 2, 5, 7, 8, 9, 10, 11

RUTLAND

I.B. Munson House Bed & Breakfast Inn

37 South Main Street, P.O. Box 427, Wallingford, 05773

I.B. Munson House

(802) 446-2856; (888) 519-3771
fax: (802) 446-3336
E-mail: stay@ibmunsoninn.com
www.ibmunsoninn.com

This 1856 Victorian mansion is nestled in a quaint, historic village. Tastefully restored and decorated with antique furnishings, the unique guest rooms feature private baths and many amenities, including deep claw-foot

soaking tubs, air-conditioning, and fireplaces. . .a pleasure for your senses. A gourmet breakfast is served in the formal dining room. This is a special place to rest and be pampered.

Hosts: Tom and Jo Ann Brem
Rooms: 7 (PB) $95-155
Full Breakfast
Credit Cards: A, B, C
Notes: 2, 3, 4, 5, 8, 9, 10, 11, 12

STOWE

Brass Lantern Inn

717 Maple Street, 05672
(802) 253-2229; (800) 729-2980
fax: (802) 253-7425
E-mail: brasslntrn@aol.com
www.brasslanterninn.com

This award-winning, traditional B&B in the heart of Stowe overlooks Mount Mansfield, Vermont's most prominent mountain. It offers period antiques, handmade quilts, local artisan wares, and air-conditioning. Most rooms have views; some have fireplaces; some have whirlpools. An intimate inn for romantics. Special packages

Brass Lantern Inn

NOTES: Credit cards accepted: A Master Card; B Visa; C American Express; D Discover; E Diners Club; F Other; 2 Personal checks accepted; 3 Lunch available; 4 Dinner available; 5 Open all year;

include honeymoon/anniversary, romance, skiing, golf, historic, and more. No smoking. A two-bedroom, fully-featured mountain cottage is also available.

Host: Andy Alrich
Rooms: 9 (PB) $80-225
Full Breakfast
Credit Cards: A, B, C
Notes: 2, 5, 8, 9, 10, 11, 12

VARIOUS CITIES

Elaine's Bed & Breakfast Selections

4987 Kingston Road, Elbridge, NY 13060
(315) 689-2082

A reservation service that lists B&Bs in the following towns: Fairlee, Killington, Poulney, and Rutland.

VERGENNES

Strong House Inn

94 West Main Street (Route 22A), 05491
(802) 877-3337; fax: (802) 877-2599
E-mail: innkeeper@stronghouseinn.com
www.stronghouseinn.com

Atmosphere abounds at the historic, 1834 Strong House Inn & Rabbit Ridge Country House. Enjoy six acres of gardens, ponds, walking trails, and wonderful mountain vistas. Please come and visit our extraordinary place in Vermont, and recapture a wonderful period of a time gone by. "Come visit and feel the spirit of Vermont."

Hosts: Mary Bargiel
Rooms: 13 (PB) $90-275
Full Breakfast
Credit Cards: A, B, C, D
Notes: 3, 4, 5, 8, 9, 10, 11, 12

WAITSFIELD

The Mad River Inn

243 Tremblay Road, P.O. Box 75, 05673
(802) 496-7900; (800) 832-8278
fax: (802) 496-5390
E-mail: madriverinn@madriver.com
www.madriverinn.com

Our inn offers 1860s country Victorian charm with picturesque mountain views and distant barns. Ten romantic guest rooms have feather beds, antiques, and private baths. Gourmet breakfast. Afternoon tea with baked goods. Elegant living room with library and comfortable couches, sun porch, ski lounge with woodstove, TV/VCR, billiards, and games. Gazebo and outdoor Jacuzzi. Next to recreation path along Mad River. Spacious and wonderful for groups and families. Great mid-week rates. Near Vermont Icelandic horse farm, Sugarbush and Mad River Glen ski resorts and hiking.

Rooms: 9 (PB) $89-135
Full Breakfast
Credit Cards: A, B, C
Notes: 2, 5, 7, 8, 9, 10, 11, 12

The Waitsfield Inn

Route100, P.O. Box 969, 05673
(802) 496-3979; (800) 758-3801
fax: (802) 496-3970
E-mail: waitsfieldinn@madriver.com
www.waitsfieldinn.com

---

6 Pets welcome; 7 Children welcome; 8 Tennis nearby; 9 Swimming nearby; 10 Golf nearby; 11 Skiing nearby; 12 May be booked through travel agent

The Waitsfield Inn

The Waitfield Inn offers gracious lodging in an elegant, 1825 parsonage located in Vermont's Mad River Valley. Relax in front of a fire in our great room, or curl up with a book in the nook. In the morning, follow the scent of fresh brewed coffee to the dining area where a delicious full breakfast awaits you in our restaurant. The restaurant also serves lunch (open to the public) and dinner on Friday and Saturday nights. Our inn is very convenient to local shops, three ski mountains, horseback riding, biking, hiking, and canoeing or kayaking.

Hosts: Pat and Jim Masson
Rooms: 14 (PB) $105-150
Full Breakfast
Credit Cards: A, B, C, D
Notes: 2, 3, 5, 7, 8, 9, 10, 11

WATERBURY

Grunberg Haus
Bed & Breakfast
& Cabins

94 Pine Street, Route 100 South, 05676
(802) 244-7726; (800) 800-7760
E-mail: grunhaus@aol.com
www.grunberghaus.com

An authentic Austrian chalet offering romantic guest rooms (with balcony, antiques, comforters, and quilts) plus secluded cabins (each with wood stove and mountain-view deck). Ideal central location for visiting Stowe, Burlington, Montpelier, and Mad River Valley (Sugarbush, Mad River Glen ski areas). Rural location—we specialize in quiet, informal relaxation. Full country breakfasts. Enjoy our warm-weather Jacuzzi, hiking/cross-country ski trails (we have snowshoes for you to borrow too), and cold-weather sauna. Outstanding golf courses, fishing (three types of trout), mountain hiking, on- and off-road biking, horses, antique stores, farmers' markets, and flea markets.

Hosts: Jeff and Linda Connor
Rooms: 14 (8 PB; 6 SB) $61-160
Full Breakfast
Credit Cards: A, B, D
Notes: 2, 5, 6, 7, 8, 9, 10, 11, 12

Inn at Blush Hill

784 Blush Hill Road, 05676
(802) 244-7529; (800) 736-7522
fax: (802) 244-7314
E-mail: blushhill@aol.com
www.blushhill.com

The Inn at Blush Hill B&B, circa 1790, sits on five acres, high on a hilltop with unsurpassed views of the mountains. Choose from five individually decorated guest rooms with private baths, featuring colonial antiques, canopy beds, down comforters, and a fireplace or Jacuzzi tub. The large common rooms are spacious and warm, filled with books, antiques, and fireplaces. A full breakfast with many Vermont specialty food products is served by the garden in summer and fireside in winter. The inn is located "back-to-back"with Ben and Jerry's ice cream factory. The skiing at Stowe and Sugarbush is only minutes away. AAA- and Mobil-rated. Children over six welcome.

Host: Pamela Gosselin
Rooms: 5 (PB) $79-150
Full Breakfast
Credit Cards: A, B, C, D
Notes: 2, 5, 7, 8, 9, 10, 11, 12

WESTON

The Colonial House

287 Route 100, 05161
(802) 824-6286
E-mail: cohoinn@sover.net
www.cohoinn.com

The Colonial House is a unique country inn and motel offering a full breakfast with its rooms. Dinner is available on Friday and Saturday nights year-round, and mid-week during the summer, fall, and winter holiday periods. Rooms are light and airy. The guest living room has an attached solarium where coffee, tea, and fresh-baked goods are offered each afternoon. Convenient to all southern Vermont attractions.

Hosts: Betty and John Nunnikhoven
Rooms: 15 (9 PB; 6 SB) $50-110
Full Breakfast
Credit Cards: A, B, D
Notes: 2, 4, 5, 7, 8, 9, 10, 11

WILMINGTON

Baked Apples
at Shearer Hill Farm
Bed & Breakfast

Shearer Hill Road, P.O. Box 1453, 05301
(802) 464-3253; (800) 437-3104
E-mail: ppusey@shearerhillfarm.com
www.shearerhillfarm.com

Wake to the aroma of our freshly brewed coffee, homemade muffins, and breads. Enjoy the quiet setting of our small working farm located on a pristine country road. We have six large rooms with private baths. In the winter ski Mount Snow and Haystack Ski Areas, or the groomed cross-country skiing trails on our property. Sleigh riding is nearby. In the summer, visit the Marlboro Music Festival just five minutes away, as well as nearby golfing, swimming, hiking, boating, horseback riding, mountain biking, and many fine restaurants. Distances: 210 miles to New York City; 120 miles to Boston; 70 miles to Albany.

Hosts: Bill and Patti Pusey
Rooms: 6 (PB) $90
Full Breakfast
Credit Cards: A, B, C, D
Notes: 2, 5, 7, 8, 9, 10, 11

WILMINGTON
(MT. SNOW/HAYSTACK REGION)

Trail's End—
A Country Inn

5 Trail's End Lane, 05363
(802) 464-2727; (800) 859-2585
fax: (802) 464-5532
E-mail: trailsnd@together.net
www.trailsendvt.com

Built as a ski lodge in 1956 when Mt. Snow was getting started, this inn is tucked away on 10 acres just off a country road. There are 15 rooms, all

---

6 Pets welcome; 7 Children welcome; 8 Tennis nearby; 9 Swimming nearby; 10 Golf nearby; 11 Skiing nearby; 12 May be booked through travel agent

Trail's End

with private baths and four with fireplaces; suites have canopy beds, fireplaces and Jacuzzis. The inn offers an outdoor swimming pool, a clay tennis court, and a stocked trout pond. Skiing, golf, boating, horseback riding, biking, and hiking are available in the area. The grounds, decorated with English flower gardens, are ideal for weddings and family gatherings. The kitchen is open to guests; lemonade and cookies are served in summer, and hot cider and cookies in winter. Children eight years and older are welcome. No pets.

Host: Kevin Stephens
Rooms: 15 (PB) $110-190
Full Breakfast
Credit Cards: A, B, C, D, F
Notes: 2, 5, 7, 8, 9, 10, 11, 12

WOODSTOCK

Barr House

55 South Street, 05091
(802) 457-3334
www.woodstockvt.com/innsd-k.htm

We are a 19th-century saltbox situated on an acre and a half in the village near the green. Our B&B overlooks golf and cross-country ski courses, but is away from busy thoroughfares. Small and unique. Two charming rooms are hosted by a sixth-generation Vermont native. Full Vermont breakfast. Public room. Gift certificates. Children over 12 welcome. Nonsmoking. No pets.

Hosts: Katharine and Jim Paul
Rooms: 2 (SB) $70-80
Full Breakfast
Credit Cards: None
Notes: 2, 5, 8, 9, 10, 11

THE BARR HOUSE

Woodstocker Bed & Breakfast

61 River Street, 05091
(802) 457-3896; fax: (802) 457-3897
E-mail: woodstocker@valley.net
www.scenesofvermont.com/woodstocker/

Nestled snugly at the foot of Mount Tom, this charming 1830 Cape Cod offers nine large, graciously appointed rooms and suites, all with private baths. Mornings at the Woodstocker begin with a sumptuous and bountiful New England breakfast. Complimen-

---

NOTES: Credit cards accepted: A Master Card; B Visa; C American Express; D Discover; E Diners Club; F Other; 2 Personal checks accepted; 3 Lunch available; 4 Dinner available; 5 Open all year;

tary afternoon refreshments feature home-baked cookies and breads. A short stroll over the covered bridge leads to the Village Green, fine dining, and shopping.

Hosts: Tom and Nancy Blackford
Rooms: 9 (PB) $85-200
Full Breakfast
Credit Cards: A, B, C
Notes: 2, 5, 7, 8, 9, 10, 11, 12

VIRGINIA

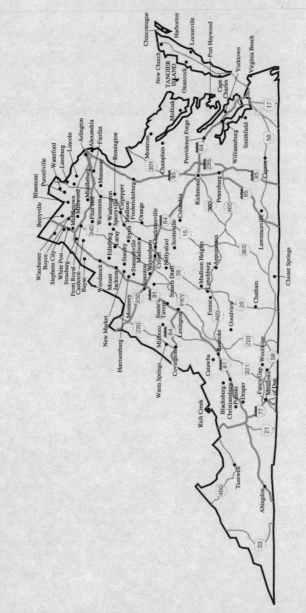

NOTES: Credit cards accepted: A Master Card; B Visa; C American Express; D Discover; E Diners Club; F Other; 2 Personal checks accepted; 3 Lunch available; 4 Dinner available; 5 Open all year;

Virginia

ABINGDON

River Garden
Bed & Breakfast

River Garden

19080 North Fork River Road, 24210
(540) 676-0335; (800) 952-4296
E-mail: wccrump@preferred.com
www.bbdirectory.com/inn/rivergarden

Located in the country, the River Garden is 15 minutes from historic Abingdon, on the banks of the Holston River's North Fork. It is decorated in antique and period furniture and offers private entrances to all rooms, and a covered deck outside facing the river, as well as a deck at the water's edge. Rooms have queen and king beds with air-conditioning and central heat. A full breakfast is served. Enjoy the recreation room, fishing and tubing.

Hosts: Carol and Bill Crump
Rooms: 4 (PB) $75-80
Full Breakfast
Credit Cards: None
Notes: 2, 5, 6, 7, 8, 9, 10, 12

ALEXANDRIA

Alexandria
Bed & Breakfast Network

P.O. Box 25319, 22202
(703) 549-3415; (888) 549-3415
fax: (703) 549-3411
E-mail: aabbn@juno.com
www.aabbn.com

Centered in Old Town Alexandria, this network offers stays in a breathtaking range of homes—1750s Old Town town houses, to 1990 luxury, high-rise apartments. We have private homes, B&Bs, inns, country inns, and boutique hotels throughout DC, Virginia, and Maryland.

Host: Leslie Garrison
Rooms: 110 (100 PB; 10 SB) $68-325
Full and Continental Breakfast
Credit Cards: A, B, C
Notes: 2, 5, 6, 7, 8, 9, 10, 12

BASYE

Sky Chalet
Mountain Lodges

Route 263, P.O. Box 300, 22810
(540) 856-2147; (877) 867-8439
fax: (540) 856-2436
E-mail: skychalet@skychalet.com
www.skychalet.com

Romantic, mountaintop hideaway in the Shenandoah Valley. Property features spectacular mountain and valley views. Rustic lodge open year-round.

---

6 Pets welcome; 7 Children welcome; 8 Tennis nearby; 9 Swimming nearby; 10 Golf nearby; 11 Skiing nearby; 12 May be booked through travel agent

Sky Chalet Country Inn
In The Heart of the Shenandoah Valley

Accommodations are simple and comfortable. Treetop Lodge features bedrooms with private baths, living rooms, fireplaces, lots of books, decks, and some kitchens. Continental breakfast is delivered to your room. We welcome honeymooners, singles, couples, groups, retreats, children, and pets (with notice). Restaurants, hiking, horseback riding, skiing, golfing, tennis, lake, caverns, vineyards, museums, antiques, crafts, creamery, corn maze, Civil War history, and deer farm are nearby. The "Mountain Lovers' Paradise" since 1937.

Hosts: Ken and Mona Seay
Rooms: 5 (PB) $34-79
Continental Breakfast
Credit Cards: A, B, D, E
Notes: 2, 5, 6, 7, 8, 9, 10, 11, 12

BERRYVILLE

Blue Ridge Bed & Breakfast Reservation Service, and, Rocks and Rills Farm Bed & Breakfast

2458 Castleman Road, 22611
(540) 955-1246; (800) 296-1246
fax: (540) 955-4240
E-mail: blurdgbb@shentel.net
www.blueridgebb.com

A lovely visit to the beautiful Rocks and Rills Farm B&B always includes a delicious, full country breakfast each morning. Located on 11 rolling acres, complete with five acres of fragrant Christmas trees, we are at the top of the beautiful Shenandoah Valley. This antique-filled, Colonial Williamsburg reproduction nestled in the foothills of the Blue Ridge Mountains is graced with a magnificent view of the mountains from a large deck suspended over a beautiful lawn and gardens. The Shenandoah River is located only two miles from this tranquil retreat on a lovely dirt road perfect for walking, hiking, or biking. Take a short drive to visit Harpers Ferry, West Virginia, or the Skyline Drive to round out the day; then return to an evening in front of a roaring fire. Children, as well as pets, are always welcome. The host speaks seven different languages including fluent Spanish. The hostess can also help you with other accommodations, as we also own and operate the Blue Ridge B&B Reservation Service. We are located just an hour and a half west of Washington, D.C., 30 minutes from Dulles International Airport, and just 20 minutes east of Interstate 81.

Hosts: Rita Z. Duncan and Rolando A. Amador
Rooms: 4 (2 PB; 2 SB) $60-100
Full Breakfast
Credit Cards: A, B, C
Notes: 2, 5, 6, 7, 8, 9, 10, 12

NOTES: Credit cards accepted: A Master Card; B Visa; C American Express; D Discover; E Diners Club; F Other; 2 Personal checks accepted; 3 Lunch available; 4 Dinner available; 5 Open all year;

BLACKSBURG

Clay Corner Inn

401 Clay Street Southwest, 24060
(540) 953-2604; fax: (540) 951-0541
E-mail: claycorner@aol.com
www.claycorner.com

Clay Corner Inn is a casual B&B with the comforts of home, the amenities of a hotel, and the friendly atmosphere of a small inn. Each guest room has a private bath, cable TV, telephone, and king or queen bed. A full, healthy breakfast is served daily. The heated pool is open May to October, and the hot tub is open year-round. The Huckleberry Trail, a six-mile walking/jogging trail, begins 100 yards from the front door.

Hosts: John and Joanne Anderson
Rooms: 12 (PB) $85-130
Full Breakfast
Credit Cards: A, B, C
Notes: 2, 5, 8, 9, 10

"Evergreen" The Bell-Capozzi House

201 East Main Street, Christiansburg, 24073
(540) 382-7372; (800) 905-7372
fax: (540) 382-0034
E-mail: evrgrninn2@aol.com
www.evergreen-bnb.com

Historic Victorian mansion located in Virginia's Blue Ridge Highlands along I-81. Private baths, central air-conditioning, inground pool; traditional Southern breakfasts are included. Teatime by reservation at $7.50 per person. Barbara is certified by Protocol School of Washington. Well-behaved teenagers are welcome.

Hosts: Rocco and Barbara Bell-Capozzi
Rooms: 7 (PB) $105-145
Full Breakfast
Credit Cards: A, B, C, D
Notes: 2, 4, 5, 9, 10

CAPE CHARLES

Chesapeake Charm Bed & Breakfast

202 Madison Avenue, 23310
(757) 331-2676
E-mail: info@chesapeakecharmbnb.com
www.chesapeakecharmbnb.com

Our family-friendly inn is located on the unspoiled eastern shore of Virginia. Enjoy all the modern conveniences of today enhanced by period antiques, individually controlled heat, and air-conditioning. See spectacular Chesapeake Bay sunsets only two blocks from the B&B. Golf, tennis, fishing, history, and hiking, are all within short distances. Awake to a culinary breakfast delight each morning. A perfect way to celebrate a special birthday or anniversary, or just to escape.

Host: Phyllis Tyndall
Rooms: 4 (PB) $75-120
Full Breakfast
Credit Cards: A, B, C
Notes: 2, 7, 8, 9, 10, 12

CATAWBA

Down Home Bed & Breakfast

5209 Catawba Valley Drive, 24070
(540) 384-6865

---

6 Pets welcome; 7 Children welcome; 8 Tennis nearby; 9 Swimming nearby; 10 Golf nearby; 11 Skiing nearby; 12 May be booked through travel agent

E-mail: dwnhmbb@rbnet.com
www.downhomebb.com

Outstanding hiking and relaxed location. Between two great day-hikes on the Appalachian Trail: McAfee's Knob and Dragon's Tooth. Minutes from the Jefferson National Forest and Craig County trout fishing. Also within walking distance of the Homeplace Restaurant. In-ground swimming pool (seasonal) and large deck for relaxing and watching birds. Private baths, guest living room, and full breakfast.

Hosts: Dave and Lucy Downs
Rooms: 2 (PB) $65 plus tax
Full Breakfast
Credit Cards: None
Notes: 2, 5, 7, 9, 10

CHARLOTTESVLE

The Inn at Monticello

1188 Scottsville Road, 22902
(804) 979-3593; fax: (804) 296-1344
E-mail: stay@innatmonticello.com
www.innatmonticello.com

A charming, country manor house built in 1850, the inn sits cradled in the valley at the foot of Thomas Jefferson's Monticello mountain. It looks out on landscaped grounds toward the mountains. Inside, we offer beautifully decorated rooms full of antique and period pieces. Some rooms have fireplaces, canopy beds, or a private porch. A gourmet breakfast is served.

Hosts: Norm and Becky Lindway
Rooms: 5 (PB) $125-145
Full Breakfast
Credit Cards: A, B
Notes: 2, 5, 8, 9, 10, 11, 12

Mark Addy

56 Rodes Farm Drive, Nellysford, 22958
(434) 361-1101; (800) 278-2154
fax: (520) 832-5277
E-mail: info@mark-addy.com
www.mark-addy.com

"We ventured into the unknown and were rewarded with bliss," say the Coles from Washington, D.C. Surrounded by the tranquility of the Blue Ridge Mountains, the Mark Addy has the adventure of Wintergreen Resort next door and the historic attractions of Charlottesville nearby. "Our bedroom with balcony. . .lovely breakfasts. . .more like a three-star hotel," say the Cowans, of Petworth, West Sussex, England. Children welcome over 12.

Host: John Storck Maddox
Rooms: 9 (PB) $90-145
Full Breakfast
Credit Cards: A, B
Notes: 2, 4, 5, 7, 8, 9, 10, 11, 12

CHINCOTEAGUE

Garden & the Sea Inn

4188 Nelson Road, P.O. Box 275,
   New Church, 23415

NOTES: Credit cards accepted: A Master Card; B Visa; C American Express; D Discover; E Diners Club; F Other; 2 Personal checks accepted; 3 Lunch available; 4 Dinner available; 5 Open all year;

(757) 824-0672; (800) 824-0672
E-mail: innkeeper@gardenandseainn.com
www.gardenandseainn.com

Casual elegance and warm hospitality await you at this European-style country inn with its romantic, candlelight, fine-dining restaurant. Near Chincoteague wildlife refuge and Assateague Island's beautiful beach, it offers large, luxurious guest rooms, beautifully designed; spacious private baths, some with whirlpools; Victorian detail and stained glass; Oriental rugs, antiques, bay windows; and patios and gardens. Mobil three-starrated. We are open mid-March to November 26.

Hosts: Tom and Sara Baker
Rooms: 8 (PB) $75-195
Full Breakfast
Credit Cards: A, B, C, D, F
Notes: 2, 3, 4, 5, 6, 8, 9, 10, 12

The Watson House

4240 Main Street, 23336
(757) 336-1564; (800) 336-6787
fax: (757) 336-5776
www.watsonhouse.com

The Watson House

Featured on the Learning Channel's "Romantic Escapes," the Watson House is a recently restored Victorian country home built in the late 1800s by David Robert Watson. Nestled in the heart of Chincoteague, it is within walking distance of favorite shops and restaurants. We have six guest rooms furnished with antiques, private baths, and air-conditioning. A full breakfast is served in the dining room or on the veranda. We offer complimentary use of bicycles, beach chairs, and beach towels to enjoy our beautiful beach. Children over 10 welcome.

Hosts: Tom and Jacque Derrickson
       David and Joanne Snead
Rooms: 6 (PB) $79-119
Full Breakfast
Credit Cards: A, B
Notes: 2, 7, 8, 9, 10

FREDERICKSBURG

La Vista Plantation

4420 Guinea Station Road, 22408
(540) 898-8444; (800) 529-2823
E-mail: lavistabb@aol.com
www.bbonline.com/va/lavista/

An 1838 Classic Revival country home nestled amid ancient tulip poplars, cedars, and hollies, surrounded by pastures, woods, and fields. The house retains its original charm, with intricate acorn- and oak-leaf moldings, high ceilings, wide pine floors, and a two-story front portico. Choose a two-bedroom apartment (sleeps six) or huge formal room with mahogany, rice-carved, king poster-bed. Both have air-conditioning, fireplaces, TV/

---

6 Pets welcome; 7 Children welcome; 8 Tennis nearby; 9 Swimming nearby; 10 Golf nearby; 11 Skiing nearby; 12 May be booked through travel agent

1838

radios, and refrigerators. Brown-egg breakfast and stocked pond.

Hosts: Michele and Edward Schiesser
Rooms: 2 (PB) $115
Full Breakfast
Credit Cards: A, B
Notes: 2, 5, 7, 8, 10, 12

HARBORTON

Harborton House

28044 Harborton Road, 23389
(757) 442-6800; (800) 882-0922
E-mail: info@harbortonhouse.com
www.harbortonhouse.com

Harborton House

Guests enjoy casual luxury at Harboton House while relaxing on the wraparound porches of the graceful Victorian home. Located in the heart of a peaceful residential fishing village, Harborton House is centrally situated close to all Eastern Shore attractions. There is a public dock and boat ramp in town.

Hosts: Helen and Andy Glenn
Rooms: 3 (PB) $79-109
Full Breakfast
Credit Cards: A, B
Notes: 2, 5, 8, 9, 10, 12

HARRISONBURG

Kingsway Bed & Breakfast

3955 Singers Glen Road, 22802
(540) 867-9696; E-mail: leamancg@juno.com

Your hosts make your comfort their priority. The home is in a quiet rural area with a view of the mountains in the beautiful Shenandoah Valley. Hosts' carpentry and homemaking skills, house plants and outdoor flowers, large lawn and the in-ground pool help make your stay restful. Just four and a half miles from downtown. Nearby is Skyline Drive, caverns, historic sites, antique shops, and flea markets.

Hosts: Chester and Verna Leaman
Rooms: 3 (1 PB; 2 SB) $60-65
Full Breakfast
Credit Cards: None
Notes: 2, 5, 7, 9, 10, 11, 12

LEESBURG

Leesburg Colonial Inn

19 South King Street, 20175
(703) 777-5000; (800) 392-1332
fax: (703) 777-7000
E-mail: saeidi@aol.com
www.leesburgcolonialinn.com

All rooms in this elegant inn are appointed in the colonial style (18th century). We have rooms with queen-size beds; also fireplaces and some suites with wet bars. Our honeymoon suites have jet tubs. We also offer private phones and cable TVs in all rooms. Three days' cancellation notice required.

Leesburg Colonial Inn

Host: Fabian Saeidi
Rooms: 10 (PB) $125-175
Continental Breakfast
Credit Cards: A, B, C, D, E
Notes: 2, 3, 4, 5, 6, 7, 8, 9, 10, 12

Norris House Inn

108 Loudoun Street Southwest, 20175
(703) 777-1806; (800) 644-1806
fax: (703) 771-8051
E-mail:inn@norrishouse.com
www.norrishouse.com

Elegant accommodations in the heart of Leesburg's historic district. Six guest rooms furnished with antiques, and three wood-burning fireplaces. Full country breakfast. Convenient location within walking distance of fine restaurants. An hour's drive from Washington, D.C., in Virginia's hunt country, rich in colonial and Civil War history, antiquing, and quaint villages. Perfect for romantic getaways, small meetings, and weddings. Open daily by reservation. Stone House Tea Room located on the inn's right.

Hosts: Pam and Don McMurray
Rooms: 6 (SB) $100-150
Full Breakfast
Credit Cards: A, B, C, D, E
Notes: 2, 5, 8, 9, 10, 12

LEXINGTON

Stoneridge Bed & Breakfast

Stoneridge Lane, P.O. Box 38, 24450
(540) 463-4090; (800) 491-2930
fax: (540) 463-6078; E-mail: rollo_va@cfw.com
www.webfeat-inc.com/stoneridge

Stoneridge B&B is a romantic, 1829 antebellum home on 36 secluded acres of fields, streams, and woodlands. Five guest rooms each have private baths, queen beds, and ceiling fans. Most feature private balconies or porches, double Jacuzzis, and fireplaces. The large front porch affords wonderful mountain views and spectacular sunsets. Virginia wines are available, and a full gourmet country breakfast is served in the candlelit dining room, or on the patio. Central

---

6 Pets welcome; 7 Children welcome; 8 Tennis nearby; 9 Swimming nearby; 10 Golf nearby; 11 Skiing nearby; 12 May be booked through travel agent

air-conditioning. Five minutes south of historic Lexington.

Stoneridge

Hosts: Norm and Barbara Rollenhagen
Rooms: 5 (PB) $95-160
Full Breakfast
Credit Cards: A, B, C, D
Notes: 2, 5, 7, 12

LURAY

The Woodruff Collection

138 East Main Street, 22835
(540) 743-1494; fax: (540) 743-1722
E-mail: woodruffbnb@rica.net
www.woodruffinns.com

"Prepare to be pampered!" Our chef-owned, 1882 fairytale Victorian offers an inclusive stay with candlelit, fireside parlors, romantic fireside Jacuzzi rooms, and our rooftop skylight fireside Jacuzzi suite. A candlelit dessert tea welcomes you. Romantic candlelit gourmet dinner is included. Two outdoor hot tubs. AAA three diamonds; Mobil three stars.

Hosts: Lucas and Deborah Woodruff
Rooms: 9 (PB) $155-295
Full Breakfast
Credit Cards: A, B, D
Notes: 2, 4, 5, 7, 8, 9, 10, 11, 12

LYNCHBURG

Federal Crest Inn Bed & Breakfast

1101 Federal Street, 24504
(434) 845-6155; (800) 818-6155
fax: (434) 845-1445
E-mail: inn@federalcrest.com
www.federalcrest.com

Recharge your spirit at this 1909 mansion in the Federal Hill District. Enjoy unique woodwork, bedroom fireplaces, private baths (some with Jacuzzis), canopy queen beds, 50s cafe and gift shop, country gourmet breakfasts, friendly hosts, and much more. Spend time rocking on our porch, strolling among the flowers, visiting Civil War sites, and Thomas Jefferson historic sites on the new D Day Memorial. Fine dining, golfing, and Blue Ridge Mountains are nearby.

Federal Crest Inn

Hosts: Ann and Phil Ripley
Rooms: 4 (PB) $109-140
Full Breakfast
Credit Cards: A, B, C, D, F
Notes: 2, 5, 7, 8, 9, 10, 11, 12

NOTES: Credit cards accepted: A Master Card; B Visa; C American Express; D Discover; E Diners Club; F Other; 2 Personal checks accepted; 3 Lunch available; 4 Dinner available; 5 Open all year;

MEADOWS OF DAN

Spangler Bed & Breakfast

1340 Mayberry Church Road, 24120
(540) 952-2454

On Mayberry Church Road bordering the Blue Ridge Parkway at milepost 180, four miles south of Mabry Mill, you'll find this 1904 farmhouse with fireplace, piano, antiques and four porches. Also available are an 1826 log cabin for one couple, and a 1985 log cabin for two couples or a family on a three-and-a-half-acre lake where guests can fish, swim, and boat.

Hosts: Martha and Harold Spangler
Rooms: 6 (2 PB; 4 SB) $60-70
Full Breakfast
Credit Cards: None
Notes: 2, 5, 7, 8, 10

MONTROSS

Porterville Bed & Breakfast

14201 King's Highway, 22520
(804) 493-9394

You'll find this cozy former Baptist parsonage in historic rural Westmoreland County, 45 miles east of Fredericksburg on Virginia State Route 3. Nearby is Stratford Hall Plantation, George Washington's birthplace, Westmoreland State Park, the county courthouse, and museum. Our two comfortable guest quarters, the Cornelia Room and the Juanita, are both on ground level for easy access. A full country breakfast is served daily,

along with a big helping of Southern hospitality.

Host: Mary Hall
Rooms: 2 (SB) $55-95
Full Breakfast
Credit Cards: None
Notes: 2, 5, 7, 9, 10

MT. JACKSON

Widow Kip's Country Inn

355 Orchard Drive, 22842
(540) 477-2400; (800) 478-8714
E-mail: widokips@shentel.net
www.widowkips.com

This stately 1830 colonial on seven rural acres in the Shenandoah Valley overlooks the Blue Ridge Mountains. A romantic getaway, it offers five rooms with fireplaces and antiques, as well as two cottages. Locally crafted quilts adorn the four-poster, canopy, and sleigh beds. Attractions include Civil War battlefields and museums, caverns, canoeing, hiking, horseback riding, golf, fishing, skiing, and swimming. A comment by a recent guest: "You have set a standard of professional excellence; we will be back."

Hosts: Betty and Bob Luse
Rooms: 7 (PB) $85-110
Full Breakfast
Credit Cards: A, B
Notes: 2, 3, 5, 6, 7, 8, 9, 10, 11, 12

ONANCOCK

76 Market Street Bed & Breakfast

76 Market Street; P.O. Box 376, 23417
(757) 787-7600; (888) 751-7600
E-mail: hosts@76marketst.com
www.76marketst.com

A Victorian 19th-century B&B inn, 76 Market Street is located in the quiet residential area of Onancock, on the beautiful Eastern Shore of Virginia. We are just four blocks from the Town Wharf with access to the Chesapeake Bay. With our easy access by car or boat, we are an ideal spot for "weekend getaways" or as a central location for activities on the Eastern Shore from Chincoteague to Cape Charles. All of our rooms are on the second floor and have private baths. Walk to excellent restaurants. Children welcome over six years of age. Central air-conditioning; smoke-free; no pets.

Hosts: Mike and Marge Carpenter
Rooms: 3 (PB) $65-95
Full Breakfast
Credit Cards: A, B
Notes: 2, 5, 7, 9, 10, 12

PROVIDENCE FORGE

Jasmine Plantation Bed & Breakfast

4500 North Courthouse Road, 23140
(804) 966-9836; (800) 639-5368
fax: (804) 966-5679
E-mail: jasmineinn@aol.com
www.bbonline.com/va/jasmine

Jasmine Plantation is a restored 1750s farmhouse that is convenient to Williamsburg, Richmond, and the James River plantations. Genuine hospitality, a historical setting, and rooms decorated in period antiques await the visitor. The home was settled prior to 1683. Guests are invited to walk the 47 acres and use their imaginations as to what events have occurred here during the inn's 300-year history. Just 2.4 miles from I-64, Jasmine Plantation offers both convenience and seclusion to travelers. Fine dining can be enjoyed nearby. Children over 12 welcome.

Hosts: Joyce and Howard Vogt
Rooms: 6 (4 PB; 2 SB) $85-140
Full Breakfast
Credit Cards: A, B, C
Notes: 2, 5, 7, 10, 12

RICH CREEK

Betty Lou's Bed & Breakfast

P.O. Box 589; 108 Summit Drive, 24147
(540) 726-3319
E-mail: bettylou@gva.net
www.gva.net/bettylousB&B

Member of Mountain State Association of Bed & Breakfast, a stay at Betty Lou's is like a visit with friends; come and enjoy the peaceful setting. Unwind on our front porch and experience our "million-dollar view!" Betty Lou's is a treat for those in search of serenity, hospitality, and a good night's sleep. Wake to the sights and sounds of our local wildlife, then make the most of the day with Giles County activities. Lunch and dinner available upon request.

Host: Perye Letsinger
Rooms: 4 (2 PB; 2 SB) $68-88
Full Breakfast
Credit Cards: None
Notes: 2, 3, 4, 5, 7, 9, 10, 11

NOTES: Credit cards accepted: A Master Card; B Visa; C American Express; D Discover; E Diners Club; F Other; 2 Personal checks accepted; 3 Lunch available; 4 Dinner available; 5 Open all year;

STANLEY

White Fence Bed & Breakfast

275 Chapel Road, 22851
(540) 778-4680; (800) 211-9885
fax: (540) 778-4773
E-mail: whifenbb@shentel.net
whitefencebb.com

This 1890 Victorian is on three acres in the beautiful Shenandoah Valley. Near Skyline Drive, the famous Luray Caverns, and 90 minutes to D.C. Two cottages and one B&B suite, all with queen beds, TVs/VCRs, fireplaces, two-person whirlpools, breakfast areas, plush robes, and CD-clock radios. Enjoy a beautiful breakfast basket delivered to your suite or a gourmet breakfast at the B&B. This is a romantic, private getaway for those who enjoy superior accommodations with impeccable attention to detail.

White Fence

Hosts: Tom and Gwen Paton
Rooms: 3 (PB) $116-149
Full Breakfast
Credit Cards: A, B, D
Notes: 2, 5, 9, 10, 11, 12

STAUNTON

Ashton Country House

1205 Middlebrook Avenue, 24401
(540) 885-7819; (800) 296-7819
fax: (540) 885-6029
E-mail: ashtonhouse@aol.com
www.bbhost.com/ashtonbnb

This Greek Revival home is surrounded by 25 explorable acres where cows roam and birds frolic in the trees. A mix of traditional and Victorian antiques grace the interior. Four of the guest rooms include a fireplace, and each is appointed individually. The inn's porches, where afternoon tea is often served, are lined with chairs for those who seek relaxation and the scenery of rolling hills. Woodrow Wilson's birthplace is among the town's notable attractions. Breakfast, afternoon tea, and evening snack are included in the rates. Air-conditioning, ceiling fans, cable TV and VCR. Handicapped-accessible. Small meetings and family reunions hosted. Antiques, fishing, parks, shopping, and water sports are nearby.

Hosts: Dorie and Vince DiStefano
Rooms: 6 (PB) $85-150
Full Breakfast
Credit Cards: A, B, C, D, F
Notes: 2, 5, 6, 7, 8, 9, 10, 11, 12

Frederick House

28 North New Street, 24401
(540) 885-4220; fax: (540) 885-5180
E-mail: ejharman@frederickhouse.com
www.frederickhouse.com

Frederick House is a small historic hotel in the European tradition. Six restored homes are situated across from Mary Baldwin College in Staunton, the oldest city in the Shenandoah Valley. You can walk to restaurants, antique shops, galleries, and museums.

Hosts: Joe and Evy Harman
Rooms: 23 (PB) $85-175
Full Breakfast
Credit Cards: A, B, C, D, E

Thornrose House at Gypsy Hill

531 Thornrose Avenue, 24401
(540) 885-7026; (800) 861-4338
fax: (540) 885-6458
E-mail: innkeeper@thornrosehouse.com
www.thornrosehouse.com

Thornrose House

Thornrose House is a turn-of-the-century Georgian Revival house with a wraparound veranda, and nearly one acre of beautiful landscaped gardens graced with two sets of pergolas with brick walkways. It is adjacent to the 300-acre Gypsy Hill Park with facilities for golf, tennis, swimming, and summer band concerts. We're conveniently located in the heart of the Shenandoah Valley presenting oppor-

tunities for hiking, biking, antiquing, historical museums, theaters including Shenandoah Shakespeare, and numerous fine restaurants. Children six and over welcome.

Hosts: Otis and Suzanne Huston
Rooms: 5 (PB) $75-95
Full Breakfast
Credit Cards: A, B, C
Notes: 2, 5, 7, 8, 9, 10

TANGIER

Shirley's Bay View Inn

16408 West Ridge Road, P.O. Box 183, 23440
(757) 891-2396
www.tangierisland.net

Enjoy a pleasant and restful visit to one of the last quiet and remote fishing villages on the Chesapeake Bay. You will stay at one of the oldest homes on Tangier Island, filled with the beauty and charm of days gone by. The beautiful beaches, sunsets, and customs of Tangier Island will make your stay a memorable one, and your hostess will make you feel you are part of the family.

Hosts: Wallace and Shirley Pruitt
Rooms: 10 (PB) $80
Full Breakfast
Credit Cards: None
Notes: 2, 5, 7, 9

VIRGINIA BEACH

Barclay Cottage Bed & Breakfast

400 16th Street, 23451
(757) 422-1956
www.barclaycottage.com

Barclay Cottage

Barclay Cottage offers casual sophistication in a warm, historic, inn-like atmosphere. Designed in turn-of-the-century style, the cottage is two blocks from the beach, in the heart of the Virginia Beach recreational area. The inn is completely restored with antique furniture to bring together the feeling of yesterday with the comfort of today. Formerly the home of Lillian S. Barclay, the inn has been a guest home for many years. We have kept the historic ambience of the inn while modernizing it significantly to meet today's needs. We look forward to welcoming you to Barclay Cottage, where the theme is "We go where our dreams take us." AAA-rated three diamonds.

Hosts: Peter and Claire
Rooms: 4 (PB) $88-118
Full Breakfast
Credit Cards: A, B, C
Notes: 8, 9, 10, 12

WARM SPRINGS

Three Hills Inn

P.O. Box 9, 24484
(540) 839-5381; E-mail: inn@3hills.com
www.3hills.com

Three Hills is perched on over 40 acres on Warm Springs mountain, unique among Bath County hostelries due to its panoramic view of Warm Springs Gap and the Alleghenies beyond. Many suites feature mountain views, fireplaces, and kitchens. The estate features boxwood gardens, extensive grounds, and acres of woods and walking trails.

Hosts: Doug and Charlene Fike
Rooms: 10 (PB) $110-189
Full Breakfast
Credit Cards: A, B, D
Notes: 6, 7, 9, 10

WARRENTON

Black Horse Inn

8393 Meetze Road, 20187
(540) 349-4020; fax: (540) 349-4242
E-mail: relax@blackhorseinn.com
www.blackhorseinn.com

In the heart of Virginia's horse country and vineyards, less than an hour from Washington, D.C., is the majestic Black Horse Inn, circa 1850. The Inn reflects the deep, rich history of

Black Horse Inn

6 Pets welcome; 7 Children welcome; 8 Tennis nearby; 9 Swimming nearby; 10 Golf nearby; 11 Skiing nearby; 12 May be booked through travel agent

Virginia. It is beautifully situated on a hill, with thoroughbred horses galloping in the surrounding fields. The Inn has nine unique rooms, each appointed with period pieces and reproductions; four rooms have fireplaces; four have whirlpool baths; one has a multispray, spa-style shower; the remainder have clawfoot tubs and showers; and most have four-poster canopy beds. A hunt-country tea is included. Children over 12 are welcome.

Host: Lynn A. Pirozzoli
Rooms: 9 (PB) $125-295
Full Breakfast
Credit Cards: A, B, C, D
Notes: 2, 5, 7, 8, 9, 10, 12

nature includes full breakfasts, fireplaces, air-conditioning, hayrides, bicycles, lawn games, VCR, and piano. Fine dining, caves, Skyline Drive, battlefields, stables, antiquing, hiking, and climbing are all nearby. Washington D.C., is 68 miles away; Washington, Virginia, just four miles. A Virginia historic landmark, the farm is listed on the National Register of Historic Places. Unwind in our new spa. Children over 12 welcome.

Host: Phil Irwin
Rooms: 2 suites (PB) $140
Full Breakfast
Credit Cards: A, B, D
Notes: 2, 5, 7, 8, 9, 10, 11, 12

WASHINGTON

Caledonia Farm—1812

47 Dearing Road, Flint Hill, 22627
phone/fax: (540) 675-3693
(800) 262-1812
www.bnb-n-va.com/cale1812.htm

Caledonia Farm-1812

Enjoy ultimate hospitality, comfort, scenery, and recreation adjacent to Virginia's Shenandoah National Park. This romantic getaway to history and

WAYNESBORO

Belle Hearth
Bed & Breakfast

320 South Wayne Avenue, 22980
(540) 943-1910; (800) 949-6993
fax: (540) 942-2443
E-mail: bellehrth@aol.com
inngetaways.net/va/belle.html

Named for its seven "belle" or beautiful fireplaces, the Belle Hearth B&B is minutes from Skyline Drive and the Blue Ridge Parkway in historic downtown Waynesboro. This early 1900s home offers traditional elegance with heart-of- pine floors, ten-foot ceilings, and Victorian furnishings. Fully air-conditioned. Backyard pool. Visit Monticello and other historical sites and museums. All outdoor activities are available, including winter skiing. Nearby George Washington National Forest and Shenandoah National Park

Belle Hearth B&B

offer a hiker's paradise. Children eight and over welcome.

Hosts: Jim and Carolyn Rodenberg
Rooms: 4 (PB) $80-110
Full Breakfast
Credit Cards: A, B, C
Notes: 2, 5, 7, 9, 10, 11

WILLIAMSBURG

Applewood Colonial Bed & Breakfast

605 Richmond Road, 23185-3539
(757) 229-0205; (800) 899-2753
fax: (757) 229-9405
E-mail: info@williamsburgbandb.com
williamsburgandb.com

Our queen bedchambers will enchant you and our location is superb. This architecturally significant home was built in 1928 by restoration craftsmen featuring a distinctive 18th-century style plus 21st-century amenities. Awake to a full breakfast served in our elegant Dining Room and enjoy complimentary afternoon refreshments plus scrumptious apple pie. Our ticket packages (Colonial Williamsburg, Jamestown-Yorktown, Busch Gardens, Ghost Tour) and Romance

package (flowers, wine, and more) will enhance your visit.

Hosts: Marty and Roger Jones
Rooms: 4 (PB) $100-175
Full Breakfast
Credit Cards: A, B
Notes: 2, 5, 8, 9, 10

The Cedars Bed & Breakfast

616 Jamestown Road, 23185
(757) 229-3591; (800) 296-3591
fax: (757) 229-0756
E-mail: cedars@widomaker.com
www.cedarsofwilliamsburg.com

Enter this three-story, brick Georgian home and the tone will be set for your visit to the 18th century. An eight-minute walk to historic Williamsburg, across from the College of William and Mary, this elegant inn offers traditional, gracious hospitality and comfort. Candlelit breakfasts are scrumptious and bountiful. Each guest chamber reflects the romance and charm of the colonial era. Canopy and four-poster beds abound. Fireplaces in parlor and cottage. Off-street parking. Williamsburg's oldest and largest B&B.

Hosts: Jim and Bróna Malecha
Rooms: 9 (PB) $95-150
Full Breakfast
Credit Cards: A, B
Notes: 2, 5, 7, 9, 10

Colonial Capital Bed & Breakfast

501 Richmond Road, 23185
(757) 229-0233; (800) 776-0570
fax: (757) 253-7667
E-mail: ccbb@widomaker.com
www.ccbb.com

6 Pets welcome; 7 Children welcome; 8 Tennis nearby; 9 Swimming nearby; 10 Golf nearby; 11 Skiing nearby; 12 May be booked through travel agent

Walk three blocks to Colonial Williamsburg, just minutes away from Jamestown, Yorktown, Busch Gardens, and Water Country USA. Antique furnishings, cozy canopied beds, private baths, in-room phones, and TV/VCR all create a rich blend of warmth, style, comfort, and convenience. Begin your day with a full cooked breakfast, and in the afternoon enjoy tea, wine, and relaxing conversation with friends new and old in our guest parlor or on the screened porch, patio, and deck. Free off-street parking. Convenience packages, discount tickets, and gift certificates are available for any occasion. Airport and Amtrack pickup. Returning guest discounts.

Hosts: Barbara and Phil Craig
Rooms: 5 (PB) $135-150
Full Breakfast
Credit Cards: A, B, C, D
Notes: 2, 5, 8, 9, 10, 12

Fox & Grape
Bed & Breakfast

701 Monumental Avenue, 23185
(757) 229-6914; (800) 292-3699
fax: (757) 229-0951
E-mail: info@foxandgrapebb.com
www.foxandgrapebb.com

Here you'll find genteel accommodations five blocks north of Virginia's restored colonial capital. This lovely, two-story colonial with its spacious wraparound porch is a perfect place to enjoy your morning coffee, plan your day's activities in Williamsburg, or relax with your favorite book. Furnishings include antiques, counted cross-stitch, duck decoys, and folk-art

Fox & Grape

Noah's arks made by your host. Pat enjoys doing counted cross-stitch; Bob carves walking sticks and makes nursery rhyme collectibles.

Hosts: Pat and Robert Orendorff
Rooms: 4 (PB) $100-115
Full Breakfast
Credit Cards: A, B, D
Notes: 5

Hites Bed & Breakfast

704 Monumental Avenue, 23185
(757) 229-4814

This charming Cape Cod is a seven-minute walk to Colonial Williamsburg. Spacious rooms are cleverly furnished with antiques and collectibles. Each room has a phone, TV, radio, coffeemaker, robes, and beautiful private bathrooms with claw-foot tubs. A suite is also available with a nice romantic setting. Guests will enjoy the parlor's antique pump organ and hand-crank victrola. Relax in the lovely garden and enjoy the swings, birds, flowers, and goldfish pond.

Hosts: James and Faye Hite
Rooms: 2 (PB) $95-110
Full Breakfast
Credit Cards: None
Notes: 2, 5, 7, 9, 10, 12

Hughes Guest Home

106 Newport Avenue, 23185
(757) 229-3493
E-mail: livesiv@aol.com

Directly opposite the Williamsburg Lodge on Newport Avenue, the Hughes Guest Home has been in operation since 1947. A lovely, two-minute stroll to Colonial Williamsburg's restored district, golfing facilities, and numerous dining facilities including the colonial taverns. The College of William and Mary, Merchant's Square, and several Colonial Williamsburg museums are also within easy walking distance. The house is decorated lavishly with family antiques. Eating facilities are across the street at the Williamsburg Lodge and Williamsburg Inn. Lodging only.

Host: Genevieve O. Hughes
Rooms: 3 (1 PB; 2 SB) $60
Credit Cards: None
Notes: 2, 7, 10

The Inn at 802

802 Jamestown Road, 23185
(757) 564-0845; (800) 672-4086
fax: (757) 564-7018
E-mail: don@innat802.com
www.innat802.com

The Inn at 802 offers you a high level of comfort, privacy, and friendly service in surroundings that reflect the quiet elegance of an earlier time. The décor in all of our guest rooms reflects colonial charm and beautifully coordinated colors. All guest rooms have private baths, writing desks, TVs, and beautiful, period-style antiques and reproductions. Our entire inn is climate-controlled for guests' comfort. We serve daily a sumptuous, homemade breakfast in our formal dining room.

Hosts: Don and Jan McGarva
Rooms: 4 (PB) $125-145
Full Breakfast
Credit Cards: A, B, C, D
Notes: 2, 5, 6, 7, 9, 10

Legacy of Williamsburg Bed & Breakfast Inn

930 Jamestown Road, 23185
(757) 220-0524; (800) 962-4722
fax: (757) 220-0524; E-mail: legacy@tni.net
legacyofwilliamsburgbb.com

An 18th-century style inn located four and a half blocks from Colonial Williamsburg. The home has six working fireplaces and candlelight throughout. All guest rooms have queen-size feather beds and private baths. A full candlelight breakfast is served each morning.

Host: Marshall G Wile
Rooms: 4 (PB) $135-190
Full Breakfast
Credit Cards: A, B
Notes: 2, 5, 8, 10, 12

Newport House Bed & Breakfast

710 South Henry Street, 23185
(757) 229-1775

A reproduction of a 1756 home, Newport House has museum-standard period furnishings, including canopy beds. Only a five-minute walk to the historic area. Breakfast with colonial recipes; colonial dancing in the ballroom Tuesday evenings (beginners welcome). The host is a historian/author (including a book on Christ)

---

6 Pets welcome; 7 Children welcome; 8 Tennis nearby; 9 Swimming nearby; 10 Golf nearby; 11 Skiing nearby; 12 May be booked through travel agent

and former museum director. The hostess is a gardener, beekeeper, 18th-century seamstress, and former nurse. No smoking.

Hosts: John and Cathy Millar
Rooms: 2 (PB) $135-160
Full Breakfast
Credit Cards: None
Notes: 2, 5, 7, 8, 9, 10, 12

North Bend Plantation

12200 Weyanoke Road, Charles City, 23030
(804) 829-5176
www.northbendplantation.com

Circa 1819 National Register property, Greek Revival-style manor house, 850-acre farm, owned and operated by descendents of original owner, Sarah Harreson, sister of ninth U.S. President. Original antiques, three porches, and pool. Lawn games, bicycles, hammock, James River plantations, Colonial Williamsburg, tennis, and golf nearby. Original Cross & Open Bible Doors, a Christian home.

Hosts: George and Ridgely Copland
Rooms: 4 (PB) $120-135
Full Breakfast
Credit Cards: A, B
Notes: 2, 5, 7, 8, 9, 10, 12

Orange Hill Bed &Breakfast

18401 The Glebe Lane, Charles City, 23030
(804) 829-6988; (888) 501-8125
E-mail: orange-hill@juno.com
www.orangehillbb.com

A cozy, turn-of-the-century farmhouse, Orange Hill sits on 50 acres of working farmland. It offers the peacefulness of the country in historic Charles City County. It is only minutes from Colonial Williamsburg, James River Plantations, Civil War sites, shopping, fishing, golf, and Colonial Downs race horse track. Features antiques. Available for weddings. Children over 12 welcome.

Orange Hill

Hosts: Mark and Kay Russo
Rooms: 3 (2 PB; 1 SB) $80-105
Full Breakfast
Credit Cards: A, B
Notes: 5, 7, 10

A Primrose Cottage

706 Richmond Road, 23185
(757) 229-6421; (800) 522-1901
fax: (757) 259-0717
www.primrose-cottage.com

A nature lover's delight. In the spring, the front walkway is lined with primroses. Thousands of tulips bloom in April and May, and even in cooler months something adds color to this award-winning garden. There are 4 rooms, all spacious, bright, and lovingly decorated with antiques. Each has its own TV and bath. Two of the bathrooms have Jacuzzis. You are invited to play the harpsichord built by the innkeeper. Wonderful, hot breakfasts are served every morning.

Host: Inge Curtis
Rooms: 4 (PB) $95-125
Full Breakfast
Credit Cards: A, B
Notes: 2, 5, 8, 9, 10, 12

Williamsburg Sampler Bed & Breakfast Inn

922 Jamestown Road, 23185-3917
(757) 253-0398; (800) 722-1169
fax: (727) 253-2669
E-mail: wbgsamper@aol.com
www.williamsburgsampler.com

This 18th-century, plantation-style colonial was proclaimed "Inn of the Year" by Virginia's governor. This is a AAA three-diamond and Mobil three-star home within walking distance of the historic area. Richly furnished bedrooms and suites with king- or queen-size beds, private baths, fireplaces, and rooftop garden. A collection of antiques, pewter, and samplers is displayed throughout the house. A "skip lunch®" breakfast is served. The Williamsburg Sampler is internationally recognized as a favorite spot for a romantic honeymoon or anniversary.

Hosts: Helen and Ike Sisane
Rooms: 4 (PB) $115-165
Full Breakfast
Credit Cards: A, B
Notes: 5, 8, 9, 10, 12

WINCHESTER

Hotel Strasburg

213 South Holliday Street, Strasburg, 22657
(540) 465-9191; (800) 348-8327
fax: (540) 465-4788
E-mail: thehotel@shentel.net
www.hotelstrasburg.com

Like stepping back in time to the 1890s, Hotel Strasburg combines Victorian history and charm to make a special place for lodging, dining, and meeting. Our new conference/banquet facility will accommodate up to 100. Tastefully decorated with many antique period pieces of furniture and an impressive collection of art, guests are invited to wander through the Inn's dining rooms and quaintly renovated sleeping rooms (Jacuzzi Suites). Nestled at the foot of Massanutten Mountain near the entrance to the breathtaking Skyline Drive, Hotel Strasburg is your most romantic stop in the Romantic Era. Inquire about pets.

Hosts: Gary and Carol Rutherford
Rooms: 29 (PB) $79-175
Continental Breakfast
Credit Cards: A, B, C, D, E
Notes: 3, 4, 5, 6, 7, 8, 9, 10, 12

6 Pets welcome; 7 Children welcome; 8 Tennis nearby; 9 Swimming nearby; 10 Golf nearby; 11 Skiing nearby; 12 May be booked through travel agent

WASHINGTON

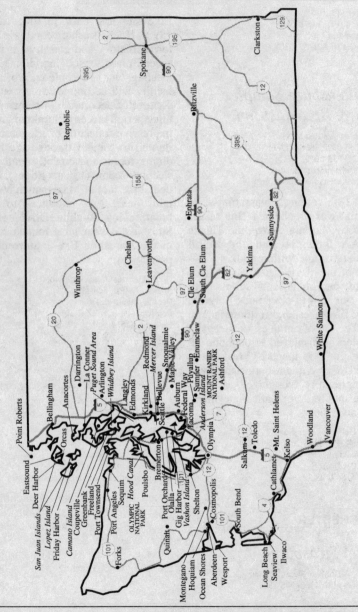

NOTES: Credit cards accepted: A Master Card; B Visa; C American Express; D Discover; E Diners Club; F Other; 2 Personal checks accepted; 3 Lunch available; 4 Dinner available; 5 Open all year;

Washington

ABERDEEN

A Harbor View Inn Bed & Breakfast

111 West 11th Street, 98520
(360) 533-7996; (877) 533-7996
fax: (360) 533-0433
E-mail: harborview@olynet.com
www.aharborview.com

Every room has a water view, private bath, and TV. Breakfast is served in the sunroom overlooking Grays Harbor. This historic 1905 home is in a historic neighborhood, close to beaches and the rainforest.

Host: Cindy Lonn
Rooms: 4 (PB) $65-95
Full Breakfast
Credit Cards: A, B
Notes: 5, 7, 8, 10, 12

ANACORTES

Sunset Beach Bed & Breakfast

100 Sunset Beach, 98221
(360) 293-5428; (800) 359-3448
www.whidbey.com/sunsetbeach/

This B&B is located on exciting Rosario Straits. Relax and enjoy the view of seven major islands from every room and deck. Stroll on the beach or walk in beautiful Washington Park, adjacent to the private gardens. Guest rooms all have private baths with a Jacuzzi shower. A hot tub is available upon request. The guesthouse is five minutes from San Juan Ferry, fine restaurants, marina, and a convenience store. The sunsets are outstanding. Children over 12 welcome. Nonsmoking.

Hosts: Joann and Hal Harker
Rooms: 3 (PB) $85-109
Full Breakfast
Credit Cards: A, B
Notes: 2, 5, 9, 10, 12

ANDERSON ISLAND

The Inn at Burg's Landing

8808 Villa Beach Road, 98303
(253) 884-9185; (800) 431-5622
E-mail: innatburgslanding@mailexcite.com

Catch the ferry from Steilacoom to stay at this contemporary log homestead built in 1987. It offers spectacular views of Mt. Rainier, Puget Sound, and the Cascade Mountains and is located south of Tacoma off I-5. Choose

---

6 Pets welcome; 7 Children welcome; 8 Tennis nearby; 9 Swimming nearby; 10 Golf nearby; 11 Skiing nearby; 12 May be booked through travel agent

The Inn at Burg's Landing

from three guest rooms, including the master bedroom with queen "log" bed, skylight above, and private whirlpool bath. The inn has a private beach. Collect seashells and agates, swim in two freshwater lakes nearby, and enjoy a game of tennis or golf. Tour the island by bicycle or on foot and watch for sailboats and deer. Hot tub. Full breakfast. Families welcome. No smoking.

Hosts: Ken and Annie Burg
Rooms: 4 (2 PB; 2 SB) $70-110
Full Breakfast
Credit Cards: A, B
Notes: 2, 5, 7, 8, 9, 10, 11, 12

CAMANO ISLAND

Inn at Barnum Point

464 South Barnum Road, 98282
(360) 387-2256; (800) 910-2256
E-mail: barnum@camano.net
www.innatbarnumpoint.com

Spectacular view on a salt water bay surrounded by mountains. Lights reflect on the water at night and the moon shines a gold or silver path across it. Guest rooms are warm and cozy in winter, and light and airy in summer. Try our luxury Shorebird

Room with separate entrance, loft, soaking tub, and deck with grill; sleeps four. All rooms have a private bath, fireplace, and TV. A full breakfast is served.

Host: Carolin Barnum Dilorenzo
Rooms: 3 (PB) $99-199
Full Breakfast
Credit Cards: A, B, D
Notes: 2, 5, 7, 8, 9, 10, 12

CHELAN

Holden Village Bed & Breakfast

21081 South Lakeshore Road, 98816
(509) 687-9695; fax: (509) 687-3375
www.holdenvillage.org

A quiet, comfortable country-style B&B with many handmade items, including quilts, pottery, weavings, tables, and a delicious family-style breakfast. A large covered porch overlooks beautiful Lake Chelan and the mountains beyond. Forest walking trails are nearby. Just three miles away, the Lady of the Lake boat heads uplake toward our parent community. Holden Village is a remote ecumenical retreat center that provides a place of healing, renewal, and refreshment for all of God's diverse people.

Rooms: 6 (SB) $36-60
Full Breakfast
Credit Cards: None
Notes: 2, 5, 7

A Quails Roost Inn

A Quails Roost Inn

121 East Highland Avenue, 98816
(509) 682-2892; (800) 681-2892
www.aquailsroostinn.com

Homesteaded in 1896, this Queen
Anne-style Victorian was finished in
1902. The home is listed on the National Register of Historic Places. The
mansion is situated on the north hill
overlooking Lake Chelan and is a
short walk from downtown or the
lake. The view is breathtaking from
the huge wraparound veranda or the
private porch off the Rose and Wicker
Rooms. All rooms are theme-decorated and hand-stenciled. During the
summer, enjoy your gourmet breakfast and fresh-ground coffee on the
veranda.

Hosts: Brad and Marilee Stolzenburg
Rooms: 3 (PB) $55-114
Full Breakfast
Credit Cards: A, B
Notes: 2, 3, 5, 7, 8, 9, 10, 11, 12

CLARKSTON

Cliff House
Bed & Breakfast

1227 Westlake Drive, 99403
(509) 758-1267
E-mail: cliffhouse@clarkston.com
www.northwestmedia.net/cliffhouse

The Cliff House offers a quiet, country atmosphere with an unsurpassed
panoramic view of the Snake River
500 feet below, surrounded by majestic hills. There are many opportunities
to observe a variety of wildlife. In this
area white-water rafting and jet-boat
trips are taken into North America's
deepest gorge, nearby Hell's Canyon.
Relax in king beds and feast on a
scrumptious breakfast. Pets welcome
in pet carriers.

Cliff House

Hosts: Yvonne and Everett Dickerson
Rooms: 2 (PB) $80-85
Full Breakfast
Credit Cards: None
Notes: 2, 5, 8, 9, 10, 11

---

6 Pets welcome; 7 Children welcome; 8 Tennis nearby; 9 Swimming nearby; 10 Golf nearby; 11 Skiing
nearby; 12 May be booked through travel agent

DEER HARBOR

Palmer's Chart House

Orcas Island, P.O. Box 51, 98243
(360) 376-4231

The first B&B on Orcas Island (since 1975) with a magnificent water view. The 33-foot private yacht Amante is available for a minimal fee, with skipper Don. Low-key, personal attention makes this B&B unique and attractive. Well-traveled hosts speak Spanish. Children over 12 welcome.

Palmer's Chart House

Hosts: Don and Majean Palmer
Rooms: 2 (PB) $60-80
Full Breakfast
Credit Cards: None
Notes: 2, 5, 7, 8, 10, 11, 12

GIG HARBOR

Rosedale Bed & Breakfast

7714 Ray Nash Drive Northwest, 98335
(253) 851-5420
E-mail: contactus@rosedalebnb.com
www.rosedalebnb.com

Let your cares slip away when you arrive at Rosedale B&B. We are located on a quiet inlet of Puget Sound. Watch the tides rise and ebb, herons take wing, and sea otters pop their heads up to peer at you. Stroll through our gardens, or read and relax by our fireplaces. The sunsets from our hot tub are spectacular. TVs/VCRs in all rooms, complementary videos, Jacuzzi tub, games, puzzles, guest library.

Hosts: Tom and Laura Yarborough
Rooms: 3 (PB) $115-145
Full Breakfast
Credit Cards: A, B, C
Notes: 2, 5, 8, 9, 10

GREENBANK

Guest House Cottages

24371 SR 525, 98253
phone/fax: (360) 678-3115
E-mail: guesthse@whidbey.net
www.whidbey.net/logcottages

Discover privacy, peace, and pampering in each of our six individually designed cottages in Greenbank, Whidbey Island. (Four of the cottages are log houses.) Each cottage has a private setting on 25 acres of island greenery, and features personal Jacuzzis, fireplaces, kitchens, and TV/VCRs. More than 500 complimentary movies, an outdoor swimming pool, and a hot tub make for a relaxing retreat for two.

Hosts: Don and MaryJane Creger
Rooms: 6 (PB) $125-295
Continental Breakfast
Credit Cards: A, B, C, D
Notes: 2, 5, 9, 10, 12

NOTES: Credit cards accepted: A Master Card; B Visa; C American Express; D Discover; E Diners Club; F Other; 2 Personal checks accepted; 3 Lunch available; 4 Dinner available; 5 Open all year;

LA CONNER

Benson Farmstead
Bed & Breakfast

10113 Avon-Allen Road, Bow, 98232
(360) 757-0578; (800) 441-9814

The Benson Farmstead is a beautiful, restored farmhouse located just minutes from the Skagit Valley, tulip fields, the historic town of La Conner, and ferries to the San Juan Islands. The Bensons are a friendly couple who serve homemade desserts in the evening, and a wonderful breakfast. They have filled their home with charming antiques, old quilts, and curios from their Scandinavian heritage. The extensive yard features an English garden, and the fields beyond are home to trumpeter swans.

Hosts: Jerry and Sharon Benson
Rooms: 4 (PB) $80-90
Full Breakfast
Credit Cards: A, B
Notes: 2, 5, 7, 8, 9, 10, 11

LEAVENWORTH

Bosch Gärten
Bed & Breakfast

9846 Dye Road, 98826
(509) 548-6900; (800) 535-0069
fax: (509) 548-3610
E-mail: innkeeper@nwi.net
www.boschgarten.com

Here at one of Leavenworth's newest B&Bs, you will find quiet elegance and warm hospitality with great mountain and garden views, spacious rooms with king beds, private baths, and cable TV. Full breakfasts feature local fruits and homemade fare; special dietary needs considered. Walk to unique Bavarian Village with many shops and restaurants. Enjoy cultural events, festivals, and popular summer theater productions. Season activities: hiking, river rafting, swimming, tennis, golf, fishing, downhill and cross-country skiing, snowshoeing, sledding, snowmobiling, and sleigh rides. Amenities include viewing decks, a Japanese gazebo with hot tub, guest living room, library, and mountain bikes. Children 12 and over welcome. No pets allowed. Two-night minimum stay required most weekends.

Hosts: Georgeanne and Denny Nichols
Rooms: 3 (PB) $102-130
Full Breakfast
Credit Cards: A, B, D
Notes: 2, 5, 7, 8, 9, 10, 11

Run of the River

P.O. Box 285, 98826
(509) 548-7171; (800) 288-6491
fax: (509) 548-7547
E-mail: info@runoftheriver.com
www.runoftheriver.com

Imagine the quintessential Northwest log B&B inn. Your suite, spacious and luxurious with sitting areas and private deck space, features handcrafted log king bed, linens of the highest quality, Jacuzzi tubs, and fireplaces surrounded by river rock. Extra touches set the tone for romance and reconnection, all designed to pamper and invigorate. From your room's log porch swing, view the Icicle River, surrounding bird refuge, and the Cascade peaks, appropriately named the Enchantments. To explore the Icicle

Valley, get off the beaten path with hiking, biking, and driving guides written just for your by the innkeepers, avid bikers and hikers. Take a spin on complimentary mountain bikes or a cruise on our new Cannondale tandem. Fun! A hearty Northwest breakfast sets the day in motion. The inn is an ideal base for side trips to Winthrop, Lake Chelan, and Gran Coulee. Very quiet, relaxing, and smoke-free. The perfect spot for a Northwest adventure.

Hosts: Monty and Karen Turner
Rooms: 6 (PB) $205-245
Full Breakfast
Credit Cards: A, B, D
Notes: 2, 5, 8, 9, 10, 11

LOPEZ ISLAND

Aleck Bay Inn

45 Finch Lane, 98261
(360) 468-3666
E-mail: abi@interisland.net
www.interisland.net/abi/abi.html

Aleck Bay Inn provides the luxurious, quiet, and personal care needed for special events, a romantic getaway, or just a relaxing time by the fireplace. The coffee is always hot, the pastry ever-present. Repeatedly visited by national and state dignitaries. The inn hosts small weddings, business meetings, retreats, and church outings. Guests can walk our beaches, hike through original forests, enjoy the game room, and watch the wildlife. Near island churches, golf courses, and tennis courts. Kayak and bike rentals available. Special breakfasts are served in our lovely dining room

or in the solarium; they begin with fresh fruit and are followed by a large portion of gourmet selections. Breakfast piano concerts on weekends. Chinese and Spanish spoken.

Hosts: May and David Mendez
Rooms: 4 (PB) $99-179
Full Breakfast
Credit Cards: A, B, C, D, E
Notes: 2, 5, 8, 9, 10

Ingham Haus Bayside Bed & Breakfast

1874 Bayshore Road, 98261
phone/fax: (360) 468-3719
E-mail: bayside@rockisland.com

Ingham Haus Bayside B&B has a lovely waterfront location on a quiet, secluded peninsula at Fisherman Bay. Enjoy gorgeous sunrises and sunsets, abundant wildlife, whale-watching, bird-watching, beachcombing, hiking, boating, biking, or just quiet moments to refresh yourself. A sumptuous, expanded continental breakfast bar of island specialties, fruit, and baked goods are served each morning, al fresco weather permitting. Spectacular views of the San Juan Islands and Olympic mountains accompany the meal. The 1100-square foot suite with partial kitchen, and two-bedroom or single rooms have adjoining patios, and are available daily or weekly. Included is a library, pool table, bicycles, and canoe.

Hosts: Bill and Norma Ingham
Rooms: 2 (SB) $65-115
Continental Breakfast
Credit Cards: None
Notes: 2, 3, 5, 7, 8, 9, 10

OLYMPIA

Swantown Inn
Bed & Breakfast

1431 11th Avenue Southeast, 98501-2411
(360) 753-9123; fax: (360) 943-8047
E-mail: swantown@olywa.ne
www.olywa.net/swantown

Located in an elegant 1893 Victorian mansion in the heart of Olympia surrounded by three-quarters acre of garden, the Swantown Inn can be your headquarters for exploring the Puget Sound region or your refuge for a quiet retreat. Queen beds with cozy down comforters, private baths, beautiful views of the sunset over the capitol dome, an inviting gazebo, and gourmet breakfasts are some of the ingredients for a memorable visit.

Hosts: Ed and Lillian Peeples
Rooms: 4 (PB) $75-115
Full Breakfast
Credit Cards: A, B
Notes: 2, 5, 10, 12

ORCAS ISLAND

Buck Bay Farm
Bed & Breakfast

716 Point Lawrence Road, Olga, 98279
(360) 376-2908; (888) 422-2825
www.buckbayfarm.com

Buck Bay Farm is located on beautiful Orcas in the San Juan Islands of Washington State. Orcas is an idyllic vacation destination with lots of outdoor fun: hiking, biking, boating or kayaking, whale-watching, golf, fishing, and much more. The B&B is a turn-of-the-century-style farmhouse.

A warm welcome and hearty, home-style breakfast await you.

Rooms: 5 (4 PB; 1 SB) $90-135
Full Breakfast
Credit Cards: A, B, C, D
Notes: 2, 5, 7, 8, 9, 10

Truffle House and Cottage
Bed & Breakfast

2098 Deer Harbor Road, Eastbound, 98245
(360) 376-2766; (877) 248-7833
fax: (360) 376-2766
E-mail: trufflehouse@interisland.net
www.interisland.net/truffleB&B

Contemporary setting on two rural acres, Truffle House B&B provides spectacular marine views from upstairs bedrooms and studio cottage. Private view balconies. Livingroom and library with satellite TV/VCR, movies, books, games. Hearty breakfast served in your room, on your balcony, or main deck. On Orcas Island enjoy whale watching cruises, kyaking, and hiking in the state's fourth largest state park. Sensible rates, seasonal discounts, and gift certificates available.

Hosts: Ray and Karen Brown
Rooms: 3 (PB) $85-115
Full Breakfast
Credit Cards: None
Notes: 2, 5, 7, 8, 10

Turtleback Farm Inn

1981 Crow Valley Road, Eastsound, 98245
(360) 376-4914; (800) 376-4914
fax: (360) 376-5329
E-mail: turtleback@interisland.net
www.turtlebackinn.com

Turtleback Farm Inn is noted for detail-perfect restoration, elegantly

---

comfortable and spotless rooms, a glorious setting, and award-winning breakfasts. You will be made welcome and pampered by the warm hospitality of Bill and Susan Fletcher and their staff. Orcas Island is a haven for anyone who enjoys spectacular scenery, varied outdoor activities, unique shopping, and superb food. As spring turns to summer, the warm days encourage your enjoyment of nature at its best. Flowers are in full bloom; birds flutter; whales, seals, and porpoises coast lazily through the shimmering waters of the sound. After a day of hiking, fishing, biking, kayaking, sailing, windsurfing, or just reading by our pond, return to Turtleback for a relaxing soak in your private bath, or a sherry on the deck overlooking the valley below. After a tasty dinner at one of the island's fine restaurants and perhaps a performance at the Orcas Center, guests can snuggle under a custom-made woolen comforter and doze off with visions of the delicious breakfast awaiting them in the morning.

Hosts: William and Susan C. Fletcher
Rooms: 11 (PB) $80-225
Full Breakfast
Credit Cards: A, B, D
Notes: 2, 3, 5, 7, 8, 9, 10, 12

PORT ANGELES

Five Seasons
Bed & Breakfast Inn

1006 South Lincoln Street, 98362
(360) 452-8248; (800) 708-0777
fax: (360) 417-0465
E-mail: info@seasons.com
www.seasons.com

Glorious, estate-like gardens surround this historic inn filled with the ambience and romance of the 1920s. Whirlpool or soaking tubs, balconies with water and mountain views. Artfully presented, gourmet candlelight breakfasts. Olympic National Park and the Victoria ferry are five minutes away. Pleasant memories are our speciality! "Best Places to Kiss;" "Best Places to Stay."

Hosts: Jan and Bob
Rooms: 5 (PB) $79-135
Full Breakfast
Credit Cards: A, B, C, D
Notes: 5, 8, 9, 10, 11, 12

PORT TOWNSEND

Ann Starrett Mansion
1889 Victorian
Bed & Breakfast Inn

744 Clay Street, 98368
(360) 385-3205; (800) 321-0644
fax: (360) 385-2976
E-mail: edel@starrettmansion.com
www.starrettmansion.com

A destination with a sense of history is a vacation with "romance." The 1889 mansion was built as a wedding gift. Authentic antiques and ambience will take you back to a gentler time. The inn won a National Trust for Historic Preservation "Great American Home Award." The lovely views and scrumptious breakfast will make you want to stay forever.

Hosts: Bob and Edel Sokol
Rooms: 11 (PB) $105-225
Full Breakfast
Credit Cards: A, B, C, D
Notes: 2, 5, 7, 8, 9, 10, 11, 12

NOTES: Credit cards accepted: A Master Card; B Visa; C American Express; D Discover; E Diners Club; F Other; 2 Personal checks accepted; 3 Lunch available; 4 Dinner available; 5 Open all year;

Baker House
Bed & Breakfast

905 Franklin Street, 98368
phone/fax: (360) 385-6673; (800) 240-0725
E-mail: hnjherrington@olympus.net

Ours is an 1898 home located in Port Townsend, Washington, one of three Victorian Seaports in America. You can leave your car at our B&B and walk three blocks to the waterfront. Our location provides gorgeous views of bays, inlets, and islands. We have four guest bedrooms, and options include private and shared baths. Breakfast is a scrumptious, three-course experience. Ours is a nonsmoking, adult-only environment. Bedrooms are equipped with Hunter ceiling fans.

Hosts: Herb and Jean Herrington
Rooms: 4 (3 PB; 1 SB) $75-85
Full Breakfast
Credit Cards: A, B
Notes: 5, 10

SEATTLE

Hill House
Bed & Breakfast

1113 East John Street, 98102
(206) 720-7161; (800) 720-7161
fax: (206) 323-0772
E-mail: visitus@seattlebnb.com
www.seattlebnb.com

This 1903 Victorian is just a 15-minute walk from downtown. It features superb gourmet breakfasts served on china and crystal, and offers seven rooms, tastefully appointed with antiques. All rooms have queen beds with down comforters and cotton sheets, fresh flowers, handmade soaps, and bath robes. Walk to numerous shops and restaurants. Located a half mile from downtown attractions such as the Convention Center and Pike Place Market. Close to transportation and off-street parking. AAA 3-diamond, *Fodors*, Seattle's "Best Places, Best Places to Kiss Northwest."

Hosts: Herman and Alea Foster
Rooms: 7 (5 PB; 2 SB) $75-165
Full Breakfast
Credit Cards: A, B, C, D, E
Notes: 5, 8, 9, 10

Hudgens Haven

9313 190 Southwest, Edmonds, 98020
(425) 776-2202; E-mail: booboona3@pol.net

Edmonds is a waterfront community on Puget Sound. Hudgens Haven is furnished with colonial antiques; large guest room has queen-size bed, two chairs, one rocker, private bath, and den with TV. Large patio and garden. We are located in a quiet neighborhood with a striking view of Puget Sound and the Olympic Mountains. Excellents restaurants and shops are nearby.

Hosts: Edward and Lorna
Rooms: 1 (PB) $70-75
Full Breakfast
Credit Cards: None
Notes: 2, 5, 6, 9

Pioneer Square Hotel

77 Yesler Way, 98104-3401
(206) 340-1234; (800) 800-5514
fax: (206) 467-0707
E-mail: sales@pioneersquare.com
pioneersquare.com

---

6 Pets welcome; 7 Children welcome; 8 Tennis nearby; 9 Swimming nearby; 10 Golf nearby; 11 Skiing nearby; 12 May be booked through travel agent

An affordable small luxury boutique hotel located in the heart of Seattle's downtown waterfront Pioneer Square Historic District. Special Internet room rates from $99.00. "Best Value in Seattle"; Home of the Pioneer Square Saloon; rated as "Seattle Best Places."

Rooms: 75 (PB) $89-149
Continental Breakfast
Credit Cards: A, B, C, D, E
Notes: 3, 4, 5, 7, 12

SOUTH BEND

Maring's Courthouse Hill Bed & Breakfast

602 West 2nd Street, P.O. Box 34, 98586
(360) 875-6519; (800) 875-6519
E-mail: maringbb@willapabay.org
www.willapabay.org/~maringbb

An 1892 church, this B&B is now a historic home with tasteful décor, offering river views, comfort, and warm hospitality in picturesque South Bend. Spacious guest rooms have queen/twin beds, cable television, and private baths. A full breakfast is served. Quiet location with wildlife. Situated 5 blocks off 101, a short walk from downtown.

Hosts: Ed and Frances Maring
Rooms: 3 (2 PB; 1 SB) $55-65
Full Breakfast
Credit Cards: A, B, C
Notes: 2, 5, 7, 8, 10

SOUTH CLE ELUM

Iron Horse Inn Bed & Breakfast

P.O. Box 629, 98943
(509) 674-5939; (800) 22TWAIN
E-mail: maryp@cleelum.com
www.ironhorseinnbb.com

Iron Horse Inn

Former 1909 Milwaukee Railroad Crew Hotel, now offering eight bright and airy rooms ranging from economical to exquisite, and including two genuine cabooses and a bridal suite with jetted tub. On the National Register, the inn has a museum-like atmosphere with an extensive collection of railroad memorabilia and artifacts. Nestled in the Cascade Mountain foothills, the house is close to cross-country skiing, hiking, biking, rafting, horseback riding, fishing, and fine dining. Only 90 minutes east of Seattle.

Hosts: Mary and Doug Pittis
Rooms: 10 (6 PB; 4 SB) $70-135
Full Breakfast
Credit Cards: A, B
Notes: 2, 5, 7, 10, 11

NOTES: Credit cards accepted: A Master Card; B Visa; C American Express; D Discover; E Diners Club; F Other; 2 Personal checks accepted; 3 Lunch available; 4 Dinner available; 5 Open all year;

VANCOUVER

Vintage Inn
Bed & Breakfast

310 West 11th Street, 98660
(360) 693-6635; (888) 693-6635
E-mail: info@vintage-inn.com
www.vintage-inn.com

Hospitality plus! One of Vancouver's original mansions built in 1903 in the heart of downtown, with elegant antiques throughout. On the National Historic Register. Large rooms with comfortable queen beds. Bountiful breakfasts. Fine restaurants, antique shops, theaters, and art galleries-all within walking distance. Fort Vancouver National Historic site seven blocks away. Easy freeway access. Fifteen minutes from downtown Portland, Oregon, and airport. No smoking, pets, or alcohol.

Hosts: Mike and Doris Hale
Rooms: 4 (SB) $89
Full Breakfast
Credit Cards: A, B
Notes: 2, 5, 7

WHIDBEY ISLAND

Cliff House & Cottage

727 Windmill Drive, Freeland, 98249
(330) 321-1566; E-mail: wink@whidbey.com
www.cliffhouse.net

On beautiful Whidbey Island, the stunning, award winning Cliff House or Gnome-like cottage. Each is yours alone in a lushly forested, waterfront hideaway with miles of driftwood beach. Unwind in luxurious seclusion.

Sumptuous feather beds, fireplaces, kitchens, TVs/VCRs, CDs, video library. Share your forest and sea retreat with deer, blue heron, racoons, squirrels, and a resident pair of nesting bald eagles, maybe even a pod of orcas! Welcome to a true oasis on this spectacular meeting of land and sea.

Hosts: Peggy Moore and Walter O' Toole
Rooms: 2 (PB) $185-450
Credit Cards: None
Notes: 2, 5, 7, 10

YAKIMA

Apple Country
Bed & Breakfast

4561 Old Naches Highway, Yakima-Naches
    98937
phone/fax: (509) 965-0344
E-mail: apple@yvn.com
www.bed&breakfastchanel.com

Warm, friendly hosts welcome you to this relaxed country atmosphere. Our remodeled 1911 farmhouse is nestled in the heart of the Yakim-Nache Valley on a working ranch. Take in the sweeping view of the valley's orchards from your spacious bedroom decorated in new and antique furniture, or garden room with private patio, queen bed, and private bath. A full luscious breakfast is served each morning. Easy access from Highway 12.

Hosts: Shirley and Mark Robert
Rooms: 2 (PB) $55-90
Full Breakfast
Credit Cards: A, B, C
Notes: 2, 5, 6, 8, 9, 10, 11

---

6 Pets welcome; 7 Children welcome; 8 Tennis nearby; 9 Swimming nearby; 10 Golf nearby; 11 Skiing nearby; 12 May be booked through travel agent

WEST VIRGINIA

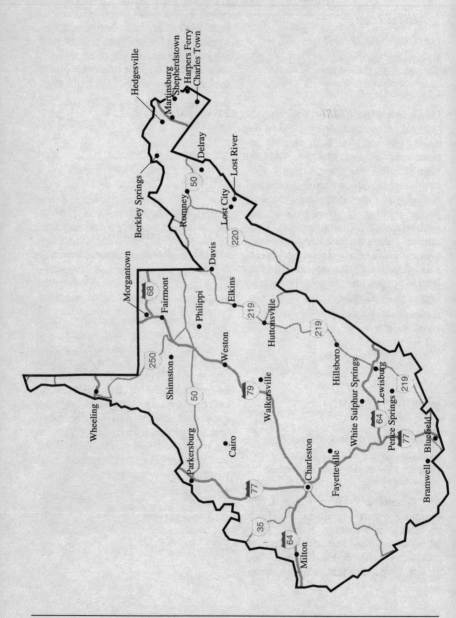

NOTES: Credit cards accepted: A Master Card; B Visa; C American Express; D Discover; E Diners Club; F Other; 2 Personal checks accepted; 3 Lunch available; 4 Dinner available; 5 Open all year;

West Virginia

BLUEFIELD

Country Chalet
Bed & Breakfast

Route 1, Box 176B, 24701
(304) 487-2120; (866) 240-8455
E-mail: maxnshar@countrychalet.com
www.countrychalet.com

Conveniently located on Route 20 between Bluefield and Princeton, the Country Chalet is surrounded by nature. The cedar shake A-frame provides a cozy, casual atmosphere sure to help busy travelers and business folks relax. Read by the large stone fireplace in the A-room with 24-foot ceiling and windowed wall, sun on the deck, stroll around the country-landscaped yard, visit the fish pond, or snooze on the shaded porch. Sharon's famous sourdough bread is the specialty of the house, and the glorious spring-to-fall flower garden is a specialty from God. Two bedrooms on the second floor are simply, yet tastefully furnished in a country motif. The queen Country Garden Room may be rented with private bath; or a party of four in two bedrooms may share the carpeted, windowed bath. A microwave, mini-fridge, phone, piano, and table games are provided. We provide a smoke-and alcohol-free environment.

Hosts: Max and Sharon Hudson
Rooms: 2 (1 PB; 1 SB) $60-70
Full Breakfast
Credit Cards: A, B
Notes: 2, 4, 5, 7, 8, 9, 10, 11

CAIRO

Log House
Homestead, L L C

Route 1, Box 223b, 26337
(304) 628-3249
E-mail: loghouse@ruralnet.org
members.ruralnet.org/loghousehomestead/
    index.htm

Step back in time at Log House Homestead. We offer two to five people at a time country seclusion with 1820s style and period furnishings, but 21st-century amenities. The whole two-story hewn log house is yours—sit in porch rockers overlooking the pond or cozy up to the stone fireplace. After a hearty breakfast, hike the North Bend Rail Trail just a quarter mile away. No phone or TV but lots of books and games. It's a museum where you stay! Whole house rented

Log House

as a unit; there are two bedrooms, a half bath, and one full bath with Jacuzzi. Well behaved children over 12 welcome. Innkeepers live adjacent to the property. Members of Mountain State Association of Bed & Breakfasts.

Hosts: Martha and Dick Hartley
Rooms: 2 (PB) $79-119
Full Breakfast
Credit Cards: A, B
Notes: 2, 5, 7, 8, 9, 10

CHARLESTON

Historic Charleston Bed & Breakfast

110 Elizabeth Street, 25311
(304) 345-8156; 877-4WVBNBS
fax: (304) 342-1572
E-mail: bed2brkst@aol.com
www.westvirginiabandb.com

This elegant, 1907 French country home is located within walking distance of the state capitol and cultural center. Rooms with queen beds and private baths. Relax in the den by the fire and when weather permits, enjoy the swing on the front porch. A full breakfast is served. We spoil our guests. Wedding couples are served breakfast in their suite. Close to hiking, biking, swimming, white-water rafting, and skiing. Come, enjoy the capital city with us!

Hosts: Bob and Jean Lambert
Rooms: 3 (PB) $75-95
Full Breakfast
Credit Cards: A, B, C
Notes: 2, 5, 7, 8, 9, 10

K.K.C. Innsitting Service

105 Ashby Avenue, 25314
(304) 342-8675
E-mail: kkcanonico@juno.com

"Getting away" for a true vacation is a common problem for B&B owners. The responsibilities of running a B&B are great and cannot be taken on by just anyone. For over five years I have offered the professional and quality service of an experienced innsitter. I will responsibly and hospitably run your B&B, using your guidelines and procedures, in the manner that has built its reputation. Member of Mountain State Association of B&Bs

CHARLES TOWN/ HARPERS FERRY

Washington House Inn Bed & Breakfast

216 South George Street, Charles Town, 25414
(304) 725-7923; (800) 297-6957
fax: (304) 728-5150
E-mail: emakus@washingtonhouseinnwv.com
www.washingtonhouseinnwv.com

In charming Colonial Charles Town, nestled in the Blue Ridge Mountains where the Shenandoah and Potomac Rivers meet, the Washington House Inn is a magnificent 1899 Victorian built at the turn of the centruy by descendants of President George Washington. The Inn welcomes and delights leisure and business travelers. "The Best of Everything" ". . .sets a benchmark for all other B&Bs" Come see us; you'll be glad you did! Mem-

---

NOTES: Credit cards accepted: A Master Card; B Visa; C American Express; D Discover; E Diners Club; F Other; 2 Personal checks accepted; 3 Lunch available; 4 Dinner available; 5 Open all year;

ber of the Mountain State Association of Bed & Breakfasts.

Hosts: Mel and Nina Vogel
Rooms: 7 (PB) $99-150
Full Breakfast
Credit Cards: A, B, C, D
Notes: 2, 5, 8, 9, 10, 12

DAVIS

Bright Morning Inn

P.O. Box 576, 26260
phone/fax: (304) 259-5119
E-mail: brightmorninginn@yahoo.com
www.brightmorninginn.com

Member of Mountain State Association Bed & Breakfasts.

Host: Susan Moore

Meyer House Bed & Breakfast

3rd Street & Thomas Avenue, P.O. Box 773, 26260
phone/fax: (304) 259-5451
E-mail: meyerhousebandb@mountain.net
www.meyerhousebandb.com

Meyer House B&B is a Victorian circa 1885 home located on top of a mountain in the Allegheny Mountain region in Davis, West Virginia. Meyer House is open year-round and offers three charming guest rooms, all with private baths, full served breakfast, and a smoke-free environment where families are always welcome. Meyer House is convenient to numerous points of interest, which are highlighted on our web site. Come join us! Member of Mountain State Association of Bed & Breakfasts.

Hosts: The Chamberlains
Rooms: 3 (PB) $75-95
Full Breakfast
Credit Cards: None
Notes: 2, 5, 7, 10, 11

DELRAY

The Menagerie at Delray

P.O. Box 171, Lick Run Road, 26714
(304) 496-8942; www.bedandbrunch.com

Private mountain getaway, 137 acres, and your choice of the farmhouse (sleeps 8) or the Glasshouse (sleeps 4). Good food, good beds, good people, and your own good time. Campfire ring and BBQ grill, peace and quiet. Member of Mountain State Association of Bed & Breakfasts.

Hosts: Kim McCracken
Rooms: 6 (2 PB; 4 SB) $65-95
Full Breakfast
Credit Cards: A, B
Notes: 2, 3, 4, 5, 7, 9

ELKINS

The Post House Bed & Breakfast

306 Robert E. Lee Avenue, 26241
(304) 636-1792
E-mail: joanbarlow@aol.com

The Post House B&B is a 1930s, Americana-style dwelling furnished with quality furniture of that period: black walnut, curly maple, and cherry. We are in the heart of the mountains where temperatures are 10 degrees cooler. Cultural and recreational facil-

---

6 Pets welcome; 7 Children welcome; 8 Tennis nearby; 9 Swimming nearby; 10 Golf nearby; 11 Skiing nearby; 12 May be booked through travel agent

ities abound at Davis & Elkins College, and the Monongahelia Forest.

Host: Jo Ann Post Barlow
Rooms: 5 (2 PB; 3 SB) $65
Continental Breakfast
Credit Cards: None
Notes: 2, 7, 9, 11

Rambling Rose Bed & Breakfast

301 Marro Drive, 26241
(304) 636-1790
E-mail: ramblingrosebb@neumedia.net
www.virtualcities.com

Get away from the noise and traffic of daily life. Relax in the homey atmosphere of the Rambling Rose B&B and join us for a full country breakfast. Dine in the formal dining room or join Rose in her country kitchen, central to her home. There are four guest bedrooms, each share two full baths, one featuring a whirlpool tub. Located only two blocks from downtown, guests can take a walking tour of Elkins, enjoy festivals at the College and Park, or go sight-seeing, biking, or antiquing in the surrounding countryside. Member of Mountain State Association of B&Bs.

Hosts: Richard and Rose Trochlil
Rooms: 4 (SB) $65-85
Full Breakfast
Credit Cards: None
Notes: 2, 3, 5, 7, 8, 9, 10, 11

Tunnel Mountain Bed & Breakfast

R.R. 1 Box 59-1, 26241-9711
(304) 636-1684; (888) 211-9123
bbonline.com/wv/tunnel

Charming three-story fieldstone home nestled on five private, wooded acres surrounded by scenic peaks, lush forests, and sparkling rivers. Finished in pine and rare wormy chestnut woodwork. Tastefully decorated with antiques, collectibles, and crafts. Near Monongahela National Forest, Blackwater Falls, Seneca Rocks, Spruce Knob, Dolly Sods, Cass Railroad, Canaan Valley, Timberline, snowshoe, cross country/downhill skiing, historic sites, festivals, and shops. Member of Mountain State Association of Bed & Breakfasts.

Hosts: Anne and Paul Beardslee
Rooms: 3 (PB) $75-85
Full Breakfast
Credit Cards: None
Notes: 2, 5, 8, 9, 10, 11

FAIRMONT

Acacia House Bed & Breakfast

158 Locust Avenue, 26554
(304) 367-1000; (888) 269-9541
E-mail: acacia@acaciahousewv.com
www.acaciahousewv.com

Shop on the premises for antiques and collectibles. Five minutes from Fairmont State College and Fairmont Hospital; 30 minutes from WVU stadium and hospital. Location: I-79, Exit 137, Route 310 to Fairmont Avenue, right on Fourth Street, right to Locust Avenue, a quarter mile on the right.

Hosts: George and Kathy Sprowls
Rooms: 4 (2 PB; 2 SB) $60-70
Full Breakfast
Credit Cards: A, B, C, D
Notes: 5, 12

NOTES: Credit cards accepted: A Master Card; B Visa; C American Express; D Discover; E Diners Club; F Other; 2 Personal checks accepted; 3 Lunch available; 4 Dinner available; 5 Open all year;

Acacia House

FAYETTEVILLE

Cozy Cottage

302 West Maple Avenue, P.O. Box 390, 25840
phone/fax: (304) 574-0134

Provides a private cottage atmosphere on the McIntosh-McCaleb estate, circa 1893. Sleeps four; has kitchen, bath, shower, TV, and air-conditioning. Continental breakfast provided in cottage. Near restaurants and all area attractions. Member of Mountain State Association of Bed & Breakfasts.

Hosts: Kenneth and Lita Eskew
Rooms: 1 (PB) $75-85
Continental Breakfast
Credit Cards: None
Notes: 2, 9, 10

Wisteria House

147 South Court Street, 25840-1525
phone/fax: (304) 574-3678

Enjoy "Southern hospitality" at its best. Three air-conditioned bedrooms, complimentary breakfast. Located in historic Fayetteville. Minutes to New River Gorge Bridge, outdoor adventures, sightseeing, fabulous restaurants, shopping, and Historic Fayette Theatre. Member of Mountain State Association of Bed & Breakfasts.

Rooms: 3 (SB) $65-85
Full Breakfast
Credit Cards: A, B
Notes: 10

HEDGESVILLE

The Farmhouse on Tomahawk Run

1828 Tomahawk Run Road, 25427
phone/fax: (304) 754-7350; (888) 266-9516
E-mail: tomahawk@intrepid.net
www.tomahawkrun.com

Nine miles west of I-81 between Martinsburg and Berkeley Springs. The Farmhouse, built during the Civil War, stands beside the Springhouse (on the National Register of Historic Places) and the foundation of the old 1740-era log cabin. Nestled in a se-

The Farmhouse

---

6 Pets welcome; 7 Children welcome; 8 Tennis nearby; 9 Swimming nearby; 10 Golf nearby; 11 Skiing nearby; 12 May be booked through travel agent

cluded valley by a meandering stream, it is surrounded by 280 acres of woods, hills, and meadows with walking paths. A stone fireplace in the large gathering room has a roaring log fire on cold evenings. A wraparound porch with rocking chairs and Jacuzzi melt away your stress, and a bountiful breakfast is served by candlelight. In addition to B&B guests, small group retreats are hosted for up to 16 persons. The hosts are also certified as leaders of marriage enrichment. Member of Mountain State Association of Bed & Breakfasts.

Hosts: Judy and Hugh Erskine
Rooms: 5 (PB) $85-140
Full Breakfast
Credit Cards: A, B, C, D, E
Notes: 2, 5, 7, 10, 12

HUTTONSVILLE

Hutton House
Bed & Breakfast

Routes 250 & 219, P.O. Box 88, 26273
phone/fax: (304) 335-6701; (800) 234-6701
E-mail: hutton@wvbandb.com
www.wvbandb.com

Welcome to our three-story Queen Anne Victorian home listed on the National Register of Historic Places, conveniently located between Elkins and Snowshoe Resort. Also near national and state forests, fishing, PGA tournament golf, train excursions into the wilderness, and Civil War and other historic sites. "Vacation" breakfasts served at your leisure. Everyone is welcome.

Hosts: Dean Ahren and Loretta Murray
Rooms: 6 (PB) $75-85

Full Breakfast
Credit Cards: A, B
Notes: 2, 5, 7, 10, 11, 12

MORGANTOWN

Fieldcrest Manor
Bed & Breakfast

1440 Stewartstown Road, 26505-2949
(304) 599-2686; (866) 599-2686
fax: (304) 599-3796
E-mail: innkeeper@fieldcrestmanor.com
www.fieldcrestmanor.com

Situated on five beautiful acres, Fieldcrest Manor offers the finest in overnight accommodations. With its beautifully manicured lawns and romantic natural landscapes, Fieldcrest is the perfect backdrop for relaxation, romance, or reconnecting with friends and family. Experience the affordable elegance waiting for you. We look forward to making your stay with us a memorable one. Member of Mountain State Association of Bed & Breakfasts.

Host: Sarah Lough
Rooms: 5 (PB) $90.
Full Breakfast
Credit Cards: A, B, C
Notes: 2, 5, 10, 11

PARKERSBURG

Avery-Savage House

420 13th Street, 26101
(304) 422-9820; fax: (304) 485-1911
E-mail: sharon@averysavagehouse.com
averysavagehouse.com

This beautiful, Victorian B&B welcomes you in 19th-century style with

---

NOTES: Credit cards accepted: A Master Card; B Visa; C American Express; D Discover; E Diners Club; F Other; 2 Personal checks accepted; 3 Lunch available; 4 Dinner available; 5 Open all year;

Avery-Savage House

West Virginia warmth. Engaging gardens, a gracious gazebo, and memorable morning meals are the hallmarks of our historic home. Listed on the National Register of Historic places, the three-story, stone and masonry house has been lovingly restored and decorated for comfort and charm. There are four guest rooms, each with original woodwork and hardwood floors. All guest rooms have private baths. Member of Mountain State Association of Bed & Breakfasts.

Host: Sharon Mace
Rooms: 4 (PB) $75-105
Continental Breakfast
Credit Cards: A, B, C, D
Notes: 2, 5, 8, 9, 10, 12

PENCE SPRINGS

Historic Pence Springs Grand Hotel

P.O. Box 90, 24962
(304) 445-2606; (800) 826-1829
fax: (304) 445-2204
E-mail: pencehotel@newwave.net
wvweb.com/www/pence_springs_hotel

Known as the Grand Hotel, this National Register inn is one of the historic mineral spas of the Virginias. A premier retreat from 1897 until the Great Depression, Pence Springs was the most popular and expensive hotel in West Virginia. This area has attracted visitors for over 200 years. From 1947 to 1985 Pence Springs was the State Prison for Women. Restoration began in 1986 and the Grand Hotel has come full circle. Pence Springs Hotel has attracted national attention in *Southern Living, Gourmet, Preservation News*, and *Goldenseal* magazines.

Rooms: 23 (15 PB; 8 SB) $75-110
Full Breakfast
Credit Cards: A, B, C, D
Notes: 2, 3, 4, 5, 6, 7, 9, 10, 11

SHINNSTON

Gillum House Bed & Breakfast

35 Walnut Street, 26431
(304) 592-0177; (888) 592-0177
fax: (304) 592-1882
E-mail: gillum@citynet.net
www.gillumhouse.com

Near I-79, in north-central West Virginia, the Gillum House is four blocks from the Ralph S. Larve West Fork River Trail, a level, scenic, 16-plus miles for biking, hiking, or horseback riding (stable facilities nearby). Tantalize your tastebuds with delicious, homemade, heart-healthy food (special diet needs accommodated). Origi-

6 Pets welcome; 7 Children welcome; 8 Tennis nearby; 9 Swimming nearby; 10 Golf nearby; 11 Skiing nearby; 12 May be booked through travel agent

nal woodwork and mantles in every room. Doll collection throughout the house. Packages available. Member: Mountainstate Association of Bed & Breakfasts.

Host: Kathleen A. Panek
Rooms: 3 (SB) $55-65
Full Breakfast
Credit Cards: A, B
Notes: 2, 5, 7, 9, 10

WALKERSVILLE

Stone Farm

Route 1, Box 36, 26447
(304) 452-8477
E-mail: sfbb@msys.net
www.msys.net/sfbb/

This restored 1910 farmhouse situated on 140 acres in the Mountain Lakes region is a step back to a slower pace and time. A time of gardening, canning, farming, or swinging on the porch. A mix of antique, not-so-old, and new in a pleasant blend. Enjoy hiking, reading, Jacuzzi, watching wildlife, or nearby attractions and activities. Escape the hectic demands of today's life.

Hosts: Lionel and Sandra Lilly
Rooms: 3 (SB) $60
Full Breakfast
Credit Cards: None
Notes: 2, 3, 4, 5, 7, 9, 10

WESTON

Ingeberg Acres Bed & Breakfast

Route 1, Box 245, V-4, 26452
(304) 269-2834 (phone/fax); (800) callWVA
E-mail: u1a00779@wvnvm.wvnet.edu
www.ingebergacres.com

A unique experience can be yours at this scenic, 450-acre horse and cattle farm. Ingeberg Acres is located in the heart of West Virginia, seven miles from Weston, overlooking its own private valley. Hiking, swimming, hunting, and fishing, or just relaxing can be the order of the day. Observe or participate in farm activities. Craft outlets and antique stores are nearby. Come enjoy the gardens, pool, and the friendly atmosphere. German spoken. We also provide boarding for horses in transit.

Hosts: John and Inge Mann
Rooms: 4 (1 PB; 3 SB) $59-80
Full Breakfast
Credit Cards: None
Notes: 2, 5, 6, 7, 9, 10

WHEELING

Bonnie Dwaine Bed & Breakfast

505 Wheeling Avenue, Glen Dale, 26038
(304) 854-7250; (800) 507-4569
fax: (304) 845-7256
E-mail: bonnie@bonnie-dwaine.com
www.bonnie-dwaine.com

Elegant romantic Victorian with all of the modern conveniences. Five guest rooms with private adjoining bathrooms, fireplaces, private phones, cable TVs, lap top connections, whirlpool tubs/showers. Gourmet breakfast weekends. The house has been professionally decorated with period furnishings and antiques. The home invites you to come inside. Relax and enjoy comfort warmth and charm in

---

NOTES: Credit cards accepted: A Master Card; B Visa; C American Express; D Discover; E Diners Club; F Other; 2 Personal checks accepted; 3 Lunch available; 4 Dinner available; 5 Open all year;

this late 1800s B&B. Member of
Mountain State Association of B&Bs

Hosts: Bonnie and Sid Grisell
Rooms: 5 (PB) $75-125
Continental Breakfast
Credit Cards: A, B, C, D, E
Notes: 2, 5, 8, 9, 10, 12

WISCONSIN

NOTES: Credit cards accepted: A Master Card; B Visa; C American Express; D Discover; E Diners
Club; F Other; 2 Personal checks accepted; 3 Lunch available; 4 Dinner available; 5 Open all year;

Wisconsin

Albany House

405 South Mill Street, 53502
(608) 862-3636; fax: (608) 862-1837
E-mail: innkeeper@albanyhouse.net
www.albanyhouse.net

Two park-like acres with flower gardens galore is the setting for this restored, 1908 three-story home. Furnished throughout with many antiques and collectibles, our bedrooms feature king and queen beds, feather duvets, and a master bedroom with a wooburning fireplace. Curl up on comfortable overstuffed seating with a good book from our large collection. After a hearty breakfast (homemade specialties include marmalade-filled muffins, classic cream scones, and iced cinnamon rolls), recover on the porch swing, stroll the grounds, or shoot a round of croquet before exploring the nearby Swiss and Amish communities. Hike or bike the Sugar River Trail or canoe the river. Smoke-free. A great reunion or retreat site. Gift certificates and customized gift baskets available. Children 10 and over welcome.

Hosts: Ken and Margie Stoup
Rooms: 6 (4 PB; 2 SB) $65-95
Full Breakfast
Credit Cards: A, B
Notes: 2, 5, 7, 8, 9, 10, 11

Oak Hill Manor Bed & Breakfast

401 East Main Street, P.O. Box 190, 53502
(608) 862-1400; fax: (608) 862-1403
E-mail: innkeeper@oakhillmanor.com
www.oakhillmanor.com

Step back in time in our 1908 manor home. Enjoy rich oak woodwork, gasoliers, period furnishings, and spacious, sunny bedrooms with queen beds. Choose a room with a fireplace, private porch, canopy bed, or claw-foot bathtub. Relax in our English country garden or read on the porch swing. Sumptuous breakfast. Canoe/fish on the Sugar River, golf/shop nearby; or ride/hike the Sugar River bike trail. Complimentary guest bikes. Inquire about the "ladies' mid-week special" (see website). Great for reunions/retreats. Smoke-free. Gift certificates available.

Hosts: Donna and Glen Rothe
Rooms: 4 (PB) $80-110
Full Breakfast
Credit Cards: A, B
Notes: 2, 5, 7, 8, 9, 10, 11

Amberwood Inn Bed & Breakfast

North 7136 Highway 42, 54201
(920) 487-3471
E-mail: innkeeper@amberwoodinn.com
www.amberwoodinn.com

---

6 Pets welcome; 7 Children welcome; 8 Tennis nearby; 9 Swimming nearby; 10 Golf nearby; 11 Skiing nearby; 12 May be booked through travel agent

Amberwood Inn

Come to Amberwood, a romantic country inn with five large, luxury waterfront suites located ten minutes from Door County. Enjoy our nearly three wooded acres, 300 feet of private Lake Michigan beach, sauna, in-room whirlpools, and spectacular breakfast. All suites offer individual lakefront deck, private bath, refrigerator, fireplace, fine antiques, and cable TV. Gift certificates available. Fall asleep to the sound of the waves; awaken to a sunrise over the water.

Hosts: Mark and Karen Rittle
Rooms: 6 (PB) $82-117
Full Breakfast
Credit Cards: A, B
Notes: 2, 5, 7, 8, 9, 10

ALMA

Gallery House

215 North Main Street, 54610
(608) 685-4975; fax: (608) 685-4977
E-mail: janbnb@nelson-tel.net
www.thegalleryhousebnb.com

The Gallery House is the oldest full standing building in Alma and listed on the National Historic Register. Our rooms are decorated in an English country manner, and boast numerous art works and historic photographs. Each of our three guest rooms have queen-size beds and private baths. Jan's gourmet breakfast and Jim's live entertainment is the highlight of any stay at the Gallery House, complimented by fresh ground coffee served strong and hot.

Hosts: Jim and Jan Furness
Rooms: 3 (PB) $85-105
Full Breakfast
Credit Cards: A, B
Notes: 2, 5, 8, 9, 10, 11

APPLETON

The Queen Anne Bed & Breakfast

837 East College Avenue, 54911
(888) 241-0419; www.bnbinns.com

The Queen Anne Bed & Breakfast is a Victorian home built circa 1895. We are located in the heart of downtown Appleton, two blocks from Lawrence University. We are 30 miles south of Greenbay and 100 miles north of Milwaukee. The Queen Anne is an intimate getaway where you can relax and enjoy a good night's sleep! Children 12 and over welcome.

Hosts: Tom and Emilie Sabol
Rooms: 4 (2 PB; 2 SB) $85-150
Full Breakfast
Credit Cards: A, B
Notes: 2, 5, 7, 9, 10

NOTES: Credit cards accepted: A Master Card; B Visa; C American Express; D Discover; E Diners Club; F Other; 2 Personal checks accepted; 3 Lunch available; 4 Dinner available; 5 Open all year;

BARABOO

Pinehaven Bed & Breakfast

E13083 Highway 33, 53913
(608) 356-3489; fax: (608) 356-0818
E-mail: pinehaven@baraboo.com
www.dells.com/pinehaven/

Located in a scenic valley with a small, private lake and Baraboo Bluffs in the background. The guest-rooms are distinctly different with wicker furniture and antiques, and queen and twin beds. Take a walk in this peaceful country setting. Area activities include Devil's Lake State Park, Circus World Museum, Wisconsin Dells, and ski resorts. Ask about our private guest cottage. No pets. No smoking. Gift certificates available. Closed in March. Children over 5 years welcome.

Hosts: Lyle and Marge Getschman
Rooms: 4 (PB); 1 cottage (PB) $89-135
Full Breakfast
Credit Cards: A, B
Notes: 2, 5, 7, 8, 9, 10, 11

BELLEVILLE

Abendruh Bed & Breakfast Swisstyle

7019 Gehin Drive, 53508
(608) 424-3808

Experience B&B Swisstyle. This highly acclaimed Wisconsin B&B offers true Swiss charm and hospitality. The serenity of this retreat is one of many treasures that keep guests coming back. Spacious guest rooms are adorned with beautiful family heirlooms. The sitting room has a high cathedral ceiling and a cozy fireplace. An Abendruh breakfast is a perfect way to start a new day or end a peaceful stay.

Host: Mathilde Jaggi
Rooms: 2 (PB) $65-70
Full Breakfast
Credit Cards: None
Notes: 2, 5, 8, 9, 10, 11, 12

CABLE

Connors Bed & Breakfast

R.R. 1, Box 255, 54821-0255
(715) 798-3661; (800) 848-3932
fax: (715) 798-3663
E-mail: info@connorsbandb.com
www.connorsbandb.com

Conners B&B

Set deep in the heart of the Chequmegon National Forest, this 77-acre estate offers spacious, clean, quiet accommodations with the convenience of state highway frontage. Access to major ski and bike trails from our door. Great wildlife viewing, bird-watching, and hiking trails. Great restaurants and antique shops nearby. Rooms available with whirl-pools or fireplaces, or choose a private log cabin.Hosts: Mona and Alex Connors

Rooms: 4 (PB) $85-105
Full Breakfast
Credit Cards: A, B, C
Notes: 2, 5, 7, 10, 11, 12

CAMBRIDGE

Country Comforts Bed & Breakfast

2722 Highland Drive, 53523
(608) 423-3097; (877) 771-1277
fax: (608) 423-7743
E-mail: info@country-comforts.com
www.country-comforts.com

Relax in the peace and quiet of the country, or wander a mile into town to shop Cambridge's historic Main Street. Renovated 100-year-old family farmhouse offers comfortable living space, quiet sleeping accommodations, and private baths. Wheelchair accessible. Four acres of lawn and gardens. Located 15 miles east of Madison, Wisconsin. Nearby attractions include: Rowe Pottery, Fireside Dinner Theatre, Glacial-Drumlin Bicycle Trail, and Cam Rock Park hiking and cross-country ski trails.

Hosts: Marian Korth, Mim Jacobson
Rooms: 4 (PB) $99-169
Full Breakfast
Credit Cards: A, B, C, D
Notes: 2, 5, 7, 9, 11

CEDARBURG

Stagecoach Inn

W61 N520 Washington, 53012
(262) 375-0208; (800) 375-0208
fax: (262) 375-6170
www.stagecoach-inn-wi.com

Visit the Stagecoach Inn, a historically restored 1853 stone building. The Inn features 12 comfortable guest rooms, some with oversized whirlpools, fireplaces, and antiques. A hearty breakfast is included. Relax in the pub and enjoy complimentary wine; visit the chocolate shop. Located in the downtown historic district within walking distance of galleries,

Stagecoach Inn

restaurants, the winery, and specialty gift shops. The Stagecoach Inn: a destination for something special, and a memorable getaway.

Hosts: Liz and Brook Brown
Rooms: 12 (PB) $80-150
Continental Breakfast
Credit Cards: A, B, C, D, E
Notes: 2, 5, 8, 9, 10, 11

CHIPPEWA FALLS

McGilvray's Victorian Bed & Breakfast

312 West Columbia Street, 54729
(715) 720-1600
E-mail: melanie@mcgilvraysbb.com
www.mcgilvraysbb.com

Experience the Midwest in this friendly, historic city. Once a booming lumber town, Chippewa Falls has many beautiful homes built at the turn of the century. Warm hospitality and a scrumptious breakfast are top priorities in this beautifully restored B&B. Relax by the fireplace on a chilly evening or enjoy one of the four porches on a summer day. There is much to do in the area: antiquing, biking, fishing, boating, skiing, and challenging golf courses. Children over 12 welcome.

Host: Melanie J. Berg
Rooms: 3 (PB) $69-99
Full Breakfast
Credit Cards: None
Notes: 2, 5, 7, 8, 9, 10, 11

CRANDON

Courthouse Square Bed & Breakfast

210 East Polk Street, 54520
(715) 478-2549; (888) 235-1665
fax: (715) 478-2753
E-mail: chousebb@newnorth.net
www.courthousesquarebb.com

Guests frequently comment about the peace and tranquillity of the setting. Enjoy birds and squirrels at the many benches placed throughout the flower

Courthouse Square

and herb gardens, or stroll down the hill to the lake through the forget-me-nots and view the wildlife. The *Rhinelander Daily News* wrote: "Traditional hospitality is emphasized at Courthouse Square Bed and Breakfast, and it's evident from the moment you enter this delightful home where tranquillity and peace abound. You will no doubt smell something delicious baking in Bess's kitchen as gourmet cooking is one of her specialties." Forty minutes from Northland Baptist Bible College. Churches are within walking distance. Inquire about children.

Hosts: Les and Bess Aho
Rooms: 3 (1 PB; 2 SB) $60-70
Full Breakfast
Credit Cards: C
Notes: 2, 5, 8, 9, 10, 11, 12

DOOR COUNTY

Also see Gills Rock and Sturgeon Bay.

Wagon Trail Resort

1041 County Road 22, Ellison Bay, 54210
(920) 854-2385; (800) 999-2466
fax: (920) 854-5278

---

6 Pets welcome; 7 Children welcome; 8 Tennis nearby; 9 Swimming nearby; 10 Golf nearby; 11 Skiing nearby; 12 May be booked through travel agent

E-mail: frontdesk@wagontrail.com
www.wagontrail.com

As you step into our pristine peaceful setting, feel the cares of life melt away. Relax and rejuvenate yourself in our whirlpool rooms, or listen to a crackling fire in our fieldstone fireplace.

Rooms: 110 (PB) $69-235
Credit Cards: A, B, D
Notes: 2, 3, 4, 5, 7, 8, 9, 10, 11

EAU CLAIRE

The Atrium Bed & Breakfast

5572 Prill Road, 54701-8121
(715) 833-9045; (888) 773-0094
fax: (715) 831-9783
E-mail: info@atriumbb.com
www.atriumbb.com

Unwind in the best of both worlds; relaxed seclusion on 15 wooded, creekside acres only minutes from downtown, shopping, and dining. Enjoy magnificent antique stained-glass windows. Hike the woodland paths along Otter Creek, or relax in the con-

The Atrium

servatory garden room with complimentary Wisconsin wines and cheeses. For your comfort, all of our guest rooms have private baths, queen-sized beds, TVs, CD players, and phones. Robes and hair dryers are provided for guest convenience.

Hosts: Celia and Dick Stoltz
Rooms: 4 (PB) $70-129
Full Breakfast
Credit Cards: A, B
Notes: 2, 5, 10, 11

Otter Creek Inn

Otter Creek

2536 Highway 12, P.O. Box 3183, 54702
(715) 832-2945; fax: (715) 832-4607
E-mail: info@ottercreekinn.net
www.ottercreekinn.net

At the Otter Creek Inn each antique-filled guest room has a double whirlpool, private bath, phone, air-conditioning, and cable TV. Our breakfast menu allows a choice of entrées and breakfast in bed! This spacious inn (more than 6,500 square feet) is a three-story English Tudor with country Victorian décor. Nestled on a wooded hill adjacent to, but high above, the Otter Creek, the inn is less than a mile from numerous restaurants and shops. Outdoor, in-ground heated swimming pool.

Hosts: Randy and Shelley Hansen
Rooms: 6 (PB) $85-175
Full Breakfast
Credit Cards: A, B, C, D, E, F
Notes: 2, 5, 8, 9, 10, 11

EXELAND

Shepherd's Loft Bed & Breakfast

166 North St. Road 40, 54835
(715) 943-2317

Quiet, lovely log home on a Columbia sheep farm east of Wisconsin Blue Hills. Each guest room has a unique loft for reading, sleeping, or children's play. Families with children are welcome. In-house gift shop specializes in lovely sheepskin rugs, and sheep and wool-related gifts. "While you are with us may you find peace as you rest in the Shepherd's presence, and when you leave may you take with you a memory which will enrich your life."

Hosts: Lorene and Elwood Shrock
Rooms: 3 (1 PB; 2 SB) $45-55
Full Breakfast
Credit Cards: A, B
Notes: 2, 5, 7, 9, 11

FORT ATKINSON

The Lamp Post Inn

408 South Main Street, 53538
(920) 563-6561
www.thelamppostinn.com

We welcome you to the charm of our 126-year-old Victorian home filled with beautiful antiques. Five gramophones for your listening pleasure. For the modern, one of our baths features a large Jacuzzi. We are located seven blocks from the famous Fireside Playhouse. You come a stranger, but leave here a friend. No smoking.

Hosts: Debbie and Mike Rusch
Rooms: 3 (2 PB; 1 SB) $70-110
Full Breakfast
Credit Cards: None
Notes: 2, 5, 7, 8, 9, 10, 11

GILLS ROCK

Harbor House Inn

12666 State Highway 42, Ellison Bay, 54210
(920) 854-5196; fax: (920) 854-9717
www.door-county-inn.com

A 1904 Victorian B&B with a New Scandinavian country "wing" overlooking the quaint fishing harbor, bluffs, and sunsets. All rooms have private baths, air-conditioning, and TV. (Most have microwaves and refrigerators.) Two cottages are also available, one with a fireplace. The most recent addition is the lighthouse suite with whirlpool and fireplace.

Harbor House Inn

---

6 Pets welcome; 7 Children welcome; 8 Tennis nearby; 9 Swimming nearby; 10 Golf nearby; 11 Skiing nearby; 12 May be booked through travel agent

Enjoy the Inn's sauna, whirlpool, beach, and gazebo. Within walking distance of Ferry Shores and restaurants.

Hosts: David and Else Weborg
Rooms: 15 (PB) $65-175
Continental Breakfast
Credit Cards: A, B, C
Notes: 6, 7, 9, 10

HAZEL GREEN

Wisconsin House Stage Coach Inn

2105 East Main, 53811
(608) 854-2233; wisconsinhuse.com

Built as a stage coach inn in 1846, the inn now offers six rooms and two suites for your comfort. Join us for an evening's rest. Dine and be refreshed in the parlor, where General Grant spent many evenings with his friend Jefferson Crawford. Most conveniently located for all the attractions of the tri-state area. Galena, Illinois, is 10 minutes away; Dubuque, Iowa, 15 miles away; and Platteville, only 20 miles away.

Hosts: Ken and Pat Disch
Rooms: 8 (6 PB; 2 SB) $55-125
Full Breakfast
Credit Cards: A, B, C, D
Notes: 2, 4, 5, 7, 8, 9, 10, 11, 12

HUDSON

Jefferson Day House

1109 Third Street, 54016
(715) 386-7111
E-mail: jeffersn@pressenter.com
www.jeffersondayhouse.com

This 1857 completely restored Italianate mansion has four guest rooms and one three-room suite. All rooms have double whirlpools, fireplaces, air-conditioning, queen beds, private bathrooms, and much more. Twenty minutes from the Twin Cities and six miles from Stillwater, Minnesota. Arrive as a guest and leave as a friend.

Hosts: Tom and Sue Tyler
Rooms: 5 (PB) $99-189
Full Breakfast
Credit Cards: A, B, C, D
Notes: 2, 5, 6, 8, 9, 10, 11, 12

LAKE GENEVA

Eleven Gables Inn on the Lake

493 Wrigley Drive, 53147
(262) 248-8393
E-mail: egielkgeneva.com
www.lkgeneva.com

Nestled in evergreen amid giant oaks in the Edgewater historic district, this quaint, lakeside Carpenter's Gothic inn offers privacy and a prime location. Romantic bedrooms, bridal chamber, and unique country cottages all have fireplaces, down comforters, baths, TVs, wet bars, or cocktail refrigerators. Some have lattice courtyards, balconies, and private entrances. A private pier provides exclusive water activities. Bike rentals are available. This charming "Newport of the Midwest" community provides fine dining, boutiques, and entertainment year-round.

Host: Audrey Milliette
Rooms: 8 (PB) $89-250
Full Breakfast

NOTES: Credit cards accepted: A Master Card; B Visa; C American Express; D Discover; E Diners Club; F Other; 2 Personal checks accepted; 3 Lunch available; 4 Dinner available; 5 Open all year;

Credit Cards: A, B, C, D, E
Notes: 5, 6, 7, 8, 9, 10, 12

LIVINGSTON

Oak Hill Farm

9850 Highway 80, 53554
(608) 943-6006

A comfortable country home with a warm, hospitable atmosphere that is enhanced by fireplaces, porches, facilities for picnics, bird-watching, and hiking. In the area you will find state parks, museums, and lakes. Open May 1 through November 1.

Hosts: Elizabeth and Victor Johnson
Rooms: 4 (1 PB; 3 SB) $50-60
Continental Breakfast
Credit Cards: None
Notes: 2, 6, 7, 8, 9, 10, 11, 12

MADISON

Annie's Garden Bed & Breakfast

2117 Sheridan Drive, 53704-3844
phone/fax: (608) 244-2224
www.bbinternet.com/annies

When you want the world to go away, come to Annie's, the quiet inn on Warner Park with the beautiful view. Luxury accommodations—a full floor of space all to yourself, including a master bedroom; a smaller bedroom; connecting full bath; whirlpool room; pine-paneled library with fireplace; and dining room opening to lovely gardens, gazebo, and shaded terrace. Miles of nature trails to lake, marshes, and woods to enjoy wildlife and sports. Only six minutes from downtown Madison and the University of Wisconsin campus. Central air-conditioning. Two-night minimum. Meet our two cats, Sparkler and Firecracker.

Hosts: Anne and Larry Stuart
Rooms: 1 (PB) $143-189
Full Breakfast
Credit Cards: A, B, C, E
Notes: 2, 5, 7, 8, 9, 10, 11

Cameo Rose Victorian Country Inn

1090 Severson Road, Belleville, 53508
(608) 424-6340
E-mail: romance@cameorose.com
www.cameorose.com

This romantic and relaxing Victorian B&B is on 120 scenic acres of woods, hills, views, and trails. Enjoy a complimentary full breakfast of home-baked treats served on antique china and lace. One room has double whirlpool; two have fireplaces. Located midway between Madison and New Glarus (America's little Switzerland). Come and be pampered!

Hosts: Dawn and Gary Bahr
Rooms: 5 (PB) $109-159
Full Breakfast
Credit Cards: A, B
Notes: 2, 5, 8, 9, 10, 11

MAIDEN ROCK

Harrisburg Inn

West 3334 Highway 35, P.O. Box 15, 54750-0015
(715) 448-4500; fax: (715) 448-3908
E-mail: ccbern@cannon.net
harrisburginn.com

6 Pets welcome; 7 Children welcome; 8 Tennis nearby; 9 Swimming nearby; 10 Golf nearby; 11 Skiing nearby; 12 May be booked through travel agent

Harrisburg Inn

Nestled on a bluff-side overlooking the Mississippi River Valley, our inn truly has "a view with a room." Every room faces the river and surrounding blufflands where birds and flowers abound. Western Wisconsin's hills invite exploration where you'll find wonderful surprises in dining, antiquing, small-town festivals, and other delights. The Harrisburg offers relaxation, romance, and great breakfasts. Welcome! Inquire about children.

Hosts: Bern Paddock and Carol Crisp Paddock
Rooms: 4 (PB) $90-135
Full Breakfast
Credit Cards: A, B, C, D
Notes: 2, 5, 7, 8, 9, 10, 11

MANITOWOC

WestPort
Bed & Breakfast

635 North Eighth Street, 54220
(920) 686-0465; (888) 686-0465
www.bbonline.com/wi/westport

Find serenity here along Lake Michigan's shoreline. Our spacious guestrooms feature private bathrooms, queen beds, double whirlpools, fireplaces, a comfortable sitting area, air-conditioning, cable TV, and refrigerator. A candlelight breakfast is served at guests' convenience in the formal dining room. WestPort is within walking distance of Lake Michigan, marina, museums, restaurants, parks, shops, and theaters. Lake Michigan car ferry is within 1.6 miles. An hour from Door County.

WestPort

Hosts: Kim and Keith Philippi
Rooms: 4 (PB) $90-135
Full Breakfast
Credit Cards: A, B
Notes: 2, 5, 7, 8, 9, 10, 11

MILWAUKEE

County Clare Inn

1234 North Astor Street, 53202-2822
(414) 272-5273; (800) 942-5273
fax: (414) 290-6300
E-mail: ctyclare@execpc.com
countyclare-inn.com

NOTES: Credit cards accepted: A Master Card; B Visa; C American Express; D Discover; E Diners Club; F Other; 2 Personal checks accepted; 3 Lunch available; 4 Dinner available; 5 Open all year;

Our guest rooms feature four-poster beds, double whirlpool baths, separate shower rooms, remote control televisions, desks, telephones, and special computer terminals. The white wainscoting and internal windows give the rooms an Irish cottage appearance. Our small intimate hotel has 30 guest rooms, 25 of which are non-smoking, and four of which are suites with a separate sitting room and sofa bed.

Rooms: 30 (PB) $109.50-139.50
Continental Breakfast
Credit Cards: A, B, C, D, E
Notes: 2, 3, 4, 5, 7

The Washington House Inn

W62 N573 Washington Avenue, Cedarburg, 53012
(262) 375-3550; (800) 554-4717
fax: (262) 375-9422
E-mail: whinn@execpc.com
www.washingtonhouseinn.com

The romance of country Victorian comes alive as you enter the Washington House Inn, Cedarburg's historic B&B inn. A lovely collection of antique Victorian furniture, a marble-trimmed fireplace, and fresh-cut flowers offer you a warm reception. Tastefully appointed in the romantic country Victorian style featuring antiques, cozy down quilts, flowers, and special touches for our guests' comfort. In late afternoon relax in front of a cheery fire, sip wine, and socialize with other guests prior to dining at one of the excellent Cedarburg restaurants. Each morning enjoy a delicious Continental breakfast in the warmth of the gathering room. Homemade muffins, cakes, and breads are baked in our own kitchen using recipes from an authentic, turn-of-the-century Cedarburg cookbook.

Host: Wendy Porterfield
Rooms: 34 (PB) $85-215
Continental Breakfast
Credit Cards: A, B, C, D
Notes: 2, 5, 8, 9, 10, 12

MINERAL POINT

Pleasant Lake
Bed & Breakfast

2238-60th Avenue, 54020
(715) 294-2545; (800) 294-2545
fax: (715) 755-3163
E-mail: pllakebb@centurytel.net
www.pleasantlake.com

Romance, relaxation, and rejuvenation of your body and spirit. Walk leisurely in the woods, watch our wildlife neighbors, canoe the lake, sit around a crackling campfire with the stars reflecting on the moonlit lake, then relax in your own fireside whirlpool. Arise to the aromas of a full country breakfast and the songs of nature.

Hosts: Richard and Charlene Berg
Rooms: 8 (PB) $89-149
Full Breakfast
Credit Cards: A, B, D
Notes: 2, 5, 9, 10, 11

REEDSBURG

Parkview
Bed & Breakfast

211 North Park Street, 53959
(608) 524-4333; fax: (608) 524-1172
E-mail: parkview@jvlnet.com
www.parkviewbb.com

---

6 Pets welcome; 7 Children welcome; 8 Tennis nearby; 9 Swimming nearby; 10 Golf nearby; 11 Skiing nearby; 12 May be booked through travel agent

Our 1895 Queen Anne Victorian home overlooks City Park in the historic district. Many of the original features of the home remain, such as hardware, hardwood floors, intricate woodwork, leaded and etched windows, plus a suitor's window. Wake-up coffee is followed by a full, homemade breakfast. Central air and ceiling fans add to guests' comfort. Located one block from downtown. Close to Wisconsin Dells, Baraboo, and Spring Green. Just three blocks from 400 Bike Trail.

Hosts: Tom and Donna Hofmann
Rooms: 4 (2 PB; 2 SB) $75-95
Full Breakfast
Credit Cards: A, B, C
Notes: 2, 5, 7, 8, 10, 11, 12

ST. CROIX FALLS

Wissahickon Farms Country Inn

2263 Maple Drive, 54024
(715) 483-3986; E-mail: wissainn@yahoo.com
wissainn.com

"Rustic country lodging with a touch of class." Located on a 30-acre hobby farm secluded by God's creative handiwork, our country inn portrays an old country store from a bygone era. Relax on the porch, enjoy the two-person whirlpool, or hike the many surrounding trails, including an ice-age trail. The "Gandy Dancer" bicycle/snowmobile trail runs right through the farm. Furnishings include a queen camelback bed, hide-a-bed sofa for two ($15 per extra person), and glider rocker. The small efficiency kitchen contains a refrigerator

and microwave. Guests have a TV with VCR. The inn is air-conditioned. No smoking; no pets. Bicycles are provided to ride the trail in summer and snowshoe in winter. With a donation to the "hay fund," Amish buggy rides are now available. Come see what the St. Croix River Valley has to offer!

Hosts: Steve and Sherilyn Litzkow
Rooms: 1 (PB) $125
Continental Breakfast
Credit Cards: A, B
Notes: 2, 5, 9, 10, 11

SPARTA

The Strawberry Lace Inn

603 North Water Street, 54656
(608) 269-7878
E-mail: strawberry@centurytel.net
www.spartan.org/sbl

Return to an era of romance and elegance. This home is an excellent example of an Italianate Victorian (circa 1875). Rest in your own private retreat with private bath, king or queen bed with mountains of pillows, and distinctive antique décor. Partake of your hosts' four-course breakfast, presented on crystal and linen. Relax by visiting, reading, or playing games on the four-season porch. Known as "the biking capital of America," the area offers bike trails, golf, water sports, antiquing, restaurants, winter sports, and many more attractions year-round.

Hosts: Jack and Elsie Ballinger
Rooms: 5 (PB) $89-145
Full Breakfast
Credit Cards: A, B
Notes: 2, 5, 9, 10, 11, 12

NOTES: Credit cards accepted: A Master Card; B Visa; C American Express; D Discover; E Diners Club; F Other; 2 Personal checks accepted; 3 Lunch available; 4 Dinner available; 5 Open all year;

SPRING GREEN

Bettinger House Bed & Breakfast

855 Wachter Avenue, (Highway 23), P.O. Box
    243, Plain, 53577
phone/fax: (608) 546-2951
E-mail: bhbb@execpc.com
bettingerbnb.com

The Bettinger House is the hostess's
grandparents' 1904 Victorian farmhouse; Grandma was a midwife who
delivered 300 babies in this house.
Choose from five spacious bedrooms
that blend the old with the new, each
named after noteworthy persons of
Plain. The home is centrally air-conditioned. Start your day with one of
the old-fashioned, full-course breakfasts for which we are famous. The
Bettinger House is located near
"House on the Rock," Frank Lloyd
Wright's original Taliesen, American
Players Theater, White Mound Park,
and many more attractions.

Hosts: Jim and Marie Neider
Rooms: 5 (2 PB; 2 SB) $60-80
Full Breakfast
Credit Cards: None
Notes: 2, 5, 7, 8, 9, 10, 11, 12

Lamb's Inn Bed & Breakfast

23761 Misslich Road, Richland Center, 53581
(608) 585-4301; fax: (608) 585-2242
E-mail: lambsinn@mwt.net
www.lambs-inn.com

Come and relax on our 180-acre farm
located in a beautiful valley. Swing in
our Amish porch swing on our
screened-in porch; feed the trout; pet
a cat. Visit Taliesen, Frank Lloyd

Wright's home; see a Shakespeare
play at the outdoor American Players
Theater, or visit the Amish. Enjoy a
full, homemade breakfast.

Hosts: Dick and Donna Messerschmidt
Rooms: 6 (PB) $85-150
Full Breakfast
Credit Cards: A, B, D
Notes: 2, 5, 12

STEVENS POINT

Dreams of Yesteryear Bed & Breakfast

1100 Brawley Street, 54481
(715) 341-4525; fax (715) 341-4248
E-mail: bonnie@dreamsofyesteryear.com
www.dreamsofyesteryear.com

Featured in *Victorian Homes* magazine and listed on the National Register of Historic Places. Your hosts are
from Stevens Point and enjoy talking
about the restoration of their turn-of-
the-century home, which has been in
the same family for three generations.
All rooms are furnished in antiques.

Dreams of Yesteryear

Guests enjoy the use of parlors,
porches, and gardens. Two blocks
from the historic downtown, antique

---

6 Pets welcome; 7 Children welcome; 8 Tennis nearby; 9 Swimming nearby; 10 Golf nearby; 11 Skiing
nearby; 12 May be booked through travel agent

and specialty shops, picturesque Green Circle Trails, the university, and more. Truly "a Victorian dream come true." Children over 12 welcome.

Hosts: Bonnie and Bill Maher
Rooms: 6 (4 PB; 2 SB) $58-149
Full Breakfast
Credit Cards: A, B, C, D
Notes: 2, 5, 7, 8, 9, 10, 11, 12

STURGEON BAY

Scofield House

908 Michigan Street, 54235
phone/fax: (920) 743-7727; (888) 463-0204
E-mail: cpietrek@doorpi.net
www.scofieldhouse.com

"Door County's most elegant B&B." This 1902 multicolored, three-story Victorian was restored in 1987 by the present hosts. Guests keep coming back for the wonderful gourmet breakfasts and homemade "sweet treats" served fresh daily. The Scofield House has six guest rooms, of which four are suites; all have private baths, color TV/VCRs, and a "free" video library. Double whirl-pools, fireplaces, and central air-conditioning. We are a smoke-free environment.

Hosts: Mike and Carolyn Pietrek
Rooms: 6 (PB) $98-202
Full Breakfast
Credit Cards: None
Notes: 2, 5, 8, 9, 10, 11, 12

White Lace Inn

16 North 5th Avenue, 54235
(920) 743-1105 ; (877) 948-5223

E-mail: romance@whitelaceinn.com
www.whitelaceinn.com

Our four historic homes are nestled in a friendly old neighborhood, bordered by a white picket fence and surrounded by gardens. The White Lace is a romantic Victorian inn with 18 wonderfully inviting guest rooms furnished in fine antiques, queen or king four-poster, or ornate Victorian beds, oversized whirlpool tub, an inviting fireplace, down comforters, and white lace. A warm welcome awaits as guests are greeted with lemonade or hot chocolate and cookies. Open year-round. Nonsmoking.

White Lace Inn

Hosts: Bonnie and Dennis Statz
Rooms: 18 (PB) $68-239
Full Breakfast
Credit Cards: A, B, C, D
Notes: 2, 5, 8, 9, 10, 11

WATERTOWN

Bradt Quirk Manor

410 South 4th Street, 53094-4526
(920) 261-7917

NOTES: Credit cards accepted: A Master Card; B Visa; C American Express; D Discover; E Diners Club; F Other; 2 Personal checks accepted; 3 Lunch available; 4 Dinner available; 5 Open all year;

Bradt Quirk Manor

Come and enjoy the warmth and charm of this 1875 Victorian home. Allow the ambiance of this stately Greek Revival manor take you back when time seemed to move more slowly and people acted more friendly. Awake with the sun streaming through a stained-glass window, freshen up in a marble sink dating back to the turn of the century, feast your eyes on antiques, lace, and other decorative accents. Each room is uniquely decorated; three have adjoining sitting rooms.

Hosts: Wayne and Elda Zuleger
Rooms: 4 (2 PB; 2 SB) $55-80
Full Breakfast
Credit Cards: A, B
Notes: 2, 5, 8, 9

WISCONSIN DELLS

Historic Bennett House

825 Oak Street, 53965
(608) 254-2500; www.historicbennetthouse.com

The 1863 home of pioneer photographer H.H. Bennett is warm and inviting in its casual elegance and wel-

coming atmosphere. Traveling with another couple? We have the ideal situation for you. Two lovely bedrooms, one with queen canopy bed and English armoire and the other with queen brass bed with wicker accents. Share a carpeted, bedroom-sized bath with Italian sinks and Bennett's claw-foot tub. You may, of course, reserve just one room. The library has become part of a two-room suite with private bath. View a favorite movie from our 100-plus collection. Savor a delicious gourmet breakfast, and visit Dells attractions: state parks; Bennett, Rockwell, Circus, and Railroad Museums; riverboat tours; skiing; and the Crane Foundation.

Hosts: Gail and Rich Obermeyer
Rooms: 3 (1 PB; 2 SB) $80-99
Full Breakfast
Credit Cards: None
Notes: 2, 5, 8, 9, 10, 11

Terrace Hill Bed & Breakfast

922 River Road, 53965
(608) 253-9363
E-mail: info@terracehillbb.com
www.terracehillbb.com

Our 100-year-old, yellow Victorian home is located atop a small bluff near the Sandstone cliffs of the Upper Dells on scenic River Road, just a block from downtown Dells. Enjoy old-world charm, browse our eclectic library, and experience serendipity. Pamper yourself with a little respite from the busy world in which we live. Private parking, private baths, in-room whirlpool, and air-conditioning. Children welcome.

---

6 Pets welcome; 7 Children welcome; 8 Tennis nearby; 9 Swimming nearby; 10 Golf nearby; 11 Skiing nearby; 12 May be booked through travel agent

Hosts: Len, Cookie, Lenard, and Lynn Novak
Rooms: 4 (PB) $85-140
Full Breakfast
Credit Cards: A, B
Notes: 2, 5, 7, 9, 10, 11

Hosts: Marty and Shionagh Stuehler
Rooms: 5 (PB) $80-165
Full Breakfast
Credit Cards: A, B, C, D
Notes: 2, 3, 4, 5, 7, 8, 9, 10, 11, 12

The White Rose
Bed & Breakfast Inn

910 River Road, 53945
(608) 254-4724; (800) 482-4725
fax: (608) 254-4585
E-mail: whiterose@jvlnet.com
www.thewhiterose.com

The White Rose

"Where the young at heart meet in the spirit of celebration." Visit our enchanting historical mansion with uniquely decorated, comfortable rooms and suites. All have TV/HBO and private baths, some with Jacuzzis. Enjoy the garden view while sitting in front of the fireplace in the parlor. Dine at our Secret Garden Café, either in the romantic Mediterranean grotto, or on the deck nestled under ancient oaks. Stroll through our incredible gardens and relax in our heated pool. We promise you an unforgettable experience.

Wyoming

**BIG HORN MOUNTAIN
BED & BREAKFAST**

BIG HORN

Spahn's
Big Horn Mountain
Bed & Breakfast, L.L.C.

P.O. Box 579, 82833
(307) 674-8150
E-mail: spahn@bighorn-wyoming.com
bighorn-wyoming.com

Towering solar electric log home and cabins on a quiet pine-forested mountainside with a hundred-mile view. The oldest B&B in Wyoming. Adjacent to one million acres of public forestland, with deer, moose and eagles on site. Gracious mountain breakfasts served with binoculars. Geologist host is a former Yellowstone Park Ranger, guides evening wildlife safaris. Twenty minutes from Sheridan and I-90. . .where you can see 100 miles from the window.

Hosts: Ron and Bobbie Spahn
Rooms: 5 (PB) $100-165
Full Breakfast
Credit Cards: None
Notes: 4, 7

BUFFALO

Historic Mansion House Inn

313 North Main Street, 82834
(307) 684-2218; (888) 455-9202
E-mail: dianem@trib.com
www.mansionhouseinn.com

Seven western Victorian guest rooms are available on historic Main Street, as well as 11 comfortable motel rooms in the annex, offering a Continental breakfast, spa, color cable TV, and air-conditioning. Located on historic Main Street and Highway 16, the scenic route to Yellowstone National Park. Open year-round.

Historic Mansion House Inn

---

6 Pets welcome; 7 Children welcome; 8 Tennis nearby; 9 Swimming nearby; 10 Golf nearby; 11 Skiing nearby; 12 May be booked through travel agent

WYOMING

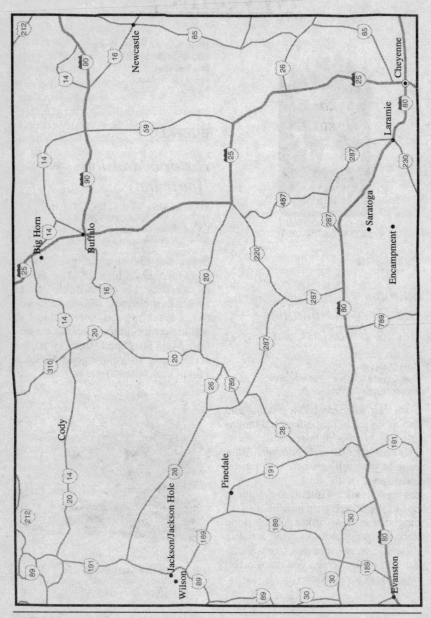

NOTES: Credit cards accepted: A Master Card; B Visa; C American Express; D Discover; E Diners
Club; F Other; 2 Personal checks accepted; 3 Lunch available; 4 Dinner available; 5 Open all year;

Hosts: Phil and Diane Mehlhaff
Rooms: 18 (PB) $45-70
Continental Breakfast
Credit Cards: A, B, D
Notes: 5, 7, 8, 9, 10, 11

CHEYENNE

A. Drummonds Ranch Bed & Breakfast

399 Happy Jack Road, 82007
phone/fax: (307) 634-6042
E-mail: adrummond@juno.com
www.adrummond.com

A. Drummonds Ranch is a quiet, gracious retreat on 120 acres near the national forest and state park with private outdoor hot tubs, incredible views, and a glorious night sky. Mountain bike, hike, cross-country ski, relax, or "take a llama to lunch." More than just a place to spend the night! Kenneled pets welcome. Children welcome with restrictions.

Host: Taydie Drummond
Rooms: 4 (2 PB; 2 SB) $70-150
Full Breakfast
Credit Cards: A, B
Notes: 2, 3, 4, 5, 6, 7, 10, 11, 12

The Storyteller Pueblo Bed & Breakfast

5201 Ogden Road, 82009
phone/fax: (307) 634-7036
E-mail: stpbandb2@sisna.com

At the Storyteller you slip into history. . . Located in a quiet residential neighborhood, this contemporary B&B blends the past with the present. Native American decor with American antiques beckon you to relax.

Over 50 Native tribes tell their stories through pottery, baskets, weavings, bead work, and Western art. The comfort of the present awaits guests with central air-conditioning, fireplaces, sitting rooms, and many amenities. Wake up to a full breakfast of the Ojibwa Nation to jumpstart the day, and enjoy complimentary snacks and beverages any time. Shopping, restaurants, museums, and theaters beckon you to visit the Old and New West of Cheyenne. Or you may want to just sit back and curl up with a good book from our historical library. We recommend reservations.

Hosts: Howard and Peggy Hutchings
Rooms: 4 (2 PB; 2 SB) $40-100
Full Breakfast
Credit Cards: None
Notes: 2, 5, 7, 8, 9, 10, 11, 12

CODY

The Lockhart Bed & Breakfast Inn

The Lockhart

109 West Yellowstone Avenue, 82435
(307) 587-6074; (800) 377-7255
fax: (307) 587-8644
E-mail: lockhart@fiberpipe.net
cruising-america.com/lockhart

---

6 Pets welcome; 7 Children welcome; 8 Tennis nearby; 9 Swimming nearby; 10 Golf nearby; 11 Skiing nearby; 12 May be booked through travel agent

Historic author's home with turn-of-the-century décor. Parlor with piano and wood-burning stove. Private dining table for breakfast. Beverages always available. Also, homemade "snackies" out at the fire, just like Grandma's house. Lots of laughter. AAA-approved. First B&B in Wyoming. Your hostess is "the oldest innkeeper in Wyoming!"

Hosts: Don Kramer and Cindy Baldwin-Kramer
Rooms: 7 (PB) $75-125
Full Breakfast
Credit Cards: A, B
Notes: 2, 7, 8, 9, 10, 11, 12

ENCAMPMENT

Rustic Mountain Lodge & Cabin

Star Route, Box 49, 82325
phone/fax: (307) 327-5539
E-mail: maplatt@union-tel.com
www.plattoutfitting.com

The Rustic Mountain Lodge offers guests rest and relaxation while enjoying graceful country living and sharing the stories of our ancestors who settled here five generations ago. Stay in a comfortable lodge or cabin with gorgeous mountain views, private fishing, and B&B service. This peaceful and scenic location is just right for retreats, reunions or workshops, and families. Captivating views, lots of Western hospitality, and nearby hot mineral springs all beckon the visitor, along with the smell of the sage and unspoiled wilderness. Call now and make reservations to enjoy all this and more!

Hosts: Mayvon and Ron Platt
Rooms: 4 (1 PB; 3 SB) $65
Full Breakfast
Credit Cards: None
Notes: 2, 3, 4, 5, 6, 7, 8, 9, 10, 11

EVANSTON

Pine Gables Inn Bed & Breakfast

1049 Center Street, 82930
(307) 789-2069
E-mail: pinegabl@allwest.net
www.cruising-america.com/pinegables

This lovely Victorian home on the National Register of Historic Places was built in 1883. Century-old antiques, hand-painted murals, and canopy beds add a special touch of elegance to each bed chamber. All rooms have TVs and phones; some have VCRs, footed tubs, and Jacuzzis. A full, hot breakfast is served to get you started each morning. Come and enjoy your home away from home at the Pine Gables Inn! Memories of a bygone time will bring you back again!

Pine Gables Inn

Hosts: Nephi and Ruby Jensen
Rooms: 6 (PB) $60-165
Full Breakfast
Credit Cards: A, B, C, D
Notes: 2, 5, 8, 9, 10, 11, 12

SARATOGA

Far Out West
Bed & Breakfast

304 North Second Street, P.O. Box 1230, 82331
(307) 326-5869; fax: (307) 326-9864
E-mail: fowbnb@union-tel.com
www.cruising-america.com/farout.html

This historic home has six guest rooms that are decorated comfortably with a country flair. All have private baths. Three rooms have king beds. We are located two blocks from downtown and a block and a half from the North Platte River where we have the best fly-fishing in the country. Each room provides color cable TV and robes. There is a large-screen TV in the great room, as well as a large, round fireplace. Open year-round. No smoking.

Hosts: Bill and B.J. Farr
Rooms: 6 (PB) $100
Full Breakfast
Credit Cards: A, B, C, D
Notes: 2, 5, 7, 9, 10

6 Pets welcome; 7 Children welcome; 8 Tennis nearby; 9 Swimming nearby; 10 Golf nearby; 11 Skiing nearby; 12 May be booked through travel agent

ALBERTA

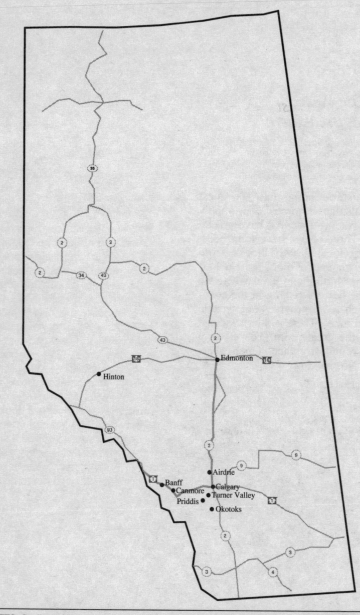

NOTES: Credit cards accepted: A Master Card; B Visa; C American Express; D Discover; E Diners Club; F Other; 2 Personal checks accepted; 3 Lunch available; 4 Dinner available; 5 Open all year;

Alberta

CALGARY

Big Springs Estate Bed & Breakfast

R.R. 1, Airdrie, T4B 2A3
(403) 948-5264; (888) 948-5851
fax: (403) 948-5851
E-mail: bigsprings@bigsprings-bb.com
www.bigsprings@bigsprings-bb.com

Big Springs Estate is situated on 35 very private pastoral acres overlooking a picturesque valley. Beautifully treed and landscaped estate gardens surround a 5,500-square foot hillside bungalow. Five distinctive decorated rooms include a Bridal Suite and Grand Executive Suite, ultra-masseur tubs, and optional romantic package. Relax in our secluded English Garden sitting room where furniture groupings are situated so that the garden atmosphere continues to the surrounding green of the outdoors. Enjoy an elegant gourmet breakfast by certified and experienced hosts. Fireplace, hot tub, piano, and "nature trail" that winds along valley rock formations. Evening snack. Extra-personal touches. Twenty minutes to Calgary and 25 minutes to the airport. Great access to Kananaskis, Banff, Lake Louise, and Calgary Stampede. Mountain Adventure and Sight-Seeing packages available.

Hosts: Earle and Carol Whittaker
Rooms: 5 (PB) $99-169 (Canadian)
Full Breakfast
Credit Cards: A, B
Notes: 5, 7, 8, 9, 10, 11, 12

Cougar Creek Inn Bed & Breakfast

240 Grizzly Crescent, Canmore, T1W 1B5
(403) 678-4751
E-mail: pdoucett@telusplanet.net
www.bbexpo.com.ab/cougarcreek.htm

Quiet, rustic, cedar chalet with mountain views in every direction. Grounds border on Cougar Creek and are surrounded by rugged mountain scenery that invites all types of outdoor activity. Hostess has strong love for the mountains and can assist with plans for local hiking, skiing, canoeing, mountain biking, and backpacking, as well as scenic drives. The inn has a private entrance with sitting area, fireplace, games, TV, sauna, and reading materials for guests. Choose from two large guest rooms, one with a double bed, a single bed, and a double futon, the other with a double bed and a single bed. Breakfasts are hearty and wholesome with many home-baked items. Open May through September.

Host: Mrs. Patricia Doucette
Rooms: 2 (PB) $75-85 (Canadian)
Full Breakfast
Credit Cards: None
Notes: 2, 3, 7, 8, 9, 10, 11

---

6 Pets welcome; 7 Children welcome; 8 Tennis nearby; 9 Swimming nearby; 10 Golf nearby; 11 Skiing nearby; 12 May be booked through travel agent

Hilltop Ranch

Hilltop Ranch Bed & Breakfast

P.O. Box 54, Priddis, T0L 1W0
(403) 931-2639; (800) 801-0451
fax: (403) 931-3426
E-mail: hilltopr@cybersurf.net
www.discoveralberta.com/hilltop/

Fifty-seven-acre hobby ranch. From the guest book: "Food was awesome," "Can we live here?" "Very quiet, peaceful time," "Our stay here was icing on the cake," "Better than any five-star hotel," "The horse and carriage ride was a real thrill!"

Hosts: Gary and Barbara Zorn
Rooms: 3 (PB) $70-120
Full Breakfast
Credit Cards: A, B
Notes: 2, 5, 6, 7, 8, 9, 10, 11, 12

Merrywood Bed & Breakfast

23 Newton Street, P.O. Box 377, Langdon,
   T0J 1X0
(403) 936-5796
E-mail: underhiswing@look.ca
mypagedirect.ca/u/underhiswing/
   merrywoodbb.html

Enjoy relaxed accommodation in a quiet hamlet east of Calgary. Easy access to airport, downtown, Calgary Stampede, Calgary Zoo, and other local attractions, including the Canadian Rockies, Banff, Lake Louise, Royal Tyrell Patlaeontology, rock hounding area, dinosaur park, Rosebud Dinner Theatre, and more. Enjoy the local birds, summer-fresh garden produce, and local crafts, and relaxing in the garden. Fenced yard for small dog.

Merrywood

Host: G.M. Chappell
Rooms: 2 (SB) $45-60 (Canadian)
Full Breakfast
Credit Cards: None
Notes: 5, 6

Paradise Acres Bed & Breakfast

Box 20 Site 2, R.R. #6, 243105 Paradise Road,
   T2M 4L5
(403) 248-4748; (866) 248-4748
E-mail: info@paradiseacres.com
www.paradiseacres.com

Come enjoy our friendly and luxurious setting with country quietness and city access. Paradise Acres features choice of breakfasts, queen-size beds,

---

NOTES: Credit cards accepted: A Master Card; B Visa; C American Express; D Discover; E Diners Club; F Other; 2 Personal checks accepted; 3 Lunch available; 4 Dinner available; 5 Open all year;

private baths, plus guest sitting rooms with TVs/VCRs. Located close to the TransCanada Highway and Calgary airport with a city and mountain view. Airport pickup available.

Hosts: Brian and Char Bates
Rooms: 5 (PB) $80 plus taxes
Full Breakfast
Credit Cards: A, B, C
Notes: 2, 5, 7, 8, 9, 10, 11, 12

Turret House Bed & Breakfast

Box 460, Nanton, T0L 1R0
(403) 646-5789; E-mail: roseptl@telusplanet.net

Come visit one of Nanton's oldest homes, close to antique shops, restaurants, sports centre, and golf course. Guest rooms and bathroom are upstairs, dining and sitting rooms are downstairs with private entrance. Nanton is a small country town near the foothills of the Rockies, halfway between Calgary and Fort MacLeadcowboy country with city amenities easily accessible. Welcome!

Turret House

Host: Sam and Rosemary Squire
Rooms: 2 (SB) $45-60 (Canadian)
Continental Breakfast
Credit Cards: None
Notes: 5, 7, 9, 10, 11

CANMORE

Stella Alpina Bed & Breakfast

1009-9th Avenue, T1W 1Z5
phone/fax: (403) 678-2119 ; (888) 548-3788
E-mail: martino@agt.net
www.stellaalpina-bb.com

Stella Alpina

Enjoy Dutch/Italian hospitality in Canmore, five minutes from Banff-National Park and 20 minutes from downtown Banff. Outdoor adventurers and former world-cruise travelers Carmelo and Anneke, avid organic gardeners, welcome you to their mountain home, close to the Bow River and downtown. Separate entrance, Jacuzzi tubs, TV, and refrigerators in-room. Gourmet breakfast. Herb and wild mushroom omelettes; excellent home base for Alpine and cross-country skiing, hiking, fishing, and bird-watching. Inquire about pets. Rated three stars by Canadian Select.

Hosts: Anneke and Carmelo Ciaramidaro
Rooms: 2 (PB) $55-80
Full Breakfast
Credit Cards: A, B
Notes: 5, 6, 7, 8, 9, 10, 11

6 Pets welcome; 7 Children welcome; 8 Tennis nearby; 9 Swimming nearby; 10 Golf nearby; 11 Skiing nearby; 12 May be booked through travel agent

BRITISH COLUMBIA

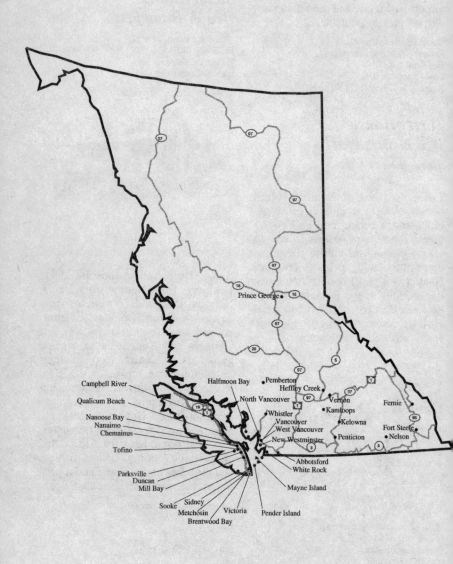

Campbell River

Qualicum Beach

Nanoose Bay
Nanaimo
Chemainus

Tofino

Parksville
Duncan
Mill Bay

Sooke Sidney
Metchosin Victoria
Brentwood Bay

Halfmoon Bay

North Vancouver

Pemberton
Heffley Creek

Whistler
Vancouver
West Vancouver
New Westminster

Abbotsford
White Rock

Mayne Island

Pender Island

Prince George

Vernon
Kamloops
Kelowna
Penticton

Fernie

Fort Steele
Nelson

British Columbia

CARIBOO CHILCOTIN COAST

PRINCE GEORGE

Beaverly Bed & Breakfast

12725 Miles Road, V2N 5C1
(250) 560-5255: (888) 522-2298
fax: (250) 560-5211
beaverlybandb.hypermart.net

Beaverly B&B is located 18 kilometers west of Prince George on 10 acres of beautiful British Columbia wilderness. You will feel very welcome and comfortable in our new home. Many trees surround us, and it is a birder's paradise. We serve a healthy, full breakfast in our country kitchen or on the deck weather permitting. Pick-up service from airport, train, or bus is available for a small fee. Follow blue B&B signs. Friendly service with a Dutch touch.

Hosts: Anneke and Adrian Van Peenen
Rooms: 3 (2 PB; 1 SB) $52-72
Full Breakfast
Credit Cards: A, B
Notes: 3, 5, 6, 7, 8, 9, 10, 11

ISLANDS

CAMPBELL RIVER

Campbell River Lodge, Fishing & Adventure Resort

1760 North Island Highway, V9W 2E7
(250) 287-7446; (800) 663-7212
fax: (250) 287-4063
E-mail: stay@campbellriverinns.com
www.campbellriverinns.com

Excitement and adventure await at our West Coast Retreat. Nestled on the banks of the famous Campbell River, operating since 1948, our modernized full service "Lodge" is the most established and unique in the area. Fabulous fishing, snorkeling, golfing, white water rafting, grizzly sightings, whale watching, black bear viewing, float plane tours and heli-fishing are some of the eco adventures available. Whether you want to resort to outdoor adventure for your holiday or just plain relaxation, the lodge has something for you. Experience our spectacular rainforest, mountains, and coastlines. Conference facilities available for corporate retreats.

Hosts: Ted and Sharon Arbour
Rooms: 28 (PB) $65-104
Continental Breakfast
Credit Cards: A, B
Notes: 3, 4, 5, 6, 7, 8, 9, 10, 11, 12

CHEMAINUS

At the Sea-Breeze

2912 Esplanade Street, Box 1362, V0R 1K0
phone/fax: (250) 246-4593
E-mail: c-breeze@telus.net
www.virtualcities.com

Turn-of-the-century home, beautifully appointed. Steps from the beach and boat ramp. Almost waterfront. Beautiful views from every room. One complete suite including kitchen. Enjoy watching sails and seals from an old-fashioned veranda. The Sea-Breeze is surrounded by clean, fresh breezes and sparkling water. *Wir sprechen Deutsch!* Picturesque town of Chemainus on Vancouver Island.

Hosts: John and Christa Stegemann
Rooms: 4 (PB) $60-65 (Canadian)
Full Breakfast
Credit Cards: None
Notes: 5, 6, 7, 8, 9, 10, 12

SIDNEY

Rose-Tree Cottage Bed & Breakfast

2514 Rothesay Avenue, V8L 2B8
(250) 655-6715
E-mail: rosetreecott@pacificcoast.net
rosetree@sidneybc.com

Situated on a no-exit avenue near the water, the Rose-Tree Cottage B&B opened June 98/99 after major renovations. The name is dedicated to a late relative, who loved roses. The quiet setting with upper deck and gardens provides a place where guests may lounge. The cottage offers marina views; reach the beach in two minutes. The hostess can arrange appointments for manicure, pedicure, massage, and reflexology for those who reserve early. Dinner available if ordered by 2:00 P.M. If you miss your garden or kitchen you can ask to help. Near many churches in the area.

Host: Nancy Jenkins
Rooms: 2 (SB) $80-95 (Canadian)
Continental Breakfast
Credit Cards: None
Notes: 2, 4, 5, 7, 8, 9, 10

SOOKE

Ocean Wilderness Country Inn

109 West Coast Road, V0X 1N0
(250) 646-2116; (800) 323-2116
fax: (250) 646-2317
E-mail: ocean@sookenet.com
www.sookenet.com/ocean

This inn offers nine guest rooms on five forested acres of oceanfront with breathtaking views. The large, beautifully decorated rooms have private baths and canopied beds. A silver service of coffee is delivered to your door as a gentle wake-up. A country breakfast of local produce is a wonderful treat. The ocean water hot tub is popular with weary travelers; book for a private soak. There are several in-room soaker tubs-for-two overlooking the ocean. Arrange a stress-relieving massage, mud facial, or seaweed/herb wrap. Perfect for small seminars, family reunions, and weddings.

Host: Marion Rolston
Rooms: 9 (PB) $75-165 (May-October)
Full Breakfast

NOTES: Credit cards accepted: A Master Card; B Visa; C American Express; D Discover; E Diners Club; F Other; 2 Personal checks accepted; 3 Lunch available; 4 Dinner available; 5 Open all year;

Credit Cards: A, B, C
Notes: 2, 5, 6, 7, 9, 10, 12

Richview House Bed & Breakfast

7031 Richview Drive, V0S 1N0
(250) 642-5520; fax: (250) 642-5501
E-mail: rvh@islandnet.com
www.islandnet.com/rvh

Richview House

This B&B is on an 80-foot cliff over-looking the Strait of Juan de Fuca and the Olympic Mountains. Each of the private suites faces the view and feature wood fireplaces, Jacuzzi tubs, or steam room. All the furniture and woodwork has been handcrafted by the owner. Expansive perennial gardens surround the property. Three-course gourmet breakfast can be served to the room or at the common breakfast table.

Hosts: Joan and Francois Gething
Rooms: 3 (PB) $150-195 Canadian
Full Breakfast
Credit Cards: A, B
Notes: 5, 8, 9, 10

VICTORIA

Battery Street Guesthouse

670 Battery Street, V8V 1E5
phone/fax: (250) 385-4632

E-mail: verduyn@telus.net
www.bbcanada.com/340.html

Lovely 1898 heritage home is in an impressive location, a 15-minute walk to the center of town. Peaceful and quiet among the trees. Once in a while a well-behaved child is welcomed.

Host: Pamela Verduyn
Rooms: 4 (2 PB; 2 SB) $75-125 (Canadian)
Full Breakfast
Credit Cards: B
Notes: 2, 5, 8, 9

A Bed & Breakfast at Swallow Hill Farm

4910 William Head Road, V9C 3Y8
phone/fax: (250) 474-4042
E-mail: swallowhillfarm@pacificcoast.net
www.victoria-bc-canada.com

You'll find a peaceful country get-away on our little Canadian farm near Vancouver on Vancouver Island's beautiful southwest coast. We offer B&B rooms and weekly/monthly accommodations at very reasonable rates. We offer king, queen and twin beds; private bathrooms; friendly conversation over scrumptious break-

A B&B at Swallow Hill Farm

6 Pets welcome; 7 Children welcome; 8 Tennis nearby; 9 Swimming nearby; 10 Golf nearby; 11 Skiing nearby; 12 May be booked through travel agent

fasts; and a spectacular ocean and mountain-sunrise view. Our B&B has a three-star Canada Select rating and is Tourism BC-approved. Children 10 and over welcome. Contact us or visit our website for more information.

Hosts: Gini and Peter Walsh
Rooms: 2 suites (PB) $55-65 (U.S.)
Full Breakfast
Credit Cards: A, B
Notes: 2, 5, 7, 8, 9, 10, 12

Dashwood Seaside Manor

1 Cook Street, V8T 5A7
(604) 385-5517

Enjoy the comfort and privacy of your own elegant suite in one of Victoria's traditional Tudor mansions. Gaze out your window at the ocean and America's Olympic Mountains. If you're an early riser, you may see seals, killer whales, or sea otters frolicking off-shore. Watch an eagle cruise by. Help yourself to breakfast from your private, well-stocked kitchen. You're minutes away from the attractions of town. Stroll there through beautiful Beacon Hill Park.

Hosts: Derek Dashwood, family, and staff
Rooms: 14 (PB) $65-240
Full Breakfast
Credit Cards: A, B, C
Notes: 2, 5, 6, 7, 8, 10, 12

Gregory's Guest House

5373 Patricia Bay Highway, V8Y 2N9
(250) 658-8404; (888) 658-8404
fax: (250) 658-4604
E-mail: gregorys@direct.ca
www.bctravel.com/gregorys.html

This early 1900s English-style home overlooks Elk Lake and features water gardens and exotic birds in a country

setting only 10 minutes from down-town and few minutes from Butehart Gardens. Bountiful complimentary breakfast. Convenient to ferrie and airport.

Hosts: Elizabeth and Paul Gregory
Rooms: 4 (3 PB; 1 SB) $79-110
Full Breakfast
Credit Cards: A, B
Notes: 2, 5, 7, 8, 9, 10, 12

Heritage House Bed & Breakfast

3808 Heritage Lane, V8Z 7A7
(250) 479-0892; (877) 326-9242
fax: (250) 479-0812
E-mail: inn@heritagehousevictoria.com
www.heritagehousevictoria.com

Award-winning registered heritage Arts and Crafts home, circa 1910. Situated on three-quarters of an acre with beautiful gardens and views of water and mountains. Private parking. Minutes from downtown by car. Close to the "Galloping Goose Trail" for the cycling and jogging enthusiast. Large, well-appointed rooms, with queen-size beds and goose-down duvets. Gourmet breakfasts served in the paneled dining room. Enjoy the host's wine by one of the fireplaces or on the old fashioned veranda. Let us help you plan your day!

Hosts: Larry and Sandra Gray
Rooms: 3 (PB) $125
Full Breakfast
Credit Cards: A, B
Notes: 5, 8, 9, 10

Humboldt House

867 Humboldt Street, V8V 2Z6
(250) 383-0152; (888) 3830327
fax: (250) 383-6402

NOTES: Credit cards accepted: A Master Card; B Visa; C American Express; D Discover; E Diners Club; F Other; 2 Personal checks accepted; 3 Lunch available; 4 Dinner available; 5 Open all year;

E-mail: rooms@humboldthouse.com
www.humboldthouse.com

Victoria's most romantic and private B&B, located two blocks from downtown Victoria. Elegant rooms with large Jacuzzi baths and wood-burning fireplaces; feast on a private gourmet breakfast. Enjoy fresh flowers, CD stereos, and goose-down linens. Complimentary champagne and choc-olate truffles on arrival. Four-star Canada Select rating.

Humboldt House

Hosts: David and Vlasta Booth
Rooms: 6 (PB) $122.50-315 Canadian
Full Breakfast
Credit Cards: A, B
Notes: 5, 8, 9, 10, 12

THOMPSON OKANAGAN

KAMLOOPS

Place Royale Bed & Breakfast

534 Robson Drive, V2E 2B6
(250) 851-1341; (866) 851-1311
fax: (250) 374-6467
E-mail: martya@telus.net
www.bbcanada.com/4349.html

Quiet, clean, affordable, luxurious, smoke- and pet-free, friendly accommodation including twin, queen, and king rooms, private baths, and picturesque mountain view. Guest lounge has fireplace and TV/VCR; outdoor hot tub and gazebo in a flower garden setting. Gourmet breakfast served on English bone china includes fresh fruit and hot entree and is served in formal dining room or the gazebo, weather permitting. Freshly baked evening dessert and afternoon tea are served. Two minutes off High-

Place Royale

6 Pets welcome; 7 Children welcome; 8 Tennis nearby; 9 Swimming nearby; 10 Golf nearby; 11 Skiing nearby; 12 May be booked through travel agent

way #1, close to golfing, fishing, hiking, and skiing.

Hosts: Frank and Marty Martens
Rooms: 3 (PB) $65-95
Full Breakfast
Credit Cards: A, B, F
Notes: 5, 8, 9, 10, 11

KELOWNA

Mountain Pines Bed & Breakfast

1250 Jackpine Road, V1P 1H6
(250) 491-1386; fax: (250) 491-0252
E-mail: coney@cheerful.com
www.bbcanada.com/1354.html

Mountain Pines

This new home is located in a secluded, peaceful mountain setting. The fully equipped suite has queen beds, a full private bath, kitchen, and private entrance. Sleeps six. An all-you-can-eat, country breakfast is served. No smoking or pets indoors; kennel available outside. Government approved accommodations. Near world-class skiing, golf, hiking, shop-

ping, and boating. Lunch and dinner available by request. Great Christian hospitality.

Hosts: Ruth Gerber
Rooms: 2 (PB) $65-95
Full Breakfast
Credit Cards: None
Notes: 3, 4, 5, 6, 7, 9, 10, 11

NOTES: Credit cards accepted: A Master Card; B Visa; C American Express; D Discover; E Diners Club; F Other; 2 Personal checks accepted; 3 Lunch available; 4 Dinner available; 5 Open all year;

VANCOUVER COAST & MOUNTAINS

ABBOTSFORD

Everett House Bed & Breakfast

1990 Everett Road, V2S 7S3
(604) 859-2944; fax: (604) 859-9180
E-mail: everettbb@bc.telus.net
www.vancouverbc.com/evertthousebb

We invite you to join us in our Victorian-style home. With easy access to the freeway and overlooking the Fraser Valley, our home is the perfect retreat, removed from the hustle of the city. It is also that "someplace special" for you while you conduct your business in the Fraser Valley. A stay at our home will provide you with a refreshing break from ordinary life.

Hosts: David and Cindy Sahlstrom
Rooms: 2 (PB) $85-135
Full Breakfast
Credit Cards: A, B
Notes: 5, 7, 9, 10, 11, 12

NORTH VANCOUVER

Sue and Simon's Victorian Guest House & Apartments

152 East 3rd Street, V7L 1E6
(604) 985-1523; (800) 776-1811
fax: (604) 983-3936

Located four blocks from the water and close to transportation, restaurants, shopping, and major attractions, Sue's Guest House features Victorian soaker tubs (no showers), antiques, quality beds and linens, TV/VCR, heaters, fans, and a party-line telephone in a welcoming and secure environment. The furnished suites next door include kitchen, bathroom, and comfortable bed-sitting room. There is a strictly enforced no-smoking policy for each property and limited off-street parking. Outside shoes off at the door please.

Hosts: Jenny, Simon, and Sue
Rooms: 7 (6 PB; 1 SB) $35-55 (U.S.)
Credit Cards: None
Notes: 5

PEMBERTON

Alpen View

7406 Larch Street, P.O. Box 636, V0N 2L0
(604) 894-6787; (877) 649-1851
fax: (604) 894-2026
E-mail: ceinarson@bigfoot.com
www.bandbwhistler.com

Guests are warmly welcomed by Fred and Christine Einarson to their quiet air-conditioned/fireside home, just off Highway 99 at the foot of the Coast Mountains and on Circle Route tours. Magnificent snowcapped mountain views are seen from the hot tub, summer jetpool, on the ten-minute stroll to the village and restaurants, or from the bedrooms. Over breakfast, guests share their experiences of Pemberton's all-season activities: golf, hiking, fishing, snowmobiling, and cross-country skiing, plus skiing and snowboarding at neighboring Whistler. Ten percent commission if booked through a travel agent. Well-

---

6 Pets welcome; 7 Children welcome; 8 Tennis nearby; 9 Swimming nearby; 10 Golf nearby; 11 Skiing nearby; 12 May be booked through travel agent

behaved children welcome. Traveler's checks accepted.

Hosts: Christine and Fred Einarson
Rooms: 3 (1 PB; 2 SB) $75-110
Continental Breakfast
Credit Cards: A, B, C, E
Notes: 5, 7, 8, 9, 10, 11, 12

VANCOUVER

Beachside Bed & Breakfast

4208 Evergreen Avenue, West Vancouver, V7V 1H1
(604) 922-7773; (800) 563-3311
fax: (604) 926-8073; E-mail: info@beach.bc.ca
www.beach.bc.ca

Experience oceanfront luxury in a quiet secluded setting. Magnificent views of city and English Bay. Perfect romantic getaway or honeymoon. Enjoy the Jacuzzi on the beach. Watch seals, sea otter, eagles, water fowl, and cruise ships from giant driftwood logs at the water's edge. Newly tiled, private baths and Jacuzzis. Fireplaces, TV/VCR, queen beds, refrigerators, and microwaves in-room. Each has a private patio. Friendly attention to detail; parking; AAA, Canada Select four stars; and 20 minutes to downtown.

Host: Joan F. Gibbs
Rooms: 4 (PB) $60-160 (U.S.)
Full Breakfast
Credit Cards: A, B
Notes: 2, 5, 7, 9, 10, 11, 12

Beautiful Bed & Breakfast Inn

428 West 40th Avenue, V5Y 2R4
(604) 327-1102; fax: (604) 327-2299

E-mail: sandbbb@portal.ca
www.beautifulbandb.bc.ca

Gorgeous colonial accommodation with antiques, fresh flowers, and views. Great central location from which guests may walk to Queen Elizabeth Park, Van Dusen Gardens, shopping, and restaurants. The bus at the end of our street runs frequently and directly to downtown Vancouver (15 minutes), Seattle (three hours), Victoria (three hours), and UBC (20 minutes). Reach the Vancouver Airport by taxi in 12 minutes. Friendly, helpful host will assist you with your plans while in Vancouver.

Hosts: Corinne and Ian Sanderson
Rooms: 6 (2 PB; 4 SB) $85-150 (U.S.)
Full Breakfast
Credit Cards: None
Notes: 2, 8, 9, 10, 11, 12

Grand Manor

1617 Grand Boulevard, V7L 3Y2
(604) 988-6719; (888) 988-6082
fax: (604) 988-4596; E-mail: donna@helix.net
www.grandmanor.net

This four-story Edwardian home is one of the original mansions on the Grand Boulevard in the heart of North

Grand Manor

Vancouver, close to shopping, skiing, swimming, tennis, Landsdale Market, and 20 min. from downtown Vancouver. Renovated rooms are clean and comfortable with mountain and ocean views. Decorated in antiques, grand manor is a place to relax and enjoy new friends in a warm, comfortable, informal atmosphere. A two-bedroom carriage house on two levels has all cooking facilities and will sleep six people.

Host: Donna Patrick
Rooms: 3 (2 PB; 1 SB) $75-130
Full and Continental Breakfast
Credit Cards: B
Notes: 5, 7, 8, 9, 10, 11

Lavender Walk

Lavender Walk

4858 8A Avenue, Delta, V4M 1S9
(604) 943-2230; fax: (604) 943-2231
E-mail: info@lavenderwalk.com
www.lavenderwalk.com

Lovely, spacious, brand-new room with French doors opens to a large private garden. Accommodations include a queen bed plus two twins. En-

suite bath with shower. Enjoy morning coffee in-room, followed by a full breakfast in the sunroom or on the patio amid wild flowers, lavender, fragrant herbs, and a small stream. Afternoon tea or sherry is also offered. Minutes to the beach, waterslides, ferries, bird-watching, and golf courses. Walk or jog the shoreline dikes. Shops and restaurants nearby. Come, enjoy our hospitality.

Hosts: Shirley and Les Shields
Rooms: 1 (PB) $85 (Canadian)
Full Breakfast
Credit Cards: B, C, F
Notes: 8, 9, 10, 11, 12

WHISTLER

Golden Dreams Bed & Breakfast

6412 Easy Street, V0N 1B6
(604) 932-2667; (800) 668-7055
fax: (604) 932-7055
E-mail: ann@goldendreamswhistler.com
www.goldendreamswhistler.com

Enjoy our world-class, year-round resort just two hours from Vancouver. Surround yourself with nature's beauty and allow us to pamper you with a wholesome breakfast, homemade jams, and fresh breads. Unique theme rooms feature cozy duvets and sherry decanters. Relax in the outdoor hot tub with mountain views! Family room with wood fireplace. Full guest kitchen. Located just a mile from village express gondolas. Valley trail system and bus route at our doorstep. Bike rentals on-site. Many seasonal activities. Now in two locations! Whistler Town Plaza is within walk-

6 Pets welcome; 7 Children welcome; 8 Tennis nearby; 9 Swimming nearby; 10 Golf nearby; 11 Skiing nearby; 12 May be booked through travel agent

VARIOUS REGIONS

Golden Dreams

ing distance of express ski lifts, fabulous restaurants, and new shops. These new condos feature gas fireplaces, entertainment centers, full kitchens, spa access, and underground parking.

Host: Ann Spence
Rooms: 3 + 2 condos; $85-145 (Canadian)
Full Breakfast
Credit Cards: A, B
Notes: 2, 5, 7, 8, 9, 10, 11

VARIOUS CITIES

AA-Accommodations West Bed & Breakfast Reservations

660 Jones Terrace, Victoria, V8Z 2L7
(250) 479-1986; fax: (250) 479-9999
E-mail: gardencity@bc-bed-breakfast.com
www.bc-bed-breakfast.com

Vancouver Island—Victoria, Duncan, Nanaimo, Parksville, Qualicum Beach. From modest to magnificent, from city to surf, cottage or country estate, we have a location to suit every request. One call, that's all! Assured comfort, quality, and cleanliness. Helpful hosts and hostesses. For efficient, caring service call Doreen between 9 A.M. and 9 P.M. Monday-Saturday, and from 2 P.M.-9 P.M. Sundays. There is no fee for this service. Free catalog on request.

Host: Doreen Wensley
Rooms: 60 (45 PB; 15 SB) $65-185
Full and Continental Breakfast
Credit Cards: A, B, C
Notes: 2, 5, 6, 7, 8, 9, 10, 12

NOTES: Credit cards accepted: A Master Card; B Visa; C American Express; D Discover; E Diners Club; F Other; 2 Personal checks accepted; 3 Lunch available; 4 Dinner available; 5 Open all year;

Manitoba

HECLA ISLAND

Solmundson Gesta Hus

Riverton, P.O. Box 76, R0C 2R0
(204) 279-2088; fax: (204) 279-2088
E-mail: holtz@mb.sympatico.ca
www.heclatourism.mb.ca

The guest house is located on private property within Hecla Provincial Park. Enjoy luxurious, European-style hospitality in a completely renovated, modern, comfortable home in an original Icelandic settlement. Relax on the veranda or in the gazebo and enjoy the beautiful view of Lake Winnipeg. Enjoy the tranquil and peaceful atmosphere while petting the dog and cats, or feeding the ducks. The host is a commercial fisherman, so feast on the catch of the day along with garden-fresh vegetables for the evening meal.

Hosts: Dave and Sharon Holtz
Rooms: 4 (1 PB; 3 SB) $55-75
Full Breakfast
Credit Cards: A, B
Notes: 2, 4, 5, 6, 7, 8, 9, 10, 11, 12

WINNIPEG

Mary Jane's Place

144 Yale Avenue, R3M 0L7
(204) 453-8104
E-mail: maryjane'splace@hotmail.com
www.bbcanada.com/516.html

Enjoy relaxed living in a three-story historic home with beautiful oak interiors and stained-glass windows close to airport, downtown, universities bus routes, and all attractions. Easy to find from all directions. Full breakfasts. Close to all Chrisitan churches. Always welcome!

Hosts: Mary Jane and Jack Zonneveld
Rooms: 4 (1 PB; 3 SB) $50-65
Full Breakfast
Credit Cards: None
Notes: 2, 5, 7, 8, 9, 10

---

6 Pets welcome; 7 Children welcome; 8 Tennis nearby; 9 Swimming nearby; 10 Golf nearby; 11 Skiing nearby; 12 May be booked through travel agent

MANITOBA

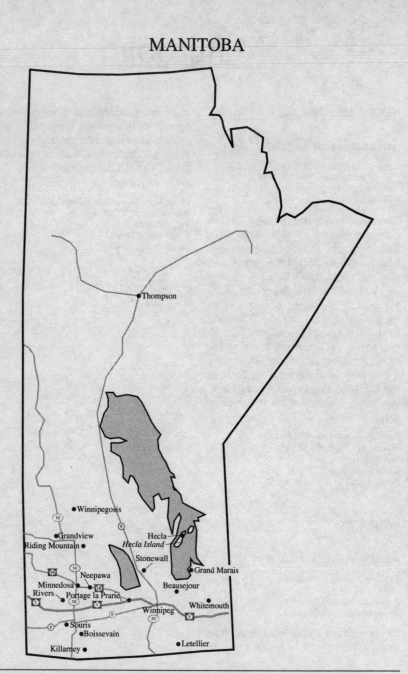

- Thompson
- Winnipegosis
- Grandview
- Riding Mountain
- Hecla
- *Hecla Island*
- Stonewall
- Neepawa
- Minnedosa
- Rivers
- Portage la Prarie
- Grand Marais
- Beausejour
- Whitemouth
- Winnipeg
- Souris
- Boissevain
- Killarney
- Letellier

NOTES: Credit cards accepted: A Master Card; B Visa; C American Express; D Discover; E Diners Club; F Other; 2 Personal checks accepted; 3 Lunch available; 4 Dinner available; 5 Open all year;

New Brunswick

HOPEWELL HILL

Peck Colonial House Bed and Breakfast

5566 Route 114, E4H 3N5
(506) 882-2114
E-mal: peckcolonial@fundyscenes.com
www.fundyscenes.com/peckcolonial

Beautiful, 200-year-old ancestral colonial home surrounded by spacious lawns and flower gardens. Enjoy a full country-style breakfast with homemade breads, jams, and our own maple syrup. Enjoy our unique tearoom, reminiscent of the original carriage house. Our seafood chowder is hard to beat!

Rooms: 3 (SB) $55-60
Full Breakfast
Credit Cards: B
Notes: 3, 4, 5, 7, 10, 11

NEW BRUNSWICK

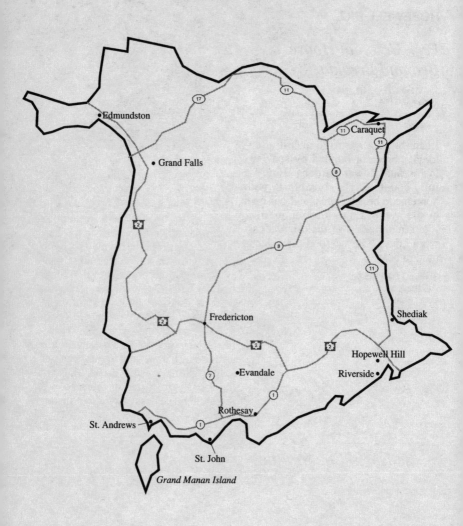

Nova Scotia

DARTMOUTH

Prince Albert Bed & Breakfast

81 Prince Albert Road, B2Y 1M1
(902) 469-0362; fax: (902) 469-0119
www.bbcanada.com/4145.html

The Prince Albert B&B is a large, century-old home with off-street parking located in downtown Dartmouth, across from the Esso garage. One ensuite with private bath, double bed, and pull-out couch; kitchen (no stove), microwave, refrigerator, coffeemaker, living room, TV/VCR, and small deck. One ensuite-private bath, queen bed, large sitting room, microwave, refrigerator, coffeemaker, and TV/VCR. Both units are suitable for families. Just a 10-minute walk to the Dartmouth/Halifax ferry.

Host: Diane Aikens
Rooms: 2 suites (PB) $65-115
Continental Breakfast
Credit Cards: B
Notes: 2, 5, 7, 9, 10

DIGBY

Thistle Down Country Inn

98 Montague Row #508, B0V 1A0
(902) 245-4490; (800) 565-8081
fax: (902) 245-6717
E-mail: thstldwn@tartannet.ns.ca
www.thistledown.ns.ca

Thistle Down Country Inn

This 1904 Edwardian home on the shore of the magnificent Annapolis Basin has splendid views of the harbor, 12 comfortable rooms (six with refrigerators), and private baths; non-smoking; full breakfast included. Lovely candlelight dinner served at 6:30 P.M. Monday through Saturday in the Queen Alexandra Dining Room by reservation. Central to many activities and attractions; whale watches arranged. Come and relax in our lovely garden on the harbor. Due to the many attractions in the area, we recommend at least two days in our town.

Hosts: Ed Reid and Lester Bartson
Rooms: 12 (PB) $85-120 Canadian
Full Breakfast
Credit Cards: A, B, C, E
Notes: 4, 6, 7, 10, 12

---

6 Pets welcome; 7 Children welcome; 8 Tennis nearby; 9 Swimming nearby; 10 Golf nearby; 11 Skiing nearby; 12 May be booked through travel agent

NOVA SCOTIA

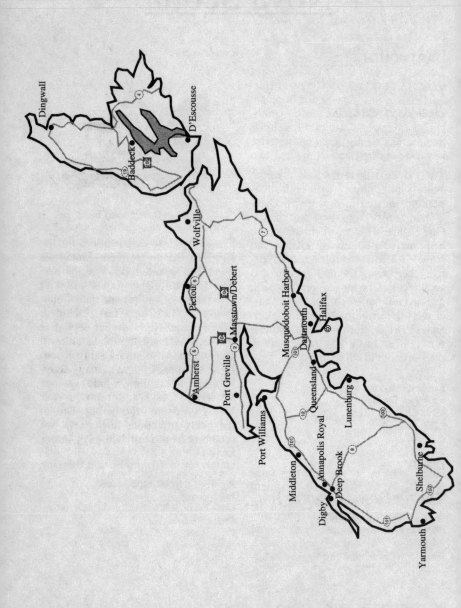

NOTES: Credit cards accepted: A Master Card; B Visa; C American Express; D Discover; E Diners Club; F Other; 2 Personal checks accepted; 3 Lunch available; 4 Dinner available; 5 Open all year;

DINGWALL

The Inlet Bed & Breakfast

P.O. Box 18, B0C 1G0
phone/fax: (902) 383-2112

Located 2.5 kilometers off the world famous Cabot Trail on Dingwall Harbour, our area offers: water frontage, sand dunes, swimming, beach combing, sailing, whale and bird watching, nature trails, both coastal and interior kayaking, canoeing, cycling, and two concerts a week in the summer. Our B&B is a family home and a former convent for 37 years. We offer vacation planning assistance. Cats on premises.

Hosts: Ann and Brian Fitzgerald
Rooms: 3 (SB) $55
Full Breakfast
Credit Cards: A, B
Notes: 4, 5, 7, 8, 9, 10, 11

MASSTOWN

Shady Maple Bed & Breakfast

11207 Highway #2, Debert, B0M 1G0
(902) 662-3565; (800) 493-5844
fax: (902) 662-3565
E-mail: emeisses@ns.sympatico.ca
www3.ns.sympatico.ca/emeisses

Come visit us on our farm in rural Nova Scotia. We have a wide variety of animals including llamas, cows, dogs, cats, sheep, pigs, and many more. Stroll through the fields or join us around the fireplace and relax. A swimming pool and hot tub are available as well. Full breakfast is served with candlelight.

Hosts: James and Ellen Eisses
Rooms: 3 (1 PB; 2 SB) $60-90
Full Breakfast
Credit Cards: B
Notes: 5, 6, 7, 9, 10, 11

QUEENSLAND

Surfside Inn

9609 St. Margarets Bay Road, B0J 1T0
(902) 857-2417; (800) 373-2417
fax: (902) 857-2107
E-mail: info@thesurfsideinn.com
www.thesurfsideinn.com

Overlooking the golden sands of Queensland Beach, the Surfside Inn has been restored to provide all of the modern amenities. An 18th-century Victorian sea-captain's home, each of our suites has cable television, mahogany beds, and a private bath with luxurious whirlpool. Start your day with a hearty breakfast, then take a stroll on the beach, or a swim in our in-ground pool. Halifax and Peggy's Cove are only minutes away. Join us for lunch or supper in our new, fine-dining restaurant where local seafood is featured on our excellent lunch and dinner menus. Romance packages, and off-season or extended stay discounts are available. Such a relaxing setting for your getaway!

Hosts: Michelle and Bill Batcules
Rooms: 6 (PB) $79-175 (Canadian)
Continental Breakfast
Credit Cards: A, B, C, D
Notes: 3, 4, 5, 7, 8, 9, 10, 11, 12

---

6 Pets welcome; 7 Children welcome; 8 Tennis nearby; 9 Swimming nearby; 10 Golf nearby; 11 Skiing nearby; 12 May be booked through travel agent

WOLFVILLE

Tattingstone

434 Main Street, B0P 1X0
(902) 542-7696; (800) 565-7696
fax: (902) 542-4427

Registered historic home (1874). Ten beautifully furnished rooms with private baths, some with Jacuzzis. Most rooms (8) have queen beds, two have two double beds. All have phones, air-conditioning, cable TVs, heated outdoor pool, gardens. Walking distance to downtown, Acadia University. Nonsmoking. Dining room features fine country dining evenings 5:30 P.M. through 9:00 P.M.

Host: Betsey Harwood
Rooms: 10 (PB)
Full Breakfast
Credit Cards: A, B, C
Notes: 3, 9, 12

Ontario

BALDERSON

Woodrow Guest Ranch & Bed & Breakfast

R.R. 1, 3062 Concession 8A Drummond,
K0G 1A0
(613) 267-1493; (800) 582-2311
fax: (613) 267-1766
E-mail: woodrowfarm@ripnet.com
www.travelinx.com/woodrowfarm

This hilltop Heritage home is located on 91 scenic acres in eastern Ontario's heartland. Offering peaceful country quiet; relax in the maple-shaded garden or stroll along our nature trail. Ottawa is just an hour away. Enjoy choice of three air-conditioned guest rooms, with king or twin beds, en suite or shared baths. Our comfortable guest lounge has a fireplace for cooler evenings and includes videos and books. Hydra and massage therapy can also be arranged at a nearby wellness spa; great after a day's riding. Also offered are one- to four-day horseback riding vacation packages.

Host: Ann Miller
Rooms: 3 (2 PB; 1 SB) $65-75 (Canadian)
Full Breakfast
Credit Cards: B
Notes: 2, 3, 4, 5, 7, 8, 9, 10, 11, 12

BARRIE

Comb & Blossom Inn Bed & Breakfast

5260 LN 6 N; P.O. Box 119, Moonstone,
L0K 1N0
(705) 835-6143; (877) 730-2097
E-mail: info@combandblossominn.com
www.combandblossominn.com

Lovingly restored, century-old, Victorian-style farmhouse with all modern amenities, including central air-conditioning. Guests have full use of the entertainment room, complete with satellite service, video library, and wood-burning fireplace. Bedrooms are bright and spacious, each with a private bathroom. A full breakfast with freshly squeezed orange juice and home-farmed honey is served in the screened-in gazebo or the country-sized kitchen. Located near many golf courses, and two ski-hills. Children welcome.

Rooms: 2 (PB) $65-75 Canadian
Full Breakfast
Credit Cards: B, E
Notes: 5, 7, 9, 10, 11

Cozy Corner

2 Morton Crescent, L4N 7T3
(705) 739-0157; fax: (705) 739-1946
E-mail: cozyc@bconnex.net
www.bconnex.net/~cozyc

This elegant city home is a 1999 Bed & Breakfast Award-Winner. Old-world courtesy and just nice folks make you feel spoiled and pampered. Two spacious suites offer Jacuzzi, queen bed, duet armchairs, coffee table, and private TV. Two other bright and comfortable double bed-

---

6 Pets welcome; 7 Children welcome; 8 Tennis nearby; 9 Swimming nearby; 10 Golf nearby; 11 Skiing nearby; 12 May be booked through travel agent

ONTARIO

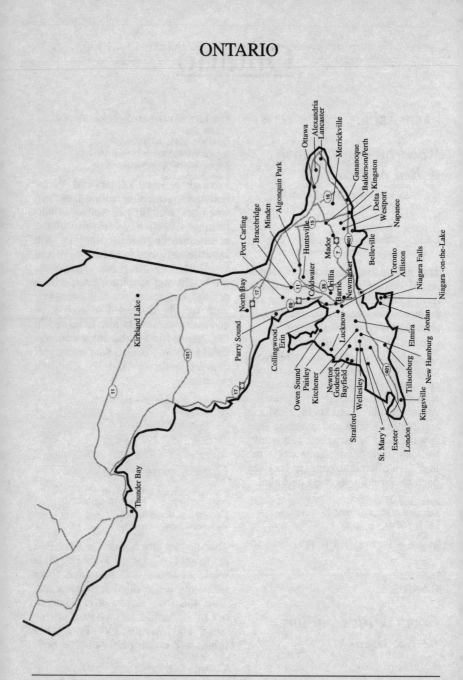

rooms have writing desks, double dressers, and private TV. We are located in the center of the Lakelands. Marvel at the pristine beauty of our surroundings, clean air, and abundant forests. Chef Kirby (retired) in residence.

Hosts: Charita and Harry Kirby
Rooms: 4 (2 PB; 2 SB) $65-110 (Canadian)
Full Breakfast
Credit Cards: B
Notes: 5, 7, 8, 9, 10, 11, 12

BELLEVILLE

Hilltop Pastures

R.R. 2, 1341 Sills Road, Stirling K0K 3E0
phone/fax: (613) 478-6078; (888) 690-3224
E-mail: hilltop@reach.net
bbcanada.com/hilltoppastures

This 1864 fieldstone home is surrounded by farmlands, and features a maple spiral staircase, oak flooring, and pine trim throughout. Organically grown market garden. "Happy chickens" and bees provide organic eggs and honey for the breakfast table. This is the heart of Quinte Country Trails. Old railway beds provide three-loop trails for multi-use recreational activities: walking, biking, bird-watching, horseback riding, cross-country skiing, and dog sledding. Come, treat yourself to an opportunity to commune with nature and revitalize the soul.

Hosts: Willie and Didi Curry
Rooms: 3 (1 PB; 2 SB) $65-75 (Canadian)
Full Breakfast
Credit Cards: A, B, C
Notes: 3, 4, 5, 7, 9, 10, 11

COLDWATER

Inn the Woods Country Inn

4240-6th Line North, Oro-Medonte, R.R. #4,
  L0K 1E0
(705) 835-6193; (800) 289-6295
fax: (705) 835-0061
E-mail: info@inn-the-woods.com
www.inn-the-woods.com

A three-level, colonial-style home located on the fringe of the Copeland forest in a tranquil, wooded setting on seven acres in the heart of the Medonte hills ski country. Inn the Woods was designed for the comfort, privacy, and relaxation of our guests and combines a peaceful, scenic ambience with nearby availability of quaint shops, fine restaurants, mountain trails, scenic country roads, and fishing streams.

Inn the Woods

Hosts: Betty and Bob Shannon
Rooms: 5 (2 PB; 3 SB) $70-100
Full Breakfast
Credit Cards: A, B, C, E
Notes: 2, 3, 4, 5, 7, 9, 10, 11

---

6 Pets welcome; 7 Children welcome; 8 Tennis nearby; 9 Swimming nearby; 10 Golf nearby; 11 Skiing nearby; 12 May be booked through travel agent

STUDIO

Pretty River Valley

COLLINGWOOD

Pretty River Valley Country Inn

R.R. #1 529742, Nottowa, L0M 1P0
phone/fax: (705) 445-7598
E-mail: inn@cois.on.ca
www.prettyriverinn.com

This cozy, quiet country inn in the scenic Blue Mountains overlooks Pretty River Valley Wilderness Park. Choose from distinctive pine-furnished studios and suites with fireplaces and in-room whirlpools-for-two. Spa and air-conditioning. Close to Collingwood, beaches, golf, fishing, hiking (Bruce Trail), bicycle paths, antique shops, and restaurants. Complimentary tea served upon arrival. Studios and suites are available. No smoking.

Hosts: Steve and Diane Szelestowski
Rooms: 8 (PB) $95-135 (Canadian)
Full Breakfast
Credit Cards: A, B
Notes: 5, 8, 9, 10, 11, 12

KITCHENER

Aram's Roots & Wings Bed & Breakfast

11 Sunbridge Crescent, N2K 1T4
(519) 743-4557; (877) 743-4557
fax: (519) 743-4166
E-mail: fay@fteal.on.ca
www.bbcanada.com/1039.html

Make yourself comfortable and relax; sit by the heated pool or Jacuzzi. Use our beautiful walking trails. This hidden little resort offers you large, comfortable rooms (king, queen, or twin beds) with ensuite/private or shared bathroom facilities. Whirlpool tubs, private entrance (two rooms), and a great full breakfast. Located in the heart of Mennonite country just minutes from the universities, St. Jacobs, Waterloo Stratford (30 minutes), and Niagara (90 minutes away). Children and pets welcome.

Host: Fay Teal-Aram
Rooms: 4 (2 PB; 2 SB) $75-100 (Canadian)
Full Breakfast
Credit Cards: A, B, C, E
Notes: 5, 6, 7, 8, 9, 10, 11, 12

Roses and Blessings

112 High Acres Crescent, N2N 2Z9
(519) 742-1280; fax: (519) 742-8428
E-mail: nmwarren@golden.net
www.bbcanada.com/rosesandblessings

Discover an "oasis"! We enjoy pampering our guests with warm Christian hospitality, cozy comfort, and renowned home-baking. We serve a sumptuous, full breakfast in our candlelit dining room, as well as an evening dessert snack. Double/queen bedrooms have private bathrooms and

---

NOTES: Credit cards accepted: A Master Card; B Visa; C American Express; D Discover; E Diners Club; F Other; 2 Personal checks accepted; 3 Lunch available; 4 Dinner available; 5 Open all year;

cable TV. Guests may use our hot tub and exercise equipment. Air-conditioned and nonsmoking. Packages available: theatre, horseback riding, and canoeing. Close to the farmers' markets, St. Jacobs, universities, and Stratford.

Hosts: Marg and Norm Warren
Rooms: 2 (PB) $70 (Canadian)
Full Breakfast
Credit Cards: A, B
Notes: 2, 5, 7, 8, 9

LANCASTER

Macpine Bed & Breakfast

Box 51, K0C 1N0
(613) 347-2003; fax: (613) 347-2814
E-mail: macpine@glen-net.ca
www.bbcanada.com/688.html

A quiet getaway on the shores of the St. Lawrence River! Welcome to our modernized, century-old farmhouse shaded with old pine trees. We have a 240-acre working Holstein dairy farm. Take a quiet walk or bike to our cottage at the river; swim, fish, canoe or watch the ocean boats. Area attractions include the Cooper Marsh Nature Walk and bird-watching, china outlet, craft and antique shops, golf, and fishing. Sightsee or shop in Ottawa, Montreal, and Cornwall. A full breakfast is served in the sunroom.

Hosts: Guelda and Robert MacRae
Rooms: 3 (SB) $45-60
Full Breakfast
Credit Cards: None
Notes: 2, 5, 7, 8, 9, 10, 11

MADOC

Camelot Country Inn

R.R. 5, K0K 2K0
phone/fax: (613) 473-0441; www.bbcanada.com

Relax in the quiet country setting of our 1853 brick-and-stone home. It is surrounded by plantings of red and white pine on 25 acres of land in the heart of Hastings County. Original woodwork and oak floors have been lovingly preserved. There are three guest rooms, two with double beds and one with twins. Breakfast may be chosen from the country breakfast, or one of two gourmet breakfasts. Dinner available upon request.

Camelot Country Inn

Host: Marian Foster
Rooms: 3 (SB) $60-70
Full Breakfast
Credit Cards: A, B
Notes: 2, 4, 5, 9, 10, 11

MIDLAND

A Wymbolwood Beach House Bed & Breakfast

533 Tiny Beaches Road South, Wymbolwood Beach, L0L 2T0
phone/fax: (705) 361-3649

---

6 Pets welcome; 7 Children welcome; 8 Tennis nearby; 9 Swimming nearby; 10 Golf nearby; 11 Skiing nearby; 12 May be booked through travel agent

E-mail: lippert@primus.ca
www.wymbolwood.com

Discover Huronia's best kept secret: A Wymbolwood Beach House, "a secluded haven, nestled in the evergreens overlooking Georgian Bay" (the new VR television). Centrally located to Midland, Penetanguishene, and Barrie, we offer a memorable getaway with all the comforts of home, including a delicious breakfast. Enjoy beautifully decorated guest rooms with cable TVs and private baths or a charming two-bedroom suite, complete with Jacuzzi tub. Experience area attractions, historic sites, boat cruises, sandy beaches. Hike, bike, or crosscountry ski through surrounding forest trails. Other features: central air-conditioning, fireplace, games room, VCR, decks—and spectacular sunsets. Open all year. Groups welcome. Weekly rates. Inquire about our seasonal packages.

Hosts: Jane and Bob
Rooms: 3 (PB) $80-90
Full Breakfast
Credit Cards: B, E
Notes: 5, 8, 9, 10, 11, 12

NIAGARA FALLS

Bed of Roses
Bed & Breakfast

4877 River Road, L2E 3G5
(905) 356-0529; fax: (905) 356-3563
E-mail: bedofrosesbb@earthlink,net
infoniagara.com/d-bed-roses.html

Christian hosts welcome you. We have two efficiency units with bedroom and living room with pull-out sofa bed, furnished kitchenette, dining

area, bath, and private entrance. A full breakfast is served "room-service-style." We are located on the famous River Road near Niagara Falls, bridges to the U.S., bike and hiking trails, golf course, and all major attractions. Free pick-up from bus and train station. Family units are suitable for up to five people. Come enjoy your stay in Niagara Falls.

Host: Norma Lambertson
Rooms: 2 (PB) $125-175
Full Breakfast
Credit Cards: A, B, E
Notes: 7, 8, 10

Gretna Green
Bed & Breakfast

5077 River Road, L2E 3G7
(905) 357-2081
E-mail: gretnagreen_zooo@hotmail.com
www.bbcanada.com/262.html

A warm welcome awaits you in our home overlooking the Niagara River Gorge. We are located close to all attractions and the famous falls. All rooms have air-conditioning and TVs. A full breakfast greets you between 8

Gretna Green

NOTES: Credit cards accepted: A Master Card; B Visa; C American Express; D Discover; E Diners Club; F Other; 2 Personal checks accepted; 3 Lunch available; 4 Dinner available; 5 Open all year;

and 9 A.M. with homemade muffins, breads, and jams. We offer pick-up service at both the train and bus stations by arrangement. Inquire about pets. Come enjoy your " Home Away From Home." Inquire about pets.

Hosts: Sue and Fran
Rooms: 4 (PB) $65-110 (Canadian)
Full Breakfast
Credit Cards: A, B
Notes: 5, 7, 10

NIAGARA-ON-THE-LAKE

Willowcreek House Bed & Breakfast

P.O. Box 1028, 288 Dorchester Street, L0S 1J0
(905) 468-9060; (877) 589-9001
fax: (905) 468-9061
E-mail: willowcreekhouse@sympatico.ca
www.niagaraonthelakebb.org

Visit our elegant Georgian home located in Old Town. Walk to shops, theaters, dining, and the golf course. All rooms have ensuite baths; for that romantic getaway, enjoy our Willowcreek Room with fireplace and Jacuzzi. We have central air-conditioning and a smoke- and pet-free environment.

Hosts: Margaret and Jake Janzen
Rooms: 3 (PB) $120-140 Canadian
Full Breakfast
Credit Cards: A, B, C
Notes: 2, 5, 8, 9, 10

OTTAWA

Australis Guest House

35 Marlborough Avenue, K1N 8E6
phone/fax: (613) 235-8461

E-mail: waters@magma.net
www.bbcanada.com/1463.html

We are the oldest-established, still-operating B&B in the Ottawa area. Located on a quiet, tree-lined street a block from the Redeau River with ducks and swans, and Strathcona Park; a 20-minute walk from the Parliament buildings. This period house boasts leaded-glass windows, fireplaces, oak floors, and unique stained-glass windows overlooking the hall. Enjoy a hearty breakfast with home-baked breads and pastries. Past winner of the Ottawa Hospitality Award and Gold Award recipient for Star of City for Tourism. Recommended by *Newsweek* and *Travel Scoop* and featured in the *Ottawa Sun* for breakfast recipes. Carol is coauthor of *The Cookbook: A Breakfast Companion of Whispered Recipes*.

Hosts: Carol and Brian Waters
Rooms: 3 (1 PB; 2 SB) $78-93
Full Breakfast
Credit Cards: None
Notes: 5

Beatrice Lynn Guest House

479 Slater Street, K1R 5C2
phone/fax: (613) 236-3904

A comfortable, owner-occupied home in downtown Ottawa, five to ten minute walk to Parliament Hill, the National Gallery of Canada, the By Ward Market, restaurants, and shopping. All rooms are shared bath, with a full breakfast provided. Children and pets welcome. Off street parking and baby-sitting available. Close to

---

6 Pets welcome; 7 Children welcome; 8 Tennis nearby; 9 Swimming nearby; 10 Golf nearby; 11 Skiing nearby; 12 May be booked through travel agent

bicycle paths. Payment by cash or travellers' cheques.

Host: Mrs. Phyllis Lyon
Rooms: 4 (1 PB; 3 SB) $70 Canadian
Full Breakfast
Credit Cards: None
Notes: 5, 6, 7

RENFREW

Glenroy Farm Bed & Breakfast

R.R. 1, Braeside, K0A 1G0
(613) 432-6248; www.bbcanada.com/1763.html

Beautiful quiet farm setting just one hour's drive from our capital, Ottawa. Situated in historic McNab Township of Renfrew County in the heart of Ottawa Valley, halfway between the towns of Renfrew and Arnprior. Smoke- and alcohol-free home. We live in an 1884 stone house, well maintained by the three generations of McGregors who built the home and lived in it. We have a produce business growing strawberries and sweet corn. Local attractions: Ottawa river rafting, Storyland, Logos Land, Bonnechere Caves, Renfrew's Swinging Bridge, Museums, Farmers' Market, and many others.

Hosts: Noreen and Steve McGregor
Rooms: 4 (SB) $50-60
Full Breakfast
Credit Cards: None
Notes: 2, 4, 5, 7, 10

The Second Tee

SOUTHAMPTON

The Second Tee

270 Tyendinaga Drive, N0H 2L0
(519) 797-3976; fax: (519) 797-1935
E-mail: barbara_misener@bwdsb.on.ca
listed@cottagelink.com

Prviate accommodation suitable for one or two couples. Occupies the ground level of a home that overlooks Chippewa Golf and Country Club. Has a separate entrance, including three sliding doors out to a gardened patio area with pond. Full kitchen and TV room includes refrigerator, stove, microwave, propane BBQ, TV with cable, and VCR. Delightful sunsets! Children welcome 10 years and older.

Hosts: John and Barbara Misener
Rooms: 2 (PB) $75
Credit Cards: None
Notes: 2, 5, 7, 8, 9, 10, 11

STRATFORD

Burnside Guest Home

139 William Street, N5A 4X9
(519) 271-7076; fax: (519) 271-0265
E-mail: burnside@golden.net
www.burnside.on.ca

Burnside is a turn-of-the-century Queen Anne Revival home on the north shore of Lake Victoria, the site of the first Stratford logging mill. The home features many family heirlooms and antiques, and is centrally air-conditioned. Our rooms have been redecorated in light, cheery colors. Relax in the gardens overlooking the Avon River while seated upon hand-crafted furniture amid the rose, herbaceous, and annual flower gardens. A home-cooked, nutritional breakfast is pro-

Burnside Guest Home

vided. Within walking distance of Shakespearean theaters and close to the Protestant and Roman Catholic churches of Stratford. Stratford is the home of a world-renowned Shakespearean festival from early May to mid-November each year. Children are welcome during the off-season.

Host: Lester J. Wilker
Rooms: 4 (SB) $50-85 (Canadian)
Full Breakfast
Credit Cards: None
Notes: 2, 5, 7, 8, 9, 10, 11

TILLSONBURG

"The English Robin" Bed & Breakfast

19 Robin Road, N4G 4N5
(519) 842-8605; E-mail: lnealon@execulik.com
www.bbcanada.com/468html

One room has a queen bed, Queen Anne chairs, TV, and patio door leading to a private deck off the bedroom, where one can relax after a long day. The other room is furnished with twin beds and comfortable chairs; the bathroom, brightened by a skylight, has a shower and bath combination for guests only.

Hosts: Tina and Tom Nealon
Rooms: 3 (1 PB; 2 SB) $55-85 (Canadian)
Full Breakfast
Credit Cards: None
Notes: 5, 8, 9, 10, 11

TORONTO

Bonnevue Manor Bed & Breakfast Place

Bonnevue Manor

---

6 Pets welcome; 7 Children welcome; 8 Tennis nearby; 9 Swimming nearby; 10 Golf nearby; 11 Skiing nearby; 12 May be booked through travel agent

33 Beaty Avenue, M6K 3B3
(416) 536-1455; (800) 603-3837
fax: (416) 533-2644
E-mail: bonne@interlog.com
www.toronto.com/bonnevuemanor

Elegant, eclectic, spacious city mansion, with a homey ambience, extraordinary breakfasts, and comfortable beds. Ideal for the young at heart and those with a taste for casual elegance.

Rooms: 3 (PB) $70-125 U.S.
Full Breakfast
Credit Cards: A, B, C
Note: 5

Toronto Bed & Breakfast Registry

Box 269, 253 College Street, M5T 1R5
(705) 738-9449; (877) 922-6522
fax: (705) 738-0155
E-mail: beds@torontobandb.com
www.torontobandb.com

Now in our 24th year, Toronto's foremost B&B reservation service of quality inspected non-smoking homes provides a high level of hospitality, cleanliness, safety, and comfort. The majority of our hosts are located in historical downtown neighbourhoods and are minutes away from public transit. Known for its personal touch, Toronto B&B is rapidly becoming a popular alternative to hotels. Free brochure available. Parking included where available.

Host: Marcia Getgood (president)
Rooms: 52 (26 PB; 26 SB) $80-135 Canadian
Full Breakfast
Credit Cards: A, B, C

Prince Edward Island

ALBANY

The Captain's Lodge

Seven Mile Bay, R.R. # 2, C0B 1A0
phone/fax: (902) 855-3106; (800) 261-3518
E-mail: captains.lodge@pei.sympatico.ca
www3.pei.sympatico.ca/captains.lodge

A quiet, secluded B&B surrounded by
flower gardens and fields of clover,
grain, and potato blossoms. A short
walk from a red sand beach; seven
kilometers from our new Confedera-
tion Bridge that links Prince Edward
Island to the mainland. Queen beds;
one room with twins. Ceiling fans,
fresh flowers, duvets, slippers, gourmet breakfasts, and evening desserts
spoil our guests. Off-season rates and
senior discounts are available. No
smoking. Resident cat, dog, and
bunny. Deposit required. Cancellation
policy. Open May 15-October 15.

Host: Jim Rogers
Rooms: 3 (PB) $85-100
Full Breakfast
Credit Cards: A, B
Notes: 2, 9, 10

---

6 Pets welcome; 7 Children welcome; 8 Tennis nearby; 9 Swimming nearby; 10 Golf nearby; 11 Skiing
nearby; 12 May be booked through travel agent

PRINCE EDWARD ISLAND

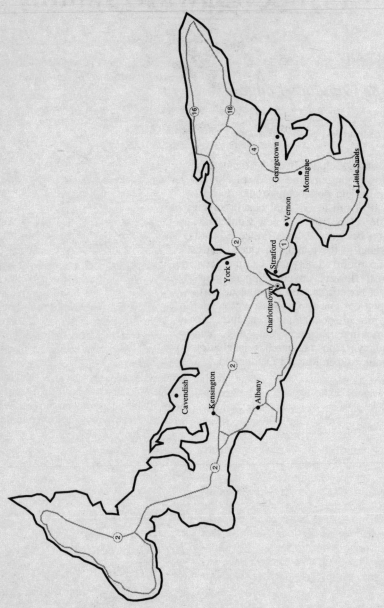

NOTES: Credit cards accepted: A Master Card; B Visa; C American Express; D Discover; E Diners
Club; F Other; 2 Personal checks accepted; 3 Lunch available; 4 Dinner available; 5 Open all year;

Quebec

MONTREAL

Auberge de la Fontaine

1301 Rachel Street East, H2J 2K1
(514) 597-0166; (800) 597-0597
fax: (514) 597-0496
E-mail: info@aubergedelafontaine.com
www.aubergedelafontaine.com

 The Auberge de la Fontaine is a nice stone house located in front of a magnificent park, newly renovated, with rooms in a warm and modern décor of unique style in Montreal. Comfortable, friendly atmosphere, and attentive, personal service are greatly appreciated by our corporate and leisure travelers. Each room is tastefully decorated. The suites with whirlpool baths, as well as the luxurious rooms, have brick walls and exclusive fabrics. You will settle in an elegant, quiet environment where duvet and decorative pillows ensure cozy comfort. Breakfast is a given at the Auberge. A delicious variety of breakfast foods are set out each morning, and you have access to the kitchen for snacks. There are no parking fees. We want our guests to feel comfortable and to be entirely satisfied with their stay. Discover the exclusive shops, restaurants, and art galleries of the Plateau Mont-Royal, which is typical of French Montreal.

Hosts: Celine Boudreau and Jean Lamothe
Rooms: 21 (PB) $115-234 (Canadian)
Continental Breakfast
Credit Cards: A, B, C, E
Notes: 5, 7, 8, 9, 10, 12

Hotel Casa Bella

264 Sherbrook Street West, H2X 1X9
(514) 849-2777; (888) 453-2777
fax: (514) 849-3650
E-mail: info@hotelcasbella.com
www.hotelcasabella.com

The Hotel Casa Bella is near the subway system in a well-located downtown area. All 20 hotel rooms are fully air-conditioned and completely renovated for your comfort. Casa Bella hospitality also includes complimentary morning coffee and croissants. For over 20 years now, the same owner has looked after the Hotel Casa Bella. She has built up a team of helpful and courteous employees who sincerely want you to enjoy your stay.

Rooms: 20 (15 PB; 5 SB) $65-89
Continental Breakfast
Credit Cards: A, B, C, E
Notes: 5, 7

NEW CARLISLE

Bay View Manor/ Manoir Bay View

---

6 Pets welcome; 7 Children welcome; 8 Tennis nearby; 9 Swimming nearby; 10 Golf nearby; 11 Skiing nearby; 12 May be booked through travel agent

QUEBEC

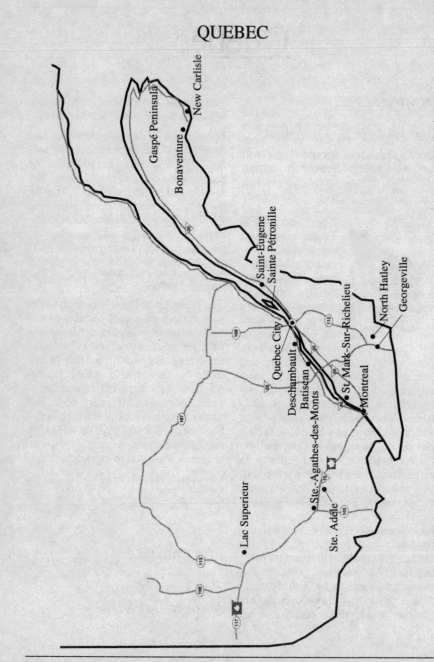

NOTES: Credit cards accepted: A Master Card; B Visa; C American Express; D Discover; E Diners Club; F Other; 2 Personal checks accepted; 3 Lunch available; 4 Dinner available; 5 Open all year;

395 Route 132, Bonaventure East, Box 21,
    G0C 1Z0
(418) 752-2725; (418) 752-6718
www.bbcanada.com/1012.html

Comfortable, two-story, wood-frame home on the beautiful Gaspé Peninsula across the highway from the beach, and beside an 18-hole golf course. The building was once a country store and rural post office. Stroll our quiet, natural beach; see nesting seabirds along the rocky cliffs; watch fishermen tend their nets and lobster traps; enjoy beautiful sunrises and sunsets; view the lighthouse beacon on the nearby point; and fall asleep to the sound of waves on the shore. Explore museums, archaeological caves, fossil site, bird sanctuary, and British Heritage Village. Hike, fish, canoe, horseback ride, or bird-watch.

Bay View Manor/Manoir Bay View

Host: Helen Sawyer
Rooms: 5 (1 PB; 4 SB) $35-45
Full Breakfast
Credit Cards: None
Notes: 5, 7, 8, 9, 10, 11

QUEBEC CITY

Hotel Manoir des Remparts

3 1/2 Des Remparts, G1R 3R4
(418) 692-2056; fax: (418) 692-1125

Located minutes from the train/bus terminal and the famed Chateau Frontenac. With some rooms overlooking the majestic St. Lawrence River, the Manoir des Remparts boasts one of the most coveted locations available in the old city of Quebec. Newly renovated, it can offer its guests a vast choice of rooms, ranging from a budget room with shared washrooms to an all-inclusive room with private terrace.

Host: Mrs. Sitherary Ngor
Rooms: 32 (23 PB; 9 SB) $45-70
Continental Breakfast
Credit Cards: A, B, C, E
Notes: 5, 7, 11, 12

6 Pets welcome; 7 Children welcome; 8 Tennis nearby; 9 Swimming nearby; 10 Golf nearby; 11 Skiing nearby; 12 May be booked through travel agent

SASKATCHEWAN

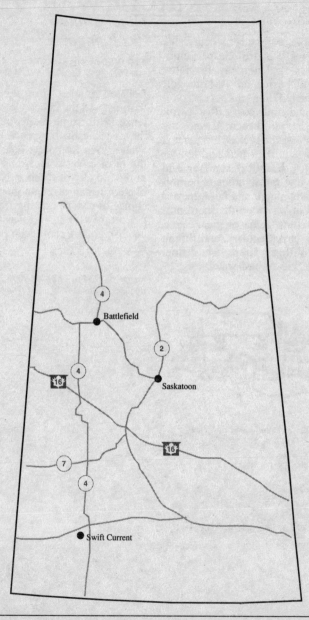

NOTES: Credit cards accepted: A Master Card; B Visa; C American Express; D Discover; E Diners Club; F Other; 2 Personal checks accepted; 3 Lunch available; 4 Dinner available; 5 Open all year;

Saskatchewan

SASKATOON

Sunshine Inn

711 5th Avenue North, S7K 2R6
phone/fax: (306) 651-1283; (800) 252-1746
E-mail: sunshineinn_711@yahoo.com
www.sunshineinnbb.com

Tastefully renovated older home located in an established neighborhood close to downtown. Our balcony suite features garden doors that open onto a large private balcony facing the treed avenue. Guest sitting room/library and dining room on the main floor. Delicious, heart-healthy breakfast.

Host: Joy Rousay
Rooms: 2 (PB) $55-75 (Canadian)
Continental Breakfast
Credit Cards: B
Notes: 2, 5, 8, 9, 10, 12

---

6 Pets welcome; 7 Children welcome; 8 Tennis nearby; 9 Swimming nearby; 10 Golf nearby; 11 Skiing nearby; 12 May be booked through travel agent

PUERTO RICO

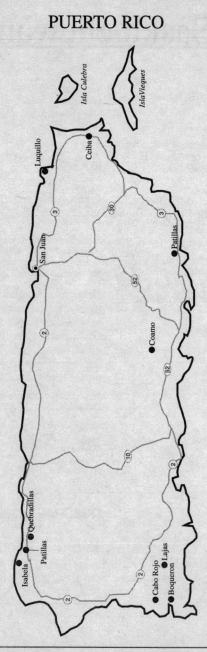

NOTES: Credit cards accepted: A Master Card; B Visa; C American Express; D Discover; E Diners Club; F Other; 2 Personal checks accepted; 3 Lunch available; 4 Dinner available; 5 Open all year;

Puerto Rico

CABO ROJO

Parador Perichi's

Road #102, Km. 14.3, Play Joyudas, Box 16310,
    00623
(787) 851-3131; (800) 435-7197
fax: (787) 851-0560
E-mail: perichi@tropicweb.net
puertoricoisfun.com

Beautiful Parador located across from the Caribbean Sea. Air-conditioned rooms with cable TV; adult's pool and children's pool; restaurant with international foods. Main beaches (Boqueron, Combate, and Buye) are just minutes away.

Rooms: 58 (PB) $55-100
Full Breakfast
Credit Cards: A, B, C, D, E
Notes: 3, 4, 5, 7, 8, 9, 10, 12

CONDADO

El Consulado Hotel

1110 Ashford Avenue, San Juan, 00907
(787) 289-9191; (888) 300-8002
fax: (787) 723-8665
E-mail: info@ihppr.com
www.ihppr.com

Localized in the best spot of Condado, this elegant European-style inn is newly remodeled and offers 29 ample bedrooms with all the amenities. Only a few steps from fine restaurants, casinos, beaches.

Rooms: 29 (PB) $85-115
Continental Breakfast
Credit Cards: A, B, C, D, E
Notes: 5, 7, 9, 11

ISABELA

Costa Dorada Beach Resort

Emilio Gonzalez #900, 00662
phone/fax: (787) 872-7595; (877) 875-0101
E-mail: info@costadoradabeach.com
www.costadoradabeach.com

Hotel in a tropical setting with palm trees on a mile-long stretch of white sand beach in the lovely town of Isabela, next to a fishing village. All oceanview rooms with air-conditioning, color cable TVs, direct-dial telephone, two pools, tennis and basketball courts, Jacuzzi, restaurant, and bar. Live music on Saturdays.

Host: Carolos R. Fernandez
Rooms: 52 (PB) $122-150
Continental Breakfast
Credit Cards: A, B, C
Notes: 3, 4, 5, 7, 8, 9, 10

QUEBRADILLAS

Parador Vistamar

Road 113N, #6205, 00678
(787) 895-2065; (888) 391-0606
fax: (787) 895-2294
E-mail: info@paradorvistamar.com
www.paradorvistamar.com

---

6 Pets welcome; 7 Children welcome; 8 Tennis nearby; 9 Swimming nearby; 10 Golf nearby; 11 Skiing nearby; 12 May be booked through travel agent

Parador Vistamar is located on a hilltop with a breathtaking view of Puerto Rico's northwest Gold Coast. Most of the rooms have ocean views, air-conditioning, color cable TV, private bath; some have balconies. Two pools, tennis, restaurant and bar. Live music on Saturdays.

Host: Mrs. Iris Myrna Cancel
Rooms: 55 (PB) $71-105
Continental Breakfast
Credit Cards: A, B, C, D
Notes: 3, 4, 5, 7, 8, 9, 10

NOTES: Credit cards accepted: A Master Card; B Visa; C American Express; D Discover; E Diners Club; F Other; 2 Personal checks accepted; 3 Lunch available; 4 Dinner available; 5 Open all year;

Virgin Islands

ST. CROIX

innparadise

1 E Golden Rock, P.O. Box 428, 00821
(340) 713-9803; (866) 800-9803
fax: (340) 713-8722
E-mail: info@innparadisestcroix.com
www.innparadisestcroix.com

innparadise is located on a quiet, semi-secluded road, conveniently located near Christensted town, nearby beaches, restaurants, and more. Spectacular harbor view. We have five newly remodeled rooms, equipped with many amenities, including complimentary beverage bar and free Internet access. Ours is a smoke-free environment. Children welcome over the age of 12.

Hosts: Tommie and Paula Broadnax
Rooms: 5 (3 PB; 2 SB) $110-175
Full Breakfast
Credit Cards: A, B, C
Notes: 2, 5, 7, 8, 9, 10, 12

Sprat Hall Plantation

Route 63 North at 58, P.O. Box 695, Frederiksted,
    St. Croix, 00841
(340) 772-0305; (800) 843-3584
E-mail: sprathall.vi@worldnet.att.net
travelto.sprathall

Sprat Hall Plantation, dating from 1650, is a country estate overlooking the sea. The furnishings of the Great House are mahogany antiques from all eras of occupation. Accommodations are in the Great House (non-smokers only), Sunset Inn Annex,

Sprat Hall Plantation

efficiencies in duplex cottages, and either one- or two-bedroom cottages. Lunch and dinner served at the beach restaurant. Enjoy the riding stables, gorgeous beach, and crystal clear turquoise water. Children welcome in cottages.

Hosts: James and Joyce Hurd
Rooms: 12 (PB) $130-150
Full Breakfast
Credit Cards: None
Notes: 2, 3, 4, 5, 7, 9, 12

ST. THOMAS

Bunker Hill Hotel

7 A Commandant Gade, Charlotte Amalie, 00802
(340) 774-8056; fax: (340) 774-3172
E-mail: bunkerhl@viaccess.net
www.bunkerhillhotel.com

The Bunker Hill Hotel is a unique, small, clean, and comfortable B&B

---

6 Pets welcome; 7 Children welcome; 8 Tennis nearby; 9 Swimming nearby; 10 Golf nearby; 11 Skiing nearby; 12 May be booked through travel agent

VIRGIN ISLANDS

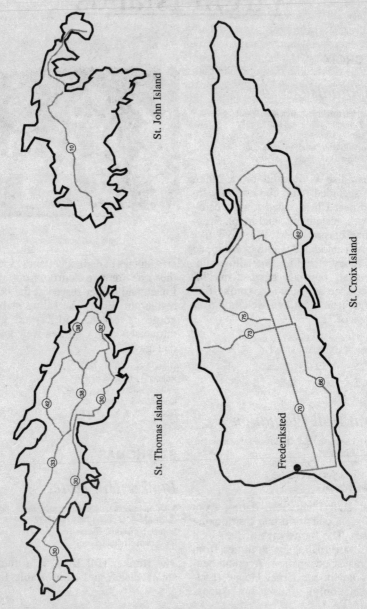

St. John Island

St. Croix Island

St. Thomas Island

Frederiksted

NOTES: Credit cards accepted: A Master Card; B Visa; C American Express; D Discover; E Diners Club; F Other; 2 Personal checks accepted; 3 Lunch available; 4 Dinner available; 5 Open all year;

inn, locted in the historic district area of Charlotte Amalie, St. Thomas, just a few minutes walking distance to many historic points of interest. Duty-free shops, restaurants, and downtown popular Main Street. All our rooms are air-conditioned with private baths, television, and telephone. Whether for business, pleasure, or relaxation, this is the convenient place to be.

Rooms: 15 (PB) $69-129
Full Breakfast
Credit Cards: A, B, C
Notes: 3, 4, 5, 8, 9, 10, 12

LOG ON TO
The CHRISTIAN
Bed & Breakfast
Directory
ON-LINE!
www.christianbedbreakfast.com

If you're looking for a quaint, old-fashioned place to stay, why not put the latest technology to work for you? The Christian Bed and Breakfast Directory is now on-line!

Log on to www.christianbedbreakfast.com for the latest information on Christian bed and breakfast lodgings. . .

- Use the special "search" function to locate the perfect lodging for your next trip. Search geographically by zip code, area code, or state. . .search according to nearby attractions (such as tennis, golf, or skiing). . .search for inns with special accommodations, for example, those that welcome children or pets.

- Check out "Today's Featured Inn," a quick overview of a randomly selected bed and breakfast—and find some great ideas for future trips.

- Enjoy the exclusive "B & B Cookbook," recipes from many of our featured inns.

www.christianbedbreakfast.com also provides a direct link to E-mail listed B & B's with questions and links to state tourism bureaus. It's the one-stop resource you need to plan your next adventure.

LOG ON AND LET YOUR IMAGINATION RUN FREE!